International Bibliography of Jewish Affairs, 1976–1977

Also of Interest

Jewish Assimilation in Modern Times, edited by Bela Vago

The Jewish Minority in the Soviet Union, Thomas E. Sawyer

**The Government and Politics of Israel*, Don Peretz

How Can People Commit the Unthinkable? Genocide: The Human Cancer, Israel W. Charny

**Religion and Politics in the Middle East*, edited by Michael Curtis

*Available in hardcover and paperback.

About the Book and Editor

International Bibliography of Jewish Affairs, 1976–1977: A Selectively Annotated List of Books and Articles Published in the Diaspora
edited by Elizabeth E. Eppler

This bibliography, a project of the Institute of Jewish Affairs, is intended as an aid to research on the historical, social, political, and cultural aspects of contemporary Jewish life and on the relationship between Jews and the non-Jewish world. The present volume covers material published in 1976 and 1977.

The Bibliography includes primarily nonfiction works published outside Israel by both Jewish and non-Jewish authors; it excludes belles lettres (with the exception of documentary novels and memoirs) and religious studies.

Entries are arranged by subject, with cross-references wherever applicable; a cumulative index of names and a list of periodicals are provided at the end of the volume.

Dr. Elizabeth E. Eppler is assistant director of the Institute of Jewish Affairs in London and archivist for the World Jewish Congress. She compiled and edited the International Bibliography of Jewish Affairs, 1966-1967 and has contributed to the Jewish Book Annual and the Guide to Eastern Literatures, among other publications.

The Institute of Jewish Affairs
gratefully acknowledges the assistance
of the Memorial Foundation for Jewish Culture,
which made the preparation and publication
of this volume possible

International Bibliography of Jewish Affairs, 1976–1977

A Selectively Annotated List of Books and Articles Published in the Diaspora

edited by Elizabeth E. Eppler

Routledge
Taylor & Francis Group
LONDON AND NEW YORK

First published 1983 by Westview Press

Published 2018 by Routledge
52 Vanderbilt Avenue, New York, NY 10017
2 Park Square, Milton Park, Abingdon, Oxon OX14 4RN

Routledge is an imprint of the Taylor & Francis Group, an informa business

Library of Congress Catalog Card Number 82-51276

ISBN 13: 978-0-367-01521-3 (hbk)
ISBN 13: 978-0-367-16508-6 (pbk)

CONTENTS

INTRODUCTION

This is the second volume of the International Bibliography of Jewish Affairs, the first having covered the years 1966-67. The ten years that elapsed between the two volumes have seen momentous events and new trends affecting Jews and Israel, both internally and externally: the aftermath of the Yom Kippur War; the Entebbe rescue operation; the politization of international organisations by the introduction of the 'Zionism equals Racism' resolution at the United Nations; the 1977 election in Israel and its consequences; the American Bicentennial and the Presidential elections; the Helsinki Conference on European Security and Cooperation which i.a. examined and placed on the international agenda the condition of Soviet Jewry; ethnic identification, particularly in the U.S.A., which led to a sharpened awareness of discrimination and prejudice against minority groups and resulted in the appearance of 'reverse discrimination'. All these and many more phenomena are mirrored in the books and articles listed.

The principles in the selection of the books and articles listed are the same as in the 1966-67 volume:

(a) Only works published outside Israel are considered.

(b) Both Jewish and non-Jewish authors are included.

(c) Fiction, drama and poetry were excluded, with some exceptions of historical novels or plays chiefly relating to the Holocaust.

(d) Also excluded were works of purely religious or theological nature (Wissenschaft des Judentums)

It is not claimed that the selection represents the whole literature on the subjects covered. The intention was to present in one volume the most important sources that may be of help to the researcher. Annotations only indicate contents and are not evaluations. Where the title clearly indicates the subject no further annotation is given. Since the Bibliography is primarily prepared for the English reader, foreign titles are translated.

The Bibliography is arranged according to subjects and within each section in the alphabetical order of authors. Transliterations of Hebrew, Yiddish, Arabic, Greek and Russian titles are according to international usage. For technical reasons diacritical signs are omitted. Editions of the same book in different countries are listed. Indexes of names and subjects serve also as cross-references. An index of journals in which listed articles have appeared is at the end of the volume.

Material has been compiled from primary and secondary sources perused at the Institute of Jewish Affairs and the compiler wishes to express her grateful thanks to Dr. S. J. Roth, Director,and her colleagues at the IJA for all the help and advice she received from them.

Last, but not least, thanks are due to Mrs. Patricia Shevah, Assistant Librarian, who helped with the checking of the entries and also prepared the indexes together with Mrs. Lena Stanley-Clamp, as well as to Miss Sharon Campbell who patiently and carefully typed the draft entries.

E.E.E.

LIST OF DIVISIONS 1976

BIBLIOGRAPHY 1976

REFERENCE

GENERAL REFERENCE BOOKS

COUNCIL OF JEWISH FEDERATIONS AND WELFARE FUNDS Directory: Jewish Federations, Welfare Funds and Commonity Councils, New York, 31p.

Guide touristique européen pour Israélites; European travel guide for Jews, Antwerp, Belgisch Israelitisch Weekflad, 142p.

KOCH, Willi A. Musisches Lexikon. Künstler, Kunstwerke und Motive aus Dichjtung, Musik und Bildender Kunst. ed. Stuttgart, Alfred Kröner, 1290 Cols., Ill, Ind.

Compendium of artists, writers composers and their works.

LEVI, John Simon. The Forefathers. A Dictionary of Biography of the Jews of Australia. 1788-1830. A Special Publication of the Australian Jewish Historical Society 1976-5737. 140p, Ill.

LIGHTMAN, Sidney. (Ed.) The Jewish Travel Guide. 1976. London, Jewish Chronicle, 296p, Ind.

LOCK, Sarah. (Comp.) Survey of Research in Jewish Subjects in Europe. London, Institute of Jewish Affairs, 1976, 61p, Ind.

Research in progress, theses and dissertations since 1970.

RUNES, Dagobert David. (Ed.) Concise Dictionary of Judaism. Westport, Conn., Greenwood P., 124p.

Reprint of the 1966 edition.

ROCKLAND, Mae Shafter and ROCKLAND, Michael Aaron. The Jewish Yellow Pages: A Directory of Goods and Services. New York, London, Schocken, 212p.

Who's Who in World Jewry. 1977. Toronto, Ont., Olive Books of Israel. xxx, 974p.

ENCYCLOPAEDIAS

AVI-YONAH, Michael. (Ed.) Encyclopaedia of Archaeological Excavations in the Holy Land, Oxford, O.U.P., 4 vols.

BIBLIOGRAPHIES

BERLIN, Charles. (Ed.) Hebrew Printing and Bibliography Studies by Joshua Bloch and others. Reprinted from the publications of the New York Public Library on the occasion of the seventy-fifth anniversary of the establishment of the Jewish Division of the New York Public Library. New York, Public Library and Ktav, 11, 518p.

BIHL, Wolfdieter. Bibliographie der österreichischen Hochschulschriften über Judentum and jüdische Persönlichkeiten 1962-74. Wien, Verband der wissenschaftlichen Gesellschaften Österreichs, 32p.

Catalogue of university theses on Jewish subjects presented at Austrian universities 1962-1974.

BUCKLEY, Joseph J. Janusz Korszak Bibliography. _Studies in Bibliography and Booklore_, 11, Nos. 1-b, 1975-76, pp 85-92.

Works of the Jewish educator who perished in Auschwitz.

CHYET, Stanley F. American Jewish Literary Productivity: A Selected Bicentennial Bibliography. _Studies in Bibliography and Booklore_, 11, Nos. 1-2, 1975-76, pp 5-24.

COHEN, Hayyim J. and YEHUDA, Zvi. (Eds.) Asian and African Jews in the Middle East 1860-1971. Annotated Bibliography. Leiden, Brill, xxvii, 453p.

CROWN, A.D. Hebrew Manuscripts and Rare Printed Books in the Fisher Library, University of Sydney, Sydney, Wentworth, 24p. Studies in Australian Bibliography, No. 20.

DELMAIRE, Jean-Marie. Elements de bibliographie du Sionisme. (ouvrages de base et publications recentes). Yod, Revue des Etudes Hebraiques et Juives Modernes et Contemporaines. 2, No. 2, pp 125-136.

DEVORE, Ronald M. (Ed.) Arab-Israeli Conflict: A Historical, Political, Social and Military Bibliography. Oxford, ABC-Clio; European Bibliographical Center. xxxv, 273p, Ind.

A bibliographical study of the Middle East Conflict containing Arab, Israeli, American and other sources.

DUBROVSKY, Gertrude W. The Farmingdale Collection. New York, Yivo, 12p.

Annotated catalogue of the Farmingdale archives of audio-tapes, tape summaries and transcripts, video tapes, papers of community organisations, news cuttings, photographs, etc. deposited in the YIVO Institute of Jewish Research in New York.

EPPLER, Elizabeth E. (Comp. and Ed.) International Bibliography of Jewish Affairs 1966-1967. A select annotated list of books and articles published outside Israel. London, Andre Deutsch for the Institute of Jewish Affairs in Association with the World Jewish Congress, ix, 401p, Indeces.

The items listed cover international Jewish affairs in all their aspects: history, sociology, politics, demography, law, literature, art and biography. Religious studies and belles lettres, with the exception of documentary works, novels and memoirs are excluded.

GOGUEL, Rudi. Antifaschistischer Widerstand und Klassen kampf. Die faschistische Diktatur 1933 bis 1945 und ihre Gegner. Bibliographie deutschsprachiger Literatur aus den Jahren 1945 bis 1973. Berlin (East) Militärverl. d. DDR, 567p.

Bibliography of anti-fascist resistance and class war.

HERMAN, Edward (Assisted by David Cohen, Lisa Landes, Marcia Posner, Fred Stern). Jewish Americans and their Backgrounds. Sources of Information. Chicago, American Library Association, 28p.

Annotated list of the major sources on American Jewish history.

HOROWITZ, Cyma M. (Comp.) The Jewish Woman in the Community: A Selected Annotated Bibliography. New York, Blaustein Library, A.J.C., 7p.

JEWISH BOOK ANNUAL Volume 34, 5737/1976-77. New York, Jewish Book Council of the National Jewish Welfare Board, viii, 235p. Bibl.

In addition to bibliographies of Jewish books published in 1975-76 in the USA, England and Israel, contains, i.a. The Jewish Writer in America: First Century by Sol Liptzin; America's Pioneer Prayer Books by Abraham J. Kamp; The New Israeli Novelists by Leon I. Yudkin; The Zionist Archives and Library by Sylvia Landress; 400 Years of Hebrew Printing in Palestine by G. Kressel; Ahad Ha'am: Wordsmith and Moral Force by Stanley Nash; Yudel Mark: 1897-1975 by Joshua A. Fishman.

LEVI, Trude (Comp. and Ed.) The Gaster Papers. A collection of letters, documents, etc. of the late Haham Dr. Moses Gaster (1856-1939). London, The Library of University College. 52p. (Mimeo)

The late Dr. Gaster's papers are kept at University College, Mocatta Library and have now been catalogued and made accessible to students of the period.

PALESTINE QUESTION: A Select Bibliography. New York, U.N.O. Dag Hammerskjold Library, iv, 63p. (Dag Hammerskjold Library, Bibliographical 22)

SADEK, Vladimir and SÉDINOVA, Jirina. De la Collection des Manuscrits du Musée Juif d'Etat de Prague (Miscellanea) Judaica Bohemiae, 12, No. 2, pp 93-125.

SCHEIBER, Sándor. Hebrew Books at the Buda Fair of 1772. (In Hungarian) Magyar Kőnyvszemle, 92, No. 4, pp 396-97.

List of Hebrew books sold at this famous fair.

A Selected Bibliography of Jewish Canadiana. Montreal. Canadian Jewish Congress.

STEINSCHNEIDER, Moritz.Jewish Literature. From the Eighth to the Eighteenth Century with an Introduction on Talmud and Midrash. New York, Sepher Hermon.

WEINRYB, Bernard D. The Khazars: An Annotated Bibliography II. Studies in Bibliography and Booklore, 11, No. 1-2, W. ppp 57-74.

WOLFE, Ann G. The Jewish Woman in the Community. A Selected Annotated Bibliography. New York, American Jewish Committee, 8p.

WOLFF, Ilse R. (Ed.) German Jewry: Its History, Life and Culture. N.e. Westport, Conn.; Greenwood P., London, Westport Publ. 229p. Ind.

Reprint of catalogue of the Weiner Library (London).

Yiddish Language Study and Standardization: A Selected Bibliography (1968-1977) Yiddishe Shprakh, 35, Nos. 1-3, pp 83-85.

YEARBOOKS

HIMMELFARB, Milton and FINE, Morris (Eds.) American Jewish Yearbook, 77. Philadelphia, Jewish Publication Society of America, New York, American Jewish Committee, 676p.

MASON, Shaindy. (Ed.) Zionist Yearbook 1976/5736-7. London, Zionist Federation of Great Britain and Ireland, 351p, Ind.

The Middle East Yearbook 1977. Prepared by the Centre for Middle Eastern and Islamic Studies, U. of Durham, London, Middle East Magazine, 288p, Ill.

Biased work which does not include Israel among the Middle East nations. The articles deal chiefly with economic questions or international relations of Arab Countries but not the Arab-Israeli conflict.

SCHEIBER, Sándor. Évkönyv. 1975/6, Budapest, Magyar Izraeliták Országos Képvisalete. 1976. 423p.

Yearbook contains essays on the history, life and literature of Hungarian Jews.

STEVENS, Elliott L. (Ed.) Central Conference of American Rabbis. Yearbook, 85, 1975. New York, 315p.

WALLACH, Michael. (Ed.) Jewish Year Book. London, Jewish Chronicle, 1976. 5736-7, xv. 310p, Ind.

WELTSCH, Robert. (Ed.) Yearbook XXI. Publications of the Leo Baeck Institute, New York, London, Jerusalem. London, Secker & Warburg, 1976, xviii, 380p, Ind, Bibl., Ill.

The Jewish Question and Antisemitism II. Contains The Anti-

Jewish Aspect of the Revolutionary Unrest of 1848 in Baden and its Impact on Emancipation by Michael Anthony Riff; The Pace of Modernisation of German Jewry in the 19th century by Steven M. Lowenstein; Jews and Antisemites in Austria at the end of the 19th century by Menachem Z. Rosensaft; The Jews and Modern Capitalism by Werner Sombart; An Analysis of Ideological Premises by Paul R. Mendes-Flohr; German Social Democracy and the Problem of Jewish Nationalism 1897-1917 by Bruce B. Frye; Historians of the German Democratic Republic on Antisemitism and Persecution by Konrad Kwiet; the Ephraim Family by Dolf Michaelis; Baron von Blankenstein - the Career of an Early 19th century Impostor by Walter Schwarz; Henriette Mandelssohn - Unresolved Conflicts of Integration by H. G. Reissner; The Zionist Organisation and the Hilfsverein - Co-operation and Conflict (1901-1914) by Moshe Rinott; Albert Einstein by Banesh Hoffman; Arnold Toynbee by Hans Liebeschuetz; Politics of Translation by Siegfried Kracauer and Walter Benjamin on the Buber- Rosenzweig Bible by Martin Jay.

PRESS/MEDIA

CAHN, Roeger. IW als Spiegel von 75 Jahren Geschichte. Israelitisches Wochenblatt für die Schweiz, 76, No. 21a, Ma. pp 15-29.

75 years of the Swiss Jewish paper.

CARR, Maurice. Israel's Daily Press, The National Jewish Monthly, 90, No. 10, pp 12.

The Early Jewish Press in Canada. A Book Lover's Ramble through Jewish Canadiana, Montreal, Canadian Jewish Congress.

LANG, Emanuel. Zur Geschichte der jüdischen Press in der Schweiz. Separatdruck aus Jüdische Rundschau Maccabi, Basel, No. 21, 20 Mai, 16p.

PAGET, Clarence. Andre Deutsch Ltd. at 25: A Hungarian emigre who made a major impact on British publishing. Publishers Weekly, 210, pp 26-27.

SCHREIBER-CHALUDE, Monique. Rencontre avec Josy Eisenberg. Regards, 12, No. 105, Jy.-Au. pp 11-15.

Rabbi Eisenberg is the producer of a Jewish programme on French television and radio.

VERGELIS, Aron. Sachaklen un oiszichtn. (Achievements and Perspectives) Sovietish Heimland, 16, No. 8, Au. pp 4-12.

The editor of the journal reviews its first fifteen years of publication and outlines the plans for the future.

REPORTS OF INSTITUTES OF JEWISH STUDIES

American Academy for Jewish Research. Proceedings. New York City, A.A.J.R., xvi, 234 + 36 p.

GILSON, Estelle. YIVO - Where Yiddish Scholarship Lives. History and Mission on Fifth Avenue. Present Tense, 4, No. 1, Aut. pp 57-65.

The Yidisher Vissenshaftlekher Institut or Institute for Jewish Research, founded more than fifty years ago in Vilna for graduate studies of East European Jewish in the Yiddish language, now in New York.

KARFF, Samuel. (Ed.) Hebrew Union College - Jewish Institute of Religion at One Hundred Years. Cincinnati, Hebrew Union College, 501p.

KASPI, A. Le Centre de Documentation Juive Contemporaine. Revue d'histoire moderne et contemporaine, 23, No. 2, pp 305-11.
Aims and activities of the Contemporary Jewish Documentation Centre in Paris.

MACIVER, R.M. (Ed.) New Horizons in Creative Thinking: A Survey and Forecast. Institute for Religious and Social Studies. Jewish Theological Seminary of America, Westport, Conn., Greenwood P.; London, Westport P., 159.
Reprint of the 1954 edition.

O'DEA, J.K. Israel With and Without Religion: An Appreciation of Kaufmann's Golah ve-Nekhar. Judaism, 25, No. 1, pp 85-97.
Analysis of Kaufmann's main problem: Jeish Survival in the Diaspora.

SACHAR, Abram L. The Great Brandeis Chair Case. Moment, 2, No. 2, pp 23-6; 47-50.

SONDHEIMER, Elizabeth. The Dorfmann Jewish Library in Lima, Ohio. Reconstructionist, 42, No. 1, pp 21-4.

PHILOSOPHY – RELIGION

ARENDT, Hannah. Die verborgene Tradition. Acht Essays, Frankfurt/M. Suhrkamp, 169p. (Suhrkamp Taschenbuch 300).
The essays include: Heinrich Heine: Schlemihl und Traumwelt-herrscher; Bernard Lazare: Der bewusste Paria; Franz Kafka: Der Mensch mit dem guten Willen; Juden in der Welt von Gestern: Franz Kafka; Aufklaerung und Judenfrage; Der Zionismus aus heutiger Sicht.

BAKAN, D. Freud e la tradizione mistica ebraica. Psicoanalisi e cabala. Comunita, 30, No. 176, pp 206-44.
Draws a parallel between Freud's instructions and the Kabbalist tradition of the Zohar.

BEN-HORIN, Meir. Jewish Secularism in Transition - Can It Return? Judaism, 25, No. 4, Fa. pp 473-88.
"Jewish Secularism has been in transition too long. Now is the time to enter the post-transition era, the era of the Trans-Secular."

BOROWITZ, Eugene B. The Prospects for Jewish Denominationalism. Conservative Judaism, 30, No. 4, pp 64-74.
Differences between various forms of Judaism are insignificant compared with the bonds that hold Jews together.

CHALIER, Catherine. Kierkegaard et le judaisme. Les Nouveaux Cahiers, 12, No. 44, Sp. pp 56-64.

DERCZANSKI, Alex. Itinéraire de Gerhard Gerschom Scholem. (English Summary) Recherches de Science Religieuse, 64, No. 2, pp 271-84.
Analyses Gerschom Scholem's road to Jewish mysticism.

FILLOUX, J.C. Il ne faut pas oublier que je suis fils de rabbin. (Summaries in English, German, Russian, Spanish) Revue Francaise de Sociologie, 17, No. 2, pp 259-66.
The importance of the father figure in Durkheim's philosophy

FRIEDMAN, Maurice. Divine Need and Human Wonder: the Philosophy of

Abraham J. Heschel. Judaism, 25, No. 1, pp 67-78.
GOLDSTEIN, Simeon. The "Jewish Position" Game. Jewish Life, 31, No. 1, W. pp 27-37.
"Judaism should not be utilized as a mirror to reflect the personal views of those who speak in its name."
GOODMAN, Saul L. The Faith of Secular Jews. New York, Ktav, viii, 301p. (Library of Judaic Learning).
GORDIS, Robert. A Basis for Morals: Ethics in a Technological Age. Judaism, 25, No. 4, W. pp 20-43.
Essay on "the need to discover a firm basis for an ethical system in a pluralistic world where religion no longer commands universal assent or can even claim a consensus."
HALPERIN, Jean and LEVITTE, George. (Eds.) Le conscience juive face à la guerre. Donnees et débats. Préface de Jean Halperin, 16e Collogue d'Intellectuals juifs de langue francaise organisé par la Section Française du Congres Juif Mondial. Paris, x, 163p.
The papers discuss Jewish attitudes to war. They are: Essay d'analyse philosophique de la guerre by Robert Misrahi; Ethique et guerre dans la pensée traditionelle juive by Elie Tomstat; Les juifs, la paix et les guerres au xxe siècle by Annie Kriegel; Analyse politique de la guerre by Stanley Hoffman; Guerre, violence agressivité et la conscience historique de la psychalanyse by Pierre Fedida; Kippour de Guerre à Jerusalem by Claude Vigee; L'etat de guerre; répercussions sur l'individu et la société by A. B. Yehoshua and Le Juif et la guerre by Elie Wiessel.
HEILMAN, Samuel C. Synagogue Life: A Study in Symbolic Interaction. Chicago, London, U. of Chicago P., xiii, 306p, Ind, Bibl.
HERTZBERG, Arthur. Dilemma of the Jewish Secularist. Congress Monthly, 43, No. 10, D. pp 6-7.
HOENIG, Sidney B. The Orthodox Rabbi as a Military Chaplain. Tradition, 16, No. 2, Fa. pp 35-60.
HRUBY, K. L'amore del prossimo nel pensiero ebraico. Humanitas, 31, No. 4, pp 259-77.
"Your neighbour" means all mankind in the Jewish tradition.
JACOBS, Louis. Hasidic Thought. New York, Behrman House, 246p.
KAPLAN, Lawrence J. The Dilemma of Conservative Judaism. Commentary, 62, No. 5, pp 44-47.
Changing Self-Concepts of Reform Rabbis: 1976. CCAR Journal, 24, No. 2, Su. pp 51-56.
KAUFMAN, William. (Ed.) Contemporary Jewish Philosophies. New York, Behrman House/Reconstructionist P., xii, 276p, Ind.
Clarifies the new forms of Jewish philosophic enquiry in response to the Holocaust, the American Jewish experience and the establishment of the State of Israel.
LEVINAS, Emmanuel. Difficile Liberté - Essais sur le Judaisme. 2nd ed. Paris, Albin Michel, 382p.
LEVINE, Baruch A. The Israelites. London, Time-Life International. 160p, Ind, Ill. (Emergence of Man S.)
Traces the history of the Israelites who "without great wealth or sweeping military conquests quietly pioneered a new kind of religious thinking that has dominated Western civilization for over 2,000 years."

LUKACS, György. Tudományos emlékülés Lukacs György születésének 90. évforduloja alkalmábol. - HERMANN István: Lukacs György gondolatainak aktualitása - LUKACS József: A vallás és az irracionalizmus vizsgálatanak néhány problémaja Lukács György életmüvében - ZOLTAI Denes: Lukács György marxista esztétikai munkássága, a hazai esztetika fejlödese - NAGY Peter: Lukács György es a magyar irodalom - UJFALUSSY Jozsef: Lukacs György es a magyar zenetudomany - MIKLOS Pál: Lukacs György és a müvészettudomany. *Acta Philosophica et Historica Academiae Scientairum Hungaricac*, 22, No. 1, pp 3-56.

Papers presented at the special session of the Hungarian Academy of Sciences to commemmorate Lukacs's 90th birthday.

MARTHE, Robert. (Ed.) Sigmund Freud - zwischen Moses und Oedipus. Die jüdischen Wurzeln der Psychoanalyse. München, List, 192p.

Essays on the founder of psychoanalysis and the specifically Jewish roots of this science.

NEUMANN, H. Superman or Last Man? Nietzsche's Interpretation of Athens and Jerusalem. *Nietzsche Studien*, 5, pp 1-28.

NEUSNER, Jacob. Invitation to the Talmud. New York, Harper & Row, 263p.

PEARL, Chaim. Orthodoxy's Political Conservatism. *Jewish Spectator*, 41, No. 2, Su. pp 23-6.

PILKINGTON, A.E. Bergson and his Influence: A Reassessment. Cambridge, UP., vii, 253p.

RACHLIS, Arnold. Struggle and Search: Reconstructionist Today. *Reconstructionist*, 42, No. 5, Ju. pp 15-19.

RAPHAEL, Fredy. Les Juifs en tant que peuple paria dans l'oeuvre de Max Weber. *Soc. Compass*, 23, No. 4, pp 397-426. (English Summary)

Weber saw the Jews only as German-Jewish assimilated intellectuals, thus underestimating the theo-political dimension of Jewish society and the idea of Jewish peoplehood.

RECONSTRUCTIONIST RABBINICAL COLLEGE ISSUE. *Reconstructionist*, 42, No. 6, Ju. pp 1-36.

Includes: Reconstructionism - A School of Thought or a Religious Denomination? by Neal Weinberg; Struggle and Search: Reconstructionism Today by Arnold Rachlis; The Reconstructionist Approach to Halakhah by Ilene Schneider.

ROSENBLOOM, Noah H. Tradition in an Age of Reform. The Religious Philosophy of Samson Raphael Hirsch. Philadelphia, Jewish Publ. Soc. of America, 490p, Bibl, Ind.

ROSENTHAL, Gilbert S. Jewish Religion in America: A Study in Mutuality. *Judaism*, 25, No. 3, Su. pp 290-300.

ROSENZWEIG, Franz. Der Mensch und sein Werk. Gesammelte Schriften, II, Der Stern der Erlösung. Haag, Nijhoff, 464p.

Re-edition of "The Star of Redemption".

RUBENSTEIN, Richard L. The Religious Imagination. A Study in Psychoanalysis and Jewish Theology. Boston, Beacon P., n.e. xviii, 246p., Ind., Bibl. (Beacon Paperback 385)

Argues that psychological mechanisms of powerlessness inherent in Jewish theology have, in the light of Auschwitz, made the traditional body of Jewish legend and belief obsolete.

RUSSELL, Bertrand. La Filosofia di Bergson. Rome, Newton Compton, 87p.

SCHOCKEN, Wolfgang Alexander. The Calculated Confusion of Calendars: Puzzles in Christian, Jewish and Muslim Calendars. New York, Vantage P. 81p.

SCHOLEM, G. On Jews and Judaism in Crisis. Selected Essays. Edited by W. J. Dannhauser. New York, Schocken Books, 306p. Interview of Scholem by Miki Tsur.

Jewish Youth Movement. Farewell: An Open Letter to Dr. Siegfried Bernfeld. Against the Myth of the German-Jewish Dialogue. Jews and Germans. S.Y. Agnon - The Last Hebrew Classic? Agnon in German: Recollections. Martin Buber's Conception of Judaism. Walter Benjamin. Walter Benjamin and His Angel. Two Letters to Walter Benjamin. Israel and the Diaspora. Reflections on Jewish Theology. On Eichmann: Eichmann. Letter to Hannah Arendt.

SCHWARTZ, Charles and Bertie G. A Modern Interpretation of Judaism. Faith Through Reason. New York, Schocken, 208p.

SCULT. Mel. The Sociologist as Theologian: The Fundamental Assumptions of Mordecai Kaplan's Thought. Judaism, 25, No. 3, Su. pp 345-52.

SIMON, H. Abraham ibn Daud. Verdienst und Grenzen. Kairos, 18, No. 1, pp 66-71.

Examines the work of the Toledo aristotelian philosopher.

SLOYAN, Gerard S. The Religious Shape of the Twenty First Century. Face to Face, 1, W/Sp. pp 15-16.

SPERO, Shubert. Encounters Between Judaism and Modern Philosophy. Tradition, 15, No. 4, Sp., pp 113-25.

STEINSALTZ, Abraham. The Essential Talmud. London, Weidenfeld & Nicolson, 208p.

Introduction to the study of Talmud.

TALMON, Shemaryahu. Martin Buber's Ways of Interpreting the Bible. Journal of Jewish Studies, 27, No. 2, pp 195-209.

------------------. Partikularismus und Universalismus aus jüdischer Sicht. Freiburger Rundbrief, 28, No. 105-8, pp 33-6.

TRUTWIN, Werner. Licht vom Licht. Religionen in unserer Welt. Dusseldorf, Patmos, 336p, Ill, Bibl.

The first, long chapter discusses the Jews.

VOGEL, Leon. Document: Moise l'egyptien ou la nevrose de Sigmund (Freud). L'Arche, 232, Jy. pp 46-55.

Refutes Freud's view that Moses was an Egyptian.

WEINBERG, Neal. Reconstructionism - A School of Thought or a Religious Denomination? Reconstructionist, 42, No. 5, Ju. p 7-15.

WEINGREEN, J. From Bible to Mishna: The Continuity of Tradition. Manchester, U.P., 164p.

WERBLOWSKY, Zwi R.J. Beyond Tradition and Modernity, Changing Religions in a Changing World. Jordan Lectures in Comparative Religion, 11th Series, London, Athlone P., ix, 146p.

WIESELTIER, Leon. Philosophy, Religion and Harry Wolfson. Commentary, 61, No. 4, Ap. pp 57-64.

WILBUR, James B. Spinoza's Metaphysics: Essays in Critical Appreciation. Assen, Van Gorcum, 176p.

BIOGRAPHIES, AUTOBIOGRAPHIES, LETTERS

ABERBACH, Moses. The Life and Letters of Doctor Jonas Friedenwald. Baltimore, Jewish Historical Society of Maryland, 30p.

ABZUG, Bella. Bella on Bella. Moment, 2, No. 6, pp 26-9.
A brief autobiographical sketch by New York's 20th Congressional District representative.

AGUINAS, Marcos. Maimonides. Buenos Aires, Congreso Judio Latinoamericano, 32p., Ill. (Biblioteca Popular Judaica, Grandes Figuras del Judaismo 97).

ALLON, Yigal. My Father's House. Tr. fr. Hebrew by R. Ben-Yosef. Ill. by Shirley Hirsch. New York, W.W. Norton, 204p.
Israel's Foreign Minister remembers his childhood and youth in a village in Galilee.

ALMANSI, Renato J. Mio Padre, Dante Almansi. La Rassegna Mensile di Israel, 42, No. 5-6, Ma.-Ju. pp 234-55.
President of the Union of Italian Jewish communities during Nazi occupation (d. 1978).

ALPERIN, Aaron. Nahum Goldmann. Tr. fr. Yiddish by Marcelo Sneh. Buenos Aires, Congreso Judio Latinoamericano. 48p., Ill. (Grandes Figuras del Judaismo 100).
Biography of the President of the World Jewish Congress.

BACH, Hans. Moses Mendelssohn. European Judaism, 10, No. 2, Su. pp 24-30.

BACHMANN, L.P. Julius Rosenwald. American Jewish Historical Quarterly, 66, No. 1, pp 89-105.
The great Jewish philanthropist, benefactor of the Blacks.

BARON, Salo W. Hannah Arendt (1906-1975) Personal Notes. Jewish Social Studies, 38, No. 2, Sp. pp 187-89.
Written on her death.

BECK, Samuel J. Karl Marx: A Psychological Portrait. Jewish Spectator, 41, No. 3, Fa. pp 14-18.
Analyses the reasons for Marx's Jewish self-hatred.

BENARI, Yehuda. Trumpeldor. Buenos Aires, Congreso Judio Latinoamericano, 40p. (Grandes Figuras del Judaismo 95)

BENJAMIN, Walter. Munich, Edition text + kritik, 92p.
Short biography.

BERKMAN, Edward O. The Lady and the Law, the Remarkable Story of Fanny Boltzmann. New York, Little, Brown, 393p.

BERMANT, Chaim. Coming Home. London, Allen & Unwin, 220p.
Autobiography of an Anglo-Jewish writer.

BIDERMAN. Israel M. Mayer Balaban. Historian of Polish Jewry. New York, Dr. I. M. Biderman Book Committee, xxv, 334p, Bibl., Indeces.

BIKOVSKIY, Lev. Solomon Izrailevich Goldelman, 1885-1974. biobibliografichni materiyali. Denver, Ukrainskiy Sukhodoloviy Institut, 293p. (English title page and summary).

BLUMBERG, Stanley and OWENS, Gwinn. Energy and Conflict. The Life and Times of Edward Teller. New York, Putnams.
Biography of the nuclear physicist, "father of the hydrogen bomb".

BLUMENFELD, Kurt. Im Kampf um den Zionismus. Briefe aus fuenf Jahrzehnten. Hg. Miriam Sambursky und Jochanan Ginat. Stuttgart, DVA, 311p., Ind. (Veroeffentlichungen des Leo Baeck Instituts).
Blumenfeld was one of Germany's most important Zionist leaders, deeply committed from an early youth; he correspondended with the leaders of the movement in the 20th century.

BRANDT. Willy. Begegnungen und Einsichten, Die Jahre 1960-75. Hamburg, Hoffman und Campe, 655p., Ill.
Memoirs of Brandt's years as Foreign Minister and Chancellor with details of his Ostpolitik, his attitude to the Arab-Israeli Conflict and meetings with Dr. Nahum Goldmann, President of the W.J.C.

BRUDE-FIRNAU, Gisela. (Ed.) Vision und Politik. Die Tagebuecher T Theodor Herzls. Frankfurt/M., Suhrkamp, 352p, Ind., Bibl., (Suhrkamp Taschenbuch 374).
Excerpts from the diaries of Theodor Herzl with annotations and an epilogue by the editor.

BUBER, Martin and SCHAEDER, Grete. Briefwechsel aus sieben Jahrzehnten. 1. 1897-1918; 2. 1918-1938; 3. 1938-1965. Heidelberg, Lambert Schneider.
Correspondence between Martin Buber and Grete Schaeder.

BURTON, Anthony. Josiah Wedgwood. London, Andre Deutsch, 240p, Ind., Ill.
Biography of the noted British politician who was a staunch supporter of Zionism.

CARPOZI, George. Bugsy: Benjamin "Bugsy" Siegal. London, Futura, 192p, Ill. (Everest Books)
Biography of the Jewish gangster.

RENE CASSIN ET L'ALLIANCE ISRAELITE UNIVERSELLE. Paris, ATU, 12p, Ill.
Memorial Brochure.

CHIERICI, Maurizio. Dayan. Novara, Istituto Geografico de Agostini, 192p.
Biography.

CHISSIN, Chaim. A Palestine Diary. Memoirs of a Bilu Pioneer 1882-1887. New York, The Herzl P., 281p.
One of the very first Jewish pioneers to settle in Palestine describes his and his comrades lives.

CHOURAQUI, Andre. René Cassin et l'aventure d'Israël. Les Nouveaux Cahiers, 12, No. 45, Su. pp 20-29.

CLARK, Ronald W. Einstein. Tr. Lydia Magliano. Milano, Rizzoli, 734p.
Biography.

CLARENS, Carlos. Cukor. London, Secker & Warburg, 224p., Ill. (Cinema One S.)
Biography of George Cukor.

COERVER, D.M. and HALL, L.B. Neiman-Marcus: Innovators in Fashion and Merchandising. American Jewish Historical Quarterly, 66, No. 1, pp 123-36.
The firm was founded by Herbert Marcus and A.L. Neiman.

COMBY, Louis. Leon Trotsky. Paris, 183p. ("Leur Vie").
Short biography.

CONSIDINE, Bob. Larger Than Life (Dr. Armand Hammer) London, W.H. Allen, 287p, Ill.
Biography of the famous art collector.

CONGDON, Lee. Karl Polanyi in Hungary 1900-1919. Journal of Contemporary History, 11, No. 1, Ja. pp 167-83.
Noted economist and anthropologist (1881-1964)

COWLES, Virginia. Die Rothschilds (1763-1973) Geschichte einer Familie. Tr. fr. English by J.J. von Koskull. Freiburg/Br. Ploetz, 304p, Ill.

DAVIDSON, Margaret. The Golda Meir Story. New York, Scribner, 211p.
Biography.

DAVIS, Richard W. Disraeli. London, Hutchinson; New York, Little, Brown, xviii, 231p, Ind.
Biography.

DAYAN, Moshe. Story of My Life. London, Weidenfeld and Nicolson, ix, 530p, Ind, Ill. (In German: Wien, München, Zurich, Fritz Molden. In French: Paris, Fayard.)
Israel's former Defence Minister and Chief of Staff reveals i.a. the background to the 1956 Suez War and the subsequent wars of 1967 and 1973.

EBON, Martin. Amazing Uri Geller. New American Library, 168p, Ill-

ELKINS, Dov Peretz. Shepherd of Jerusalem: A Biography of Rabbi Abraham Isaac Kook. New York, Shengold, 136p, Ill.

ENGELBOURG, S. Edward A. Filene: Merchant, Civic Leader and Jew. American Jewish Historical Quarterly, 66, No. 1, pp 106-22.
A very assimilated Jewish businessman.

ENGELMAN, Edmund. Sigmund Freud's Home and Offices, Vienna 1938. Photographs and Memoir. Intro. by Peter Gay. New York, Basic Books, 144p.

FEINGOLD, S. Norman and SILVERMAN, William B. (Eds.) Kivie Kaplan: A Legend in His Own Time. New York, Union of American Hebrew Congregations, vii, 258p.
A staunch supporter and national president of the National Association for the Advancement of Coloured People, a dedicated member of the Reform Jewish movement.

FEUER, Lewis S. Recollections of Harry Austryn Wolfson. American Jewish Archives, 28, No. 1, Ap. pp 25-50.
Historian of Philosophy.

FISHER OF CAMDEN, LORD. (Samuel Fisher). Brodetsky - Leader of the Anglo-Jewish Community. Leeds U.P. 28p. (The Seventeenth Selig Brodetsky Memorial Lecture delivered in the University of Leeds on 17 May)
The President of the Board of Deputies of British Jews on Prof. Selig. Brodetsky, one of his eminent predecessors.

FOGELIN, Robert J. Wittgenstein. London, Routledge, 239p.
Monograph of the philosopher.

FOWLES, Edward. Memories of the Duveen Brothers. (Ed. by Colin Simpson) London, Times Books, 215p.
The Duveen brothers were great art dealers.

FOX, M. Law and Ethics in Modern Jewish Philosophy: The Case of Moses Mendelssohn. Proceedings of the American Academy of Jewish Research, 43, pp 1-13.

FREUD, Ernst, FREUD, Lucie, GRUBRICH-SIMITIS, Ilse. Sigmund Freud, sein Leben in Bildern und Texten. Eingeleitet von K.R. Eissler, Gestaltet von Willy Fleckhaus, Frankfurt/M., Suhrkamp, 352p.
Published for the centenary of Freud's birth.

FREUD, Martin, Freud mon père. Paris, Denoël.

FRIEDMAN, Maurice. Martin Buber: The Life of Dialogue. Chicago, U. of Chicago P., xviii, 322p.

GELLER, Uri. My Story. Hollywood, Warner Bros., Ill. 272p.
An Israeli who claims he has extra-sensory powers.

GIRARD, Patrick. Isaac de la Peyrere. Les Nouveaux Cahiers, 12, No. 44, Sp. pp 36-45.
French Sephardi rabbi (died 1728) as chazan of a Marrano fugitive community in Bayonne.

GLASER, Hermann. Sigmund Freuds zwanzigstes Jahrhundert. Seelenbilder einer Epoche. Munchen, Hanser, 512p.

GOLDMEIER, Harold. Changing Views of God Among American Jews. Religious Education, 71, No. 1, Ja/F. pp 57-67.
Attitudes of Conservative Jewish Parents, who may believe in God but not the Covenant.

GRUNENBERG, Antonia. Bürger und Revolutionär. Georg Lukacs, 1918-1928. Foreward: Frank Benseler. Frankfurt/M., Europ, 300p.

HALTER, Marek. Le fou et les rois. Paris, Albin Michel. 288p.
Autobiography. The author escaped from the Warsaw Ghetto to Russia, lived in a kilkhoz and in 1949 went to France where he became a painter of some repute. After the Six Day War he formed the International Committee for Peace in the Middle East and published the journal 'Elements'.

HART, Dorothy. Thou Swell, Thou Witty: The Life and Lyrics of Lorenz Hart. New York, Harper & Row, 192p. Ill.

HAUSER, Martin. Auf dem Heimweg; aus den Tagebüchern eines deutschen Juden, 1929-1945. Bonn, Hohwacht, 228p. Ill.

HELFET, Arnold. Immanuel Jakobovits. Chief Rabbi of the United Hebrew Congregation of the British Commonwealth. Jewish Affairs, 31, No. 1, Ja. pp 23-25.

HERZEN, Alexander. Memoirs. Tr. fr. Russian J.D. Duff. Westport, Conn., Greenwood P.; London, Westport P., xvi, 384p.
Facsimile of the 1923 edition.

HOFFMAN, Michael J. Gertrude Stein. London, G. Prior, 185p. (World Authors S.)
Monograph.

IRWIN, William Henry. House that Shadows Built: Biography of Adolph Zukor. New York, Arno, 260p, Ill.
Biography of the motion picture pioneer.

ISRAEL, Gerard. René Cassin, grandeur et servitude. Les Nouveaux' Cahiers, 12, No. 44, Sp. pp 2-4.
In memory of the Nobel Laureate.

JAMES, Robert Rhodes. Victor Cazalet. A Portrait. London, Hamish Hamilton, xiv, 306p, Ind.
Victor Cazalet, a Conservative Member of Parliament, was a vehement champion of the Zionist cause, a friend of Dr. Weizmann and a leading British anti-Nazi, who died in the same plane crash as General Sikorski.

KAGANOFF, N.M. The Business Career of Haym Salomon As Reflected in His Newspaper Advertisements. American Jewish Historical Quarterly, 66, No. 1, pp 36-47.
Best-known Jew in 18th century America.

KAHN, Lothar. Ludwig Börne. First Jewish Champion of Democracy. Judaism, 25, No. 4, Fa. pp 420-34.

KEEL, O. Yohanan Aharoni. 1919-1976. Leben und Werk eines führenden israelischen Biblikers und Archäologen. (Y.A. Vie et ouvre d'un bibliste et archeologue israelien remarquable). Judaica, 32, No. 2, pp 70-75.
Biography of the excavator of Ramat Rahel and Hazor.

KEENE, Raymond D. Leonard Stein. Master of Attack, London, Hale, 154p.
Biography.

KOMLOS, Aladár. Kritikus számadás. (Critical Reckoning) Budapest, Szepirodalmi, 663p.
Selection of the author's essays written over 50 years and published to mark his 85th birthday.

--------------. Tárgyi bizonyitékok. (Pályam emlékezete sorozat). Ujlras, 15, No. 7, Jy. pp 121-28.
Memoirs of a Jewish writer and literary historian.

KUNZLI, Arnold. Karl Marx - Eine Psychographie. Wien, Europaverlag. 872p.

LAPPIN, Ben. The Legacy of Dr. Samuel B. Hurwich. Viewpoints, 9, No. 4, Fa./W. pp 63-68.
Canadian Jewish Physician, labour Zionist.

LATTES, Dante. Scritti. Rassegna Mensile di Israel, 42, Nos. 9-10, Se-O, 428p.
Special centenary issue devoted to the Italian Jewish scholar.

LAWRENCE, David Herbert. Letters to Thomas and Adele Seltzer. Ed. by Gerald M. Lacy. Santa Barbara, Black Sparrow P., xiv, 284p, Ill.

LERNER, R. Leo Strauss (1899-1973) American Jewish Yearbook, 76, pp 91-97.
Biography and works of the historian and philosopher.

LEVENBERG, S. 35 Years Since the Death of Simon Dubnow. Jewish Frontier, 43, No. 9, N. pp 20-26.

LEVIN LEE, Alexandra. Henrietta Szold Baltimorean. Baltimore, Associated Jewish Charities and Welfare Fund. The Jewish Historical Society, 20p.
A Bicentennial Publication of the Jewish Historical Society of Maryland.

LICHTEN, Joseph. The Life, Work and Message of Abrahm Joshua Heschel. Angelicum, 52, No. 4, pp 531-40.

LITVINOFF, Barnet. Weizmann, Last of the Patriarchs. London, Hodder & Stoughton, 288p, Ill., Ind., Bibl.

LOEWE, L.L. Basil Henriques: A Portrait. Based on his Diaries. Letters and Speeches Collated by his widow Lady Rose Henriques. London, Routledge, 193p, Ill.

LOWENTHAL, Marvin. Henrietta Szold, Life and Letters. Westport, Conn., Greenwood P., ix, 350p, Ill.
Reprint of the 1972 edition.

Georg Lukacs. Munich, text + kritik, 90p.
Life and work.

LUXEMBURG, Rosa. Briefe an Freunde. Ed. B. Kautsky, Köln, Europäische Verlagsanstalt, 172p.

MACDONALD, Malcolm. Schoenberg. London, Dent, 300p, Ill, (Master Musicians S.)
Monograph.

MCKENNA, Marion. Myra Hess. London, Hamish Hamilton, 320p, Ill.
Biography of the Pianist.

MALKA, Victor. Pierre Mendès France: Mes Origines. <u>L'Arche</u>,19, No. 228, Ma. pp 36-40.
 Interview.
MANZONI, Giacomo. Arnold Schoenberg. L'uomo, l'opera i testi musicali. Milano, Feltinelli, 417p.
 Biography of the composer with a hitherto unpublished early work.
MARX, Arthur. Goldwyn: Man Behind the Myth. London, Bodley Head, 376p, Ill.
 Biography of Sam. Goldwyn.
MARX, Groucho. The Grouchophile. An Illustrated Life. New York, Bobbs-Merrill, Ill.
MARX, Groucho with ARCE, Hector. The Jewish World in Groucho. New York, Putnam.
MARX, Harop and BARBER, Rowland. Harpo Speaks. London, Robson, 456p, Ill.
 Biography.
MARX, Samuel and CLAYTON, Jan. Rodgers and Hart: Bewitched, Bothered and Bedeviled! An Anecdotal Account. New York, Putnam, Ill.
MAYER, Sir. Robert. My First Hundred Years. Gerrards Cross, Van Duran, 140p, Ill.
 The great Jewish music lover's memoirs.
MEDALIA, Leon S. My First Ninety Years: A Doctor's Odyssey. New York, Fountainhead, xix, 396p.
MEIJER, Jaap. Victor van Vriesland als Zionist. Een vergeten hoofstuk uit de geschiedenis van het Joods nationalisme in Nederland. Heemstede, 78p.
 Van Vriesland was an important Dutch Zionist.
MENDES-FRANCE, Pierre. La vérité guidait leurs pas. Paris, Gallimard 258p. (Coll. "Temoins")
 Autobiography.
MÖLLER, Dietrich. Karl Radek in Deutschland. Revolutionär Intrigant, Diplomat. Köln, Wissenschaft und Politik, 303p.
 The Russian Jewish revolutionary who became a victim of the Stalinist purges of the 30's.
NAGIEL, Isy. Nahum Goldmann: l'homme - l'action les idees. <u>Regards</u>, 12, No. 105, Jy-Au. pp 5-10.
NARDI, Shulamith. The Writer-President Zalman Shazar (1889-1974). <u>Jewish Affairs</u>, 31, No. 1, Ja. pp 41-43.
Nel Primo centenario della Nascita di Dante Lattes. <u>La Raseegna Mensile di Israel</u>, 42, No. 9-10, S-O. (Special Issue)
 Essays and articles on the Italian Jewish scholar (1876-1965)
NEUMANN, Emanuel. In the Arena. An Autobiographical Memoir. New York, Herzl P., xx, 374p, Ind.
 Emanuel Neumann, a leading figure in American Zionism was involved in negotiations with the Emir Abdullah during the Mandate period and was one of the chief protagonists in the drama of the partition negotiations at the UN.
NOREN, Catherine. The Camera of my Family. New York, Knopt and Random House, 240p.
 A German Jewish family.

PFABIGAN, Alfred. Karl Kraus und der Sozialismus. Eine politische Biographie. Wien, Zurich, München, Europa, 364p.
Political biography of the Austrian Jewish socialist.
POLIER, Shad. In Memoriam. Congress Monthly, 43, No. 7, S. pp 3-6.
On the death of the American and World Jewish Congress leader, son-in-law of Stephen Wise.
POLLACK, Herman. A Forgotten Fighter for Justice: Ben Goldstein-Lowell. Jewish Currents, 30, No. 6, Ju. pp 14-18.
POSZLER, György. Emlekezeses meditacio. (Memory and Meditation) Nagyvilag, 21, No. 5, My. pp 749-53.
Commemmorates the 75th birthday of the Hungarian Jewish literary historian and novelist, killed by the Nazis in 1944.
POTTER, Jeffrey. Men, Money and Magic. The Story of Dorothy Schiff. New York, Coward, McCann & Geoghegan, 352p, Ill.
PRYCE-JONES, David. Elie Kedourie's Achievement. Encounter, 46, No. 2, F. pp 54-57.
Essay on the noted Middle East political scientist.
REIF, Adalbert. Gespraeche mit Hannah Arendt. Munchen Piper, 127p, Ind., Bibl. (S Piper 138)
Includes the biographical television interview with Gunther Gaus and the short interview with Thilo Koch on the Eichmann case.
REIK, Theodor. Trente ans avec Freud. (Suivi de la correspondence inédité de Freud a Reik) Brussels, Editions Complexe, 110p.
Describes his work at Freud's side and publishes his correspondence with him.
ROAZEN, Paul. Freud and His Followers. London, Allen Lane; New York, Knopf, 614p, Ill. (In German: Bergisch Gladbach, Lubbe)
ROSENBAUM, E. and SHERMAN, A.J. Das Bankhaus M.M. Warburg & Co. 1798-1938. Hamburg, Hans Christians. 235p, Ill.
History of the famous bank.
ROSENBERG, M.J. Mordecai Noah. Diplomat, Showman, Prophet. National Jewish Monthly, 90, No. 11, Jy-Au. pp 7-14.
ROSENSTEIN, Neil. The Unbroken Chain. Biographical Sketches and the Genealogy of Illustrious Jewish Families from the 15th-20th Century. New York, Shengold, 716p.
ROTH, Cecil. The House of Nasi: Dona Gracia. Westport, Conn., Greenwood P., xiii, 208p, Ill.
Reprint og the 1948 edition.
RUBENSTEIN, Hilary. Complete Insomniac. London, Coronet, 224p.
Autobiography of literary agent.
SACHAR, Abram Leon. A Host at Last. Boston, Mass., Little, Brown, 308p, Ill.
Memories of the author's incumbency as President of Brandeis University.
SCHEIN, Clarence J. Surgeon at Work. New York, Stein & Day.
SCHOEPS, Joachim Hans. Aron Bernstein, ein liberaler Volkaufklärer, Schriftsteller und Religionsreformer. Zeitschrift für Religious und Geistesgeschichte, 28, No. 3, pp 223-44.
Biography of founded of Volks-Zeitung, (earlier Urwähler Zeitung) and reformer of Jewish political life.

SCHRAGER, F. Oyfn rand fun tsvey tkufes (zikhroynes). En marge de deux époques. Paris, Author, 328p.
Memoirs by an East European Jew about his childhood and years in a Hebrew School, his studies and political activities in France, POW camp and resistance movement and ending with his activities in ORT after the war.

SCHUR, Max. Il Caso di Freud. Torino, Boringhieri, 470p.
Biography of Freud written by his physician who attended him during his long fight with cancer.

SCHWEITZER, Gertrude. The Herzog Legacy. New York, Doubleday,
On Yaaoov Herzog.

SEGRE, Victor. Vita et Morte di Trotskij. Bari, Laterza, 360p.

SELIGMAN, Ceasar. Erinnerungen (1860-1950). Ed. by Erwin Seligman, Frankfurt/M., Waldemar Kramer, 207p.
Autobiography.

SHARF, Andrew. The Universe of Shabbetai Donnolo, Leiden, Brill, 232p, Ill.
A Jewish doctor born in Southern Italy in 913AD. The author of a herbal and traditionally one of the founders of Europe's first medical school at Salerno.

SOLOMON, Joseph. Autobiography. American Jewish Archives, 28, No. 1, Ap. pp 51-58.

SOWDEN, Dora. He Knows How to Put Things. Jewish Affairs, 36, No. 7, Jy. pp 31-32.
On Yigal Allon.

SPADA, James. Barbara, the First Decade: Films and Career of Barbara Streisand. New York, Citadel P., 224p, Ill.

SPANDER, Rose. Lillian Wald, Mother of Nursing Services. Condensed from Emanu-El Jewish Center Bulletin. Jewish Digest, 21, No. 8, My. pp 14-15.

STEINER, Edward A. From Alien to Citizen: The Story of My Life in America. New York, Arno P., 332p, Ill. (Modern Jewish Experience S.)
Facsimile of 1914 edition.

STOESSINGER, John G. Henry Kissinger: The Anguish of Power. New York, Norton, x, 234p.

SWALLOW, Norman. Eisenstein: Documentary Portrait. London, Allen & Unwin, 156p, Ill.

SWARTZ, Helen M. and SWARTZ, Marvin (Eds.) Disraeli Reminiscences. Braincliff Manor, New York, Stein & Day; London, Hamish Hamilton, 256p.

SZAPIRO, E. Archives Debré. Archives Juives, 12, Nos. 1-2.
Family documents from the 18th-20th centuries, supplied by Prof. Debré.

SZEKELYHIDI, Vilmos: Zala-Karlstein-Moszkva. Hamburger Jenö (1883-1936). E'lét es Tudsmá'ny, 10D, pp 2355-59.
Life and work of Jeno" Hamburger.

SZILARD, Leo levelei. (Letters of L. Szilard) Comp. Lászlo Timár. Tr. Judit Elek. Kritika, 12, No. 7, Jy. pp 5-8.

EMLEKEIM SZILARD LEOROL. D. Hawkins professzorral beszelget Kunfalvi Rezsö. Fizikaitzem le, 86, No. 9, S. pp 353-56.
Professor D. Hawkins' memoirs of the atomic physicist Leo Szilard.

TAMANI, G. A. Firkovic, archeologo bibliofilo e scrittore caraita. Studia Pataviana, 23, No. 2, pp 337-49.
Biography of Abraham Firkovic (1786-1874) archaelogist and expert on the Karaites.

TEENSMA, B.N. L'autobiographie d'Abraham Perelgrino alias Manuel Cardosa de Macedo (in Dutch with English Summary) Studia Rosenthaliana, 10, No. 1, pp 1-36.
Annotated biography of Portuguese proselyte

TROTSKY, Leon. Diary in Exile, 1935. Tr. fr. Russian by E. Zarudnaya. Cambridge, Mass., London, Harvard, U.P., xviii, 218p, Ill. Ind.,
A reissue of a book first published in 1958. Introduction by Jean van Heijenoort, Trotsky's personal secretary 1932-39.

TWERSKY, Isadore. Harry Austryn Wolfson (1887-1974) American Jewish Yearbook, 76, pp 99-111.
Historian of ideas, critic of the contemporary disintegration of Jewish consciousness.

UROFSKY, Melvin I. and LEVY, David W. (Eds.) Brandeis, Louis Dembitz (1856-1941) Letters. Vol. 5, 1922-1941, Elder Statesman 1976, Albany, New York State U.P.

VERGELIS, Aron. Reizes, Dertseilungen un Lider (Travels, Stories and Songs) Moscow, Sovietsky Pisatel, 455p.
Trips to Europe and America made by the editor of Sovietish Heimland over the past 15 years.

VONO, Piero di. Baruch Spinoza. Firenze, La Nuova Italia, 137p. (Collana Strumenti)

WALL, B.M. Leon Godchaux and the Godchaux Business Enterprises. American Jewish Historical Quarterly, 66, No. 1, pp 50-66.
Leon Godchaux from Lorraine became a great financier in New Orleans.

WALTER, Bruno. Von der Musik und vom Musizieren. 2nd ed. Frankfurt/M., S. Fischer, 256p.
Sequel to the conductor's shorter volume of reminiscences 'Theme und Variationen'.

WEILL, Georges. Cerf Berr, militant de l'emancipation. Les Nouveaux Cahiers, 12, No. 45, Su. pp 30-42.

WENZEL-BURCHARD, Gertrud. Granny Greta Warburg und die Ihren. Hamburger Schicksale. Hamburg, Christian, 238p, Ill.

WEYNE, Arthur. The First Jewish Governor: Moses Alexander of Idaho. Western States Jewish Historical Quarterly, 0. pp 21-42.
Portrait of the first Jew to be elected, by popular vote, a chief executive of an American commonwealth.

ZUDIKIER, Jacobo. Ludwig Lazare Zamenhof. Creador del Esperanto. Buenos Aires, Congreso Judio Latinoamericano, 40p. Ill. (Biblioteca Popular Judia, Grandes Figuras del Judaismo 93)
Short biography of the inventor of Esparanto.

SOCIETY

BERMAN, Gerald S. The Adaptable American Jewish Family: An Inconsistency in Theory. The Jewish Journal of Sociology, 18, No. 1, Ju. pp 5-16.
Attempts to answer the question: How has the Jewish group advanced so well economically while maintaining cohesive family ties?

COHEN, Jack Simcha. Changing Neighbourhoods: The Drive to the Sea. Jewish Life, 31, No. 1, W. pp 29-33.
The Jewish community must come to grips with all issues affecting neighbourhood stabilization.

DES PRES, Terrence. The Survivor: An Anatomy of Life in the Death Camps. Oxford, O.U.P., 218p, Bibl.
The author employs first-hand accounts to examine the origins and extent of the 'will to live' exhibited in Hitler's and Stalin's concentration camps.

GOLDBERG, A.L. The Relevance of Cosmopolitan/Local Orientations to Professional Values and Behaviour. Sociology of Work and Occupations, 3, No. 4, pp 331-56.
The author tested his hypothesis that cosmopolitan/local was the optimum condition for experiences in Israel.

HARRIS, Monford. Ecology: A Covenantal Approach. CCAR Journal, 24, No. 3, Su. pp 101-8.
"Jewish tradition affirms the reality of covenantal relationship between the Israelite and beings in nature."

RUPPIN, Arthur. The Jewish Fate and Future. Tr. by E.W. Dickes. Westport, Conn., Greenwood P., xi, 386p.
Reprint of the 1940 edition.

ETHNOGRAPHY

ARMSTRONG, John A. Mobilized and Proletarian Diasporas. The American Political Science Review, 59, No. 2, pp 393-408.
Suggests a typology of the more significant types of diasporas. Groups discussed are Jews, Greeks, Armenians and Germans.

DAOUD, Yaqub Ibn. Un rameau vivant: le caraisme. Les Nouveaux Cahiers, 12, No. 45, Su. pp 49-53.
On the Karaites - a living sect.

Ethnic Lobbying: An American Tradition. Institute of Human Relations, New York, 5p.

FISHMAN, Joshua. The Future of Ethnicity in America. Yiddish, 2, Nos. 2-3, W/Sp. pp 1-3.

GLASER, R. The Greek Jews in Baltimore. Jewish Social Studies, 38, Nos. 3-4, pp 321-36.
Six families were examined by questionnaire. Results showed that customs tended to vary as a result of contact with Baltimorians.

GREELEY, Andrew M. Ethnicity, Denomination and Inequality. Beverley Hills/London, Sage, 85p, Bibl. (Sage Research Papers in the Social Sciences. Studies in Religion and Ethnicity 29)
Based on a composite sample of 12 NORC surveys to trace basic outlines of the achievements of American denominational and ethnic groups. Among the conclusions are that there are major cultural differences between Jews and Gentiles that account

for differences in the level of education and achievement.

KOSMIN, Barry, A., BAUER, Marzy and GRIZZARD, Nigel. Steel City Jews. A Study of Ethnicity and Social Mobility in the Jewish Population of the City of Sheffield, South Yorkshire. With an Historical Introduction by Kenneth Lunn. London, Reeearch Unit, Board of Deputies of British Jews, 28p, Map.

KRICKUS, Richard. Pursuing the American Dream: White Ethnics and the New Populism. Garden City, New York, Anchor P., 424p.

LAVENDER, Abraham D. and FORSYTH, John M. The Sociological Study of Minority Groups as Reflected by Leading Sociological Journals: Who Gets Studied and Who Gets Neglected. Ethnicity, 3, No. 4, D. pp 388.

In view of the small amount of attention given to non-black ethnic groups in the sociological literature, this paper suggests that it is no wonder that so little is known about ethnic-ethnic, ethnic-black, and ethnic-dominant society relations.

LOPATA, Helena Znaniecki. Polish Americans. Status Competition in an Ethnic Community. Englewood Cliffs, New Jersey, Prentice Hall, 174p, Ind., Bibl. (Ethnic Groups in American Life S.)

Deals also with Jewish Poles.

SCHWARTZ, Barry (Ed.) The Changing Face of the Suburbs. Chicago, London, Univ. of Chicago P., ix, 355p, Ind.

Papers in this volume deal with the changes in metropolitan life and their ramifications, i.a. on the religious life of suburban dwellers.

SHAROT, Stephen. Judaism, A Sociology. Newton Abbot, London and Vancouver, David and Charles; New York, Holmes and Meier, 224p, Ind.

Study of the differences in custom and religious observances in Jewish communities, looking at the dominant non-Jewish environments, wider social structures and Jewish-Gentile relations and their influence on Jewish Organisation and practice.

STATISTICS

BENSIMON, D. and DELLA PERGOLA, S. Sondage socio-économique auprès des Juifs en France. Resultats preliminaires pour Paris. Pofetudes, YOD, 1, No. 2, Ja. pp 4-24.

BENSION-DONATH, Doris. Socio-Démographie des Juifs de France et d'Algerie, 1867-1907. Paris, Presses Orientalistes de France,376p.

MAYER, K. Die jüdische Bevölkerung der Schweiz im Spiegel der Volkzählung 1970. (French Summary) Schweizerische Zeitschrift für Soziologie, 2, No. 2, pp 128.

The Jews of Switzerland in the light of the 1970 census.

PERGOLA, Sergio. della. Anatomia dell'ebraismo italiano: Caratteristiche demografiche, economiche, sociali, religiose e politiche di una minoranza. Assisi, Roma, Carucci, 358p, Bibl. (Collana di cultura ebraica 4)

Demographic and sociological study of Italian Jewry.

------------------------. La Conguintura Demografica dell'ebraismo Itàliano. La Rassegna Mensile di Israel, 42, Nos. 3-4, Ma-Ap. pp 149-67.

----------------------. and TAGLIACOZZO, Amedeo. Gli Italiani in Israele: Presentazione di un 'indagine socio-demografica. *La Rassegna Mensile di Israel*, 42, Nos. 11-12, N-D. pp 437-52.

La Población israelita de la provincia de Tucáman. Tucaman, Socieded Union Israelita, 87p.

Second census of the Jewish population of Tucaman (Argentina).

REED, John Shelton. Needles in Haystacks: Studying "Rare" Populations by Secondary Analysis of National Sample Surveys. *Public Opinion Quarterly*, 40, No. 1, W. pp 514-22.

The possibilities and pitfalls of using secondary analysis are examined in an attempt to locate a representative sample of Southern Jews.

Zero Population Growth and the Jewish Community: A Symposium. *Analysis*, N-D. pp 1-12.

Examines the ramifications of declining fertility rates over the coming decades, paying special attention to the consequences for synagogues and Jewish education. The discussants are George E. Johnson, Harold S. Himmelfarb and Mordecai Waxman.

OCCUPATIONAL STRUCTURE

AUERBACH, J.S. From Rags to Robes: The Legal Profession, Social Mobility and the American Jewish Experience. *American Jewish Historical Quarterly*, 66, No. 2, pp 219-84.

PERLMAN, Mark. Jews and Contributions to Economics: A Bicentennial Review, *Judaism*, 25, No. 3, Su. pp 301-11.

POLGE, H. Pourquoi les Juifs ne peuvent etre agriculteurs. *Archives Juives*, 12, No. 1, pp 13-14.

Quotes the argument of Mathieu de Dombasle of 1840 that their many festivals stop Jews from working in agriculture.

CLASS AND STATUS STRUCTURE

ELAZAR, Daniel and FRIEDMAN, Murray. Moving Up. Ethnic Succession in America. With a case history of the Philadelphia School System. New York, Institute on Pluralism and Group Identity, x. 60p, Ill., Bibl.

"As liberal Protestant elites allied with blacks in support of the system for preferential treatment, the Jews and Italians became fearfut that their struggles for upward mobility would be stalemated".

SOCIAL WELFARE AND POVERTY

BERGER, G. American Jewish Communal Service 1776-1976: From Traditional Self-Help to Increasing Dependence on Government Support. *Jewish Social Studies*, 38, Nos. 3-4, pp 225-46.

BLOCH, Harry. Jewish Welfare in Colonial Times. *Jewish Digest*, 21, No. 10, Jy.-Au. pp 20-22.

Condensed from *New York State Journal of Medicine*, 72, No. 12.

BRODSKY, Irving. Serving the Jewish Aged - the Center's Changing Role. New York, Associated YM-YWHAs of Greater New York, 16p.

BUBIS, Gerald B. Professional Education for the Jewish Component in Casework Practice. *Journal of Jewish Communal Service*, 52, No. 3, Sp. pp 270-77.

GOLDIN, Milton. Why They Give: American Jews and their Philanthropies. New York, Macmillan, 261p.

HOFSTEIN, Saul. Integration of Jewish Commitment into the Treatment Process. Journal of Jewish Communal Service, 52, No. 3, Sp. pp 259-69.

KLUTZNICK, Philip M. Fund-Raising and Jewish Priorities. Jewish Digest, 21, No. 9, Ju. pp 3-5.

KORN, Bertram W. The Struggle for the First Jewish Military Chaplain. Jewish Digest, 21, No. 10, Jy-Au. pp 44-50.
Condensed from Jewish Exponent.

LEVY, Charles S. Social Work and the Jewish Community Centre. Journal of Jewish Communal Service, 53, No. 1, Fa. pp 44-51.

National Conference of Jewish Communal Service. The new pluralism and social work education: a challenge to the profession of social work. New York, Various pagings.
Includes: I. The new pluralism and social work education by Donald Feldstein and Joseph Giordano. II. The new pluralism and social work education: the historical and contemporary political and social context by Murray Friedman.

ZEFF, David. The Jewish Aging: Problem Dimensions, Jewish Perspectives and the Unique Role of the Family Agency. Journal of Jewish Communal Service, 53, No. 1, Fa. pp 81-87.
Because the elderly are largely hidden and are constitutionally incapable of militant action, the agencies must become their advocates - not only in the direct services they provide, but in representing their interests in the general community.

ZUKERMAN, Karl D. Government, Voluntarism, Jewishness and Accountability: An Essay on Principle and Principal. Journal of Jewish Communal Service, 52, No. 4, Su. pp 365-73.
The Jewish communal agency's mission is to be an instrument of the community to continue Jewish identity, heritage and life. The implications of government funding affects its core.

JEWISH IDENTITY AND IDENTIFICATION

ALLOUCHE-BENAYOUN, Joëlle. Minorité et Racisme. 1: Une Condition minoritaire: La condition Juive vécu par de jeunes Juifs de 17 a 30 ans. 2: annexes. Thèse pour le Doctorat de 3ème cycle, Psychologie Sociale. Paris, Ecole des Hautes Etudes en Sciences Sociales. 461 + 110p, Bibl. (Mimeo.)
Identification among young Jews in France. Doctoral thesis in social psychology based on questionnaires.

AUERBACH, Jerold S. Dual Loyalty (Again). Moment, 1, No. 7, Ap. pp 53-57.
The choice may never be necessary; if it is, it is by no means certain that all American Jews would, or should, choose as Americans rather than Jews.

BERL, Fred. Jewish Identity: Its use for Clinical Purposes. Journal of Jewish Communal Service, 52, No. 4, Su. pp 344-54.

BERMANT, Chaim. Odd Men (and Women) Out. "One Can Sell Anglo-Jewry Anything Except Culture." Present Tense, 4, No. 1, Au. pp 66-71.
Jewish intellectuals in Britain are indifferent to the community and the community is largely indifferent to them.

CHARLES, Daniel. "Breira": Alternative of Surrender. *The American Zionist*, 67, No. 3, No. pp 12-17.

"Dissent, substantively as well as formatively, is at the heart of the Breira phenomenon. American Jews are in accord that dissent is a vital democratic freedom. What troubles the Jewish community is not the right itself, but its abuse. No one seems to be debating the right; it is rather timing and means of communication that are being challenged.

DASHEFSKY, Arnold. (Ed.) Ethnic Identity in Society. R.e. New York, Rand McNally, xiv, 252p, Ind., Bibl.

Collection of essays in which many references are made to Jewish Americans, to Antisemitism including a paper "American Students in Israel the Changing Salience of an Ethnic Role" by Simon N. Herman.

GLOCK, Charles Y. and BELLAH, Robert N. (Eds.) The New Religious Consciousness. Berkeley, Cal., U. of California P., xvi, 391p, Ind.

With a chapter on "Jewish Identity and Counter-culture" by Thomas Piazza.

GOSS, Isaac. Can We Produce Jewish Intellectuals? *Jewish Affairs*, 36, No. 9, S. pp 69-72.

JAKOBOVITS, Immanuel. To Be Equal or To Be Different. *European Judaism*, 10, No. 1, W. 1975/76, pp 7-14.

Jewish identity in free society.

JANNER, Greville. "I Doubt That I Could Muster a Minyan". *Present Tense*, 4, No. 1, Aut. pp 16-19.

A Jewish M.P. in the House of Commons.

KARP, Abraham J. Ideology and Identity in Jewish Group Survival in America. *American Jewish Historical Quarterly*, 65, No. 4, Ju. pp 310-34.

Traces Jewish group survival in American through many phases.

---------------. Ideology as Strategy in Jewish Group Survival in America. Rochester, New York, 62p. (Mimeo.)

LADD, Everett Caroll Jr. and LIPSET, Seymour Martin. The Divided Academy: Professors and Politics. New York,MacGraw-Hill, xv, 407p, Ind., Bibl.

In the chapter 'Intellectuality and Social Background: The Liberalism of Jewish Academics', the political liberalism of American Jews; Politics of the Jewish academics; Religious and irreligious faculty etc.

LERMER, Arthur. Jewish Identification and the problem of Integration into an Open Democratic Society. *Viewpoints*, 9, No. 4, Fa-W. pp 31-39.

LOR, Aaron A. Identity. *Viewpoints*, 9, No. 4, Fa-W. pp 27-30.

PELLI, Moshe. Jewish Identity in Modern Hebrew Literature. *Judaism*, 25, No. 4, Fa. pp 447-60.

If there is a definition of Jewish identity, it is no longer absolute, just as Judaism, by itself, has become a relative concept.

PETRUSAK, F. and STEINERT, S. The Jews of Charleston: Some Old Wine in New Bottles. *Jewish Social Studies*, 38, Nos. 3-4, pp 337-46.

American Jews are acculturated rather than assimilated.

PLOTNICOV, L. and SILVERMAN, M. How the Jews Identify Themselves and Why. Paper read at the American Anthropological Association, 75th Annual Meeting, Washington, D.C. Nov. 1976.

Discusses ethnic signalling or the intentional display of ethnic identification among the American Jews.

Responses to Richard Marienstras. European Judaism, 10, No. 1, W. 1975/76. pp 3-6.

Answers to articles published in the journal by Paul Flohr, Alan Montefiore and Morton Narrowe.

Translating Commitment into Practice. If Not Now, When? Symposium. Jewish Education, 46, Fa-W. pp 31-41.

Includes: The Crisis of Identity in the Dynamics of Jewish Life by Ellis Rivkin. - Community and Nation_ Basis for Jewish Commitment by Arthur Hertzberg. - Educational Planning for Commitment by Hyman Chanover.

ASSIMILATION, ACCULTURATION

FAIA, Michael A. Secularization and Scholarship Among American Professors. Sociological Analysis, 37, No. 2, Sp. pp 63-77.

Recent studies comparing Catholics with Protestants and secularized Jewish academicians with their non-secularized Jewish colleagues, have led to contradictory conclusions about the impact of secularization on scholarship.

FRANKEL, William. The Jewish Press and the Acculturation of Anglo-Jewry. New Community, 4, No. 4, W/Sp. 1975/76, pp 467-70.

GREENBERG, Irving. The End of Emancipation. Conservative Judaism, 30, No. 4, Su. pp 47-63.

The end of emancipation is necessary because the dominance of the modern threatens Jewish existence through assimilation and deculturation as well as paralysis in situations like the Holocaust.

HELMREICH, William B. Jewish Marginality and the World Struggle for Equality: Some Historical Causes and Consequences. The Journal of Intergroup Relations, 6, O. pp 37-40.

Identified suspicion of motive by others and a lack of self-respect by many Jews as key factors that may account for the negative image of the Jew among certain segments of society despite his active involvement in various social causes.

HERST, Roger E. Jewish Careers and Life Styles. Congress Monthly, 43, No. 7, S. pp 13-14.

Is it possible to have a professional life style, a high degree of Jewish observance and a nuclear family structure at the same time?

HYMAN, Paula. Challenge to Assimilation: French Jewish Youth Movements Between the Wars. The Jewish Journal of Sociology, 18, No. 2, D. pp 105-14.

JICK, Leon A. The Americanization of the Synagogue 1820-1870. Hanover, N.H., U.P. of New England for Brandeis U.P., ix, 247p, Ind., Bibl.

Professor Jick's subject is the experience of 200,000 German-Jewish immigrants who came to the USA between 1830-60 and gradually shed their Jewish and German traditions, to become truly American.

KALLNER, Rudolf. Herzl und Rathenau, Wege jüdischer Existenz an der Wende des 20. Jahrhunderts, Stuttgart, Ernst Klett, 450p, Ind., Bibl. M.

Presents the two men who perhaps best typified the assimilationist and Zionist Jew at the turn of the century, but both of whom contributed to the political thought of the 20th century.

KATZ, James, E. and MURASKIN, Lana D. The Assimilation of Jewish Young Adults Through the New York City Young Men's Hebrew Association. Adult Education, 26, No. 4, Su. pp 226-234.

KAUTSKY, Karl. Are the Jews a Race? Westport, Conn., Greenwood P., 255p.

An example of Jewish self-hatred, first published in 1926.

KRIEGEL, Annie. L'assimilation à la francaise. Les Nouveaux Cahiers, 12, No. 45, Su. pp 43-48.

MAYKOVICH, Minako K. To Stay or Not to Stay: Dimensions of Ethnic Assimilation. International Migration Review, 10, No. 3, Fa. pp 377-87.

Deals i.a. with aliyah-motivation.

MOORE, Deborah Dash. Jewish Ethnicity and Acculturation in the 1920's: Public Education in New York City. The Jewish Journal of Sociology, 18, No. 2, D. pp 96-104.

REINHARZ, Jehuda. Fatherland or Promised Land. The Dilemma of the German Jew. 1893-1914. U. of Michigan P., 328p.

RISKIN, S. Orthodoxy and Her Alleged Heretics. Tradition, 15, No. 4, pp 34-44.

The real enemy or Orthodoxy is assimilation and ignorance.

SANDLER, Robert. Why Jewish Academicians Leave the Synagogue. Condensed from Sh'ma, 6, No. 105. Jewish Digest, 22, No. 2, pp 49-51.

SCHNAPPER, D. Quelques réflexions sur l'assimilation comparee des travailleurs émigrés italiens et des Juifs en France. Bulletin de la Société Francaise de Sociologie, 3, No. 7, pp 11-18.

Assimilation of Italian and Jewish immigrant workers in France.

MIXED MARRIAGES

ALSTON, Jon P., McINTOSH, William A and WRIGHT, Louise M. Extent of Interfaith Marriages Among White Americans. Sociological Analysis, 7, No. 4, Fa. pp 261-64.

The General Social Survey Program conducted by the National Opinion Research Center shows that seventeen per cent of the white population have spouses with different religious preferences.

BERNSTEIN, Saul. Is It The Worst of Times? Or the Best of Times? Jewish Life, 31, No. 1, W. pp 40-46.

Warns of the danger of mixed marriage and assimilation.

COHN, W. Jewish Outmarriage and Anomie: A Study in the Canadian Syndrome of Polarities. (French Summary) Canadian Review of Sociology and Anthropology, 13, No.1, pp 90-105.

The proportion of intermarriage follows other social phenomena: divorce, suicide, crime.

HOLLANDER, David B. Intermarriage By Jews. Perspective, 3, No. 1, Su. pp 14-18.

The only solution to the peril of intermarriage is a

commitment to the discipline and authority of the Torah.

Intermarriage. The Jewish Observer, 12, Ma. pp 3-5.
"How can the American Jewish establishment lead the fight against intermarriage, if it has led the way to its threshold by speeding up the assimilation process?" (Takes a critical look at the AJC's study on intermarriage.)

KOMINSKY, Neal. Rabbinic Ethics and Mixed Marriage: An Exercise in 'Catch 22". CCAR Journal, 22, No. 4, Aut. pp 64-66.

MALLER, Allen S. Intermarriage and Jewish Continuity. Congress Monthly, 43, No. 8, O. pp 14-15.
Rapid rise of mixed marriages where the wife is Jewish.

----------------. Jewish-Gentile Marriage: Another Look at the Problem. CCAR Journal, 24, No. 1, W. pp 65-74.
A Reform viewpoint.

SELTZER, Sanford. Jews and non-Jews. Falling in love. An informal guide to interfaith marriage for couples, their families and the rabbis who counsel them. New York, Union of American Hebrew Congregations, 42p.

CONVERSION

ALSTAT, Philip R. The Nun who returned to Judaism. Condensed from Jewish Week, Jewish Digest, 21, No. 9, Ju. pp 63-65.

EICHHORN, David Max. Hebrew Christianity. Jewish Spectator, 41, No. 3, Fa. pp 33-35.
They should not be given publicity but at the same time a major educational effort must be made to obviate their influence.

JOB, F. Baptêmes de juifs dans le Duché de Lorraine au XVIIIe. (de 1713 a 1771). Conversions in Lunéville, Pont à Mousson et Toul. Archives Juives, 12, No. 3, pp 44-48.

MECHOULAN, H. Nouveaux éléments dans la controverse des statuts de pureté de sang en Espagne au XVII siècle. (English Summary) Studia Rosenthaliana, 10, No. 2, pp 142-50.
The "purity of blood" controversy in 17th century Spain.

MOORE, Kenneth. Those of the Street. The Catholic-Jews of Mallorca. A study in urban cultural change. Notre Dame, London, U. of Notre Dame P., 218p, Ill.
Anthropologial study of the Xuetas, Catholics who maintained the Jewish tradition in Mallorca.

MOULINAS, R. Conversions et baptêmes chez les Juifs d'Avignon et du Comtat aux XVII et XVIII siècles. Archives Juives, 12, No. 2, pp 19-29.
Relatively high numbers of Jews converted to Christianity in the 17th-18th centuries.

SALOMON, H.P. Haham Saul Levi Morle'ria and his Portuguese New Christians. (In Dutch with English Summary). Studia Rosenthaliana, 10, No. 2, pp 127-41.
The famous rabbi was born in Portugal and practiced Catholicism before converting to Judaism in France. Did not believe in the Judaism of Marranos.

SILVERLIGHT, John. My Father and I: Confessions of a Convert's Son. Present Tense, 3, No. 2, pp 52-56.

English journalist whose father, born Jewish, was an Anglican priest.

SOLA-SOLE, José Maria. Judíos y conversos an la poesía contesana del sigli XV: el estilo poligloto do Fray Diego de Valencia. Hispanic Review, 44, No. 4, pp 371-85.
Study of poem written against the convert Juan de Espana of León containing many Hebrew words.

COMMUNITY STUDIES

BERGER, Graenum. Innovation by Tradition. New York, Commission on Synagogue Relations. Fed. of Jewish Philanthropies of New York, 335p.

BERNSTEIN, Samuel J. From Moving Up to Moving Out. Jewish migrations in New York reflect the fortunes of the city. National Jewish Monthly, 90, No. 6, F. pp 10-12.

KATLEAN, Ferne and SPRINGER, Selma. (Eds.) A Manual for Jewish Family Living Programs. Los Angeles, Jewish Centers Association, 174p.

KLUTZNICK, Philip M. Vital Issues in the Jewish Community. Interviewer: Max F. Baar. Washington, C.C., B'nai Brith Youth Organisation, 80p. (The Judaism Pamphlet S.)
"In order to revitalise the Jewish community, first we need more effective fact finding and research as to the changing nature of this community - local, national and world."

ROSENFELD, Max. Secularism and Our Heritage. A Surprise of Legends. Jewish Currents, 30, No. 3, Ma. pp 26-35.

WOMEN

AMERICAN ZIONIST FEDERATION. Zionism and Social Progress: Women for Zionism. New York, 36p.

BAUM, Charlotte, HYMAN, Paula and MICHEL, Sonya. The Jewish Woman in America. New York, Dial, 290p.

BLEICH, David J. Women on Synagogue Boards. Tradition, 15, No. 4, Sp. pp 53-67.

COHEN, Steven M., DESSEL, Susan C. and PELAVIN, Michael A. Women's Power and Status in Jewish Communal Life: A Look at the UJA. Response, 10, No. 1, W. pp 59-66.
"With regard to women's rights, the organisation is neither a progressive force in Jewish or American society, nor is it the most tradition and resistant to change."

DAVIS, Sarah. Jews in Politics: Where are the Women? Council Woman, Ja. pp 5-7.
"Only four Jewish women have ever served in the House of Representatives. None has ever served in the Senate or the Cabinet."

ELKIN, Lillian. The Jewish Woman: Myths and Facts. Congress Monthly, 43, No. 2, F. pp 15-18.
An essay-review of The Jewish Woman in America by Charlotte Baum, Paula Hyman and Sonya Michel. (Dial Press, 1976)

FEMME JUIVES. Les Nouveaux Cahiers, 11, No. 46, pp 64-88.
Literary essays by Liliane Atlan, Elizabeth de Fontenay, Clara Malraux, Nime Moati and Jacqueline Sudaka on the condition of Jewish women. Les Nouveaux Cahiers, 11, No. 47,

pp 1-6. Responses to the foregoing by Colette Baer, Linette Lehmann and Odette Azria.

FRIESAND, Sally. Judaism and the New Woman, New York, Behrman House,

GERTEL, Elliot. Passivity, Equality and the Jewish Woman, *Congress Monthly*, 43, No. 9, N. pp 13-15.

GLANZ, Rudolf. The Jewish Woman in America. Two Female Immigrant Generations 1820-1929. New York, Ktav and the National Council of Jewish Women. 2 vols: Vol. 1: The Eastern European Jewish Woman. xiii, 213p, Ind., Bibl., Ill. Vol. 2: The German Jewish Woman. xiii, 213p, Ind., Bibl., Ill.

Analyses the social and creative background of Jewish women who formed a large part of immigrant Jews at the turn of the century. One of the most striking developments is the emergence of a new class - the unmarried working girl.

GREENBERG, Blu. Feminism: Is It Good or Bad for the Jews? *Hadassah Magazine*, 58, No. 4, Ap. pp 10-11.

"Feminism for all its worth in upgrading the status of Jewish women, does not bode well in its entirity for Jewish survival. Some of its directions may be wrong or even destructive when judged from a Jewish perspective."

The Jewish Woman. Special Issue, *Davka*, No. 17, pp 1-66.

Includes: Halachah and the Jewish Woman by Marty Ballonoff; New Notes on the Pulpit: L.A's Women Cantors; Women in the Resistance by Susan Gordon; The Rabbinate: A New Image by Laura Geller and Sandy Eisenberg Sasso.

KAPLAN, Marion A. German-Jewish Feminism in the Twentieth Century. *Jewish Social Studies*, 38, No. 1, W. pp 39-53.

The League of Jewish Women, founded 1904.

KOLTUN, Liz. (Ed.) The Jewish Woman. New Perspectives. New York, Schocken, xx, 294p, Bibl.

Collection of essays and articles on the position of women in Judaism and the Jewish community.

KRAMER, Sydelle and MASUR, Jenny. (Eds.) Jewish Grandmothers. Boston, Beacon P., 174p, Bibl., Ill.

Personal accounts of ten Jewish immigrant women confronted with the American experience.

KRASZ, Judy. The Women's Involvement in Israel. *The Jewish Digest*, 21, No. 5, My. pp 33-37.

LERNER, A.L. Who Hast Not Made Me A Man: The Movement for Equal Rights for Women in American Jewry. *American Jewish Yearbook*, 76, pp 3-38.

LOCKETT, D.R. Feminist Footholds in Religion. *Foundations*, 19, No. 1, pp 33-39.

Includes Judaism.

MULHER em ISRAEL, 1975 Ano Internacional de Mulher. Sao Paulo, Organizacao das Pioneiras, 118p.

"Women in Israel" published for the UN International Year of Women.

NEIDLE, Cecyle S. Great Immigrant Women, New York, Triangle, 312p.

Includes Jewish women.

PETERS, Barbara and SAMUELS, Victoria. (Eds.) Dialogue on Diversity A New Agenda for American Women. New York, Institute on

Pluralism and Group Identity, 88p, Ill.
A selection of papers on women's rights and aims of feminist movements, including "The Jewish Woman" by Ann Wolfe (pp 42-50)

PINCUS, Cynthia. Beyond Feminist Politics: The Israeli Woman. School Review, No. 8, Au. pp 564-71.
The problems that beset the American woman will not seriously engage the Israelis in the near future.

POUPKO, Chana K. and WOHLGELERNTER, Devora L. Women's Liberation - An Orthodox Response. Tradition, 15, No. 4, Sp. pp 45-52.
Calls for promotion of a strong sense of pride in women coupled with a conviction that what they do is religiously significant.

ROSENBERG, Joel. The Feminine Through a (Male) Glass Darkly: Preface to a Demythology. Response, 10, No. 1, W. 1975/76, pp 67-88.
"Sexual discrimination in Jewish law may have to go the way of concubinage, sacrifices, tithing, active priesthood."

SCHAPPI, L. Die Stellung der Frau im Judentum, im Islam und im Christentum. Ein Vergleich. Judaica, 32, No. 3, pp 103-12.
Compares the status of women in the three great monotheistic religions.

SCHEPPS, David. Remarkable Women of the Scriptures, Philadelphia, Dorrance, 210p.

SCHERR, Lilly. La Femme juive a travers les siecles. Les Nouveaux Cahiers, 12, No. 46, Aut. pp 24-35.
The status of Jewish women in Talmud, the Middle Ages and in contemporary society.

STILLER, Nikki. Peace Without Honor: The Battle of the Sexes in Israel. Midstream, 22, No. 5, My. pp 33-41.
Social pressures in Israel are formidable and the women of Israel act in accord with those pressures.

SWIDLER, Leonard. Women in Judaism: The Status of Women in Formative Judaism. New York, Scarecrow; Folkestone, Bailey Bros. vi, 242p, Ind.
Treats of the place of women in Judaism from the 2nd century B.C.E. to the 5th century C.E.

WOLFE, Ann G. No Room at the Top. Council Woman, No. 1, Ja. pp 3-4.
Male domination in the Jewish communal structure has deprived women of the chance to share leadership, but today women are demanding equal participation.

Women in Jewish and Christian Tradition: Special Section. Sidic, 9, No. 3, pp 4-18.
Three articles: A Feminist Perspective on the Jewish Woman by Lucy Y. Steinitz; Christian Tradition on Women by Sandra M. Schneiders; The God of Rebekah by Piet van Boxel.

WOHLMANN-MEYER, Claire. Was hat sich geändert? Der Weg der Schweizer Jüdin 1901-1976. Israelitisches Wochenblatt fur die Schweiz, 76, No. 21a, Ma, pp 65-69.

DISCRIMINATION
AND PREJUDICE

FRYSHMAN, Bernard. Affirmative Action and Equal Opportunity: An Overview. New York, Commission on Legislation and Civic Action, Agudath Israel of America, 27p.
Agudath Israel activity opposing discriminatory practices and quotas resulting from improper implementation of Affirmative Action.

GINGER, Ann Fagan. (Ed.) DeFunis Versus Odegaard and the University of Washington: The University Admissions Case, The Record, Dobbs Ferry, Oceana, 3 vols.
The DeFunis Case was the first use in the courts of the application of "reverse discrimination" in admissions to American Universities.

GLAZER, Nathan. Affirmative Discrimination: Ethnic Inequality and Public Policy. New York, Basic Books, 248p.

MIDDLETON, Russell. Regional Differences in Prejudice. American Sociological Review, 11, No. 2, pp 94-117.
1964 national survey reveals that residents of the South displayed a much higher level of anti-black prejudice than residents of the non-South, but the regions differed only slightly on measures of anti-Semitism and anti-Catholic and anti-immigrant prejudice and on certain psychological measures; authoritarianism, anomia and psychic distress.

MORSE, J. Mitchell. Prejudice and Literature. Philadelphia, Temple U.P., 192p.
Examples of how literature can foster racial and religious prejudice.

MARRIAGE
AND DIVORCE

BAR-ZEV, Asher. ZPG and the Jewish Problem. Conservative Judaism, 30, No. 1, Sp. pp 76-82.
Zero population growth is against the interests of Jewry but Jews will have to adopt moral world standards.

BERKOVITS, Eliezar. A Jewish Sexual Ethics. Jewish Life, 3, No. 4, Fa. pp 19-28.
"Within Judaism, man is acknowledged in his bio-psychic reality. This is the basis of Jewish sexual ethics. It excludes primitive biological sexuality as well as sophisticated ascetism."

BERMAN, S. Value Perspectives on Jewish Family Life. Social Casework, 57, No. 6, pp 366-372.
The author sees Jewish law as divided into three categories of behaviour which embody the fundamental value of interpersonal interaction with the family unit. In Sherman's comment to Berman's essay, he discusses weakened familism and the tilt towards identification with the larger community. For some Jews, Sherman notes, the collectivity has been solely Judaism; for others: social, political or humanitarian movements.

BUBIS, Gerald. The Changing Jewish Family: Address at the 45th General Assembly, Philadelphia, Nov. 10-14th, 1976, New York,

Council of Jewish Federations and Welfare Funds, 10p. (Assembly Papers)

---------------. The Single Parent Family. Reconstructionist, 43, No. 2, F. pp 7-10.

Indicates areas where the synagogue can more consciously address itself to the needs of the single-parent family.

BULKA, Reuven. Divorce: The Problem and the Challenge. Tradition, 16, No. 1, Su. pp 127-33.

Discusses the break-up of an increasing number of Jewish marriages, even among the Orthodox.

SCHLESINGER, Benjamin. The Jewish Family, Toronto,

---------------------. Reflections on Family Breakdown Among Jewish Families. Journal of Psychology and Judaism, 1, No. 1, Fa. pp 45-53.

Increasing divorce and general disintegration can be countered by serious application to the meaning of marriage and family. An understanding of the classical Jewish family and how it functioned can be useful in countering the problems faced by the modern Jewish family.

WEINBERGER, Bernard. The Growing Rate of Divorce in Orthodox Jewish Life. Jewish Life, 31, No. 1, Sp. pp 9-14.

We must concede that a problem does exist, even if its magnitude is uncertain, examine the causes and determine whether we can reverse the trend.

YOUTH

BACHMAYER, Bernice. Youth Problems in the Jewish Community of Johannesburg. Jewish Affairs, 36, No. 9, S. pp 73-76.

BECKER, T. Self, Family and Community. A Cross Cultural Comparison of American and Israeli Youth. Youth and Society, 8, No. 1, pp 45-66.

CHARTOCK, Lewis C. How Teen Workers View Their Practice. An evaluation of a JWB National Teen Training Institute. New York, Florence G. Heller-JWB Research Center, vii, 39p.

FURST, Max. Fefilte Fisch. Eine Jugend in Königsberg. Munich, DTV, 280p.

Experiences of a Jewish youth leader who returned from Israel to Germany.

LEVINE, Norman and BROOKS, William C. The Effect of Outreach on Participation by Teens. Reeearch Digest. New York, Florence G. Heller-JWB Research Center. A Research Project in Co-Operation with Jewish Community Center of San Diego, 14p.

MAYMAN, Muriel. Historical and Contemporary 'Havurot': A Comparison. Journal of Jewish Communal Service, 52, No. 4, Su. pp 361-64.

The model of the 'havura' was taken from the example of Yeshivot where students study in pairs or in groups.

MORRIS, Sylvia Jean. Is Youth Against Zionist? The Jewish World, 1, No. 7, Ju. pp 2-5.

REIMER, Joseph. Looking Back at the Havura. Response, 10, Nos. 2-3, Su/Fa. pp 243-46.

ROTHSCHILD, Sylvia. A Great Happening in Boston. A Revolt of the Young. Present Tense, 3, No. 3, Sp. pp 21-26.

SHAPIRA, Ariella. Competition, cooperation and conformity among city and kibbutz children in Israel. Ann Arbor, Mich., U. Microfilms, x, 111p. Tables.
Dissertation - U. of California, 1970.

TAYLOR, Joseph L. An Approach to the Treatment of Children in Group Residences. *Journal of Jewish Communal Services*, 52, No. 3, Sp. pp 286-92.

Trends in Jewish Child Care. *Journal of Jewish Communal Services*, 53 No. 1, Fa. pp 93-102.

SOCIO-MEDICAL PROBLEMS

ABRAMS, William. A Jewish Approach to Leisure. *Viewpoints*, 9, No. 4, Fa/W. pp 55-62.
"I venture to suggest that the modern Jew would expect of his leisure time the satisfaction of three fundamental desires: to experience joy and fulfillment, to achieve wisdom (that is to understand the meaning of his life and his approaching death) and to leave the world a better place than he found it, so that his life will not have been in vain."

BIRNBAUM, L. Death of Young Sons and Husbands. *Omega: The Journal of Death and Dying*, 7, No. 2, pp 171-75.
Discusses the reactions of bereaved persons who after the Yom Kippur War came to non-directive group counselling.

BARDFIELD, Philip A. Jewish Medical Ethics. *Reconstructionist*, 42, No. 6, S. pp 7-12.
"The concerned Jewish layman should try to understand the ethical sensitivity and human compassion that has determined all Jewish bio-ethical decisions, and play an active role with the physician in the application of these decisions to current problems."

BAR-ZEV, Asher. Homosexuality and the Jewish Tradition. *Reconstructionist*, 42, No. 5, My. pp 20-24.
"Whether we think of homosexual behaviour merely as a personal preference or as a pathological state, in neither case can it be accepted within the Jewish religion."

BEN-VERED, Amos. Mucolipidosis IV: A New Jewish Genetic Disease. *Hadassah Magazine*, 58, No. 11, O. pp 12-13; 34-45.
A recently discovered congenital disease affecting children whose both parents are Ashkenazi Jews of Southern Polish ancestry.

BLOCH, Harry. Early American Jewish Physicians. *Jewish Currents*, 30, No. 9, O. pp 16-18.

FURSTENBERG, Rochelle. Abortion in Israel: Pros and Cons. *Hadassah Magazine*, 58, No. 3, Ma. pp 20-21; 38.
A new abortion law is almost certain to pass this year but the dilemma stays on the personal and national level.

EPSTEIN, Carol B. Conservative Judaism and the Problem of Birth Control. *Viewpoints*, 9, No. 4, Fa/W. pp 40-54.
"The practical difference between Orthodox and Conservative Judaism, particularly in an area such as birth control, is that Conservative rabbis would urge strict adherence to a lesser degree by giving more weight to modifying circumstances. The laws are basically the same."

GOLDFARB, Daniel C. The Definition of Death: In the Common Law and Jewish Tradition. Conservative Judaism, 30, No. 1, W. pp 10-22.
"The decision to withdraw extraordinary support devices from patients whose conditions have deteriorated past the point of any reasonable expectation of recovery is, in accordance with Jewish law, and should receive our support and guide us in our counselling."

GREENBERG, Blu. Abortion: A Challenge to Halakhah. Judaism, 25, No. 2, Sp. pp 201-8.
"As a community, we should support liberalized legalized abortion; we should do so with regrets, perhaps, and with grave reservations; we should do so with a sense of urgency to inform our people, and society at large, of our own value system."

PANETTI, Charles. (Ed.) The Geller Papers. Scientific Observations on the Paranormal Powers of Uri Geller. New York, Houghton Mifflin.

PFEFFER, Leo. Abortion and Religious Freedom. Congress Monthly, 43, No. 6, Ju. pp 9-12.

ROSEN, David. Euthanasia - A Jewish View. Zionist Record and South African Jewish Chronicle, Supplement, 17, Se. pp 10-11.

ROSNER, Fred. Tay-Sachs Disease: To Screen or not to Screen. Tradition, 15, No. 4, Sp. pp 101-2
Tay-Sachs Disease occurs chiefly among Jews.

SIEGEL, Seymour. Updating the Criteria of Death. Conservative Judaism, 30, No. 4, W. pp 23-30.
On the basics of ethics and Halakhah he would support updating the criteria of death. Followed by a discussion by several rabbis.

SILFEN, P. Clinical Criminology in Israel. International Journal of Offender Therapy and Comparative Criminology, 20, No. 1, pp 18-25.
Experience of a group of Israeli criminologists (psychiatrist, psychologist, two sociologists and two lawyers) in therapy, research and teaching.

SIMON, I. Les connaissances odontologiques bibliques et talmudiques comparées à celles des peuples de l'antiquité. (Suite) Revue d'histoire de la Medicine Hébraique, No. 119, pp 61-64.
Dental hygiene among Jews in antiquity.

SPERO, Moshe Halevi. On the Relationship Between Psychotherapy and Judaism. Journal of Psychology and Judaism, 1, No. 3, Fa. pp 15-33.
Although religion may itself be therapeutic at times, and psychotherapy can promote religious growth, psychotherapy, at present, seemsill-equipped to replace religion as a new belief system.

RACE, RACISM, GENETICS

DECTER, Moshe. Arms Traffic with South Africa: Who is Guilty? New York, American Jewish Congress, 36p.

-------------. Black Africa: Nations in Glass Houses. Moment, 2, 2, No. 2, N. pp 60-64; Jewish Tradition, 43, No. 8, O. pp 18-23.

GREEN, Philip. Race and IQ: The Fallacy of Heritability. Dissent, 23, No. 2, Sp. pp 181-96.

HEUSE, Georges A. Races, racismes, antiracismes. Nouvelle Ecole, No. 29, My.
Expounds the views of the "New Right".

KATZ, Phyllis. (Ed.) Towards the Elimination of Racism. New York, Pergamon Press, xiv, 444p, Ind. (Pergamon International Library of Science, Technology, Engineering and Social Studies, 14)
The essays deal with various aspects of combating racism.

KATZNELSON, Ira. Black Men, White Cities: Race, Politics and Migration in the United States, 1900-30 and Britain, 1948-68. London, Phoenix Books, U. of Chicago P., n.e. 219p, Ind.
Argues that the connection between national and local patterns of race relations show similarities.

PINNER, Hayim. Time is Running Out in Southern Africa. Jewish Frontier, 43, No. 8, O. pp 28-29.
Jews and apartheid.

POLIAKOV, Leon. Il mito ariano. Storia di un'antropolgia negativa. Milano, Rizzoli, 377p.
Italian version of "The Aryan Myth".

--------------, DELACAMPAGNE, Christian and GIRARD, Patrick. Le Racisme. Paris, Seghers, 155p, Ill., Bibl. (Collection 'Point de depart')
Survey of the origins and forms of racism, singling out antisemitism as a special case.

RABINOVE, Samuel. Human Relations Laboratory: Personal Reflections from a Jewish Perspective. Journal of Intergroup Relations, 6, No. 1, O. pp 30-6.
The AJC's legal director describes an all-day residential laboratory in community relations and community dynamics sponsored by the Boston University Human Relations Laboratory, North Andover, Mass.

SCHNALL, David J. The Myth of the Jewish Race. Jewish Quarterly Review, 66, No. 3, Ja. pp 181-85.

SHAHAK, Israel. Nature raciste du sionisme et de l'Etat d'Israel. Lettre, No. 209, pp 3-6.
Chairman of the Israeli League of Human Rights maintains there is racial discrimination in Israel.

THURLOW, Richard C. Racial Populism in England. Patterns of Prejudice, 10, No. 4, Ju/Au. pp 27-33.
There is a similarity in the ideology of racial populist groups in England since the First World War - changes relate to the Second World War which discredited antisemitism - and the Race Relations Acts have forced a moderation on extremist racist outbursts in recent years.

EDUCATION

ABRAMOVITCH, Stanley. Jewish Education in Iran. Jewish Education, 46, No. 2, pp 35-42.
Jewish organisations and the Jewish community are deeply involved in the process of modernisation and are making great efforts to assure the continuation of an independent Jewish education program for the ten thousand children in Jewish Day Schools.

ALLOUCHE, Jean-Luc. Une école juive à la rue, L'Arche, 19, No. 237, D. pp 71-72.

AMERICAN ASSOCIATION FOR JEWISH EDUCATION. Dept. of Statistical Research and Information. Trends in Jewish School Enrollment in the United States, 1974-75. New York, 28p.

ARON, Isa, GREENSPAN, Jay, ROUS, Janice and WOLF, Michael. Alternative Jewish Education: The Havurah Model. Response, 10, Nos. 2-3, Su/Fa. pp 152-92.

BASS, Hyman. Jewish Education at the Crossroads. The World of Yiddish, Bulletin No. 9, pp 1-20.

BEN-HORIN, Meir. Re-Schooling American Jewry. Journal of Jewish Communal Service, 52, No. 3, Sp. pp 278-80.

BLASI, Joseph Raphael. The Kibbutz as a Learning Environment. Education and Community, A Radical Critique of Innovative Schooling. by Donald W. Oliver. Berkeley, Cal. McCutchen, pp 201-14.

BROOKE, Marcus S. It is my Aim to Change all This. Present Tense, 3, No. 4, Su. pp 10-12.

Describes Carmel College, a Jewish Public School in England, founded by Rabbi Kopul Rosen.

ELKINS, Dov Peretz. To Learn, to do, to Fulfill: Humanistic Education for Jewish Life. Religious Education, 11, No. 2, Ma/Ap. pp 187-201.

"If the emphasis were on the joy of learning, education would be more effective."

ESKOW, Seymour. Let Israel be the Curriculum: Notes on Strategies for Increasing the Flow of Students to Israel and Improving the Quality of their Education, Rockland, Community College 4.

THE FRIENDS OF THE ZIONIST FEDERATION EDUCATIONAL TRUST. The Zionist schools 1976, a year of consolidation in the midst of crisis, Annual Survey, 18p, Ill.

FUCHS-KREIMER, Nancy. Religious Studies in the Public Schools: The Jewish Response. Analysis, 0. pp 1-11.

Suggests some of the ways in which Jewish organisations, rabbis and parents can, without renouncing a commitment to church-state separation, participate positively in the development of religious studies for public schools.

GOLDMAN, Israel M. Jewish Law and Jewish Learning. Jewish Spectator, 41, No. 3, Fa. pp 24-33.

HALEVY, Zvi. Jewish Schools Under Czarism and Communism. A Struggle for Cultural Identity. New York, Springer, vi, 298p, Ind., Bibl.

In seven chapters: Origins and Socio-economic status of Russian Jewry since the Polish Partitions; Traditional Jewish Education; The Secular Yiddish School Movement before and after the Russian Revolution; The Secular Hebrew School Movement; The Development of the Soviet Communist School in Yiddish; The Curriculum of the Soviet Communist School in Yiddish; Yiddish Schools in annexed areas, 1939-40.

KAMINETSKY, Joseph. A Program for the Day School Movement in the '70's and Beyond. Tradition, 16, No. 1, Su. pp 120-26.

KATZ, M.E. Seventy-five Years of Jewish Education in the Cape. Jewish Affairs, 31, No. 1, Ja. pp 17-21.

KAUNFER, Neal. Retraining Jewish Teachers, Response, Vol. 1, Nos. 2-3, (30-31) Su/Fa. pp 193-99.

KRAMER, Doniel Zvi. The History of Impact of Torah Umesorah and Hebrew Day Schools in America, Ann Arbor, Mich., U. Microfilms, 381p. Bibl.

Ph. D. Dissertation, Yeshiva University, New York.

KRONISH, Ronald. The Influence of John Dewey on Jewish Education: Preliminary Findings. Conservative Judaism, 30, No. 1, pp 44-57.
Jewish education is in need of a realignment of theory with practice.

LASKER, Arnold. What Parents Want from the Jewish Education of their Children. Journal of Jewish Communal Service, 52, No. 4, Su. pp 393-403.
Parents consider that they and their home have a greater effect in helping their children as Jews than does the school. The resources of the home can be mustered and integrated with the resources of the school for the harmonious Jewish development of the child.

MISHEIKER, Ronnie. Jewish Education in Johannesburg. A brief and historical survey. Jewish Affairs, 36, No. 10, O. pp 21-23.

OUT OF THE DEPTH. London, JNF Education Dept., n.d. 32p. Bibl.
Guide for the commemoration of 'Heroes' and 'Martyrs' Day.

PODET, A.H. Secular Studies and Religious Uniqueness: A View of Hanukkah. Religious Education, 71, No. 6, pp 596-602.
Plea for giving Hanukkah an historical and social meaning.

PRESTON, David L. The German Jews in Secular Education, University Teaching, and Science: a Preliminary Inquiry. Jewish Social Studies, 38, No. 2, Sp. pp 99-116.

RELIGION IN THE SCHOOLS: Symposium. Religious Education, 71, No. 1, Ja/F. pp 68-95.
The Search for Common Definitions of Religious Studies and Public Education, by Guntram G. Baschoff. - Objectivity in the Teaching of Religion Studies in Public Schools, by David E. Engel. - Implementing the Study of Religion in High Schools: One State's (Michigan) Experience by Paul J. Will.
Discusses the problem in a country where there is complete separation of Church and State.

ROME, David. On the Jewish School Question In Montreal, 1903-31. Montreal, Canadian Jewish Congress, 152p, (Canadian Jewish Archives)

SCHIFF, Alvin I. Communal Planning and Jewish Education: Editorial Essay. Jewish Education, 46, No. 1, Sp/su. pp 3-13.
The convergence between national planning and local implementation will strengthen the structure of Jewish education and culture in America. The product of that convergence will be the improvement of its substance and consequences.

SEGAL, Kenneth I. Ethical Values of Jewish Youth: The Implication for our Schools. CCAR Journal, 24, No. 1, W. pp 57-64.
Results of a study of 245 teenagers at the Rodef Shalom Religious School in Pittsburgh, Pa.

SHERWIN, Byron L. Restructuring Jewish Education. Congress Monthly, 43, No. 9, No. pp 10-13.
"Under present conditions the focus of Jewish education ought to be upon the people requiring education rather than upon supporting and sustaining institutions which are structured to deal with problems relevant to past generations."

SILBERMAN, Charles E. Where are our Children? Moment, 1, No. 4, pp7.
State of Jewish education.

SILVER, Daniel Jeremy. The American University and Jewish Learning. Judaism, 25, No. 3, Su. pp 281-89.

SINGER, David. The Yeshivah World. Commentary, 52, No. 10, O. pp 70-73.

SLESINGER, Zalman. Toward a Contemporary and Community-Wide Perspective of Jewish Education. Jewish Frontier, 43, No. 7, Au/S. pp 20-25.

The present situation calls for a perspective of Jewish education that not only reflects the social-cultural dynamics of our times, but also recognises the cultural interdependence, the educational needs and the spiritual well-being of the total Jewish community in the U.S.A.

STRASSFIELD, Michael and Sharon. (Eds.) The Second Jewish Catalog: Sources and Resources. Philadelphia, Jewish Publication Society of America, 464p, Ill.

The success of the first "Jewish Catalog" prompted the publication of this volume of educational materials.

THABAULT, R. Le Maroc à l'Heure du Vichysme. Les Nouveaux Cahiers, 11, No. 43, pp 16-20.

The author was responsible for public education in the Protectorate, Describes the fate of the Alliance Israélite Universalle schools.

WILSON, Marvin R. The Jewish Concept of Learning: A Christian Appreciation. Christian Scholar's Review, 5, No. 4, pp 350-65.

Analyses the concept of Jewish learning and draws from biblical, Talmudic, medieval, modern and Chasidic sources.

WOLPIN, Nisson. The American Hebrew Day School Movement Comes of Age.- A Report and an Analysis. The Jewish Observer, No. 1, O. pp 3-10.

A survey on trends in Torah education.

ZOHAR, Haim. Jewish Education in the Diaspora. L'Eylah, 1, No. 1, W. pp 35-40.

A survey.

STUDENTS

HAAG, John. Blood on the Ringstrasse: Vienna's Students 1918-33. Wiener Library Bulletin, 29, N.S. No. 39/40, pp 29-33.

Clashes between the progressive and Jewish students and Nazis.

HASLER, Alfred A. Das Ende der Revolte. Aufbruch der Jugend 1968 und die Jahre danach. Zurich, Ex Libris, 336p, Ind, Bibl., SF.

Analyses factors that motivated the student revolution in 1968 and its consequences.

HAVE YOU SOLD OUT? A Response Symposium. Veterans of the Jewish Student Movement. Response, 10, No. 1, Sp. pp 33-86.

A retrospective view of the Jewish student movement. David Twersky, William Novak, Lucy Y. Steinitz and Jack Nusan Porter, are or have been active or influential in the movement over the past decade.

SCIENCE AND SCIENTISTS

CARMELL, Aryeh and DOMB, Cyril. (Eds.) Challenge: Torah Views of Science and Its Problems. New York, Feldheim, Association of Orthodox Jewish Scientists of Great Britain. 538.

HOFFMAN, Banesh and DUKAS, Helen. Einstein, Schöpfer und Rebell. Biographie. Tr. Jeanette Zehnder. Zürich, Stocker-Schmid; Stuttgart, Belser, 320p.

HUXLEY, Thomas Henry. Science and Hebrew Tradition: Essays, Westport, Conn., Greenwood P.; London, Westport P., xvi, 372p.
  Reprint of 1896 edition.

MALLOW, Jeffrey V. Jews and Science. Response, 10, No. 1, Sp. pp 19-31.

SPERO, Samuel W. and SLOE, Menachem. "Computing" Jewish Law. Jewish Life, 31, No. 3, Fa. pp 5--57.
  Describes a project at Bar Ilan University in Ramat Gan, Israel creating a data bank of the Rabbinic Responsa literature.

YORK, Herbert F. The Advisors. Oppenheimer, Teller and the Superbomb. San Francisco, W.H. Freeman, 175p.

LITERATURE

CISMARU, Alfred. Ionesco as Apologist of Jewish Causes. Midstream, 22, No. 6, Ju/Jy. pp 73-76.

FINESTEIN, Israel. Matthew Arnold and the Jews. Jewish Quarterly, 23, No. 4, W. pp 10-17.

HAYWARD, Max. and LABEDZ, Leopold. Literature and Revolution in Soviet Russia 1917-1962. A Symposium. Westport, Conn., Greenwood P.; London, Westport P., xx, 235p.
  Reprint of 1963 edition. Includes Jewish writers, the Jew in Soviet literature.

MAYO, Louise Abbie. Herman Melville, the Jew and Judaism. American Jewish Archives, 28, No. 2, N. pp 172-79.
  Melville is the only major American writer in the nineteenth century to include a serious consideration of Jews and Judaism in his works.

MICHELSON, H. The Jew in Early English Literature. New York, Sepher Hermon, 186p. Ill.
  Reprint of the 1926 edition.

MITCHELL, Gina. British Novels Present a New Image of the Jews. Patterns of Prejudice, 10, No. 5, S/O. pp 26-32.
  Examines popular fiction published since 1945, with particular attention to the works of Len Deighton, Robert Shaw, Muriel Spark and Leslie Thomas.

JEWISH LITERATURE

CASSUTO, Umberto. Storia della letteratura ebraica postbiblica. Assisi, Roma, Carucci, 215p. (Collana di cultura ebraica).

FRIEDLANDER, Albert H. Kafka's Ape. Meditation on Religious Dialogue. European Judaism, 10, No. 1, W. pp 30-36.

FRIEDMAN, M.J. The Schlemiel: Jew and non-Jews. Studies in Literary Imagination. 9, No. 1, pp 139-53.
  The anti-hero in contemporary American Jewish fiction.

RAPHAEL, Chaim. The Litvak Connection and Hasidic Chic. Commentary, 61, No. 5, My. pp 48-53.
On contemporary Jewish writing.

SHOWALTER, D.E. A River of Blood and Time: Images of Jewish-Gentile Relations in Contemporary Pulp Culture. The South Atlantic Quarterly, 76, No. 1, pp 12-30.
The image of the Jew in non-Jewish literature and that of the gentile in Jewish novels in the USA.

WISSE, Ruth R. American Jewish Writing, Act II. Commentary, 61, No. 6, Ju. pp 40-45.
The world of American Jews has lent itself to the production of satire, but not so far as any nobler art.

ZINBERG, Israel. A History of Jewish Literature. The Science of Judaism and Galician Haskalah. Tr. and ed. by Bernard Martin. Cincinnati, Hebrew Union College P.; New York, Ktav, vols. 8-10.

JEWISH WRITERS

ALBARET, Celeste. Monsieur Proust as told to Georges Belmont. Tr. Barbara Bray. London, Collins and Harvill P., 387p., Ind., Ill.
Memoirs of Marcel Proust by his housekeeper and closest companion for the last nine years of his life.

ALEXANDER, Edward. The Destruction and Resurrection of the Jews in the Fiction of I.B. Singer. Judaism, 25, No. 1, W. pp 98-106.

ANGOFF, Charles. How "Jewish" are Jewish Writers in America. Tradition, 16, No. 2, Fa. pp 24-34.

BENJAMIN, J.C. Israel Zangwill: A Re-evaluation. Jewish Quarterly, 24, No. 3, Au. pp 3-5.

BRESLIN, John B. Elie Wiesel. Survivor and Witness. America, 133, 19 Ju. pp 537-39.
"Elie Wiesel has fashioned from his survival a witness that speaks far more of love and prayer than of rancor and malediction." Based on an interview.

BROD, Max. Heinrich Heine: The Artist in Revolt. Tr. J. Witriol. Westport, Conn., Greenwood P.; London, Westport P., 355p, Ill.
Facsimile of the first edition.

Elias Canetti. Munich text + kritik, 59p.

CARGAS, Harry James. In Conversation with Elie Wiesel. New York, Paulist P., ix, 126p.
Portrait of the man who writes the legends of the Holocaust.

-------------------. Elie Wiesel and the Holocaust. Commonweal, 100 10 S. pp 594-96.
"Wiesel's works can be distinguished from the writings of others because they are acts of faith."

CSUKLY, László: Emlékezés Révész Béla-ra. Uj Forrás, No. 1, pp 127-36.
Memories of the Hungarian Jewish writer and critic on the centenary of his birth. Revesz was killed by the Nazis.

Das Ja des Neinsagers. Karl Kraus und seine geistige Welt. Munchen, Richard Boorberg, 248p.

DUERR, Volker and MOLNÁR, Geza. (Eds.) Versuche zu Goethe. Festschrift fuer Erich Heller zum 65. Geburtstag, Heidelberg, L. Siehm, 383p, Bibl.
Jubilee volume in honour of German exile literary critic and essayist, now Professor at the North-western University, which

contains, in addition to the many Goethe studies, a short essay on Karl Kraus by Friedrich Torberg and a bibliography of Heller's works.

DUKORE, Bernard. F. Where Laughter Stops: Pinter's Tragicomedy. U. of Missouri P., 96p.

Monograph.

FENYŐ, Mario D. Writers in Politics: The role of Nyugat in Hungary, 1908-19. Journal of Contemporary History, 11, No. 1, Ja. pp 185-98

Nyugat was a high-quality literary monthly with many Jewish avant-garde writers around it.

GOTTLIEB, Freema. Leonard Woolf: The Pride, the Shame. European Judaism, 10, No. 1, W. pp 24-30.

Heinrich Heine. Munich, Edition text + kritik, 80p.

HINCHCLIFFE, Arnold P. Harold Pinter, London, McMillan, 192p.

Monograph.

JAFFIN, David. Joseph Roth, the Poet of Silence. European Judaism, 10, No. 1, W. pp 47-48.

KUNA, Franz. (Ed.) On Kafka: Semi-centenary Perspectives. London, Elek, 208p.

Monograph.

Le CLECH, Guy. Malamud et l'école judéo-americaine du roman. L'Arche, 19, No. 230, My. pp 39-40.

KAUFMAN, Shirley. Charles Reznikoff, 1894-1976. An Appreciation. Midstream, 22, No. 7, Au/S. pp 51-6.

KAGAN, Robert. The Sweeter Welcome: Voices for a Vision of Affirmation: Bellow, Malamud and Martin Buber. Needham Heights, Mass., Humanities P., 169p.

KERMODE, Frank. (Ed.) Erich Heller: Frank Kafka, Moderne Theoretiker. Munich, DTV, Forras.

LACKO, Miklós. Osvát Ernő. Forras, 15, No. 4, Ap. pp 92-101.

Osvat was a prominent Jewish writer of the 1920's, editor of the avant-garde literary monthly Nyugat.

MOREAU, J.L. Vallomás Radnótiról. Nagyvilag, 21, No. 12, D. pp 1860-71.

On Miklos Radnóti.

Nelly Sachs. Munich, text + kritik, 51p.

Evaluation of the Nobel Laureate poet.

PAINTER, George. Proust Known and Unknown. Adams International Review, 40, Nos. 394-96, pp 12-14.

PERLMANN, M. Levanda's Jubilee, 1885. Proceedings of the American Academy of Jewish Research, 43, pp 167-82.

Lev Osipovich Levanda (1835-1888) wrote in Russian.

PETRANYI, Ilona. A drámairó Pap Károly. Irodalom törtehet. 64, No. 3, pp 566-688.

Dramatic works of the Hungarian Jewish writer.

PINSKER, Sanford. The Comedy that 'hoits' - An Essay on the Fiction of Philip Roth. U. of Missouri P., vi, 144p.

On Abraham Klein. The Jewish Spectator, 41, No. 1, Sp . pp 24-26.

PIZER, Donald. Novels of Theodore Dreiser: A Critical Study. Minneapolis, U. of Minnesota P., 382p.

POMOGATS, Béla. A Tudatos Költő. Nagyvilág, 21, No. 12, D. pp 1860-71.

On Miklós Radnóti.

ROSENTHAL, M.L. On Being a Jewish Poet. Memories and Associations. Present Tense, 3, No. 2, W. pp 27-32.

ROVNER, Ruth. Charles Reznikoff - A Profile. Jewish Frontier, 43, N. pp 14-18.

SALAMON, George. Arnold Zweig. New York, Twayne; London, G. Prior, 200p.

SCHNITZLER, Arthur. in Selbstzeugnissen und Bilddokumenten. Hamburg, Rowohlt, 158p, Ill.
Autobiographical sketches, letters, photos of the Austrian Jewish writer.

SCHWARTZ, Howard. Charles Reznikoff: Dean of American Jewish Poets. Jewish Quarterly, 24, Nos. 1-2, Sp/Su. pp 29-30.

SPANN, Meno. Franz Kafka. London, G. Prior, 175p. (World Authors S.)
Monograph.

STERNBERGER, Dolf. Heinrich Heine und die Abaschaffung der Sünde. Frankfurt, Suhrkamp, 448p, Ind, Ill. (Suhrkamp Taschenbuch 308)
Heine's pleas for the abolition of sin.

STRONG, Alexandra. Albert Cohen at 81. Jewish Quarterly, 24, No. 1-2, Sp/Su. pp 23-25.

TIGER, Virginia. William Golding: The Dark Fields of Discovery. London, M. Boyars, 244p.
Monograph.

WIRKNER, Alfred. Kafka und die Aussenwelt. Quellenstudien zum 'Amerika' - Fragment. Stuttgart, Klett 113p.
America in Kafka's world.

WIZNITZER, Manuel. Arnold Zweig et le pays d'Israel: Patrie ou exil? Paris, 338p.
Thesis submitted to Paris University on Zweig's ambivalent attitude to Zionism and Israel.

WOODCOCK, George. Mordecai Richler. Toronto, McClelland & Stewart, 62p, (Bantam)
Biography.

WUNDHEILER, Luitgard N. Paul Celan, Poet of the Holocaust. World-view, 19, No. 12, D. pp 24-26; 35-56.

ZELK, Zoltan. Egy magyár költö utolso eve. (Pásztor Béláról, 1908-1943). Kritika, No. 11, N. pp 17-19.
In memory of Béla Pásztor, martyred Jewish poet.

------------. hetvenevés. Illyés Gyula, Mándy Iván, Beladi Miklos es Szabo István irasa. Kritika, No. 12, D. pp 16-17.
Contemporaries celebrate 70th birthday of Hungarian Jewish poet.

ZOHN, Harry B. Gertrud Kolmar: German-Jewish poet. Jewish Quarterly 24, No. 1-2, Sp/Su. pp 26-28.

-------------. (Ed. and Trans.) KRAUS, Karl. Half-Truth and One-and-half Truth. Selected Aphorisms. Montreal, Engendra Press,

ZWEIG, Stefan. Die Monotonisierung der Welt. Aufsätze und Vorträge. Ausgewählt und mit einem Nachwort von Volker Michels. Frankfurt/M. Suhrkamp, 140p.
Essays and lectures on contemporary problems by the noted Austrian Jewish writer who committed suicide in exile in Brazil in 1942.

YIDDISH

DREESSEN, W.O., RÖLL, W. and TIMM, E. Jiddische Drucke vor 1800. Hilfen für den Umgang mit einem neuen Quellenverzeichnis. Zeitschrift für Deutsches Altertum und Deutsche Literatur, 105, No. 4, pp 310-17.

Concordance helping to identify works listed by H. Dinse (1974) M. Steinschneider (1852-60), W. Steerk and A. Leitzmann (1923).

FISHMAN, Joshua A. Sociolinguistic Perspective on the Jerusalem Conference on Yiddish Language and Culture. Yiddishe Shprakh, 35, Nos. 1-3, pp 16-31.

GOLDSMITH, Emanuel S. Architects of Yiddishism at the Beginning of the Twentieth Century. A Study in Jewish Cultural History. Rutherford, Madison, Teaneck, Fairleigh Dickinson U.P.; London, Associated U.P., 309p, Ind., Bibl., Ill.

Keeping in mind the importance of Yiddish during a crucial period in Jewish history, the author explores the Yiddish language movement in its attempt to secure a position of primacy for Yiddish and Yiddish culture.

KORN, Yitzhak. Problemen far der velt-konferents far Yiddishe Kultur. Di Tsukunft, 82, No. 2, F. pp 62-65.

LIFSHUTZ, Ezekiel. The Yiddishe Gazeten (1874-1928) Yiddish, 2, Nos. 2-3, W/Sp., pp 32-38.

ROSENFELD, Lulla. Bright Star of Exile. Jacob Adler and the Yiddish Theater. New York, Viking P., 240p, Ill.

SELAVAN, Ida Cohen. The Yiddish Press in Pittsburgh: Agency for Americanziation or Ethnic Identification. Yiddish, 2, Nos. 2-3, W/Sp., pp 49-54.

SINGER, Isaac Bashevis. The Case for Yiddish. Condensed from Judaica Book News. Jewish Digest, 22, No. 2, N. pp 40-45.

YIDDISH LANGUAGE

COPELAND, Robert M. and SUSSKIND, Nathan. (Eds.) The Language of Herz's Esther: A Study in Judeo-German Dialectology. University, Ala.: The U. of Alabama P., 439p. (Judaic Studies S.)

FALKOVITCH, E. Sprachliche bamerkungen. (Linguistic Notes) Sovietish Heimland, 16, No. 7, Jy. pp 169-77.

Yiddish usage today.

-------------. Sprachliche bamerkungen. (Linguistic Notes) Sovietish Heimland, 16, No. 10, O. pp 135-43.

Notes on Yiddish linguistics and syntax.

HAIBLUM, Isadore. Yiddish in the Underworld. Where the Shamus is Never Kosher and Sex Spells Danger. The National Jewish Monthly, 90, No. 10, Ju. pp 18-25.

KOBRIN, Leon. From "Daytchmerish" to Yiddish in America. Yiddish, 2, Nos. 2-3, W/Sp. pp 39-48.

RUDIN, Neil. Yiddish Literature: A Path to Ethnic Awareness. Tradition, 16, No. 1, S. pp 77-82.

SONNTAG, Jacob. Jerusalem Conference on Yiddish. Jewish Quarterly, 24, No. 3, Au. pp 16-18.

SPIVAK, E. Idiom un vertl in Sholem Aleichem's fraseologie. (Idiom and anecdote in Sholem Aleichem's phraseology.) Yiddish Kultur, 38, No. 5, My. pp 22-29.

URBACH, Rachel. Congrès pour la langue yiddish: reflexions d'une deleguee belge. Regards, 12, No. 107, O. pp 45-48.

YIDDISH LITERATURE

ARONTCHIK, Judes. Wegn einer a lid (About a Poem) Sovietish Heimland, 16, No. 2, F. pp 162-65.
An actress of the Yiddish theatre remembers the poet David Hofstein.

BERGELSON, David. Proletarishe proze-kunst. (Proletarian prose). Sovietish Heimland, 16, No. 1, Ja. pp 56-62.
Reprint of an article on Note Lurie's Di stepp ruft (The steppe calls), first published in the Minsk journal Oktober in 1932.

BERIOZKIN, H. Harz un velt. (Heart and World). Sovietish Heimland, 16, No. 1, Ja. pp 149-55.
Discusses the work of the Yiddish poet Motl Grubian.

BRUKAJ, Mayer. Einer fun di ershte. (One of the first) Sovietish Heimland, 16, No. 3, Ma. pp 79-81.
On the Yiddish poet Moishe Yadovin.

CHAMETSKY, Jules. The Yiddish Fiction of Abraham Cahan. Yiddish, 2, Nos. 2-3, W/Sp. pp 7-22.

FINKELSTEIN, Aba. Y. L. Peretzes verk un verk vegn Peretzn, dershinen in sovietfarband in di yorn 1917-74. (Bibliography of works by and on J. L. Peretz published in the USSR 1917-74) Sovietish Heimland, 16, No. 5, My. pp 192-97 and No. 6, Ju. pp 182-88.

GOLDBERG, B.Z. Recollections of Maurice Samuel. Yiddish, 2, Nos. 2-3, W/Sp. pp 58-61.

GORALNIK, Aron. Di muze fun flamiker satire. (The muse of flaming satire) Sovietish Heimland, 16, No. 1, Ja. pp 156-60.
The influence of Saltikov-Shchedrin (1826-89) on 19th century Yiddish literature.

--------------. Di sovietish literature taum 25. parteitsuzamenfor. Sovietish Heimland, 16, No. 2, F. pp 166-70. (Soviet literature for the 25th Party Congress).
Problems of Russian and Yiddish literature to be raised at the 25th Party Congress.

LIBEDINSKAYA, Lidya. A begegnish mit der yungt. (Meeting the Youth) Sovietish Heimland, 16, No. 3, Ma. pp 17-20.
Impressions of a visit in Birobidzhan, where the author met young Yiddish writers.

LUBOMIRSKY, Y. Peretz Markishes dramas. (The dramas of Markish) Sovietish Heimland, 16, No. 1, Ja. pp 161-66.

MARGOLIN, Moishe. Der didter Avrom Shlonsky Sovietish Heimland, 16, No. 12, D. pp 140-48.

MARK, Berl. Di literatur in getto vi an element fun vidershtand. (Literature of the ghetto as an element of resistance) Sovietish Heimland, 16, No. 4, Ap. pp 3-7.
Reprint of an article first published in the Warsaw journal Yiddishe Shriftn in 1963, to commemmorate the 20th anniversary of the uprising.

MOSKOWITZ, Moshe. Chaim Grade and the Jewish Ego. Judaism, 25, No. 3, Su. pp 331-40.

PILCH, Judah. Shimon Frug (1860-1916) Jewish Frontier, 43, No. 5, My, pp 14-16.
RASKIN, A. Bamerkungen vegn Bergelsons shafund. (Notes on Bergelson's works) Sovietish Heimland, 16, No. 7, Jy. pp 141-49.
---------. Di hayntseitige yiddishe novelle. (The Contemporary Yiddish short story) Sovietish Heimland, 16, No. 8, Au. pp 94-104.
REMENIK, Hersh. Sholem Aleichems realizm. (The realism of Sholem Aleichem.) Sovietish Heimland, 16, No. 10, O. pp 114-22.
ROTENBERG, Yehoshua. Yiddish literature un Yiddishe Geschichte, Di Tsukunft, 82, No. 1, Ja. pp 7-11.
SEREBRIANI, Yisroel. Goldfadens gastrol - reize in die frie achtsiger yorn. (Goldfaden's guest role - a journey in the early 80's). Sovietish Heimland, 16, No. 10, O. pp 126-34.
SHULMAN, Abraham. Doestoevski Couldn't Compete With Sholem Aleichem. Condensed from Workmen's Circle Call. Jewish Digest, 22, No. 2, N. pp 75-77.
TAUBE, Herman. I. L. Peretz - An Inspiration for Generations. Jewish Frontier, 43, No. 5, My. pp 17-18.
WEINER, Leo. The History of Yiddish Literature in the Nineteenth Century. New York, Sepher Hermon,
Reprint of 1899 edition.
WISSE, R. Di Yunge and the Problem of Jewish Aestheticism. Jewish Social Studies, 38, Nos. 3-4, pp 265-76.
Di Yunge was the group of American Yiddish writers who followed the path of L'art pour l'art, advocating "art for art's sake" which gave Yiddish literature undeniable formal perfection.

HEBREW

BAKER, William. George Eliot and Hebrew: Some Source Materials. Studies in Bibliography and Booklore, 11, Nos. 1-2, W. pp 75-84.
BRILLING, Bernhard. Zur Geschichte der Hebräischen Buchdruckereien in Altona. Studies in Bibliography and Booklore, 11, Nos. 1-2, W. pp 41-56.
Altona was an important place for Hebrew publishing in the 17th/18th century.
DRIVER, Godfrey Rolles. Semitic Writing: From Pictograph to Alphabet. Oxford, U.P., 286p, Ill. (Schweich Lectures)
Hebräische Schrift von der Steinschrift zum Poster. Zurich, Museum of Folk-Art, 68p. Ill.
Catalogue of the exhibition in Zürich Kunstgewerbemuseum, 17 S.-24 O.
IVRY, Isaac. "Conscience" for Zion and Hebrew. Midstream, 22, No. 8, O. pp 49-51.
The editor of Hadoar discussed the failure of the Hebrew language in America.
LAVY. Jaacov. (Ed.) Langenscheidts Handwörterbuch: Hebräisch-Deutsch. Berlin, Langenscheidt, 639p.

HEBREW LANGUAGE

BEN-ABBA, Dov. Iwrit für einen Trip durch Israel. Hebräischer Sprachführer. Tr. by D. Rosenberg. Düsseldorf, Polyglotte, 141p.
Pocket Hebrew phrase-book.

BLAU, Joshua. A Grammar of Biblical Hebrew. Wiesbaden, Otto Harrassowitz, xi, 209p. (Porta Linguarum Orientalium 12)
COLE, Peter. Studies in Modern Hebrew Syntax and Semantics. London, North-Holland Pub. Co. xii, 286p.
LANDMANN, Michael. Reform of the Hebrew Alphabet. Tr. David J. Parent. Foreword by James W. Marchand. Norman, Ill. Applied Literature P., Ann Arbor, Mich., U. Microfilms Intern.
MANSOOR. Menahem. Contemporary Hebrew. New York, Behrman House.
ROSEN, Halim B. Textbook of Israeli Hebrew. 2 R.C., Chicago, U. of Chicago P., xvi, 404p.
ST. JOHN, Robert. Tongue of the Prophets: The Life Story of Eliezer Ben Yehuda. Westport, Conn., Greenwood P., 377p.
 The pioneer of Hebrew revival. Reprint of 1952 edition.
SAWYER, John F.A. Modern Introduction to Biblical Hebrew. New York, Oriel P., 230p.
WILLIAMS, Ronald J. Hebrew Syntax: An Outline. Toronto, U. of Toronto P., 122p.

HEBREW LITERATURE

GINZBURG, Simon. The Life and Works of Moses Hayyim Luzzatto, Founder of Modern Hebrew Literature. Westport, Co., Greenwood P., vii, 189p.
 Reprint of the 1931 edition.
GOLDSMITH, Samuel J. Abraham Mapu. Padre de la moderne literature hebrea. Buenos Aires. Congreso Judio Latino americano. (Biblioteca Popular Judia, Grandes Figuras del Judaismo 98) 32p. Ill.
 Monograph of the Hebrew writer.
KLAUSNER, Joseph. Ed. by Leon Simon. A History of Modern Hebrew Literature (1785-1930). Tr. Herbert Danby. Westport, Conn., Greenwood P., v, 204p.
 Reprint of the 1932 edition.
SILBERSCHLAG, E. The Thrust of Hebrew Letters in America. A Panoramic View. Jewish Social Studies, 38, Nos. 3-4, pp 277-88.
 Hebrew literature in the USA reached its peak in the inter-war years. Will there be a renaissance?
WINEHOUSE, Bernard. Naftali Herz ('Hertzele') Imber. Jewish Quarterly, 24, No. 3, Au. pp 6-9.
YUDKIN, Leon. Fate and Faith in Amichai's Poetry. Jewish Affairs, 31, No. 6, Ju. pp 43-45.

JUDEO-ARABIC, LADINO

Poslovice i izreke sefardskih jevreja Bosne i Hercegovine (Proverbs and Sayings of the Sephardi Jews of Bosnia and Herzegovina) Beograd, Federation of Jewish Communities in Yogoslavia and Ben-Zvi Institute of the Yad Izhak Ben-Zvi and the Hebrew University, Jerusalem, 96p, Ill.
 Ladino proverbs and sayings from Bosnia and Herzegovina, ordered alphabetically with an introduction and preface in Serbo-Croat, English and Hebrew.
SALA, Marius. Le Judeo-Espagnol. Paris, Hague Mouton, 117p.
 Ladino.

JEWS AND GENTILES

AGUS, Jacob B. Judaism and the New Testament. Journal of Ecumenical Studies, 13, No. 4, Fa. pp 80-97.

ANGELL, Charles. The Jewish-Christian Dialogue on Israel is a Monologue. Interchange, 1, No. 9, My. pp 6-7.

ATLAN, Henry. Israel and the Gentiles. Jewish Spectator, 41, No. 3, Su. pp 14-18.

"Jewish particularism, as all other particularisms, is a contradiction in terms and contrary to Jewish self-interest. Rather than cultivate such a particularism, the Jews endure exile and dispersion among the nations so as to rediscover Jewish universality."

BLENKINSOPP, Joseph. Judaism and Teaching the Old Testament. The Living Light, 13, No. 3, Fa. pp 360-71.

Study of the Old Testament will ensure a positive approach.

BUREN, Paul. M. van. The Burden of Freedom: Americans and the God of Israel. New York, Seabury P., 114p.

Christian-Jewish relations in the U.S.A.

COHON, Samuel S. Reflections on Judaism and Christianity. Jewish Spectator, 41- No. 3, Fa. pp 19-23.

THE COMPLEX REALITY OF JUDAISM: Special Issue. Sidic, 9, No. 1, pp 1-35.

Includes: The Complexity of Contemporary Judaism, by Kurt Hruby. The Complexity of Jewish Existence by Jonathan Magonet. On the Jewish-Christian Dialogue (Part II) by Mayer Jais.

DUPUY, B. Que represente l'éxistence juive pour un chretien? Recontre, 10, pp 13-22.

ERLICH, Ernst Ludwig. Judaica et Christiana. Bern, Frankfurt, Herbert Lang, 52p.

FIORENZA, Elizabeth Schüssler. (Ed.) Aspects of Religious Propaganda in Judaism and Early Christianity. Montreal, Notre Dame P., 195p, Bibl.

The essays contained in the book discuss the response of Judaism and early Christianity to the Greco-Roman world and its religious propaganda.

FLANNERY, Edward H. The Next Century of Jewish-Christian Relations. Face to Face, 1, W/Sp., pp 3-4.

FLEISCHNER, Eva. Judaism in German Christian Theology since 1945: Christianity and Israel Considered in Terms of Mission. Folkestone Scarecrow P., xviii, 237p. (American Theological Library Association Monograph 8)

GOLLINGER, Hildegard. Juden und Judentum im christlichen Religionsunterricht. 2. "Zielfelderplan für den katholischen Religionsunterricht" - eine Chance für den jüdisch-christlichen Dialog? Freiburger Rundbrief, 28, Nos. 105-8, pp 46-50.

GOLLWITZER, Helmut. Vietnam, Israel und die Christenheit, München, Chr. Kaiser, 104p.

Essay on the responsibility of Christians in crises like Israel and Vietnam.

GORDIS, Robert. Judaism and World Community. Congress Monthly, 43, No. 2, F. pp 10-11.

An address delivered at a Conference on World Religions, Hinduism, Buddhism, Judaism, Christianity and Islam.

GRANT, Michael. Jesus. London, Weidenfeld & Nicolson, 288p.
--------------. Paul The Discontented Jew. Midstream, 22, Nos. 8-9, Au/S. pp 32-40.
Suggests that, had it not been for Paul, Judaism might eventually have conquered the Roman empire instead of Christianity.
HOMMEL, Gisela. Der Siebenarmige Leuchter. Erster Blick aufs Judentum für Christen. Ein Erfahrungsbericht. München, J. Pfeiffer, 156p, Bibl.
JEWISH-CHRISTIAN RELATIONS: LOOKING TO THE TWENTY-FIRST CENTURY: Special Issue. Face to Face, 1, W/Sp., pp 1-20.
Includes: The Next Century of Jewish-Christian Relations by Edward H. Flannery. Starting Points on the Road to Understanding by Claire Huchet-Bishop. A Crisis of Faith by Franklin H. Littell. Jewish-Christian Dialogue - Prospects and Future by Seymour Siegel.
JOHNSON, Paul. A History of Christianity. London, Weidenfeld, vii, 556p, Ind, Bibl.
A world history of Christianity with references to Christian anti-semitism, attitudes to Jews, Judaism, the Nazi persecution of Jews and the changes that have taken place since World War II.
KUNG, Hans and KASPER, Walter. (Eds.) Christians and Jews. New York, Seabury P., 93p.
---------- and LAPIDE, Pinchas E. Jesus in Widerstreit. Ein jüdisch-christlicher Dialog. München, Kösel; Stuttgart, Calwer, 51p.
LANGE, Nicholas R.M. de. Origen and the Jews: Studies in Jewish Christian Relations in Third-century Palestine. Cambridge U.P., x, 240p. (Oriental Publications.)
LAPIDE, Pinchas E. Ist das nicht =osephs Sohn? Jesus im heutigen Judentum. München, Kösel; Stuttgart, Calwer, 167p.
-----------------. Two Famous Rabbis. Annual of the Swedish Theological Institute, 10, pp 97-100.
MARTY, Martin E. A National of Behavers. Chicago, U. of Chicago P., xi, 239p, Ind.
Religious attitudes in contemporary American society. In the group 'Mainline Religion', Professor Marty deals with the Jewish-Christian experience.
MATT, Hershel Jonah. The People Israel and the World as Reflected in the Jewish Prayer Book. Face to Face, 21, No. 2, Su/Fa. pp 11-2.

DIALOGUE

BRONSTEIN, Herbert. Jewish-Christian Dialogue: Problems and Prosepcts. Criterion, 15, No. 2, Sp. pp 16-19.
The problems of dialogue are threefold: (1) Christians are still too silent about anti-semitism, Israel and UN Declarations (2) Jews today are becoming more concerned about their own needs, in education, etc; (3) Dialogue is often very superficial. Yes, the prospects are good.
CUPITT, Don. Jesus the Jew. Christian Attitudes on Jews and Judaism 49, Au. pp 6-8.
"Most modern theologians have held that what Christians believe in is not the historical Jesus but the Christ of faith, the

divine Christ of the Church. I am saying the exact opposite. I am saying we should go back to before the split between Jews and Christians, back to Jesus himself, and start from there."

DER, Suzanne. La fin du drama entre juifs et chretiens. Marsiglia, 75p.

Le dialogue entre Juifs et Chretiens. Istina, 21, No. 1, W. pp 65-93

Several documents on the relation between Judaism and Christianity by D. Flusser, P. Dabosville, Rabbi Henry Siegman and the U.S. Bishops Conference's pastoral message.

FLESSMAN-VAN LEER, Ellen. Pre-Dialogue Talks. Christian Attitudes on Jews and Judaism, 48, Ju. pp 11-16.

Dialogue will become a possibility when Christians have learned to live with and accept their feelings of guilt and Jewish national existence is no longer threatened from the outside.

HENRIX, Hans Hermann. Der Dialog mit dem Judentum als Aufgabe ökumenischer Theologie. Una Sancta, 31, No. 2, Ju. pp 136-45.

Rabbi Jacob Petuchowski has pointed out that Jewish-Christian dialogue requires a return to a theological dimension. There is need for a Jewish theology of Christianity and a Christian theology of Judaism. Unfortunately, this call has remained without an echo.

HUDDLESTON, Trevor and MACCOBY, Hyam. Christian Jewish Dialogue. B'nai B'rith Journal, Su. pp 2-4,;Jewish Quarterly, 23, No. 4, W, 1975/76, pp 1-4.

LIPNER, J. Truth Claims and Inter-Religious Dialogue. Religious Studies, 12, No. 2, pp 217-30.

MAURIER, Henri W.F. The Christian Theology of the Non-Christian Religions. Lumen Vitae, 31, No. 1, pp 59-79.

A consistent problem in establishing dialogue with non-Christian religions is a tendency on the part of Christians to posit Christianity as an absolute. By creating a paridigm of action-reaction rather than superior-inferior, the partners can see each religion as related to and involving the other.

MAYER, Reinhold. Franz Rosenzweig. Eine Philosophie der dialogischen Erfahrung. München, Kaiser, 188p. (Abhandlungen zum christlich-jüdischen Dialog).

Reapplication of Rosenzweig's philosophy in the Christian-Jewish dialogue.

NEHER, Andre. Réparation et pardon. Rencontre, 10, pp 165-77.

Christian-Jewish relations after the Holocaust.

PAWLIKOWSKI, John T. Sinai and Calvary. A Meeting of Two Peoples. New York, Benziger, 229p.

Christians and Jews in the Holy Land.

------------------. The Theological Significance of the State of Israel for Christians. Engage/Social Action, 3, No. 12, D. pp 34-40.

Church statements on Judaism usually exclude any mention of Israel, viewing it solely as a 'political issue'. The exclusion of Israel from the Jewish-Christian dialogue agenda seriously impoverishes the encounter.

PIERRARD, P. Le dialogue judéo-chrétien. Un demisiècle de progrès (1926-1976) Rencontre, 10, pp 23-49.

RIBIERE, G.G. La conscience chretienne face a la solitude d'Israel.

Rencontre, 10, pp 84-86.

RIVKIN, Ellis. Jewish-Christian Relations in the Next Hundred Years. Face to Face, 1, W/Sp. pp 12.

ROTTENBERG, Isaac C. A Dialogue that Almost Died. Worldview, 19, No. 9, S. pp 35-38.

RUETHER, Rosemary. The Future of Christian Theology about Judaism. Christian Attitudes on Jews and Judaism, 49, Au. pp 1-5;8.

SCHAEFFER, Edith. Christianity is Jewish. Eastbourne, Sussex, Coverdale House, 190p.
For better interfaith relations.

SIEGEL, Seymour. Jewish-Christian Dialogue - Prospects and Future. Face to Face, 1, No. 1, W/Sp. pp 13-15.

Judaism and Eastern Orthodox Theological Relations. Journal of Ecumenical Studies, 13, No. 4, Fa. pp 63-69.

SILVER, Samuel M. Explaining Judaism to Jews and Christians. New York, Arco; London, Barrie & Jenkins, 118p, Ill.

SIMPSON, William W. Light and Rejoicing. A Christian's Understanding of Jewish Worship. Belfast, Christian Journals, 138p.
A Methodish Minister, former secretary of the Council of Christians and Jews, attempts a simple introduction to Judaism as a living religion.

SLOYAN, Gerard S. Jesus on Trial: The Development of the Passion Narratives and Their Historical and Ecumenical Implications. Intro. by John Reumann, New York, Fortree P., 156p.

STENDAHL, Krister. Saint Paul and the Jews. Engage/Social Action, 3, No. 24, D. pp 19-25.

-----------------. Widening the Perspectives of Jewish-Christian Relations. Face to Face, 1, No. 4, W/Sp. pp 17-18.

STYLIANOPOULOS, Theodore. New Testament Issues in Jewish-Christian Relations. Journal of Ecumencial Studies, 13, No. 4, Fa. pp 70-79.

TALMAGE, F.E. (Ed.) Disputation and Dialogue. Readings in the Jewish Christian Encounter. New York, Ktav, Anti-Defamation League of B'nai B'rith, xix, 411p, Ind.

TANENBAUM, Marc H. Religious Values in an Age of Violence. Milwaukee Theology Dept., Marquette U., 57p. (The 1976 Pere Marquette Theology Lecture)
Christians and Jews should engage in a massive effort to establish a 'new humanism' on a global basis.

THOMAS, Clemens. (Ed.) Zukunft in der Gegenwart: Wegweisungen in Judentum und Christentum. Bern, Frankfurt/M., Lang, 241p.

TOWNSEND, John T. "The Reproaches" in Christian Liturgies. Face to Face, 2, Su/Fa. pp 8-11.

VERMES, Geza. Jesus the Jew: Historical Reading of the Gospels. London, Fontana, 286p.

WERNER, Eric. Tribus Agathas (The Good Way) Journal of Ecumenical Studies, 13, No. 4, Fa. pp 143-54.

WIGODER, Geoffrey. Problems of Interfaith in Israel. Jewish Affairs, Au.; Jewish Digest, 21, No. 6, Ma. pp 68-71.

WILL, Herman, Israel and Christian-Jewish Relations, Engage/Social Action, 3, No. 24, D. pp 41-43.

WYSHOGROD, Michael. The Future of Jewish-Christian Relations. Face to Face, 2, No. 1, W/Sp. pp 19-20.

ZUIDEMA, W.H. Quedoesja - de vraag naar de joodse levensstijl (Kedusha - the Inquiry concerning the Jewish Style of Life). Ter herkonning, 4, No. 1, F. pp 4-11.
Judaism is a religion strongly geared toward life and experience. In Judaism, holiness regulates one's daily behaviour but it is also a social program.

CATHOLICS AND JEWS

BOKSER, Ben-Zion. New Statement on Christian-Jewish Relations. Congress Monthly, 43, No. 3, Ma. pp 12-14.
Discusses the new Guidelines to the Second Vatican Council's "Nostra Aetate" in 1965.

CATHOLIC-JEWISH HARMONY. Christian Attitudes on Jews and Judaism, 48, Ap. pp 13-16.
Text of a pastoral message approved by the Roman Catholic Bishops of the United States at their Conference in Washington, November, 1975. It was prepared in conjunction with the tenth anniversary of "Nostra Aetate".

CUCHETTI, Carlos. Del Concilio Ecumenico Vaticano II al Encuentro Judeo - Catolico de Jerusalem. Buenos Aires. OJI, Boletin Informativo, No. 17, 10p.
Lecture delivered at a Conference of the Argentinian-Israeli Cultural and Scientific Institute.

DUBOIS, Marcel. Israele: Il suo significato per le relazioni fra ebrei e cristiani. Documenti e Fatti, Nos. 16-17, Jy-O. pp 2-7.

DULLES, Avery. Jewish-Christian Relations since Vatican II: Problems and Prospects. Catholic Mind, 54, No. 3, Ma. pp 43-54.
Address delivered as the Fourth Annual King Christian X Memorial Lecture, in Washington, 28th October, by a theology professor at the Catholic University of America.

ETCHEGARAY, R. With Jews of Marseilles. Encounter Today, 11, Nos. 2-3, Su/Aut. pp 105-6.
The Archbishop of Marseilles addressed the Jews of the town.

FISHER, Eugene Joseph. A Content Analysis of the Treatment of Jews and Judaism in Current Roman Catholic Religion Textbooks and Manuals on the Primary and Secondary Levels. Ann Arbor, Mich., U. Microfilms, 366p. Bibl.
Ph.D. Dissertation, New York U.

GARBER, George. The Impact of the Establishment of the State of Israel on the Attitude of the Catholic Church Towards Israel During the Years 1948-1975, as reflected in American Catholic periodicals. Ann Arbor, Mich., Xerox Microfilms, 203p., Bibl.
Dissertation - New York U.

LEVENTMAN, P.G. and LEVENTMAN, S. Congressman Drinan S.J. and His Jewish Constituents. American Jewish Historical Quarterly, 66, No. 2, D. pp 215-48.

LIENART, Cardinal. Vatican II. Mélanges de Science Religieuse, 33, Special Issue, 155p., Ind., Ill.
Cardinal Lienart's evaluation of the Second Vatican Council.

MOELLER, Charles. Aus einem Kommentar zum 10 Jahrestag von "Nostra aetate", Freiburger Rundbrief, 28, Nos. 105-8, p. 12; Encounter

Today, 11, Nos. 2-3, Su/Aut. pp 72-76.
Address by the vice-president of the Vatican Commission for Religious Relations with the Jews, delivered as a conclusion to the national celebration of the tenth anniversary of the Vatican II declaration.

POLIAKOV, Leon. The Catholic Church and the Jews: The Vatican's New Guidelines. Midstream, 22, No. 8, O. pp 29-35.

RIJK, Cornelius A. Kerk en Judendum. (Church and Judaism) Kosnars and Oekumene, 10, Nos. 3-4, pp 85-93.
The Vatican declaration "Nostra Aetate" was not just an act of rehabilitation of the Jews but a first step towards rehabilitating the Church's own identity.

SIEGMAN, Henry. Ten Years of Catholic-Jewish Relations: A Reassessment. Encounter Today, 11, Nos. 2-3, Su/Aut. pp 77-88. Freiburger Rundbrief, 28, Nos. 105-8, pp 3-11; Rencontre, 10, pp 87-111.

SLOYAN, Gerard S. The Jews and the New Roman Lectionary. Face to Face, 2, Su/Fa. pp 5-7.

JEWISH-CATHOLIC DIALOGUE: Special Section, by Eric Werner and Monika K. Hellwig. Journal of Ecumenical Studies, 13, No. 2, Sp. pp 125-40.
Four articles: The Eucharist in Hebrew Literature During the Apostalic and Post-Apostalic Epoch. Catholic Response. The Christian Eucharist in Relation to Jewish Worship. Jewish Worship.

PROTESTANTS AND JEWS

BEYERHAUS, Peter and BETZ, Ulrich. (Eds.) Ökumene im Spiegel von Nairobi '75. Durch die Wuste zur Welteinheit. Bad Liebenzell, Verl. der Liebenzeller Mission, 376p. Ind., Ill. (Telos Dokumentation).
Report of the Fifth Conference of the World Council of Churches held in Nairobi in December, 1975. Discusses, i.a. the Protestant Churches' relations to Jews and other non-Christians' attitudes to the Middle East conflict and to Israel.

GUTTERIDGE, Richard. Open thy Mouth for the Dumb: the German Evangelical Church and the Jews, 1879-1950. London, Blackwell, 374p, Ind.

HAMMERSTEIN, Franz von (Ed.) Vorurteilen zum Verständnis. Dokumente zum jüdisch-christlichen Dialog. Frankfurt/M., Otto Lembeck, 164p.
"From prejudices to understanding"

MAISCH, Ingrid. Juden und =udentum im christlichen Religionsunterr-icht. 1. Bilanz der Reformbemühungen. Bericht über eine Tagung in der Evangelischen Akademis Arnoldshain. 14-16 Februar 1977. Freiburger Rundbrief, 28, Nos. 105-8, pp 44-45.
Jews in Lutheran religious education.

NELSON, J. Robert and PANNENBERG, Wolfhart. (Eds.) Um Einheit und Heil der Menschheit. 2e. Frankfurt/M. Otto Lembeck, 342p, Ind., Bibl.
Papers delivered at the conference of the Faith and Order commission of the WCC in 1967; includes Humanity, Israel and the nations in Hebrew Tradition by Mosche Greenberg.

SCHONEVELD, Coos. Dialogue with Jews. Jewish Spectator, 41, No. 4, Fa. pp 44-48.

Leading Protestant thinker's view.

STARK, Rodney, FOSTER, Bruce D., GLOCK, Charles Y. and QUINLEY, Harold E. Wayward Shepherds: Prejudice and the Protestant Clergy. New York, Harper and Row, 130p.

American Protestant attitude to Jews.

VOGLER, B. La Réforme et les Juifs. Rencontre, 10, pp 214-28.

WOLF, Arnold Jacob. Rabbi in Nairobi. Worldview, 19, No. 3, Ma. pp 23-25.

The Director of Hillel and Jewish Chaplain at Yale writes of his attendance at the latest Assembly of the World Council of Churches, held in Nairobi during November and December 1975.

ORTHODOX AND JEWS

ANKORI, Zvi. Greek Orthodox-Jewish Relations in Historical Perspective - The Jewish View. Journal of Ecumenical Studies, 13, No. 4, Fa. pp 17-57.

BEBIS, George S. The Influence of Jewish Worship on Orthodox Christian Worship. Journal of Ecumenical Studies, 13, No. 4, Fa. pp 136-42.

CONSTANTELOS, Demetrios J. Greek Orthodox-Jewish Relations in Historical Perspective. Journal of Ecumenical Studies, 13, No. 4, Fa. pp 6-16.

Orthodox-Christian-Jewish Dialogue. Journal of Ecumenical Studies, 13, No. 4, Fa. pp 1-156.

Includes: Introduction to Greek Orthodox-Jewish Publications by Nomikos Michael Vaporis and Marc H. Tanenbaum. Judaism and Eastern Orthodoxy: Theological Reflections by Seymour Siegel. Judaism and the New Testament by Jacob C. Agus. The Influence of Jewish Worship on Orthodox Christian Worship by George S. Bebis.

ISLAM AND JUDAISM

COON, Carleton S. Caravan: The Story of the Middle East. New York, Chicago, San Francisco, Holt Rinehart and Winston, 386p, Ind, Bibl.

Survey of Islamic civilization in the Middle East, taking into account also other cultures, like the Jews.

LEWIS, Bernard. (Ed.) The World of Islam. Faith, People, Culture. London, Thames & Hudson; New York, Knopf, 360p, Ind., Ill.

Contributors to the volume include, in addition to the editor: A. Shiloah, A.I. Sabra, E. Itzkowitz, and Elie Kedourie. Many references to Muslim-Jewish relations.

--------------. The Return of Islam. Commentary, 52, No. 1, Ja. pp 39-49.

Stresses the universality and centrality of religion in the lives of Muslim people.

--------------. Terugkeer van de Islam: een studie over de invloed van de Islam in de huidige Arabische wereld. Den Haag, Centrum voor Informatie en Documentatie Israel, 25p.

MAHOMET ET ISRAËL. (Les Citations du Coran, favourables a Israël, avec un article d'Andre Zaoui). Sens, No. 2, Fa. (Special Issue.)

MINTJES, H. Muslim en Jood: Vriend of Vijand? Kampen, Kok, _Verkenning en bezinning_, 10, No. 3, pp 42.
Muslims and Jews - Friends or enemies? Study prepared for Commission on Jewish-Christian relations.

RODGERS, Michael. The Spread of Islam. London, Phaidon, 152p, Ill.

VRIES, Wilhelm de. Arab Christians in the Middle East. _Christian' Attitudes on Jews and Judaism_, (London), No. 48, Ju. pp 17-19.
Civil equality in a constitutionally Islamic state presents a basic problem.

ZAOUI, André C. Mohammed and Israel. _CCAR Journal_, 23, No. 1, W. pp 27-34.
According to this Israeli rabbi, good Moslems cannot call themselves anti-semitic nor by extension anti-Zionist, because to do so would be outrageously contradictory to Moslem tradition and honor.

SECTS/CULTS

DAVIS, Rex and RICHARDSON, James T. The Organization and Functioning of the Children of God. _Sociological Analysis_, 7, No. 1, W. pp 321-39.
Summarizes the early history of the sect in America and elsewhere and presents a description and analysis of the current international organizational structure. Also discussed decision making mechanisms and everyday life in a typical colony.

RAAB, Earl. Reverend Moon and the Jews - The San Francisco Experience. _Congress Monthly_, 43, No. 10, D. pp 8-12.
Moon does not attract Jews by calling them to Christ, but by adopting the 'consciousness movement' style.

RUDIN, A. James. Jews and Judaism in Rev. Moon's Divine Principle: A Report. New York Interreligious Affairs Dept., A.J. Committee, 8p.

SILVERBERG, David. "Heavenly Deception": Rev. Moon's Hard Sell. _Present Tense_, 3, No. 3, pp 49-56.
Just as young Jews played no uniquely Jewish role when they joined the Church, so American Jewry will not play a unique role in its demise. The rise and fall of Moon in this country is a basically secular American drama.

SIMMONDS, Robert B., RICHARDSON, James T., HORDER, Mary N. A Jesus Movement Group: An Adjective Check List Assessment. _Journal for the Scientific Study of Religion_, 15, No. 12, D. pp 323-337.
Personality assessment study of members of a commune showing a 'maladaptive' pattern of self-conceptions.

ZIONISM

ANGELL, Charles. Zionism: Why Call It Racism? Jewish Digest, 21, No. 7, Ap. pp 48-52. Condensed from National Catholic Reporter, 12, No. 14, Ja. 30.

ARNONI, M.S. Zionism as a Movement of National Liberation. Congress Monthly, 43, No. 1, D. 1975/ J. 1976, pp 30-34.

AVINERI, Shlomo. Zionism as a Movement of Liberation. Jewish Affairs, 36, No. 9, S. pp 49-52.

BARGAD, Warren. Zionism in Israeli Culture and Society. American Zionist, 67, No. 2, O. pp 17-20.

BOROCHOV, Ber. Nationalism and the Class Struggle: A Marxian Approach to the Jewish Problem. Intro. by Abraham G. Duker. Westport, Conn., Greenwood P.; London, Westport P., 205p.

Reprint of the 1937, first English edition of Borochov's formulation of Zionist-Socialism.

BRANDEIS, Louis D. The Jewish Problem and How to Solve It. Congress Monthly, 43, No. 1, D. 1975/J. 1976, pp 36-38.

Reprint of one of Justice Brandeis's articles on Zionism.

BULAWKO, Henry. Le sionisme a-t-il échoué? Regards, 12, No. 103, My. pp 10-11.

Calls for a reassessment of Zionism.

COHEN, Mitchell. The Jewish Question Becomes the Zionist Question. Response, 10, Nos. 2-3, Su/Fa. pp 47-55.

COHEN, Naomi W. American Zionism - A Retrospective View. The American Zionist, 46, No. 6, F. pp 20-24.

COOPER, Elias. Brief History of Zionism. The American Zionist, 67, No. 1, Ja. pp 7-16.

Attempts to alter the Arabs' concept of Zionism "as a movement linked with imperialism and based on racist perceptions."

-------------. Portrait of a National Liberation Movement. Brief History of Zionism. New York, Zionist Organisation of America, 22p

Answer to the equation of Zionism with racism.

DELMAIRE, Jean-Marie. 1891: Vers le sionisme politique. Yod, Revue des Etudes Hebraiques et Juives Modernes et Contemporaines. 2, No. 2, pp 51-66.

DUPUY, B. The Christian Facing Zionism. Encounter Today, 11, Nos. 2-3, Su/Aut. pp 102-4.

ELATH, Eliahu. Zionism at the UN: A Diary of the First Days. Philadelphia, Jewish Publication Society of America, 352p, Ind,Ill.

The author was Israel's first representative at the United Nations.

ELON, Amos. Morgen in Jerusalem (The Pride and the Pity) Theodor Herzl, sein Leben und Werk. Tr. Traudl Lessing. München, Molden, 431p, Ind., Bibl.

FAUR, Jose. Early Zionist Ideals among Sephardim in the Nineteenth Century. Judaism, 25, No. 1, W. pp 54-64.

GOLDMANN, Nahum. Israel muss umdenken! Die Lage der Juden 1976. Mit einem Gespräch zum deutschjüdischen Verhältnis. Reinbeck Hamburg Rowohlt, 121p.

The President of the World Jewish Congress expressed his views of the Middle East conflict in "Ou va Israel?" (Paris 1976) of which this is a translation with an added chapter in the form of a conversation with Freimut Duve on German-Jewish relations. In Norwegian: Kvar gar Israel? Oslo, Norske; In Spanish: Adonde va Israel? Buenos Aires, Timerman.

----------------. Israel Cannot Be A Country Like all Others. Jewish Quarterly, 24, Nos. 1-2, Sp/Su. 1976, pp 3-6.

The veteran Zionist leader would like to see a return to the original Zionist vision of the Jewish state as one of a special character. Translation of a chapter from the author's book, published in French Ou va Israel? (Whither Israel?) and in a Hebrew edition (L'an Israel?)

GOODMAN, (Lord) Arnold. Divided Loyalties. AJA Review, 19, No. 1, Sp. pp 3-6.

GORVINE, Harold. To be a Zionist. Reconstructionist, 43, No. 5. My. pp 7-12.

A brief history of Zionsim.

GOTTGETREU, Eric. When Uganda Was to be Named New Palestine. Jewish Affairs, 36, No. 8, Au. pp 12-14.

GRIESSMAN, B. Eugene. Philo-Semitism and Protestant Fundamentalism: The Unlikely Zionists. Phylon, 37, No. 3, Fa. pp 197-211.

Looking ahead, fundamentalists see wonderful events for both Christians and Jews. The return of the Jews to Israel represents an essential part of their dream - the great biblical event that ends a 1900-year hiatus.

GRONER, Arlene Pianko. Sh'ma: Journal and Community. No editorial line, no institutional backing, no pretensions. National Jewish Monthly, 90, No. 5, Ja. pp 20-26.

HARRAP, Louis. The Zionist Movement Revisited. New York, Jewish Currents, 31p. (Jewish Currents Reprints 11).

Examines the Zionist movement in the light of the claims of the Palestinians.

HALPERIN, Vladimir. La Suisse, le mouvement sioniste et l'Etat d'Israël. Israelitisches Wochenblatt fur die Schweiz, 76, No. 21a, Ma. pp 46-47.

HERTZBERG, Arthur. Zionism and the Jewish Past. Congress Monthly, 43, No. 1, D. 1975/Ja. 1976, pp 21-3; 26.

HOFFMAN, Martha. Theodor Herzl - Werden und Weg. Munich, Israelitische Kultusgemeinde,

JAKOBOVITS, Immanuel. Zionism Today: Vision, Illusion and Reality. L'Eylah, 1, No. 1, pp 17-22; PAI News, 46, Ap. pp 3-12.

KAHANE, Meir. Open Letter to Joseph Alsop. The American Zionist, 46, No. 6, pp 12-19.

KALLEN, Horace M. Zionism and Liberalism. Congress Monthly, 43, No. 1, D. 1975/Ja. 1976, pp 34-36.

Essay written in 1919.

----------------. Zionism and World Politics: A Study in History and Social Psychology. Westport, Conn., Greenwood P.; London, Westport P., xii, 345p.

Reprint of work first published in 1921.

KAPLAN, Jacob. Judaisme francais et sionisme. Paris, Albin Michel, 267p.

A selection of statements, articles, sermons and lectures on Zionism, Israel and the Middle East conflict by the Chief Rabbi of France.

KIRCHE UND JUDENTUM. Zionismus, Stuttgart, Evangelische Kirche in

Deutschland.
KOLLIN, Gilbert. The Emergence of Zionism. Jewish Spectator, 41, No. 2, Su. pp 58-61.
KORN, Itzhak. The 29th Zionist Congress: A Testing Time for the World Zionist Movement. Jewish Frontier, 43, No. 5, My. pp 9-12.
LEHMAN-WILZIG, Sam N. Proto-Zionism and its Proto-Herzl: The Philosophy and Efforts of Rabbi Zvi Hirsh Kalischer. Tradition, 43, No. 3, Ma. pp 4-6.
LUCAS, Noah. Zionism: Cause and Effect. Olam, Su/Aut. pp 16-20.
MAGONET, Jonathan. Is Zionism Messianic? European Judaism, 10, No. 2, Su. pp 12-14.
MEMMI, Albert. Judaism, Zionism and Socialism. Israel Horizons, 24, No. 8, O. pp 22-27.
Interview.
MENDES-FLOHR, R. Paul. Martin Buber's Concept of the Centre and Social Renewal. The Jewish Journal of Sociology, 18, No. 1, Ju. pp 17-26.
MOUTET, Anne-Elizabeth. Les francais et le sionisme. L'Arche, No. 230, My. pp 31-35.
NEHER, Andre. Die Haltung Israels gegenüber Staat, Land und Volk. Freiburger Rundbrief, 28, Nos. 105-8, pp 56-69.
The Jewish attitude to State, land and people.
NEWMAN, Aubrey. Zionism and Nationalism (Review Article). The Jewish Journal of Sociology, 17, No. 1, Ju. pp 57-60.
NISAN, Mordechai. The Idea of a Jewish State Reconsidered. Viewpoints, 9, No. 3, Sp/Su. pp 21-25.
ORLAND, Nachum. Vladimir Jabotinski und die innerjüdischen Parteienkämpfe in der Vorgeschichte der Staatsgründung Israel. Saeculum, 27, No. 4, pp 376-414.
Life and work of Jabotinski (1880-1940) before the establishment of the Jewish State.
PFISTERER, Rudolf. Der Zionismus - die nationale Befreiungabewegung des jüdischen Volkes. Aus Politik und Zeitgeschichte, 4, D. pp 18-39.
Maintains that Zionism is the national liberation movement of the Jewish people.
PINSKER, Lev Semenovich. Road to Freedom. Intro. by B. Natanyahu. Westport, Conn., Greenwood P.; London, Westport P., 142p.
On Zionism. Reprint of the 1944 edition.
PIPERNO, Giorgio. (Ed.) Ebraismo, Sionismo, Halutzismo. Preface Joel Barromi. Rome, Carrucci, 318p. (Collana di cultura ebraica 7)
Essays on Judaism, Zionism and the pioneer movement.
POPPEL, Stephen M. German Zionism and Jewish Identity. The Jewish Journal of Sociology, 18, No. 2, D. pp 115-22.
QU'EST-CE QUE LE SIONISME? (après le colloque prétendument théologique de Tripoli, et les nouvelles calomnies contre le sionisme, la vérité rétablie par des articles de Pierre Daboville, Yves Chevalier, Emile Touati) Sens, Special Issue, No. 3, Ma.
REITER, Alexandre. Le Sionisme. Paris, France-Israël Information, 20p.
RENDTORFF, Rolf. Die religiönsen und geistigen Wurzeln des Zionismus. Aus Politik und Zeitgeschichte, 4, D. pp 3-17.
Christian theologian's view of the religious and spiritual roots of Zionism.

ROMANO, Giorgio. Il Sionismo in ITalia fino alla seconda guerra mondiale. La Rassegna Mensile di Israel, 42, Nos. 7-8, Jy-Au. pp 341-54.

ROSENBLATT, Bernard Abraham. The American Bridge to the Israel Commonwealth. Westport, Conn., Greenwood P.; London, Westport P., 128p.

Non-Jewish Zionists, reprint of 1959 edition.

ROSENTHAL, David. About Zionist Congresses and the Crisis in Zionism. Jewish Frontier, 43, No. 8, O. pp 9-14.

Zionism, the national liberation movement of the Jewish people, finds itself everywhere in retreat. So it might be worthwhile that the movement, in its search for solutions to the crisis, should return to the basics of its teachings, which once gave it its outer splendor and its inner moral and revolutionary strength.

ROTENSTREICH, Nathan. The State of Israel and Zionism. The American Zionist, 67, No. 3, D. pp 7-15.

The particular character of the State of Israel which brings into prominence its relationship to the ideology which created the state and to the obligations emanating from that ideology.

SCHAPPES, Morris and BLOOMFIELD, Eugene. The Arms Race, Israel and "Breira". Jewish Currents, 30, No- 11, D. pp 16-18.

SCHMIDT, Sarah. Horace M. Kallen and the 'Americanization' of Zionism. American Jewish Archives, 28, No. 1, Ap. pp 59-73.

--------------. Horace M. Kallen and the 'Progressive' Reform of American Judaism. Midstream, 22, No. 10, D. pp 14-23.

Kallen was correct when he wrote in 1973 of the many American Jews who 'regard Israel as an ideal bet on a future of equal liberty and equal safety under law ...' a bet which must have the generous support of American Jews as Americans and also as Jews.

--------------. Messianic Pragmatism: The Zionism of Horace M. Kallen. Judaism, 25, No. 2, Sp. pp 217-29.

SHAPIRO, Yonathan. Leadership of the American Zionist Organisation. 1897-1930. Chicago, U. of Illinois P., 295p.

First published in 1971.

SHIPTON, Sidney L. Towards a Practical Zionism: a handbook on the tasks and work of a Zionist society. 3.e. London, The Zionist Federation of Great Britain and Ireland, 13p.

SIMON, Leon and STEIN, Leonard. (Eds.) Awakening Palestine. Westport, Conn., Hyperion, viii, 318p, Ind. (The Rise of Jewish Nationalism and the Middle East S.)

First published London, 1923. Contributors: Sir Alfred Mond, Ramsay Macdonald, Millicent Garret Fawcett, Patrick Geddes, A.M, Hyamson, Chaim Weizmann, J. Lurie, Canon Danby, W. Ormsby-Gore, S. Tolkowsky, M.D. Eder, A. Ruppin, N. Wilbush, S. Hoofien, Jacob Thon, S.E. Soskin, Herbert Sidebotham and the editors.

SPITAELS, G. Les socialistes belges et le sionisme. Regards, 12, No. 100, Ja. pp 45-47.

TEKOAH, Yosef. What Is Zionism? Congress Monthly, 43, No. 1, D. 1975/Ja. 1976, p. 20.

WALK, Joseph. Das Deutsche Komittee Pro Palestina 1926-55. Bulletin des Leo Baeck Instituts, No. 15, pp 162-95.

The pre-Nazi Zionist sympathisers.

WAS IST ZIONISMUS? erarbeitet von der Studienkommission. "Kirche und Judentum" der Evangelischen Kirche in Deutschland. Stuttgart, Evangelische Zentralstelle für Weltanschauungsfragen, 26p. (Information Nr. 66)
Contents: "Zionismus" in der Weltpolitischen Auseinandersetzung; Zionsliebe und Zionssehnsucht; Der Zionismus in der Neuzeit; Der Staat Israel; Der Vorwurf des Rassismus; Christliche Solidaritätmit den Juden

WERBLOWSKY, Zwi R.J. Israel: Il Popolo e la Terra. La Rassegna Mensile di Israel, 42, Nos. 3-4, Ma-Ap. pp 122-29.
The traditional relationship between the Jewish people and the Land of Israel.

WHARTMAN, Eliezer. Israel: A Magnet? Reconstructionist, 42, No. 1, F. pp 7-9.
Questions the essence of Zionism in the U.S. if it advocates aliyah.

WILL, George E. The Roots of Zionism Aren't Racist. Israel's Right to Exist is Anchored in History. Congress Monthly, 43, No. 1, D/Ja. p 16.

WIRNIK, Rachmiel. (Ed.) What You Should Know About Zionism, Israel and Racism. New York, World Union of General Zionists, 80p.

YATZIV, Gadi. In Defence of an Undistorted Zionism. Jewish Quarterly, 23, No. 4, W. pp 5-9.

YEHOSHUA, A.B. Dispersing the Fog over Zionism. Israel Horizons, 24, No. 10, O. pp 21-28.
Despite the problems that face us, despite the failures and the catastrophies in Israel, life in Israel is more moral, healthier and normal than that of the Jew in the diaspora.

ZEMER, Hannah. The Universal Message of Zionism. The Socialist-Society, Bombay, 3p.

ZIONISM: Special Section. Moment, 1, No. 4, pp 37-44.
Includes full text of Ambassador Patrick Moynihan's address during the General Assembly debate, the text of the resolution, the vote and an abridged version of "Theses of Zionism" from Walter Lacqueur's A History of Zionism (Holt, Rinehart & Winston, 1972)

ZIONISM: THE CRITIQUE FROM WITHIN - Special Section, Olam, pp 2-12.
Three articles: Zionism and the Arabs by Nahum Goldmann. My Zionism: A Reflection on First Principles by Gadi Yatziv. The Real Threat to Israel by Meir Pa'il.

ZIONISM, ISRAEL AND THE JEWISH PEOPLE; Special Issue. Congress Monthly, 42, No. 1, D. 1975/Ja. 1976. pp 1-47.
Five Sections: Appraising the UN. Anti-Zionism IS Anti-Semitism. Zionism as Idea, Program and Movement. Arabs and Jews. Women's Division Mission to Israel.

ANTI-ZIONISM

ASTRACHAN, Anthony. The Twilight of Reason. The UN's Unholy Alliance. Present Tense, 3, No. 2, W. pp 36-40.
The Zionism-Racism issue

AVINERI, Shlomo. Jews and Anti-Zionists. Jewish Digest, 22, No. 4, D. 1976, pp 66-69. Condensed from Crossroads, (7, No. 3)

BANKI, Judith Hershcopf. The UN's Anti-Zionism Resolution: Christian Responses. New York, The American Jewish Committee, Institute of Human Relations. 58p.

BAUM, Phil. Politics as Theater: The United Nations and What to do About it. Congress Monthly, 43, No. 1, D. 1975/Ja. 1976, pp 5-9.
The Zionism-Racism Resolution.

BERGER, Elmer. Memoirs of an Anti-Zionist Jew. Journal of Palestine Studies, 5, Nos. 1-2, Au. 1975/W. 1976, pp 3-55.

BROWNFIELD, Allan C. Zionism under the Spotlight. Middle East International, 56, F. pp 12-14.

CONFEDERACION DE ASOCIACIONES ISRAELITAS DE VENEZUELA (CAIV). OFICINA DE DERECHOS HUMANOS. La opinion publica venezolana ante la resolucion de la ONU sobre el Sionismo. Caracas, 64p, Ill.
Venezualan public opinion reaction to the Zionism-Racism Resolution.

DECALO, Samuel. Africa and the UN Anti-Zionism Resolution: Roots and Causes. Cultures et Developement, 8, No. 1, pp 89-118.

EHRLICH, A. Crise en Israël: Menace fasciste? Khamsin, No. 3, pp 27-66.
Anti-Zionist viewpoint.

ETTINGER, SHMUEL. Anti-Zionism and Anti-Semitism. Insight, 3, No. 5, My. 8p.
The Soviet attitude.

GANGING UP ON ISRAEL. The New Republic, 175, 11 D. pp 5-8.
Examines some of the actions recently taken against Israel at the UN.

GOLDSTEIN, Judith. (Ed.) Transcript: The Debate on Zionism and Racism in the United Nations Third Committee, 16-17 O. New York, American Jewish Committee,

GORDON, Murray. UN's Anti-Israel actions: The Political Fallout. Congress Monthly, 43, No. 1, D. 1975/Ja. 1976, pp 9-12.

GROSS, Leo. Voting in the Security Council and the PLO. American Journal of International Law, 70, No. 3, Jy. pp 470-91.
"One would have been justified in expecting that the United States and other minority members, particularly those which are permanently members of the Security Council, would have been on their toes to prevent the contagion of unbridled majoritarianism from infecting that principal organ of the United Nations. This, regrettably, has not been the case."

HANNAUER, Edmund R. Continuing the Discussion: Zionism and Racism. Christianity and Crisis, 36, No. 6, Ap. pp 79-82.
Response to the discussion of the United Nations resolution on Zionism and racism. It was disappointing to note that the participants, all thoughtful people, tended to evade, if not distort the issues.

IDINOPULOS, Thomas A. The Zionism and Racism Controversy: Historical Perspective on the Issues. The Christian Century, 93, 28 Ja. pp 68-72.
"The General Assembly of the United Nations has presented us with a new chapter in the dreary spectacle of the Jew as international scapegoat."

JASTROW, Morris. Zionism and the Future of Palestine. The Fallacies and Dangers of Political Zionism. Westport, Conn., Hyperion P., xix, 159p. M. (The Rise of Jewish Nationalism and the Middle East S.)

Reprint of work first published in 1919. A sharp critique of Zionism.

KNEE, Stuart E. The Impact of Zionism on Black and Arab Americans. Patterns of Prejudice, 10, No. 2, pp 21-28.

"Israel has been identified by Arab American activists, black militants and the radical left as 'guilty of everything the United States is guilty of."

KOREY, William. Hitler's Heirs at the United Nations. Representation Without Taxation. Hadassah Magazine, 57, No. 6, F. pp 18-37.

The monolithic Arab bloc with 20 strategically crucial votes provides less than 1% of the UN budget.

--------------. News, Views, Reviews. B'nai B'rith and Mexico. National Jewish Monthly, 90, No. 8, Ap. pp 32-38.

Action at the International Women's Year Conference.

--------------. Orwell at UNESCO. Midstream, 22, No. 8, O. pp 5-9.

Totalitarians of George Orwell's 1984 created a new language - 'Newspeak' - in which words would mean the very opposite of their commonsense definition. Today a coalition of totalitarian regimes in both Communist and Third World countries are busily engaged in inverting language fnr purposes of manipulating thought.

LATAPIE, J.P. La politisation à l'Unesco. Rencontre, 10, pp 250-56.

The antizionist resolutions at the UNESCO General Conference.

LEWIS, Bernard. The Antizionist Resolution. Foreign Affairs, 55, No. 1, O. pp 54-64.

LOVSKY, F. Le sionisme est-il une forme du racisme? Foi et Vie, 75, No. 3, pp 22-52.

Condemns the Zionism-Racism Resolution.

LUND, May Brit. Antisionisme og antisemitisme. (In Norwegian) Kobenhaven, 2p.

Argues that anti-Zionism is but a new form of antisemitism.

MOYNIHAN, Daniel Patrick. The Terrible Lie - The Terrible Consequences. (Excerpt from the statement at the UN) Congress Monthly, 43, No. 1, D. 1975/Ja. 1976, pp 12f.

1976-1933? (apres les votes de l'ONU et de l'UNESCO assimilant sionisme et racisme, avec un article de Jacques Ellul) Sens, No, 1, Ja. (Special Issue)

OSTERREICHER, John M. The Wicked Lie. Congress Monthly, 43, No. 1, D. 1975/Ja. 1976, pp 17-18.

On the UN Zionism-Racism Resolution.

PARZEN, H. The Purge of the Dissidents. Hebrew Union College and Zionism, 1903-7. Jewish Social Studies, 37, Nos. 3-4, pp 291-322.

Includes Max Margolis's letter of resignation of 1907, due to his Zionist reputation.

RAAB, Earl. The Two Anti-Zionisms. Midstream, 22, No. 3, pp 52-58.

Contends that anti-Zionism is "a carry all anti-semitism which is the cutting edge of a clever ideological offensive against the United States."

RACHLINE, Michel. Un juif libre. Paris, Guy Authier, 472p, Bibl.

Views of a secularist, anti-Zionist Jew.

RODINSON, Maxime, SHAHAK, Israel and LOBEL, E. Judaisme et sionisme ... *Khamsin*, No. 3, pp 67-81.
Anti-Zionist articles.

RODNER, Jan B. Lognere Iblant Oss. En Analys av den Anti-Sionistiske Propagandaen. (In Norwegian) Oslo, Exodus,
Demonstrates that anti-Zionism is a new form of antisemitism.

SHOENBERG, Harris. The Debasement of the United Nations. *Jewish Affairs*, 36, No. 9, S. pp 57-62.

----------------. The Debasement of the United Nations. *Midstream*, 12, No. 5, My. pp 18-25.

SHAHAK, Israel. Lettre ouverte à un sionist: une critique de l'apologie d'Irène Gendzier. *Khamsin*, No. 3, pp 90-100.
Anti-Zionist attack.

SHATTAN, Joseph. The Mad Hatter's UN Tea-Party. *Midstream*, 22, No. 1, Ja. pp 55-61.
The former director of the Youth Institute for Peace in the Middle East writes a personal account of the General Assembly debate equating Zionism with racism.

SILLS, Joe Byrnes. Fever Chart of the UN. *Worldview*, 19, No. 10, O. pp 9-12.
Analysis of a series of public opinion polls questioning the effectiveness of the UN, US participation, and the Zionism/racism resolution, among other issues.

SORGE, B. Sionismo e razzismo. *Rivista di Studi Politici Internazionali*, 43, No. 1, Ja/Ma. pp 96-102.

TARTAKOWER, Aryeh. Fun a Natsionaler Haym biz Sinas Yisroel. (From National Home to the Hatred of Israel) *Di Tsukunft*, 82, No. 3, My. pp 92-93.

TAYLOR, Alan. The Theory and Practice of Zionism. Paper delivered at Symposium on Zionism. Baghdad University.
Anti-Zionist.

TOMEH, George J. (Ed.) Les Resolutions des Nations Unies sur la Palestine et le conflit israelo-arabe 1947-74. Beirut, Institute of Palestine Studies, Kuwait, Ministry of Information, xxvi, 284p, Map.

United Nations General Assembly Resolution 31/20 (November 29 1976) Question of Palestine. *Review Egyptienne de Droit International*, 32, pp 205-6.
The Zionism/Racism Resolution.

UN Declaration: Zionism is a racist movement (symposium) *Pakistan Horizon*, 29, No. 1, pp 47-58.
Includes speeches by Mukhtar Zuman and Qutubuddin Aziz.

B'NAI BRITH INTERNATIONAL COUNCIL. B'NAI B'RITH ISRAEL COMMISSION. The UN and Zionism. Washington, 9p.

VITTA, Edoardo. Nazioni unite e sionismo. *La Rassegna Mensile di Israel*, 42, Nos. 5-6, My-Ju. pp 227-33.

VOGT, Ernst. Israel - Kritik von Links. Dokumentation einer Entwicklung. Wuppertal, Peter Hammer, 230p, Bibl.
Analyses the development that led from the support of Israel to the violent anti-Israel stance of the Left.

WISTRICH, Robert S. The Myth of Zionist Racism. London, World Union of Jewish Students, 38p.
Pamphlet produced in the wake of the UN resolution condemning Zionism as racism, examining the myth and any elements of truth.

World Reaction to the UN resolution on Zionism. Geneva, Centre d'information et de documentation sur le moyen-orient. No pagination, Ill.

Zionism, a form of racism and racial discrimination. On the occasion of the meeting of the Summit Conference of the non-aligned countries, August 1976 in Colombo, Sri Lanka, Baghdad, Ministry of Information, Iraq Today Magazine, 28p.

ISRAEL

ELLISON, Henry L. Mystery of Israel. N.e. London, Paternoster P., 117p.
"Recent events in the Middle East have led many Christians to re-assess what the Bible says about the place of the Jewish people in world history."

ELON, Amos. Understanding Israel: A Social Studies Approach. New York, Behrman House, vii, 242p, Ind, Ill.
Textbook with available educational materials listed by Morris J. Sugarman.

FALK, RUNNE, Arne. Auf Abraham's Spuren. Graz-Stuttgart, Stocker, 296p, Ill.

-----------. Salome Tante. Graz-Stuttgart, Stocker, 303p, Ill.
Pilgrimages to the Holy Land.

ISRAEL IN THE YEAR 2000. A Symposium. Tr. Dr. Albert Waldinger. The Jewish Spectator, 41, No. 1, Sp. pp 57-71.

Israel. Tourope Urlaubsberater. No. 602. Lübeck, Geo. Center,100p.
Guidebook.

KENNEDY, K. Impressions of Israel. Administration, 24, No. 4, pp 425-66.

LAPIDE, Pinchas E. Israel für Pilger. Munich, Israelitische Kulturgemeinde.

LARSEN, Elaine. Israel. New York, Hastings House; London, Batsford, 176p, Ill, M.
Description.

MELZI D'ERIL. Gian Paolo. Terra Antica Stato Moderno. Israele. Milano, Cavallotti. 195p, Ill.
"Old country, Modern State: Israel" Experiences of the author in Israel.

PLESSIX GRAY. Francine du. A Reporter at Large: Jerusalem Journal, The New Yorker, 76, 14 Ju. pp 38-76.
Diary of impressions and conversations with Israelis from different areas of society.

PRAWER, Joshua and MEYER, Peter. Heiliges Land in Text und Bild. Stuttgart, Hallwag,

SCHEWE, Heinz. Darf ich für dich die Harfe Sein? Momentaufnahmen aus einem bedrohten Land. Hamburg, Christians, 325p, Ind, Ill.

HISTORY

ABCARIUS, Michel Fred. Palestine Through the Fog of Propaganda. Westport, Conn., Hyperion P., 240p.
Reprint of the 1946 edition.

AL-JADER, Adel Hamed. The Policies of Granting Concessions to Large Scale Operations in Palestine during the Mandate. In Arabic. Palestine Affairs, 55, pp 184-205.

ANDREWS, Fanni Fern. The Holy Land under the Mandate. Westport, Conn., Hyperion, 2 vols. (The Rise of Jewish Nationalism and the Middle East S.)

Reprint of the 1931 edition, published by Houghton-Mifflin, New York.

BADI, Joseph. The Ben-Gurion period in the history of Politics of the State of Israel. 1948-65. Ann Arbor, Mich., U. Microfilms. iv, 207p, Bibl.

Dissertation - New York University, 1968.

BERNADOTTE af WISBORG, Folke Greve. To Jerusalem. Tr. from the Swedish by Joan Bulman. Westport, Conn., Hyperion; London, Hodder & Stoughton, viii, 280p, Ind, Bibl.

Count Folke Bernadotte's book was first published in 1951.

BELL, J. Bowyer. Terror Out of Zion. The Violent and Deadly Shock Troops of Israeli Independence 1929-49. New York, St. Martin's P., xi, 374p, Ind.

Describes the activities of the Irgun Zvi Leumi and the Stern Gang and the Haganah.

BURSTEIN, Moshe. Self-Government of the Jews in Palestine Since 1900 Westport, Conn., Hyperion P., 298p, Ind, Bibl. (The Rise of Jewish Nationalism and the Middle East S.)

First published as the author's Ph.D. thesis at Columbia University, New York, in 1934.

CAMERON, James. The Making of Israel. London, Secker & Warburg,104p Ind, M.

As a foreign correspondent the author witnessed the birth of Israel, both at the UN and in England and was present at the declaration of independence.

THE FUTURE OF PALESTINE. Prepared by the Arab Office, London, Westport, Conn., Hyperion P., 166p. (The Rise of Jewish Nationalism and the Middle East S.)

Reprint of the Arab Office's official publication of 1947.

GRANOVSKY, Abraham. Land Policy in Palestine. Westport, Conn., Hyperion P., xv, 208p, Ind. M.

Reprint of book originally published by Block, New York, 1940.

HUREWITZ, Jacob Coleman. The Struggle for Palestine. N.e. New York, Schocken, x, 408p, Ind, Bibl.

Reprint of 1950 edition with a new introduction.

IANCU, C. Une lettre inedite d'Eleazar Rokeach sur les debuts du mouvement Yisub Eres Yisrael (1880). <u>Revue des Etúdes Juives</u>, 135, Nos. 1-3, pp 177-83.

Rokeach (1854-1914) asked and received support of the Alliance Israelite Universelle for his Yishuv Eretz Israel Movement.

JEWISH AGENCY FOR ISRAEL. Memorandum Submitted to the Palestine Royal Commission on Behalf of the Jewish Agency for Palestine, Westport, Conn., Greenwood P., 323p.

Reprint of document submitted to the Peel Commission in 1936.

KENYON, Kathleen M. Archaeology in the Holy Land. London, Ernest Bean, xxx, 365p, Ill, 4.r.e.

SWIRSKI, S. Community and the Meaning of Modern State: The Case of Israel. <u>Jewish Journal of Sociology</u>, 18, No. 2, D. pp 123-40.

YEHOSHUA, A.B. A State of Siege. <u>Olam</u>, Su/Au. pp 10-15.

State of Mind of the Israelis.

GENERAL DESCRIPTION

AVI-YONAH, Michael and SHATZMAN, Israel. Illustrated Encyclopaedia of the Classical World. Maidenhead, Sampson Low, 509p, Ill, Ind.
Standard reference work taking into consideration the most up-to-date archaelogical discoveries.

BERMAN, Susan. Driver Give a Soldier a Lift. New York, G.P. Putnams, 252p.
Life in Israel.

LANDES, David S. Palestine Before the Zionists. Commentary, 52, No. 2, F. pp 47-56.
Discusses the condition of Palestine, and of the Jews there, before the immigration of secular Zionists toward the end of the last century.

DONATH, Doris Bensimon. L'Education en Israel. Paris, C. Lowy, 200p.

IDINOPULOS, Thomas. A Study in Love and Law in Israel. The Christian Century, 93, 17 N. pp 1010-1013.
A report on the ultra-Orthodox Jews of Mea Sherim in Jerusalem.

LITERATUR UND KRITIK. No. 105, Sondernummer: Literatur aus Israel. Salzburg, Otto Müller, pp 257-316.
Special issue on Israeli literature with an article on the solitude of the German-speaking writer in Israel by Alice Schwarz.

PELED, Yoav. ... and the Israelis. On the Daily Press in Israel: Formal and informal Censorship. Interchange, 2, No. 4, D. pp 4-5.

RAHMANI, L.Y. and LARSON, Peter. The Museums of Israel. London, Secker & Warburg; New York, Rizzoli, 239p, Ill.
Guide to all the museums of Israel with their history by the Chief Curator, Israel Department of Antiquities and Museums and with photographs by Peter Larson.

REED, Judith. (Ed.) Impressions of Education in Israel; a report of the Educational Staff Seminar Study Mission, February 13-29, 1976, Washington D.C., George Washington U., xi, 123p, Ill.

SCHIFF, Gary S. The Socialization of Values in Israel's Educational System. Jewish Education, 46, No. 1, Sp/Su. pp 57-67.
The socialization of values in Israel's educational system reflects the continued highly politicized nature of the society. Despite claims and legal provisions to the contrary, the three school networks - especially the two religious ones - remain essentially party-dominated.

UCKO, Sinai. A Theological Case Study from Israel. Judaism, 25, No. 4, W. pp 79-84.
The current religious scene in Israel.

YARON, Zvi. So Much Hate in the Name of Love. Religious Kibbutz Journal of Gush Emunim. Israel Horizons, 24, No. 5, My. pp 17-18.
Attacks Gush Emunim.

INTERNAL POLITICS

BARNEA, Nahum. Israel's 'New Politics'. The Third Generation of Leaders Scorns Party and Ideology. National Jewish Monthly, 90, No. 6, F. pp 1-23.

BERNSTEIN, Marver H. The Politics of Israel. The First Decade of Statehood, Westport, Conn., Greenwood P.; London, Westport P., xiv, 360p. M.

BERSOHN, Maurice. Israel: Structures Politiques et Socialies. Paris La Documentationa Francaise. 220p.

BURSTEIN, Paul. Political Patronage and Party Choice among Israeli Voters. The Journal of Politics, 38, No. 4, N. pp 1024-32.

DAVIS, Uri Hyman. Israel: Utopia Incorporated. A Study in Class. State and Corporate Kin Control. Ann Arbor, Mich., U. Microfilms, 1976, 274p. Bibl.

GINIEWSKI, Paul. La Storia d'Israele comporta una quarta dimensione: A Sua vita contemporanea e Politica. La Rassegna Mensile di Israel 42, Nos. 5-6, My-Ju, pp 267-80.

GLASS, Charles. Jews Against Zion: Israeli Jewish Anti-Zionism. Journal of Palestine Studies, 5, Nos. 1-2, Aut. 1975/W. 1976, pp 56-81

HOFFMITZ, Laible. Two Years of the Rabin Government and the Situation in the Israel Labour Party. Jewish Frontier, 43, No. 10, O. pp 24-27.

Interview with Meir Zarmi, Secretary General of the Israel Labor Party.

ISAAC, Rael Jean. The Land of Israel Movement: A Study in Partial Deinstitutionalization. Ann Arbor, Mich., U. Microfilms, vi, 372p. M. Bibl.

Ph.D. Dissertation - City University of New York, 1971.

----------------. Israel Divided. Ideological Politics in the Jewish State. Baltimore, Ma.; London, Johns Hopkins. x, 227p, Ind., Bibl, M.

Discusses the extremist fringes of the Israeli Political Spectrum and the possibility of a Kulturkampf.

LOCKMAN, Zachary. The Left in Israel: Zionism vs. Socialism. MERIP Reports, No. 49, Jy. pp 3-22.

LOUVISH, Misha. Histadrut and Government. (Letter from Israel) Jewish Frontier, 43, No. 7, Au-S. pp 7-9.

The role of the Histadrut as a "State Within a State".

--------------. Labor in Crisis (Letter from Israel) Jewish Frontier 43, No. 5, Ap. pp 5-7.

NACHMIAS, D. The Right-Wing Opposition in Israel. Political Studies 24, No. 3, Su. pp 268-80.

NAHAS, Dunia. The Israeli Community Party. London, Croom Helm, 113p Ind, Bibl.

ORLAND, Nachum. Die Parteien Israels und ihre Geschichte. Emuna/ Israel-Forum, 11, Nos. 5-6, pp 31-45.

Description and history of Israeli Political parties; their importance in the Country's life.

REESE, K.M. Left-Right Responses in Israel. Reprint from Chemical and Engineering News. 22 S. 1975. Jewish Digest, 21, No. 6, Ma. pp 57-58.

ROTH, A. Israel auf der Suche nach dem Nationalen. Politische Studien, 27, No. 227, S-O. pp 530-34.

RUBENSTEIN, Aryeh. Religious Party Politics in Israel. Midstream, 22, No. 1, Ja. pp 27-41.

Focuses on Mafdal (an acronym for ha-Miflaga ha-Datit Leumit, the National Religious Party) which has 100,000 registered members, is the third largest Knesset faction and has particip- ated in the government almost uninterruptedly since the establishment of the State.

SCHONEVELD, J. The Bible in Israeli Education. A Study of Approaches to the Hebrew Bible and its Teaching in Israeli Educational Literature. Assen, Amsterea. 304p, Ind. (Theological Library 50)

SELIGER, K. Rakach und Maki. Die zwei kommunistische Parteien Israels. Osteuropa, 26, No. 4, Ap-My.

SHEPHERD, Naomi. Israel's Doves. People are Beginning to Listen. Present Tense, 4, No. 1, Aut. pp 31-37.

---------------. Red Star Over Nazareth. Present Tense, 3, No. 3, Sp. pp 5-9.

---------------. Turning Right in Israel? Times (and Politics) are Changing. Present Tense, 3, No. 2, W. pp 19-26.

SLANN, Martin. Tolstoyan Pacifism and the Kibbutz Concept of Haganah Azmit. (Self-Defence) Reconstructionist, 42, no. 7, O. pp 11-17.

TALMI, Meir. The Future of the Alignment Does not Depend on us Alone. Israel Horizons, 25, No. 8, O. pp 10-13.

TARNOV, Jacques. Les Nostalgiques du Grand Israël. L'Arche, No.232, Jy. pp 26-28.

TULIN, David. Mapam and the Dilemma of Israel's Progressives. Israel Horizons, 20, No. 9, S. pp 14-19.

Israel's left-wing labor-Zionist party holds the key to a reunified progressive force capable of changing government policy in the direction of peaceful accommodation and a society of true Jewish character.

TWERSKY, David. The Crisis in Israel. Response, 10, Nos. 2-3, Su/Fa pp 13-46.

Political Shifts in Israel. Dissent, 23, No. 1, W. pp 16-20.

The crucial task of Israeli statecraft is to find a balance between what Israel can control and what she can be forced to do.

ZELNIKER, S. and KAHAN, M. Religion and Nascent Cleavages: The Case of Israel's National Religious Party. Comparative Politics, 9, No. 1, pp 21-48.

ZUCKER, Norman L. and FLINK, Naomi. Piety and Politics. Challenging Israel's Orthodox. Present Tense, 3, No. 2, W. pp 63-69.

LEGAL SYSTEM

DORNSTEIN, M. Compliance with Legal and Bureaucratic Rules: The Case of Self-Employed Tax Payers in Israel. Human Relations, 29, No. 11, pp 1019-34.

Based on a random sample of independent workers.

Equality of Treatment under the Law in Israel. New York, American Jewish Committee, 2p.

GOLDWATER, Chaim Ivor. Issue Estoppel by Foreign Judgment in Israeli Law. The International and Comparative Law Quarterly. 25, Part 4, O. pp 869-72.

KLICH, Ignacio. The Grounds of Land Tenure in Palestine. Olam, Su/Aut. pp 51-55.

KRAINES, Oscar. The Impossible Dilemma: Who is a Jew in the State of Israel? New York, Bloch, x, 156p, Ind.

Treats the subject in all its complex aspects: political, legal, racial and social.

NAKLEH, Khalil. The Multiplicity of Legal Systems in Israel: The Case for Legal Heterogeneity. Third World Review, 1, No.1,pp 28-38

SAMUELSON, Maurice. Israel's Deep Divide. Middle East International No. 65, N. pp 6-8.
Internal conflict over activities of Gush Emunim.
SHAPIRO. A.E. Law in the Kibbutz: A Reappraisal. Law and Society Review, 10, No. 3, pp 415-42.
Answers R.D. Schwartz's Social Factors in the Development of Legal Control: A Case Study of Two Israeli Settlements. (Yale Law Journal 1974)
YADIN, U. La nouvelle loi israeliénne sur l'indemnisation des victimes d'accidents de la circulation. Revue internationale de Droit Compare, 20, No. 3, pp 475-86.
Comments on the new Israeli law on the indemnification of victims of road accidents.

MINORITIES

THE AMNESTY INTERNATIONAL REPORT 1 June 1975 - 31 May 1976. London, Amnesty International, 220p.
Includes AI activities on behalf of Soviet Jews, Jews in Arab countries and minorities in Israel.
BEN-DOR, Gabriel. Intellectuals in Israeli Druze Society. Middle Eastern Studies, 12, No. 2, My. pp 133-58.
CHOMSKY, Noam. The Arabs in Israel. Monthly Review, 27, No. 11, Ap. pp 20-30.
LERNER, Natan. Las Minorias en Israel. Su regimen legal 1976. Buenos Aires, Congreso Judio Latinoamerican, 40p. (Hechos de la Historia Judia 85)
Discusses the rights of minorities in Israel (Arabs, Druze, Christians)
LOUVISH, Misha. Israel's Arab Citizens. (Letter from Israel) Jewish Frontier, 43, No. 5, My. pp 4-8.
MARYUMA, N. The Arabs in Israel; nationalism and its limits. (In Japanese) Chuto Sugo kenkyu, 5, Su. pp 25-36.
SHOHAM, S., SEGAL, Esther and RAHAV, Giora. Secularization Deviance and Deliquency among Israeli Arab Villagers. Human Relations, 28, No. 7, Jy. pp 661-74.
TSIMHONI, Daphna. The Christian Communities in Jerusalem and the West Bank, 1948-67. Middle East Review, 9, No. 1, Fa. pp 41-46.
WASSERSTEIN, David. The Druzes and Circassians of Israel. London, Anglo-Jewish Association, 24p. (Anglo-Israel Association Pamphlet, 55)
ZARKABI, Zahi, A Communist Mayor of Nazareth. World Marxist Review, 19, No. 196, pp 99-102.
YARON, Zvi. Religion in Israel. American Jewish Yearbook, 76, pp 41-90.
Religion's role in nationalist ideology, in Israeli life and as a political force.
ZAYAD, Kassem. I Will Struggle Against Discrimination Unceasingly. An Arab Israeli Spells Out Certain Views. Israel Horizons, 24, No. 3, Ma. pp 19-20.
-------------. Am I a 'Positive' or a 'Negative' Arab? Israel Horizons, 24, No. 6, Ju-Jy. pp 9-12.
For Arab-Jewish co-existence in Israel.

-------------. Israel's Arabs no longer Need be Treated as Wards. Israel Horizons, 24, No. 4, Ap. pp 24-25.

-------------. Land Expropriations: Test Case of Relations Between Israel and her Arab Citizens. Israel Horizons, 24, No. 5, My. pp 10-12.

ZAYYAD, Tawfiq. The Fate of the Arabs in Israel. Journal of Palestine Studies, 6, No. 1, Aut. pp 92-103.
  Anti-Israel stance.

ZUREIK, Elia T. Transformation of Class Structure Among the Arabs of Israel: From Peasantry to Proletariat. Journal of Palestine Studies, 6, No. 1, Aut. pp 39-66.

JERUSALEM AND THE HOLY PLACES

AVI-YONAH, Michael. Jerusalem, The Holy. New York, Schocken, 130p. Ill.
  Archaeology of Jerusalem.

BENVENISTI, Meron. Jerusalem, Jerusalem. Moment, 2, No. 3, D. pp 10-14; 51-54.
  The Deputy Mayor of Jerusalem discusses the city since its reunification.

-----------------. Jerusalem: The Torn City. Minneapolis, U. of Minnesota P., 407p.
  The struggle over Jerusalem between Jews and Arabs and its effects.

BHUTANI, S. Jerusalem and the United Nations. India Quarterly, 32, No. 4, pp 447-55.

COHEN, Saul B. Geopolitical B asis for the Integration of Jerusalem. Orbis, 20, No. 2, Su. pp 287-314.
  Israel policymakers and the public tend to defer the Jerusalem issue until a framework for peace has been accepted by Arabs and Jews. For Israel to fail to take the initiative now would be to continue a policy of reaction that has led alternately from stalemate and crisis to war, not peace.

GOICHON, A.M. Jerusalem. Fin de la Ville Universelle. Paris, Maisonneuve et Larose, ix, 378p, Ind, Ill, Bibl.
  Prejudiced in favour of a Jordanian administration of Jerusalem, the author argues that under Israeli rule the city will lose its universal character.

GUGGENHEIM, Willy and MEIER, Annemarie. Jerusalem. Ger Atlantis, 186p, Ill.

KENYON, Kathleen M. Digging Up Jerusalem. London, Ernest Benn, 288p Ill, M.

KUH, Katherine. UNESCO and the Jerusalem Digs. Saturday Review, 24 Ja. pp 40-42.
  Investigates the archaeological brouhaha in the Holy City.

LANDESBILDSTELLE. Zentrum für audio-visuelle Medien. Jerusalem - Stadt der Menschheit; Fotoausstellung der Landesbildstelle im Schloss Charlottenburg. Berlin, 48p, Ill.

LELYVELD, Arthur. J. Jerusalem. CCAR Journal, 24, No. 3, Su. pp1-13.
  Our history and the experience of the years of Israel's return to the Holy City testify to the fact that we can count on its current custodians to care respectfully for its sanctities. For

the first time in two thousand years, to open them to all to come in reverence and peace.

N.D.S. "All my Sources are in thee, City of God". Echoes from the ICCJ Conference in Jerusalem. Encounter Today, 11, Nos. 2-3, Su/Aut. pp 46-71.

The International Council of Christians and Jews discussed the status of Jerusalem.

SCHNEIDER, Peter and WIDOGER, Goeffrey. (Eds.) Jerusalem Perspectives A Nineteenth and Twentieth Century Outline of the Holy City. Arundel, London, Rainbow Group,42p, Bibl.

The London Rainbow Group has been established as an experiment in Jewish-Christian theological dialogue. The brochure contains papers read in a one-day seminar on Jerusalem, together with a chronology of the city.

SOFER, Haim. The Political Status of Jerusalem in the Hashemite Kingdom of Jordan 1948-67. Middle Eastern Studies, 12, No. 1, Ja. pp 73-94.

THUBRON, Colin and the Editors of Time and Life Books. Jerusalem. Amsterdam, Time and Life Books, 200p, Ind., Ill, Bibl. (The Great Cities S.)

Jerusalem presented as the city of the major religions, with photographs by Jay Miasel.

WERBLOWSKY, Zvi R.J. Gerusalemme Celeste e Terrana. Documenti e Fatti, No. 15, Ma-Ju. pp 2-6.

Jerusalem in the Jewish tradition.

FOREIGN RELATIONS

ALPAN, Moshe. Israeli Trade and Economic Relations with Africa. In: Israel and the Third World, pp 100-10.

AMIR, Shimeon. Challenge and Response: Israel's Development Cooperation: 1974-75. In: Israel and the Third World. pp 234-43.

-------------. Israel's Development Cooperation: Youth Programs. In: Israel and the Third World, pp 111-17.

AVRIEL, Ehud. Israel's Beginnings in Africa. In: Israel and the Third World, pp 69-74.

BARROMI, Joel. Latin American States' Conduct at the UN Assembly on Issues Affecting Israel. In: Israel and the Third World, pp 270-88.

BEN, Philippe. L'enfant maudit de l'ONU releve la tete. L'Arche, 19, No. 233, Au. pp 21-22.

Israel at the UN.

BRECHER, Michael. Israel and China: A Historic "Missed Opportunity". In: Israel and the Third World, pp 218-33.

CURTIS, Michael and GITELSON, Susan Aurelia. (Eds.) Israel and the Third World. New Brunswick, N.J., Transaction Books, 410p, Ind.

Articles in this volume are listed under the names of their authors.

DECALO, Samuel. Afro-Israeli Technical Cooperation: Patterns of Setbacks and Successes. In: Israel and the Third World, pp 81-89.

DECTER, Moshe. Israel and South Africa. Congress Monthly, 43, No. 9 N. pp 3-4.

EGER, Akiva. Histadrut: Pioneer and Pilot Plant for Israel's International Cooperation with the Third World. In: Israel and *the Third World*, pp 75-80.

GITELSON, Susan Aurelia. Africans re-assessing Israel and Arabs. *Patterns of Prejudice*, 10, No. 5, S-O. pp 3-7.

African countries behaviour at the Ivory Coast meeting of ECOSOC 30 Ju-9 Jy.

------------------------. Israel's African Setback in Perspective. In: *Israel and the Third World*, pp 182-99.

------------------------. Unfulfilled Expectations: Israeli and Arab Aid as Political Instruments in Black African United Nations Voting Behaviour. *Jewish Social Studies*, 38, No. 2, Sp. pp 159-75.

HOROWITZ, Irving Louis. From Pariah People to Pariah Nation: Jews, Israelis and the Third World. In: *Israel and the Third World*, pp 361-91.

KANOVSKY, Eliyahu. Can Israel Serve as a Model for Developing Countries? In: *Israel and the Third World*, pp 45-51.

KAUFMAN, Edy. Israel's Foreign Policy Implementation in Latin America. In: *Israel and the Third World*. pp 120-46.

KEARNEY, Vincent S. Israel and South Africa: Strange Alliance. *America*, 133, 25 S. pp 158-161.

"If Israel has the real key to the puzzle, it is keeping quiet. Or is it that Israel is no longer overly concerned about its Third World image?"

KOCHAN, Ran. Israel in Third World Forums. In: *Israel and the Third World*. pp 247-69.

-----------, GITELSON, Susan Aurelia. and DUBEK, Ephraim. Black African Voting Behaviour in the UN on the Middle East Conflict: 1967-72. In: *Israel and the Third World*. pp 289-317.

KREININ, Mordechai E. Israel and Africa: The Early Years. In: *Israel and the Third World*. pp 54-68.

LORCH, Netanel. An Israeli View of the Third World. In: *Israel and the Third World*, pp 27-30.

LUMER, H. Israel and South Africa. *Jewish Affairs*, 6, No. 3, My-Ju. pp 7-11.

MEDZINI, Meron. Asian Voting Patterns on the Middle East at the UN General Assembly. In: *Israel and the Third World*, pp 318-24.

--------------. Reflections on Israel's Asian Policy. In: *Israel and the Third World*, pp 200-11.

NE'EMAN, Yuval. What is to be Done - *American Zionist*, 67, No. 1, S. pp 7-14.

RIVLIN, Benjamin. and FOMERAND, Jacques. Changing Third World Perspectives and Policies Towards Israel. In: *Israel and the Third World*. pp 325-60.

SEGRE, D.V. The Philosophy and Practice of Israel's International Cooperation. In: *Israel and the Third World*, pp 7-26.

SHAPIRA, Yoram D. External and Internal Influences in Latin American -Israeli Relations. In: *Israel and the Third World*, pp 147-81.

Israel's International Cooperation Program with Latin America. The Political Angle. Inter-American Economic Affairs, 30, No. 2, pp 3-31. Tab.

Assessment of Israeli cooperation with Latin American countries, the motives and criteria of Israeli development aid.

SHARON, Ariel. Israel and America: A Realistic Appraisal. *The American Zionist*, 67, No. 3, N. pp 7-8.

SHIMONI, Yaakov. Israel, the Arabs and Africa. Africa Report, 21, No. 4, Jy-Au. pp 51-55.
Interview.

---------------. Israel and the People's Republic of China. In: Israel and the Third World, pp 212-17.

SHEH, Nahum. Nahum Goldmann Makes Some Pointed Remarks on Israel's Present Position. Israel Horizons, 24, No. 2, F. pp 18-20. (From Al Hamishmar, Dec. 1975)

South Africa and Israel. Congress Monthly, 43, No. 7, S. pp 7-8.
Exchange of letters between Bayard Rustin, director of the Black Americans to Support Israel Committee, and Arthur Hertzberg, President of the American Jewish Congress, concerning the visit to Israel by Prime Minister Vorster of South Africa and the announcement of plans to expand commercial and other relations between the two countries.

TEITLEBAUM, Raul. Israel ... and the Israelis. Why Israel Needs the 500 Million Dollars Ford Does Not Want to Give. Interchange, 1, No. 10, Ju. pp 6-7.

TOLPIN, Jacob G. We and the Third World. Jewish Frontier, 43, No.6, Ju-Jy. pp 8-12.
Technology transfer to the Third World countries cannot be overcome very soon, but progress is being made and this weakens the influence of the Arab countries in the Third World and favours a chance for Israel to return to its favourable position in the area. In Yiddish: In Di Tsukunft, 82, No. 2, F. pp 92-96; 82, No. 3, Ma. pp 81-87.

WARSZAWSKI, Paul. Israel, the Jews and the Third World. Olam, Su/Aut. pp 3-9.
"Quite probably the nadir in relations between the Third World, the Jewish people and the State of Israel has as yet not been reached. It is equally probable that in the immediate future, international gatherings of the non-aligned group as well as meetings of the United Nations will witness the continuation of an apparent monolithic stand of the Third World on this subject"

ISRAEL-DIASPORA RELATIONS

ALTER, Robert. Israeli Culture and the Jews. Commentary, 62, No. 5, N. pp 59-65.
There has been a more pronounced degree of involvement, especially among intellectuals, with Israel on the part of American Jews, accompanied by a greater readiness to exercise critical freedom from official Zionist positions in defining a relationship with Israel.

America and Israel: Three Perspectives. Response, 10, No. 8, W. pp 9-39.
Contains: New Diaspora, New Israel by Arthur Waskow. American Olim and the Politics of Israel by David Twersky. Democratic Socialism, Israel and the Jews: An Interview with Michael Harrington by Mitchell Cohen.

AVI-HAI, Avraham. Israel-Centrism and Diasporism. The Jewish Journal of Sociology, 18, No. 1, Ju. pp 43-56.
Israel-Diaspora relationships will continue to be determined by social and international realities rather than by ideology.

BOROWITZ, Eugene. Are American Jews Allowed to Dissent on the Policies of Israeli Governments. Israel Horizons, 24, No. 8, O. pp 14-19.
On certain conditions - yes.

----------------. For Dissent on Israeli Policy. Parts 1 and 2. Sh'ma, 6, Nos. 116 and 117, 5 and 17 S. pp 123-36.
Advocates the absolute right of Jews to dissent from Israeli policies, provided the critics are loyal and no dissent is voiced in times of danger; responses in part 2.

BRICKNER, Balfour. Credo of a Dove Zionist. Worldview, 19, Nos.7-8, Jy-Au. pp 4-8.
"The Zionist doves are no more traitors to Israel or America than the American doves of the Vietnam war days were traitors to America. It is because we are interdependently connected to Israel that we seek to be heard."

COHEN, M. Democratic Socialism. Israel and the Jews: An Interview with Michael Harrington. Response, 9, No. 4, W. pp 33-39.

DAVIS, Moshe. Meditations on the Bicentennial-America and the Holy Land. New York, United Jewish Appeal, 24p.
Third Annual Louis A. Pincus Memorial Lecture, United Jewish Appeal 1976, National Conference, December 13th 1975.

EPSTEIN, Gary. Could Judaism Survive Israel? Tradition, 16, No. 1, Su. pp 41-55.
"Israel serves as a source of pride and commitment and identity. We may have come close, however, to making the State the sole source of these essential tributes. A world without Israel would be horrifying to contemplate and difficult to live in. It need not also be a world without Judaism."

FEIN, Leonard and HELLER, Mark. An Interview with Shimon Peres. Moment, 1, No. 7, F. pp 12-18.
An interview with Israel's Minister of Defence, during his visit to New York in late December.

GLAZER, Nathan. American Jews and Israel: The Last Support. Inter change, 2, No. 3, N. pp 1; 6-8.
The delicate relationships between the two.

GOLDSMITH, Sam J. The Public Relations Chaos. London, Calmus, 9p.
First published in the American Zionist monthly magazine of the Zionist Organisation of America, Ju, 1975, S. 1975 and F. 1976.

GORDIS, Robert. The Unbreakable Bonds to the Holy Land. Congress Monthly, 43, No. 1, D. 1975/Ja. 1976. pp 27-29.

HARRINGTON, Michael. How Does the Left View Israel and Why? Israel Horizons, 24, No. 3, Ma. pp 10-13.

HOWE, Irving. For Free Discussion in the Jewish Community. Interchange, 1, No. 10, Ju. pp 1; 7-8.
Claims the right to express candid views on Israel.

JACOBSON, Sheila and GEPNER, Gurit. Let's do Business with Israel. Hadassah Magazine, 58, No. 11, N. pp 19-38.
How to seek out investment opportunities that make good business sense and how to enjoy the benefits of an Israel Government program designed to encourage foreign capital investment in the country's many-faceted industrial infrastructure.

LESSING, Abba. Jewish Impotence and Power. Midstream, 22, No. 8, O. pp 52-58.
Israel does not guarantee safety and security, but it is the one

and only structure which safeguards Jews against humiliation and powerlessness in the future.

LUZZATO, Guido L. Simone de Beauvoir e la Solidarità con Israele. La Rassegna Mensile di Israel, 42, Nos. 7-8, Jy-Au. pp 378-80.

MANDELKORN, Philip. Should American Jews Criticise Israel? Condensed from Baltimore Jewish Times; Jewish Digest, 22, No. 1, S. pp 17-22.

MOSHER, Lawrence. Israel Worries American Jews. Middle East International, 60, Ju. pp 4-5.

PRINZ, Joachim and NURZBURGER, Walter S. Dissent: Two Views. Moment, 2, No. 3, D. pp 59-68.

Exchange of views on Israel-Diaspora relations between the vice-president of the World Jewish Congress and the president of the Rabbinical Council of America, with a reply by Leonard Fein, Moment's editor.

RABINOWITZ, Stanley. Bicentennial Reflections on America and Israel. Conservative Judaism, 30, No. 4, Su. pp 39-46.

SCHWARTZ, Helen J. Israel Versus the Diaspora. Jewish Spectator, 41, No. 2, Su. pp 43-46.

SIEGMAN, Henry. For Zion's Sake. Moment, 1, No. 4, Ja. pp 13-17.

American Jews and Israeli policy.

SURKIS, Reuven. What Are the Israelis Telling their Kids About Us? Interchange, 2, No. 2, O. pp 1; 6-8.

VIORST, Milton. Israel-Diaspora Relations. This is Not the Way to Talk to Our Friends. Interchange, 2, No. 4, D. pp 2ff.

VITAL, David. Israel and Jewry: Digging In. Midstream, 22, No. 9, N. pp 33-48.

WASKOW, Arthur. New Israel, New Diaspora. European Judaism, 10, No. 2, Su. pp 15-22; Response, 9, No. 4, pp 9-24.

WAXMAN, Chaim I. The Centrality of Israel in American Jewish Life. A Sociological Analysis. Judaism, 25, No. 2, Sp. pp 175-87.

WEISS-ROSMARIN, Trude. The Right to Criticize: Editorial. The Jewish Spectator, 41, No. 2, Su. pp 3-6.

It would be an insufferable loss if freedom of speech, of the right of dissent and criticism, were to disappear altogether from the American Jewish scene.

WIGODER, Geoffrey. Israel - public debate is irresponsible. Sh'ma, 6, No. 118, O. pp 137-39.

Criticises the Breira movement.

ISRAEL DEFENCE FORCES

BECKETT, Brian. Israel's Nuclear Options. Middle East International 65, N. pp 12-15.

CREVELD, M.van. Israel and Nuclear Weapons. Wiener Library Bulletin, 30, N.S. nos. 41-42, pp 57-61.

DOWTRY, Alan. Israel and Nuclear Weapons. Midstream, 22, No. 9, N. pp 7-22.

What is the evidence regarding Israel's nuclear capability? Are nuclear weapons likely to be useful to Israel?

FENWICK. Jean-René. Les vedettes de Cherbourg. une action du S.R. israelien en France. Lausanne, Elsevier, 261p, Ind, Ill.

Description of the dramatic 'escape' of gunboats ordered by Israel from France but not delivered due to De Gaulle's embargo.

SCHIFF, Zeev. Generals vs. the Israeli Government. Midstream, 22, No. 7, Au-S. pp 24-31.

------------. The Israeli Air Force. Air Force Magazine, 59, No. 8, Au. pp 31-38.

SHIROM, A. On Some Correlates of Combat Performance. Administration Science Quarterly, 21, No. 3, pp 419-32.
Enquiry conducted among Israeli military personnel on the Golan Heights.

SHLAIM, Avi. Failures in National Intelligence Estimate: The Case of the Yom Kippur War. World Politics, 28, No. 2, Ap. pp 348-80.
National defence plans must take into consideration the element of surprise.

TALMOR, David. Examination of Soldiers' complaints in the Israel Defence Forces. (IDF) Revue de Droit Penal Militaire et de Droit de la Guerre, 15, Nos. 1-2, pp 9-13.

WEIZMAN, Ezer. On Eagles' Wings. London, Weidenfeld and Nicolson; New York, Macmillan, 340p, Ill.
A former commander of the Israel Air Force accounts for the growth of the air force from its beginnings.

The Zionist Nuclear Menace - A Threat Against the West. Palestine, 3, No. 1, Ja. pp 61-65.

ECONOMIC AND SOCIAL PROBLEMS

ASAD, T. Class Transformation in Palestine under the Mandate. MERIP Reports, No. 53, D. pp 3-8.

BURSTEIN, Paul. Social Networks and Voting: Some Israeli Data. Social Forces, 54, No. 3, Ju. pp 833-97.
"The data presented demonstrates for the first time in a multivariate analysis that network variables have a significant impact on party choice independent of background attributes, and are important as mediators between background attributes and party choice as well."

CHETKOW, B. and KATAN, J. Interrelations between Community Workers and Politicians: An Israeli Example. International Review of Community Development, 19, Nos. 35-36, pp 137-56.

CRIDEN, Yosef and GELB, Saadia. The Kibbutz Experience. Dialogue in Kfar Blum. London, New York, Schocken, 224p, Ill.

CROMER, G. The Israeli Black Panthers: Fighting for Credibility and a Cause. Victimology, 1, No. 3, pp 403-13.

DANIEL, Abraham. Labor Enterprises in Israel. Vol. 1: The Comparative Economy. Vol. 2: The Institutional Economy. New Brunswick, N.J. Transaction Books, 312p; 232p.

DASSAL, Georges. La Santé du Moyen Orient. Politiques ou medicine? Geneve, Centre.
Compares Medical care in Israel with other Middle Eastern countries.

FRIEDMAN, A. Union Structure and Rank and File Revolt: The Israeli Experience. (French Summary) Industrial Relations, 31, No. 2, pp 261-82.
Explains the heavy toll the serious strikes have taken in the last six years and their reasons.

GINSBERG, Eli. Manpower Policy in Nation Building: Lesson from Israel. In Israel and the Third World, pp 31-36.

GITELMAN, Zvi and NAVEH, David. Elite Accommodation and Organizational Effectiveness: The Case of Immigrant Absorption in Israel. The Journal of Politics, 38, No. 4, N. pp 963-86.

GONEN, A. and WEINTRAUB, D. Community Characteristics and Differential Regional Participation. Sociologica Ruralis, 16, Nos. 1-2, pp 7-27. (French and German Summaries)

Pilot studies on the emergence and function of voluntary cooperation in an Israeli region.

HOFFMITZ, Laible. North African Jewry in Israel. Jewish Frontier, 43, No. 2, F. pp 17-21.

Israel's Military Industries. Condensed from Aviation Week and Space and Technology. Jewish Digest, 22, No. 1, S. pp 77-79.

KATZ, Eliahu and GUREVITCH, Michael. The Secularization of Leisure, Culture and Communication in Israel. London, Faber and Faber, 288p, Ind.

An empirical study of the use of leisure in Israel and the viability of the traditional prescribed uses of leisure time in Judaism.

KELLNER, Peter. Israel's Economy on the Brink. Middle East International, 56, F. pp 6-8.

KONOPNICKI, M. and SZESKIN, A. Structures Cooperatives et Système de crédit en milieu rural israelien. Revue des Etudes Cooperatives, No. 184, pp 113-39.

The crisis in Israeli cooperatives.

KRAMER, Ralph. The Voluntary Service Agency in Israel. Berkeley, Institute of International Studies, U. of California, 94p, Bibl.

LEON, Dan. Reflections on Israeli Society in the '70s. Letter from Israel. Jewish Quarterly, 24, No. 3, Aut. pp 19-25.

LERMAN, Robert. A Critical Overview of Israeli Housing Policy. Jerusalem, Brookdale Institute of Gerontholgy and Adult Human Development. American Joint Distribution Committee in Israel, 89p, Ill.

LOMRANZ, J. Cultural Variations in Personal Space. Journal of Social Psychology, 99, No. 1, pp 21-27.

Experiments with 45 Israeli secondary school students of Argentinian, Iraqi and Russian origin who immigrated the year before to study the variations of social distance of their specific ethnic group.

LOWDERMILK, Walter Clay. Palestine: Land of Promise. Westport, Conn., Greenwood P., vi, 244p, Ill.

The author was a member of the Anglo-American Inquiry Commission. This work was first published in 1944 and stresses the agricultural potential of the country provided there was enough water.

MARIAMPOLSKI, H. Changes in Kibbutz Society: Their Implications for the Situation of the Sexes. International Review of Modern Sociology, 6, No. 1, pp 201-16.

MARS, L. The Position of the Administrator in an Israeli Cooperative Village(French and German Summaries). Sociologia Ruralis, 16, Nos. 1-2, pp 41-55.

Relations with the Jewish Agency, with the political party to which the village belongs and the villagers themselves - all sources of conflict.

MARX, Emanuel. The Social Context of Violent Behaviour: A Social Anthropological Study in an Israeli Immigrant Town. London, Routledge, 130p, Ind, Bibl. (Routledge Direct Editions)

After two years of anthropological fieldwork in a community of Moroccan immigrants in a new Israeli town, the author concluded that the violent person is very much aware of the reaction to his act. He, therefore, uses this means to achieve his end, or at least uses it to inform the public of the problem that needs attention.

NEIPRIS, Joseph. Some Origins of Social Policy in a New State: The Formation of Policy Concerning Aged Immigrants in Israel, 1948-55. Ann Arbor, Mich., U. Microfilms, iv, 256p, Bibl.

Dissertation - U. of California, Berkeley, 1966.

PHILIPPE, Beatrice. Des Israelites tres conformistes. Les Nouveaux Cahiers, 12, No. 44, Sp. pp 29-35.

RABKIN, Leslie Y. In Israel's Radical Communes: The Institution of the Family is Alive and Well. Psychology Today, No. 2, F. pp66-73.

Tracks the change of the Israeli Kibbutz from socialist vision to capitalist reality. In three successive generations, the family and private property have risen again.

RAPAPORT, C. and others. Early Child Care in Israel. London, Gordon, 211p, Ill.

ROTER, R. and SHAMAI, N. Die Reform des Steuertransfersystems in Israel. Internationale Review der Sozialen Sicherheit, 29, No. 4, pp 393-412.

Tax-transfer reform in Israel.

SCHINDLER, Ruben. The Pioneering Ideology and the Roots of Social Welfare in the Pre-State Period of Israel. Journal of Jewish Communal Service, 52, No. 4, Su. pp 384-92.

SHUMSKY, Abrahm. The Clash of Cultures in Israel, a problem for Education. Westport, Conn., Greenwood P.; London, Westport P., xi, 170p.

Reprint of 1955 edition.

SMOOHA, Sammy. Ethnic Stratification and Allegiance in Israel: Where do Oriental Jews Belong? Il Politico, 41, No. 4, pp 635-51.

Examines Israel as a three-tier society: Ashkenazim occupying the highest level, Arabs placing the lowest extreme and the Orientals in between these two groups.

SPILERMAN, Seymour and HABIB, Jack. Development Towns in Israel: The Role of the Community in Creating Ethnic Disparities in Labor Force Characteristics. American Journal of Sociology, 81, No. 4, pp 781-812.

Examines the new towns "strategic" role in the solution of problems created by ethnic stratification.

TAMARIN, George R. Israeli Society: Authoritarian Traditionalism Versus Pluralist Democracy. In: Case Studies on Human Rights and Fundamental Freedoms. II, pp 101-36.

The Sabra phenomenon, Orthodox domination, Postition of Women, Arab-Jewish relations. Ashkenazim and Sephardim.

TEICHER, Morton I. Social Planning in Israel. Journal of Jewish Communal Service, 52, No. 4, Su. pp 374-83.

Criticises the multiplication of institutions and individuals engaged in social planning which is cumbersome and inefficient.

TORGOVNIK, E. Urban Political Integration in Israel: A Comparative Perspective. Urban Affairs Quarterly, 11, No. 4, Ju. pp 469-88.

WEINGROD, Alex. Israel: Group Relations in a New Society. Westport P., London, Greenwood Reprints, 82p.
Reprint of 1965 edition.

ZAHN, Ulf. Der Fremdenverkehr in israelischen Kooperativen und kollektiven Siedlungen. Ein Beispiel für den Fremdenverkehr im ländlichen Raum. Mitteilungen der Georgraphischen Gesellschaft in München. 61, pp 181-204.
Tourism as a kibbutz-industy has been introduced in only 10% of the communal settlements but it is expanding.

MIDDLE EAST

AJAMI, Fouad. Between Cairo and Damascus. Foreign Affairs, 54, No. 3, Ap. pp 444-61.

Arms in the Middle East: Special Report. Moment, 2, No. 3, D. pp 15-20.
Introduction by Ira Silverman. Arms in the Middle East by Seth Carus. A Concluding Observation by Edward N. Luttwak.

BEAUMONT, Peter. et a. Middle East: A Geographical Study, London, Wiley, 560p, Ill.

CAMPBELL, John C. (Ed.) The Middle East. New York, Arno P., ix, 435p. Ind., M. (Great Contemporary Issues S.)
Reprints of newspaper cuttings relating to the Middle East from World War I to 1975.

A Chronological Compilation of United Nations action on the Palestine Question 1947-1975. New York, International Chronologies 2 parts. (various pagings) in English and French.

DEVLIN, John F. The Ba'ath Party: A History from Its Origins to 1966. Stanford, Cal. Hoover Institution, 372p, Ind, Bibl.
Deals also with the Party's attitude to Jews, Israel and the Palestine question.

DRABECK, Anne Gordon and KNAPP, Wilfred The Politics of African and Middle Eastern States. An Annotated Bibliography. Oxford, Pergamon International Library, x, 192p, Bibl.
Handbook for students in the field.

DUCLOS, L.J. Les forces militaires au Moyen-Orient. Maghreb-Machrek, 74, O-D. pp 8-12.
Report on the military strength of Israel and the Arab states 1973-1976 including personnel, armour, aircraft and the respective defence expenditure.

Ethnic and Religious Minorities in the Middle East. Middle East Review, 9, No. 3, Fa. pp 1-77.
Partial contents: The Christians of Lebanon - I. The Lebanese Identity by Kamal S. Salibi. II. Lebanese Strife Sours Maronites by Jonathan C. Randal. Egypt's Christian Minority by Thomas W. Lippman. The Christian Communities in Jerusalem and the West Bank, 1948-1967 by Daphna Tsimhoni. The Kurdish Struggle for Independence by Omran Yahya Feili and Arlene R. Fromchuk.

FISHER, Sydney Nettleton. (Ed.) Social Forces in the Middle East. Westport, Conn., Greenwood P.; London, Westport P, xvi, 282p, M.
Reprint of the 1955 edition.

FREYMOND, Jacques. Guerres, revolutions, Croix-Rouge. Reflections sur le rôle du Comite International de la Croix-Rouge. Geneve, Institut Universitaire de Hautes Etudes Internationales, xii, 222p. (HEI Presse 3)

Study of the Red Cross's role in war and revolution with a brief historical introduction and including Red Cross action in the Middle East (application of the Geneva Convention) and assistance to hostages.

GITELSON, Susan Aurelia. Arab Aid to Africa. Midstream, 22, No. 8, O. pp 22-28.

GLUBB, Sir John Bagot. Story of the Arab Legion. n.e. London, Da Capo; Eurospan, 371p.

HARRIMAN, Averell. Special Envoy to Churchill and Stalin 1941-46. London, Hutchinson; New York, Random House. xii, 595p, Ind, Ill.

Discussions on the Middle East.

HURNI, F. Von Nasser zu Sadat: Sozialismus, Nationalismus und Pragmatismus in der arabischen Welt. Schweizer Monatshefte, 56, No. 4, Jy. pp 293-306.

The changes in Arab policies from Nasser to Sadat.

ISMAEL, Jacqueline S. and TAREQ, Y. The Holy Land: The American Experience. The Arab Americans and the Middle East. Middle East Journal, 3, No. 3, Su. pp 390-405.

KHAWAM, Rene R. (Tr.) Le Livre des Ruses, la strategie politique des Arabes. Paris, Phebus, 447p, Ind.

Demonstrates, by translating the original Arabic texts, how Arab policies are formulated.

KIRKBRIDE, Alec. From the Wings. Amman Memoirs 1947-1951. London, Frank Cass, 159p, Ind.

Sir Alec Kirkbride was British Minister plenipotentiary in Amman at the end of the British Mandate in Palestine.

KOCK, Gert. Der "Europäisch - Arabischer Dialog": Hintergründe und Merkmale. Deutsche Aussenpolitik, 21, No. 6, Ju. pp 890-902.

LANDAU, Jacob M. Middle Eastern Themes: Papers in History and Politics. London, Frank Cass, 309p.

LEWIS, Jesse W. The Strategic Balance in the Mediterranean. Washington D.C., American Enterprise Institute for Public Policy Research, 169p, M.

MANSFIELD, Peter. The Arabs. London, Allen Lane, 572p, Ind.

The author, a historian and journalist, wrote this book with the aim of presenting a concise and authoritative introduction to the social, political and historical facets of the modern Arab world.

MASOOD, M. (Ed.) The Middle East 1975. (Special Issue) Pakistan Horizon, 28, No. 4, Karachi, Pakistan Institute of International Affairs, 251p.

MEDZINI, Meron. The Arab World: After the Interim Agreement. Midstream, 22, No. 2, F. pp 28-34.

MIDDLE EAST INSTITUTE. The Process of Development in the Middle East: goals and achievements, a summary record, the 30th annual conference. Washington, 15-16 O. 1976, Washington, 1976, 51p, (Mimeo)

NARAYAN, B. Sadat and the pan-Arab Movement. Indian Journal of Politics, 10, No. 2, pp 60-69.

NORTON, A. Nuclear Terrorism and the Middle East. Military Review, 56, No. 4, Ap. pp 3-11.

PAYNE, Robert. The Splendor of the Holy Land: Egypt, Jordan, Israel, Lebanon. New York, Harper & Row, 196p.

PRITTIE, Terence. Israel and the Lebanon. Britain and Israel, 60, S. 4p.

REED, David. Syria's Assad: Pivotal New Force in the Middle East. Reader's Digest, No. 8, Au. pp 138-44.

"While still a revolutionary socialist who sides with the Soviets, he now welcomes Western nations and will play a major role in Arab-Israeli relations."

RETI, Ervin. Libanon Egy valsag tortenelmi gyokerei. E'let es Tudomany, 21, 12 Ma. pp 502-8.

Historical roots of the crisis in Lebanon.

SALIBI, Kamal S. Crossroads to Civil War. (Lebanon). London, Ithaca P., viii, 178p, Ind, Ill.

The armed conflict in Lebanon has inextricably connected, internally with social pressures resulting from rapid urbanisation, and externally with the Arab-Israeli conflict.

SCHWARZFUCHS, Stephen. Quand les juifs de France s'inquietaient des Chretiens du Liban. L'Arche, No. 232, Jy. pp 34-36.

French Jews' concern for Lebanese Christians.

SINAI, Anne and POLLACK, Allen. (Eds.) The Syrian Arab Republic. A Handbook. New York, American Academic Association for Peace in the Middle East. 190p, Ind, Bibl. (The Middle East Confrontation S.)

Contents: Syria, Past and Present by Joseph Neyer. Government and Ideology by A. R. Kelidar. Economy and Population Including the Status of Jews in Syria; Syria and the Soviet Union by Yaakov Ro'i, Roger F. Pajak and Drew Middleton. Syria and ssrael by Jacob Ascher and Irving Heymont. Syria and the International Community by Elizabeth L. Conroy. Syrian Views (including on Israel and Zionism) and a Syrian Political Directory.

SMART, Ian. Future Political Patterns in the Middle East. The World Today, 32, No. 7, Jy. pp 243-50.

STRATEGIC SURVEY 1975. London, International Institute for Strategic Studies, 130p.

Discusses new factors in security; decolonization; the super-powers; Europe, the Middle East and the Gulf; Asia after Vietnam; Arms control, with chronologies.

TAIEB, Jacques. A L'origine de la tragédie libanise. Les Nouveaux Cahiers, 12, No. 45, Su. pp 8-19.

YOUNGER, Sam. The Syrian Stake in Lebanon. The World Today, 32, No. 11, N. pp 399-406.

MIDDLE EAST POLICY OF POWERS

ABEDISEID, Mohammad. Die deutsch-arabischen Beziehungen Probleme und Krisen. Stuttgart, Seewald. Bibl. (Zeitpolitische Schriftenreihe 15)

A Palestinian analyses Germany's role in the Middle East, recognizing her difficult situation between Arabs and Israelis.

ALROY, Gil Karl. The Kissinger Experiment: American Policy in the Middle East. New York, Horizon, 189p.

ATHERTON, Alfred I. Jr. The United States and the Middle East. *The Department of State Bulletin*, 2 Au. pp 174-79.
Address by the Assista-nt Secretary for Near Eastern and South Asian Affairs, before the 108th annual convention installation banquet of B'nai B'rith at Omaha, Nebr. on June 30th.

BEN, Philippe. U.S.A.: Le Président Ford soutiendra Israël en 1977. *L'Arche*, No. 232, Jy. pp 22-23.

BEN-AVI, Abraham. Middle East Flashback: 1950-1976. *Midstream*, 22, No. 10. D. pp 6-13.
Review of the U.S. Middle East policy.

BROWNFIELD, Allan C. Carter and Israel. *Middle East International*, No. 64, O. pp 14-15.

BRUZONSKY, Mark A. A United States Guarantee for Israel? Washington D.C., Georgetown University Center for Strategic and International Studies, 57, 5p.
Discusses whether the U.S. should undertake any guarantees for Israel's security and if so, what form such guarantee should take.

-----------------. Perspective: Waiting on Washington, *Moment*, 2, No. 2, N. pp 5-10.
"After years of divisiveness in Washington, the State Department and an increasingly independent Congress are getting ready for what many in Washington are convinced may be a crucial year of decision regarding the future of Arab-Israeli relations and, by implication, of American-Israeli relations."

-----------------. What Think-Tank Think About the Middle East. The fifth branch of government steps up its production of mideast studies. *The National Jewish Monthly*, 91, No. 4, D. pp 12-23.

-----------------. U.S.-Israeli Policies: Reading the Signs for '77. *Worldview*, 19, No. 9, S. pp 4-9.
"Israel faces an increasingly clear choice for 1977 - accept the urgent necessity to come forth with a new approach toward return of the occupied territories, recognize the national rights of the Palestinians and develop an overall approach to a reasonable settlement ... or risk a major schism with the United States."

CANADA-ISRAEL COMMITTEE. Canadian Foreign Policy in the Middle East. A Summary review. Montreal, 68p.

CARMICHAEL, Joel. Blackmail on the Cheap: Editorial. *Midstream*, 22, No. 1, Ja. pp 3-6.
"Soviet penetration can be frustrated only by an enduring peace between Israel and its neighbours, which in the wake of a possible split in the Arab front is entirely conceivable."

COHEN, Samy. Le "giscardisme" et Israël. *Les Nouveaux Cahiers*, 12, No. 45, Su. pp 1-7.

CURTIS, Michael. American Interest and the Middle East. *Middle East Review*, 8, Sp/Su. pp 13-19.

DAR, S. The Kamazan War and Pakistan. *Pakistan Horizon*, 29, No. 2, pp 59-74. (The Yom Kippur War)

Du BROFF, Sidney. Germany - Foundering Again? The American Zionist 67, No. 2, N. pp 24-27.

Germany is under threat, both economically and politically. Democratic Germany can join with her Left and her Right to make common cause in blaming Israel for all her problems.

----------------. Henry Kissinger - The Great Jewish Disaster. Jewish World, 1, No. 8, Jy. pp 2-7.

Criticises Kissinger's Middle East policy.

EBAN, Abba. A New Look at Partition. Jewish Frontier, 43, No. 7, Au-S. pp 10-13.

"Israel's sovereignity came to birth through partition. It would dwindle with partition's death. We must tell the nation frankly that an agreed new partition is a 'concession' not only to Arab demands but also to Israeli interest and conceptual truth."

ELLERIN, Milton. Rising Arab Influence in the U.S. New York, Trends Analyses Division, A.J. Committee, 15p.

FENYVESI, Charles. The American Achievement in the Middle East. A Conversation with Joseph Sisco. The National Jewish Monthly, 90, No. 8, Ap. pp 22-28.

FREEDMAN, Robert O. Détente and Soviet Policy Toward the Middle East. Middle East Review, 8, Sp-Su. pp 25-41.

FREEMAN, R. Soviet Policy Toward the Middle East Since the October 1973 Arab-Israeli War. Naval War College Review, 29, No. 3, pp 61-103.

FRIEDRICH, Carl Joachim. American Policy Toward Palestine. Westport Conn., Greenwood P.; London, Westport P., vi, 106p.

Pre-State period. Reprint of the 1944 edition.

GLASSMAN, Jon D. Arms for the Arabs: The Soviet Union and War in the Middle East. Baltimore: Johns Hopkins U.P., 243p.

GOLAN, Matti. The Secret Conversations of Henry Kissinger. Step-by-Step Diplomacy in the Middle East. New York, Quadrangle, N.Y. Times, Bantam, 280p, Ind.

The author is chief diplomatic correspondent of Ha'aretz, and he examines the motives of Kissinger's 'step-by-step' diplomacy in the Middle East.

GORDON, Max. Issues and Candidates '76. Jewish Currents, 30, No. 9 O. pp 4-11.

Includes the Middle East policy of candidate for the President of the U.S.A.

GORDON, Murray. Carter and the Middle East. Congress Monthly, 43, No. 9, N. pp 5-6.

GREAT BRITAIN AND PALESTINE. 1915-1945. Westport, Conn., Hyperion, xii, 178p, Ind, M. (The Rise of Jewish Nationalism and the Middle East S.)

First published in 1946 in London as Information Paper No. 20 of the Royal Institute of International Affairs.

GRIFFITH, W. Soviet Influence in the Middle East. Survival, 18, No. 1, Ja.-F. pp 2-9.

HALPERN, Ben. Kissinger's Parting Fanfare. Midstream, 22, No. 9, pp 3-6.

HAZAN, Baruch A. Soviet Propaganda. A Case Study of the Middle East Conflict. New York, Toronto, London, John Wiley & Sons, x, 293p, Ind., M.

HORELICK, Arnold L. Moscow's New "Time of Troubles" in the Middle East: Soviet Optimism for Staying in the Game. *Middle East Review* 8, No. 2, Sp/Su. pp 42-51.

HUFF, Earl Dean. Zionist Influences Upon U.S. Foreign Policy: A Study of American Policy Toward the Middle East from the time of the Struggle for Israel to the Sinai Conflict. Ann Arbor, Mich., U. Microfilm, v, 297p. Bibl.

Ph.D. Dissertation - U. of Idaho, 1971.

ISSA, K. and YOUSSEF, A. Soviet Policy in the Middle East after the October War. (In Japanese) *Chuto-tsuho*, No. 238, My. pp 32-40.

KAHN, Lothar. The Further Adventures of "Dr. K." *Jewish Spectator*, 41, No. 3, Fa. pp 38-42.

Kissinger's policy in the Middle East.

KARASOVA, T. Israel's Labour Party (MAI) in the Service of Reaction and Aggression. (In Russian). *Narodi azii i Afriki*, 16, No. 6, pp 47-59.

KEDOURIE, Elie. In the Anglo-Jewish Labyrinth: McMahon-Husayn Correspondence and its Interpretation, 1914-39. Cambridge U.P. 333p, Ind.

KIMCHE, Jon. Soviet Military Shifts and the Destruction of Lebanon. *Midstream*, 22, No. 3, Ma. pp 45-51.

KISSINGER, Henry. American Resolve and the Security of Israel. *The Department of State Bulletin*, 16, 7 Ju. pp 720-25.

Address given in Baltimore on May 9th, upon receiving the Chizuk Amuno Synagogue Distinguished Leadership Award.

KNIGHT, John and PATZ, Günther. (Eds.) Australia and the Middle East: Papers and Documents. Canberra, Australian Institute of International Affairs, v, 106p.

KOHLER, Foy D., GOURE, Leon and HARVEY, Moase L. The Middle East in Soviet Global Strategy. Miami, Centre for Advanced International Studies.

KRYNEN, D. De Gaulle, la France et Proche-Orient. *Revue Politique et Parliamentaire*, 82, Ma-Ap. pp 16-35.

KULSKI, Wladislaw Wazebor. Germany and Poland. From War to Peaceful Relations. Syracuse, N.Y., U.P., xxiv, 336p, Ind, Bibl,M

Traces German-Polish relations from 1939 to date, i.e. the consequences of the Warsaw Treaty of 1970. Deals extensively with the implications of the two countries' relations on the Jews and on Israel.

KURKCOUGLU, O. Turkey's Attitude Towards the Middle East Conflict. *Dis. Polit*, 5, No. 4, pp 23-33.

MCDERMOTT, Anthony. Japan and the Arabs. *Middle East International* No. 63, S. pp 12-14.

MANN, Daniel. Israel and America 1977. *Jewish Frontier*, 44, No. 7, F. pp 15-17.

MANUEL, Frank Edward. The Realities of American-Palestine Relations. Westport, Conn., Greenwood P.; London, Westport P., viii, 378p.

Reprint of 1949 edition.

MIDDLE EAST OPINION TRENDS IN FRANCE AND GREAT BRITAIN. *Facts*, 23, No. 1, O. pp 575-85. Foreign Report of A.D.L.

Uses I.J.A. Research Report, Great Britain 8.

MIERLO, Harry Van. Macht en manipulatie in het Midden-Oosten. Bussum, Agathon, 200p.

The role of the great powers in the Middle East conflict.

MILENKOVIC, M. Events in the Middle East. Review of International Affairs, 27, No. 625, 20 Ap. pp 13-41.; 19-20.

The conflict viewed from Yugoslavia.

MOSHER, Lawrence. Special Relationship Wearing Thin. Middle East International, No. 57, Ma. pp 4-6.

On U.S.-Israel relations.

----------------. U.S. Middle East Policy: A New Direction. Middle East International, No. 63, S. pp 4-5.

MUSALLAM, Sami Fayex Khalil: Zum Araberbild in der bundesrepublikanischen Presse am Beispiel des IV Nahostkrieges. Orient, 320p. (Diss. U. of Bonn)

THE NATIONAL BIENNIAL CONVENTION OF THE AMERICAN JEWISH CONGRESS - THEMES AND ADDRESSES: Special Issue. Congress Monthly, 43, No. 5, My. pp 1-23.

We will Never Abandon Israel by Henry A. Kissinger. Judaism and the Democratic Ideal by Robert Gordis. Policies of Peace by Edward M. Kennedy. Crises and Commitments by Simcha Dinitz.

PELED, Mattiyahu. Israel ... and the Americans. Danger Signs. Interchange, 1, No. 10, Ju. pp 5-6.

PRIMAKOV, E. Israel Versus the Arab States. International Affairs, 22, No. 11, N. pp 44-52.

RA'ANAN, Uri. The Soviet-Egyptian "Rift". Commentary, 52, No. 6, Ju. pp 29-35.

REICH, B. Az Egyesült Államok politikája a Közel-Keleten. (U.S. Policy in the Middle East) Nemzetközi Szemle, 20, No. 5, My. pp 21-35.

ROSTOW, Eugene V. Detente and the Political Situation in the Middle East. Middle East Review, 8, No. 1, Sp/Su. pp 9-13.

RUBIN, Barry. Latin America and the Arab-Israel Conflict. Weiner Library Bulletin, 29, New Series 37/8, pp 30-39.

"At the peak of the oil embargo, Latin America magazine predicted that 'expressions of sympathy for Arab positions will not be slow to come from a number of capitals in Central America that have customarily aligned themselves with the Israeli cause.' This has not happened; indeed most of the small and poor Central American and Caribbean countries have been the most steadfast."

-------------. West Europe and the Middle East. The Nation, 45, No. 15, My. pp 584-87.

Even-handed the Europeans may be in spirit, but in fact they are balancing friendly solicitude for Israel against a heavy respect for the Arab weapon of oil.

RUGH, William A. Arab Perceptions of American Foreign Policy During the October War. Washington, Middle East Institute, 51p. (Special Study 2)

Based on an examination of Arab media reflecting views on the October 1973 war.

SCHIFF, Zeev. The New Balance of Power. Midstream, 22, No. 1, Ja. pp 7-15.

Changes in the regional balance of power and in the attitudes of countries and great powers since the Yom Kippur war.

SHLAIM, Avi and YANNOPOULOS, G. (Eds.) The EEC and the Mediterranean Countries. London, Cambridge U.P., vii, 352p, Ind.

Systematic examination of economic relations between Mediterranean countries and the EEC. The papers include: Trade agreements between the EEC and Arab countries of the Eastern Mediterranean and Cyprus by G.V. Vassiliov and The EEC and Israel by Sergio Minerbi.

SHORROCK, William I. French Imperialism in the Middle East. The failure of policy in Syria and Lebanon, 1900-1914. Wisconsin, U. of Wisconsin P., x, 214p, Ind, Bibl, M.

Uses unpublished French documents in an account of French presence in the Middle East and the implications for Palestine.

SIEGEL, Seymour. Why I am Voting for Gerald Ford. Sh'ma, 6, No. 120, 29 D. pp 153-55.

SLONIM, Shlomo. American Pressures on Israel. The American Zionist, 76, No. 6, F. pp 7-11.

The Ford Administration Policy.

SMETTAN, M. Probleme und Politik der NATO im Ostlichen Mittelmeer. Deutsche Aussenpolitik, 22, No. 2, F. pp 49-62.

STOOKEY, Robert W. The Holy Land: The American Experience I. The Christian American Concern. Middle East Journal, 30, No. 3, Su. pp 351-68.

19th Century American travellers in Palestine were motivated by purely religious considerations. US Political interest in the Middle East occurred only after World War I.

TRICE, Robert H. Interest groups and the foreign policy process: US Policy in the Middle East. Beverley Hills; London, Sage, 80p.

UNITED STATES-SOVIET DETENTE AND THE MIDDLE EAST: Special Issue. Middle East Review, 9, No. 2. Sp/Su. pp 1-60.

Includes: Detente and the Political Situation in the Middle East by Eugene V. Rostrow. American Interest and the Middle East by Michael Curtis. Has the Middle East Conflict Overturned the Super-power Balance? by Bernard Schechterman. Detente and Soviet Policy Toward the Middle East by R. Freedman

U.S. DEPARTMENT OF STATE. United States Policy in the Middle East. September 1956-June 1965; Documents. Westport Conn., Greenwood P.; London, Westport P., xiv, 425p.

Reprint of the 1957 edition.

U.S. Congress. Senate. Committee on Foreign Relations. Foreign Policy Choices for the Seventies and Eighties. Hearings: 10 S. 1975 - 20 S. 1976. Washington, U.S. Govt. Print O., 2 vols, 730p.

Includes Middle East and East-West Issues.

THE U.S. AND THE ARAB WORLD: Special Issue. Race and Class, 17, No. 3, W. pp 221-342.

Six articles including: 'A World Restored' Revisited American Diplomacy in the Middle East by Eqbal Ahmad. Reaction and Revolution in the Middle East: Arab Perspectives by Mohammed Hussanein Heikal and others. Gunboat in the Arab Gult by Michael Klare.

VLADIMIRSKY, V. Middle East: Need for an Immediate Settlement. International Affairs, (Moscow) No. 7, Jy. pp 99-103.

VÖLKER, Edmond. (Ed.) Euro-Arab Cooperation. Proceedings of the Colloquium on the Changing Political and Economic Relations Between Western Europe and the Arab Countries of the Middle East. Amsterdam, October 29-31, 1975. Leiden, Sijthoff, xvii, 228p, Ind.
Proceedings of a colloquium organized by the Europa Instituut of Amsterdam University.

WELL, Günther van. Le developpement d'une politique commune des Neuf au Proche-Orient. Politique Etrangere, 41, No. 2, Ma, pp 113-26; In German: Europa Archiv, 31, No. 4, 25 F. pp 119-28.
Evaluation of the common Middle East policies of the EEC.

YAFFE, Richard. The American Scenario for the Mideast. Israel Horizons, 24, No. 4, Ap. pp 5-7.

--------------. Israel's Role in America's Mideast Policy. Israel Horizons, 24, No. 5, My. pp 6-9.

--------------. Will Either the Democrats or Republicans Solve Our Problems? Israel Horizons, 24, No. 8, O. pp 6-7.
Pre-election speculation on how U.S. Democrats or Republicans will deal with the Middle East conflict.

YAPP, M.E. The Soviet Union and the Middle East. Asian Affairs, 63 No. 1, F. pp 7-18.
Soviet Motives in the Middle East and the methods of intervention. U.S. distrust of Soviet Middle East policies.

ARAB-ISRAELI CONFLICT

The Arab-Israeli Conflict. Bulletin of Peace Proposals. Special Issue, No. 4, pp 291-384.

The Arab World and Israel. World Affairs Report, 6, No. 3, Su. pp 288-99.

ARURI, Naseer. (Ed.) Middle East Crucible: Studies on the Arab-Israeli War of October 1973. Wilmette, Ill., Medina U.P.

ASAQI, Fawzi. Some Geographic Elements in the Arab-Israeli Conflict. Journal of Palestine Studies, 6, No. 1, Aut. pp 67-91.

AZIZ, M. The October War and International Politics: A Systems Approach. Indian Journal of Politics, 10, No. 1, Ja-Ju. pp 91.

BEAUCE, Thierry de Trois fonds arabes de cooperation. Politique Etrangère, 41, No. 1, pp 43-56.
Funds of Arab aid for countries affected by the Arab-Israeli conflict 1967-73.

BEIT-HALLAHMI, Benjamin. Some Psychological and Cultural Factors in the Arab-Israeli Conflict. A Review of the Literature. Journal of Conflict Resolution, 16, No. 2, pp 269-80.

BELLOW, Saul. To Jerusalem and Back: A Personal Account. New York, Viking; London, Alison P., Secker & Warburg. 182p. French edition: Paris, Flammarion.
Notes and conversations during a four-months' stay in Israel. Bellow seeks to findan answer to the many paradoxes Israel presents.

------------. Reflections (The Middle East) The New Yorker, 76, 12 and 19 Jy.

BIVORT, Lawrence Harwood de. The Establishment of Israel and the Arab-Israeli Conflict: A Legal Analysis, London, U. Microfilms, 503p, Bibl.
Ph.D. Thesis, Johns Hopkins University, Baltimore.

BLITZER, Wolf I. (Ed.) Myths and Facts 1976. A Concise Record of the Arab-Israeli Conflict. Washington D.C. Near East Report, viii, 119p, M.

The fourth such volume (the first was published in 1964). It takes into account the developments since 1973.

BULL, Odd. War and Peace in the Middle East. The Experiences and Views of a U.N. Observer. London, Cooper, xvi, 205p, Ind.

First published in Norwegian in 1973, an objective analysis of the Middle East conflict by the commander of UNTSO 1963-70.

BRECHER, Michael. Ein Gespräch in Kairo. Fragen und Antworten zum arabisch-Israelischen Verhältnis. Aus Politik und Zeitgeschichte, 49, 4D. pp 40-55.

A Jewish political scientist discusses the Arab-Israeli conflict with Egyptian colleagues.

BUTTERWORTH, Robert Lyle with Margaret E. Scranton. Managing Interstate Conflict 1945-74. Data with synopses. Pittsburgh, U. Center for International Studies, vii, 535p, Ind.

Among the cases cited and analysed are many relating to Israel and the Middle East conflict, beginning with Israel's independence.

CATTAN, Henry. Palestine and International Law: Legal Aspects of the Arab-Israel Conflict. 2 R.e. London, Longman, 388p.

Slanted in favour of the Palestinians and Arabs in general, highlighting "Israel's violations of international law". Includes all the relevant UN resolutions since 1973.

CHOMSKY, Noam. Riflessioni sul Medio Oriente. Torino, Einaudi,182p.

Addresses to Arab students in American Universities 1969-74.

COOPER, Leo and SEELEY, . Crisis in the Middle East: The Arab-Israeli Dispute and its effect on the Western Alliance. London, Royal United Services, Institute for Defence Studies.

DANN, Urien. Grundfaktoren und Grundhaltungen im Palästinakonflikt. Aus Politik und Zeitgeschichte, B. 24, 12 Ju. pp 3-9.

Analysis of the Arab-Israeli conflict.

DEUTSCH, László and BRODIE, Harry. A Place to Live and a Place to Die. London, Corgi, 256p, M.

What Israel was like during the Yom Kippur War.

DIVINE, D. Why This War? International Journal of Middle East Studies, 7, No. 4, O. pp 523-43.

On Egyptian policy in the October 1973 War.

DOUGHY, . Qu'est-ce qu'on sémites. Juifs et Arabs. (preface by Jean Lacoutre) Paris, J.C. Lattes, 40p, Ill.

Cartoons on the Arab-Israeli conflict, some of which were published in the Israeli weekly Ha'olam Ha'zeh.

DÜRRENMATT, Friedrich. Zusammenhänge. Essay über Israel. Eine Konzeption. Zurich, Arche, 240p.

The noted Swiss dramatist confronts the basic differences between Arabs and Jews that form the background to this almost insoluble problem.

EL-ASMAR, F. L'agression sioniste contre le terre en Israël/ Palestine. Situations Moyen-Orient, 15, My/Ju. pp 14-18.

ERRARA-HOECHSTETTER. Chronologie du conflit israel-arabe. Maghreb-Machrek, No. 74, O-D. pp 69-78.

FEIN, R., GILBERT, E.M., KATZ, B., NATAY, B. and RIEMER, J. Le Conflit Israelo-arabe. Geneva, Documents de Politique du Moyen-Orient, 8p.

GHALI, Bhutros. The October War and the new balance of forces in the Arab World. (In Japanese) *Chuto-tsuho*, No. 238, My. pp 17-24.

GILBERT, Martin. The Arab-Israeli Conflict: Its History in Maps, R.e., London, Weidenfeld & Nicolson, 120p.

GOLAN, Matti. Mideast Perspectives. *Midstream*, 22, No. 4, Ap. pp 7-15.

    the root of the matter will still be that the Arab countries cannot yet completely find it in their hearts to coexist with Israel, if not in peace then at least as good neighbours.

GRIFFIN, Kenyon N., MARTIN, John C. and WALTER, Oliver. Religious Roots and Rural Americans' Support for Israel During the October War. *Journal of Palestine Studies*, 6, No. 1, Aut. pp 104-14.

HALPERIN, Daniel. Entre la guerre et la paix, quelques notes sur le symposium strategique de Jerusalem. *Revue Militaire Suisse*, 20, No. 2, F. pp 70-82.

HAQQI, S. The Fourth Arab-Israeli War: New Challenges and Possibilities. *Indian Journal of Politics*, 10, No. 1, Ja-Ju. pp 76-90.

HARKNESS, Georgia and KRAFT, Charles F. The Biblical Backgrounds of the Middle East Conflict. Nashville, Tenn., Abingdon, 208p.

    The authors conclude that in order to understand the Middle East conflict one has to go back to Biblical times and have sympathy for both sides.

HEIKAL, Mohamed. The Road to Ramadan. The Inside Story of how the Arabs Prepared for, and almost won, the war of October 1973. London, Fontana, 283p, Ind, Ill.

    Paperback edition of book published by Collins in 1975.

HOLST, Johan Jörgen. Lehren der Nahost-Krise von 1973 für das Atlantische Bündnis. Struktur und Prozedurprobleme in Hinblick auf neuartige Konfliktsituationen. *Europa Archiv*, 31, No. 7, Ap. pp 205-14.

    Lessons of the Yom Kippur War for NATO.

HORDES, Jess N. Evolving U.N. approaches to and the role of UN machinery in the Arab-Israel conflict: 1947-56. Ann Arbor, Mich., U. Microfilms, 299p.

    Ph.D. Dissertation, Johns Hopkins U. Baltimore.

International Symposium on the 1973 October War. Cairo, Ministry of War, Bibl.

JENDGES, Hans. Der Nahostkonflikt. Neue Version. Berlin, Colloquium, 128p, Bibl. M. (Landeszentrale fuer politische Bildungsarbeit Berlin in Verbindung mit dem Fachbereich Politische Wirtschaft der Freien Universitaet Berlin; *Zur Politik und* Zeitgeschichte 30)

    Reviews the position as of 1976 and considers whether peace is finally in sight.

JONAH, James O.C. Peacekeeping in the Middle East. *International Journal*, 31, No. 1, W. pp 100-22.

KAPELIUK, Amnon. The Arab Armies and the Yom Kippur War. Some Misconceptions of Arab Capability. Tr. Jack Stone. *Israel Horizons*, 24, No. 1, Ja. pp 11-15.

KAPLOWITZ, Noel. Psychopolitical Dimensions of the Middle East Conflict: Policy Implications. The Journal of Conflict Resolutions. 20, No. 2, pp 279-318.
Found two straightforward Arab orientations toward Israel - open acceptance and total rejection. Among Israelis, we found orientations of totalism, hard bargaining and conciliation.

KHOURI, Fred. J. The Arab-Israeli Dilemma. 2 ed. Syracuse, New York, Syracuse U.P. 480p.

LAMBERT, Lance. Battle for Israel. London/Eastbourne, Coverdale House, 128p.
A Christian friend of Israel discusses the spiritual and political background tothe Arab-Israeli conflict.

LAQUEUR, Walter Z. (Ed.) Israel-Arab Reader. London, Bantam Books, 608p.
Paperback edition of the documentary volume.

LOFFLER, Paul. Arabische Christen im Nahostkonflikt. Christen im Politischen Spannungsfeld. Frankfurt/M. Otto Lembeck, 98p.
Surveys the attitude of Arab Christians to the Middle East conflict and publishes the relevant documents.

McKENZIE-SMITH, R. Crisis Decision-Making in Israel: The Case of the October 1973 Middle East War. Naval War College Review, 29, No. 1, pp 39-52.

NAPOLI, Domenico di. Medio Oriente: Anatomia di una crisis. Pescara, Libreria dell'Universita. 282p.

MALIMANN, Wolfgang. Die israelisch-arabische Aufrüstung 1967-74. Bonn, U. of Bonn.
Unpublished Doctoral thesis.

MANSFIELD, Peter. Sadat's "Controlled Experiment" Middle East International, No. 66, D. pp 13-14.

----------------. Wind of Change in Egypt. Middle East International, No. 63, S. pp 14-16.
On the interim agreement with Israel.

MASSOUD, Muhammad Said. I Fought as I Believed: An Arab Canadian Speaks Out on the Arab-Israeli Conflict. Montreal, Ateliers des Sourd, xiv, 724p.

MEIR, Golda. Arab Aspirations, Jewish Hopes. Congress Monthly, 43, No. 1, D.1975/Ja. 1976, pp 41-42.
Views after the Yom Kippur War.

MOLLER-RASMUSSEN, Lars. Copenhagen, Information, 211p. (In Danish) Israel-Palestina Konflikt uden ende?

MYTHS AND FACTS 1976. A Concise Record of the Arab-Israeli Conflict Washington D.C., Near East Report, viii, 119p.

NARKISS, Uzi. La Batalla de Jerusalem. Tr. by Isidor Niborski. Buenos Aires, Congreso Judio Latinoamerica. 32p, Ill. (Hechos de la Historis Judia 86).
Account of the battle for Jerusalem in 1967 by the Commander of the forces involved.

nassar, Husni. Harb al-Salam. Alexandria, 236p, (In Arabic)
On the October1973 War.

NATSUME, T. A Diary of Life in the Battlefield During the Ramadan (October) War: in Syria during the Middle East Conflict.(In Japanese) Chuto-tsuho, NO. 234, Ja. pp 30-36.

NIELSEN, Jorgan S. et al (Eds.) International Documents on Palestine 1973. Beirut, Institute for Palestine Studies; Kuwait, U. of Kuwait, xxxv, 592p, Ind.

NISAN, Mordechai. A Strategy for Israel: Confrontation or Conciliation? American Zionist, 66, No. 7, My-Ju. pp 19-21.

NUTTING, Anthony. Suez in Retrospect. Middle East International, No. 64, O. pp 16-18.

PELED, Mattityahu. Israel ... and the Arabs. Sadat's News is Good News. Interchange, 2, No. 4, D. pp 3-5.

PICARD, Elizabeth. La Syrie du 'redressement' et les chances de paix au Proche-Orient. Politique Etrangere, 41, No. 2, Ma, pp 169-80. In German: Europa Archiv, 31, No. 8, Ap. pp 248-56.

PINEAU, Christian. 1956 Suez. Paris, Laffont, 233p.

Discloses Anglo-French-Israeli connection.

PODHORETZ, Norman. The Abandonment of Israel. Commentary, 52, No. 7, Jy. pp 23-31.

"If a nuclear war should ever erupt in the Middle East, then, be it on the heads of all those in the United States and elsewhere ... who under cover of self-deceptions and euphemisms and outright lies are 'negotiating over the survival of Israel'"

PRANGER, Robert J. and TAHTINEN, Dale R. Implications of the 1976 Arab-Israeli Military Status. Washington, D.C. American Enterprise Institute for Public Policy Research, 50p. (Foreign Affairs Studies, 34)

The authors outline the four zones of possible warfare and consider the likely uses of the major weapons now in the arsenals of the two sides.

RAMSELAAR, A.C. Schillebeeckx over de problematiek van Israel. (Schillebeeckx on the Problematic of Israel.) ter herkenning, 4 No. 4, O. pp 103-10.

The author summarizes the main ideas of a short but essential article by Schillebeeckx: "Reflections on the Mid-East Conflict" written in 1974.

Schillebeeckx holds a fervent plea for the detheologizing of the Mid-East problem on the political level.

Religious Roots and Rural Americans' Support for Israel during the October War. Journal of Palestine Studies, 6, No. 1, Ja. pp 104-14

ROSENTHAL, David. The Arab-Israeli Conflict: Some Truths. Jewish Frontier, 43, No. 2, F. pp 10-16.

SCHATTEN, Fritz. Entscheidung in Palestina. Koexistenz oder Katastrophe. Stuttgart, Seewald, 206p, Ind, Maps.

Analyses the psychological and historical background to the Arab-Israeli conflict which the author sees as the conflict between two national liberation movements in the same area, but which in his view is capable of peaceful solution.

SCHECHTERMAN, Bernard. Has the Middle East Conflict Overturned the Superpower Balance? Middle East Review, 9, No. 1, Sp/Su. pp 20-24.

SCHENKER, Avraham. Israel is at a Fateful Moment in Its History. Israel Horizons, 24, No. 6, Ju-Jy. pp 20-26.

SEWELL, T. The War of Atonement - and its Lessons. The Army Quarterly and Defence Journal. 106, No. 1, Ja. pp 47-71.

Military and strategic considerations.

SILVER, S. Medinas yisroel un di arabishe velt. (Israel and the Arab World) Sovietish Heimland, 16, No. 5, My. pp 162-65.
Review of Aharon Cohen's book of the same title, published in Israel.

SHABATH, Heskel and STARR, Ralph. Jewish-Arab Conflict in the Middle East: Is It Reconcilable? Viewpoints, 9, No. 3, Sp/Su, pp 16-20.

SICHERMAN, Harvey. The Yom Kippur War: End of Illusion? Beverly Hills/London, Sage, 91p. (The Foreign Policy Papers published by the Foreign Policy Research Institute, Philadelphia, V.1. No. 4)
Describes the Israeli and American illusions that contributed to their surprise at the outbreak of the October 1973 War.

SID-AHMED, Mohamed. Lebanon and the Arab-Israeli Conflict. Middle East International, No. 63, S. pp 6-8.

Some Reflections on the Arab-Israeli Conflict. London, British Council of Churches, 16p.
Study paper prepared by the Division of International Affairs of the British Council of Churches and the Conference of British Missionary Societies.

A Survey of the Attitudes of Americans Towards the Arab-Israeli Conflict and Toward Jews in the United States. New York, Louis Harris, 97p. (Study No. 2530) Mimeo.

VICKER, Ray. From Damascus. The Times - and Attitudes - Are Changing. Present Tense, 4, No. 1, Aut. pp 24-28.

WAKEBRIDGE, C. A Tank Myth or a Missile Mirage. Military Review, 56, No. 7, Jy. pp 3-11.
On the Arab-Israeli Conflict.

WELLER, J. Tanks in the Middle East. Military Review, 56, No. 5, My. pp 11-23.
On the Arab-Israeli Conflict.

YOST, Charles. The Middle East: Alternative to Stalemate. Saturday Review, 3 Ap. pp 14-21.
U.S. Diplomat calls upon both sides to negotiate now as time is running out fast for both Arabs and Israelis.

ZEIDAN, Abdel-Latif M. United Nations Emergency Force 1956-67. Stockholm, Almqvist, xii, 268p.
Peacekeeping in the Middle East.

ARAB BOYCOTT

The Arab Boycott - An Analysis. New York, Anti-Defamation League of B'nai B'rith. 18p.

BOUMAN, Johan. Roots of Arab Intolerance. American Zionist, 66, No. 7, My-Ju. pp 7-15.
The psychological-cultural background of the Arab world, Islamic traditionalism and Israel, and the Arab progressives and Israel.

CANADA-ISRAEL COMMITTEE. The Arab Boycott: Implications for Canada. Montreal 62p.

CHILL, Dan S. The Arab Boycott of Israel: Economic Agression and World Reaction. New York, Praeger, 121p.

KESTENBAUM, L. The Antitrust Challenge to the Arab Boycott: per se theory, Middle East Politics and United States v. Bechtel Corporation. Texas Law Review, 54, No. 7, N. pp 1411-31.

MASLOW, Will. How You Can Fight the Boycott. Moment, 2, No. 3, D. pp 55-58.
Example of application of method evolved by the American Jewish Congress.

NOONAN, John T. Bribes and the Boycott: The Responsibilities of American Lawyers. American Bar Association, 55, No. 12, D. pp 1606-9.

PRITTIE, Terence. The Secondary Arab Boycott and Britain. Middle East Review, 9, No. 1, W. pp 46.

----------------. Trade Boycott and Antisemitism. AJA Review, 19, No. 1, Sp. pp 15-17.

ROSENFELD, Stephen S. Washington Report. Money, Morality and the Boycott. Present Tense, 3, No. 2, W. pp 16-18.

ROTH, Etienne. La Lutte Contre le Boycotte Arabe. L'Arche, No. 231 Ju. pp 34-36.

RUBIN, Barry. Challenging the Arab Boycott. The Nation, 215, No. 11 S. pp 205-8.
Despite some lapses, administration strategy seems to be to condemn direct discrimination while closing its eyes to other aspects of the boycott.

SHIRMAN, Shalom. The History of the Arab Boycott. Middle East Review, 9, No.1, W. pp 40.
Condensed in Jewish Digest, 21, No. 8, My. pp 41-5.

SCHWARTZ, L. The Arab Boycott and American Responses: Antitrust Law or Executive Discretion. Texas Law Review, 54, No. 6, Au. pp 1260-88.

SHAPIRO, Manheim S. Whose Boycott? Jewish Digest, 21, No. 9, Ju. pp 80.

SHORT, Martin. Trading with the Enemy. Middle East International, No. 60, Ju. pp 11-13.

STEINER, H. International Boycotts and Domestic Order: American Involvement in the Arab-Israeli Conflict. Texas Law Review, 54, No. 7, N. pp 1355-1410.

TIMBERG, S. Sovereign Immunity and Act of State Defences Transnational Boycotts and Economic Coercion. Texas Law Review, 55, No. 1, pp 1-37.

Twelve Questions and Answers on the Arab Boycott. New York, American Jewish Committee, 16p.

U.S. CONGRESS. House Committee on the Judiciary. Arab Boycott. Hearings Before the Subcommittee on Monopolies and Commerical Law ... on H.R. 5236, H.R. 12383 and H.R. 11488; Arab Boycott, 9 Ju. 1975 and 8 Ap. 1976. Washington, U.S. Govt. Print. Off. 185p.

U.S. CONGRESS. House Committee on Interstate and Foreign Commerce. The Arab Boycott and American Business. Report by the Subcommittee on Oversight and Investigations ... An inquiry into the nature and scope of the Arab trade boycott, its impact on domestic commerce, the applicability of Federal laws to foreign imposed boycott practices. S. Washington, U.S. Govt. Print. Off., 115p.

U.S. CONGRESS. House Committee on Government Operations. Effectiveness of federal agencies' enforcement of laws and policies against compliance, by banks and other U.S. firms, with the Arab boycott. Hearings before a Subcommittee of the ... 8-9 Ju. Washington, U.S. Govt. Print. Off., 178p.

U.S. CONGRESS, Senate. Committee on Banking, Housing and Urban Affairs. Export administration amendments, foreign boycotts, and domestic and foreign investment improved disclosure acts of 1976; a report. Washington, U.S. Govt. Print. Off., 49p.

U.S. CONGRESS, Senate. Foreign Boycotts and Domestic and foreign investment improved disclosure acts of 1975; a report, Washington, U.S. Govt. Print. Off., 33p.

YAFFE, Richard. Blocking Arab Blackmail. The National Jewish Monthly, 90, No. 3, Ma. pp 18-19.

OCCUPIED TERRITORIES

AMAD, Adnan. (Ed.) Israeli League for Human and Civil Rights. (The Shahak Papers) Beirut, Near East Bureau for Information and Interpretation.

Pro-Palestinian work claiming violations of human and civil rights in the occupied territories.

BOURDET, C. La colonisation isréalienne, obstacle à la paix. Situations Moyen Orient, No. 15, My-Ju. pp 19-22.

Protests against the settlements on the West Bank.

GAVRON, Daniel. On Patrol in Gaza. The Watchword was Honor and Suspect the tocals. National Jewish Monthly, 91, No. 1, S. pp 42-52.

GRUEN, George E. U.S. Policy on Jerusalem and the Territories; does Ambassador Scranton's speech mark a shift. New York, American Jewish Committee, 14p.

HILAL, J. Class Transformation in the West Bank and Gaza. MERIP Reports, eo. 53, D. pp 9-15.

KOTLER, Yair. Building Boom in Gaza. Midstream, 22, No. 5, My. pp 26-32.

LOUVISH, Misha. Trouble in the West Bank. (Letter from Israel) Jewish Frontier, 43, no. 6, Ju-Jy. pp 4-7.

LUMER, H. Zionist Robbery and Brutality in the West Bank. Jewish Affairs, No. 2, Ma-Ap. pp 9-12.

NUTTING, Anthony. Gloom on the West Bank. Middle East International No. 55, Ja. pp 17-18.

PURY, A. de. La promesse patriarchale: origines, interpretations et actualisations. Etudes Théologiques et Religieux, 51, No. 3, pp 351-66.

Argues that Biblical promises to the Patriarchs cannot serve as a basis for israel's territorial claims.

SMITH, Terence. Life on a Volcano. The New York Times Magazine, 14 Ma. pp 14-15; 40.

Despite the perils of the Syrian border, the residents of Merom Golan kibbutz keep their cool - and their determination to stay.

STERN, Gavriel. An Unfortunate Decision and Its Consequences. Some Causes for the Recent Disturbances in the West Bank. Israel Horizons, 24, No. 4, Ap. pp 8-10.

STONE, Jack. Arabs Restless Under Israeli Rule. Israel Horizons, 24, No. 5, My. pp 13-16.

TARNOV, Jacques. Mourir pour la Judee-Samarie? L'Arche, No. 231, Ju. pp 26-27.
The West Bank's future.

UNITED NATIONS. Report of the Special Committee to Investigate Israeli Practices affecting the Human Rights of the Population of the Occupied Territories. Note by the Secretary-General to the General Assembly 31st Session Agenda item 55. 1 O. 118p. M.

VAN AGGELEN, J. Protection of Human Rights in the Israeli held territories since 1967 in the light of the Fourth Geneva Convention. Revue Egyptienne de Droit International, 32, pp 83-124.
Alleges violations of the Geneva Conventions.

WALZER, Michael. Israeli Policy and the West Bank, Dissent, 23, No. 3, Jy. pp 234-36.

WEITZMANN, Kurt. The Monastery of Saint Catherine at Mount Sinai. The Icons: From the Sixth to the Tenth Century. Princeton, U.P., 276p. Ill.
Description.

JEWS AND ARABS

ARAB-JEWISH UNITY. Testimony Before the Anglo-American Inquiry Commission for the Ihud (Union) Association by Judah Magnes and Martin Buber. Westport, Conn., Hyperion, 96p. (The Rise of Jewish Nationalism and the Middle East S.)
Reprint of the book first published by Victor Gollancz, London, in 1947.

ARAB TREATMENT OF JEWS. Myths and Facts. Washington, D.C., pp 80-85.

BALLAS, S. Le personnage israélien dans la littérature arabe. Les Nouveaux Cahiers, 12, No. 44, Sp. pp 46-52.
The image of the Israeli in Arab literature.

BUBER, Martin, MAGNES, Judah L. and SIMON, Ernst. (Eds.) Toward Union in Palestine, Essays on Zionism and Jewish Arab Cooperation. Westport, Conn., Greenwood P.; London, Westport P., 124p.
The three main propagators of Arab-Jewish coexistence and leaders of Brit Shalom put forward their ideas, work first published in 1947.

GINAT, J. A Rural Arab Community in Israel: Marriage Patterns and Women's Status. Salt Lake City, U. of Utah.
Ph.D. thesis. U. of Utab, U.S.A.

GOTTEIN, Shlomo Dov. Jews and Arabs: Their Contacts Through The Ages. New York, Schocken, 263p. 3 N.E.

GOTTHEIL, Fred. Arab Immigration into Pre-State Israel: 1922-31. Middle East Studies, 9, No. 3, pp 315-24.

HAMMAMI, S. and MACHOVER, M. Vivre ensemble. Khamsin, No. 3, pp7-26.
Interview.

HOFFMITZ, Laible. Dynamite on the Campus. (The Jewish-Arab Relations in the Israeli Universities) Jewish Frontier, 43, No. 3 Ma. pp 15-18.

HOFMAN, John E. and ROUGANA, Nadim. Young Arabs in Israel: Some Aspects of a Conflicted Social Identity. The Journal of Social Psychology, 47, No. 99, pp 75-86.

JIRYIS, Sabri. The Arabs in Israel. Tr. Inea Bushnaq. New York, Monthly Review Press, 314p. M.

The Koenig Report: Demographic Racism in Israel. MERIP Reports, No. 51, pp 11-14.

The Koenig Report: "Memorandum-Proposal-Handling the Arabs of Israel" Journal of Palestine Studies, 6, No. 1, Aut. pp 190-200.

LEVI, A.M. and BENJAMIN, A. Jews and Arabs Rehearse Geneva: A Model of Conflict Resolution. Human Relations, 28, No. 4, N. pp 1035-44.

Describes a structured model of conflict resolution illustrated with examples from two workshops which brought together young adult Israeli Jews and Arabs.

LEVINE, Naomi. Israel and its Arab Minority. Congress Monthly, 43, No. 1, D1975/Ja.1976, pp 43-44.

MANDEL, Neville J. The Arabs and Zionism Before World War I. U. of California P., 265p.

MOGANNAM, Matiel. E.T. The Arab Woman and the Palestine Problem. Westport, Conn., Hyperiod P., 319p, Ind, Ill, M. (The Rise of Jewish Nationalism and the Middle East S.)

Reprint of the book published in 1937, when the author saw the only solution to the problem if the Jews were to give up their "extreme ideas" and content themselves to live with the Arabs in a Palestine state, friendly with the British, that would be formed and admitted to the League of Nations if that body continued to exist.

Recent Developments in Arab-Jewish Relations in Israel. New York, American Jewish Committee, 19p. (Reports on the Foreign Scene 16)

ROSENBERG, William G. Israeli Arabs: The Mayor of Nazareth. The Atlantic Monthly, 31, No. 8, Au. pp 16-22.

Toufik Zayed.

ROSENFELD, Henry. The Class Situation of the Arab National Minority in Israel. Paper presented at the AAA meeting in Washington, D.C. November 17-21.

RUBENSTEIN, Daniel. Israel Arabs. Moment, My-Ju. 1, No. 10, pp 21-26.

Interviews two representative Israeli Arabs on what it means to be an Arab in the Jewish State.

SERENI, Enzo and ASHERY, R.E. (Eds.) Jews and Arabs in Palestine. Studies in a National and Colonial Problem. Westport, Conn., Hyperion, 315p. (The Rise of Jewish Nationalism and the Middle East S.)

Reprint of essays first published in 1936 by Hechalutz Press, New York. Contributors include: Haim Arlosoroff, Zev Abromowitz, David Hurwitz, M. Nemirovsky, David Ben Gurion, Moses Beilinson, Berl Katznelson, Eliezer Liebenstein, Yakov Hazan, Hayim Greenberg, Alexander S. Kohansky and the editors.

SOEN, D. Arabs, Social Change and Ethnicity in Israel. Orient, 17, No. 4, D. pp 109-22.

TAMARIN, George R. Jewish-Arab Relations in Israel Following the 1973 War. Plural Societies, 7, No. 4, W. pp 27-46.

TERRY, Janice. Zionist Attitudes Toward Arabs. Journal of Palestine Studies, 6, No. 1, Aut. pp 67-78.

PALESTINIANS

AGHA, Hussein J. What State for the Palestinians. Journal of Palestine Studies. 6, No. 1, Aut. pp 3-38.

AHMAD, N. The Lebanese Crisis: the role of the PLO. Pakistan Horizon, 29, No. 1, pp 31-46.

AKSENTIJEVIC, M. The Security Council and the Palestinian Question. Review of International Affairs, 27, No. 621, 20 F. pp 24-26.

AMERICAN JEWISH COMMITTEE. Some Questions on the PLO and Israel. New York, AJC, 2p.

Arafat: Effective Ruler of Lebanon. In the 11 years since Arafat's first raids into Israeli occupied territory there have been heroic deeds as well as tactical mistakes for which his movement has paid. Events, 19 N. pp 13-16.

AVINERI, Shlomo. Something has Changed in America's Policy Toward the Palestinians. Israel Horizons, 24, No. 2, F. pp 20-25.

BERTELSEN, Judy. The Palestinian Arabs: A non-State Nation. Systems Analysis. Beverly Hills/London, Sage, 81p, Bibl. (Sage Professional Papers in International Studies, 43)

Examines both the strategies and goals adopted by the Palestinian Arabs, and some of the points where their strategies are likely to erupt into the international context.

BRUZONSKY, Mark A. The U.S., the P.L.O. and Israel. Commonwealth, 100, My. pp 326-30.

"The American attitude towards the Palestinians is changing." Contends that "the U.S. is moving toward some form of P.L.O. recognition."

----------------. and SINGER, Israel. Dependent Israel: The Two Options. Worldview, 19, No. 4, Ap. pp 42-47.

"The time has come for Israel to let everyone know its territorial and security requirements for a real peace. then the burden will be on the Arab states and on the Palestinians to reach a reasonable settlement; and on the U.S. to understand."

-----------------------------------. Israel and the Palestinians: Time for Decision. Israel Horiøons, 24, No. 5, My. pp 19-27.

Call for some accommodation between the two.

CANAAN, Tewfik. For the Record. (Text of Lecture given in Jerusalem published in Palestine and Jordan 29 Au. 1936) Middle East International, No. 65, N. pp 27-31.

COHN, J.P. and PETIT, G. L'organisation de la liberation de la Palestine. Annuaire du Tiers-Monde, pp 122ff.

Description of the PLO, its aims, structure and activities.

DRUMMOND, William J. and ZYCHER, Augustine. The Fourth Estate: Arafat's Press Agents. Harper's, No. 3, Ma. pp 24-27;30.

"In spite of their good intentions, the media are playing into the hands of the P.L.O."

EL-RAYYES, Riad and NUHAS, Dunia. Guerrillas for Palestine. London Croom Helm, 160p. Italian ed. Milano Epistone, 167p.

Pro-Arab book.

EPP, Frank H. The Palestinians: Portrait of a People in Conflict. Toronto, McClelland and Stewart; London Books, Canada. 242p, Bibl, Ill.

Pro-Palestinian work based on interviews with Palestinians in North America and the Middle East.

FAHOUM, Khaled. Entretien avec le President du Conseil National Palestinian. France-Pays Arabes, No. 64, pp 31-33.

the aims of the P.L.O.

FRADE, F. La cuestion palestina hoy. Revista de Politica International, 25, No. 145, My/Ju. pp 41-66.

GEFFNER, Ellen Joyce. The Arab View of the Loss of Palestine. Israel Horizons, 24, No. 1, Ja. pp 7-10.

Their defeat in 1948 meant that the Israelis, i.e. the Zionists, robbed them of their chance to develop and they feel that they can regain national identity only by regaining Palestine.

GENDZIER, Irene L. Behind the Zionist Position. The Nation, 215, 14 F. pp 169-72.

"While a number of Israelis close to, or in government circles are coming to realize the inevitability of dealing with the Palestinian issue on a political level, their American supporters, unable or unwilling to face the question, remain mired in the dangerous fantasies of military solutions."

GERVASI, Frank. The Rights of the Palestinians: Myths and Realities. The Nation, 215, 1 My. pp 530-32.

"For all their endorsements of the revolutionary aims of the PLO at Rabat, the Arab states are not sincerely concerned with self-determination for the Palestinians, but with fulfilling their own expansionist ambitions in the area that formerly was Palestine - all of it."

GOLLIN, J.H. Nasserism and the Palestinians. Olam, Su/Aut. pp41-45

Suggests that "the emergence of a tragic pattern of Egyptian and inter-Arab politics which seems to persist in the region to this very day: Arab regimes are wont to promote and support the Palestine movement to varying degrees in order to control and use it for their own political machinations, while confrontation with Israel and the fulfillment of the aspiration of the Palestine movement tend to be secondary and often negative considerations.

GORDON, Murray. The Security Council "Debate": The Tangle Behind It. Midstream, 22, No. 3, Ma. pp 19-29.

"In the current confusion over the question of Palestinian nationalism, the Security Council may have produced some of the building blocks from which to build an Israel-Palestinian dialogue."

HARKABI, Yehoshafat. Strategies Against Israel. Jewish Digest, 22, No. 3, N. pp 3-8. (Condensed from Ma'ariv, and Crossroads 7, No. 2)

Chiefly PLO and Arab terrorist organisations.

HUGHES, Edward. Yasser Arafat's Fight for the Palestinians. Reader's Digest, No. 4, Ap. pp 116-20.

"After years of directing terrorist attacks against the Israelis, the leader of the Palestine Liberation Organisation appears ready to compromise his goals."

Israel and the Palestinians. A Symposium. *Moment*, 1, No. 8, Ma. pp 33-48.

ISRAEL, Gerard. French Policy on the Palestinian Issue. *AJA Review*, 19, No. 1, Sp. pp 10-13.

ISSA, Mahmoud (alias Selim). Je suis un Fedayin. En collaboration avec Huguette Cuchet-Cheruzel. Paris, Stock, 288p, (Coll. Temoigner)

Memoirs of a Palestinian who fought in King Hussein's 'Black September', was a prisoner of the King's Bedouin, participated in the terrorist attack in Athens, was imprisoned there and finally fought in the streets of Beirut.

JETHMALANI, R.B. Aims of the P.L.O. *Congress Monthly*, 43, No. 1, D.1975/Ja. 1976, pp 13.

KATZ, Samuel. Israël face au mythe de la Palestine, Paris, Albatross, 240p, M.

Adduces irrefutable proof of the continuous Jewish presence in Palestine, the origins of recent Arab claims to the land and puts the whole problem into an international perspective. He blames chiefly Great Britain and the Soviet Union for supporting Arab dreams of the destrüction of Israel.

KENNEDY, R. Scott. The Mideast's Fearful Symmetry of Violence. *The Christian Century*, 93, 4-11 Au. pp 684-6.

"If the Middle East is to move off its present course of no war/no peace, all of us must attend to the fact that true peace is not possibile unless it includes the Palestinians.

KHADER, Bichara and Naïm. (Eds.) OLP, Al-Fatah, FPLP, FDPLP. Testi Della Rivoluzione Palestinese 1968-76. Tr. G. Feletto and C. Moretti. Verona, Bertani, 400p, Bibl.

Italian edition of "Textes de la révolution palestinienne", a collection of statements made and documents issued by the PLO, Al-Fatah, FDLP and FDPLP.

KIERNAN, Thomas. Arafat. The Man and the Myth. New York, Norton, 281p. Ind.

Biography, based on the author's personal acquaintance of Yassir Arafat.

---------------. Yassir Arafat: Fraud. *Moment*, 1, No. 10, My-Ju. pp 16-20; 60-64.

"He does not represent the Palestinians in general, or even any specific segment of the Palestinians; he represents his superiors in the Syrian regime."

KOTLER, Yair. Two "Palestines" in Israel. *Midstream*, 22, No. 6, Ju-Jy. pp 7-16.

KURTZER, Daniel Charles. Palestine Guerrilla and Israeli Counter-insurgency Warfare: The Radicalization of the Palestine Arab Community to Violence.

Ph.D. Thesis, Columbia U, New York.

LANDA, R. From the History of the Palestinian Resistance Movement. 1967-1971. (In Russian) *Narodi Azii i Afriki*, 5, pp 18-31.

--------. The Present State in the Palestine Resistance Movement. 1971-1976. (In Russian) *Narodi Azii i Afriki*, 5, pp 15-29.

LANGER, Felicia. La Repressione di Israele Contro I Palestinesi. Minalo, Teti 220p.

LE GAC, Daniel. Au nom de la Palestine. Paris, J.C. Lattes,

LIEBMAN, M. Rapport Final du 'Colloque Palestine'. Situation Moyen Orient, 15, No. 3, My-Ju, pp 4-8.

LOUVISH, Misha. Israel and the Palestinians. Jewish Frontier, 43, No. 2, F. pp 7-9.

MANOR, Yohanan. La Politique Palestinienne d'Israël. Politique Etrangere, 41, No. 5, My. pp 485-506.

MANDELSON, Peter. Palestinians on Israel's Conscience. Middle East International, No. 55, Ja. pp 19-20.

MILSON, Menahem. Arabs and Israeli Attitudes. Dissent, 23, No. 4, Fa. pp 332-37.

"The value of the Palestinian situation from the Jewish point of view is that we shall not assume the distorted image that our enemies attribute to us. We must reserve to ourselves the right to determine the aims of Zionism, and not leave it to Yassir Arafat to define them."

MISRAHI, Robert. Israel et les Palestinians. Geneve, Centre diinformation et de Documentation sur le Moyen Orient, 96p.

The last, fourth chapter of the author's book La Philosophie Politique et l'Etat d'Israel (1975) setting out his views on friendly cooperation between Jews and Arabs as the only constructive solution of the Middle East conflict.

MUSLIH, Muhammed Y. Moderates and Rejectionists Within the Palestinian Liberation Organisation. The Middle East Journal, 30, No. 2, Sp. pp 127-40.

Shows that the moderates within the PLO are prepared to accept an interim agreement for the Palestine problem. Should they fail to achieve the establishment of a Palestinian state, they will either be overtaken by the radicals or perhaps turn to radicalism.

NAKLEH, Issa. A Palestinian Viewpoint. Saturday Evening Post, No. 3, Ma. pp 20-23; 36+

By a leading Palestinian Arab intellectual who describes himself as a "Christian Arab", a member of the Palestinian Bar, chairman of the Palestinian Arab Delegation, and permanent representative of the Arab Higher Committee for Palestine in New York.

OGUSHI, T. The Present Status of the Palestinian Problem and a View of Future Developments. (In Japanese). Chuto-tsuho, No. 234, Ja. pp 3-11.

OKAKURA, T. The History and Organisation of the PLO. (In Japanese) Chuto-tsuho, No. 234, Ja. pp 21-29.

ONODY, Gyorgy. Palesztina és a Palesztinok. Budapest, Kossuth, 106p. (Nemzetkozi Zsebkonyvtár)

Hungarian propaganda work in favour of the Arabs, described as the nation that has suffered most since the end of World War II Based entirely on Arab and East European sources.

OREN, Stephen. Syria, the Palestinians and the UN. Anatomy of Bluff. Jewish Frontier, 43, No. 1, Ja. pp 8-10.

PAOLINI, M. La questione palestinese nel contesto interarabo. Nuovi contenuti del programma di transizione. Politica Internazionale, 8, No. 2, My. pp 25-32.

PELED, Mattityahy. Israel ... and the Palestinians. The Palestinians Have Spoken: Is Anyone Listening? Interchange, 1, No. 9, My, pp 3-4.

The Politics of the Palestinian Question: Views on Recognition and Negotiations. Analysis, S. pp 1-11.

The American Jewish public need to formulate a response to the diplomatic offensives and threats posed since 1973 by the Arab world.

PRITTIE, Terence. Arafat: The Man and his Methods. Britian and Israel, 55, Ma. pp 4.

----------------. PLO or Palestinians. Which? Britain and Israel, No. 61, O-N. pp 4.

EL-RAYYES, Riad and NAHAS, Dunia. Guerrillas for Palestine. London, Croom Helm, 155p, Ind.

Maintains that the identity of the Palestine people has only been asserted with the rise of the guerrillas, i.e. the PLO.

RANA, S. The Objectives and Strategy of the Palestine Liberation Organisation. India Quarterly, 32, No. 2, Ap/Ju. pp 153-68.

RICHMOND, Sir John. What Should the Palestinians Do Next? Middle East International, No. 66, D. pp 15-16.

Argues for the Palestinians.

ROZENBLOOM, Doron. We Must Shatter the Myth of Fear of a Palestinian State. Israel Horizons, 24, No. 4, Ap. pp 12-16.

The Israel Council for Israeli-Palestinian Peace was formed by public figures and intellectuals such as Urie Avneri, Amos Keynan, Mati Peled, Liova Eliav, David Shaham and others. Includes excerpts from their manifesto delineating the lines for a peace dynamic between Israel and the Palestinian peoples.

SAKRAN, Frank C. Palestine: Still a Dilemma. Ardmore, Whitmore, 185p, M.

SALPETER, Eliahu. Israel's View of the Palestinian Question: Examining the Realities. The New Leader, 1 Ma. pp 8-10.

A Jordan-West Bank Federation or Palestinian autonomy within a Jordanian confederation would provide Israel with more physical and psychological security than any other solution short of continued direct Israeli control of the West Bank.

SANZ, Luis. Guerra y revolución en Palestina: la lucha Palestina, la revolución y el problema nacional. Bilbao, Zero, 135p. (Colleccion Lee y Discute, Serie R 69).

"War and revolution in Palestine: The Palestinian struggle, the Arab revolution and the national problem."

SAYIGH, Rosemary. The Palestinian Experience Viewed as Socialization. Unpublished MA Thesis. American U. of Beirut.

SCHOENBERG, Harris O. The UN Palestinian Committee and its Report: Diplomacy or Deceit? New York, The B'nai B'rith International Council, 32p.

Some Questions on the PLO and Israel. New York, American Jewish Committee, 2p.

SOUSTELLE, Jacques, GOTTLIEB, G. and GROSE, P. Palestine and Evian. Foreign Policy, No. 23, p 64ff.

Symposium sur le sionisme. Bagdad, Novembre 1976. France-Palestine, No. 63, Supplément de France-Pays Arabes. No. 12, D.

TURKI, Fawaz. The Palestinian Estranged. Journal of Palestine Studies, 5, Nos. 1-2, Aut.1975/W.1976, pp 82-96.

United States Calls for Support for UNRWA. State Department Bulletin, 75, No. 1957, 27 D. pp 755-6.

Statement by US Representative to General Assembly Pearl Bailey

US Congress. House Committee on International Relations. Problems of World War II and its aftermath; Part 2, The Palestine Question, problems of postwar Europe. Washington, US Govt. Print. Off.374p.

YASSINE, Abdel-Quader. Palestinians Alone. Middle East International, No. 63, S. pp 16-19.
Contends that the Palestinians are isolated.

ZAHLAN, Antoine. The Economic Viability of a West Bank State. Middle East International, No. 66, D. pp 20-21.
Argues for a Palestinian State on the West Bank.

TERRORISM

ALEXANDER, Yonah. (Ed.) International Terrorism. National, Regional and Global Perspectives. New York, Praeger in assoc. with the Ralph Bunche Inst. on the U.N. xx, 392p, Ind, Bibl.
The papers included in the volume deal with all aspects of terrorism with contributions by L.C. Green, B.K. Johnpoll, R.E. Butler, J.T.E. Hachey, R.O. Freedman, S. Quershi, E.S. Efrat, Y. Alexander, E. Weisbrand, D. Roguly and S.M. Finger. The authors deal with Canada; political terrorism in the USA, in Latin America, Ireland; Soviet policy towards international terrorism (attitude and support for the PLO); South-east Asia, South Africa; from terrorism to war: the anatomy of the birth of Israel; Palestinian terrorism: violence, verbal strategy, and legitimacy; and international terrorism and the United Nations.

America-Israel Friendship League. "A Legend is Born". What Americans Have Said and Written about the Israel Defence Forces' Rescue Operation at Entebbe Airport in Uganda on July 4. 47p.

BEN-PORAT, Yoram. Thunderball. New York, Dell, 260p. French ed: Paris, Hachette.
The Entebbe raid.

BOWYER-BELL, J. On Revolt. Strategies of National Liberation. Cambridge, Mass., London, Harvard U.P., xv, 272p, Ind, Bibl, Ill.
Beginning with the war for Israel's independence, the author examines the examples of guerrila warfare employed by national liberation movements in Africa and Asia.

EISENBERG, Dennis and LANDAU, Eli. Carlos: Terror International. London, Corgi, 286p.
A novel on the life and activities of Carlos, also known as the Jackal, one of the most notorious international terrorists, who was behind the Lod and Munich massacres, and many others.

FOCUS ON TERRORISM: Special Section, Orbis, 2, W. pp 1213-1680.
Includes: The Politics of International Terrorism by Andrew J. Pierre. Controlling Political Terrorism in a Free Society by John B. Wolf. Negotiating for Hostages: A Policy Dilemma by Edward R. Mickolus.

HONDERICH, Ted. Political Violence: A Philosophical Analysis of Terrorism. Ithaca, New York, Cornell U.P., x, 118p.

IRNBERGER, Harald. Die Terror-Multis. Wien, Jugend und Volk, 330p.
Young urban terrorists, including neo-nazis.

HOSTAGES, HIJACKING AND THE SECURITY COUNCIL. America, 133, 4 S. pp 94-97.
The inability of the UN to act against international terrorism.

KREIS, Karl Markus. Der internationale Terrorismus. Ein unbewältigtes Problem der Staatengemeinschaft. *Europa Archiv*, 31, No. 11, 10 Ju. pp 367-75.

The international community's failure to combat terrorism.

LAQUEUR, Walter. The Continuing Failure of Terrorism. *Harper's*, No. 11, N. pp 69-74.

"Although acts of terrorism command the headlines, they fail to achieve their social and political objectives."

---------------. The Futility of Terrorism. *Harper's*, No. 3, Ma. pp 99; 102-5.

"Terrorists change the make-up of the front page, but not the lives of their people."

MOYNIHAN, Daniel Patrick. The Totalitarian Terrorists. *New York*, 27 Jy. pp 38-40.

Argues for an international force against terrorism.

OFER, Yehuda. Operation Thunder: The Entebbe Raid. The Israelis' Own Story. Tr. by Julian Meltzer. Harmondsworth, Penguin, 141p, Ill, M. In Afrikaans: Kapstad, Hollandsch-Afrikaansche.

Dramatic account of the Israeli rescue action.

PARRY, Albert. Terrorism: From Robespierre to Arafat. New York, Vanguard, xvi, 624p, Ill.

PIERRE, Andrew J. Coping with International Terrorism. *Survival*, 18, No. 2, Ma-Ap. pp 60-67.

ROSS, Philip. The Illustrated Story of the Great Israeli Rescue. *New York*, 2 Au. pp 26-38.

Account of the rescue of hostages by Israeli forces on July 4th in Uganda. Based on interviews.

SCORER, Catherine. The Prevention of Terrorism Acts 1974 and 1976. London, National Council of Civil Liberties, 39p.

Monitoring report of the operation of the Act which was introduced in Britain as a result of the emergency in Northern Ireland.

SICKER, Martin. A New Look at the Father of the Stern Gang. *Jewish Digest*, 21, No. 7, Ap. pp 65-72. Condensed from *The American Zionist*.

On Yair Stern.

SMITH, Colin. Carlos. Portrait of a Terrorist. London, Deutsch and Sphere Books, 304p, Ill.

Illich Ramirex Sanches, who has adopted the name Carlos Martinez is one of the most wanted men among all terrorists. He was responsible for the kidnapping of OPEC oil ministers, the shooting of Mr. J. Edward Sieff and the rocket attack on an El-Al aircraft in Orly airport.

STEVENSON, William. (with material by Uri Dan.) 90 Minutes at Entebbe. London, New York, Toronto, Bantam; Corgi Jet Special. 216p, Ill. In German: Berlin, Ullstein; in Italian: Milan, Sonzagro.

SYRKIN, Maris. After Entebbe - What? (Editorial) *Midstream*, 22, No. 7, Au-S. pp 3-6.

TINNIN, David. Hit Team. London, Weidenfeld & Nicolson, 256p.

The 1972 Munich Olympiad massacre of Israeli athletes.

TOPHOVEN, Rolf. (Ed.) Guerrilla und Terrorismus heute. Politik durch Gewalt. Bonn, Wehr und Wissen, 173p. (Beitraege zur Wehrforschung 25)

The eight contributors include an analysis of the theoretical basis of guerrilla and terror activities of the Palestinians and others.

WATSON, Francis M. Political Terrorism: The Threat and the Response. Washington, New York, Luce, viii, 248p, Ind.
Examines how terrorism works using as illustrations Black September, the Tupamaros, the Japanese Red Army, etc.

WILLIAMSON, Tony. Counterstrike Entebbe. London, Collins, 184p, Ind. In French: Paris, Plon.
Dramatic account of the Entebbe operation of the Israel Defence Forces to free the hostages from Uganda.

MIDDLE EAST OIL

CASADIO, Gian Paolo. The Economic Challenge of the Arabs. Lexington, Mass; London, Heath, xi, 216p, Ind, Bibl.
Discusses the impact of higher oil prices on both the Arab world and the oil consumers.

EL-RASHIDI, G. The Oil Weapon in World Politics. Arab Quest for Self-Reliance and National Development. Indian Journal of Politics, 10, No. 2, D. pp 1-16.

HAMILTON, Adrian D. OPEC Puts on the Pressure. Middle East International, No. 64, O. pp 9-11.

IREWITZ, Jacob Coleman. Oil, The Arab-Israeli Dispute and the Industrial World: Horizons of Crisis. Boulder, Col, Westview P., 344p, Ind, Bibl.

LAGADEC, J. La politique petroliere arabe. In: Annuaire du Tiers-Monde, pp 95ff.

LENCZOWSKI, George. Middle East Oil in a Revolutionary Age. Washington, D.C. National Energy Project, American Enterprise Institute for Policy and Research, 36p.
Evolution of the legal and economic position of the international oil industry in the Middle East against the background of political unheaval and economic change in the area.

LIEBER, Robert J. Oil and the Middle East War: Europe in the Energy Crisis. Cambridge, Mass, Harvard, vii, 75p. (Harvard Studies in International Affairs 35)

MIKDASHI, Zuhayr and SHLAIM, Avi. OPEC and the New Economic Order. Middle East International, No. 55, pp 7-9.
Favouring the Arab stance.

PRICE, D.L. Oil and Middle East Security. Beverly Hills, London, Sage, 84p, M.

PRITTIE, Terence. The Arab Oil-War and Britain. Britain and Israel, No. 56, Ma-Ap. 4p.

REMBA, Oded. Arab Oil Power and America's Energy Dilemma. Midstream, 22, No. 6, Ju-Jy. pp 28-41.
Contends that Americans view the energy crisis too complacently.

SAMUELSON, Robert. Too Little Too Late: The Oil Policy we Needed but Didn't Get. The New Republic, 175, 3-10 Ja. pp 12-19.
Two years after the Arab oil embargo, America is still without an oil policy that deserves the name.

SANKARI, F. The Arab Oil Embargo: Impact on United States Behaviour Toward the Arab-Israeli Conflict. Middle East Journal, 30, No. 3, pp 33-50.

SHERBINY, Naien A. and TESSLER, Mark A. (Eds.) Arab Oil Impact on the Arab Countries and Global Implications. New York, London, Praeger, xi, 327p, Ill.

SHIHATA, . Arab Oil Policies and the New International Economic Order. Virginia Journal of International Law, 16, pp 261ff.

STERN, Sol. On and Off the Arabs' List. The New Republic, 125, 27 Ma. pp 7-12.

Since 1972, by its own diplomatic behavior, the government has demonstrated that in the scramble for Arab petrodollars anything goes.

The Uses of Arab Oil Power. Middle East Review, Special Issue, 9, No. 1, W. pp 3-75.

Includes: The Media and the Middle East by Barry Rubin. Arab Petropower and American Public Opinion by George E. Gruen (AJC's director of Middle East Affairs). The History of the Arab Boycott, 1921-75 by Shalom Schirman. The Secondary Arab Boycott and Britain by Terence Prittie.

UNDOVITCH, Abraham L. (eds.) The Middle East: Oil, Conflict and Hope. Lexington, Mass., Lexington Books, xxi, 557p, Ind. (Critical Choices for Americans Vol. 10)

Collection of essays, including an introduction by the Editor and Bent Hansen, Monroe Berger, P.J. Vatikiotis, Elie Kedourie, Shimon Shamir, Boutros Ghali, Walter Laqueur, Albert H. Hourani, John Waterbury and Ben Halpern.

WILLIAMS, Maurice J. The Air Programs of the OPEC Countries. Foreign Affairs, 54, No. 2, Ja. pp 308-24.

How important has OPEC aid been in helping non-oil developing countries to meet their increased oil bills? The role it plays in the politics of the OPEC Governments and the contribution they are likely to make to the development of the non-oil Third World.

ZARB, Frank G. US Energy Policy. World Today, 32, No. 1, Ja. p 1ff

MIDDLE EAST SETTLEMENT

AHMED, Mohamed Sid. Apres Kissinger: un grand pas au Moyen-Orient? Jeune Afrique, No. 828, 19 N. pp 24-27.

The Tunisian writer is not too optimistic of a settlement.

------------------. Quand les canons se eeront. Paris, Belfont, English Ed: London, Croom Helm, 192p.

On the future of the Middle East after the settlement of the Arab-Israeli conflict.

ALLON, Yigal. Israel: The Case for Defensible Borders. Foreign Affairs, 55, No. 1, O. pp 38-53. In Italian: Rivista di Studi Politici Internazionali, 43, No. 4, O-D. pp 596-608.

"While credible military quarantees or pacts can fulfill a positive function in a settlement of the Middle East conflict it will have to be a supplementary function to Israel's own strength, to its defensible borders, and in no way a substitute for them!"

AVINERI, SHlomo. An Exchange on Mideast Guarantees. Foreign Policy 6, No. 1, W. pp 212-23.

The third in a series of major action proposals on a Middle East settlement. Followed by responses from the authors of the previous articles.

BECKER, Abraham S. Moscow and the Middle East Settlement: A Role for Soviet Guarantees? Middle East Review, 8, Sp/Su. pp 52-57.

BRUZONSKY, Mark A. Carter and the Middle East: After His Campaign Promises. The Nation, 215, 11 D. pp 615-21.

"Assuming the settlement in Lebanon holds and the Arabs resume their demands for a political agreement with Israel in exchange for the return of territory and a solution of the 'Palestinian problem', the United States will press and cajole Israel to put its own cards on the table at Geneva or some other forum."

CHOMSKY, Noam. The Interim Sinai Agreement. New Politics, 11, No. 3, W. pp 4-33.

"The Intarim Agreement is not an interim agreement. Rather, it will establish a new and extraordinary dangerous states quo based on unending military confrontation between the States of the region and an escalating arms race."

GEIST, Benjamin. Israel's Options in the Middle East Conflict. The World Today, 32, No. 11, N. pp 407-12.

"Recent shifts in the attitudes of some Arab countries towards the Palestinian problem have given rise to a heated debate in Israel on the prospects for a settlement."

GORDON, Murray. The Sinai Accord: One Year Later. Congress Monthly 43, No. 8, O. pp 4-6.

--------------. Midstream, 22, No. 8, O. pp 10-21.

"Israel and its supporters should not believe they would be powerless in resisting demands for complete withdrawal provided Israel puts before American and world public opinion a peace plan of its own that is morally defensible and politically sound."

GOTTLIEB, Gidon. Palestine: An Algerian Solution. Foreign Policy, 6, No. 1, W. pp 198-211.

"The Evian Agreement of 1962 which ended the war between France and the Algerians is a model that Israel and the Palestine Liberation Organisation could follow if they can be prevailed upon to meet."

HELBIG, Fritz. Naher Osten - Faktoren för eine politische Lösung. Deutsche Assenpolitik, 21, No. 3, Ma, pp 398-419.

KERR, Malcolm H. (Ed.) Elusive Peace in the Middle East. London, Hodder, 354p, Ill.

Essays on the Middle East conflict.

LAQUEUR, Walter. Is Peace Possible in the Middle East? Commentary, 61, No. 3, Ma. pp 28-33.

"All one can hope for is the absence of war."

LATHAM, Aaron. Kissinger's Bluff is Called. New York 2 Ap, pp 30-5

As hostilities ease, as even Arabs and Israelis improve communications, his game of allying himself with both sides begins to break down.

LUMBER, H. Who Blocks a Just Peace. Jewish Affairs, 6, No. 1, Ja.-F. pp 31-37.

In the author's Communist view, Israel.

McPEAK, Merrill A. Israel: Borders and Security. Foreign Affairs, 64, No. 3, Ap. pp 426-43.

KÖZEL-KELET, Megállapodás Egyiptom és Izraél között (1975 Szeptember 1.) Külpolitika, 1, No. 2, pp 125-38.

The 1 S. 1975 partial agreement between Egypt and Israel.

NES, D. The Sinai Agreement, the US and Egypt, 1952-75. (In Japanese). *Chuto-tsuho*, No. 238, My. pp 25-31.

PELCOVITS, N.A. Security Guarantees in a Middle East Settlement. Beverly Hills, London, Sage, 69p. (Foreign Policy Papers V.2, No. 5)

Published by the Foreign Policy Institute, Philadelphia. Discusses the issue in the light of the events following the Yom Kippur War.

POLISH, David. Who Are the Intransigents? *Jewish Frortier*, 43, No. 3, Ma. pp 7-15.

In order to achieve peace both sides need to make concessions.

The Prospects of Peace in the Middle East. (In Japanese) *Chuto-tsuho* No. 238, My. pp 3-14.

RABIN, Yitzhak. Our Driving Goal: Peace. *Congress Monthly*, 43, No. 3, F. pp 8-10.

Excerpt from the address delivered by the Prime Minister of Israel before the Special Joint Session of the US Congress in Washington, Jan 28.

RENTDORFF, Rolf. Chances of Peace in the Middle East. *Christian Attitudes on Jews and Judaism*, No. 47, Ap. pp 1-4.

Any one-sided solution is not only a bad solution from the political point of view but it is a deeply un-Christian solution.

RIEBENFELD, Paul. Israel, Jordan, Palestine. *Midstream*, 22, No. 3, Ma. pp 30-44.

"If the two peoples of Palestine - Jews and Arabs - are to have peace, it is between Jerusalem and Amman that peace will have to be established - whoever is in Amman."

RONEN, D. Reaching for Peace in the Middle East: A Borrowing from Polany's Notion of 'Marketing' and 'Reciprocity'. *Co-Existence*, 13, No. 3, O. pp 221ff.

ROSEN, Steven J. and INDYK, Martin. The Temptation to Pre-empt in a Fifth Arab-Israeli War. *Orbis*, 20, No. 2, Su. pp 265-85.

"The Middle East environment of the future is apt to place a premium on pre-emption in a crisis, a premium that will seriously detract from the stability necessary for a negotiated settlement to the Arab-Israeli conflict."

ROSENFELD, Alvin. Secret Protocols and Authorized Leaks. On the vital questions, there are more agreements than disagreements in their books on Henry Kissinger's Mideast diplomacy. *The National Jewish Monthly*, 90, No. 10, Ju. pp 10-16.

ROSENFELD, Stephen S. From Washington. On the Way to '77. *Present Tense*, 3, No. 4, Su. pp 16-18.

"In Washington the sentiment is that neither Israel's present policies nor its basic view of the Arabs permits territorial concessions large enough to be swapped for the political concessions Israel demands and deserves."

SAFRAN, Nadav. Do the Arabs Prefer Peace? *Moment*, 2, No. 1, S. pp 13-18; 55-59.

"The assumption that the Arabs have no interest in peace can cause Israel to overlook such real possibilities of peace as may exist."

SAM'O, E. The Sinai Agreement and Beyond. *World Affairs*, 139, No. 1, pp 40-52.

SASSOLI, Domenico. E possibile una soluzione parziale nel Medio Oriente? Politica Internationale, 8, No. 3, Ma.
On the viability of a practical solution.
SCHWARTZ, Jacques. Why our Doves are Pigeons. Israel Horizons, 24, No. 8, O. pp 23-26.
For a peaceful solution of the Arab-Israel conflict.
SHEEHAN, Edward R.F. Step by Step in the Middle East: How Kissinger Did It. Foreign Policy, 24, No. 2, S. pp 3-70.
Based on extensive talks with American, Arab and Israeli officials on three continents, this analysis presents a comprehensive account of Kissinger's diplomatic efforts over the last few years towards peace in the Middle East.
------------------. The Arabs, Israelis and Kissinger, New York, Reader's Digest, (Crowell, Dist.) xiii, 287p, Ind, M.
Comprehensive history of 'step-by-step' diplomacy.
SHERER, Emanuel. Mit a ponim tsua sholem. Unzer Tsait,37, No, 1, Ja. pp 1-7.
"Face to Peace"
SID-AHMED, Mohamed. After the Guns Fall Silent. Peace or Armageddon in the Middle East. Foreward by Lord Caradon. London, Croom Helm, 144p, Ind.
Contends that the October 1973 war and detente have fundamentally changed the basis of the conflict.
SIMPSON, D.J. Döntőév Izráelben. (Year of Decision in Israel) Nemzetközi Szemle, 20, No. 5, My, pp 21-35.
On the possibility of an agreement.
SISCO, Joseph. 1977: Year of Opportunity. American Zionist, 67, No. 3, N. pp 9-11.
SLAIEH, E. The October War and Sadat's Year of Decision. Indian Political Science Review, 10, No. 2, Jy. pp 167-69.
STEINBERG, Bluma. Super Power Conceptions of Peace in the Middle East. Viewpoints, 9, No. 3, Sp/Su. pp 5-11.
STODDART, Curwen. The New Stage in the Mideast Political Struggle. Israel Horizons, 24, No. 1, Ja. pp 27-29, 10, 26.
"Deals with the sudden turn of events brought on by the Syrian counter-offensive, against the Sinai Accord, backed by the Soviet Union and using the Palestinian issue as a spearhead.
SYRKIN, Marie. Kissinger: Blunder or Design. Midstream, 22, No. 4, Ap. pp 3-6.
TEKOAH, Yosef. In the Face of the Nations: Israel's Struggle for Peace. New York, Simon and Schuster, 284p.
Collection of speeches, essays and lectures by Israel's former Ambassador to the United Nations reflecting Israel's foreign policies.
TURNER, B.S. Avineri's View of Marx's Theory of Colonialism: Israel. Science and Society, 40, No. 1, pp 385-409.
Critique of Avineri's analysis of Marx's theories of colonialism and their application in Israel and the Arab world and the prospects of a Middle East settlement.
TYRRELL, R. Emmet, Jr. Chimera in the Middle East. Harper's, N. pp 35-38.
There is no reasonable solution agreeable to both sides.
United Nations General Assembly Resolution 31/62 (ja. 3, 1977) Peace Conference on the Middle East. Revue Egyptienne de Droit

International, 32, pp 211-12.

U.S. Congress. House. Committee on International Relations. The Palestinian Issue in Middle East peace efforts. Hearings before the Special Subcommittee on Investigations. S.-O. and 12 N. 1975. Washington, U.S. Govt. Print. Off. 293p.

U.S. Congress. Senate. Committee on Foreign Relations. Middle East peace prospects. Hearings before the Subcommittee on Near Eastern and South Asian affairs. 19 My.-7 Ju. , 21 Ju, 30 Ju.. 19 Jy. and 26 Jy. Washington, U.S. Govt. Print. Off.

WALZER, Michael. Israeli Arabs: The Rabin Government's Dilemma. The New Republic, 17 Ap. pp 11-13.

Israel "must make clear to its own people and to the Palestinians that, at some point, the West Bank will be returned to Jordan or established as an independent entity."

WASKOW, Arthur I. The Middle East: A Way to Peace. The Progressive 76, My. pp 17-20.

"Only if an American public committed to a joint peace in the Middle East is prepared to press its own government to put peace before the maximisation of American power will the U.N. Security Council become a usable took to break the Israel-Palestine deadlock."

WHARTMAN, Richard. At Last, a Basis for a Dialogue. Yigal Allon's Plan for the Occupied Territories. Israel Horizons, 24, No. 9, N. pp 21-24.

HISTORY

PACHTER, Henry. Nostalgia and Revision: The Vogue of Weimar Culture. Dissent, 23, No. 3, Jy. pp 279-83.

JEWISH HISTORY

APPEL, John J. Popular Graphics as Documents for Teaching and Studying Jewish History. Waltham, Mass., American Jewish Historical Society; New York, Ktav, 45p, Ill.

A Bicentennial Festschrift for Jacob Rader Marcus.

BEN-SASSON, Hayim Hillel. (Ed.) A History of the Jewish People. London, Weidenfeld and Nicolson, xii, 1170p, Ind, Bibl, Ill.

Professor Ben-Sasson who edited this major work also wrote the chapter on the Middle Ages, Professor Abraham Malamat wrote the chapter on Origins and the Formative Period, Professor Hayim Tadmor the Period of the First Temple, The Babylonian Exile and Restoration- Professor Menahem Stern, the Period of the Second Temple; Shmuel Safrai, the Era of the Mishnah and Talmud (70-640) and Professor Shmuel Ettinger, the Modern Period.

GOLDBERG, M. Hirsch. The Jewish Connection. The Incredible ... ironic bizarre ... funny and provocative in the story of the Jews. New York, Stein and Day, 252p.

Jewish personalities who made contributions to civilisation in various fields.

GOLDMANN, Nahum. Le paradoxe juif. Conversations en francais avec Léon Abramowicz. Paris, Stock, 261p.

The views of Dr. Goldmann on topical issues, expressed during long hours of conversation with L. Abramowicz.

GREENSTONE, Julius Hillel: The Messiah Idea in Jewish History. Westport, Conn., Greenwood P., 347p.
Reprint of the 1906 edition.

GROSSMAN, Edward. Koestler's Jewish Problem. Commentary, 62, No. 6, D. pp 59-64.
On Koestler's theory of the Khazar origins of European Jewry.

HIRSCHSON, Niel. Neusner and Jewish History. Jewish Affairs, 31, No. 6, Ju. pp 47-48.

HRUBY, K. La complexite du judaisme contemporain. Sidic, 9, No. 1, pp 4-13.
From the Middle Ages to the present and the impact of the Jewish State.

KOBLER, Franz. Napolean and the Jews. New York, Schocken, 220p.
Presents Napolean as the initiator of Jewish emancipation; maintains that it was his Near Eastern campaign that encouraged he idea of the Jews restoration to the Holy Land.

KOESTLER, Arthur. The Thirteenth Tribe. (The Khazar Empire and Its Heritage) London, Hutchinson; New York, Random House, 255p. French edition: Paris, Callman-Levy, German edition: Munich, Zurich, Fritz Molden.
Argues that the European Jewry originate from the Khazars.

LAERSI, Rufus. (Israel Goldberg). Israel: A History of the Jewish People by Rufus Learsi. Westport, Conn., Greenwood P., 715p. M.
Reprint of the 1949 edition.

LEWIS, Bernard. The Meaning of Jewish History. In a Land of Immigrants. The American Jewish Experience. B'nai B'rith Commission on Adult Education, 26p.

PATAI, Raphael. Ethnohistory and Inner History: The Jewish Case. Jewish Quarterly Review, 67, No. 1, Jy. pp 1-15.
External history, for the Jews, consisted of all those events, processes and conditions, which were imposed upon them by the Gentile majority in whose midst they lived; while their inner history comprised in the main the autonomous region of their preoccupation with religious life, practice, belief and study.

POLACK, Albert I. and LAWRENCE, Joan. Cup of Life. A Short History of Post-Biblical Judaism. London, SPCK, vii, 187p, Bibl.
Highlights of major events in Jewish history written jointly by a Jew and a Christian, introduced by the Archbishop of Canterbury.

ROTENSTREICH, Nathan. On Cyclical Patterns and their Interpretation. The Interpretation of Judaism in the Wake of Vico and Hegel. Hegel Studien, No. 11, pp 181-208.
Interpretations of the relationship between Judaism and Jewish history.

RUNES, Dagobert David. (Ed.) The Hebrew Impact on Western Civilisation. Westport, Conn., Greenwood P.; London, Westport P., xiv, 922p.
Reprint of the 1951 edition.

SHAPIRO, Harry Lionel. The Jewish People: A Biological History. Westport, Conn., Greenwood P, 84p.
Reprint of the 1960 edition.

VILLIERS, Douglas. (Ed.) Next Year in Jerusalem. Portraits of the Jew in the Twentieth Century. New York/London, Viking P./Douglas Villiers Publishing, 352p, Ill.

Contributions by R.H. Crossman, Isaac Bashevis Singer, George Steiner, Walter Laqueur, Arthur Koestler, Isaiah Berlin, Michael Horowitz, Leo Rosten, Stephen Aris, Harry Golden, Nicholas Faith, Philip French, Ronald Saunders, Albert Goldman, Chaim Bermant, Edward Lucie-Smith, David Daiches, Rudolf Peierls Peter Stadlen, Yehudi Menuhin, Elie Wiesel on Jewish contribution to all aspects of civilisation in the 20th century.

WOUK, Herman. This is My God. London, Fontana, 320p, N.e. Bibl.

Paperback reprint of work first published in 1959.

WURMBRAND, Max and ROTH, Cecil. Le Peuple juif. Quatre mille ans de survivance. Paris, Albin Michel, 480p, Ill.

French translation of work published in English in 1975.

HISTORIOGRAPHY

GARTNER, Lloyd P. Idea of Jewish History (Review Article) The Jewish Journal of Sociology, 18, No. 1, Ju. pp 61-65.

GILBERT, Martin. Jewish History Atlas, Rev. ed. london, Weidenfeld & Nicolson, 152p, 121 Maps.

GOLDIN, Judah (Ed.) The Jewish Expression. London, Newhaven, Conn., Yale U.P., 470p.

A collection of essays in which contemporary Jewish scholars examine and interpret 3,000 years of Jewish history with a long introductory essay by Professor Goldin.

HANDLIN, Oscar. A Twenty-Year Retrospect of American Jewish Historiography. American Jewish Historical Quarterly, 65, No. 4, Ju. pp 295-309.

KOESTLER, Arthur. Le Royaume Juif des Khazars. L'Arche, 19, No. 230, My. pp 47-55.

Critique of The Thirteenth Tribe.

KORN, B.W. (Ed.) Bicentennial Festschrift for Jacob Rader Marcus. Leiden, Brill in association with the American Jewish Historical Society.

RAPHAEL, Chaim. The Judaism of History. Commentary, 61, No. 3, Ma. pp 51-54.

RODREGUEZ, Carlos Del Valle. El Mundo Judio. Madrid, Universidad Nacional de Educacion a Distancia, 408p.

Textbook for extra-mural studies.

SCHORSCH, Ismar. On the History of the Political Judgment of the Jew. New York, Leo Baeck Institute. 23p. (Leo Baeck Memorial Lecture 20)

VARDY, Steven Béla. Modern Hungarian Historiography. New York, London, Columbia U.P., x, 333p, Ind, Bibl. (East European Monographs, No. xvii)

Includes the historiography of the Holocaust, antisemitism, Jews.

WOLF, K. Hans Kohn's liberal nationalism. The historian as prophet. Journal of History of Ideas, (U.S.) 37, pp 651-72.

ANCIENT HISTORY

AVI-YONAH, Michael. The Jews of Palestine. A Political History from the Bar Kochba War to the Arab Conquest. Oxford, Blackwell, xviii, 286p, Ind, Bibl, Ill. (Blackwell's Classical Studies)

The author demonstrates how, despite the destruction of the political organisation, the Jews of Palestine have maintained their national and religious identity in the face of the pressures from Roman and Christian Governments.

CALLAWAY, J. Excavating Ai (el Tell): 1964-1972. *The Biblical Archaelogist*, 39, No. 1, pp 18-30.

Account of the excavation of Joshua'a Ai, four kilometres east of Beth El.

COMAY, Joan. The Hebrew Kings. London, Weidenfeld & Nicolson; New York, Morrow, viii, 468p, Ind, Ill.

Relates the history of the Kings of Israel from Saul to the destruction of the kingdom of Judah.

DE VAUX, Roland. The Early History of Israel. Vol. 1: From the beginnings to the Exódus and Eovenant of Sinai. Vol. 2: From the Entry into Canaan to the Period of the Judges. Tr. David Smith, London, Darton Longman & Todd; New York, Westminster P., 496p, 412p.

FARMER, William Reuben. Maccabees, Zealots and Josephus: An Inquiry into Jewish Nationalism in the Greco-Roman Period. Westport, Conn., Greenwood P., 239p.

Reprint of the 1956 edition.

FASOLA, U.M. Le due catacombe ebraiche di Villa torionia. *Rivista di Archeologia Cristiana*, 52, Nos. 1-2, pp 7-62, Ill.

Development of the Jewish Catacombs in Villa Torlonia II-IV centuries.

FEUCHTWANGER, Leon. A zsidó háboru I-II. Tr. Terenyi Istvan. Budapest, Europa, 860p.

Hungarian edition of *The War of the Jews*. Feuchtwanger's work, based on Josephus.

FRANK, Harry Thomas. How the Dead Sea Scrolls Were Found. Condensed from *The Biblical Archaeology Review*, D. 1975. *Jewish Digest*, 21, No. 6, Ma. pp 44-52.

HARRIS, H.A. Greek Athletics and the Jews. Ed. I.M. Barton and A.J. Brothers. Aberystwith, U. of Wales P., 124p, Ill, M.

HENDIN, D. A Guide to Ancient Jewish Coins. With Values by H. Kreindler. New York, Attic, 134p.

MAZZOLENI, D. Les sepultures souterraines des Juifs d'Italie. The Jewish catacombs of Rome, Monteverde, Vigna Randanini, Vigna Cimarra, Via Appia, Pignatelli, Via Labicana, Villa Torlonia, Venosa, Sicile, Sardinia, (San Antonia). *Les Dossiers d l'archaelogie*, No. 19, pp 82-99.

PEARLMAN, Moshe. In the Footsteps of Moses. Leon Amiel. New York, Crowell, 230p, Ill, Ind.

RABIN, Chaim. Qumran Studies. New York, Schocken; London, Wildwood House, 135p.

RATTEY, B.K. Short History of the Hebrews. From the Patriarchs to Herod the Great. Oxford, U.P., 144p, Ill, M.

ROSE, D.B. and TOOMBS, L.E. Tell el-Hesi 1973 and 1975. *Palestinian Exploration Quarterly*, 108, No. 1, pp 41-54.

SAFRAI, S. and STERN, M. (Eds.) in cooperation with FLUSSER, D. and van UNNIK, W.C. The Jewish People in the First Century. Historical Geography, Political History, Social, Cultural and Religious Life and Institutions, V.2. Assen, Van Gorcum, xii, 561-1283p. Inds. (Compendia Rerum Iudaicarum ad Novum Testamentum)

Second volume of the first section of the Compendium Series. It describes the social and economic structure, religious and cultural life and institutions of Palestinian and diaspora Jewry in the First Century.

SCHUBERT, Kurt. The Dead Sea Community: Its Origins and Teachings. Tr. John W. Doberstein. Westport, Conn., Greenwood P.; London, Westport P., 178p.

Reprint of the 1959 edition.

SCHURER, E. A History of the Jewish People in the Time of Jesus Christ.

Reprint of the 1891 edition.

SMALLWOOD, B. Mary. The Jews under Roman Rule. From Pompey to Diocletian. Leiden, Brill, 595p, Ind, Maps. Bibl. (Studies in Judaism in Late Antiquity 20)

Comprehensive history of the period ending with a study of Palestine and the Diaspora in the third century A.D.

USSISHKIN, O. Royal Judean Storage Jars and Private Seal Impressions. Bulletin of the American School of Oriental Research No. 223, pp 1-13.

Excavations in Tell Lakish.

YADIN, Yigael. Hazor. Die Wiederentdeckung der Zitadelle König Salomos. Tr. from English by Maria Poetchau. Hamburg, Hoffman und Campe, 282p, Ill.

-------------. Beersheba: The High Place Destroyed by King Josiah. Bulletin of the American School of Oriental Research, No. 222, pp 5-17.

Analyses the excavations of Yehuda Aharoni (1973-74)

MEDIEVAL JEWISH HISTORY

BERTIN, D. Deux constructions juives du Xii siècle: une découverte récente à Rouen. Archives Juives, 12, No. 4, pp 55-60.

In August 1966 remains of a 12th century synagogue and school were discovered in Rouen.

BARON, Salo Wittmayer. A Social and Religious History of the Jews. Late Middle Ages and Era of European Expansion (122-1650). V.16. Poland and Lithuania 1500-1650. Philadelphia, Jewish Publication Society of America, 400p, Ind.

CHAZAN, Robert. (Ed.) Medieval Jewish Life. Studies from the Proceedings of the American Academy for Jewish Research, New York, KTAV, xiv, 463p.

IANCU, Danielle. L'expulsion des Juifs en Provence medievale. Ph.D. Thesis. U. of Aix-en-Provence.

---------------. Préoccupations intellectuelles des medicins juifs au Moyen Age: inventaires de bibliothèques. Provence Historique, 26, No. 103, pp 21-44.

Descriptive bibliography of the libraries of medieval Jewish physicians.

KRIEGEL, M. Un trait de psychologie sociale dans les pays mediterranéens du bas Moyen Age: le Juif comme intouchable. (English Summary) Annales Economies, Societes, Civilisations, 31, No. 2, pp 326-30.

The Jew as 'untouchable' in medieval Mediterranean countries.

LEVIN, Jack L. Judaic Roots of the American Revolution. Congress Monthly, 43, No. 8, O. pp 10-11.

The total Jewish population of the colonies at the time is estimated at 2,500, yet they made a great contribution to the Revolution.

MARCUS, Jacob Rader. The Jews in the Medieval World. A Source Book (315-1791). Westport, Conn., Greenwood P.; London, Westport P, xxiv, 504p.

Reprint of the1938 edition.

PARKES, James William. The Jew in the Medieval Community. A Study of his political and economic situation. 2.e. with a new introduction. New York, Hermon P., xxii, 440p, Ind. (The Judaic Studies Library,3)

Study of the economic and social conditions of Jews in medieval Europe. Contemporary documents in the Appendix.

PEREZ-HERRERO, E. La necropolis hispano-hebrea de Puente Castro. (Leon). Studium Legionense, No. 17, pp 177-99.

The Jewish burial site of Puente Castro (Leon) in Spain proves the present of a large Jewish community in the 10-12th centuries.

WEAKLAND, J.E. Pastorelli, Pose, and Persecution: A Tragic Episode in 1320. Jewish Social Studies, 38, No. 1, pp 73-76.

Persecution of Jews in Southern France by the Pastorals in 1320. Based on Vatican Sources, Bibl.

WIESELTIER, Leon. You Don't Have to be Khazarian. The New York Review of Books, O. 28, pp 33-36.

Criticises Arthur Koestler's The Thirteenth Tribe: The Khazar Empire and Mts Heritage (Random House, 1976)

YERUSHALMI, Yosef H. (Ed.) Bibliographical Essays in Medieval Jewish Studies. The Study of Judaism, V.2. New York, Ktav for Anti-Defamation Leage of B'nai B'rith, ix, 392p, Bibl.

contents: The Jews in Western Europe: Fourth to Sixteenth Century by Ivan G. Marcus. The Church and the Jews: From St. Paul to Paul VI by Kenneth R. Stow. The Jews Under Islam: From the Rise of Islam to Sabbatai Zevi by Mark R. Cohen. Medieval Jewish Religious Philosophy by Lawrence V. Berman. Medieval Jewish Mysticism by Jochanan H.M. Wijnhoven. Minor Midrashim by John T. Townsend.

-------------------. The Lisbon Massacre of 1506 and the Royal Image in the Shebet Yehudah. Cincinnati, Hebrew Union College, xiii, 91p, Annual Supplements 1.

JEWISH HISTORY TO 1914

BARON, Salo Wittmayer. The Jewish Community. Its History and Structure to the American Revolution. Westport, Conn., Greenwood P., 3 vols, Ind., Bibl.
Reprint of work first published in 1942.

BEINART, Haim. La Inquisition Espanola. Buenos Aires, Congreso Judio Latinoamericano, 48p. (Biblioteca Popular Judia, Hechos de la Historia Judia)

BLUMENKRANZ, Bernhard and SOBOUL, Albert. (Eds.) Les Juifs et la Revolution Francaise. Problemes et aspirations. Paris, Privat, 231p, Ind.,Ill.
Documents and essays on the Jews and the French Revolution.

CHYET, Stanley F. George Washington and the Jews. Jewish Digest, 21, No. 5, My, pp 10-12.

EISENBACH, Arthur. Wielka Emigracja wobec Kwastii Zydowskiej 1832-1949. Warsaw, Panstwowe Wydawnictwo Naukowe, 476p, Ind.,Ill.
The "Great Emigration" from Poland and the Jewish question. Historical-sociological study.

EISENBERG, Josy. Une histoire des Juifs. Paris, Fayard, 506p, Bibl. (Livre de Poche 4797) Spanish edition: Buenos Aires, Acervo Cultural 430p.
Short history of the Jews.

FEUERWERKER, David. L'Emancipation des juifs en France de L'Ancien Regime a la fin du Second Empire. Paris, Albin Michel, 777p, Ind. Bibl. (Coll. L'evolution de l'humanite)
Monumental work on the emancipation of French Jewry, that in many respects led to emancipation movements in other European countries.

LIAMGOR, Alberto. Marginalidad y judaismo en Cristobal Cólon. Buenos Aires, Congreso Judio Latinoamericano, 40p, Ill. (Biblioteca Popular Judia, Hechos de la Historia Judia 81)
On the possible Jewish ancestry of Columbus.

MOSSE, Werner E. and PAUCKER, Arnold. (Eds.) Juden im Wilhelminischen Deutschland 1890-1914. Ein Sammelband. Tübingen, Mohr.xiv, 786p. (Schriftenreihe wissenschaftlicher Abhandlungen des Leo Baeck Instituts 33)
This is the concluding volume in the Leo Baeck' Institute's history of German Jewry in the post-emancipation period. Contents: Emanzipation und Kriese - Zur Geschichte der 'Judenfrage' in Deutschland vor 1890 by Reinhard Ruerp; Die Juden in Wirtschaft und Gesellschaft by Werner E. Mosse; Die Rathenaus-Zwei Generationen judischen Anteils and der industriellen Entwicklung Deutschlands by Ernst Schulin; Die juedische Beteiligung and der Politik by Peter Pulzer; Begegnung mit der Moderne - Deutsche Juden in der deutschen Kultur by Peter Gay: Wilhelm II. und die Juden by Lamar Cecil; Die gesellschaftliche Bedeutung der christlichjuedischen Differenz - Zur Situation im deutschen Katholizmus by Hermann Grieve; Struktur und Funktion das deutschen Antisemitismus by Werner Jochman; Zur Problematik einer juedischen Abwehrgeschichte in der deutschen Gesselschaft; Die geistigen und religioesen Stroemungen in der deutschen Judenheit by Pinchas E. Rosenblueth; Theologische Debatte um das "Wesen" des Judentums by Uriel Tal; Die umkaempfte national-

juedische Idee by Yehuda Eloni and Die schleichende Krise der juedischen Identitaet - Ein Nachwort by Robert Weltsch.

NAHON, G. The relations between the Sepahrdic communities in France and the Sephardic community in Amsterdam in the 17th and 18th centuries. Studia Rosenthaliana, 10, No. 1, Ja. pp 37-38 and No. 2 Jy. pp 151-88.

NOZEK, Bedrich. Soziale Differenzierungen und Streitigkeiten in jüdischen Kultusgemeinden der Böhmischen Ländern im 17. Jahrhundert und Entstehung der "Landesjudenschaft". Judaica Bohemiae, 12, No. 2, pp 59-92.
Internal conflicts in 17th century Bohemian Jewish community.

RAISIN, Jacob Saemon. The Haskalah Movement in Russia. Westport, Conn., Greenwood P.: London, Westport P., 355p, Ill.
Reprint of basic work published in 1931.

La Revolution francaise et les juifs. Annales historiques de la Revolution Francaise, 48, No. 223, pp 1160.

REZNECK, Samuel. Jews in the American Revolution. Jewish Digest, 21 No. 10, Jy-Au. pp 23-27.
Condensed from book "Unrecognized Patriots" (Greenwood)

SAMUEL, E.R. Sir Thomas Shirley's Project for Jews - The Earliest Known Proposal for Resettlements. Transactions of the Jewish Historical Society of England, 24, pp 195-97.
Proposal to James 1 in 1607 for the resettlement of Jews in order to obtain revenue.

SCHOLEM, Gershom. Sabbatai Zevi, The Mystical Messiah, 1626-76. Tr. R. J. Zwi Verblowsky. Princeton, U.P., 1027p, Ill. (Bellingen S 93)

SEMENOV, Evgenii Petrovich. The Russian Government and the Massacres, a page of the Russian Counter-Revolution. Tr. from French with intro. by Lucien Wolf. Westport, Conn., Greenwood P.: London, Westport, P., xxvi, 265p.
On the pogroms in Kishinev, first published in 1907.

SPICEHANDLER, Ezra. The Persecution of the Jews of Isfahan under Shah Abbas II (1642-1666) Hebrew Union College Annual, 1975, 46, pp 331-56.

SPRINGER, A. Gavrill Derzhavin's Jewish Reform Project of 1800. Canadian-American Slavic Studies, 10, No. 1, pp 1-23.
The project which the noted poet presented to the Tsar was basically not hostile to Jews.

JEWISH HISTORY 1914-1939

APT, Leon J. The Plight of the American Jewish Community During World War I. Intellect, 61, No. 2, F. pp 290-4.
"The First WorldWar exposed the strengths and weaknesses of the American Jewish community."

BROOK-SHEPHERD, Gordon. Anschluss: The Rape of Austria. Westport, Conn., Greenwood P., 222p, Ill.
The 1938 Anschluss and its consequences. Reprint of book first published in 1963.

FEJES, Judit. A magyar - német gazdasági és politikai kaposolatok kérdésehez az 1920-as évek fordulóján. Történelmi Szemle, 18, No. 3, Ma. pp 361-84.
Hungarian-German relations in the late 1920s and early 1930s.

LIPTAK, Dorottya. A Gömbös kormány külpolitikájának egyes kérdesai a magyar történeti irodalom tükreben. Acta Universitatis Szegediensis de Attila József nominatae, Acta Historica, 57, pp 61-70.
Some questions of foreign relations of the Gömbös (fascist) Government in the light of historical writings. Deals with Hungary's adherence to the Axis.

MARX, Julius. Kriegs-Tagebuch eines Juden. Munich, Israelitische Kultusgemeinde.
World War I.

MEISSNER, Hans Otto. 30. January '33. Hitler's Machtergreifung, Esslingen, Bechtle, 453p, Ind, Bibl. Ill.
The author, whose father was a high official in the Weimer and Naxi Germany, witnessed Hitler's coming to power in 1933 and gives an historical account.

NAGY, Zsuzsa. A liberális pólgari ellenzék pártjai es szervezetei (1919-1944) Tortenelmi Szemle, 18, No. 3.
Parties of liberal bourgeois opposition and their organisations (1919-1944). Discusses their role in the anti-fascist struggle.

RABI, Wladimir. L'Affaire Grynszpan. L'Arche, No. 231, Ju. pp 46-59.
Recalls the murder of vom Rath by Heroz Grynszpan in Paris 1938 which was followed by Kristallnacht.

SZABÓ, Miklós. A magyar girondistáktol" az ebredö magyarokig. Az 1919-es ellenforradalmi kurzus elötörteneteböl. Vilagossa'g, 17, No. 3, N. pp 151-60.
From the "Hungarian Gironde" to the awakening Hungarians. The antecedents of the 1919 counter-revolution - a right-wing anti-Semitic movement.

JEWISH HISTORY
1939 - 1945

AINSZTEIN, Rueben. Hitler's Generals and Vlasov's 'Volunteers'. Jewish Quarterly, 24, No. 3, Aut. pp 32-41.
Originally published in Midstream.

BETHELL, Nicholas. The War Hitler Won: September 1939. N.e. London, Futura Publ., 480p.
The Polish campaign, including the persecution of Jews.

BLUM, John Morton. V Was for Victory, Politics and American Culture During World War Two. New York, Harcourt Brace Jovanovich, xii, 372p, Ind.
Professor Blum's study of America's involvement in the war concentrates on the home front. He deals extensively with the Jews' reaction to their persecution, anti-Jewish prejudice, the impact of Zionism, etc.

BOTZ, Gerhard. Die Eingliederung Österreichs in das Deutsche Reich: Planung und Verwirklichung des politisch-administrativen Anschlusses (1938-1940) 2 R.e. Linz, Europa, 194p. (Schriftenreihe des Ludwig Boltzmann Instituts für Geschichte der Arbeiterbewegung 1)
The political and administrative measures for the incorporation of Austria into the Third Reich.

BURRIDGE, Trevor. British Labour and Hitler's War. London, Andre Deutsch, 206p, Ind, Bibl.

Examines the Labour Party's role in the formulation of British Foreign Policy during World War II. That is done in broad outline but with very few references to the Labour Party's attitude to the persecution of Jews and the Palestine Question.

COLE, Wayne S. Charles A. Lindbergh and the Battle Against American Intervention in World War II. New York, Harcourt Brace Jovanovich, 298p.

GOSZTONY, Peter. Hitlers fremde Heere. Das Schicksal der nichtdeutschen Armeen im Ostfeldzug. Düsseldorf, Econ. 548p, Ind, Bibl.

Deals i.a. with the Jewish forced labour battalions in Hungary who were taken to the Eastern Front.

JABOTINSKY, Vladimir. Evgen'evich. The Jewish War Front. Westport, Conn, Greenwood P.: London, Westport P., 255p.

Reprint of the 1940 edition.

JONG, Louis de. Het koninkrijk der Nederlanden in de tweede wereldoorlog. The Hague, Nijhoff for Rikjsinstituut voor Oorlogsdocumentatie, Vols. 4-7.

V.4	1.	May 1940	-	March 1941.	vii.	495p.
V.4.	2.	May 1940	-	March 1941	vii.	497-992p.
V.5.	1.	March 1941	-	July 1942	viii.	616p.
V.5.	2.	March 1941	-	July 1942	vii.	617-1171p.
V.6.	1.	July 1942	-	May 1943	viii.	515-911p.
V.6.	2.	July 1942	-	May 1943	vii.	519-911p.
V.7.	1.	May 1943	-	June 1944	viii.	688p.
V.7.	2.	May 1943	-	June 1944	vi.	689-1442p.

Further volumes of the complete history of the German occupation of Holland based on documents which are also published.

KULKA, Erich. Czechoslovak Jews in the 'Svoboda Army'. <u>Jewish Quarterly</u>, 23, No. 4, W. pp 29-32.

MASLOWSKI, Jan. Pielegniarki w drugiej wojnie swiatowej (Nurses in the Second World War) Warsaw, Panstwowy Zaklad Wydawniotw Lekarskich, 231p, Ind.

The author describes the activities of nurses during hostilities and under Nazi occupation, in the ghettoes, in the camps, with the partisans and the army. Material about Jews is scattered all over the book.

NEWMAN, Simon. March 1939: The British Guarantee to Poland. Oxford, Clarendon P., 253p, Ind, Bibl.

Based on the diplomatic papers at the Public Record Office and other hitherto unpublished sources. Deals with antisemitism.

ORY, Pascal. Les collaborateurs 1940-45. Paris, du Seuil, 316p, Bibl.

RENAUDOT, Francoise. Les Français et l'Occupation. Paris, Laffont, 254p.

The behaviour of all Frenchmen and women was not without reproach.

THE HOLOCAUST

ALBRECHT, Dieter. (Ed.) Katholische Kirche im Dritten Reich. Eine Aufsatzsammlung zum Verhältnis von Papsttum Episkopat und deutschen Katholiken zum National-sozialismus 1933-1945. Mainz, Grünewald. viii, 272p, Ind, Bibl. (Topos Taschenbucher 45)

Collection of papers examining the relationship between the Catholic Church and the Third Reich, and German Catholics and the Vatican during the Nazi era. There are many references to the persecution of Jews.

ALEXANDER, Edward. The Holocaust in American-Jewish Fiction: A Slow Awakening. Judaism, 25, No. 3, Su. pp 320-30.

American Jewish Committee. William E. Weiner Oral History Library. A Study in American Pluralism Through Oral Histories of Holocaust Survivors. Submitted by ... to the National Endowment for the Humanities. New York, 251p.

Apres l'holocauste: oublier? pardonner? Rencontre, 10, No. 46, pp 147-205.

To forgive and forget after the Holocaust? Views of R. Braun, G. Ribiere, G. Passelecq, A. Neher, V. Jankolevich.

ARNDT, Ino and SCHEFFLER, Wolfgang. Organisierter Massenmord an Juden in nationalsozialistischen Vernichtungslagern. Ein Beitrag zur Richtigstellung apologetischer Literatur. Vierteljahresbefte für Zeitgeschichte, 24, No. 2, pp 105-55.

BBING, Axel. Auschwitz. Unterrichterrichtseinheit für den Schulgebrauch. Frankfurt/M. Röderberg, 40p, Ill.

Teaching aid on Auschwitz for sixth-formers in West German comprehensive schools.

BOSCHENSTEIN, Hermann. Ein Nachwort zur "unbewältigten Vergangenheit" Israelitisches Wochenblatt fur die Schweiz, 76, No. 21a, Ma. pp 53-57.

The Holocaust and its aftermath in Germany.

Times of the Holocaust 1933-45. No excuse for Apathy. Literature of the Holocaust Seminar. Cleveland Heights, Ohio, High School, 24p, Ill.

Teaching aids.

DAVIDOWICZ, Lucy S. La Guerre contre les juifs, 1933-45. Paris, Hachette, 472p.

French edition of "The War Against the Jews 1933-44" (1975)

------------------. A Holocaust Reader. New York, Behrman House, xiv, 379p, Ind. (Library of Jewish Studies)

Selected documents and accounts relating to the destruction of European Jewry with an introduction and annotations.

ECKHARDT, Alice and Roy. Christentum und Judentum: Die theologische und moralische Problematik der Vernichtung des europäischen Judentums. Evangelische Theologie, 36, No. 5, pp 406-26.

Answers to questions sent to individuals and organisations participating in the Jewish-Christian dialogue on the theological and moral problematic of the 'Final Solution'.

----------------------. How German Thinkers View the Holocaust. Christian Century, 93, No. 3, Ma. pp 249-52.

Their stay in Germany made them sensitive to the potential for the repetition of that event.

EISENBERG, Azriel. (Ed.) Earth, be not silent. Personal and Eyewitness Accounts of the Holocaust. Resistance and Rebirth. New York, Hebrew Publ. Co., (Sanhedrin Books) 576p.

EPSTEIN, Helen. Children of the Holocaust. Searching for a Past - and a Future. Present Tense, 3, No. 4, Su. pp 21-25.

"I do not yet know what form my relationship to the Holocaust will take in the future, whether it will be central or peripheral to my life and work. I do know that I want to decide not out of obligation to my ancestors, my parents or the Jewish people - but obligation to myself."

ERIS, Alfred. Portrait of the Artist as a Mass-Murderer. Midstream, 22, No. 2, F. pp 50-60.

"A closer look at the writing of some of the great writers (T.S. Eliot, William Carlos Williams, Ezra Pound, George Orwell, Graham Greene, Evelyn Waugh and George Bernard Shaw) in those years before and during the inexpressible ordeal of 1933-45 may be useful as an index to the feelings of both Jews and Gentiles at a time when overt expression of hatred could be waved away as 'fashionable.'"

FASS, Moshe. Theatrical Activities in the Polish Ghettos During the Years 1939-42. Jewish Social Studies, 38, No. 1, W. pp 54-72.

FENELON, Fania. Sursis pour l'orchestre. Temoignage eceuilli par Marcelle Routier. Paris, Opera Mundi, Stock, 397p.

In the women's camp at Auschwitz-Birkenau the Nazis set up an orchestra of the prisoners conducted by Alma Rose, Gustav Mahler's niece. One of the surviving members of the orchestra describes the orchestra that had to play whenever a trainload of deportees arrived for selection by the notorious Dr. Mengele.

FLEISCHNER, Eva. The Crucial Importance of the Holocaust for Christians. Engage/Social Action, No. 24, D. pp 26-33.

FREEMAN, Elayne. Holocaust Literature for Young Readers. Viewpoints 9, No. 3, Sp/Su. pp 44-56.

FRIEDLANDER, Albert Hosehander (Ed.) Out of the Whirlwind: Reader of Holocaust Literature. New York, London Schocken, viii, 536p.

FUNKE, Manfred. (Ed.) Hitler, Deutschland und die Maechte Materialen zur Aussenpolitik des Dritten Reiches. Duesseldorf, Droste, 848p. (Bonner Schriften zur Politik und Zeitgeschichte.)

Forty-three papers by experts discuss the various aspects of Nazi foreign policy and the Third Reich's relations with major and minor powers. Of special interest: "Die 'Endoeslung' und das deutsche Ostimperium," also "Kernstueck das rassenideologischen Programms des Nationalsocialismus" by Andreas Hillgruber in which he discusses the place of the Final Solution in Nazi Germany's plans in Eastern Europe.

HILBERG, Raul. German Railroads/Jewish Souls. Society, 6, No. 10, D. pp 60-74.

The role of the German railroads in the destruction of the Jews.

JANKELEVITCH, Vladimir. L'impardonnable. Rencontre, 10, No. 46, 4p.

Holocaust: the unpardonable deed.

Holocaust and Affirmation: Moment, 1, No. 5, F. pp 33-51.

Three articles: The Holocaust Dybbuk by Harold Schulweis. Chorus of Comforters by Nelly Sachs. The Edge of Decency by Terrence des Pres.

IRANEK-OSMECKI, Kazimierz, LICHTEN, Joseph L. and RACZYNSKI, Edward. The Polish Government in Exile and the Jewish Tragedy during World War II. *Wiener Library Bulletin*, 29, 37/8, pp 62-66.

Reply to an earlier contribution by Avi Avital (New Series, Nos. 33-34, 1975) about the attitude of the Polish Government in exile to the Jewish question, by three men who had an inside knowledge of the events described in this article.

IVRY, Itzhak. The Conspiracy of Silence Surrounding the Holocaust. *Jewish Frontier*, 43, No. 1, Ja. pp 12-14.

"In the State of Israel, the fighting soldier ... will not permit anyone to weave around him the conspiracy of silence which was woven around the Jew in Europe during World War II."

JELINEK, Yeshayahu. The Parish Republic. Hlinka's Slovak People's Party, 1939-45. New York, Columbia U.P., viii, 206p, Ind, Bibl. (East European Monographs, NO. 14)

Deals in great detail with the persecution of the Jews.

KANTER, Isaac. Social Psychology and the Holocaust. *Journal of Psychology and Judaism*, Fa. pp 55-56.

KAUNFER, Neal. An Inquiry as a Focus for Teaching the Holocaust. *Jewish Education*, 46, No. 2, Sp/Su. pp 31-34.

The purpose is to engage students intellectually as well as emotionally in learning about and from the Holocaust.

KELLEN, Konrad. Seven Beauties: Auschwitz - the Ultimate Joke? *Midstream*, 22, No. 8, O. pp 59-66.

LANDESVERBAND DER JUDISCHEN GEMEINDEN IN NIEDERSACHSEN UND DIE NIEDERSACHSISCHE LANDESZENTRALE FUR POLITISCHE BILDUNG. Zum Gedenken Bergen-Belsen 1945-75.

LEVINE, Herbert S. A Jewish Collaborator in Nazi Germany. The Strange Career of Georg Kareski, 1933-37. *Central European History*, 9, pp 251-81.

LEWIS, Theodore S. Living by Jewish Law under the Nazis. *Jewish Spectator*, 41, No. 2, Su. pp 65-67.

LINCOLN, Timothy Dwight. Two Philosophies of Jewish History after the Holocaust. *Judaism*, 25, No. 2, Sp. pp 150-57.

MELTZER, Milton. Never to Forget. The Jews of the Holocaust. New York, Harper & Row, 217p.

MICHEL, Jean. Dora. Paris, J.C. Lattes, 304p.

The author was captured by the Nazis in 1943 and spent two nightmare years in the subterranean concentration camp where missiles were made.

MOLLO, Andrew. A Pictorial History of the SS. 1923-45. London, MacDonald and Janes, 192p, Ill.

Includes their participation in the 'Final Solution'.

NACHMAN, Larry David. Reflections on the Holocaust. *Reconstructionist*, 41, No. 10, Ja. pp 13-18.

OIKOUMENIKOS. Two Kinds of People Confronted with the Nazi Persecution. *Encounter Today*, 11, Nos. 2-3, Su/Aut. pp 108-9. In French: *Rencontre*, 10, pp 195-97.

ORBACH, William. The Destruction of the Jews in the Nazi-Occupied Territories of the USSR. *Soviet Jewish Affairs*, 6, No. 2, pp 14-51.

Estimates vary between 500,000 and 1 million.

OZICK, Cynthia. vs. SCHULWEIS, Harold. The Holocaust Dybbuk Debate, *Moment*, 1, No. 10, My-Jy. pp 77-80.

PRESSER, Jacob. La notte dei girondini. Tr. fr. Dutch by Primo Levi, Milano, Adelphi, 116p.

Originally published in Holland as 'De nacht der Girondijnen' documents how the Nazis utilized Jewish self-hatred to carry out their plans in the concentration camps.

RABINOWITZ, Dorothy. Portrait of a Survivor. Commentary, 62, No. 4, O. pp 38-47.

-------------------. Survivors of the Holocaust Living in America. New York, Knopf, 242p.

ROSENBAUM, Irving. The Holocaust and the Halakha. New York, Ktav and Yeshiva University, x, 177p, (Library of Jewish Law and Ethics)

Applies halachic standards to the interpretation of the Holocaust.

ROTH, Francoise. Retour a Vichy: le Professeur Minkowski temoigne. L'Arche, No.232, Jy. pp 17-20.

The Vichy Government and the Jews.

SCHADT, Jörg. Verfolgung und Widerstand unter dem Nationalsozialismus in Baden. Die Lageberichte der Gestapo und des Generalstaatsanwalts Karlsruhe 1933-40. Stuttgart, Berlin, Köln, Mainz, W. Kohlhammer, 354p. Ind. (Schriftenreihe des Stadtarchivs Mannheim, Band 3)

Documentary study of persecution and resistance in Baden (Germany) based largely on the material preserved in the City Archives of Mannheim.)

SCHREIBER, Bernard. The Men Behind Hitler. A German Warning to the World. London, H. and P. Tadeusz, 160p.

Deals with the several ways in which the 'Final Solution' was carried out by the Nazis and warns that the forces behind the diabolical plan are still alive in Germany.

STEINITZ, Lucy Y. and SZONYI, David M. (Eds.) Living after the Holocaust: Reflections by the Post-war generation in America. New York, Bloch, iv, 149p, Ill.

Anthology with contributions by young American Jews who do not consider the Holocaust as part of history and aim with helping their contemporaries to come to terms with it.

STERN, David. Imagining the Holocaust. Commentary, 52, No. 7, Jy. pp 46-51.

Like literature in general, the literature of the Holocaust is about the dilemmas of moral choice, its temptations, triumphs and failures.

Three Christian Views of the Holocaust. Judaism, 25, No. 1, pp 135-66.

Contents: Holocaust Interpretations and Religious Assumptions by Hans O. Tiefel. Two Philosophies of Jewish History by Timothy Dwight Lincoln. Visit to Majdanek (Concentration Camp) near Lublin by Frank Parker.

TIEFEL, Hans O. Holocaust Interpretations and Religious Assumptions. Judaism, 25, No. 2, Sp. pp 135-49.

VELD, N.K.C.A. in 'T. De SS en Nederland. Document uit SS-archieven, 1939-45. 's Gravenhage, Martinus Hijhoff, 2 vols.

Documentation on SS action in Holland.

VETH, D. Giltay and VAN DER LEEUW, A.J. Het Weinrebrapport. Rapport door het Rijksinstituut voor oorlogsdocumentatie uitgebracht aan den Minister van Justitie inzake de activiteiten van des. F. Weinreb gedurende de jaren 1940-45 in het licht van nadere gegevens bezien. 's-Gravenhage, Staatsuitgeverij. 2, 1683p.

F. Weinreb, a Dutch Jew, was accused of collaboration with the Nazis.

WIESEL, Elie. The Ever Mysterious Holocaust. Condensed from Sh'ma, No. 100, Jewish Digest, 21, No. 7, Ap. pp 37-39.

WINOGRAD, Leonard. Double Jeopardy. What an American Army Officer, a Jew, remembers of prison life in Germany. American Jewish Archives, 28, No. 1, Ap. pp 3-17.

Second World War memoirs.

ZIMMELS, Hirsch Jacob. The Echo of the Nazi Holocaust in Rabbinic Literature. London, Marla, 371p.

PERSECUTION

AIGNER, Silvia. Die Judenverfolgung in Wien 1938-1945. Wien, Lehramtsprufüng Hauptschulen an der Pädagogischen Akademie des Bundes in Wien, 36p.

KA-TZETNIK, 135633. Sunrise Over Hell. London, W.H. Allen, 215p.

Nazi persecution of Jews in Poland.

KIMMICH, Christoph M. Germany and the League of Nations. Chicago, U. of Chicago P., xii, 264p, Ind, Bibl.

Chapter 9 deals i.a. with the Nazi persecution of the Jews, notably with the Bernheim Petitions against anti-Jewish legislation.

RUTKOWSKI, Adam. Directives allemandes concernant les arrestations et les deportations des Juifs en Avril-Aout 1944. Le Monde Juif, 32 , No. 82, Ap-Ju. pp 53-65.

ZEVI, Bruno. Commemorazione del 16 Ottobre 1943. Roma, Comunita Israelitica, 17p.

Memorial address delivered on the anniversary of 16 October 1943, the Nazi razzia of Rome's Jews.

RESCUE

DRUKS, Herbert. Why the Death Camps Were Not Bombed. The American Zionist, 67, No. 3, D. pp 18-21.

British and American officials were reluctant and unwilling to help stop the killers from killing Jews. Jewish leaders were badly divided and they could not present a united front as to what they wanted.

QUINT, Rena. Franklin D. Roosevelt - Protector of the Jews: or Co-Conspirator Against Them? Jewish Life, 31, No. 1, W. pp 48-54.

As President of the United States, Roosevelt could have used his exalted office to aid the victims of Nazi persecution. Instead he shut his ears and eyes to their plight.

STEIN, Joshua Berton. Britain and the Jews of Europe, 1933-1939. Ann Arbor, Michigan, U. Microfilms, viii, 387p, M.

Ph.D. Dissertation: St. Louis University, 1972.

--------------------. Great Britain and the Evian Conference 1938. Wiener Library Bulletin, 29, N.S. 37-38, pp 40-52.

WAR CRIMES

BLANEY, Michael S. Herbert Pell, War Crimes and the Jews. American Jewish Historical Quarterly, 18, No. 2, Ju. pp 335-52.

Examines the role of Herbert Claiborne Pell, the American representative on the U.N. War Crimes Commission established in 1943, and the events leading up to the Nuremberg Trials of Nazi war criminals following the Second World War.

BLUM, Howard. The Hunt for an American Nazi. Esquire, 46, No. 10, O pp 71-74; 144ff.

An account of the efforts of Charles Kremer, a New York Dentist, to deport Bishop Valerian Trifa, a former member of the Rumanian Iron Guard, now head of the Rumanian Orthodox Episcopate of America.

------------. The Wanted Book: The Search for Nazis in America. New York, Quadrangle; N.Y. Times, 256p.

Describes the hunt for Nazis who escaped to the U.S.A. Among the agencies assisting the authorities was the World Jewish Congress, Institute of Jewish Affairs.

COSTE-FLORET, M. Application dans le temps de la Loi du 26 décembre 1964 sur l'Imprescriptibilité des creimes contre l'humanitié. Gazette du Palais, No. 6, (2e sem) Doctrine, 653-55.

Application of the Statute of Limitations to war crimes.

GLUECK, Sheldon. The Nuremberg Trial and Aggressive War. New York, Kraus Reprint, 121p.

Reprint of work written as background to the Nuremberg Trials of major war criminals. First published in 1946.

---------------. War Criminals, their Prosecution and Punishment. New York, Kraus Reprint, 260p, Ind.

Reprint of work on the international legal provisions for the prosecution of war criminals in preparation for post-World War II trials, first published in 1944.

GREEN, Leslie C. Superior Orders in National and International Law. Leiden, Sijthoff, xix, 374p, Ind.

Professor Green has made a special study of domestic and international law dealing with the question of 'superior orders' which, ever since the war crimes trials following World War II, has been used as a defence to an allegation of war crimes. A chapter deals with Israel.

HAREL, Isser. Das Haus in der Garibaldistrasse. München, Propyläen, 288p, M, Ill. Italian ed: Milan,Mondadori, 362p.

The chapter of Adolf Eichmann.

HARROWER, Molly. Were Hitler's Henchmen Mad? Psychology Today, 9, No. 7, Jy. pp 76-80.

When experts rated Nazi responses to the Rorschach ink-blot test, the Nuremberg defendants looked like any group of Americans

HAUSNER, Gideon. Le Proces du Siecle. L'Arche, 19, No. 229, Ap. pp 50-59.

The Eichmann trial.

HEYDECKER, Joe Julius and LEEB, Johannes. Nuremberg Trial: History of Nazi Germany as Revealed Through the Testimony at Nuremberg. N.e Westport, Conn., Greenwood P.; London, Westport P., 398p.

HEYDRICH, Lina. Leben mit einem Kriegsverbrecher. Mit einem Anhang von Werner Maser. Pfaffenhofen, W. Ludwig (Ilmgau) 211p, Ind, Ill.
The widow of the Nazi war criminal, Reinhard Heydrich, murdered by the resistance in Czechoslovakia, wrote her memoirs, to which Werner Maser has written a lengthy comment correcting some of Mrs. Heydrich's statements.

KLARSFELD, Serge. Le cas du SS Unterscharführer Ernst Heinrichsohn. Le Monde Juif, 32, No. 82, Ap-Ju. pp 66-70.

KUPFERMAN, F. Pierre Laval. Paris, Masson, 192p. (Leur Vie S.)

MIALE, Florence R. and SELZER, Michael. The Nuremberg Mind. The Psychology of the Nazi Leaders. New York, Quadrangle/N.Y. Times Book Co., xiv, 302p. Bibl. Ill.
At the time of the Nuremberg Trials of major war criminals Dr. Gustave M. Gilbert - who also wrote the introduction - carried out Rorschach tests on 16 Nazi criminals. His records were again analysed and written up by the authors. The Rorschach test of Eichman has been added in appendix.

OPPITZ, Ulrich-Dieter. Strafverfahren und Strafvollstreckung bei NS-Gewaltverbrechen. Ulm/Donau, Braunland, xxix, 318p, M. Bibl. (Forschungsunternehmen der Humboldt-Gesellschaft, 9)
Survey of Nazi criminals' trials in the Federal German Republic up to 1973.

SEGRE, Augusto. Kappler. Condannato dalla Storia. La Rassegna Mensile di Israel, 42, Nos. 11-12, N-D. pp 395-400.
Kappler, responsible for the massacre and deportation of Rome Jews, condemned to life imprisonment, escaped from a prison hospital.

DAS SIEGER-TRIBUNAL. Nürnberg 1945-46. Dreissig Jahre danach. Referate und Arbeitsergebnisse des zeitgeschichtlichen Kongresses der Gesellschaft für freie Publizistik von 21 bis 23 Mai 1976, in Kassel. Coburg, Nation Europa, 128p.
Neo-Nazi attempt to discredit the Nuremberg Tribunal.

WEISS, Avraham. Spotlight on Nazi War Criminals in USA. Jewish Currents, 30, No. 11, D. pp 8ff.

RESISTANCE

BILOVITCHUS, Elie. Zi hot makriv geven dos lebn farn glik fun di mentchen. (She dedicated her life to the happiness of mankind) Sovietish Heimland, 16, No. 10, O. pp 107-13.
Hessie Glezerite's activities in the Vilna ghetto during Nazi occupation.

FOOT, M.R.D. Resistance: European Resistance to Nazism 1940-45. London, Eyre Methuen, 346p.

GROBMAN, Alex. The Warwar Ghetto Uprising in the American Jewish Press. Wiener Library Bulletin, 29, N.S. 37-38, pp 53-61.
"The Uprising brought forth little response, although the rebellion was well known ... An analysis of the newspapers and periodicals of that period, shows a paucity of editorial comment ... American Jewry, both membership and leaders, had failed to give adequate constructive reactions."

HAESTRUP, Jorgen. The Fourth Arm - Basic Features of the History of Resistance Movements in Europe 1939-45. Odense, U.P. (In Danish) Den 4 vabenart - Hovedtrek af de europaeiske modstrandsbevaegelsers historie 1939-45) Denmark: Odense Universitets forlag. 1976.

HAWES, Stephen and WHITE, Ralph. (Eds.) Resistance in Europe 1939-45 (Based on the proceedings of a Symposium held at the University of Salford, March 1973) Harmondsworth, Penguin, 234p, Bibl.

Resistance in general, but includes Jewish participation in resistance movements without a specific paper on Jewish resistance as such.

INTERSIMONE, Guiseppe. Cattolici nella resistenza Romana. Rome, Cinque Lune, 117p.

Account of Catholic resistance to the fascists and Nazis in Rome, including the rescue of Jews.

KURZMAN, Dan. The Bravest Battle: The 28 Days of the Warsaw Ghetto Uprising. New York, Putnam, 386p.

LANG, Berel. "Why Didn't They Resist?" Reconstructionist, 41, No. 10, Ja. pp 7-12.

It is time to recognise how ingeneous the question is, how idle, and finally, how perverse.

LOPEZ, Guido. La Resistenza e gli Ebrei. La Rassegna Mensile di Israel, 42, Nos. 3-4, Ma-Ap. pp 202-11.

Jews in the Italian resistance during World War II.

MARK, Berl. Uprising in the Warsaw Ghetto. London, New York, Schocken, 209p.

NOVITCH, Myriam. Sobibor. La révolte du 14 Octobre 1943. Paris, Centre de publication Asie Orientale, 300p, Ill.

The revolt in Sobibor extermination camp.

RANZ, John. Chapters of Jewish Resistance. Jewish Currents, 30, No. 4, Ap. pp 5-13.

ROSNER, Raphaël. Réflexions sur l'insurrection du Ghetto de Varsovie, Le Monde Juif, 32, No. 82, Ap-Ju. pp 37-52.

ROTHFELS, Hans. The German Opposition to Hitler, an Appraisal. Westport, Conn., Greenwood P., 166p.

Reprint of the 1962 edition.

SCHADT, Jörg. (Ed.) Verfolgung und Widerstand unter dem Nationalsozialismus in Baden; Die Lageberichte der Gestapo und des Generalstaatsanwalts Karlsruhe, 1933-1940. Hrsg. von Stadtarchiv Mannheim. Stuttgart: Kolhammer, 1976, 354p. Bibl. (Veröffentlichungen des Stadtarchivs Mannheim, Bd. 3)

STROOP BERICHT. Es gibt keinen jüdischen Wohnbezirk in Warschau mehr. Foreward by Andrzej Wirth. Darmstadt, Neuwied, Luchterhand, n.e. 15p + 126p of photographs.

Photographic account of the destruction of the Warsaw ghetto in 1943 made by the SS Commander in charge: Jürgen Stroop.

SUHL, Yuri. (Ed.) They Fought Back: Story of the Jewish Resistance in Nazi Europe. New York, Schocken, 328p.

SWEETS, John F. The Politics of Resistance in France 1940-44. A History of the "Mouvements unis de la résistance." Dekalb, Northern Illinois U.P., xii, 260p, Ill, Ind, Bibl, M.

Traces the history of the Mouvements Unis; based on documents, contemporary press, memoirs, discusses attitudes to persecution of the Jews.

TURCHI, Emma. La felicita è lá lotta. Venezia, Marsilio, 221p.
Memoirs of antifascist resistance in Italy.

TURKOW, Jonas. Los ninos del ghetto. Su heroisme y martirio. Buenos Aires. Congreso Judio Latinoamericano. 32p. Ill. (Biblioteca Popular Judia. Hechos de la historia judia 82)
Children in the Warsaw ghetto.

GERMANS AND JEWS

HARTLE, Heinrich. Deutsche und Juden. Studien zu einem Weltproblem. Leoni, Druffel, 325p, Ind, Ill.
the author discusses the Jewish question with antisemitic prejudice by maintaining that the Jewish 'race' is, by its claim to superiority and uniqueness aiming at world conquest.

LOWENTHAL, E.G. Juden in Deutschland: Gegenwart im Rückblick. Israelitisches Wochenblatt für die Schweiz, 76, No. 21a, Ma. pp 83-84.

LUTH, Erich. Die Friedensbitte an Israel 1951. Eine Hamburger Initiative. Mit Beitraegen von Rudolf Kustermeier, Dr. Moshe Tavor und Norbert Wollheim. Hamburg, Hans Christians, 160p, Ind, Bibl. Ill.
Two journalists, the author and Köstermeier have started a reconciliation movement between Germans and Jews in 1951, before Chancellor Adenauer's famous Bundestag declaration on moral and financial reparations. This is an account of their work and its consequences.

MICHEL, Ernest. W. Germany Revisited. Condensed from a Jewish Telegraphic Agency Feature, Jewish Digest, 21, No. 6, Ma. pp 53-6.

ROSENBLÜTH, Pinchas E. Friedrich Meineckes Anschauungen uber Juden und Judentum. Bulletin des Leo Baeck Instituts, No. 15- pp 93-123.

SCHALLENBERGER, E. Horst and STEIN, Gerd. Jewish History in German Textbooks. Patterns of Prejudice, 10, No. 5, S-O. pp 15-17; 21.
No outright antisemitism in W. German history schoolbooks, but there is no continuity in the treatment of Jewish history.

SCHATZKER, Chaim. Das Deutschlandbild in den israelitischen Geschichtsbüchern. Aus Politik und Zeitgeschichte, 9 O. pp 3-11.
The presentation of Germany in Israeli schoolbooks.

UTHMANN, Joerg von. Doppelganger, du bleicher Geselle. Zur Pathologie des deutsch-juedischen Verhaeltnisses. Stuttgart, Seewald, 188p.
A German diplomat who served with the first German Ambassador to Israel, makes an honest attempt to explain the psychodynamics of the curious love-hate relationship between Jews and Germans.

INDIVIDUAL JEWISH COMMUNITIES

ALGERIA

CHEMOUILLI, Henri. Une Diaspora méconnue: Les juifs d'Algerie. Paris, IMP, 327p, Bibl.
The author, himself an Algerian Jew, describes history and life of a now virtually non-existent Jewish community.

ARAB COUNTRIES

ABBOU, G. Les Juifs de l"Empire ottoman vus par les voyageurs et diplomates occidentaux. Yod, 1, No. 2, Ja. pp 25-34.

GILBERT, Martin. Jews of Arab Lands: Their History in Maps. London, Board of Deputies, 36p, Ill. In French: London, World Organisation of Jews from Arab Countries.

KIRSHNER, Sheldon. Diary of Egyptian and Syrian Jewry. Midstream, 22, No. 9, pp 23-32.
Interviews with Cairo and Damascus Jews in June 1975.

LITTMAN, David. Douze siècles et cinquante ans de persécutions arabes. L'Arche, 19, No. 229, Ap. pp 36-42.
Jews in Arab countries.

MEMMI, Albert. Did Jews in Arab Countries Fare Better Than Their European Compatriots? Israel Horizons, 24, No. 3, Ma. pp 16-18.

ARGENTINA

BLANKSTEIN, George I. Peron's Argentina. N.e. U. of Chicago P., xvi, 478p, Ind. Bibl.
Professor Blankstein was a State Department adviser on Inter-American affairs and worked in Argentina as a Social Science Research Fellow. He deals extensively with antisemitism and Nazism in Argentina under Peron.

KLEIN, Alberto. Cinco Siglos de Historia: Una crónica de la vida judía en la Argentina. Beunos Aires, cuadernos de Estudios Judios, Publicacion del Comité Judio Americano, 56p.
Five hundred years of Jewish history in the Argentine - a summary by years and major events.

LIEBERMANN, José. Aportes de la Colonizacion agraria Judia a la Economia Nacional. Buenos Aires, Comite Judió Americano, 39p. (Cuadernos de Estudies Judios).
Contributions of Jewish agrarian colonies to the national economy of the Argentine - a historical survey.

La población israelita de la Provincia de Tucamán. Censo Segundo. Tucamán, Sociedad Union Israelita. 87p.
Second census of the Jewish population of Tucaman.

SEGAL, Bernard. A Mostly Open Door: Argentina's Jews and Argentine Pluralism. Ethnicity. 3, No. 3, Ma. pp 82-97.
The Jews of Argentina are relatively prosperous, but are reluctant to take much public credit for their part in helping to build an economic system now is disrepute, held to be in league with great powers against the aspirations of the Argentine masses.

WARSZAWSKI, Paul. Argentina: Anti-semitismo a Subversão. A propósito de situacao dos judeus na Argentine. Shalom, 12, No. 137 O. pp 24-27.

WEISBROT, Robert. Jews in Argentina Today. Judaism, 25, No. 4, Fa. pp 390-401.

While many Jewish youth have been simply swallowed up by the Argentine 'New Left' others - cut off from Jewish knowledge, institutions and observance are seeking new forms of Jewish expression. Whether the elements of militant Zionism, liberalized religion and ethnic pride coalesce into a revitalized heritage, or whether ignorance, isolation and inertia lead ultimately to total assimilation is the community's crisis.

AUSTRALIA

EXECUTIVE COUNCIL OF AUSTRALIAN JEWRY. Symposium: "Australian Jewry in the Next Twenty Five Years". Sunday 13th Monday 14th June 1976 at Beth Weizmann, Melbourne, Melbourne, 96p.

LEVI, John S. A Tale of Australia's First "Rabbi". Condensed from Australian Jewish Historical Society Journal, N. 1975, 7, No. 2. Jewish Digest, 21, No. 9, Ju. pp 27-31.

BELGIUM

BOK, Willy. Apercu des tendances actuelles du Judaisme Belge. Regards, 12, No. 100, Ja. pp 68-77.

LOTTMAN, Herbert R. Diamonds in the Shtetl. 'The City is a Family' Present Tense, 3, No. 2, W. pp 44-50.

On the Jewish quarter of Antwerp.

BRAZIL

FRIEDLER, Egon. Brazil's Jews After the UN Anti-Israel Vote. Israel Horizons, 24, No. 9, N. pp 26-29.

HIRSCHBERG, Alice Irene. Desafio a Resposta. A História da Congregacao Israelia Paulista, desde a sua Fundaçao. Saõ Paulo, Congregacao Israelita Paulista, 238p, Bibl.

History of the Jewish community of Sao Paolo, Brazil including their present status and structure.

NICOLAIEWSKY, Eva. Israelites no Rio Grande do Sul. N.p. Brazil.

SOBELL Henry J. Judaism in Brazil. New Elul, (WUB) My-Ju.

BULGARIA

ASTRUKOV, Y. Yidn in Bulgarie (Jews in Bulgaria). Sovietish Heimland, 16, No. 7, Jy. pp 5-9.

By the Chairman of the Social and Cultural Organisation of Bulgarian Jews.

OCHSCHLIES, Wolf. Bulgarien - Land ohne Antisemitismus. Erlangen, Ner Tamid, 168p, Ill.

A concise study of Bulgarian-Jewish relations of which almost half is devoted to the period of World War II; a further score of pages describe the situation after the war.

CANADA

BROWN, Michael Gary. Jewish Foundations in Canada: The Jews, the French and the English to 1914. Ann Arbor, Mich., U. Microfilms, 425p, Bibl.
Ph.D. Dissertation, U. of New York at Buffalo.

COHEN, Stanley M. An Interview with Saul Hayes. Viewpoints, 9, No. 4, Fa. pp 5-25.
A discussion with the former Executive Vice-President of the Canadian Jewish Congress on the contemporary Jewish scene in Canada.

KURELEK, William and ARNOLD, Abraham. Jewish Life in Canada. Edmonton, Alberta, Hurtig, 91p, Ill. (Colour)
Historical study of Canadian Jewry with reproductions of the paintings of W. Kurelek.

CZECHOSLOVAKIA

Delegierten - Tagung der jüdischen Religionsgemeinschaft in der Slowakischen sozialistischen Republik wählte eine neue Leitung. Informations Bulletin, No. 4, D. pp 3-6.

FEDER, Richard. Zivot a odkaz. (Life and Heritage) Praha, Council of Jewish Communities of the Czech Socialist Republic, 217p, Ill.
Sermons and historical papers, relating to the Jews in Czechoslovakia by the late Chief Rabbi.

MUNELES, Otto. Kommentare zu den ausgewählten Grabinschriften vom Alten jüdischen Friedhof in Prag. Judaica Bohemiae, 12, No. 1, pp 3-30.
Explanations to selected tombstones in the Old Jewish Cemetery of Prague.

SADEK, Vladimir. The Restorations of the Old Jewish Cemetery in Prague Were Started. Judaica Bohemiae, 12, No. 2, pp 55-58.

EASTERN EUROPE

MEYER, Peter and others. The Jews in the Soviet Satellites. Westport, Conn., Greenwood P., viii, 637p, Ind, Bibl.
Reprint of the 1953 edition.

SCHEPS, Samuel. Ostjudentum im Rückblick. Israelitisches Wochenblatt für Die Schweiz. 76, No. 21, Ma. pp 80-82.
The legacy of East European Jewry.

EGYPT

ST. JOHN, Robert. The Treasures of Cairo's Karaite Jews. Jewish Affairs, 31, No. 2, F. pp 37-38. From the Jewish Digest.

FAR EAST

FRANKL, Ludwig August. The Jews in the East. Tr. Rev. P. Beaton. Westport, Conn., Greenwood P.; London, Westport P., 2 vols.
Reprint of the 1959 edition.

FRANCE

ALLOUCHE, Jean-Luc. Les rapatriés, 15 ans apres. L'Arche, 19, No. 244, Jy. pp 33-39.
Algerian Jews in France.

EISENBACH, Artur. L'Hôtel Lambert - et la question juive a la veille du Printemps des peuples. (In Polish with French and Russian Summaries) Przeglad Historyczny, 67, No. 3, pp 369-98.
In 1832 and 1849 the Polish emigré leaders tried to persuade Polish Jews and Jews in the West to support the independence movement.

GIRARD, Patrick. Les Juifs de France de 1789 à 1860: de l'emancipation à l'égalite. Paris, Callman-Lévy, 299p, Ind, Bibl.
Analysis of the changes and debates within French Jewry since the Revolution, with individual emancipation to the founding of Alliance juive, regarded as a model for development by other' communities. Examines the adaptation to Gentile society.

HILDESHEIMER, F. Les Juifs a Nice au XVII siecle. Archives Juives, 12, No. 1, pp 1-12.
17th century Jews in Nice were tolerated on temporary safe-conducts but common law applied to them.

KERNER, S. Franco-Judaica dans la presse russe, 1836 a 1889. Archives Juives, 12, No. 3, pp 49-53.
Articles on French Jewry published in Russia, 1836-89.

LEWI, Monique. Histoire d'une communauté juive: Roanne, Etude historique et sociologique d'un judaisme. Roanne, Horvath, 181p, Ill, M.
Thesis presented at Lyons University, on the history of the Jewish community of Roanne (Lyonnais) France. There is a young community reconstituted only 40 years ago.

Le manuscrit Valabrègue: documents judeo-comtadins du XVIII siecle. Archives Juives, 12, No. 4, pp 61-70.
Communal organisation in the combat Venaissin region of France in the 18th century.

NAHON, G. Rapport sur les inscriptions hébraiques médiévales de l'Alsace et de la Lorraine, avec le texte des inscriptions inedites de Nancy. Archives Juives, 12, No. 3, pp 37-43.
Inscriptions in Nancy, Molsheim, Hagenau, Strasbourg.

GERMANY

KATTERMANN, Hildegard. Geschichte und Schicksale der Lahrer Juden. Eine Dokumentation. Stadtverwaltung, Lahr. 43p.
A Jewish community in Germany.

KNAUSS, Erwin. Die jüdische Bevölkerung Giessens 1933-45. Eine Dokumentation. 2.e. Wiesbaden, Kommission für Geschichte der Juden in Hessen, 192p.

MARWEDEL, Gunther. Die Privilegien der Juden in Altona. Hamburg, Hans Christians, 432p, Ind. (Hamburger Beiträge zur Geschichte der Deutschen Juden 5)
Statutes and privileges of Jewish medieval communities were the foundation of their existence. This work deals with those of the Jews of Altona, near Hamburg.

REISSNER, Hanns. Aus der Geschichte der Berliner Jüdischen Gemeinde. Reprint from 'Jüdische Rundschau' 25 Au. 1936 and 23 S. 1938. Nachrichtenblatt, 16, No. 3, S. pp 4-7.

RICHARZ, Monika (Ed.) Jüdisches Leben in Deutschland. Selbstzeugnisse zur Sozialgeschichte 1780-1871. Veröffentlichung des Leo Baeck Instituts. Munich, DVA, 500p, Ind.

Extracts from memoirs of German Jews of the period, held in the Leo Baeck Institute, New York. The introduction deals with the social, cultural, economic and religious background of the personalities chosen.

SCHULTE, Klaus H.S. Bonner Juden und ihre Nachkommen bis um 1930. Eine familien - und a zial - geschichtliche Dokumentation. Bonn, Ludwig Röhrscheid, 724p, Ind. (Veröffentlichungen des Stadtarchivs, Bonn, 16)

History of the Jews in Bonn up to the rise of Nazism, based on material in the Bonn City Archives.

GIBRALTER

SHAMASH, Ruby. Jews on the Rock. Condensed from Canadian Jewish News, 23 My, 1975. Jewish Digest, 21, No. 6, Ma. pp 13-14.

Jews in Gibralter.

MORSY, M. Les Juifs marocains à Gibralter au 18e siècle: histoire d'une minorité manipulée. Pluriel-Débat, No. 6, pp 47-60.

At the mercy of the authorities, 18th century Gibralter Jews were a political tool of both the Moroccans and the British.

GREECE

MARKS, Ilona. The Jewish Community in Rhodes. Menorah, 3, No. 1, pp 42-48.

HUNGARY

Studien zum Ungarischen Judentum. Ed. by Österreichlisches Jüdisches Museum in Eisenstadt. Eisenstadt, Roetzer, 80p. (Studia Judaica Austriaca 3)

Three essays on Hungarian Jewish History: Jewish Laws in Burgenland from St. Stephen to Maria Teresia (1001-1780) by Ivan Hacker. Hungarian Jewish 1780-1914 by Wolfdieter Bihl. Assimilation and Emancipation of Hungarian Jewry in the mid-19th century by Wolfgang Häusler.

INDIA

LORD, James Henry. The Jews in India and the Far East. Westport, Conn., Greenwood P.; London, Westport P., iii, 120 + 17p.

Reprint of classic, first published in 1907.

LOTTMAN, Herbert R. The Last Indian Jews. Present Tense, 3, No. 4, Su. pp 7-9.

The Bene Israel.

RENFORD, Raymond. India's Fading Jewish Community. The Jewish Digest, 21, No. 5, pp 75-76.

IRAQ

HAIM, Sylvia G. Aspects of Jewish Life in Baghdad Under The Monarchy. Middle Eastern Studies, 3, No. 2, My, pp 188-208.
ROSENFIELD, Ray. In a Sea of Hate. Present Tense, 3, No. 3, Sp. pp 9-11.
The Jews of Iraq.

ITALY

ELIE, H. Le statut des juifs en Italie à la fin du XVIe siecle. Rencontre, 10, pp 229-33.
ROTH, Cecil. A History of the Jews in Venice. London, New York, Schocken, N.e. x, 380p.

JAMAICA

HOLZBERG, Carol S. The Social Organisation of the Jamaican Political Economy: Ethnicity and the Jewish Segment. Paper read at the Canadian Sociology and Anthropology Association in Quebec, My 26-29.
Explores the disproportionate representation of the Jewish community among the national entrepreneurial elite of Jamaica.

JAPAN

KRANZLER, David. Japanese, Nazis and Jews. New York, Yeshiva U.P., 644p.

LATIN AMERICA

ELKIN, Judith Laikin. History of the Jews of Latin America in the Nineteenth and Twentieth Centuries. Ann Arbor, Michigan., U. Microfilms.
Ph.D. Dissertation, U. of Michigan.
ITZIGSOHN, Jose A. The Jewish Communities of Latin America: An Analysis. Olam, Sp. pp 19-22.
"Their future is of concern not only to Jews but also the people of Latin America, of which the Jews are proportionally small but a very active component and a ready ally for their inevitable movements toward national liberation."
RAUCH, Eduardo. Latin American Jewry: Help, but how? Response, 10, Nos. 2-3, Su/Fa. pp 129-33.

LEBANON

Jews in Lebanon: A Report from the Paris Office of the American Jewish Committee. Paris, 2p.

MEXICO

CHEUSE, Alan. Not Quite At Home. Enigma in Mexico. Present Tense, 3, No. 4, Su. pp 33-38.
Position of Jews in a country of great economic disparity.
KOLACK, Shirley and Sol. The Jews of Mexico. Jewish Digest, 22, No. 1, S. pp 49-52. Condensed from The Jewish Advocate.

MOROCCO

BOWIE, L. An Aspect of Muslim-Jewish Relations in Late Nineteenth Century Morocco: A European Diplomatic View. International Journal of Middle East Studies, 7, No. 1, pp 3-19.
Activities of naturalised and protected Jews, based on British and French archives.

KHAYYAT, S.L. Moroccan Jewry: An Ethno-Cultural Study. Jewish Quarterly Review, 67, No. 1, pp 55-58.
Review article of book edited by I. Ben Ami, Jerusalem, 1975.

LITTMAN, David. Jews under Muslim Rule - 2: Morocco 1903-12. Wiener Library Bulletin, 29, N.S. 37-38, pp 3-19.
Based on letters received by the Alliance Israelite Universelle.

MALKA, Victor. Les Bons Juifs du roi Hassan II. L'Arche, 19, No. 231, Ju. pp 28-31.

-------------. Le defí du Maroc nouveau. L'Arche, 19- No. 233, pp 23-25.
The Jews of the new Morocoo.

-------------. De l'inquiétude à la sérénité. Les Nouveaux Cahiers, 11, No. 43, pp 4-55.
Moroccan Jewry today.

MULTIPLE COMMUNITIES

ABRAMOVICH, Stanley. The Other Jews. Jewish Life, 31, No. 1, Sp. pp 16-25.
Brief reports on the Jewish communities in several countries of Eastern Europe, the Middle East and Africa.

NETHERLANDS

FISHMAN, Joel. The Jewish Community in Post-War Netherlands. 1944-1975. Midstream, 22, No. 1, Ja. pp 42-54.

FUKS, Lajb. New Data Concerning the Amsterdam Chief Rabbi David Lida and the Council of the Four Countries. (In Dutch with English Summary) Studia Rosenthaliana, 10, No. 2, Jy. pp 189-94.
Two letters from the Polish Council of the Four Countries (1684) addressed to the Sephardi and Ashkenazi communities in support of Lida for whom they made difficulties.

GOLB, N. In Search of the Original Home of the Great Mahzor of Amsterdam. Studia Rosenthaliana, 10, No. 2, Jy. pp 195-211.

KOEN, E.M. Notarial Records relating to the Portuguese Jews in Amsterdam up to 1639. Studia Rosenthaliana, 10, No. 1, Ja. pp 96-104 and No. 2, Jy. pp 212-31.

VAN HAASTERT, J. The Ashkenazic Cemetery is Oosterhout. (In Dutch with English Summary) Studia Rosenthaliana, 10, No. 1, pp 79-94.
Cemetery of the Jewish communities of Breda, Oosterhout and Geestreudenberg now returned to the State.

PANAMA

SASSO, Dennis C. One Century of Jewish Life in Panama. Reconstructionist, 42, No. 6, S. pp 18-24.

POLAND

DIAMOND, Sigmund. Journey to the East. Different Communities - Different Jews. Present Tense, 3, No. 3, Sp. pp 60-67.
A visit to Poland and the Soviet Union.

FISHMAN, Chuck. I See Poland Clear. Present Tense, 3, No. 3, Sp. pp 56-59.
Photo-story of the remaining 8,000 Jews.

KORN, David. Polish Jewry: The End of a 1000 Year History. Jewish Digest, 21, No. 8, My. pp 64-69. Condensed from The Jewish Week, (Washington, 4-10 S. 1975)

SILVAN, Gabriel. A 'Kiddush Ha-Shem" in Communist Poland. Jewish Affairs, 36, No. 4, Ap. pp 39-42.

WEINRYB, Bernard P. The Jews of Poland: A Social and Political History of the Jewish Community in Poland from 1100 to 1800. Philadelphia, Jewish Publication Society of America, xiv, 424p.

ZAMOYSKI, Adam. The Jews in Poland: Part I; 1264-1795. History Today, 26, No. 2, F. pp 73-82. Part II: 1795-1930. Ibid, 26, No. 3, M. pp 194-200.

PORTUGAL

MALKA, Victor. Le Portugal Demain. L'Arche, 19, No. 230, My. pp 17-20.
The Jews in Portugal after the Salazar dictatorship.

ROMANIA

FARB, Nathan. A Sadness of the Spirit. Photographs of Romania. Present Tense, 3, No. 2, W. pp 41-43.

IANCU, Carol. L'Antisémitisme et L'Emancipation des Juifs en Roumanie (1866-1919).
Ph.D. Thesis, U. of Aix-en-Provence.

------------. Un Comité de secours pour les Juifs de Roumanie à Strasbourg en 1900. Archives Juives, 12, No. 1, pp 16-18.
With documents, published in the annexe from the Archives of the Alliance Israélite Universelle.

------------. Le serment "More Judaico" en Roumanie. Revue des Etudes Juives, 135, Nos. 1-3, Ja-S. pp 169-76.

SOUTH AFRICA

HERRMAN, Louis. A History of the Jews in South Africa from the Earliest Times to 1895. Westport, Conn., Greenwood P.; London, Westport P., 288p, Ill.
Reprint of the 1935 edition.

NEUSNER, Jacob. With the Jews of South Africa. Moment, 2, No. 2, N. pp 18-22.
"I went to South Africa to learn about the potentialities of Judaism on the moral frontier of humanity. I left ashamed to be a human being but ineffably proud to be a Jew."

NORWICH, I. Johannesburg - Beginnings and Jewry's First Years. Jewish Affairs, 36, No. 10, O. pp 8-14.

SARON, Gus. Early Days of Johanessburg Jewry. Beginnings of the Park Synagogue and Tribulations of the Park Synagogue. Jewish Affairs, 31, No. 2, F. pp 6-10 and No. 3, Ma. pp 35-41.

----------. From Immigrants to South Africans. A Sketch of South African Jewry. Jewish Affairs, 36, No. 11, N. pp 20-29.
----------. The 'Lost' History of Jewish Kimberley. Zionist Record and South African Jewish Chronicle. Supplement, 17 S. pp 11-13.
----------. A Visual History of Early Jewish Johannesburg. Jewish Affairs, 36, No. 10, O. pp 15-20.
WHARTMAN, Eliezer. The Forgotten Pioneers. Jewish Affairs, 36, No. 7, Jy. pp 15-16.
Early Jewish settlers in South Africa.

SPAIN

ARONSFELD, C.C. Letter From a Late Holiday in Spain. Jewish Frontier, 43, No. 5, My. pp 23-25.
BELLER, Jacob. Remnants of Spain's Jewish Past. Jewish Digest, 22, No. 2, O. pp 28-32. Condensed from Viewpoints, 9, No. 2.
ROTH, N. The Jews and the Muslim Conquest of Spain. Jewish Social Studies, 38, No. 2, pp 145-58. In his Chronicon Mundi Lucas de Tuy of St. Isadoro's Monastery in Leon (written between 1197 and 1204) alleges betrayal by the Jews of Toledo to the Moslem invaders. This was pure invention.

SWEDEN

ROVNER, Ruth. Living in Sweden. It's Practically Perfect. Present Tense, 4, No. 1, Aut. pp 38-45.

SWITZERLAND

VADNAI, G. Survol des communautés romandes. Les trois quarts de siècle: 1901 à 1976. Israelitisches Wochenblatt für die Schweiz, 76, No. 21a, Ma. pp 48-49.
Jewish communities in French-speaking Switzerland.

SYRIA

GRUEN, George F. The Present Status of Syrian Jewry: a Fact Sheet. New York, American Jewish Committee, 4p.

TUNISIA

PARFITT, Tudor. Passover in Djerba. Powerless on a Tunisian Island. Present Tense, 3, No. 3, Sp. pp 68-71.

TURKEY

SCHACHTER, Hindy L. Three Days in Istanbul. Jewish Frontier, 43, No. 6, Ju-Jy. pp 13-14.
The Jews in Turkey.

UNITED KINGDOM

ABRAHAMS, David. Spotlight Southend - Alive, Well and Expanding. Jewish World, 1, No. 9, Au. pp 7-19.
FISHMAN, W.J. East End Jewish Radicals. London, Duckworth, 348p, Ill.
Re-emergence of organised labour among immigrant Jews at the turn of the century.

LEVIN, Hilary S. and Salmond S. Jubilee at Finchley, 1926-1976. The Story of a Congregation, London, Finchley Synagogue, 29p, Ill.

MOONMAN, Jane. The Gilded Ghettos. London Style. Present Tense, 3, No. 3, Sp. pp 11-16.

Jewish life in England.

WEISMAN, Malcolm. The Aberdeen Hebrew Congregation. Menorah, 3, No. 1, Su. pp 53-56.

WILLIAMS, Bill. The Making of Manchester Jewry 1740-1875. Manchester, Manchester U.P.; New York, Holmes and Meier. 448p, Ind, Bibl.

The origins and development of one of Britain's largest provincial Jewish communities and the varying attitudes of Manchester people to this minority.

U.S.A.

ALPERIN, Aaron. Seventy Years of Labor Zionism in America. Tr. Irving Heller. New York, Labor Zionist Alliance, 23p. (Current Jewish Affairs Pamphlet 6)

AMERICA - A NOVUM IN JEWISH EXPERIENCE - Bicentennial Issue. Judaism, 25, No. 3, Su. pp 259-384.

Includes: The Jew on the College Campus by Alfred Jospe. Jews and Contributions to Economics by Mark Pearlman. The Jewish Contribution to American Politics by Henry L. Feingold The Holocaust in American-Jewish Fiction: A Slow Awakening by Edward Alexander. The Anti-Semitic 'Imaging' of the Jew in America by Michael Dobkowski.

AMERICAN BICENTENNIAL. Papers presented at the Annual Meeting of the Conference on Jewish Social Studies Held in Conjunction with the Academic Committee of the World Jewish Congress. 26 April at the School of International Affairs, Columbia University, New York. Jewish Social Studies, 38, Nos. 3-4, Su/Fa. (Special Issue)

BARBARASH, Ernest E. The Birth of Two Nations: A Historical Account of a Nation Born and a People Reborn. Published on the occasion of the Bicentennial. New York, American-Israel Friendship League, 23p, Ill.

AMERICAN JEWISH BUSINESS ENTERPRISE: Special Bicentennial Issue. American Jewish Historical Quarterly, 66, No. 3, S. pp 1-178.

Includes: Some Aspects of the New York Jewish Merchant and Community 1654-1820 by Leo Hershkowitz. Julius Rosenwald by Lawrence P. Carosso. Neiman-Marcus: Innovators in Fashion and Merchandising by Don. M. Coerver and Linda B. Hall. The Jewish Businesswoman in America by Irene D. Neu.

AMERICAN JEWS AND THE LABOR MOVEMENT: Special Bicentennial Issue. American Jewish Historical Quarterly, 66, No. 2, Ma. pp 200-85.

Includes: Jewish Unions and the American Federation of Labor Power Structure, 1903-35 by Robert Asher. The American Federation of Labor Zionism and the First World War by Sheila Stern Polishook. Education and Economic Mobility: The Jewish Experience in New York City, 1880-1920 by Selma C. Berrol.

AMERICAN JEWS AND THE WORLD: VISIONS AND ISSUES: Special Double Issue. Response, 10, Nos. 2-3, Su/Fa. pp 1-256.
Includes: The Case for Conflict in Communal Life by Steven Martin Cohen. The Jewish Question Becomes the Zionist Question by Mitchell Cohen. Soviet Jewry: Growth of a Movement by Paul S. Appelbaum. Latin American Jewry: Help, but How? by Eduardo Rauch. Where Are the Jewish Journalists? by Neil Reisner. Retraining Jewish Teachers by Neal Kaunfer.

ANGEL, Marc D. Thoughts About Early American Jewry. Tradition, 16, No. 2, Fa. pp 16-23.

ARON, William S. A Disappearing Community: Jewish Life on New York's Lower East Side. Jewish Life, 37, No. 4, Fa. pp 40-47.
A photo-essay.

BARON, J.M. The Bicentennial: The Jewish Experience in America. Introductory Remarks. Jewish Social Studies, 38, Nos. 3-4, pp 193-94.
Introductory remarks to the Seminar arranged by Jewish Social Studies and the Academic Committee of the World Jewish Congress.

BAUM, Phil. A Letter To The National News Council. Congress Monthly, 43, No. 3, Ma. pp 8-11.
Deals with the CBS-AJCongress dispute over part of the February 4 1975 "60 Minutes" programme devoted to the question of Syria and Syrian Jewry.

BEN, Phillipe. Ford ou Carter? Le Vote Juif aux U.S.A. L'Arche, 19, No. 231, Ju. pp 24-25.

BLAU, Joseph Leon. Judaism in America: From Curiosity to Third Faith. U. of Chicago P., xiv, 156p. (Chicago History of American Religion)

BUCHWALD, Art. For us, the American Dream Has Come True. Jewish Chronicle Colour Magazine, 3 S. pp 41ff.
Jews in the U.S.A.

CAROSSO, V.P. A Financial Elite: New York's German-Jewish Investment Bankers. American Jewish Historical Quarterly, 66, No.1 pp 67-88.
Their role in American finance and philanthropy.

COHEN, Steven Martin. The Case for Conflict in Communal Life. Response, 10, Nos. 2-3, Su/Fa. pp 5-12.
Discusses public dissent in American Jewish life.

COMMISSION ON SOCIAL ACTION OF REFORM JUDAISM. The Candidates Speak: Report of a non-partisan consultation with 1976 presidential candidates. Washington, D.C., Jan 21-22, 1976, New York, 16p.

COOPER, Martha R. What Electoral College Reform Could Mean to American Jewry. Analysis, 55, Ja. 7p. Jewish Digest, 21, No. 8, My. pp 19-26.

ELAZAR, Daniel J. Community and Policy. The Organisational Dynamics of American Jewry. Philadelphia, Jewish Publication Society of America, xv, 421p, Ind, Bibl.
Survey of the structure and functions of the American Jewish community, and how it should be understood as a body politic. Discusses American Jewry's relation to Israel which is now the prime focus of Jewish identity.

----------------. Jews in the U.S: The Jewish Community - changing patterns; address at the 45th General Assembly, Philadelphia, 10-14 N., New York, Council of Jewish Federations and Welfare Funds, 18p. (Assembly Papers)

EVANS, Eli N. The Provincials: A Personal History of the Jews in the South. New York, Atheneum; London, Transatlantic, 368p, Ind, Bibl.
The author grew up in North Carolina where he, his family and his forebears were involved in the Zionist movement, the Civil Rights movement and other communal activities.

FACING DOMESTIC ISSUES IN THE ELECTION. Sh'ma, 6, 14 My. pp 106-12.
Hyman Bookbinder, Marvin Braiterman, Leslie Gottlieb, Charlotte Jacobson, I.L. Kenen, Joseph Polak, Earl Raab and Gerald Serotta discuss what they see as the domestic issues of greatest concern to American Jews.

FAGIN, Lois. Jewish Roots in Indian Territory. Jewish Digest, 21, No. 10, Jy-Au. pp 28-31. (Condensed from Oklahoma Today, 26, No. 1)

FEIN, Isaac M. Boston - Where It All Began: A Historical Perspective of the Boston Jewish Community, Boston, Jewish Bicentennial Committee, 83p, Ill.

FEIN, Leonard. Jackson and the Jews: Mixed Marriage or Mixed Blessing? Moment, 1, No. 10, Ap. pp 22-27.
Not intended as a rejection or an endorsement of any particular candidate but as an illustration of the ways in which we need to go about making up our political minds.

FEINGOLD, Henry L. The Condition of American Jewry in Historical Perspective - A Bicentennial Assessment. American Jewish Year Book 76, pp 3-41.

-----------------. The Jewish Contribution to American Politics. Judaism, 25, No. 3, Su. pp 312-19.

FEUER, Leon I. The Birth of the Jewish Lobby. A Reminiscence. American Jewish Archives, 28, No. 2, pp 107-18.

FRANCK, Isaac. The American Jewish Experience. Midstream, 22, No. 2, Ma. pp 7-18.
Assessment of 200 years.

FRANK, Ben. G. Jews from Arab Lands: At Home in Brooklyn. Congress Monthly, 43, No. 3, Ma. pp 15-16.
The 25,000 Syrian, 1,000 Egyptian and several hundred Lebanese Jews, all living within a several mile radius of Ocean Parkway.

GEFFEN, David. (Ed.) Jewish Delaware. History, Sites, Communal Services. Jewish Federation of Delaware, Jewish Historical Society of Delaware, 52p, Ill, Bibl.

GLAZER, Nathan. Different, but Equal. Jewish Chronicle Colour Magazine, 3 S. pp 53-56.

GORDIS, Robert. America - a Novem in Jewish Experience. Judaism, 25, No. 3, Su. pp 261-69.

GORDON, Albert Isaac. Jews in Suburbia. Westport, Conn., Greenwood P.; London, Westport P., 264p.
A 1959 study reprinted.

GORDON, Haim. Jewish Outposts in Dixie. Jewish Digest, 21, No. 10, Jy-Au. pp 69-72. Condensed from Haddassah Magazine, 56, No. 6.

Guide to Jewish Chicago. 3.e. Chicago, A.J. Congress, 41p.

HALPERN, Ben. The Roots of American Jewish Liberalism. American Jewish Historical Quarterly, 66, No. 2, pp 190-214.
Sephardi and Ashkenazi origins of liberalism among American Jews, a political attitude to change.

HENDERSON, Thomas M. Tammany Hall and the New Immigrants: The Progressive Years. New York, Arno P., 314p.

Political behaviour of Manhattan's four largest ethnic groups (including Jews) during the period of Charles Murphy's leadership of Tammany Hall (1902-24)

HERSCHER, Uri D. The Metropolis of Ghettos. The Journal of Ethnic Studies,

The Lower East Side between 1880 and 1920. Based on personal conversations during 1972, with individuals of immigrant stock, all of whom had grown up in this area.

HERTZBERG, Arthur. The American Jewish Experience: An Interpretation. Congress Monthly, 43, No. 7, S. pp 10-12; Jewish Chronicle Colour Magazine, 3 S. pp 17-18.

Jewish community of East European extraction is the only minority in America which has survived now into the fourth generation of recognizable cultural and political difference in the U.S.

-----------------. Celebrating Jewish New York. Congress Monthly, 43, No. 6, Ju. pp 4-6.

HIMMELFARB, Milton. Carter and the Jews. Commentary, 52, No. 8, Au. pp 45-48.

"Carter need not worry very much about his Jewish vote. I hope Jewish voters need not worry very much about him."

HIRSHHAUT, J. Groisshtetishe Migratsies un Yiddishe Gemeindes. (A Problem fun Yiddish Amerikanishn Lebn.) Di Tsukunft, 82, No. 3, Ma. pp 94-97.

Problems created by internal migration in American Jewish communities.

HOWE, Irving. The Immigrant Glory. Midstream, 22, No. 1, Ja. pp 16-22.

From his book "World of Our Fathers".

------------. The Immigrant Jews of New York, 1881 to the present. London, Routledge & Kegan Paul. xx, 714p, Ind, Ill, Bibl. (Littman Library of Jewish Civilisation); (World of our Fathers, New York, Harcourt Brace Jovanovitch)

Social and literary history of New York Jews based on Yiddish and English newspapers, memoirs and other source materials.

KARP, Abraham J. (Ed.) Golden Door to America: The Jewish Immigrant Experience. New York, Viking; London, Hodder, 271p. (B'nai B'rith Jewish Heritage Classic)

---------------. How Jewry has Served America. Jewish Digest, 21, No. 10, Jy-Au. pp 77-83.

---------------. Jewish Perceptions of America: From Melting Pot to Mosaic. Syracuse, New York, Syracuse U.P., iv, 20p. (B.G. Rudolph Lectures in Judaic Studies)

KISLOV, A. and RAGOV, S. Notitsen fun dem yiddishen yishuv in USA. (Notes of the Jews in the USA). Sovietish Heimland, 16, No. 6,Ju. pp 6-19.

KLEIN, Walter F. What's Jewish About It? A Perspective on American Jewish Community Reactions to Public Issues. Journal of Jewish Communal Service, 52, No. 4, Su. pp 355-60.

Roughly since 1945, American Jewry, in an institutional and organized manner has 'gone public' on a range of issues which on the surface, at least, appear to have something less than a direct connection to our security and well-being as Jews. Beyond that, there are sometimes issues on which individuals, acting as citizens, might have legitimately differing views."

KRAMER, William. Much cause for pride, little to regret. Jewish Chronicle Colour Magazine, 3 S. pp 20-24.
Bicentennial jubilee celebration by the Synagogue Council of America at the Turo Synagogue, Newport, Rhode Island.

KRANZLER, G.G. The Changing Orthodox Jewish Community. Tradition, 16, No. 2, Fa. pp 61-72.
Decline in numbers but greater influence.

LACHMAN, Seymour P. The American Jewish Community and the Bicentennial. Jewish Education, 46, No. 1, Sp/Su. pp 25-30.
We must begin to build an American culture that is based upon substance as well as symbol, and which can lead to a knowledgeable, proud and confident American Jewish community of the future.

LIETZMANN, Sabina. New York - Die wunderbare Katastrophe. Hamburg, Hoffman und Campe, 319p, Ind, Bibl.
Portrait of New York with a special chapter and many references to the Jews.

LOOKSTEIN, Jospeh H. Coalitionism and Separatism in the American Jewish Community. Tradition, 15, No. 4, Sp. pp 233-43.
Calls on Orthodox Jews to show more understanding and solidarity with Jews adhering to other versions of Judaism

MARCUS, Jacob R. The Beginnings of American Jewry. Jewish Digest, 21, No. 10, Jy-Au. pp 9-19.

MASLOW, Will. Jewish Political Power: An Assessment. American Jewish Historical Quarterly, 66, No. 2, D. pp 349,62.

MELTZER, Milton. Taking Root: Jewish Immigrants in America. New York, Farrar, Straus and Giroux, x, 262p, Ind.
Survey of conditions under which millions of East European Jewish immigrants lived in America between 1880-1920.

---------------. World of our Fathers. The Jews of Eastern Europe. New York, Dell, 222p, Ind, Bibl. M.
Popular account of Eastern European Jewry until World War I.

MENDELSOHN, Ezra. (Ed.) Essays on the American Jewish Labor Movement. New York, Yivo Institute for Jewish Research, vii, 423p, (YIVO Annual of Jewish Social Science, V. 16)
Contents: From Sweatshop to Stability: Jewish Labor Between Two World Wars; The Russian Roots of the American Jewish Labor Movement by E. Mendelsohn. Some Remarks on Jewish Labor and American Public Opinion in the pre-World War I Era by Rudolph Glanz. The Jewish Socialists and the American Jewish Congress Movement; the Cultural Dimension of the American Jewish Labor Movement by Isaiah Trunk. Another Great Prize: The Jewish Labor Movement in the Context of American Labor History.

MEYER, Isidore S. (Ed.) The American Jew in the Civil War. New York, Kraus-Thomson. Catalog of the Exhibit of the Civil War Centennial Jewish Historical Commission. "Reprint of the Publication of the American Jewish Historical Society Quarterly, 50, No. 4.
Published in facsimile for the American Bicentennial.

NARELL, Irena Penzik. The Jewish 49ers. Jewish Digest, 21, No. 10, Jy-Au, pp 51-57. Condensed from Women's American Ort Reporter,25, 2.

NEUSTADT-NOY, Isaac. The unending task: efforts to unite American Jewry from the American Jewish Congress to the American Jewish Conference. Ann Arbor, Mich., U. Microfilms, 511p.

Ph.D. Dissertation, Brandeis U.

OLASHANSKY, Bernard. The Changing Jewish Community, Journal of Jewish Communal Services, 53, No. 1, Fa. pp 29-43.

Characterization of the American Jewish community.

PIERCE, Lorraine, E. The Jewish Settlement on St. Paul's Lower West Side. American Jewish Archives, 28, No. 2, pp 143-61.

POSTAL, Bernard. American Jewry's Long Fight for Equality. Jewish Digest, 21, No. 8, My. pp 29-34. Condensed from Pioneer Woman, 21, No. 1, Ja.

---------------. The First U.S. Town Names for a Jew. Jewish Digest 21, No. 10, Jy-Au. pp 41-43. Condensed from Judaica Post, 4, No. 2

RAAB, Earl. American Jewry in the Next 25 Years. Jewish Digest, 21, No. 10, Jy-Au. pp 84-85. Condensed from San Francisco Jewish Bulletin.

RACKMAN, Emanuel. The Future of American Jewry. Jewish Digest, 21, No. 10, Jy-Au. pp 86-93. Condensed from JWB Circle, 31, No. 3.

RAPHAEL, Chaim. The View from Here. Jewish Chronicle Colour Magazine, 3 S. pp 26-28.

RICHMOND, Michael E.M. Carter and the Jews. Does Carter's down-home born-again evangelicalism make Jews uneasy. Christian Century, 93, No. 34, 27 O. pp 926-28.

The issue of Carter and the Jews is insubstantial.

ROCHLIN, Harriet. Pioneer Jews of Arizona. Hadassah Magazine, 58, No. 10, pp 14-15;28+

A look at various prominent Jews among the several thousand that lived in Arizona during the territorial years between 1863 and 1912.

ROSENBAUM, Irving. A Jewish "Gallup Poll". Jewish Digest, 21, No. 7, Ap. pp 21-23. Condensed from The Sentinel (Chicago) Ja. 15.

ROSENSWAIKE, Ira. The Founding of Baltimore's First Jewish Congregation: Fact vs. Fiction. American Jewish Archives, 28, No. 2, N. pp 119-25.

RUBIN, Ronald I. Help for the Republicans: The Jewish Vote. New York, 6 D. pp 9-12.

"If the Republicans are willing to allocate the needed outlays in positions, in time and in party presence, Jews can be edged even further from the Democratic spectrum."

SAMUELSON, Myron. The Story of the Jewish Community of Burlington, Vermont. Burlington, Private,vi, 187p,Ill, Bibl.

---------, Robert. How the American Jewish Community Could be Democratic: A Political Model. Interchange, 1, No. 8, Ap, pp 1;6-7.

SANDERS,Ronald. The Downtown Jews. N.e. New York, Signet, xxi, 395p.

SARNA, D. Jonathan. Jewish Immigration to North America: The Canadian Experience (1870-1900). The Jewish Journal of Sociology, 18, No. 1, Ju. pp 31-41.

From 1870, immigrants to the United States settled overwhelmingly in East Coast cities, and were concentrated in a fairly narrow range of trades. In Canada, Jews from the same areas in Europe were far more widely diffused geographically and occupationally.

SCHAPPES, Morris U. (Ed.) Documentary History of the Jews in the United States. 1654-1876. R.e. New York, Schocken, London, Wildwood House, 766p.

------------------. Reflections on the Bicentennial Address at Jewish Currents Dinner, 16 My. Jewish Currents, 30, No. 7, Jy-Au. pp 26-31.

------------------. Some Jewish Foremothers of '76. Jewish Currents 30, No. 3, Ma. pp 18-21.
American Jewish women two centuries ago - address to the Emma Lazarus Federation of Jewish Women's Clubs in International Women's Year.

SHULMAN, Abraham. The New Country. New York, Scribners, 208p.
Photographic account of Jewish life in America with a long introduction.

SKLARE, Marshall. American Jewry - The Ever-Dying People. Midstream 22, No. 6, Ju-Jy. pp 17-27.
Jews might believe that theirs is a dying people, yet they have gone about implementing heroic and extraordinary measures to prolong Jewish life.

----------------. Diversity Jealously Guarded. Jewish Chronicle Colour Magazine. 3S. pp 30-36.

STEINITZ, Hans. Wandlungen und Entwicklungen im amerikanischen Judentum. "Tempel" und "Schul" haben zusammengefunden. Israelitisches Wochenblatt fur die Schweiz, 76, 21 May. pp 71-72.
Changes and developments in American Jewry.

STERN, Malcolm H. New York's Early Jews: Some Myths and Misconceptions. A lecture, with response by Marc D. Angel. New York, Jewish Historical Society, 29p.

STONE, Amy and SZONYI, David. Jews in Congress. Moment, 1, No. 10, My-Ju. pp 27-32.
The presence and behaviour of 21 Jews in the U.S. Congress shows that American Jewry has come of age of politically.

TOBIN, Gary Allan. Ethnic mobility in a suburban community (St. Louis, Mo.) Ann Arbor, Mich., U. Microfilms, 453p.
Ph.D. Dissertation, U. of California, Berkeley.
Includes Jews.

TUCHFELD, Barry S. The "Involuntary" Voluntary Organisation: Social Control in a Southern Jewish Community. Contemporary Jewry, 1, No. 2, Fa/W.
Participation in Jewish voluntary organisations is highly related to women. Comments from respondents implied that participation in voluntary organisations served as a means of social control within the Jewish community ... Males showed less concern. The community studies is Knoxville, Tennessee.

UNITED STATES AND OTHER COUNTRIES. American Jewish Year Book, 76, pp 115-442.
Events in Jewish communities of U.S.A., Canada, Latin America, U.K., Germany, Austria, U.S.S.R., Czechoslovakia, Yugoslavia, Israel, South Africa, Australia.

WARSHAW, Mal. Tradition. Orthodox Jewish Life in America. New York, Schocken in association with the exhibition 'Tradition' at the Brooklyn Museum. 24 S. - 28 N. 118p.

WHITEMAN, Maxwell. The Jewish Peddler in Colonial Times. Pioneers of American Merchandising. Jewish Digest, 21, No. 10, Jy-Au. pp 3-8. Condensed from Studies and Essays in Honor of Abraham A. Neuman.

Why the Jewish Vote is Crucial for Presidential Candidates. Events, 19 N. pp 22-24.

Arab view of the 'Jewish vote'.

WIERNIK, Peter. History of the Jews in America, from the Period of the Discovery of the New World to the Present Time. 2.e. Westport, Conn., Greenwood P.; London, Westport P., xxxii, 475p, Ill.

Reprint of 1931 edition.

WIESELTIER, Leon. Only in America. New York Review of Books, 15 Jy. pp 22-28.

The world of our Fathers was a doomed world and it died. Whether their descendants can overcome complacence and reform their own world remains to be seen.

WOLF, Arnold Jacob. American Jewish Community. Fritz Mondale Visits the Jews. Interchange, 2, No. 3, pp 3ff.

YAFFE, Richard. From Commerce to Beneficience. Jewish Chronicle Colour Magazine, 3 S. pp 43-48.

U.S.S.R.

DERIENSKO, Petria. Af der birobidzhaner erd. (On Birobidzhan soil) Sovietish Heimland, 16, No. 3, Ma. pp 21-24.

A Moldavian writer describes her visit.

ERRERA, Leon Abram. Russian Jews: Extermination or Emancipation? Tr. from French: B. Lowry. Westport, Conn., Greenwood P.; London, Westport P., x, 206p, M.

Reprint of 1894 edition.

FISHER, Wesley. Kol Kidre in Moscow: A Soviet Specialist's Lament. Response, 10, Nos. 2-3, Su/Fa. pp 163-67.

GILBERT, Martin. The Jews of Russia. Their History in Maps and Photographs. London,National Council for Soviet Jewry of the U.K. and Ireland. 78p, Ill, M.

GREENBERG, Louis. Jews in Russia: Struggle for Emancipation 1772-1917. 2 vols in 1. R.e. New York, London, Schocken, 214p.

LEVIN,S. Among the Remains (Tourist Guide of Lithuania, discovered among numerous old documents left behind by his parents). Jewish Affairs, 36, No. 11, N. pp 31-32.

RIVINA, I. Der denkmol in Babij-Yar. (The Babi-Yar Memorial) Sovietish Heimland, 16, No. 1, Ja. pp 121-23.

Article first published by Novosti describing the events in Babi Yar as seen by the last 15 who eventually escaped murder.

SHAPIRO, L. Sachaklen un prespektiven. (Results and Perspectives) Sovietish Heimland, 16, No. 3, Ma. pp 10-16.

The Secretary of the Communist Party Central Committee in Birobidzhan surveys the achievements of the Jewish region.

SHKOLNIK, Leonid. Der veg fun yorhundert. (The Way of the Century) Sovietish Hiemland, 16, No. 1, Ja. pp 4-61.

History of the Birobidzhan settlement.

SHUSTER, Y. Kovner Melodies. (Kovno melodies) Sovietish Heimland, 16, No. 9, S. pp 156-62.

Jewish life in Kovno.

WINCELBERG, Shimon and Anita. The Samurai of Vishograd. The Notebooks of Jacob Marateck. Philadelphia, Jewish Publication Society of America, 206p.

YEMEN

HABSUS, Hayyim. Immagine dello Yemen. Ed. Gabriella Moscate Steidler. Napoli, Istituto Orientale, xxiv, 167p.
Includes the Jews of Yemen.

JEWISH ORGANISATIONS

AMERICAN JEWISH COMMITTEE. Decades of Decision: A Brief History of the American Jewish Committee, New York, 19p.
------------------------. The First Seventy Years, New York, 18p.
AMERICAN JEWISH JOINT DISTRIBUTION COMMITTEE. Annual Report 1975. New York, 20p.
ANTI-DEFAMATION LEAGUE OF B'NAI B'RITH. An Ethnic Dimension in American History: a unit of immigration, industrialization, urbanisation and imperialism, 1880-1920: resource guide. New York, 85p.
BLINDERMAN, Abraham. The Vanishing Landsmanschaften. What They Meant to Jewish Life. Jewish Digest, 2, No. 1, Jy-Au. pp 73-76.
Groups of Jewish immigrants from the same area formed Landsmanschaften.
CLAWAR, Stanley S. Neo-Vigilantism in America: An Analysis of the Jewish Defence League. Ann Arbor, Mich., U. Microfilms, 391p, Bibl.
Ph.D. Dissertation, Bryn Mawr College.
COHEN, Richard. Background to Brussels II: The Struggle for Soviet Jewry Enters a New Phase. Congress Monthly, 143, No. 2, F. pp 3-5.
Report by the chief press officer of Brussels I and Brussels II on the situation confronting Soviet Jews on the eve of the World Conference and on the new phase of activity on behalf of Soviet Jews that will be inaugerated at Brussels.
--------------. World Jewry: United in Solidarity With the Jews of The U.S.S.R. Congress Monthly, 43, No. 3, Ma. pp 4-7.
A report on the Second World Conference on Soviet Jewry, which took place in February in Brussels.
Compassion in Action: A Continuing Task. A Study of the American Jewish Joint Distribution Committee, Inc., New York, AJJDC, 42p, Ill.
DECTER, Moshe. Crisis in the Soviet Jewry Movement. Moment, 1, No. 4, Ap. pp 33-48.
Criticises the leadership of the movement in America and Israel.
EPSTEIN, David M. Working With Federation as a Strategy for Jewish Social Change. Response, 10, Nos. 2-3, Su/Fa. pp 71-80.
FEINGOLD, Henry L. The Illusion of Centrality. National Jewish Monthly, 90, No. 11, Jy-Au. pp 30-31.
"Jewish objectives are ill-defined and out of reach."
GENOOTSCHAP NEDERLAND-ISRAEL. AFDELING Z.W. - VELUWE Dokumentatie en handleiding. Heelsum, 57p.
The Netherlands-Israel Friendship League's work.

GENERAL FEDERATION OF JEWISH LABOUR IN ISRAEL. Executive Committee. Documents and Essays on Jewish Labour Policy in Palestine. Westport Conn., Greenwood P.; London, Westport P., 239p.
Contemporary papers, reprint of the 1930 edition.

GRONER, Irwin, HIMMELFARB, Milton and SIDORSKY, David. Jewish Communal Organization: Democracy and Leadership. Journal of Jewish Communal Service, 52, No. 3, Sp. pp 235-39.

HADASSAH: The Women's Zionist Organisation of America. 1975/76 Hadassah annual projects report, 62nd National Convention, Au.15-18 1976, Washington, 40p.

HOROWITZ, Benjamin. Hakoah in New York (1926-32) A New Dimension for American Jewry. Judaism, 25, No. 3, Su. pp 375-82.

LEVIN, Morris. Needed - A New Institution. Journal of Jewish Communal Service, 52, No. 3, Fa. pp 52-62.
Jewish institutions have changed probably less than their constituents.

MILLER, Charles. An Introduction to the Jewish Federation. New York, Council of Jewish Federations and Welfare Funds, 32p.

NEUSNER, Jacob. Facing the Future in the Present. Jewish Affairs, 31, No. 6, Ju. pp 16-20.
An Address to the 29th National Congress of the South African Jewish Board of Deputies.

REISMAN, Bernard. An Alternative Perspective on Training Jewish Communal Workers. Journal of Jewish Communal Service, 52, No. 4, Su. pp 338-43.
In the Jewish field the additional requirement of weaving in a Jewish component adds to the complexity of designing a training programme.

ROME, David. The Congress Archival Record of 1934. Montreal, Canadian Jewish Congress, 131p, Ind, (Mimeo) (Canadian Jewish Archives, 6)
A year in the history of the Canadian Jewish Congress.

ROSENBAUM, Fred. Free to Choose: The Making of a Jewish Community in the American West. The Jews of Oakland, California from the Gold Rush to the Present Day. Berkeley, Ca. Judah L. Magnes Memorial Museum, 164p.

SCHWAB, Walter M. B'nai B'rith. Fifty Years of Achivement 1926-76. London, B'nai B'rith District of Great Britain and Ireland. 80p, Ind, Ill.
Short history of the BB Lodges in the U.K.

VINCENT, Sidney Z. The Jewish Federation: Reflections on the American Institution. Waltham, Mass., Philip W. Lown Graduate Center in Contemporary Jewish Studies, Brandeis U., 14p.

WORLD JEWISH CONGRESS: 40 Years in Action. A record of the World Jewish Congress 1936-76. Ed. by George Garai. Geneva, London, 62p, Ill. (Also in French)

SEPHARDI AND
ORIENTAL JEWS

ANGEL, Marc D. Sephardim in America. Present Tense, 4, No. 1, Aut. pp 12-14.

Despite manifestations of a revival of interest, doubts that a real renaissance of a living Judeo-Spanish culture will take place.

BIRNBAUM, Ruth. The Uniqueness of the Early Sephardic Community in America. Judaism, 25, No. 1, W. pp 44-53.

ROUMANI, Maurice M. The Case of the Jews from Arab Countries: A Neglected Issue. In: Case Studies on Human Rights and Fundamental Freedoms. A World Survey. Vol, 5, The Hague, M. Nijhoff, pp 69-100.

Emigration of Jews from Arab countries since 1948 and their settlement in Israel. Persecution of Jews in the Arab states.

SOEN, D. Oriental Ethnic Groups and Their Place in the Social Stratification of Israel. Sociology, 26, No. 1, pp 51-65.

ZIMMELS, Hirsch Jacob. Askenazim and Sephardim. 3.e. London, Marla, xiv, 347p.

LEADERSHIP

CUTTER, William. Thoughts on Jewish Professional Training. Journal of Jewish Communal Service, 52, No. 4, Su. pp 331-37.

Any curriculum grounded exclusively in theoretical concerns about professional life, or in pure academic study in bound to be inadequate. The Jewish professional needs Jewish knowledge and consciousness and the ability to think originally.

EDELSBERG, Herman. Beyond Israel and Quotas. Soviet Jewry and Arab Boycott, there are broader considerations of leadership and trust. National Jewish Monthly, 91, No. 1, S. pp 22-34.

"LEADERSHIP DEVELOPMENT" A 10 week Training Program for Jewish Community Centers and Y's. A Project of the JWB Leadership Development Committee and the Jewish Community Center of Cleveland, Ohio, New York, National Jewish Welfare Board, 35p. (Mimeo.)

VINCENT, Sidney Z. Shaping a More Creative and Responsive Community - The Role of Leadership. New York, Council of Jewish Federations and Welfare Funds, 10p.

LEGAL PROBLEMS

DERSCHOWITZ, Alan M., SILVERGATE, Harvey A., BAKER, Jeanne. The JDL Murder Case. "The Informer Was Our Own Client." The Civil Liberties Review. No. 2, Ap-My. pp 43-60.

"In any particular case, especially one as serious as the Hurok bombing, the cost may be excessive; but considering how rarely the courts impose such costs, every decision like that rendered in the Siegel (the murder defendant) case is a victory for civil liberties."

MORRIS, J.B. The American Jewish Judge: An Appraisal on the Occasion of the Bicentennial. Jewish Social Studies, 38, Nos. 3-4, pp 195-223.

Jewish contribution to justice in the U.S.A

RAMBAUD, Patrick. La définition de l'agression par l'organisation des Nations Unies. Revue Générale de Droit International Public, 80, No. 3, Jy-S. pp 835-61.

JEWISH LAW

FUSS, Abraham M. (Ed.) Studies in Jewish Jurisprudence. Vol. IV: Criminal Law. New York, Sepher Hermon, 312p.

GAMORAN, H. Talmudic Usury Laws and Business Loans. Journal for the Study of Judaism in the Persian, Hellenistic and Roman Period, 7, No. 2, pp 129-42.

Shows how the Rabbis interpreted the scripture injunction against interest in order to permit commercial transactions that would violate the law.

GOLDFARB, Solomon D. Who is a Jewish Child? Conservative Judaism, 30, No. 4, Su. pp 3-9.

JACKSON, B.S. Essays in Jewish and Comparative Legal History. Leiden, Brill, 264p. (Studies in Judaism in Late Antiquity, X)

MEISLIN, Bernard J. Jewish Law in American Tribunals, New York, Ktav. 233p.

Precedents where American Courts applied Jewish Law.

PEASE, Louis Edwin. After the Holocaust: West Germany and material reparation to the Jews - from the Allied occupation to the Luxemburg agreements. Ann Arbor, Mich., U. Microfilms, 605p.

Ph.D. Dissertation, Florida State University.

INTERNATIONAL LAW

MEISSNER, Boris., FRENZKE, Dietrich, CHILECKI, Erika. (Eds.) Sowjetunion und Völkerrecht 1963-73. Wissenschaft und Politik. 530p.

GENOCIDE

HOROWITZ, Irving Louis. Genocide: State Power and Mass Murder. New Brunswick, N.J. Transaction Books, 80p, Ind, Bibl.

Asserts that genocide is not an accident of history but mass murder conducted with the approval of the State apparatus.

U.S. Congress. House. Committee on International Relations. Investigation into certain past instances of genocide and exploration of policy options for the future. Hearings before the Subcommittee on Future Foreign Policy Research and Development... 11 My. - 30 Au. Washington, U.S. Govt. Print. Off., 275p.

HUMAN RIGHTS

BOSSUYT, Marc. L'Interdiction de la Discrimination dans le Droit International des Droits de l'Homme. Brussels, Emile Bruylant, xi, 262p, Ind, Bibl.

Commentary on the prevention of discrimination in international legislation on Human Rights, published when the UN Human Rights Covenants came into force.

GOODMAN, Lenn Evan. Equality and Human Rights: The Lockean and the Judaic Views. Judaism, 25, No. 3, Su. pp 357-62.

HENKIN, Louis. Judaism and Human Rights. Judaism, 25, No. 4, Fa. pp 435-46.

Human Rights in Jewish religious thought. The Jewish Experience and the Protection of Human Rights. The Jewish Contribution to Human Rights, Law and Institutions. Disappointment and Reviving Fears in Recent Years.

Human Rights Around the World: The U.S. and the U.N.: Special Issue Freedom at Issue, Ja-F. pp 1-32.

Includes: Middle East: Optimism and Despair Commingled by Don. Peretz.

LUCA, Costa. (Pseud.) Legal Discrimination Among Arabs. Patterns of Prejudice, 10, No. 4, pp 1-14.

Written by a prominent Arab businessman who travels extensively in the Middle East and knows the problems discussed from personal observation, as well as scholarly study.

MAWDUDI, Abul A'la. Human Rights in Islam. London, Newsmedia, 43p.

THE ORGANISATION OF AMERICAN STATES AND HUMAN RIGHTS. Activity of the Inter-American Commission on Human Rights 1969-70. Washington, D.C. Secretariat of the Inter-American Commission on Human Rights, vii, 547p, Ind, Bibl.

Papers on the protection of human rights in Latin America.

VEENHOVEN, Willem A., GRUM EWING, Winifred and others (Eds.) Case Studies on Human Rights and Fundamental Freedoms. A World Survey. The Hague, Nijhoff for Foundation for the Study of Plural Societies, 3, xiii, 579p; 4, xi, 568p; 5, x, 589p, M.

Of special interestin Vol. 3_ Homogenity and Pluralism in the Middle East: The Case of Lebanon by Moshe Ma'oz which deals extensively with the Palestinians and America's Minorities by S. J. Makielski, Jr. which deals extensively with the Jews. In Vol. 4: The Problems of National Minorities in the USSR by Edward J. Rozek and The Persecution of Christians in the USSR by Michael Bordeaux.
In Vol. 5: The Case of the Jews from Arab Countries: A Neglected Issue by Maurice A. Roumani.

RELIGIOUS RIGHTS

THE AMERICAN JEWISH CONGRESS: COMMISSION ON LAW, SOCIAL ACTION AND URBAN AFFAIRS. Docket of Pending Cases affecting Freedom of Religion and Separation of Church and State No. 19. New York, American Jewish Congress, 62p.

LALIGANT, M. Problématique actuelle du droit à la liberté religieuse. In: La Casas et la politique des droits de l'homme, Aix-en-Provence, 12, 13, 14 O. 1974. Institut d'Etudes Politiques d'Aiz, pp 321-44.

Difference in conception of religious liberty according to religious domination.

SHOHAM, Gilbert L. Religion in a Democratic Society. Reconstructionist, 42, No. 7, O. pp 7-10.

SORAUF, Frank J. The Wall of Separation: The Constitutional Politics of Church and State. Princeton, N.J., U.P.; New York, Columbia U.P., xiii, 394p.

WHARTMAN, Eliezer. Freedom of Religion. Jewish Affairs, 31, No. 6, Ju. pp 39-41.

RACIAL DISCRIMINATION

LEAR, Elmer N. Affirmative Action: An International Perspective. American Zionist, 66, No. 7, My-Ju. pp 16-18.

MINORITY RIGHTS

DINSTEIN, Yoram. Collective Human Rights of Peoples and Minorities. International and Comparative Law Quarterly, 25, No. 1, Ja. pp 102-20.

HAGOPIAN, Elaine. Minority Rights in a Nation-State: The Nixon Administration's Campaign Against Arab Americans. Journal of Palestine Studies, 5, Nos. 1-2, Aut. 1975/W. 1976, pp 97-114.

SACUIK, Olena and YASEN, Bohdan. (Eds.) SAHAYDAK, Maksym (Comp.) Intro. by Robert Conquest. Ethnocide of Ukrainians in the USSR. Baltimore, Paris, Toronto, Smolosky, 209p, Ind.

It appears that the new Ukrainian nationalism, as it is expressed here, has rid itself of its notorious antisemitism and "has actually come to regard the Jewish population with special friendship, as fellow-sufferers under the same oppression." (R. Conquest.)

UIBOPUU, Henn-Jüri. The International Legal Status of Soviet Minorities Today. Review of Socialist Law, 2, No. 4, pp 217-31.

INDEMNIFICATION

BÖHM, Franz. Das deutsch-israelische Abdommen 1952. Offprint from "Konrad Adenauer und seine Zeit". Politik und Persönlichkeit des ersten Bundeskanzlers. Beiträge von Weg- und Zeitgenossen. Stuttgart, Deutsche Verlags-Anstalt. pp 437-65.

Professor Böhm played a major role in bringing about the German-Israeli reparations agreement of 1952.

POLITICAL PROBLEMS, PARTIES, MOVEMENTS

NAZISM

ADLER, H. G. Die Freiheit des Menschen. Aufsätze zur Soziologie und Geschichte. Tübingen, J.C.B. Mohr. (Paul Siebeck) 358p, Ind.

Essays on human liberty, nationalism, Nazism, persecution and allied subjects.

BINION, Rudolph. Hitler Among the Germans. New York, Oxford, Amsterdam, Elsevier, xiv, 208p, Ind, Bibl.

Exploration of the psychodynamics of Hitler's rise to power and his rule of Germany. The author devotes a large part of the book to the study of Hitler's antisemitism.

Biomedical Ethics and the Shadow of Nazism: Special Supplement. The Hastings Center Report, New York, Au.

A Conference on the proper use of the Nazi analogy in ethical debate, 8 Ap. 1976. Participants included Lucy S. Davidowicz, Milton Himmelfarb and Telford Taylor.

BOTZ, Gerhard. National Socialist Vienna: Antisemitism as a Housing Policy. Wiener Library Bulletin, 29, N.S. Nos. 39-40, pp 47-55.

BRACHER, Karl Dietrich. Zeitgeschichtliche Kontroversen um Faschismus, Totalitarianismus, Demokratie, Muenchen, Piper, 159p. (serie Piper 142)

German political scientist and expert on national-socialism argues that contemporary critics of nazism, especially on the Left fall into the trap of viewing Nazism as a purely socio-economic phenomenon and by generalising historical and political issues they commit the mistakes of the 20s and 30s. The second half of the book discusses the consequences of the Nazi regime for the Federal German Republic.

BYTWERK, Randall T. Julius Streicher and the Impact of Der Stürmer. Wiener Library Bulletin, 29, N.S. NOs. 39-40, pp 41-46.

DALEY, Robert. The Case of the SS Hero. The New York Times Magazine, 7 N. pp 32-33; 102+

For former Nazi Col. Joachim Peiper, World War II ended violently on July 4, 1976 in a remote French village, Or did it?

DENKLER, Horst und PRUMM, Karl. (Eds.) Die deutsche Literatur im Dritten Reich. Themen - Traditionen - Wirkungen, Stuttgart, Reclam, 556p, Ind.

Collection of essays analysing the destructive nature of literature in the Third Reich, including antisemitic elements.

GROSSER, Alfred. Dix leçons sur le nazism. Paris, Fayard, 251p.

HAUSCHILD, Hans. Erzieher im Dritten Reich. München Gladbach, Elsbeth Rutten, 175p.

Reminiscences of a German teacher of the Nazi years before the war and the systematic indoctrination of children and youth.

HENRY, Clarissa and HILLEN, Marc. Children of the SS. London, Hutchinson, Tr. by Eric Mosbacher, 256p, Ind, Ill.

First published in French in 1975. Study of the Nazi's attempt to develop a controlled human breeding stock.

HORN, Daniel. The Hitler Youth and Educational Decline in the Third Reich. History of Education Quarterly, 16, No. 3, pp 425-47.

HUDAL, Alois C. Römische Tagebücher. Lebensbeichte eines alten Bischofs. Graz, Leopold Stocker, 316p, Ind, Ill.

Bishop Hudal was, from 1923, Rector of Anima, the college of the German National Foundation. Under the impact of Italian Fascism, he published "The Fundamentals of Nationalism-Socialism" which was the beginning of his dedicated work to build a bridge between the Catholic Church and the Nazis.

HUMBEL, Kurt. Nationalsocialistische Propaganda in der Schweiz 1931-39. Einige Hauptaspekte der mittel. Technik, Inhalte, Methoden und Wirkungen der deutschen Propaganda gegenüber Auslanddeutschen und Deutschschweizern sowie behördliche Abwehrmassahmen. Bern, Paul Haupt. 295p, (Res publica helvetica)

Important study on Nazi influence in Switzerland prior to the outbreak of World War II.

INFIELD, Glenn B. Leni Riefenstahl: The Fallen Film Goddess. A Study of the Filmmaker who Gained Notoriety During the Third Reich. New York, T. Y. Crowell.

MASER, Werner. Hitler's Letters and Notes. Tr. by Arnold Pomerans, New York, London, Bantam, xi, 390p, Ind, Ill.

Paperback English edition of the book published in 1973.

MÜLLER-MEHLIS, Reinhard. Die Kunst im Dritten Reich. 2.e. Munchen, Wilhelm Heyne, 230p, Ill.

Dissects Nazi art, chiefly architecture.

PACHTER, Henry. Heidegger and Hitler. The Incompatibility of Geist and Politics. Boston University Journal, 24, No. 3, pp 47-55.

PRYCE-JONES, David. Unity Mitford. A Quest. London, Weidenfeld & Nicolson, 276p, Ind, Ill, Bibl.

Biography of Sir Oswald Mosley's sister-in-law who was an ardent follower of the Nazis.

RIPPLEY, La Vern J. German Americans. New York, Twayne, London, G. Prior, 271p.

Includes their behaviour during World War II and their attitude to Nazism.

ROXAN, David and WANSTALI, Ken. Jackdaw of Linz: Story of Hitler's Art Thefts. London, White Lion, N.e. xii, 196p, Ind, Ill.

SANDMANN, Fritz. L'Osservatore Romano e il nazional-socialismo, 1929-39. Roma, Cinque Lune, viii, 403p, Ind, Bibl.

The enciclical "Mit brennender Sorge" of Pius XI and Nazi anticlericalism. The Vatican's policies.

SEABURY, Paul. The Wilhelmstrasse: A Study of German Diplomat's under the Nazi Regime. Westport, Conn., Greenwood P.; London, Westport P., 217p, Ill.

Examines the Foreign Office involvement in Nazi crimes.

STEINER, John M. Power Politics and Social Change in National Socialist Germany. A process of escalation into Mass Destruction. Hague, Paris, Mouton, xx, 466p, Ind, Bibl.

Analysis of the inner attitudes and motivations of Nazis leading to their genocidal actions. Deals extensively with the mass-murder of Jews. Based on hitherto unpublished documents, question of over 450 former SS and soldiers. Memoirs of notorious Nazi leaders.

STIERLIN, Helm. Adolf Hitler: A Family Perspective. New York, Psychohistory P. for the Institute of Psychohistory. 163p, Ind, Bibl.

Analysis of Hitler's psychological make-up, seeking to explain his behaviour by his mother-fixation and desire to avenge his mother's death.

THIESS, Jochen. Architekt der Weltherrschaft. Die "Endziekle" Hitlers. Duesseldorf, Droste, 221p, Ind, Bibl.

Contends, on the basis of his research, that Hitler did not aim at Germany's equality with other great powers, but sought to establish a racially 'pure' base from which he was to rule the world.

TOLAND, John. Adolf Hitler. New York, Doubleday, London, Trans-atlantic Book Service, x, 1035p, Ind, Ill.

Biography, based on partly new documents and 150 taped interviews with persons directly involved with Hitler.

UNITED STATES, DEPARTMENT OF STATE, DIVISION OF EUROPEAN AFFAIRS: National Socialism: Basic Principles. Their Application by Nazi Party's Foreign Organisation and the Use of Germans Abroad for Nazi Aims. Westport, Conn., Greenwood P.; London, Westport P., vi, 510p.

Reprint of the 1943 edition.

NEO-NAZISM

ALLEN, Charles R. Jr. The Hitler Boom and Fascism. New York, Jewish Currents, 44p, Bibl.

Reprint of articles published in Jewish Currents on the recent emergence of interest in the Nazis and the emergence of neo-Nazi literature.

ARONSFELD, C.C. The National Front - Progress and Prospects. Jewish Frontier, 43, No. 8, O. pp 14-16.

A British neo-Nazi movement.

ASHKENAZI, Abraham. Modern German Nationalism. New York, London, Sydney, Toronto, John Wiley and Sons, xvi, 222p. (A Halstead Press Book)

Contends that German authoritarianism and nationalism has survived National Socialism in the Federal Repuhlic. In the last chapter he gives a content-analysis of three Right-wing newspapers in an election situation. Deutsche Nachrichten, Deutsche National-Zeitung. Bayern-Kurier.

BARBIERI, Daniele. Agenda nera. Trent'anni di neofascismo in Italia. Roma, Coines, 340p, Ind, (Universale Coines 35)

Analyses the rebirth and evolution of neo-fascism in Italy, its international ramifications and impact on Italy's political life since the end of the war. The work is based on neo-fascist periodicals, of which there is an index, as well as an index of the national and international fascist organisations.

BULAWKO, H. Les néo-nazis belges s'agitent. Regards, 12, No. 108, N.-D. pp 15-16.

BUTZ, Arthur R. The Hoax of the Twentieth Century. Richmond, Surrey. Historical Review Press, 315p, Ind, Bibl.

Antisemitic work; trying to show that the Nazi murder of six million Jews is a myth.

CHRISTOPHERSEN, Thies. Die Auschwitz-Lüge, 2.e. Mohrkirch, Kritik, Die Stimme des Volk, Nr. 23, 62p. In Spanish: Buenos Aires, Ed. Milicia (Biblioteca de Formation Doctrinarria)

Antisemitic neo-Nazi pamphlet denying the Holocaust.

CORDOVA-CLAURE, Ted. Swastikas in Argentina. Atlas World Press Review, 11, No. 11, N. pp 14-16.

"A resurgent neo-Nazi movement finds fertile ground" Reprinted from the newsmagazine Resumen of Caracas.

L'epidemie néo-nazie et antisémite s'étend. Regards, 12, No. 108, N.-D. pp 8-12.

FUTTERKNECHT, Franz. Das Dritte Reich im deutschen Roman der Nachkriegszeit. Untersuchungen zur Faschismus-theorie und Faschismusbewältigung. Bonn, Bouvier, 342p, Ind, Bibl. (Literature und Wirklichkeit, 17)

The author analyses some of the major novels published in Germany since the end of World War II, whose authors show the true face of the Third Reich. This phenomenon is part of the wish to overcome the Nazi past.

KARDELL, Hennecke. Das oeffentliche Aergernis, und die antibürokratische Sehnsucht. Geneve, Marve, 354p.

Attacks the Federal German Republic's bureaucracy for its attitude to Nazis and neo-Nazis and for being too friendly to Jews and Israel.

MURCIA, Pier Guiseppe. Ritorneremo! Storia e cronaca de fascismo dopo la resistenza. Milano, Sugar, 413p.
"We shall Return" Post-War fascism in Italy.

RUDEL, Hans Ulrich. Trotzdem. Kriegs-und Nachkriegszeit. Preuss, Oldenorf, K.W. Schütz, 474p, Ill.
A hero of neo-Nazis, Rudel has returned to Germany from self-imposed exile in Argentina. These are his memoirs of war and aftermath and thoughts on present-day Germany.

THADDEN, Adolf von. Die Erbschaft der Giganten. Adolf Hitler und Josef Stalin. Weltbeweger - Partner - Antagonisten. Leoni, Druffel, 256p, Ind, Ill, Bibl.
The author is now the leader of the neo-Nazi party NPD in Germany.

FASCISM

ARISMENDI, R. A fasizmus Latin-Amerikában. Nemzetközi Szemle, 20, No. 10, O. pp 48-59.
Fascism in Latin America. A Hungarian view.

BONFANTI, Guiseppe. Il Fascismo: 1. La conquista del potere. Documenti e testimonianze di storia contemporanea. Brescia, La Scuola, 192p, Ill, Bibl.
Documented study of the Fascist conquest of Italy. Includes a study of Fascist racialist policies.

CIANFLONE, Geppina and SCAFOGLIO, Domenico. Fascismo sui Muri, Le scritte murali neofasciste di Napoli. Napoli, Guida, 113p, Ill. (La Terra Deportata 1.)
Description and analysis of the neofascist grafitti that appear on Naples walls. It would appear that the presence of neofascism in Naples with all its complexities might give the impression that it was one of the most vocal political movements in the city.

ERDMANN, Karl Dietrich. Nationalsozialismus, Faschismus, Totalitarismus. Geschichte in Wissenschaft und Unterricht, 27, No. 8, Au. pp 457-69.

DE FELICE, Renzo. (Ed.) Antologia sul Fascismo. Il Guidizio Storico. Bari, Laterza, 279p. (Tempi Nuovi Laterza S.)
Selected texts on the many apsects of fascism written from a variety of viewpoints and annotated by Professor De Felice.

----------------. Fascism: An Informal Introduction to its Theory and Practice. New Brunswick, N.J. Transaction Books, 128p. Tr. from Italian: "Intervista sul fascismo", Bari, Laterza.
Professor de Felice, outstanding scholar on fascism, briefly summarizes its basic tenets.

HOFFMAN, Gerard H. Canadian Fascist Movements in the thirties. Jewish Frontier, 43, No. 1, Ja. pp 26-28.

KÜHNL, Reinhard. Aspekte der Faschismusdiskussion. Historische Aufarbeitung und aktuelle Bedeutung. Für Wolfgang Abendroth zum 70. Geburtstag. Blätter für deutsche und internationale Politik, 21, pp 531-49.

LAQUEUR, Walter. Fascism - The Second Coming. Commentary, 52, No.2, F. pp 57-62.
"Seen in historical perspective, European fascism may have been not so much the end of an era as the precursor of a new dark age."

MAIOCCHI, Maria Antonietta. La Donna "Nera". "Consenso" femminile e fascismo. Milano, Feltrinelli, 1-2p.
Social, historical and psychological motives of women who in their masses joined the Fascist Movement in Italy.

NEMES, Dezső . A fasizmus kérdéséhez. Budapest, Magvető, 147p. (Gyorsuló Idő)
"On the Question of Fascism" by a member of the Politbureau of the Hungarian Communist Party. Deals with Italian and German fascism, the class-quality of fascism, on the debates relating to fascism and with the fascist era in Hungary, with special emphasis on its antisemitic nature.

NESTI, A. La question catholique et le fascisme. (English Summary) Social Compass, 23, No. 3, pp 171-96.
Analyses the relationship between Catholicism and fascism in different periods.

ORMOS, Mária and INCZE, Miklos. Európai fasizmusok 1919-39. Budapest, Kossuth, 312p, Ind, Bibl. (Magyar Tudományos Akademia Törtenettudomanyi Intézete)
Treats fascism as a manifestation of bourgeois society and details the fascist movements in Europe country by country.

QUAZZA, Guido. (Ed.) Fascismo e Antifascismo nell'italia repubblicana. Torino, Stampatori, 189p.
Proceedings of a Seminar in contemporary history discussing Fascism and anti-Fascism in post-war Italy.

RABINBACH, Anson G. Marxistische Faschismustheorian. Ein Überblick. Aesthetik und Kommunikation, 7, No. 26, pp 4-19.

REBATET, Lucien. Les mémoires d'un fasciste. V.1. Les décombres 1938-40. V.2. 1941-47. Paris, Pauvert, 610p and 268p.
Rabatet was a French fascist journalist and political writer, a collaborator, whose racialist book was first published during the occupation in 100,000 copies. He was sentenced to death, pardoned, released in 1952 and died in 1972.

SAAGE, Richard. Faschismustheorien. Eine Einfuehrung. Muenchen, C.H. Beck, 184p, Bibl. (Beck'sche Schwarze Reihe 141)
In contrast with other critics of fascism, the author presents the socio-economic dimensions of national-socialism and does not analyse the personalities or the demonology of fascist ideology.

SANTANGELO, Antonio. Analisi del comportamento fascista. Milano, Moizzi, 124p.
Illustrates the regressive structure of society as presented by a fascist model.

SCHIEDER, Wolfgang. (Ed.) Faschismus also soziale Bewegung. Hamburg, Hoffman und Campe, 216p, Ind. (Historische Perspectiven 3)
Essays on fascism as a social movement in Italy and Germany, presented at the German Historians' Conference in 1974. Contributions by Michael H. Kater, Hans Mommsen, Ernst Nolte, Jens Petersen, Wolfgang Schieder, Heinrich August Winkler.

SCOPPOLA, Pietro. La Chiesa e il facismo. Documenti e interpretazione. Bari, Laterza, xiv, 415p, Bibl.
The Vatican and Mussolini, annotated documents relating to the Lateran Treaty.

Theories of Fascism: Special Issue. Journal of Contemporary History, 11, No. 3, O. pp 1-282.
Includes: German Society, Hitler and the Illusion of Restoration 1930-33 by Heinrich A. Winkler. French Fascism and Modernization by Klaus-Jürgen Müller. The Cult of the Duce in Mussolini's Italy by Piero Melograni.

TOGLIATTI, P. A fasizmusról. A fasiszta diktatúra fo jellemvonásai. Dokumentumok. Történelmi Szemle, 18, No. 3, Ma. pp 439-57.
Analysis of the main characteristics of Fascist dictatorship.

VAGDA, Mihaly. Fascism as a Mass Movement. London, Allison & Busby, 140p, Ind.

VESPIGNANI, Renzo et al. (Ed.) Faschismus. Neue Gesellschaft für bildende Kunst und Kunstamt Kreuzberg. Berlin, Hamburg, Elefanten P.,xvi, 167p, Ill.
Illustrated documentation on fascist and Nazi culture and propaganda directed against "subversives" including Jews.

WIPPERMAN, Wolfgang. Faschismustheorien. 3.e. Darmstadt, Wissenschaftliche Buchgesellschaft, x, 183p, M.
Essays.

WISTRICH, Robert S. (Ed.) Theories of Fascism. London, Beverley Hills, Ca., Sage 220p.
Essays.

RADICAL RIGHT

DUPRAT, Francois. Les mouvements d'extrème droits en France. Paris, Revue d'histoire du fascisme, V.1. 1940-41; V.2. 1942-44, 104p.

INNERE SICHERHEIT. Informationen des Bundesministeriums des Innern, Bonn., 25 Ju. 44p.
The Federal German Minister of the Interior's report on Right and Left Radical Movements.

VERHOEYEN, E. L'Extrème-droiteen Belgique. Bruxelles, C.R.S.P. 3 vols.
Documentation on the Belgian extreme Right.

WALENDY, Udo. Die Methoden der Umerziehung. Norderstedt, Nordland-Buchdienst Dettner, 40p.
Suggests ways to re-educate Germans so as to obviate the rise of the Radical Right.

ZORATTO, Brune and LECHNER, BRUNHILDE. Italiens Neue Rechte. Homberg/Ohm, Buchvertrieb (Klaus Jahn) 79p.
Origins and development of Italy's neo-Fascist movement.

ANTI-FASCISM/ ANTI-NAZISM

ZANI, Luciano. Italia Libera. Il primo movimento antifascista clandestino 1923-25. Bari, Laterza, 185p.
The beginnings of the anti-Fascist movement in Italy.

RADICAL LEFT

LEVIN, Nora. Jewish Socialist Movements 1871-1917. New York, Schocken, 554p, Bibl. Ind.

LEVINE, Norman. On the Necessity of a Jewish-Marxist Dialogue. Judaism, 25, No. 1, W. pp 107-14.

LEWIS, Aubrey. Jewish Socialists in England Speak Out. Jewish Currents, 30, No. 5, My. pp 14-17.

LIEBMAN, A. The Ties that Bind: The Jewish Support for the Left in the United States. American Jewish Historical Quarterly, 66, No. 2, pp 285-321.

Since World War II Jewish support for the Left tends to weaken.

WALD, A.M. The Menorah Group Moves Left. Jewish Social Studies, 38, No. 3-4, pp 289-320.

History of the Left-wing intellectual Menorah Society and its Menorah Journal in the face of problems raised by Marxism.

WISTRICH, Robert. Ferdinand Lassalle: The Gladiator. European Judaism, 10, No. 1, W. pp 15-23.

Socialist leader who, though never converted, denied Judaism which he considered a separate entity.

----------------. The Jews and Socialism. Jewish Spectator, 41, No. 4, Fa. pp 13-21.

----------------. Revolutionary Jews from Marx to Trotsky. London, Harrap, 254p, Ind, Ill, Bibl.

Surveys the role Jews played in 19th and 20th Century revolutionary movements.

COMMUNISM

HAK, A. A mishpockhe fun alte bolshevikes. (A family of old Bolsheviks.) Sovietish Heimland, 16, No. 6, Ju. pp 122-34.

About Rozovskaya, a close collaborator with Lenin during the Revolution.

LOWY, M. Marxists and the National Question. New Left Review, 96, pp 81-100.

Critique of the classical Marxist position.

OFFENBERG, Mario. Kommunismus in Palästina. Nation und Klasse in der antikolonialen Revolution. Meisenheim/Glan, Anton Hain, 369p. (Marburger Abhandlungen zur Politischen Wissenschaft 29)

The role of nation and class in the anti-colonial revolution.

COMMUNIST POLICY ON JEWS

L'Acte Final d'Helsinki et les droits des Juifs d'URSS. Regards, 12, No. 100, Ja. pp 29-32.

AGURSKY, Mikhail. Russian Neo-Nazism - A Growing Threat. Midstream, 22, No. 2, F. pp 35-42.

ALSHANSKIY, Naum. Russian Antisemitism. Jewish Quarterly, 23, No. 4, W. pp 33-36.

AXELBANK, Albert. From Birobidzhan. A "Jewish National State?" Present Tense, 4, No. 1, Aut. pp 20-23.

CARLEBACH, Julius. Karl Marx and the Radical Critique of Judaism. London, Routledge and Kegan Paul, 370p.

DU BROFF, Sidney. East Germany, The Nazis Again Rule - as Communists. Jewish World, 1, No. 9, Au. pp 2-5.

ELLEINSTEIN, Jean. Les Juifs en Union Soviétique. Reflexions sur les Juifs en URSS. Séries d'articles parus dans la "Presse Nouvelle Hebdomadaire. Paris, Presse Nouvelle, 39p.

A collection of articles by the French Jewish Communist which appeared in the Presse Nouvelle Hebdomadaire. M. Elleinstein has harsh words for the Soviet treatment of its Jewish population.

-----------------. The Stalin Phenomenon. London, Laurence and Wishart, 221p, Ind.

Includes Stalin's treatment of the Jews.

JACOBS, Everett M. Jewish Representation in Local Soviets, 1959-73. Soviet Jewish Affairs, 6, No. 1, pp 18-26.

Jews are significantly underrepresented in urban Soviets (councils) and that the number of Jews elected to kray (territory)/oblast (province)/okrug (regions) and rayon (large rural area) soviets is substantially below what one could expect.

KOREY, William. Updating "The Protocols of the Elders of Zion." Midstream, 22, No. 5, My. pp 5-17.

"The imminent danger for Soviet Jewry posed by the enormously stepped-up anti-Zionist campaign, now given international sanction and justification through a United Nations resolution, is self-evident."

KRIEGEL, Annie. Les Juifs d'Urss et la Strategie de Moscou (Conference de Bruxelles) L'Arche, 19, No. 22, Ma. pp 22-27.

LISKOFSKY, Sidney. Testimony before the Subcommittee on International Organisations of the Committee on International Relations, USH of Representatives, IIF, New York, American Jewish Committee, 10p.

On violations of human rights of Russian Jews.

LITVINOFF, Emanuel. The Future of Judaism in the Soviet Union. Condensed from Insight, 1, No. 9, (1975) Jewish Digest, 21, No. 6, Ma. pp 6-12.

MARKOVITS, Andrei S., KAPLAN, Cynthia S. From Minsk to America: Socialism and the Jews. Response, 10, Nos. 2-3, Su/Fa. pp 57-64.

MATZ, Judith and SANFORD, Margery. (Eds.) Separated Soviet Families. A Collection of Case Histories. Miami, Fla. Greater Miami Jewish Federation, S. Florida Conference on Soviet Jewry, 145p.

Cases of 69 separated Soviet Jewish families are presented, with photographs and addresses.

NATIONAL INTERRELIGIOUS TASK FORCE ON SOVIET JEWRY. A Report on the Second World Conference of Jewish Communities on Soviet Jewry, Brussels, 17-19 F. Chicago, 6p.

PELIKAN, Jiri. Ein Frühling, der nie zu Ende geht Erinnerungen eines Prager Kommunisten. Frankfurt/M. S. Fischer, 332p.

In his reminiscences of the 'Prague Spring' of 1968 the author speaks of antisemitic motives of the Soviet invaders.

POSPIELOVSKY, Dimitry V. Russian Nationalist Thought and the Jewish Question. Soviet Jewish Affairs, 6, No. 1, pp 3-17.

On the one hand, there is approval of the ready acceptance of foreigners into Russian nationality; on the other hand, many of Russia's 'tragedies' are blamed ... on the over abundance of non-Russians in Russian key government positions.

Progressive Jewish Editors. Memorandum to Soviet Officials on the Soviet Jewish Situation. Jewish Currents, 30, No. 11, D. pp 9-15.

REINHOLD, O. and RYZHENKO, F. Contemporary Anti-Communism: Policy and Ideology. Tr. fr. Russian, London, Central Books, 344p.

Mentioned as anti-Soviet ideological centres are the United Jewish Appeal, World Zionist Organisation and World Jewish Congress while "Today the bulwarks of neocolonialism are the racists of South Africa and Rhodesia and the Zionists in Israel" Originally published in Russian, 1973 in Moscow.

SHNEIDERMAN, S.L. The Ghost of Emes Walks in Pravda. Midstream, 22, No. 10, D. pp 51-56.

SOSIN, Gloria Doene. Russian Report: Respected Comrades! Present Tense, 3, No. 3, Sp. pp 17-20.

SVIRSKY, Grigory. Hostages. The Personal Testimony of a Soviet Jew. Tr. fr. Russian by Gordon Clough. London, Bodley Head; New York, Knopf. xi, 305p. In Russian: Polyarnaya tragedia. Beckenham, Kent.

The author writes from personal experience of antisemitism in the U.S.S.R. Having left that country in 1972, Svirsky was, a year later, chief prosecution witness in a successful suit for slander against the Soviet Embassy in Paris.

USSR '76. Moscow, Novosti Press Agency, 246p, Ill.

A richly illustrated handbook of the USSR. There is some information on the Jews as a Soviet nationality and a religious community, though otherwise the material on Soviet nationalities is rather scarce in the text, as different from illustrations.

U.S. Congress. House. Committee on International Relations. Anti-Semitism and reprisals against Jewish emigration in the Soviet Union. Hearing before the Subcommittee on International Organisations ... 27 My. Washington, U.S. Govt. Print. Off. 26p.

WINTER, Wolfgang. Wer füllt Korb drei der KSZE-Akte. Aussenpolitik, 27, No. 4, pp 367-82.

"Basket Three" of the Helsinki Final Act deals with human rights issues affecting chiefly the Jews in the USSR.

COMMUNIST POLICY ON ZIONISM AND ISRAEL

BONDAREVSKI, G. In a netz fun vidershpruchn tsvishn di imperialistishe meluches. (In a net of contradictions between the imperialist regimes). Sovietish Heimland, 16, No. 11, N. pp 3-10. and No. 12, D. pp 159-67.

Criticises Zionism, its history and the State of Israel.

DADIANI, L. Di komunistishe partein kegn tsionism. (Communist parties against Zionism.) Sovietish Heimland, 16, No. 5, My. pp 122-29.

----------. Di tsionism is kegn der entshpanung. (Zionism is against Detente.) Sovietish Heimland, 16, No. 4, Ap. pp 176-78.

Attacks the foreign policy of Israel and Zionism.

Di Gesise Fun Der Alie. (The Agony of Aliyah) Sovietish Heimland, 16, No. 4, Ap. pp 13-27.

Collection of articles attacking both the immigration policy and economy of Israel.

GOZHANSKE, Tamar. Sakone fun fashizm in yisroel: di ultra-rechte shtremungen in der medine. (Danger of fascism in Israel_ ultra-right tendencies in the land) Sovietish Heimland, 16, Nos. 1-2, Ja., F., pp 108-16; 141-47.
An Israeli communist warns that the right-wing parties in Israel may turn fascist.
GRAZHDAN, V. Who are the Pentecostalists - Zionists? Lywdina I Svit 9, S. pp 53-57.
GROSHEV, E. Der kamf kegn di iberbleibechtzen funem natsionalism. (The Struggle against the remnants of nationalism) Sovietish Heimland, 16, No. 3, Ma. pp 4-9.
Describes the fundamentals of communism, attacks both religion and Zionism.
KRIEGEL, Annie. Lénine et le Sionisme. L'Arche, 19, No. 226, Ja. pp 56-63.
MAROM, Ran. The Bolsheviks and the Balfour Declaration 1917-1920. Wiener Library Bulletin, 29, N.S. 37-38, pp 20-29.
STERN, August. (Ed.) Un procès "ordinaire" en URSS, Le Dr. Stern devant ses juges. Tr. Ania Chevallier. Paris, Gallimard, 340p.
A transcript of the celebrated trial of Dr. Shtern in Vinnitsa in December 1974. He was sentenced to eight years' imprisonment on various charges of professional corruption but was released on 14 March 1977 and left the USSR a month later.
VERGELIS, Aron. A bankrote ideologie in shpigl fun undzere teg. In shayches mitn 29-ten Tsionistishn Kongres. (A banknote ideology in the mirror of today. In connection with the 29th Zionist Congress.) Sovietish Heimland, 16, No. 12, D. pp 37-48.
Attacks Zionism and Israel.
--------------. Der tsionism un die yiddishe kultur. (Zionism and Jewish Culture) Sovietish Heimland, 16, No. 10, O. pp 6-19.
Critique of Zionism and its relation to Jewish culture.
VLADIMIROV, G. Di tsionistishe organisatsie. (The Zionist Organisation) Sovietish Heimland, 16, No. 9, S. pp 122-33.
ZIMANAS, G. Der tsionizm un di yidn. (Zionism and the Jews) Sovietish Heimland, 16, No. 6, Ju. pp 20-25.

COMMUNIST POLICY ON RELIGION

ACZEL, György. A szocialista állam és az egyházak Magyarországón. (The Socialist State and the Churches in Hungary) Vilagossag, 17, No. 10, O. pp 601-7.
Includes the Jews.
BOURDEAUX, Michael. White Book on Restriction of Religion in the USSR Brussels, Committee for the Defence of Human Rights in the USSR, 66p.
A mimeographed booklet in seven parts, each accompanied by documents: The Law; Rossian Orthodox Church; Baptists; Roman Catholics; The Jews; Moslems; Buddhists.
------------------, HEBLY, Hans, VOSS, Eugene. (Eds.) Religious Liberties in the Soviet Union. WCC and USSR. A Post-Nairobi Documentation. Keston, Kent, Keston College, 96p, Ill. (Keston Books 7)
Collection of materials on the situation of the Christian churches in the USSR.

DAVIS, Moshe. Jewish Spiritual Life in the USSR. (Some Personal Impressions) Menorah, 3, No. 1, Su. pp 16-20; Religion in Communist Lands, 4, No. 4, W. pp 20-23.
MEERSON-AKENOV, M. Religious Renaissance in the USSR. Diakonia, No.11.
Soviet Persecution of Religion in Ukraine. Toronto, World Congress of Free Ukrainians, 54p, Ill.
Brochure, containing many interesting photographs (including a Jewish cemetery in Kiev in present sad state.)

DISSENT IN THE USSR
AND EASTERN EUROPE

APPELBAUM, Paul S. Soviet Jewry: Growth of a movement. Response, 10, Nos. 2-3, Su/Fa. pp 121-28.
DAVIDOVICH, Efim. The Making of a Dissident. Commentary, 62, No. 6, D. pp 47-53.
Part of the autobiography of a Soviet Jewish refusenik.
DEUTSCHER, Tamara. Intellectual Opposition in the USSR. New Left Review, 16, No. 96, pp 101-13.
Analysis of the principal tendencies of intellectual opposition in the USSR, based on Samizdat.
FEIFER, George. Moscow Farewell. London, Cape, 446p.
The author's experience in Russia, including his encounters with dissidents and Jewish activists.
GOLDSTÜCKER, Eduard. Dissidents in the Soviet Union. The Center Magazine, Ja/F. pp 77-78.
"The present situation created by the Soviet Union produces an instinctive national resistance, articulated again, in the first instance, by the intellectual dissident." Written by a political exile from Czechoslovakia.
JICK, Leon A. From Minsk. Do they Remember us? Present Tense, 3, No. 4, Su. pp 19-20.
On Col. Yefim Davidovich, a leading Jewish activist who died on 24 April.
KANFER, Irene. A travers le Samizdat juif. Les Nouveaux Cahiers, 11 No. 43, pp 49-52.
KHODOROVICH, Tatyana. (Ed.) The Case of Leonid Plyushch. Writings by the victim of one of the most horrifying cases of political psychiatry in the USSR. London, Hurst, 160p, Ill.
KOPOLEW, Lew. Aufbewahren für alle Zeit! Autobiographie. Hamburg, Hoffman und Campe. Tr. from Russian by Heddy Pross-Weerth and Heinz Dieter Mendel. 618p, Ill. In French: A conserver pour l'eternite. Paris, Stock, (Temoins de notre temps)
MATHON, Tania and MARIE, Jean-Jacques. L'affaire Pliouchtch. Paris, Le Seuil, 176p, Ind, (Coll. Combats) In German: Wien, München, Molden, 132p, Ind.
MEDVEDEV, Roy. Demain L'URSS. L. Pliouchtch, etc. Paris, Syros, 175p.
The noted dissident describes some of the activists and their aims.
The Moscow Symposium on Jewish Culture. Reoonstructionist, 42, No. 8, N. pp 5-6.
NATIONAL COUNCIL ON SOVIET JEWRY. SOVIET JEWRY RESEARCH BUREAU. Colonel Yefim Davidovich. Comp. by Jonathan Schenker. New York, 30p.

NEUBERG, Paul. The Novels of György Kndrad. Index on Censorship, 5, No. 4, W. pp 43-48.
Konrad is a Hungarian dissident writer of Jewish origin.

RASS, Rebecca. With the collaboration of Morris Brafman. From Moscow to Jerusalem. The Dramatic Story of the Jewish Liberation Movement and its Impact on Israel. New York, Shengold, 256p.

REDDAWAY, Peter. Dissent in the Soviet Union. Dissent, 23, No. 2, Sp. pp 136-54.

SCHARLACH, Bernice. Art is our Aliyah: Underground Soviet Jewish Artists Defy the KGB. Hadassah Magazine, 58, No. 3, pp 10-11;50-51.

TARNOR, Norman. Inside the Jewish Gulag. Hadassah Magazine, 58, No. 12, D. pp 16-17; 31-32.
The diary of a Professor's trip to the Soviet Union in November 1975. He had been invited to speak to a group of Jewish scientists in Moscow on his speciality, Hebrew literature of the past two hundred years.

TOKES, Rudolf. (Ed.) Dissent in the USSR: Politics, Ideology and People. Baltimore and Cordon, Johns Hopkins U.P., xiv, 453p, Ind.

Twelve from the Soviet Underground. Juddah L. Magnes Museum, Berkeley, Ca. 40p, 55 items and figures.
Exhibition catalogue.

ULAM, Adam B. Ideologies and Illusions: Revolutionary Thought from Herzen to Solzhenitzen. Cambridge, Mass.; London, Harvard, U.P., viii, 335p, Ind.

VORONEL, Alexandr. Les conditions sociales de l'eveil national juif d'URSS. Regards, No. 100, Ja. pp 34-42.

EMIGRATION/ALIYAH FROM THE USSR

BAUM, Phil. Rethinking Jackson-Vanik: New Approaches to Soviet Jewish Emigration? Congress Monthly, 43, No. 6, Ju. pp 7-9.
"The longer we content ourselves with waiting for something to happen ... the longer Russian Jews will wait for the issuance of exit visas."

GINSBURGS, G. Current Legal Problems of Jewish Emigration from the USSR. Soviet Jewish Affairs, 6, No. 2, pp 3-13.
Details the legal provisions introduced since 1973. For previous years see ibid, 3, No. 1, pp 3-19.

JOHNSON,George E. Which Promised Land? The Realities of American Absorption of Soviet Jews. Analysis, No. 47, 2p.

KASSOW, Samuel. Are We Doing the Right Thing for Soviet Jews? Interchange, 2, No. 4, D. pp 1;6-8.

KOREY, William. Soviet Decision-Making and the Problems of Jewish Emigration Policy. Survey, 22, No. 4, W. pp 112-31.
"When we look at the concrete circumstances of the Jewish emigration issue we find, that the government makes reasonable and calculated choices based on national purposes and foreign policy goals."

KUZNETS, Simon. Immigration of Russian Jews to the US:Background and Structure. Cambridge, Mass., Charles Warren Center for Studies in American History, 35-125p.

LACKS, Roslyn. Trying to Make it in the USA. New Emigres, New Problems. Present Tense, 3, No. 4, Su. pp 45-51.

LEVIN, Arthur. A Soviet Jewish Family in Calgary. The Jewish Spectator, 41, No. 1, Sp. pp 36-40.

LITVINOFF, Emanuel. The Russian 'Drop-Outs' Condensed from Insight, 2, No. 1. Jewish Digest, 22, No. 2, N. pp 31-34.

MAKOVSKA, Lina. A Second Life. Council Woman, No. 1, Ja. pp 12-13.
A Soviet Jewish woman doctor talks about the struggle to build a new life in the United States.

Quo Vadis? Policy on Russian Jewish Emigration. New York, National Jewish Conference Center. 12p.

RADITSA, Leo. Letter from Rome. Midstream, 22, No. 10, D. pp 24-31.
On the Russian Jews who are waiting for emigration overseas.

ROTH, Étienne. Juifs d"URSS. Des "Olim" a contre-Courant. L'Arche, No. 237, D. pp 20-21.

RUBIN, Burton S. Absorbing Russian Jews in America. Jewish Digest, 21, No. 7, Ap. pp 3-6, Condensed from Journal for Jewish Communal Service, 52, No. 2, W.

Russian Jews in Rome. Jewish Digest, 21, No. 7, Ap. pp 7-10. Condensed from Shamir, No. 4, W.

SANFORD, Margery. Orphans of the Exodus. Separated Soviet Families. A Collection of Case Histories. Miami, South Florida Conference on Soviet Jewry in cooperation with the National Conference on Soviet Jewry. 107p, Ill.

SNYDER, Janet. Our Meetings with the Refuseniks. To Feel What It's Like to Live in a Cage! Jewish Digest, 21, No. 8, My. pp 10-13.

TAYLOR, Telford with DERSHOWITZ, Alan. FLETCHER, George, LIPSON, Leon and STEIN, Melvin. Courts of Terror. Soviet Criminal Justice and Jewish Emigration. New York, Knopf, x, 188p, Ind, Ill.

VASAK, Karel and LISKOFSKY, Sidney. (Eds.) The Right to Leave and to Return. Papers and Recommendations of the International Colloquium held in Uppsala, Sweden, 19-20 June 1972. New York, American Jewish Committee, The Jacob Blaustein Institute for the Advancement of Human Rights, The International Institute of Human Rights, Uppsala University, Faculty of Law, xi, 570p.
Includes: L. Pettite: Right to Leave and to Return in the USSR and E. Litvinoff: The Emigration of Soviet Jews.

VORONEL, Alexander. The Aliyah of Russian Intelligentsia. Midstream 22, No. 4, Ap. pp 28-35.
The existence of Israel influences everything that is best in Russian Jewry.

COMMUNIST PURGES AND TRIALS

CARMICHAEL, Joel. Stalin's Masterpiece: Show Trials and Purges of the 1930s; The Consolidation of the Bolshevik Dictatorship. London, Weidenfeld & Nicolson; New York, St. Martins P., viii, 238p. Ind.
Refers also to the anti-Jewish element in the purges.

EAST-WEST
RELATIONS/DETENTE

JACKSON, G.S. Jews and Detente. Jewish Currents, 30, No. 3, Ma. pp 4-10.
Discusses the Jackson-Vanik amendment.

LIEDERMANN, Helmut. Die Schlussakte der Konferenz Über Sicherheit und Susammenarbeit in Europa KSZE. Osterreichische Zeitschrift fur Aussenpolitik, 16, No. 1, pp 3-22.

LISKOFSKY, Sidney. Conference on Security and Cooperation in Europe. (The Helsinki Final Act) New York, American Jewish Committee, Ja. 27p.
Deals chiefly with Basket Three.

MORGENTHAU, Hans J. Detente: Reality and Illusion. Middle East Review, 8, Sp/su. pp 5-9.

POTTER, Philip A. The Churches and Religious Liberty in the Helsinki Signatory States. The Ecumenical Review, 28, No. 4, O. pp 442-59.

ROTH, Stephen J. The Helsinki "Final Act" and Soviet Jewry. London, Institute of Jewish Affairs, 24p.
Analysis of the Jewish aspects of the Final Act signed at the end of the Conference on European Security and Cooperation.

RUSSELL, Harold S. The Helsinki Declaration: Broddingnag or Lilliput? American Journal of International Law, 70, No. 2, Ap. pp 242-72.

SMITH, Hehdrick. Alien in Russia, a bit of a Russian Abroad. Ambivalence, secret pride and self-affirmation after decades of self-denial. National Jewish Monthly, 90, No. 5, Ja. pp 28-34.

SOBEL, Lester A. (Ed.) Facts on File, Kissinger and Detente. New York, 202p, Ind.

SOLZHENITSYN, Aleksandr. (and others) Detente: Prospects for Democracy and Dictatorship. New Brunswick, Transaction, 112p, (Issues in Contemporary Civilisation)

URBAN, George R. (Ed.) Detente. London, Maurice, Temple Smith; New York, Universe Books, 368p.

MIGRATION AND REFUGEES

ANGLADE, Jean. Des immigres en France de 1919 a nos jours. Paris, Hachette, 221p, Bibl.
Discusses the problems of immigrants in France between 1968-73, during which period their numbers grew by about 1 million. No mention is made of Jews but it may be assumed that they are included among Algerians, Moroccans, Poles, Russians and Tunisians.

BAILLET, Pierre. Les Rapatriés d'Algerie en France. Paris, Documentation Francaise, Notes et Etudes Documentaires, Nos. 4275-4276. 79p.
Analyses the integration of Algerian repatriates into French society. The chapter on Jews concludesthat the migration of Algerian Jews was successful. (pp 46-50)

BEN GAD, Yitschak. Forgotten Refugees: Jews from Arab Lands, American Zionist, 67, No. 2, O. pp 23-24.

DINNERSTEIN, Leonard and REIMERS, D.M. Ethnic Americans. A History of Immigration and Assimilation. New York, Harper & Row, 184p, Ind.
Concise account of the reasons and composition of immigrant waves to America and of their integration into American society since 1840.

JONES, Maldwyn A. Destination America. London, Weidenfeld & Nicolson in assoc. with Thames Television; New York, Holt, Rinehart & Winston, 256p, Ill.
Based on research and interviews and illustrated with historic photographs and documents, this volume focuses on those who voluntarily contributed the most to the United States - The Irish, British, Germans, Scandinavians, Italians and east-European Jews. Concentrates on the century between 1815 and 1914 but immigrations of later years are included: World War II refugees, Cubans, Mexicans, Asians, among others. Also treats the anti-immigration movement and the immigration heritage.

RISCHIN, Moses. (Ed.) Immigration and the American Tradition. Indianapolis, Bobbs-Merrill, 511p, (American Heritage Series)

THOMAS, Gordon and MORGAN-WITTS, Max. Voyage of the Damned: Voyage of the 'St. Louis'. N.e. London, Coronet, 320p, Ill.

TIMÁR, Laszlo. Amiről többet kellene beszélnünk! Magyar Tudosók Nyugaton. Látohátar, 5, No. 6, Ju. pp 205-16.
Hungarian scientists and other scholars abroad, among them many Jews.

ALIYA/YERIDA

AVRIEL, Ehud. Aprite le Porte. Milano, Mondadori, 379p.
Account of "illegal immigration" (Aliyah Bet)

BOWERS, Faubion. Only - and Lonely - in America. The New York Times Magazine, 26 S. pp 24-25; 27.
"The new immigrants from the Soviet Union, most of them Mews or partly Jewish, complain about America. and delight in their right to do so."

EBAN, Abba and TEKOAH, Yosef. The Soviet Dropout Issue. Congress Monthly, 43, No. 10, D. pp 5-6.

ELIZUR, Dov. and SHYE, Samuel. The Inclination to Reimmigrate: A Structural Analysis of the Case of Israelis Residing in France and the U.S.A. Human Relations, 29, No. 1, pp 73-83.
Reimmigrants were motivated by the spiritual "Israel of the future", more so in the U.S.A. than in France.

GIDWITZ, Betsy. Problems of Adjustment of Soviet Jewish emigres. Soviet Jewish Affairs, 6, No. 1, pp 27-42.
"Soviet Jewish immigrants appear to experience greater difficulties in adjustment than many other settlers, even more than those from other totalitarian societies. Doubtless a major element in their problems has been their long isolation from the rest of the world."

Israel: A Dream Gone Sour for Jews Who Return to Arab Countries. Events, 19 N. pp 25-27.
On the return of some Moroccan Jews - as it later transpired - for a visit only.

LEKET, Yechiel. The Validity and Importance of Aliyah in the 1970s. Jewish Frontier, 43, No. 9, N. pp 11-19.

LOUVISH, Misha. Reorganising the Absorption Machinery. Jewish Frontier, 43, No. 9, N. pp 5-7.
Problems of aliyah.

NAHSHON, Gad. Israelis in America - Moral Lepers. Midstream, 22, No. 8, O. pp 46-49.
"From a non-Zionist point of view, it should be said that Israelis are being treated the same as the Jewish new immigrants were treated by established American Jews throughout American Jewish history."

PILCH, Judah. Aliyah in Reverse. Jewish Frontier, 43, No. 1, Ja. pp 15-18.
"A new approach is needed in our relationship with the yordim (Israeli emigrants) as well as a new procedure for recruiting American olim (immigrants)

RIVLIN, Helen Ann B. The Holy Land: The American Experience. American Jews and the State of Israel: A Bicentennial Perspective. Middle East Journal, 30, No. 3, Su. pp 369-89.
"American Jews have participated in ... the creation of a nation composed of a complex combination of separate groups bound together by a network of interlocking institutions that foster unity while protecting diversity.

TUREN, Nina. Return to Zion: Characteristics and Motivations of Returning Emigrants. Social Forces, 54, No. 3, Ma. pp 546-58.
Data shows that return migration from the U.S. to Israel is non-selective and that reimmigrants are motivated mainly by the attraction of the country of destination.

ARAB REFUGEES

PETERS, Joan. An Exchange of Populations. Commentary, 52, No. 8, Au. pp 38-44.
A balance has not been struck by Jewish immigration to and Arab emigration from Israel.

TEKOAH, Yosef. Refugees: Arab and Jews. American Zionist, 67, No. 1, S. pp 19-22.

NATIONALISM, NATIONAL MINORITIES

AVINERI, Shlomo. Socialism and Nationalism in Moses Hess. Midstream 22, No. 4, Ap. pp 36-44.

BARON, Salo Wittmayer. Nationalism and Religion in the Contemporary World. Journal of Ecumenical Studies 13, No. 4, Fa. pp 117-35.
Religions no longer play a major role in nationalist movements motivated by the oppression of ethnic minorities. The task of the major faiths should be the promotion of ethnic, cultural and religious pluralism.

HAIM, Sylvia G. (Ed.) Arab Nationalism: An Anthology, N.e. U. of California P., 300p.

KAMENKA, E. (Ed.) Nationalism, The Nature and Evolution of an Idea. London, Edward Arnold, vi, 135p, Ind, Bibl.
Includes: Mass Politics and the Political Liturgy of Nationalism by George L. Mosse and Political and Social Aspects of Israeli and Arab Nationalism by Shlomo Avineri.

WATT, W. Montgomery and CACHIA, Pierre. Who Is An Arab? Worldview, 19, Nos. 1-2, pp 20-21.

WADDY, Charis. The Muslim Mind. London; New York, Longman, xviii, 205p, Ind, Ill.

Introduction to Islam by a Christian Arabist scholar, born in Australia who grew up in Jerusalem in the years following the First World War. She puts the questions raised by oil, by the Palestinians and by Britain's immigrant communities in the perspective of Muslim outlook.

ANTISEMITISM

AMERY, Jean. Der ehrbare Antisemitismus. Eine Rede. Merkur, 30, pp 533-52.

The veteran German thinker against antisemitism.

Antisemitic Irritations in South Africa. Patterns of Prejudice, 10, No. 4, Jy-Au. pp 20-22;33.

Part of the South African Jewish Board of Deputies 1974-76 Report.

AVINERI, Shlomo. The Reemergence of Antisemitism. Congress Monthly, 43, No. 1, D.1975/Ja. 1976. pp 14-16.

---------------. Le nuove forme dell'antisemitismo. La Rassegna Mensile di Israel, 42, Nos. 3-4, Ma-Ap. pp 13-35.

Includes anti-Zionism.

BARON, Salo W. Changing Patterns of Antisemitism. Jewish Social Studies, 38, No. 1, W. pp 5-38.

The dislike of the unlike will continue. Its degree and quality will depend on general socio-economic, cultural and religious conditions prevailing in the different areas and periods.

BERMAN, H. Political Antisemitism in Minnesota during the Great Depression. Jewish Social Studies, 38, Nos. 3-4, pp 247-64.

Antisemitism was a means of fighting federal intervention in favour of poor sectors.

BIBERSTEIN, J. von. Die These der Verschwörung 1776-1945. Philosophen, Freimaurer, Juden, Liberale und Sozialisten als Verschwörer gegen die Sozial-Ordnung. Berne, H. Lang, Frankfurt/M. P. Lang.

History of the "idea of a conspiracy" judeo-Freemasonry, originating in the 18th century.

BRODER, Henryk M. Linke Tabus - Linker Kitsch. Linker Opportunismus. Linker Antisemitismus. Berlin, Klaus Bär, 115p.

BUSI, Frederick. Céline, the Wild Man of French Literature, Midstream, 22, No. 6, Ju-Jy. pp 69-72.

The French antisemitic writer.

---------------. The Dreyfus Affair and the French Cinema. Wiener Library Bulletin, 29, N.S. Nos. 39-40, pp 56-59.

---------------. The Dreyfus Case: An Affair Without End. Judaism, 25, No. 1, W. pp 8-19.

Narrates the principal events in the case and highlights "the remarkable similarities between the French scandal and its American counterpart (Watergate) particularly the motivation which led otherwise decent men to commit crimes for the sake of 'loyalty' or 'national security'.

CAFFAZ, L'antisemitismo italiano sotto il Fascismo. Firenze, La Nuova Italia. 131p.

COUDENHOVE-KALERGI, Richard. (Ed.) Anti-semitism Throughout The Ages by Heinrich Johann Maria Graf von Coudenhove-Kalergi. Tr. by Angelo S. Rappoport. Westport, Conn., Greenwood P., 288p, Ill.
Reprint of the 1935 edition.

DOBKOWSKI, Michael Nachin. Ideological anti-Semitism in America: 1877-1927. Ann Arbor, Mich., U. Microfilms, 592p, Bibl.
Ph.D. Dissertation, New York University.

------------------------. The Anti-Semitic "Imaging"of the Jew in America. Judaism, 25, No. 3, Su. pp 363-74.

------------------------. Populist Antisemitism in U.S. Literature. Patterns of Prejudice, 10, No. 3, Ma-Ju. pp 19-27.
Populism certainly was not alone, but merely one important architect in the developing blueprint of American antisemitism.

ECKERT, Willchad Paul. L'antisemitisme en republique fédérale allemande en 1975. Rencontre, 10, pp 234-37.

ELBAZ, André E. Correspondence d'Edmond Fleg pendant l'affaire Dreyfus, Paris, A.G. Nizet.

EPSTEIN, Lawrence J. Zionism and Anti-Semitism. Reconstructionist, 42, No. 6, S. pp 12-16.
"Anti-semitism will not disappear until the number of Jews in Israel and other countries constitutes a large enough proportion of the world's population as to render national anti-Semitism politically unfeasible."

European Antisemitism: 1890-1945. Special Issue. The Wiener Library Bulletin, 29, N.S. Nos. 39-40, pp 1-62.
Includes: Georg von Schoenerer and the Genesis of Modern Austrian Antisemitism by Robert S. Wistrich. Julius Streicher and the Impact of Der Stürmer by Randall T. Bytwerk. Nationalist Socialist Vienna: Antisemitism as a Housing Policy by Gerhard Botz. The Dreyfus Affair and the French Cinema by Frederick Busi.

FINEBERG, Solomon Andhil. To Avoid the Quicksands of Anti-Semitism. CCAR Journal, 24, No. 1, pp 35-41.
Discusses Jewish protest to statements like that of General Brown, who feels that Jews over-react thereby doing more harm than good.

FORSTER, Arnold. The Trouble-Makers: An Anti-Defamation League Report. Westport, Conn., Greenwood P.; London, Westport P., 317p.
Antisemitism in America. Reprint of the 1952 edition.

--------------- and EPSTEIN, Benjamin R. Cross-Currents. Westport, Conn., Greenwood P., 382p.
Antisemitism in America. Reprint of the 1956 edition.

FRIEDMAN, Norman L. Anti-Semitism and American Jewry. Congress Monthly, 43, No. 9, N. pp 7-9.
Manifestations of antisemitism 1973-76 and their effects on American Jewry.

FRIEDMAN, Saul S. Pogromchik: The Assassination of Simon Petlura. New York, Hart, xiv, 414p, Ind, Ill, M.
The Paris trial proceedings and other pertinent data relating to the anti-Jewish pogroms in the Ukraine under Petlura's rule.

----------------. Universal Antisemitism. Jewish Frontier, 43, 8-9, Au-S. pp 14-18.

GELTMAN, Max., DAVIE, Donald, GREENBERG, Clement, KRAMER, Hilton, ROSENBERG, Harold and MACCOBY, Hyam. The Poetry and Politics of Hate. Symposium. Midstream, 22, No. 6, Ju-Jy, pp 57-68.

Antisemitism in the Poetry of Ezra Pound.

GLOUBERMAN, Emanuel. Vasilii Rozanov: The Antisemitism of a Russian Judeophile. Jewish Social Studies, 38, No. 2, Sp. pp 117-44.

GOLDSTEIN, David L. Dostoievski et les juifs. Paris, Gallimard, 340p, Bibl. (Idees)

Examines the chapter in Dostoievski's diary devoted to the Jews and the motives why he had found it necessary to take a position on the subject. The author also studies the place of Jews in Dostoievski's work generally and his attitude to Jews as a persecuted group.

GOTTGETREU, Eric. Light on Dreyfus. Jewish Affairs, 36, No. 9, S. pp 53-56.

HIRSCHSON, Niel. Anatomy of Antisemitism. Jewish Affairs, 31, No. 2, F. pp 27-30.

JELEN, Christian. Un modele d'antisemitisme (1947-53) Les Nouveaux Cahiers, 12, No. 44, Sp. pp 29-35.

KNECHT, E. Le Mythe du Juif errant. Romantisme, 3, No. 12, pp 95-102.

Bibliography of the subject of the "Wandering Jew"

WAGNER, Richard. Die Kunst und die Revolution, Das Judentum in der Musik, Was ist deutsch? Ed. T. Kneif. München, Rogner und Bernhard, 136p.

Antisemitic essay on Jews in music.

KORZEC, Pavel and ROSEN, Léon. Le cinéma polonais, "terre promise" de l'antisémitisme. Les Nouveaux Cahiers, 12, No. 44, Sp. pp 5-16.

KRANE, Edna. Shakespeare's Shylock - Symbol or Stereotype. Jewish Quarterly, 24, Nos. 1-2, Sp/Su. pp 10-15.

KUBINSKY, Judit. Politikai Antiszemitizmus Magyarorszagon. (1875-90) Budapest, Kossuth, 273p, Ind, Bibl.

Political antisemitism in Hungary, nurtured on medieval superstitions and religious prejudices, first showed itself in the 1870s as a result of foreign, chiefly German, influence. The movement reached its climax in 1882-83 when in the wake of the trumped-up Tiszaeszlar case, it invited nationwide anti-Jewish riots. The author presents the phenomenon as a consequence of the decline of the middle classes and of the landed gentry.

LEVINGER, Lee Joseph. Anti-Semitism in the United States: Its History and Causes. Westport, Conn., Greenwood P.; London, Westport P., 120p.

Reprint of 1925 deals chiefly with the impact of mass Jewish emigration.

LEMIS, David L. The Public Image of Henry Ford: An American Folk Hero and His Company. Detroit, Wayne State U.P., 598p.

Discusses, i.a., Ford's antisemitism.

MCCARTHY, Patrick, Céline. New York, Viking, 352p, Ind.

Biography and analysis of the works of the French antisemite.

MACCOBY, Hyam. The Jew as Anti-Artist: The Anti-Semitism of Ezra Pound. Midstream, 22, No. 3, Ma. pp 59-71.

Pound was the modern representative and exponent of aganism and saw the Jew as his chief ideological enemy.

MARTCHENKO, Borys. Simon Petlura. Paris, Bibliotheque Ukrainnienne. 80p, Ill, Bibl.
With a chapter "Petlura and the Pogroms."

MILLER, Judith. The Agnew/Brown Syndrome. Present Tense, 4, No. 1, Aut. pp 9-12.
The presidential campaign in America and the impact of the antisemitic remarks of Vice-President Agnew and Secretary of Defence Brown.

MORAIS, Vamberto. A Short History of Anti-Semitism. New York, Norton, ix, 300p, Ind, Bibl.
Discusses the subject from a psychological, moral and philosophical viewpoint.

MOSLEY, Leonard. Lindbergh. A Biography. London, Hodder & Stoughton New York, Doubleday, xxx, 446p, Ind, Ill.
Definitive biography of Charles Lindbergh with many references to his antisemitic attitude.

PARKES, James William. The Emergence of the Jewish Problem 1878-1939 Westport, Conn., Greenwood P., xxiv, 259p.
Reprint of the 1946 edition.

PAWLIKOWSKI, John T. Anti-Zionism = Anti-Semitism: Fact or Fable? Worldview, 19, Nos. 1-2, pp 15-19.
If a critic of Israel's policies remains committed to the survival of the Jewish State, he cannot be termed antisemitic.

PERLMUTTER, Philip. Anti-Semitism Today. Reconstructionist, 42, No. 6, S. pp 16-18.
"The best defense against anti-semitism is a determined Jewish community which will not allow itself to become apathetic or indifferent to the threats or challenges to it."

PEVZNER, Sam. Antisemitism in Argentina. Jewish Currents, 30, No. 11, D. pp 4-8.

PIORO, Maurice. Vigilance! Le monstre de la haine vit toujours! Regards, 12, No. 108, N-D. pp 20-24.
Antisemitism in Belgium.

POLIAKOV, Leon. Presentation de quelques reflexions de Durkheim sur l'antisemitisme. (Extrait de Henri Dagan Enquete sur l'antisemitisme, 1898) Yod, 1, eo. 2, Ja. pp 49-52.

--------------. Storia dell'antisemitismo. Rome, La Nuova Italia, 4 vols. (Biblioteca di Storia 9)
Italian version of "History of Antisemitism"

RABI, Wladimir. Retour d'Amiens: Le Procès Goldman. L'Arche, No. 231, Ju. pp 36-37.
The case of Pierre Goldman, accused of murder.

RAPHAEL, Fredy. Conditionnements socio-politiques et socio-psychologiques du satanisme. Revue des Sciences Religieuse, 50, No. 2, pp 112-56.
The best examples for the process of diabolisation are witchcraft and the idea of the Jew-devil. Both appear in societies shaken in their spiritual and economic foundations.

REICHMAN, Eva G. Hostages of Civilisation: The Social Sources of National Socialist Anti-Semitism. Westport, Conn., Greenwood P., 281p.
Reprint of fundamental work, first published in 1951.

RIEBER-MOHN, H. and EITINGER, Leo. Retten til a overleve. Norge, Cappelen, 151p. (In Norwegian)

RIFF, Michael A. Czech Antisemitism and the Jewish Response Before 1914. Wiener Library Bulletin, 29, N.S. No. 39-40, pp 8-19.

ROGGER, Hans. Government, Jews, Peasants and Land in Post-Emancipation Russia. The Pre-emancipation Background: Stirrings and Limits of Reform. Cahiers du Monde Russe et Contemporaine, 17, No. 1, pp 5-25.

Antisemitism in Tsarist Russia.

ROSENTHAL, Morton M. Argentinian Jews in Danger, ADL Bulletin, 33, No. 11, N. pp 4-15.

In the midst of general repression and turmoil, an anti-Semitic campaign has reached peak intensity.

RUBIN, Lawrence. Analysing Anti-Semitism: Indifference is Cause for Concern. Civil Rights Digest, W/Sp. pp 30-38.

Despite the assurances of the pollsters that anti-Semitism is not a serious problem, the Jewish community is gripped by a sense of urgency and uncertainty.

SAFRAN, Willy. Louis-Ferdinand Celine. Bruxelles, University, 205p.

The Belgian psychiatrist concludes that the French antisemitic writer was a sado-masochist.

ST. JOHN, Robert. A Hate Maestro is Dead. Jewish Affairs, 36, No. 7, Jy. pp 17-18.

Gerlad L.K. Smith, the notorious American antisemite.

SANDÓR, Iván. A Vizsgálat Iratai. Tudositás a tiszaeszlári per Körulmenyeiröl. Budapest, Kozmosz. 206p.

Report on the circumstances surrounding the blood-libel trial. Surveys the evidence of the notorious 1883 case of which both the prosecution and the defence published records and on which much has been written since.

SCHERR, Lilly. Le juif Süss. POF-Etudes, Yod, 1, No. 2, Ja. pp 53-72.

The Jew Süss as an antisemitic stereotype.

SEVENSTER, J.N. De wortels van het heidense antisemitisme in der Dudheid. Kampen, Uitgeversmaatschappij J.J. Kok, 32p. Verkenning en bizinning SV.10, No. 1, Ju.

Discusses the roots of antisemitism in the pagan world.

SILBERMAN, Alphons. Antisemitismus in der Bundesrepublik Deutschland, Bild Der Wissenschaft, 13, No. 6, Ju. pp 68-72.

------------------ and SALLEN, Herbert A. Latenter Antisemitismus in der Bundesrepublik Deutschland. Teil: Aus dem Leben der Forschung. Offprint from Heft 4, Kölner Zeitschrift für Soziologie und Sozialpsychologie, pp 706-23.

SLAVIN, Stephen L. Bias in U.S. Big Business Recruitment. Patterns of Prejudice, 10, No. 5, S-O. pp 22-25.

The present system of corporate recruitment effectively excludes Jews from most sectors of the American economy.

SZARAZ, György. Egy elöitélet nyomában. Budapest, Magvetö. 287p. (Byorsulo idö)

Antisemitism in Hungary.

TALMON, Jacob L. The New Anti-Semitism. The New Republic, 175, No. 12, 18 S. pp 18-23.

"There is still the fundamental truth that somehow the Jewish right to live and exist on a basis of genuine equality, as a right and not on sufferance or in return for some special excellence is not yet taken for granted by the world."

U.S. Dept. of Defense. Defence Race Relations Institute. Anti-Semitism: A handout. Patrick Air Force Base, Fla 248p.
A compilation of previously published material.

WARDI, Dh. La caricature antisémite dans les Fables de J. Anouilh. Yod, POF-Etudes, 1, No. 2, Ja. pp 73ff.

WILSON, Stephen. Antisemitism in France during 'La Belle Epoque'. Wiener Library Bulletin, 29, N.S. No. 39-40, pp 2-7.

WISTRICH, Robert S. George von Schoenerer and the Genesis of Modern Austrian Antisemitism. Wiener Library Bulletin, 29, N.S. No. 39-40, pp 20-28.

ZISENWINE, David W. (Ed.) Anti-Semitism in Europe: Sources of the Holocaust. Introduced by Robert Chazan. New York, Behrman House, x, 110p. (The Jewish Concepts and Issues Series.)
Collection of primary sources tracing the developments of antisemitism in Europe from the 17th century to the Nazi period.

ANTISEMITIC PUBLICATIONS

APP, Austin J. The Curse of Anti-Anti-Semitism. Making Pontius Pilates out of Politicians. Takoma Park, Maryland, Boniface P. 66p.

ARETZ, Emil. Hexen-Einmal-Eins einer Luege. N.E. Paehl b. Weilheim/Obb. Verl. Hohe Warte, Franz v. Bebenburg, 392p, Ind, Bibl.
The author vigorously contests that the figure of six million Jews killed by the Nazis is true and goes to great lengths to disprove this 'lie'.

Britain First. The Nation Wreckers: The Zionist Conspiracy against British Nationalism. Croydon, Britain First.

CHAIJ, Julio. El Judaismo Según la Biblia. Origenes y Fundamento de la Mentalidad Judia. Ensayo analitico de las Narraciones Biblicas. Buenos Aires, Editorial Milicia, 134p. (Biblioteca de Formacion Doctrinaria, 16).
Antisemitic pamphlet.

ROOSTER, Conrad. Der Luegenkreis um die deutsche Kriegsschuld. Offenbach/Main, Bund fuer deutsche Wiederverinigung, 40p, Ind, Ill.
Right-wing pamphlet, designed to clear Nazi Germany of responsibility for World War II and blaming the British, the Americans, Russians, Jews, Freemasons instead.

ROSENFELD, Anatol. Mistificacoes Literárias: "Os Protocols deo Sábios de Sião". Sao Paulo, Perspective, 65p.
Critique of the Protocols of the Elders of Zion.

ROTH, Heinz. Varför fötiger man Sanningen. (Warum werden wir Deutschen belogen?) Odenhausen, Author, 58p, Ind. Bibl.
Denial of the holocaust.

STREICHER, Julius and MONNIOT, Albert. Los crimenes rituales. Una patrana antisemita? Prologo: Edouard Drumont. Buenos Aires, Editorial Milicia. Biblioteca de Formacion Doctrinairia, 19) 232p, Ill.
Neo-Nazi translation of antisemitic work on ritual murder.

TURKOW, Mark. The Upsurge of Anti-Semitic Literature in Argentina. Israel Horizons, 20, No. 9, S. pp 20-22.
A brief survey.

CHRISTIAN ANTISEMITISM

EHRMAN, Albert. The Origins of the Ritual Murder Accusation and Blood Libel. Tradition, 15, No. 4, Sp. pp 83-90.

EPSTEIN, Benjamin R. and FORSTER, Arnold. "Some of My Best Friends ..." Westport, Conn., Greenwood P.: London, Westport P., 274p.
Christian sources of antisemitism. Reprint of 1962 edition.

FLANNERY, Edward H. All Christians are Antisemitic. Christian Attitudes on Jews and Judaism, No. 48, Ju. pp 1-6.
1. Antisemitism is a disease ingrained in the Christian psyche.
2. Antisemitism forms an integral part of Christian history.
Followed by responses from U.S. subscribers.

------------------. L'angoisse des Juifs. Paris, Mame, 332p.
Antisemitism in Christian teaching.

GLASSON, T. Francis. Antisemitism and the Cross. Common Ground, 30, No. 3, Aut. pp 4-6.

IDINOPOLOS, Thomas A. Old Forms of Anti-Judaism in theNew Common Book of Prayer, Christian Century, 93, No. 25, 4-11 Au. pp 680-84.
Liturgists of the Episcopal Church are adopting the "Reproaches" hymn for Good Friday service from the traditional Roman Catholic rite just at a time when Roman Catholics are re-examining their liturgy to eliminate from it precisely those attitudes in error about, or prejudicial to, Jews and Judaism.

ISAAC, Jules. Gesu e Israel. Nardini, Centro Internazionale del Libro. 461p.
Italian translation of the author's fundamental work on the Christian roots of antisemitism.

KAMEN, Henry. The Spanish Inquisition. n.e. London, White Lion, 334p, Ind.
Reprint of the original, 1965 edition. An attempt at writing the definitive history and the truth behind the Inquisition.

KOHNER, Hans. Der Antisemitismus der Kirche. Genese. Geschichte und Gefahr. Zurich, Die Waage, 215p, Bibl.

MACCOBY, Hyam. Is the Political Jesus Dead? Encounter, 46, No. 2, F. pp 80-89.
The sources of Christian antisemitism.

OESTERREICHER, John M. Anatomy of Contempt: a critique of Dr. R. Ruether's "Faith and Fratricides". South Orange, N.J. The Institute of Judaeo-Christian Studies, Seton Hall, 45p (Institute Paper No. 4)
In her book Dr. Ruether attempted to uncover the "theological roots" of Christian antisemitism. Professor Osterreicher contends that she failed to do so.

PARKES, James William. The Bible in Public Worship: A Source of Antisemitism. Face to Face, 2, Su/Fa. pp 3-5.

PAWLIKOWSKI, John T. Anti-Semitism in the Christian Tradition. Learning With, 4, No. 1, Ja. pp 15-17.
Takes up the question of anti-Semitism in the New Testament which he feels harbors strong anti-Judaism but not clear-cut anti-Semitism. Anti-Judaism represents an attitude towards Jews and Judaism that is negative in tone and places Judaism in an inferior position relative to Christianity, but does not Jews nor wish upon them suffering and extermination.

RENDTORFF, Rolf. Die neutestamentliche Wissenschaft und die Juden. Zur Diskussion zwischen David Flusser und Ulrich Wilckens. Evangelische Theologie, 36, No. 2, Ma-Ap. pp 191-200.

NEGRO ANTISEMITISM

DINER, Hasia Rona. Black-Jewish Relations. In the Almost Promised Land: Jewish Leaders and Blacks 1915-1935. Ann Arbor, Mich, U. Microfilms, 451p, Bibl.

Ph.D. Dissertation, U. of Illinois.

TSUKASHIMA, Ronald Iadao and MONTERO, David. The Contact Hypothesis: Social and Economic Contact and Generational Changes in the Study of Black Anti-Semitism. Social Forces, 55, No. 1, S. pp 149-65.

Literature suggests that intimate, equal-status contact is related to racial tolerance but this is only true for the oldest blacks. The effects of perceived economic mistreatment demonstrates that the correlation between this variable and antipathy towards Jews becomes more strongly related with each younger generation of Blacks.

GERSHMAN, Carl. Blacks and Jews. Midstream, 22, No. 2, F. pp 8-17.

"Today American Jews are less interested in the problems of Blacks tban they were a decade ago. Yet there can still be a useful and effective Black-Jewish alliance, based less on Jewish liberal commitments and more on enlightened self-interest"

THE ARTS

The Arts in Jewish Life: Special Issue: Reconstructionist, 4, No. 4, Ap. pp 1-32.

Includes: Jews and Visual Arts in America by Alfred Werner. Jewish Creativity in Music by Leon Stein. Jewish Education and the Arts: A Dilemma: Design for Jewish Survival by Harold E. Katz.

AUSLANDER, Nochem. 100 yor yiddisher teater. Sovietish Heimland, 16, No. 11, N. pp 136-38.

Material relating to the history of the Yiddish theatre in the USSR, followed by shorter contributions, including an article by Shlomo Michoels.

BALÁZS, István. A megvalosithatatlan fömu. (Schönberg: Mózes és Áron c. operajarol) Világosság, 17, Nos. 2 and 10, F. and O.

"The Unproducable work: Schonberg's Opera "Moses and Aron".

BENJAMIN, Cynthia Pearlman. Modern Hebrew Calligraphy. The Ketuba. Response, 10, Nos. 2-3, Su/Fa. pp 207-10.

BERCOVICI, Israel. Hundert yor yidish teater in rumenya 1876-1976. (A Hundred Years of Yiddish Theatre in Rumania) Bucharest, Kriteron 318p, Ill.

A richly illustrated volume by the Principal dramatist of the Bucharest Jewish Theatre.

BIALER, Y.L. Jewish Life in Art and Tradition. Based upon the Collection of the Sir Isaac and Lady Edith Wolfson Museum, Hechal Shlomo, Jerusalem, London, Wiedenfeld & Nicolson; New York, Putnams, 144p, Ill.

BROD, Max. Die Musik Israels. Revidierte Ausgabe mit einem zweiten T Teil. Werden und Entwicklung der Musik in Israel, by Yehuda Walter Cohen. Basel, Tours, London, Bätenreiter, 164p, Ind, Ill.
Discussion of Jewish music, its history and the development of Israeli music.

CLARK, Kenneth. Rembrandt and the Bible. The Listener, 12 Au. pp 174-77.
Printed version of T.V. talk.

COHN, Anna and BLUE, Jeff. Treasures of Parchment, Silver and Linen. The B'nai B'rith Klutznick Museum reopens its collection of Jewish ceremonial and Folk Art. The National Jewish Monthly, 90, No. 9, My. pp 8-12.

DAVIS, Lionel B. Jewish Music in America before 1800. Jewish Currents, 30, No. 3, Ma. pp 12-15.

FREUDENHEIM, Tom L. The (Jewish) Jewish Museum. Moment, 2, NO. 2, N. pp 27-29;51-52.
The Jewish Museum of New York.

FRIEDENBERT, Daniel M. Jewish Minters and Medallists. Philadelphia, Jewish Publication Society of America, 131p.

HAIK-VANTOURA, Suzanne. La musique de la Bible revelee. Paris, Robert Dumas, 503p.

KOZLOFF, Max. Jewish Art and the Modernist Jeopardy. Art Forum, 14, No. 2, Ap. pp 43-47.

HAUSER, Arnold. Látogatoban Hauser Arnoldnál. A beszélgetest vezeti: Nyiri Kristóf. Kritika, 12, Nos. 4 and 5, Ap-My. 5-9;16-18.
Arnold Hauser, a student of art and society interviewed in his native Hungary.

LEVEEN, Jacob. The Hebrew Bible in Art. The Schweich Lectures of 1939 with a new preface and Addenda and Corrigenda, New York, Sepher Hermon.
Reprint of the 1944 edition.

PAVON-MALDONADO, B. Un problema arqueologico en la sinagoga de El Transito. Seferad, 36, No. 1, pp 141-42.'
Thinks that some parts of the Transito in Toledo built in 1357 originate in the 11th and 12th century.

METZGER, T. La représentation du capiste dans les manuscripts libreax médiévaux. Journal des Savants, No. 1, pp 32-53.
The illustration of the scribe in 14th and 15th century European Hebrew manuscripts.

ROSEN, Charles. Arnold Schoenberg. New York, Viking, (Modern Masters Series)

The Ludwig Rosenberger Collection of Judaica. A selection exhibited at the Joseph Regenstein Library, University of Chicago, 9th March-3rd May. Catalogue introduced by Pobert Rosenthal, text by Paul Silverman and Richard Peiser, 24p.

SCHUBERT, U. Die Erschaffung Adams in einer spanischen Haggadah-Handschrift des 14. Jahrhunderts. (Br. Mus. Or. 2884) und ihre spätantike jüdische Bildvorlage. Kairos, 18, No. 3, pp 213-17.
The image of the creation of Adam was drawn in the high Middle Ages.

-----------. Die Miniaturen des Ashburnham Pentateuch im Lichte der Rabbinischen Tradition. Kairos, 18, No. 3, pp 191-213.

SED-RAJNA, Gabrielle. L'Art Juif. Paris, Falmmarion, Ill.

SHECHORI, Ran. Art in Israel. New York, Schocken, 200p, Ill.
STEIN, Leon. Jewish Creativity in Music. Jewish Affairs, 36, No. 9, S. pp 87-93.
De Tempel van Salomo. Exhibition at Rijksmuseum in honour of opening of old synagogue. 1976. Catalogue in Dutch includes articles by J.F. Van Agt, "Portuguese Synagogen in Den Haag", Judith Belenfante, A. K. Oggenberg and F. J. Hoogewond on Solomon's Temple. 100p, 31 figs.
TCHEBOTARIOV, S. Groisse humanistishe kunst. (Great Humanist Art) Sovietish Heimland, 16, No. 9, S. pp 131-41.
On Shostakovich's works on Jewish themes.
WALBE, Joel. Der Gesang Israels und seine Quellen. Hamburg, Christian, 358p.
The sources of Jewish liturgical music.
WERNER, Alfred. Jews and Visual Arts in America. Reconstructionist, 42, No. 3, Ap. pp 7-12.
WERNER, Eric. A Voice Still Heard ... The Sacred Songs of the Ashkenazic Jews. University Park, Penn., Pennsylvania State U.P., xiii, 350p, Ind. (Leo Baeck Institute S.)
Study of the history, liturgical, musical, social and political background of Ashkenazic Synagogue music.
------------. (Ed.) Contributions to a Historical Study of Jewish Music. New York, Ktav, 287p.
Scholarly essays and introduction.
ZISKIND, Ivan. Synagogue Architecture in South Africa. Story and Drawings. Jewish Affairs, 36, No. 10, O. pp 28-30.

JEWISH ARTISTS

BECKER, Heinz and Gudrun. (Eds.) Giacomo Meyerbeer. Breifwechsel und Tagebücher. Bd. 3, 1837-45. Berlin, New York, Walter de Gruyter, 851p.
BLAUKOPF, Kurt and ROMAN, Zoltán. Mahler. A Documentary Study. London, Thames and Hudson, 288p, Ill. In German Wien, Universal.
Study of the composer, Gustav Mahler.
CREMER, Robert. Lugosi: The Man Behind the Cape. Chicago, Regnery.
EDMUNDS, Sheila. A Note of the Art of Joseph Ibn Hayyim. Studies in Bibliography and Booklore, 11, Nos. 1-2, W. pp 25-40.
Illuminator of the Kennicott Bible (Oxford, Bodlean Library)
EISNER, Lotte H. Fritz Lang. Tr. by Gertud Mander and Ed. by David Robinson, London, Secker & Warburg, 416p, Ill.
Biography of a film director.
FEIN, Irving A. Jack Benny. An Intimate Biography. New York, Putnams; London, W.H. Allen, 319p.
FEJES, György: Töredekek Reinitz Bélaról. Magyar Zene, No. 1, pp 42-71.
On Bela Reinitz, the Jewish composer murdered by the Nazis.
FERENCZIK, János: Bruno Walter centenáriumára. Muzsika, No. 11, N. pp 1-3.
Hungarian conductor pays homage to Walter on his centenary.
FIFIELD, William. Modligliani: The Biography. New York, Morrow, 162p, Ill.
FREEDLAND, Michael. Fred Astaire. London, W.H. Allen, 277p, Ill.
Biography.

FRIEDLER, Egon. ARnold Schoenberg. Pionero de la Musica Contemporanea. Buenos Aires, Congreso Judio Latina Americano, 40p, Ill. (Grandes Figuras del Judaismo 99)

Biography of the composer.

GETLEIN, Frank. Chaim Gross. New York, Jewish Book Club. 238p, Ill.

Life and work of the American sculptor.

GIURGOLA, Romaldo and MEHTA, Jaimini. Louis Kahn. Boulder, Ore. Westview P., 253p, Ill.

Life and work of the noted American architect.

HICKEY, D. and SMITH, Gus. Prince: Laurence Harvey. His Public and Private Lives. London, Star Books, 224p, Ill.

Biography of the actor.

JORDAN, Rene. Streisand. (Barbra Streisand) London, W.H. Allen, 253p.

KRAUS, Wolfgang. (Ed.) Schreiben in dieser Zeit. Fuer Manes Sperber. Wien, Europa, 197p.

Festschrift for Manes Sperber with contributions by Heinrich Boell, Carlo Schmid, Hermann Kesten, Eugene Ionesco, Raymond Aron, Andre Malraux, Jean Amery, Friedrich Israel Torberg, Pierre Emmanuel, E.M. Cioran, Siegfried Lenz, Elie Wiesel, Francois Bondy and a bibliography of Sperber's writings.

LEINSDORF, Erich. Cadenza. A Musical Career. Boston, Mass.

Autobiography of the conductor.

LEVY, Alan. The Bluebird of Happiness. The Memoirs of Jan Peerce. New York, Harper & Row, 325p, Ill.

LIPMAN, Samuel. Copeland as American Composer. Commentary, 61, No. 4, Ap. pp 70-74.

Anna Mahler - Her Work. Introduced by Ernst H. Gombrich. Essay by Anna Mahler, New York, A. Schram.

LYUBOMIRSKI, Yeshua. Der aktor Elie Traktovenko. Sovietish' Heimland, 16, No. 11, N. pp 145-58.

Pen-portrait of the Yiddish actor.

METKEN, Gunter. (Yaacov) Agan. New York, Abrams, 84p, Ill. (Modern Artist Series)

MYERS, Carmel. Recollections of An Early Jewish Movie Star. Jewish Digest, 21, No. 7, Ap. pp 55-58. Condensed from Western States Jewish Historical Quarterly, 7, No. 2, Ja.

PASSUTH, Krisztina: Amos Imre szimbolumrendszere. Ars. Hungarica, No. 1, pp 65-91.

The symbolism of the Hungarian Jewish graphic artist.

PIATAGORSKY, Gregor. Cellist. New York, Doubleday, 256p. Ill, Ind, Discography.

PRATT, Davis. (Ed.) Photographic Eye of Ben Shahn, N.E. Cambridge, Mass, Harvard U.P., xvi, 147p.

RATTNER, Abraham. And There Was Light. Studies for the stained glass window, Chicago Loop Synagogue, Catalogue of an exhibition held at the National Collection of Fine Arts, Smithsonian Institute, 23 Ja- 28 Ma. 1976, 32p.

RYBACK, I. The Shtetl and Other Paintings. With an introduction by A. Werner, Leiden, Brill.

SOUVERBIE, Marie-Therese. Chagall. Tr. fr. French, G. Possiger, Munchen, Schuler, 136p, Ill.

Monograph of the painter.

SUTRAHN, Joan. Carvalho. Artist-Photographer-Adventurer-Patriot. Portrait of a Forgotten American. New York, Richwood Publ. Co., 226p, Ill.

Born in 1815 in Charleston, the son of Sephardic Jews, Solomon Nunes Carvalho was one of the 19th century's most dashing personalities - as a portraitist, photographer, explorer, historian, inventor and Jewish community leader.

WALDENBERG, Patrick. Max Ernst. München, Schuler, 134p, Ill.

Evaluation of the artist.

WERNER, Alfred. Chaim Gross: Skill and Sagacity. Jewish Frontier, 43, No. 10, D. pp 15-17.

FOLKLORE

COHEN, N.G. Jewish Names as Cultural Indicators in Antiquity. Journal for the Study of Judaism in the Persian, Hellenistic and Roman Period, 7, No. 2, pp 97-128.

While the names of Patriarchs were seldom used in Biblical times in post-Biblical times certain names became commonplace in certain regions, e.g. Abraham in Persia, Shimon in Greek domains, Ruben in Roman areas and Asia Minor.

DOLEZELOVA, Jana. Questions of Folklore in the Legends of the Old Jewish Town Compiled by Leopold Wiesel (1804-1870). Judaica Bohemiae, 12, No. 1, pp 37-50.

DRODZYNSKI, Alexander. Jiddische Witze und Schmonzes. Mit Zeichnungen von Szymon Kobylinski. Dusseldorf, Droste, 240p.

An introductory essay on Jewish humour precedes the collection of Jewish jokes and sayings grouped in categories.

DRUKER, Irme. "Der pinkes is ofn, un di hant shraibt" (The Notebook is open and the hand writes) From the book Michoel-Yoysef Guzikov. Sovietish Heimland, 16, No. 11, N. pp 1-4;22.

Guzikoff (1802-1837) was a maker of musical instruments and musician, descendant of a long line of klezmerim.

GLUCK, Solomon L. The Jewish Postcard: Images of Nostalgia. Jewish Digest, 22, No. 1, S. pp 53-54.

GOLDMAN, Albert. Jewish Comics. Moment, 1, No. 4, Ja. pp 18-24.

A discussion of the changing nature of Jewish comedy and comics in America. Excerpt from Next Year in Jerusalem, by Douglas Villiers, to be published by Viking Press.

LANDMANN, S. Exorzismen in der jüdischen Tradition. Zeitschrift für Religions - und Geistesgeschichte. 28, No. 4, pp 357-66.

The examples of An-Ski's dybbuk, The Book of Exorcisms of Manasseh ben Israel and The Dybbuk of Korez (17th century Ukraine)

LAX, Eric. On Being Funny: Woody Allen and Comedy. New York, Charterhouse, 243p.

LIEBMAN, Malvina W. Jewish Cookery from Boston to Bahgdad. Miami, Fla, 256p, Ill.

LOEB, L.D. Sense Stimulation and Ritual Response: Classifying the Religious Symbolism of the Perisan and Yemenite Jews. The Realm of the Extra-Human Agents and Audiences, World Anthropology, pp 167-77.

Compares Jewish traditions in Shiraz (Persia) and Sana (Yemen) in the use of 45 ritual objects by views, touch, smell and taste.

MARCUSE, F.L. The Ethnic and the Anti-Ethnic Joke. Jewish Currents, 30, No. 7, Jy-Au. pp 17-21.

POLLACK, Herman. Jewish Folkways in Germanic Lands. 1648-1806. N.e. Boston, MIT, xx, 410p.

POSTAL, Bernard. Jewish Landmarks. Congress Monthly, 43, No. 8, O. pp 12-13.

---------------. Jews on the Map. Geographical Place Names for Jews. Jewish Digest, 21, No. 10, Jy-Au. pp 32-35. Condensed from Pioneer Woman, 43, No. 6.

RACHLEFF, Owen. Chukkat Hagoy. Jewish superstition. Midstream, 22, No. 1, Ja. pp 67-71.

A look at the Jewish adaptation of the occult explosion.

--------------. Jewish Comics. Midstream, 22, No. 4, Ap. pp 51-56.

Deplores lack of taste by Jewish comics.

ROSE, Evelyn. Complete International Cookbook. London, Robson, 320p. Ill.

ROSEN, Naftali. Das Jüdische Jahr. Exhibition of the Jüdisches Museum der Schweiz in Basel. Aspects of Jewish life throughout the year. Catalogue, 72p.

ROSENBLUM, Doron. What's So Funny. MOment, No, 9, Ma. pp 28-32.

Humour in Israel since 1973.

ROTH, June. Healthier Jewish Cookery: The Unsaturated Fat Way. New York, Aroo; London, Barrie & Jenkins, 256p.

RYDE, David. What's in a (Jewish) Name. B'nai B'rith Journal,

SPALDING, Henry D. Keeping Up with the Kohnses: A Book of American Jewish Humour. Jonathan David, xvii, 429p.

LIST OF DIVISIONS 1977

BIBLIOGRAPHY 1977

REFERENCE

BOWDEN, Henry Warner. Dictionary of American Religious Biography. Westport, Conn., Greenwood P., 575p.
Biographies of 425 men and women, Protestant, Catholic, Jewish.

GENERAL REFERENCE BOOKS AND DICTIONARIES

KAGANOFF, Benzion C. Dictionary of Jewish Names and Their History. New York; London, Schocken, 250p.

LIGHTMAN, Sidney. (Ed.) The Jewish Travel Guide 1977. London, Jewish Chronicle, 304p, Ill, Ind.
World-wide guide for Jewish travellers, listing places of Jewish interest, hotels, restaurants, etc.

POSTAL, Bernard and KOPPMAN, Lionel. American Jewish Landmarks. A Travel Guide and History. New York, Fleet P., 670p, Ind, Ill.
Published for the American Bicentennary.

ENCYCLOPAEDIAS

ROTH, Cecil and WIGODER, Geoffrey. (Eds.) The New Standard Jewish Encyclopaedia. London, W.H. Allen, 2027p, Ind.

BIBLIOGRAPHIES

Analytical Articles on the Palestine Problem and Arab-Israeli Conflict. Journal of Palestine Studies, 6, No. 2, pp 167-79.
Bibliography.

BRICKHAN, William W. The Jewish Community in America. An Annotated and Classified Bibliographical Guide. New York, Burt Franklin & Co., xxvii, 396p, Ind.
Useful compilation of sources of American Jewish history.

CARGAS, Harry James. The Holocaust: An Annotated Bibliography. Haverford Pa., Catholic Library Assoc. 86p.
Useful list of material relating to the Holocaust.

DAVIES, Norman. Poland: Past and Present: A Select Bibliography of Works in English. Newtonville, Mass., Oriental Research Partners, Wellingborough, Northants. Collets, 220p.
Includes material on Polish Jewry.

ENSER, A.G.S. A Subject Bibliography of the Second World War. Books in English 1939-74. London, Deutsch; New York, Academic P., 592p, Ind.,
Useful reference work, grouping the titles according to subject.

FINKELSTEIN, Louis. A Bibliography of the Writings of ... New York, Jewish Theological Seminary of America, 30p.

GIRODANO, Joseph and PINEIRO, Grace. The Ethno-Cultural Factor in Mental Health; a literature review and bibliography. New York, Institute on Pluralism and Group Identity, American Jewish Committee 51p, Bibl.

GREENBERG, Simon. The Ethical in the Jewish and American Heritage. New York, Jewish Theological Seminary of America, xvi, 327p. (Moreshet Series Studies in Jewish History, Literature and Thought 4)

HALPERN, Joel M. (Ed.) From Shtetl to Destruction: The Jewish Experience in Eastern Europe. Comp. by Eliyahu Matzozky. Monticello, Ill, Council of Planning Librarians, 39p. (Exchange Bibliography No. 1240)
Bibliography.

HNIK, Thomas. (Ed.) European Bibliography of Soviet, East European and Slavonik Studies, 1, 1975. Birmingham, U. of Birmingham, xxxvii, 437, Ind.
Bibliography of books, articles from periodicals, symposia and scholarly reviews which appeared in 1975 on the subject in Britain, France, Belgium, French-speaking areas of Switzerland, FGR and Austria.

IOB. International Ecumenical Bibliography Volume 10/11. 1971/72. München, Chr. Kaiser; Mainz, Matthias-Grünwald, 587p, Ind, Bibl.
Important reference book for the study of inter-faith relations.

KAGANOFF, N.M. and KATZ-HYMAN, M.B. Judaica Americana. American Jewish Historical Quarterly, 67, No. 2, pp 162-71.
Current bibliography.

KINGMA, J. and OFFENBACH, A.K. Bibliography of Spinoza's Works Up to 1800. Studia Rosenthaliana, 11, No. 1, Ja. pp 1-31.

KNECHT, E. Le mythe du Juif errant. VI. Echos et survivances (1862-1960). Romantisme, 7, No. 16, pp 101-15.
The myth of the "Wandering Jew". Third part of an annotated bibliography, the first two appeared in 1969 and 1973.

MEISSNER, Boris, FRENZKE, Dietrich et al. (Eds.) Sowjetunion und Völkerrecht 1962-1973. Bibliographie und Analyse. Köln, Wissenschaft & Politik, 575p, Ind. (Dokumente zum Ostrecht, Bd. 9)
Bibliography of the literature on the USSR and international law

NOSEK, Bedrich. Auswahlkatalog hebräischer Drucke Prager Provenienz aus dem 18 Jahrhundert in den Sammlungen des Staatlichen jüdischen Museums in Prag. III. Teil: 1700-1799. Judaica Bohemiae, 13, No. 2, pp 96-120.
18th century Prague Hebrew printing.

PENNIE, David A. (Eds.) with biographical notes by Sidney Sugarman and Diana Bailey (Comp.) Bibliography of the printed works of James Parkes with selected quotations. Southampton, U. of Southampton, xvi, 132p, Ind, Bibl.
The Rev. James Parkes has made notable contributions to the fight against antisemitism and the promotion of good Christian-Jewish relations.

Publikationen des Leo-Baeck Instituts. Aus zwei Jahrzehnten. (Hrsg. von Max Kreuzberger unter Mitarb von Irmgard Foerg.) Jerusalem, London, New York, xi, 119p.
Bibliography.

SADEK, Vladimir. Aus der Handschriftensammlung des Staatlichen jüdischen Museums in Prag. Eine auf das Revolutionsjahr 1848 bezügliche Handschrift. Judaica Bohemiae, 13, No. 1, pp 44-46.
A document of 1848 in the Prague Jewish Museum.

SEDINOVA, Jirina. From the MSS Collection of the State Jewish Museum in Prague (Manuscripts of Liturgical Content) Judaica Bohemiae, 13, No. 2, pp 74-95.

SANDOR, Ivan. (Ed.) Magyar néprajztudrmányi bibliográfia (1850-70) Tanulmányok és adatok a Karpát medence etnográfiájához. Budapest, Akademiai.

Hungarian ethnographic bibliography. Many Jewish data drawn from the contemporary Jewish press: Magyar Izraelita, Izraelita Közlony, Ben Chananja and Statistics of Jews from Hazank es a Külföld, 1866.

SCHEICHL, Sigurd Paul. Bibliografie Karl Kraus. Kommentierte Bibliografie, München, Ed. Text und Kritik, 88p.

Annotated bibliography of the works of Karl Kraus.

SCHMELZER, Menahem H. Jewish Scholarship in the United States: Selections from the Literature, 1973-1975. American Jewish Yearbook, 77, pp 182-228.

Annotated Bibliography.

SINAI, J. A Bibliographical Review of the Modern History of Israel. Middle East Review, 10, No. 1, pp 66-72.

SINGERMAN, Robert. Jewish and Hebrew Onomastics: A Bibliography. New York, Garland, 144p.

Studies in Bibliography and Booklore II, New York, Library of Hebrew Union College, Jewish Institute of Religion, 103p.

WOLFE, Ann G. About 100 Books ... a gateway to better intergroup understanding. 8.e. New York, American Jewish Committee, 40p.

YEARBOOKS

The American Jewish Calendar. New York. Hebrew Publishing Co., 12p.

With photographs of early American Jewish settlements.

Annual V. 11. 1976. Sofia, Central Board of the Social, Cultural and Educational Organisation of the Jews in the People's Republic of Bulgaria. 326p, Ill.

Contains, apart from articles on the XI Party Congress and July Central Committee plenum, studies on the language of Bulgarian Jews, on Bulgarian Jews in the International Brigade, on Jewish cultural figures, etc.

BENVENISTY, David. (Ed.) Annual. Volume 12. Sofia Social, Cultural and Educational Organisation of the Jews in the People's Republic of Bulgaria, Central Board, 293p, Ill.

The volume contains articles on the Jewish Bulgarian Communist newspaper Bratstve (1921-23) and Evreiski vesti (1944-76) on the social differentiation of Bulgarian Jewry in the 16th-18th centuries, on the World War II period, and many others. It also includes excerpts from the diaries of L. Lulchev and B. Filev introduced and annotated by D. B. Cohen.

COHEN, Isaac. (Ed.) Irish-Jewish Year Book, 5738 (1977-78). Dublin, Office of the Chief Rabbi, 76p.

FINE, Morris, HIMMELFARB, Milton and JELENKO, Martha. (Eds.) American Jewish Yearbook, V. 77, New York; Philadelphia, American Jewish Committee, Jewish Publication Society of America, xi, 676p, Ind.

Contains: Who Hast Not Made Me a Man: The Movement for Equal Rights for Women in American Jewry by Anne Lapidus Lerner. Politics and Intergroup Relations by Oscar Cohen. The United States, Israel and the Middle East by George E. Gruen. UN Resolution on Zionism by Sidney Liskofsky. The American

Jewish Community Responds to Issues of the Day: A Compendium by Geraldine Rosenfeld. Second World Conference on Soviet Jewry by David Geller. Soviet Jews in the United States: A Profile by Joseph Edelman. Jewish Scholarship in the United States: Selections from the Literature 1973-1975. Jewish Population in the United States, 1976 by Alvin Chenkin. Trends in U.S. Jewish Education: National Jewish Population Findings by Fred. Massarik. A Reader in the Demography of American Jews by Jack J. Diamond. Articles on the Jewish Communities of Canada, Argentina, Brazil, Great Britain, France, Belgium, Italy, Federal Republic of Germany, German Democratic Repuhlic, Soviet Union, Poland,Israel, South Africa, tables of the world Jewish population, directories of Jewish organisations and press in Canada and the U.S.A.

Jewish Book Annual. V. 35 5738/1977-78. New York, Jewish Book Council, 276p, Ill, Bibl.

In addition to the annual Bibliographies, it also includes: Saul Bellow: Jewish Writer by H.V. Ribalow. The Holocaust in Jewish Novels by Edward Alexander. Amsterdam, Center of Hebrew Printing in the 17th Century by H.C. Zafren. Judaica and Hebraica in Book Catalogs by L.S. Gold. Some of Israel's Research Institutes by S.G. Levi. Melech Ravitch: In Memoriam by I. Yanasowicz. Jewish Nationalist Thought in Yiddish by E. S. Goldsmith. On Dov Sadan by J. Kabakoff. Jewish Juvenile Book Awards: Survey on Sephardic Jewry by M. D. Angel. Recent Literature on Jewish Women by B. Greenberg. Jewish Characters in Early American Fiction by R.S. Klein. The Judaica Collections of Yale University Library by E.A. Jajko. Alexander Marx by M. Schmelzer. The World of Charles Angoff by J.T. Benton. Eisig Silberschlag by Z. Ravid. Jewish Literary Anniversaries 1978 by T. Wiener.

KEETON, G.W.and SCHWARZENBERGER, G. (Eds.) Yearbook of World Affairs, V.31, London, Stevens, Sweet & Maxwell, vii, 364p, Ind.

Includes: Kissinger's System of Foreign Policy by R.J. Vincent. Recent Developments in United Nations Peace Keeping by Alan James. The United Nations: Out of Control or Out of Touch by Charles William Maynes. International Terrorism: A Political Analysis by W.H. Smith.

MOONMAN, Jane. (Ed.) Zionist Year Book 1977, London, Zionist Federation of Great Britain and Ireland, 343p, Ind, Ill.

STEINBACH, A. Alan and GOODMAN, Philip. (Eds.) Jewish Book Annual, V.34, 5735/1976-77. New York, Jewish Book Council of the National Jewish Welfare Board, viii, 235p, Bibl.

In addition to Bibliographies of new books in English, Yiddish and Hebrew, also contains: The Jewish Writer in America: First Century by Sol. Liptzin. America's Pioneer Prayer Books by Abraham J. Karp. The New Israeli Novelists by Leon I. Yudkin. On the Art of Translation by A. Alan Steinbach. The Zionist Archives and Library by Sylvia Landress. 400 Years of Hebrew Printing in Palestine by G. Kressel (In Hebrew) and others.

WELTSCH, Robert. (Ed.) Year Book XXII. Political and Religious Ferment. An Annual Collection of Essays on the history and activity of Jews in Germany during the past century. London, Secker & Warburg, Leo Baeck Institute, xix, 361p, Ind, Bibl. Ill.

Contents: Between Baden and Luxembourg - Jewish Socialists on the Eve of World War I by W. T. Angress. Anti-Capitalism or Anti-Semitism? The Case of Franz Mehring by R. Wistrich. Types of Jewish Municipal Rights in German Townships - the Problem of Local Emancipation of J. Toury. German Nationalism and Jewish Assimilation - The Bismarck Period by G. R. Mork. Aspects of Hebrew Enlightenment Satire by Saul Berlin. Involvement and Detachment by M. Pelli. From Wolfenbüttel to Wissenschaft - The Divergent Paths of Isaak Markus Jost and Leopold Zunz by I. Schorsch. On an Unpublished Letter of Isaac Markus Jost by N.N. Glazer. Abraham Geiger and Samuel Holdheim - Their Differences in Germany and Repercussions in America by J. J. Petuchowski. From Relativism to Religious Faith - The Testimony of Franz Rosenzweig's Unpublished Diaries by P. R. Mendes-Flohr and J. Reinharz. Yitzchak Baer - A Reappraisal of Jewish History by P. E. Rosenblüth. Three Chapters of German-Jewish Banking History by K. Grunwald. German and Austrian Jews in the Financial Modernisation of the Middle East by J. O. Ronall. Jewish Surnames - Further Researches by W. Stern. Gottfried Semper and German Synagogue Architecture by H. Rosenau. The Prague Origins of the Güntherian Converts (1800-1850) by T. W. Simons, Jr. Julius Preuss: Father of Hebrew Medical Research by F. Rosner.

Zidovska ročenka 5738. Rada zidovskych nabozenskych obci 1977-78. Prague, Zidovska, Nabozenska, 140p.

Yearbook of the Jewish community of Czechoslovakia.

REPORTS OF INSTITUTES OF JEWISH STUDIES

The Jacob Blaustein Institute for the Advancement of Human Rights of the American Jewish Committee. A Six Year Report. New York American Jewish Committee, Institute of Human Relations, 14p.

The Jewish Quarterly Review. Special Volume commemorating the 70th anniversary of the Dropsie University, In Honor of the late Prof. Solomon Zeitlin. Philadelphia, Pa., Dropsie.

SHAPIRO, David S. Amicus Platoni. Amicior Veritati. Judaism, 26, No. 3, Su. pp 334-38.

On the Jewish Theological Seminary.

SIGAL, Phillip. Unfinished Business. Judaism, 26, No. 3, Su. pp 309-20.

The 90th anniversary of the Jewish Theological Seminary.

STEIN, Jacob. Promis, Performance and Problems. Judaism, 26, No. 3, Su. pp 296-300.

On Conservative Judaism and the Jewish Theological Seminary.

TOAFF, Elio. (Ed.) Annuario di Studi Ebraici 1975-76. Rome, Collegio Rabbinico Italiano, 172p.

PHILOSOPHY – RELIGION

ADAMS, Charles J. (Ed.) A Reader's Guide to the Great Religions. 2.e. New York, Free Press, 521p.
Includes Judaism.

BENAMOZEGH, Elié. Israël et l'humanité. N.r.e. Preface d'Aimé Pallière. Paris, Albin Michel, 390p.
Judaism as a universalist religion.

BLOCH, Jochanan. Die Aporie des Du. Probleme der Dialogik Martin Bubers. Heidelberg, Lambert Schneider, 355p, (Phronesis, Eine Schriftenreihe, 2)
Analysis of Buber's existentialism.

BULKA, Reuven. Setting the Tone: The Psychology-Judaism Dialogue. Journal of Psychology and Judaism, 1, No. 1, pp 3ff.

CHERCHEVSKY, Mireille. Le Judaïsme. Paris, Seghers, 219p.
Introduction to Judaism.

COHEN, Gerson D. The Present State of Conservative Judaism. Judaism 26, No. 3, Su. pp 268-73.

A Commentary on "Reform Judaism, A Centenary Perspective" CCAR Journal, 25, No. 1, Sp. pp 1-80.
Includes: One Hundred Years: What We Have Taught by Alfred Wolf. One Hundred Years: What We Have Learned by Gerald A. Goldman. Our Obligations: Religious Practice by Jack Stern, Jr. Our Obligations: The State of Israel and the Diaspora by Ronald B. Sobel.

Conservative Judaism on its Ninetieth Birthday. Judaism, 26, No. 3, pp 261-325.
Series of articles on Conservative Judaism since the foundation of the Jewish Theological Seminary (1866)

DAVIS, Moshe. Emergence of Conservative Judaism: Historical School in 19th Century America. N.e. Greenwood P.; London, Westport P., xiv, 527p, Ill.

ECKERT, W.P., GOLDSCHMIDT, H.L. and WACHINGER, L. Martin Bubers Ringen um Wirklichkeit. Konfrontation mit Juden, Christen und Sigmund Freud. N.e. Stuttgart, Katholosches Bibelwerk, 152p.
Three studies on Buber's confrontation with Jews, Christians and Freud.

EISENSTEIN, Ira. Inherent Contradictions in Conservatism. Judaism, 26, No. 3, Su. pp 339-42.

ELKINS, Dov Peretz. Clarifying Jewish Values, Rochester, New York, Growth, 92p.

------------------. Humanizing Jewish Life: Judaism and the Human Potential Movement. New York, A.S. Barnes; London, Yoseloff, 264p, Ind. Bibl.
Collection of articles, speeches and activities in and about fellowship groups and family cluster units at Temple Beth-El of Rochester, New York, organised by the author.

FREUD, Sigmund. L'uomo Mosé e la religione monteista. Torino, Boringhieri, 150p.
Itálian version of "The Man Moses and the Monotheistic Religion."

GLATZER, Nahum N. (Ed.) Modern Jewish Thought: A Source Reader. New York, Schocken, 240p.

KAREL, Piotr. Swietz izraelskie i zydowskie. Jednota, 21, Nos. 7-8 pp 20-28.
Jewish and Israeli festivals.

KATSH, Abraham I. The Biblical Heritage of American Democracy. New York, Ktav,
An explanation of how Jewish ideas and values influenced the development of democratic ideals and principles.

KATZ, Steven T. Jewish Ideas and Concepts. New York; London, Schocken, 326p.

KELMAN, Wolfe. In Defense of Conservative Judaism. Judaism, 26, No. 3, Su. pp 286-89.

LANGER, Jiri. Nine Gates to the Chassidic Mysteries. Tr. Stephen Jolly. New York, Behrman House, xxxiv, 266p. (A Jewish Legacy Book)
The author was a companion of Franz Kafka, who travelled to Belz and lived for a while among the Chassidism.

LEVINE, Arthur J. Needed - A Definition, Judaism, 26, No. 3, Su. pp 292-95.
Conservative Judaism.

LEVY, Hyman. Spinoza - Emancipator of Reason. The Jewish Quarterly, 25, No. 2, Su. pp 23-24.

LOOKSTEIN, Joseph A. A Critique and a Plea. Judaism, 26, No. 3, Su, pp 326-30.
Orthodox View of Conservative Judaism.

MARMUR, Dow. The Wisdom of Insecurity. On the Role of Progressive Judaism Today. European Judaism, 11, No. 1, W. pp 16-20.

MECHOULAN, Henry. Quelques Remarques sur Le Marranisme et la Rupture Spinoziste. Studia Rosenthaliana, 11, No. 2, Jy. pp 113-25.

MISRAHI, Robert. Spinoza face au christianisme. Revue Philosophique de la France et de l'Etranger. 102, No. 2, pp 233-68.
Contests Christian attempts to adopt Spinoza whose doctrine is Jewish rather than Christian.

MOORE, Albert D. Iconography of Religions: An Introduction. London SCM P., 344p, Ill.
Generously illustrated guide, begins with primal religions and covers all major religions of the world, including Judaism.

MORRIS, Henry David. Is Reconstructionism a Form of Religious Humanish? Reconstructionist, 43, No. 5, pp 7-13.
The familiar definition is: a philosophy of Judaism that views it as an evolving religious civilization, that works to realize the organic Jewish community that conceives of God in a non-supernaturalistic way.

NEHER, André. Copernicus in the Hebraic Literature from the Sixteenth to the Eighteenth Century. Journal of the History of Ideas, 38, No. 2, pp 211-26.
The majority of Jewish scholars accepted the heliocaustic system of the 18th century.

NOVAK, David. The Distinctiveness of Conservative Judaism, Judaism, 26, No. 3, Su. pp 305-408.

PATAI, Raphael. The Jewish Mind. New York, Scribner's xi, 624p.Ind.
Considers the Jewish mind as a product of Jewish culture and Jewish culture as a product of the Jewish mind.

PERRY, Ruth. Striking a Balance. Judaism, 26, No. 3, Su. pp 301-4.
Conservative Judaism between Orthodoxy and Liberalism.

PETUCHOWSKI, Jakob J. Conservativism - its Contribution to Judaism. Judaism, 26, Su. 3, Su. pp 352-57.

--------------------. From the Viewpoint of Contemporary Judaism. Face to Face, 3-4, Fa/W. pp 12-13.

--------------------. Die religiöse Grundlage des Pluralismus. Freiburger Rundbrief, 29, Nos. 109-12, pp 33-36.
Opening address at the third National Workshop on Christian-Jewish Relations in Detroit, 19-21 Ap. 1977.

PRIJS, Leo. Die jüdische Religion. Eine Einführung. München, Verlag. J. Pfeiffer, 134p, Ill, Bibl.
Introduction to Judaism, chiefly for Christians.

PUCCIARELLI, Eugenio. Entrega del Premio Baroch Spinoza. Buenos Aires, Museo Judio del Buenos Aires, 30p, Ill.
The Buenos Aires Jewish Museum presented the Spinoza prize.

RABINOWITZ, Stanley. Where do we Stand Now? Judaism, 26, No. 3, Su. pp 274-78.
The President of the Rabbinical Assembly on Conservative Judaism.

RAPHAEL, David D. In Memory of Spinoza. European Judaism, 11, No. 2, Su. pp 2-4.

RAPHAEL, Frédy. and WEYL, Robert. Juifs en Alsace, Culture, Société, Histoire. Paris, Private, 458p, Ind, Ill. (Collection France-Judaica.)
Documented, illustrated history of the Jews of Alsace.

RAPPAPORT, S. Spinoza's Spiritual Worth. Jewish Affairs, 37, No. 2, F. pp 11-14.

The Resurgence of Fundamentalism: A Symposium. The Humanist, 37, No. 1, Ja-F. pp 36-43.
The New Religiosity by Sidney Hook. Religion in America by Anthony Flew. Religion Today by Joseph L. Blau.

RISKIN, Shlomo. Conservativism and the Orthodox Resurgence. Judaism, 26, NO. 3, Su. pp 331-33.

ROSENFELD,Max. Secularism and Our Heritage. Jewish Currents, 31, No. 1, Ja. pp 22-25; No. 2, F. pp 27-20; No. 10, N. pp 27-30.

-------------- and KOBRIN, Leon. Secularism and our Heritage. Jewish Workers 75 Years Ago. Jewish Currents, 31, No. 5, My. pp 28-30.

RUBENSTEIN, Peter J. and ZINNERMAN, Sheldon. Congregational Perceptions: The Tale of the Tapes. CCAR Journal, 25, Su, pp 3-17.
Interviews with more than twenty members of six congregations in three different cities indicate how present-day Reform Jews view themselves and their relations to Reform Judaism.

RUTMAN, Herbert S. Ritual, Uniformity and Reform Judaism. CCAR Journal, W. pp 89-91.
"The greater use of Jewish ritual poses a danger which, for the sake of the preservation of Reform Judaism's uniqueness, must be avoided."

SCHOLEM, Gershom G. Les Grands Courants de la Mystique Juive. Tr. M.M. Davy, Paris, Payot, 432p.

SCHWARZ, Sidney H. A Rationale for Reconstructionism. Reconstructionist, 43, No. 5, Ju. pp 14-20.
"The test of Reconstructionism is whether it can continue to subject Judaism to the most stringent evaluation against the standards of the Jewish tradition and suitability to our American environment."

SPINOZA, Benedict De. Dictionary Ed. Dagobert D. Runes. Westport, Conn., Greenwood P.; London, Westport P., xiv, 309p.
Facsimile of the 1951 edition.

Spinoza vu par Nahum Goldmann (propos receuillis par Joël Askenazi) Les Nouveaux Cahiers, 13, No. 50, Aut. pp 27-29.

STEVENS, Carey, BLANK, Arthur and POUCHINSKY, Greg. Religion as a Factor in Morality Research: A Cross-Sectional analysis of older adolescents, young adults, middle age and senior citizens. Journal of Psychology and Judaism, 1, No. 2, pp 61ff.

TRIMBLE, Virginia L. Masada, Suicide and Halakhah. Conservative Judaism, 31, No. 2, W. pp 45-55.

TWORUSCHKA, Udo. (Ed.) Religionen Heute. Themen und Texte für Unterricht und Studium. München, Kösel; Frankfurt/M., Diesterweg, 184p, Ind.
Teachers' handbook on world religions. Of special interest: Religion und Politik im Judentum and Frieden im Judentum both by Hans-Jürgen Loth.

UNGAR, André. Judaism for our Time. London, The Reform Synagogues of Great Britain, 28p.

WAXMAN, Mordecai. The Basic Issues - An Analysis. Judaism. 26, No. 3, pp 279-85.
The failure of Conservative Judaism in America.

WOLFSON, Harry Austryn. From Philo to Spinoza. Two Studies in Religious Philosophy. Intro. by Isadore Twersky. New York, Behrman House, 64p.
Professor Wolfson, who died in 1974, was one of the greatest scholars and humanists of the 20th century specialising in medieval religious philosophy.

ZAC, Sylvain. Kant et le probleme du judaisme. Les Nouveaux Cahiers, 13, No. 49, pp 32-49.

BIOGRAPHIES, AUTOBIOGRAPHIES, LETTERS

ADAMS, Larry L. Walter Lippman. New York, Twayne Publ. 229p.

ADLER, Mortimer J. Philosopher at Large: An Intellectual Autobiography. New York, Macmillan, 349p, Ind, Ill, Bibl.

ALMANY, Abraham. Menahem Begin: A Memoir. Midstream, 23, No. 7, Au. S. pp 39-40.

ALPERT, David B. The Man from Kovno. American Jewish Archives, 29, No. 2, N. pp 107-15.
Rabbi Abraham Alpert made many efforts to improve the lot of immigrant life in Boston.

AMERONGEN, Martin Van. Kreisky und seine unbewältigte Gegenwart. Graz, Wien, Köln, Styria. 128p.
The author, a Dutch journalist analyses the Kreisky-Wiesenthal controversy. Austrian politics, particularly as reflected in the problem of Nazis and in the attitude of Jews, and the qualities of the two antagonists are presented.

APP, Austin J. Autobiography. German-American Voice for Truth and Justice. Takoma Park, Maryland, Boniface P., 308p, Ind, Ill.
App is a leading American Nazi.

ARONSON, Theo. Victoria and Disraeli. The Making of a Romantic Partnership. London, Cassell, xii, 212p, Ind, Ill, Bibl.

BASSO, Lelio (Ed.) Per conoscere Rosa Luxemburg. Milano, Mondadori, xxii, 351p.

BEGIN, Menachem. White Nights. London, Vallentine, Mitchell, n.e. 240p.
Memoirs.

BERGMAN, G.F.J. The Bizarre Life Story of Mordecai Moses. Australian Jewish Historical Society, 8, No. 3, pp 100-8.

BLUMENTHAL, Ernst Pinchas. Diener am Licht. Eine Biographie Theodor Herzls. Frankfurt/M. Europäischer Verlag, 325p.
A new biography.

BENYOSEF, I.A. Albert Einstein and Judaism. Jewish Affairs, 32, No. 6, Ju. pp 17-20.

BONDY, Ruth. The Emissary. A Life of Enzo Sereni. Tr. fr. Hebrew by Shlomo Katz. Foreword by Golda Meir. Boston, Atlantic-Little, Brown, 265p, Ill.

BUBER-NEUMANN, Margarete. Milena, Kafkas Freundin. München, Langen-Müller, 320p.
Biography of Milena Jesenska, Franz Kafka's friend, who, although not Jewish, was killed in a concentration camp.

CANOVAN, Margaret. The Political Thought of Hannah Arendt. London, Methuen University Paperback, n.e. 144p.

CHAIN, Ernst. Profile of a Ben Brith. B'nai B'rith Journal, 10, Sp. pp 13-16.

CLARK, Ronald W. The Man Who Broke 'Purple'. The Life of the World's Greatest Cryptologist, Colonel William F. Friedman. London, Wiedenfeld & Nicolson, 224p, Ill.

COHEN, Mitchell. Ber Borochov: Towards a Portrait of a Socialist Zionist. Response, 11, No. 2, Fa. pp 5-28.

COHEN, Trevor. The Honourable Vaiben Louis Solomon. Australian Jewish Historical Quarterly, 8, No. 3, pp 89-99.

COOPER, Elias. Spinoza - A Tercentenary Appreciation. The American' Zionist, 67, No. 8, Jy. pp 21-25.

COOVER, Robert. The Public Burning. New York, Viking P., 534p.
The Rosenberg case.

CROSS, John A. Sir Samuel Hoare: A Political Biography. London, Cape, xiv, 416p, Ind, Ill.
Sir Samuel Hoare (Lord Templewood) was Home Secretary in the Chamberlain Government and was involved with Jewish refugees from Nazi Germany.

DANIEL, Jean. Le refuge et la source. Paris, Grasset, 117p.
Autobiography with childhood and youth in Algiers.

DASHEFSKY, Arnold. The three faces of Ber Borochov. Jewish Frontier 44, No. 8, O. pp 15-25.

DOR, Moshe. An Interview with Aba Kovner: Poet, Partisan, Pioneer. The Jewish Quarterly, 24, No. 4, pp 21-23.

DREYFUS, Alfred. Five Years of My Life. The Diary of Captain Alfred Dreyfus. Intro. by Nicholas Halasz. New York, London, Peebles P., (Bobbs-Merrill), 253p, Ill.

The work has been out of print since 1901 and is reproduced in its complete, original form.

DREYFUS, Pierre. Album de famille. L'Arche, 20, No. 243, Ju. pp 32-35.

Recollections of Captain Dreyfus' family.

DRINNON, Richard and Anna Maria (Eds.) Nowhere at Home: Letters of Emma Goldman and Alexander Berkman. New York, Schocken, xxviii, 282p, Ill.

DUBINSKY, David and RASKIN, A.H. David Dubinsky. A Life with Labor. New York, Simon and Schuster, 351p, Ill.

EASTWOOD, Granville. Harold Laski. Intro. by James Callaghan. Oxford Mowbray, x, 173p.

Biography of the noted political scientist whose views on Israel and Jewish problems are highlighted.

ELEK, Helene. La mémoire d'Hélène. Paris, Maspero, 311p. (Actes et memoires du Peuple)

Memories of a Hungarian Jewish ex-communist and members of the resistance, now living in France.

ENGELMAN, Edmund. Berggasse 19. Sigmund Freud's Home and Offices. Vienna, 1938. Stuttgart, Belser, 156p, Ill.

FEIN, Irving. Jack Benny. New York, Pocket Books, 319p.

Biography of the American-Jewish comic.

FIREMAN, Morton C. Dr. James Parkes - An Affectionate Statement on his Eightieth Birthday. CCAR Journal, 25, No. 1, W. pp 81-88.

Tribute to the eminent scholar in Jewish-Christian relationships Jewish history, Judaism and Zionism.

MENDES-FRANCE, Pierre. Liberté, liberté, chérie. Paris, Fayard, 428p, Ind.

Autobiographical account of his role in the Resistance.

FRANK, Ben G. Simone Veil - French Jewish Stateswoman. Jewish Affairs, 32, No. 10, O. pp 21-23.

FRANKS, Viktor E. ... trotzdem. Ja zum Leben sagen. Ein Psychologe erlebt das Konzentrationslager. Münich, Kösel, 200p.

Memoirs of a noted psychologist who survived the concentration camps.

FREEDLAND, Michael. Fred. Astaire. New York and Dunlop, 277p, Ill.

Biography, first published in England, 1976.

FREUDENTHAL, Berthold. Ich habe mein Land gefunden. Frankfurt/M, Josef Knecht, 1977. 207p.

Memoirs.

GELLER, Uri. My Story. N.e. London, Corgi, 288p, Ill.

Biography.

GLUCKEL OF HAMELIN. The Memoirs of ... Tr. Marvin Lowenthal. New York, Schocken, 205p.

GOLDEMBERG, Isaac. The Fragmented Life of Don Jacobo Lerner. Tr. Robert S. Picciotto. New York, Persea Books; London, Sidgwick & Jackson, 186p.

GOLDSTEIN, Mortiz. Berliner Jahre. Erinnerungen 1880-1933. München, V. Dokumentation, 269p. Ill. (Dortmunder Beiträge zur Zeitungsforschung, 25)

Memoirs of a German-Jewish journalist.

GOURDON, Alain. Mendès France ou le rêve francais. Paris, Ramsey, 562p.

Biography.

GREENFIELD, Richard Pierce and GREENFIELD, Irving A. The Life Story of Menachem Begin. New York, Manor Books, 242p.

HANNAM, Charles. A Boy in Your Situation. London, Deutsch, 216p.

Story of a Jewish boy in Nazi Germany.

HECHT, Ben. A Child of the Century. Brooklyn, New York, Jewish P.,

WILL HERBERG: A Tribute. National Review, 29, 5 Au. pp 880-86.

Six articles: A Biographical Sketch by Seymour Siegel. Herberg as Sociologist by Nathan Glazer. Herberg as Political Philosopher by Lewis S. Feuer. Herberg as Theologian of Christianity by Bernhard W. Anderson. Herberg as Jewish Theologian by Fritz A. Rothschild. Herberg as Teacher by Donald G. Jones.

HILDESHEIMER, Wolfgang. Mozart. Stuttgart, Suhrkamp, 420p, Ind, Ill.

Biography with many references to his Jewish librettist, Da Ponte and Jewish Interpreters of his music.

HOENIG, Sidney B. Jewish Law and Lore: The Scholarship of Dr. Samuel Belkin. New York, Yeshiva U.P., 136p.

HURWITZ, Harry. Menachem Begin. Johannesburg, Jewish Herald, 173p, Ill.

Israels Ambassade, about Menachem Begin. Israel's Prime Minister. Kobenhaven, 24p.

JANNI, Tina. Ernst Bloch Visto Da Gershom Scholem. La Rassegna Mensile di Israel, 43, Nos. 11-12, N.-D. pp 667-71.

Scholem's view of Bloch.

JENKINS, David and VISOCCHI, Mark. Mendelssohn in Scotland. London, Chappell, 160p, Ill.

Felix Mendelssohn-Bartholdy.

JOSEFSBERG, Milt. Jack Benny as a Jew. Jewish Digest, 23, No. 1, S. pp 63-64.

Excerpts from book The Jack Benny Show: The Life and Times of an American Entertainer. New Rochelle, N.Y. Arlington House.

KISSINGER, Henry A. Golda Meir: A Universal Conscience. Congress Monthly, 44, No. 8, N. pp 5-7.

KLAIDMAN, Stephen. The Talmudist of the Twentieth Century. A Conversation with Rabbi Adin Steinsaltz. National Jewish Monthly, 91, No. 7, Ma. pp 6-12.

KLUNCKER, Karlhaus. (Ed.) Karl und Hanna Wolfskehl Breifwechsel mit Friedrich Gundolf 1899-1931. Amsterdam Castrum Peregrini, 2 vols. 700p, Ind.

Wolfskehl and Gundolf were German Jews, outstanding critics and writers of the period preceding the Nazi era. Some of their correspondence discusses the influence of Judaism on Western civilization.

KONVITZ, Milton. Emanuel Neumann - A Tribute. Midstream, 23, No. 2, F. pp 58-60.

KOSTELANETZ, Richard. Gershom Scholem. The Mystics' Medium. Present Tense, 4, No. 3, Sp. pp 29-33.

KOSZARSKI, Richard. (Ed.) Hollywood Directors 1914-40. Oxford U.P. 384p.

Many Jews among them.

KOTLAN-WERNER, Henriette. Kunst und Volk, David Josef Bach 1874-1947. With a foreword by Hertha Firnberg. Wien, Europa for Ludwig Boltzmann Institut für Geschichte und Arbeiterbewegung,174p, Ill. (Materialien zur Arbeiterbewegung, 6)

Life and work of the Jewish Austrian Social Democrat.

KRAFT, Werner. Das Ja des Neinsagers. Karl Kraus und seine geistige Welt. München, Edition und Kritik, 248p.

Monograph of Kraus.

KUPFERBERG, Herbert. Die Mendelssohns. Tr. Klaus Leonhardt. Tübingen, Rainer Wunderlich, 304p, Ill.

Monograph of the Mendelssohn family.

KUSSEL, Sallie. The Jerusalem of Dorem Afrika. Jewish Affairs, 32, No. 11, N. pp 34-36.

LACOUTURE, Jean. Léon Blum. Paris, Le Seuil, 600p, Ill.

LARSEN, Egon. Weimar Eyewitness. London, Bachman & Turner, 192p, Ill, Ind, Bibl.

Memoirs of the post-war years in Germany, Austria and Czechoslovakia by a Jewish journalist.

LAZARUS, Mary. E.L. Zox. M.L.A. 1837-1899. Australian Jewish Historical Society, 8, No. 3, pp 109-21.

LEFKOWITZ, Bernard. Goodbye to Dolly's. New York Post, Did Mother Really Know Best? Present Tense, 4, No. 4, Su. pp 54-55.

Dorothy Schiff, owner-editor of the New York Post, died in November 1976.

LEIBOVICI, Sarah. Cet étrange Christophe Colomb. Les Nouveaux Cahiers, 12, No. 50, Aut. pp 56-58.

On the myth that Colombus was of Jewish extraction.

LEOR, Haim. Josef Sprinzak el padre del parlamentarismo israeli. Tr. Isidoro Niborski. Beunos Aires, Congreso Judio Mundial. Congreso Judio Latinoamericano, 40p, (Grandes Figuras del Judaismo 103.)

LEVENBERG, Shneier. Simon Dubnow (1860-1941) The Historian of Russian Jewry. The Jewish Quarterly, 24, No. 4, W. pp 30-37.

LIEBERMANN, Mischket. Aus dem Ghetto in die Welt. Berlin, Verlag der Nation, 360p, Ill.

Autobiography of a Jewish woman who lived in Weiman Germany and the USSR.

LINK-SALINGER, (Hyman) Ruth. Gustav Landauer. Philosopher of Utopia with a Scholarly Bibliography. Ed. by Prof. Arthur Hyman. Indianapolis, Hackett,xiv, 171p, Bibl.

LINKSZ, Arthur. Visszanezek ... ifjukorom Magyarorszagon. New York Twenty-first Century Hungarian Publishing Co., 380p, Ill.

Memories of a Hungarian Jewish ophthalmic surgeon who, in 1939, emigrated to the United States.

LIPSCHUTZ, Robert. The President's Lawyer. The Jewish Veteran, 81, My-Ju. pp 10-13.

The magazine's editor, Stephen Barlas, interviews the White House Counsel, who comments on contemporary issues.

LUCE, Clare Booth. Golda Meir: Last Link to Israel's Founders. Jewish Digest, 22, No. 9,My. pp 39-43. Condensed from The New Republic, 174, No. 16,

MACDONALD, Edgar. (Ed.) The Education of the Heart: The Correspondence of Rachel Mordecai Lazarus and Maria Edgeworth. Chapel Hill, North Carolina, U. of North Carolina, xxiii, 341p.

McGUIRE, William. (Ed.) The Freud/Jung Letters. The Correspondence between Sigmund Freud and C.G. Jung. Tr. by Ralph Manheim and R.F.C. Hull. London, Routledge & Kegan Paul, in association with Hogarth P., 692p, Ill. U.S. Edition: Princeton U.P., 650p.

MAGNES, Beatrice L. Episodes. Berkeley, Judah L. Magnes Memorial Museum, 124p.

Memories of Judah L. Magnes' widow.

MAGNES, Judah L. Pioneer and prophet on two continents. A Pictorial Biography. Berkeley, Ca., Judah L. Magnes Memorial Museum, 56p.

MALKA, Victor. Menahem Begin. La Bible et le Fusil. Paris Media, 200p, Ill.

Biography and analysis of Begin's policies.

MÁNDI, Teréz. Nagy Endre centénariumá. Szinhaz, No. 5, My. pp 39-42.

Nagy was born in 1877. He was the founder of political cabaret in Hungary and bringing to it a flavour of Jewish humour.

MARROW, Alfred J. Kurt Lewin - Leben und Werk. Tr. Hainer Kober. Stuttgart, Klett-Cotta, 260p, Ill, M.

One of the most renowned psychologists of his generation.

MASKELL, R.E. Alexander Marks, 1838-1919. Australian Jewish Historical Society, 8, No. 3, pp 122-25.

MATT, Hershel J. Will Herberg: A Tribute. Conservative Judaism, 31, No. 2, W. pp 5-14.

MELADY, Thomas and Margaret. Idi Amin: Hitler in Africa. Kansas, Sheed Andrews, 184p, Ill.

The last US Ambassador to Uganda describes Amin's antisemitism, admiration of Hitler and contacts with the PLO.

MENUHIN, Yehudi. Unfinished Journey. London, Macdonald & Janes; New York, Knopf; München, Ripes, 426p, Ill.

Autobiography.

MERLIN, Samuel. Menahem Begin: Orator, Commander, Statesman. Has the Call to Power come 29 Years Late? The National Jewish Monthly, 91, No. 11, Jy-Au. pp 6-11.

MICHAEL, Reuven. (Ed.) Heinrich Graetz. Tagebuch und Briefe. Tübingen, J.C.B. Mohr, xiv, 469p. (Schriftenreihe wissenschaftlicher Abhandlungen des Leo Baeck Instituts 34)

MIRSKY, Jeanette. Sir Aurel Stein. Archaeological Explorer. Chicago; London, U. of Chicago P., 585p, Ind, Ill.

Biography of the Jewish explorer.

MIRSKY, Mark Jay. My Search for the Messiah. Studies and Wanderings in Israel and America. New York, Macmillan, 240p.

MORABI, Alfred. Un docteur juif dans la cité musulmane mediévale: Maimonide. Les Nouveaux Cahiers, 13, No. 49, Su. pp 50-60.

MORRIS, Roger. Uncertain Greatness. Henry Kissinger and American Foreign Policy. London; Melbourne; New York, Quartet, viii, 312p. Ind.

The author was briefly on Kissinger's staff and adds useful information on Kissinger's character and U.S. foreign policy.

MOSLEY, Diana. A Life of Contrasts. London, Hamish Hamilton, 304p, Ill.
Autobiography of Sir Oswald Mosley's wife.
MOSLEY, Oswald. My Life. N.e. London, Sanctuary P., 500p. Ill.
NARAYAN, B.K. Anwar El-Sadat: Man with a Mission. New Delhi, Vikas Publ. 160p.
OBER, Kenneth H. Meir Goldschmidt. New York, Twayne, 146p, (World Authors)
OLAN, Levi A. Forward to the Fundamentals. Judaism, 26, No. 3, Su. pp 348-51.
On Isaac Luser and Isaac M. Wise.
PALGI, Arieh. The Man and his Paradoxes. An Interview with Nahum Goldmann. Israel Horizons, 25, No. 2, F. pp 6-8.
PANITCH, Victor. In shturmedike yoren (in stormy years) New York, Cyco, 639p.
Autobiography.
PAPP, Janós. A Kner-könyvkiadás történétebõl. A könyvmûvészeti kisérletezés évei. Békési Élet. No. 3, pp 307-22.
History of the Jewish printing family Kner in Hungary.
Extract from a work in preparation.
PARKINSON, G.H.R. Georg Lukács. London, Routledge & Kegan Paul, vii, 205p, Ind, Bibl.
Monograph.
PAYNE, Robert. The Life and Death of Trotsky. New York, McGraw-Hill, viii, 498p, Ind, Ill, Bibl.
PETREMENT, Simone. Simone Weil: A Life. Tr. Raymond Rosenthal. New York, Pantheon; London, Mowbrays, 577p.
Biography of the noted Jewish philosopher who converted to Catholocism.
PFEFFER, Leo. Issues that Divide: The Triumph of Secular Humanism. Journal of Church and State, 19, Sp. pp 203-16.
Examines the positions taken by religious groups on the issues which divide them.
PIERRARD, Pierre. Interroge le Grand Rabbin Jacob Kaplan. Justice pour la foi juive. Paris, Le Centurion, 288p.
Memoirs of the Chief Rabbi of France in the form of a long interview.
PIERRE-BLOCH, Jean. Le temps d'y penser encore. Ed. Jean-Claude Simeon, Paris, 26p.
PILCH, Judah. Between Two Generations. Rochester, N.Y. Growth, 199p.
Memoirs of a Jewish educator.
PORRIER, Herbert Le. Der Arzt aus Cordoba. Wien, Hamburg, Paul Zsolnay, 352p.
Biography of Moses Maimonides.
-------------------. Maimodide, Medicin. L'Arche, 20, No. 239, F. pp 46-55.
PRAUSE, Gerhard. Herodes der Grosse. König der Juden. Hamburg, Hoffman und Campe, 374p, Ind, Ill, M.
Authoritative account of Herod and his times.
PREMINGER, Otto. An Autobiography. New York, Doubleday, 430p, Ill.
PRINS, Willy. Die Himmelsleiter. Hamburg, Christians Verlag, 208p.
Biography of David Shaltiel, Chief of Haganah Intelligence and later Israeli diplomat.

PRITTIE, Terence. Through Irish Eyes. London, Bachman & Turner, 309p, Ill.
Autobiography describing his involvement with Israel and the Zionist idea.

RABI, Wladimir. L'Homme qui est entré dans la loi: Pierre Goldmann. (Supplément à "Les Temps modernes) Paris, La pensee sauvage, 60p.
A Jewish gangster's prosecution was construed as antisemitism.

RADDATZ, Fritz J. Heine. Ein deutsches Märchen, Essay. Hamburg, Hoffman und Campe, 200p.
Attempts to destroy the many legends around Heine.

RIES, Wiebrecht. Transzendenz als Terror. Einereligions-philosophische Studie über Franz Kafka. Heidelberg, Verlag Lambert Schneider. 159p, (Pronesis, 4)
Analysis of Kafka's "logic of fear" which influenced Camus in his theory of metaphysical revolt.

RIESS, Curt. Rolf Liebermann. Nennen Sie mich einfach Musiker. Hamburg, R. Glöss, 300p, Ill.
The Director of the Paris Opera.

ROAZEN, Paul. La Pensée Politique et Sociale de Freud. Brussels, Complexe, 256p.

ROSEN, Philip. Franz Boas, Father of Anthropology. Jewish Currents, 31, No. 6, Ju. pp 14-19.

ROSENBLATT, Samuel. Days of My Years. New York, Ktav, 207p.
Autobiography.

ROSENFELD, Lulla. Bright Star of Exile. Intro. by H. Clurman. New York, Crowell, 384p, Ill.
Biography of Jacob Adler as a backdrop to the History of the Yiddish Theatre.

ROSENFELD, Steven S. From Washington: The Kind of Role Jack Javits Plays. Present Tense, 4, No. 4, Su. pp 12-16.

ROTHSCHILD, Sylvia. Rav Soloveitchik: Talmudic Scholar and Philosopher. Present Tense, 4, No. 4, Su. pp 39-44.

ROTHSCHILD, Lord Nathaniel Mayer Victor. Meditations of a Broomstick. London, Collins, 192p, Ind, Ill.
Autobiography of Lord Rothschild, who for several years headed the "Think Tank" established by Edward Heath when he was British Prime Minister.

RUBENSTEIN, Aryeh. Isaac Mayer Wise: A New Appraisal. Jewish Social Studies, 39, Nos. 1-2, W/Sp. pp 53-74.

SADEK, Vladimir; SEDINOVA, Jirina. Peter Beer (1758-1838) Penseur eclaire de la vieille ville juive de Prague. Judaica Bohemiae, 13, No. 1, pp 7-28.

ST. JOHN, Robert. L'eretico. Bologna, Esculapio, 367p.
Biography of Elieser ben Yehuda.

SALLIS-FREUDENTHAL, Margarete. Ich habe mein Land gefunden; autobiographischer Rückblick. Frankfurt/M., Josef Knecht, 207p,Ill
Autobiography.

SCHALLENBERGER, Horst and SCHREY, Helmut. Im Gegenstrom; für Helmut Hirsch zum siebzigsten. Wuppertal, Peter Hammer, 248 (4) p.

SCHEPS, Samuel. Armand Lévy, compagnon de Mickiewicz, revolutionnaire romantique. Pref. Andrzej Vincenz, tondon, Poets' and Painters' P., 53p.

SCHLIPP, Paul A. (Ed.) Albert Einstein: Philosopher-scientish. New York, Open Court Publ. Co., 781p.

---------------. Philosophy of Karl Popper. New York, Open Court Publ.Co., 2 vols.

---------------. and FRIEDMAN, Maurice (Eds.) Philosophy of Martin Buber. New York, Open Court Publ. Co., 811p.

SCHOLEM, Gershom. Von Berlin nach Jerusalem. Jugenderinnerungen. Frankfurt/M., Suhrkamp, 230p, Ind.

Memoirs of the Jewish philosopher, of his childhood and youth in Berlin and his first years in Jerusalem (1897-1925)

SCHUMACH, Murray. The Life and Times of Irving Spiegel: A Farewell to Spizzy. The National Jewish Monthly, 91, No. 6, Ju. pp 28-33.

Specialist on Jewish affairs for The New York Times who died in March.

SCHUR, Max. Sigmund Freud. Leben und Sterben. Frankfurt/M., Suhrkamp, 696p.

SCHWARZ, Leo W. Wolfson of Harvard: Portrait of a Scholar. Philadelphia, Jewish Publication Society of America, 283p.

SHANE, A.L. Rabbi Jacob Judah Leon (Templo) of Amsterdam (1603-75) and his Connections with England. Transactions of the Jewish Historical Society of England, 25, pp 120-36.

His model of the Temple of Solomon is held by the Masonic Grand Lodge of London.

SIGNORET, Simone. La nostalgie n'est pas ce qu'elle etait. Paris, Seuil, 378p.

Autobiography.

SILVERMAN, Robert. Samuel David Luzzatto - The Dilemma of a Conservative Jew. European Judaism, 11, No. 2, Su. pp 5-12.

SIMON, Ernst. Sigmund Freud el Judió. Tr. from Hebrew by Iehoschua Faigon. Buenos Aires, Congreso Judió Latinoamericano, Congreso Judio Mundial, 48p, Ill. (Grandes Figuras del Judaismo, 104)

SIMONOVITS, István. Emlékézes dr. Weil Emilre. Párttörteneti Közlémenyek, 21, No. 7, Ju. pp 180-87.

Dr. Weil a prominent Jewish physician, was an important Communist leader.

SIMOR, Andras. Igy elt Korvin Otto. Budapest, Mora, 192p.

Korvin was a leader of the Hungarian Proletariat Dictatorship of 1919.

ŠKLOVSKIJ, Viktor. Sergej M. Ejzenštejn. Tr. Manfred Dahlke. Hamburg, Rowohlt, 360p, Ill. In Hungarian: Budapest, Gondorlat, 350p.

SLATER, Robert. Rabin of Israel. London, Robson Books, 224p, Ill.

SOWDEN, Dora. René Shapshak. South African Emigres Bump Abroad. Jewish Affairs, 32, No. 3, Ma. pp 39-43.

SPERBER, Manes. Bis man mir Scherben auf die Augen legt. All das Vergangene. Zürich, Europa, 378p.

Third volume of autobiography.

--------------. Ces temps-la. (II) Le Pont inacheve. Paris, Calmann-Levy, 269p.

Second volume of memoirs.

SPYCHKET, Jerome. Clara Haskil. Eine Biographie. Foreward by Herbert von Karajan. Tr. Erika and Gerald Turner. Bern, Hallwag, 256p, Ill.

Biography of the Rumanian Jewish pianist.

STEINBACH, U. Menachem Begin. Orient, 18, No. 2, F. pp 7-10.

------------. Yigael Yadin, Orient, 18, No. 3, Ma. pp 5-8.
THOMPSON, Kenneth and MYERS, Robert J. (Eds.) Truth and Tragedy: A Tribute to Hans J. Morgenthau. With an intellectual autobiography by Hans J. Morgenthau. Ed. with the assistance of Robert Osgood and Tang Tsou. Washington, The New Republic, 336p.
TREPPER, Leopold. The Great Game. Memoirs of a Master Spy. London, Michael Joseph; New York, McGraw-Hill, 422p, Ind, Ill.
Upon the defeat of Hitler, Trepper who had founded and led the famous Rote Kapelle underground network, was imprisoned in a Soviet jail. Released after Stalin's death, he returned to Poland where he became enmeshed in the antisemitic events of 1968.
TUCHMAN, Barbara W. The Assimilationist Dilemma: Commentary, 63, No. 5, My. pp 58-61.
The story of Hans Morgenthau.
WEHR, Gerhard. Der deutsche Jude - Martin Buber. München, Kindler, 287p, Ind.
Monograph, published on the centenary of Buber's birth.
WERNER, Alfred. An Appreciation. Midstream, 23, No. 6, Ju-Jy. pp 43-48.
The noted Jewish historian.
WEXLEY, John. The Judgment of Julius and Ethel Rosenberg. New York, Ballantine, 230p, Ill.
Who is Menahem Begin? A Documentary Sketch. Beirut, Institute for Palestine Studies, 61p. (Memoranda S. 13)
Arab propaganda brochure.
WIESMANN, Sigrid. (Ed.) Gustav Mahler in Vienna. Tr. Anne Shelley. London, Thames & Hudson; New York, Rizzoli, 167p, Ill.
WINCZAKIEWICZ, Anna. J'ai Survecu. Tr. Kazimierz Piekarec. Paris. Ed. La Pensee Universelle, 123p.
A survivor of the Warsaw ghetto.
WISTRICH, Robert. The Jewish Origins of Rosa Luxemburg. Olam, No. 3, W/Sp. pp 3-10.
YAFFE, Richard. An Interview with Nahum Goldmann. Israel Horizons, 25, No. 10, Fa/W. pp 6-10.
ZOGRAPHAKI, Georgion K. (Ed.) Mordechai Fritze. The Jewish Colonel and first Greek higher-officer who fell in the Greek-Italian war on 5.12.1940. (In Greek) Athens, Central Board of Jewish Communities in Greece, 63p, Ill.
ZORINSKY, Senator Ed. Good News on Capitol Hill. The Jewish Veteran, 81, Ma-Ap. pp 6-9.

PRESS/MEDIA

FOX, Stuart. (Comp.) Jewish Films in the United States. A Comprehensive Survey and Descriptive Filmography. Boston, G.H. Hall, 359p.
FRANKEL, Edith Rogovin. Israel's Russian Press is Booming. Present Tense, 5, No. 1, Aut. pp 11-14.
KOTZIN, Miriam. What is Jewish Film? Congress Monthly, 44, No. 7, O. pp 16-17.
LEVENTHAL, Lionel. Jerusalem Book Fair. More Exhibits and Visitors Than Ever. The Bookseller, 21 My. pp 2522-25.

Nicht nur Bücher - auch Kultur ... Interview mit dem Leiter der Buchmesse, Rafi Aldor. Börsenblatt, 32, 24 Ap. pp 67-69.
The Jerusalem Bookfair.

NORTON, Wesley. Religious Newspapers in the Old Northwest to 1861: A History, Bibliography and Record of Opinion. Athens, Ohio, Ohio U.P., xi, 196p.
Among the newspapers discussed are Isaac M. Wise's The Israelite and Die Deborah.

NOWAK, William. Commentary: The Good, The Bad and the Ugly. Interchange, 2, No. 1, S. pp 7-12.
A critical review of three decades of Commentary Magazine's growth.

QUDSI, S. Israeli Papers (In Arabic) In: Al-Marifa, No. 181, Ma. pp 34-51.
Analysis of the Israeli press.

ROGOVIN-FRANKEL, Edith. The Russian Press in Israel. Soviet Jewish Affairs, 7, No. 1, pp 47-68.

ROSENBLATT, Gary. The Jewish De-Press. Moment, 3, No. 1, N. pp 46-50.
Report on the English-lan guage Jewish newspapers in the United States.

SAHM, Uri. Papier und Anzeigen werden gemeinsam gekauft. Was die Deutschen von den Israelis lernen können. (Der Israelische Verlagerverband und sein Prasident) Borsenblatt, 32, 22 Ap. pp 70-72.
The advertising policy of Israeli publishers.

SCHATZ, Julius. Images of the Jewish Experience in Film and Television. Jewish Digest, 22, No. 9, My. pp 63-65.

STRAUS, Peter R. His Daughter's Father: Otto Frank. Moment, 3, No. 2, D. pp 27-30.

STRAUSS, Richard and ZWEIG, Stefan. A Confidential Matter. The Letters of Richard Strauss and Stefan Zweig 1931-35. Tr. Max Knight. Berkeley, Ca. Los Angeles, New York, London, California U.P. 153p, Ill.

STUCKENSCHMIDT, H.H. Arnold Schoenberg: His Life, World and Work. London, J. Calder, 584p, Ind, Ill.
Biography and analysis of his works.

WIENER, Markus. Pro Kopf die meisten Titel der Welt. Ein Land, das für die internationale Verlegerschaft immer interessanter wird. (Der Buchmarkt in Israel: Alles ganz anders) Börsenblatt, 32, 22 Ap. pp 9-14.
Report on the book trade in Israel.

SOCIETY

ROSE, Peter I. Strangers in Their Midst: Small Town Jews and their Neighbors. Merrick, N.Y. Richwood Publ. Co., 224p.
Sociological study of Jews living in small towns and small communities in the U.S.A.

ROSKIES, David C. Shtetl Society. Jewish Spectator, 42, No. 3, Fa. pp 44-46.

ROSNER, Menachem. The Kibbutz as a Way of Life. Cambridge, Mass., Institute for Cooperative Community, 150p.

ROZENKIER, A.B. Continuité et/ou discontinuité dans les attitudes de la seconde generation du Kibboutz. Doctoral Thesis, University of Paris V, Ecole des Hautes Etudes en Sciences sociales, Centre de Recherches cooperatives, 538p, Bibl.

ETHNOGRAPHY

ELLMAN, Yisrael. The Ethnic Awakening in the United States and its influence on Jews. Ethnicity, 4, No. 2, Ju. pp 133-35.
  Affords the Jews new prospects enabling them to preserve their identity.

Ethnic Conflict in the World Today. The Annals of the American Academy of Political Science. Special Issue, S. pp 1-219.
  Includes: Ethnicity in the Soviet Union by Teresa Rakowska-Harmstone. Majorities and Minorities: A Comparative Survey of Ethnic Violence by Christopher Hewitt.

LAWRENCE, Daniel. The Continuing Debate on Heredity and Environment. Patters of Prejudice. 11, No. 3, pp 5-9.
  "The debate on the relative contributions of 'nature' and 'nurture' to the development of intelligence will continue... Despite the large measure of agreement between "the experts" there are many respected academics who judge that the hereditarian case is based on such shaky conceptual foundations that it can never be established however much research is carried out."

PERGOLA, Sergio della and TAGLIACOZZO, Amedeo. Gli Italiani in Israele: Parts 2-5. La Rassegna Mensile di Israel, 43, Nos. 1-2, Ja-F. pp 16-32; Nos. 7-8, Jy-Au. pp 356-75; No. 9, S. pp 437-60; No. 10. O. pp 525-46.
  Study of Italian Jews in Israel.

REINES, Chaim W. Human Relationships in the Jewish Tradition. Judaism, 26, No. 3, Su. pp 358-66.
  The forms of special relationships recorded in Biblical and Rabbinic literature:gregariousness, greetings and friendly receptions, friendship, hospitality and feasts, weddings and funerals and attitudes to them.

ROSENSTOCK, Michael. A Genetic Portrait of the Jewish People. AJR Information, 32, No. 2, F. pp 1-2.

SELLER, Maxine. To Seek America: A History of Ethnic Life in the United States. Englewood, N.Y., Jerome S. Ozer, 328p.
  Includes Jews.

STATISTICS

FOWLER, Floyd J. 1975 Community Survey: A Study of the Jewish Population of Greater Boston. Boston, Combined Jewish Philanthropies of Greater Boston, xiii, 125p, M.
  Demographic survey, based on a structured questionaire, follow up to an earlier 1965 survey. There are important new features in the community.

MARGOLINSKY, Ju. Jødiske Dødsfald i Danmark 1693-1976. (Jewish Deaths in Denmark 1964-1976) Lyngby, Dansk, Historish Handbosforlag, 400p.

"STANOVNIŠTVO" 3.4.74. Izdavač Institut društvenih nauka. Centar za demografska istraživanja Beograd. pp 169-84. (Marko Peric. Posebno demografsko istraživanje jevrejske zajednice u Jugoslaviji)

POPULATION

The Jewish Population Study of the Greater Kansas City area. Jewish Federation of Greater Kansas City. Kansas City, 54p.

LUBINSKY, Menachem. Neighborhood growth and development and the problems of Jewish neighborhoods, New York, Agudath Israel of America, 16p.

OCCUPATION

ETZIONI-HALÉVY, Eva and HELÉVY, Zvi. The 'Jewish-Ethic' and the 'Spirit of Achievement'. Jewish Journal of Sociology, 19, No. 1, Ju. pp 49-66.

Critical examination of theories explaining social success among Jews. Review of the Weber-Sombart controversy on Jewish contribution to the development of modern capitalism in the light of recent experience.

TOLL, William. American Jewish Families: The Occupational Basis of Adaptability in Portland, Oregon. The Jewish Journal of Sociology, 19, No. 1, Ju. pp 33-47.

CLASS AND
STATUS STRUCTURE

SKLARE, Marshall. (Eds.)Jews, The: Social Patterns of an American Group. N.e. Westport, Conn., Greenwood P., 669p.

SOCIAL WELFARE

American Jewish Philanthropy: Special Issue. Moment, 3, No. 6, Ju. pp 1-72.

Partial contents: The Outs and Ins of Federation by Leonard Fein. Where Are The Women by Elsa Solender. The Youngers of Zion: UJA's Leadership Cabinet and How it Got That Way by Gary Rosenblatt. Jewish Leadership, Now and Then by Nahum Goldmann.

KATZ, Harold, KATZ, Lucille B., TROPPER, Pearl K. (Eds.) The Jewish Older Population of Birmingham. Birmingham, Ala., Jewish Community Center. 230p.

Field study of work and retirement, financial security, health conditions, medical needs and service, housing, personal relationships, education and leisure activities of the Jewish aged.

KELLNER, Jacob. Formative Years of Jewish Social Welfare (1842-1869) Journal of Jewish Communal Service, 53, No. 4, Ma. pp 228-34.

LEVY, Charles S. Justice, Justice Shalt Thou Pursue. Wurzwiler School of Social Work. iv, 176p.

Selected letters, editorials and commentaries written by Charles S. Levy between 1958-1976 which address themselves to social issues during that time.

LURIE, Abraham. Social Work Services to Patients in the Jewish Institution. Journal of Jewish Communal Service, 53, No. 4, Ma. pp 282-88.
There is no entity as sectarian medicine, but there is a set of institutional values which have motivated the existence of Jewish institutions at some level.

MEIER, Levi. Filial Responsibility to the Senile Parent: A Jewish Approach. Journal of Psychology and Judaism, 2, No. 1, Fa. pp 45-54.

SCHINDLER, Ruben. Unemployment Assistance During the Period of the Yishuv: Philanthropy, Productivity and Mutual Aid. Journal of Jewish Communal Service, 53, No. 4, Su. pp 356-61.

SILVERBERG, David. The "Old" Poor - and the "New". What's Happening to Them? Present Tense, 4, No. 3, Sp. pp 59-64.

IDENTITY AND IDENTIFICATION

AGUS, Jacob. Jewish Identity in an Age of Ideologies. New York, Sepher Hermon, 463p.

BLU, K.L. Varieties and Ethnic Identity: Anglo-Saxons, Blacks, Indians and Jews in a Southern County. Ethnicity, 4, No. 3, pp 263-86.
The claims of ethnicity of Blacks, Indians and Jews against Protestant White Anglo-Saxon Americans.

CHUTZPAH: A Jewish Liberation Anthology. Chutzpah Collective, San Francisco, New Glide Publ. 191p.
Jewish radicals discuss a number of current issues affecting them as Jews.

DAWIDOWICZ, Lucy S. The Jewish Presence: Essays on Identity and History. New York, Holt,Rinehart & Winston, 308p.

DIAMENT, Mario. Conversaciones con un Judío. Buenos Aires, Timerman 197p.
On Jewish identification.

DOLGIN, Janet L. Jewish Identity and the JDL. Princeton, U.P., xi, 189p, Ind, Bibl.
The author has made a personal study of the Jewish Defence League in New York and in Israel and analyses relationships between its members and their relation to American society.

DUBB, Allie. Jewish South Africans: A Sociological View of the Johannesburg Community. Grahamstown, S.A. Institute of Social and Economic Research, Rhodes U., xi, 190p, Bibl. (Occasional Paper No. 21)
Deals chiefly with Jewish identification in South Africa.

EISENSTADT, S.N. Jüdische Identitätsmuster. Schweizer Monatshefts, 57, No. 8, N. pp 613-30.
Models of Jewish identification.

EMORY UNIVERSITY, Address and Response at the inaugeration of the Jay and Leslie Cohen Chair of Judaic Studies, 23 Ja. Atlanta, 41p.
Contents:"Being Jewish" and Studying About Judaism by Jacob Neusner. Judaic Studies: An Exercise in the Humanities by David R. Blumenthal.

ESTEBAN, Fernando Diaz. Tensiones en el hebreo contemporaneo. Sefarad, 30, No. 2, pp 366-82.

FINESTEIN, Israel. Secular Jew: Does He Exist and Why? *Jewish Journal of Sociology*, 19, No. 2, D. pp 185-95.

An essay review based on "Faith of Secular Jews" edited by Saul L. Goodman (1976)

FRIMER, Norman E. "Who is a Jew" in the Vilna Ghetto? *Tradition*, 16, No. 5, Fa. pp 55-62.

GILDIN, Leon H. Response: Jewish Secularism Revisited. *Jewish Frontier*, 44, No. 5, Ma. pp 24-25.

GOLDSMITH, Emanuel S. Jewish Secularism Revisited. *Jewish Frontier*, 44, No. 3, Ma. pp 13-16.

HEILMAN, Samuel C. Inner and Outer Identities: Social Ambivalence Among Orthodox Jews. *Jewish Social Studies*, 39, No. 3, Su. pp 227-40.

The modern Orthodox Jew has learned to live with the sociological ambivalence inherent in his dualistic identity.

HERMAN, Simon N. Jewish Identity: A Social Psychological Perspective London, Sage; New York, Herzl P., 264p.

HOENIG, Sidney B. Jewish Identity in a Changing World: An Historical Survey. *Jewish Education*, 47, W. pp 39-48.

Jewish identity in the context of the historical background, contemporary confrontation and suggestions for positive continuity.

HURVITZ, Mark. How Does One Join the Jewish People. *Reconstructionist*, 42, No. 10, Ja. pp 17-23.

Questions of Jewish identity.

KALLEN, Horace M. Cultural Pluralism and the Jews. *Jewish Spectator* 42, No. 3, Fa. pp 11-15.

KOVACS, Malcolm Louis. The dynamics of commitment: the process of resocialization of Baalei Teshuvah, Jewish students in pursuit of their identity at the Rabbinical College of America (Lubavitch). Ann Arbor, Mich., U. Microfilms, 311p, Bibl.

Ph.D. Dissertation, Union Graduate School.

KRAUSZ, Ernest. Le facteur religieux dans la formation de l'identité juive. *Revue Internationale des Sciences Sociales*, 29, No. 2, pp 272-83.

Examines the question whether religion helps contemporary Jews to find their identity.

LAZERWITZ, Bernard. The Community Variable in Jewish Identification. *Journal for the Scientific Study of Religion*, 16, No. 9, D. pp 361-69.

Measures identification by three factors: locality of residence, environment, influence of the community.

MANN, Theodore R. Jewish Identity and Jewish Community Relations. *Congress Monthly*, 44, No. 4, My. pp 5-7.

RABI, Wladimir. L'intellectual juif dans la societe contemporaine. *Les Nouveaux Cahiers*, 13, No. 48, Sp. pp 6-14.

Do Jewish intellectuals play an ethical role in society?

ROBERT, Marthe. From Oedipus to Moses. Freud's Jewish Identity. Tr. Ralph Manheim. London, Routledge & Kegan Paul. 229p, Ind. (Littman Library of Jewish Civilization)

Traces the relationship between Freud's Jewish background and the ultimate genesis of his theory of psychoanalysis.

SILBERMAN, Helen M. The New Seekers: A Search for Identity. Reconstructionist, 43, No. 4, My. pp 7-14.
Looks at the new cults, offers reasons for their appeal and contrasts them and Judaism.

SOWDEN, Dora. Intellectuals in Politics. Jewish Affairs, 32, No. 9, S. pp 53-56.

SPERO, Moshe Halevi. Erik Erikson's Jewishness. Midstream, 23, No. 6, Ju-Jy. pp 76-82.
Psychoanalyst who made a study of identity and the roots of antisemitism.

TEICHER, Morton I. Some Notes on the Madrich. A Child-Care Worker in Israel. Journal of Jewish Communal Service, 53, No. 4, Ma. pp 238-41.

UROFSKY, Melvin I. To be American and Jewish. Jewish Spectator, 42, No. 3, Fa. pp 31-35.

VORSPAN, Albert. What Kind of Jews Will we be? Present Tense, 4, No. 2, W. pp 72-73.

WIESEL, Elie. Un juif aujourd'hui. Recits, Essais, Dialogues, Paris, Le Seuil, 256p.
Essays on Jewish identification after the Holocaust and in the light of the reality of Israel.

ZAKI, M. L'identité juive: ses processus de changement et ses particularités a travers l'études des conflits d'identité chez les jeunes juifs de Lyon. U.de Lyon, II, Lyon, 96p.
Doctoral thesis.

ACCULTURATION, ASSIMILATION

BENSIMON, Doris. Indicateurs de marginalisation et d'integration a la societé francaise: le judaisme. In; Eglises et groupes religieux dans la societé française. Integration ou marginalisation, Strasbourg, Cerdic, pp 211-23.
The position of Jews in French society.

BERGMAN, Elihu. The American Jewish Population Erosion. Midstream, 23, No. 4, O. pp 9-19.

DUKER, Abraham G. and BEN-HORIN, Meir. Emancipation and Counter-Emancipation: A Jewish Social Studies Reader. New York, Ktav, and the Conference on Jewish Social Studies, 413p.

JAKOBOVITS, Immanuel. The Challenge of Secularization. Tradition, 16, No. 5, Fa. pp 23-41.
Paper delivered at the Conference on Anglo-Jewry.

KAHANE, Meir. Why be Jewish. Intermarriage, Assimilation and Alienation. New York, Stein & Day, x, 251p, Ind.
Contends that intermarriage and assimilation is compounded by a general alienation from Jewishness.

KRIEGEL, Annie. Les juifs et le monde moderne. Essai sur les logiques démancipation. Paris, Seuil, 255p.
Emancipation and tradition in Judaism in the last two centuries. Compares Negro and Jewish emancipation movements and the relations between Judaism and socialism.

LOWENBERG, Robert. The Theft of Liberalism - a Jewish Problem. Midstream, 28, No. 5, My. pp 19-33.

MARKOVITS, Andrei S. Jewish Struggle in the Diaspora. Response, 11, No. 2, Fa. pp 83-90.
Questions of identity, assimilation and survival.

MARRUS, Michael R. European Jewry and the Politics of Assimilation: Assessment and Reassessment. Journal of Modern History, 49, No. 1, Ma. pp 89-109.

MEVORAH, B. Johann Kaspar Lavaters Auseinandersetzung mit Moses Mendelssohn über die Zukunft des Judentums. (La controverse de J.K. Lavater et de M. Mendelssohn sur l'avenir du judaïsme) Zwingliana, 14, No. 8, Au. pp 431-50.
The Mendelssohn-Lavater controversy about the future erosion of Jewish identity by integration or total assimilation by conversion.

MIRSKY, Norman B. Unorthodox Judaism. Columbus, Ohio State U.P. 213p.

MIXED MARRIAGES

BENSIMON, Doris and LAUTMAN, Francoise. Un marriage, Deux traditions:Chrétiens et Juifs. Bruxelles, Editions de L'Universite Bruxelles; Paris, Centre National de la Recherche Scientifique, 248p, Bibl.
Sociological inquiry into Christian-Jewish mixed marriages. The sample was 145 couples in Paris and the Paris region in 1972/73.

COHEN, Steven Martin. Socioeconomic Determinants of Intraethnic Marriages and Friendship. Social Forces, 56, No. 3, Ju. pp 997-1010.
"Findings lend support to the melting pot view that higher social class (indexed by higher education) and some forms of ethnic identification are incompatible ... Among the more recently arrived immigrant groups, assimilation (as manifest in marriage outside the ethnic group or in diminished sentimental attachment to the ethnic group) seems most advanced among the better-educated individuals."

MARMUR, Dow. Intermarriage. London, Reform Synagogues of Great Britain. 12p (Judaism in Our Time)

MARTIN, Bernard. Contra Mixed Marriages: Some Historical and Theological Relations. CCAR Journal, 25, Su. pp 75-85.
"Our only hope of significantly diminishing mixed marriages, and the threat to Jewish survival inherent therein, is to raise future generations of Jews who will respond not only to the voice of Auschwitz but to the voice of Sinai."

ROSENBLATT, Garry. Coping with Intermarriage. Jewish Digest, 23, No. 1, S. pp 9-12. Condensed form The National Observer.

SANDMEL, Samuel. When a Jew and Christian Marry. Philadelphia, Fortress P., 128p.

SILVER, Samuel M. Mixed Marriage Between Jew and Gentile. New York, Arco, 107p, Ind.

CONVERSION

COHEN, Stanley M. Jewish Converts in Quebec. Jewish Digest, 22, No. 9, My. pp 16-23. Condensed from The Canadian Zionist, 46,No.3.

DAUM, Annette. A Sixteen Unit lesson plan on Reform Judaism's response to "Hebrew/Christian" Missionary movements and the cults. Experimental ed. New York, Dept. of Interreligious Affairs, Union of American Hebrew Congregations. 1 vol.various pagings.

GLASER, Samuel Z. On Making Missions to Jews Possible. Sh'ma, 7, 16 S. pp 142-43.
It should cause us to ask whether we have allowed our belief to permeate the institutions of Jewish life.

HOENIG, Sidney B. The Historical Jewish Response to Christian Proselytization. Face to Face, 3-4, Fa/W. pp 9-12.

JACOBS, Steven S. Are Your Children Immune from Missionaries? Jewish Digest, 22, No. 4, D. pp 10-12. Condensed from Brotherhood, 11, No. 1.

JONES, Kenneth. Converting in Israel: Being a Jew May Be Hard - Becoming One is Harder Still. Moment, 2, No. 7, pp 19-22.
An American student now living in Israel, describes his two conversions, first in the U.S. and then in Israel.

LEVY, Richard N. The Case Against 'Quickie Conversions'. Jewish Digest, 22, No. 9, My. pp 10-15. Condensed from Davka.

MALAMED, Gad. How to Answer Street Missionaries. Jewish Digest, 22, No. 6, F. pp 49-51. Condensed from Kol Yavneh, 4, No. 5.

MARTIN, Walter T. and POSTON, Dudley L. Differentials in the ability to convert Education into Income: The Case of the European Ethnics. International Migration Review, 11, No. 2, Su. pp 215-31.
Includes the Jews.

VAN EEGHEN, I.H. Les enfants de Hansken Hangebroeck. (In Dutch) Studia Rosenthaliana, 11, No. 1, pp 33-39.
Conversion of a Protestant family to Judaism in 18th century Amsterdam.

COMMUNITY

ALBERT, Phyllis Cohen. The Modernization of French Jewry: Consistory and Community in the Nineteenth Century. Hanover N.H., Brandies U.P., xxii, 450p. Ind.
Development of French Jewry between the era of Napolean and the Dreyfus affair and History of the Consistoire, one of the most important Jewish institutions in France, based on hitherto unpublished documents.

BERNSTEIN, Irving. "We are one": The Challenge Facing the Jewish Community. Conservative Judaism, 31, No. 2, W. pp 70-75.

FEIN, Leonard. The war inside the Jews. A painful breakdown of the liberal consensus. New Republic, 177, No. 1, 15 O. pp 16-18.

KOLTUN, Elizabeth and SCHECHTER, Neil. The Jewish Urban Crisis. Interchange, 2, No. 7, Ma. pp 1;6-8, Jewish Digest, 23, No. 1, S. pp 24-29.
Disintegration of the Flatbush community caused by lack of response to community problems.

LERNER, Natan. Los judiós como comunidad. El Olivo, No. 2, Ap-Ju. pp 5-10.

LEVITZ, Irving N. Crisis in Orthodoxy: The Ethical Paradox. Jewish Life, 32, No. 1, W. pp 23-28.

"Organizational irregularities reflecting a dearth of ethical leadership, corrupt and criminal practices in the kashrus industry, unethical practices in yeshiva administrations, a cynical attitude toward secular law, dishonest business practices, and neglect of the aged - these are but a sampling of some of the many scandals that have become public."

MEDDING, Peter Y. Towards a General Theory of Jewish Political Interests and Behaviour. The Jewish Journal of Sociology, 19, No. 2, D. pp 115-44.

Demonstrates that the political liberalism of Jews is a particular variant of Jewish political behaviour, occuring only under specific historical and social conditions, rather than a universal phenomenon.

RAAB, Earl. The End of Jewish Community Relations? Journal of Jewish Communal Service, 53, No. 1, W. pp 107-15.

There is a tendency on the part of the Jewish community to turn away from the American arena, which would be suicidal. It is around this focus that ethnocentric and Israelocentric Jewish life can be integrated with American life.

RAPHAEL, Marc Lee. The Genesis of a Communal History: The Columbus Jewish History Project. American Jewish Archives, 29, No. 1, Ap. pp 53-69.

The Columbus, Ohio project as a joint undertaking of the Columbus Jewish Federation, the Ohio Historical Society and the Ohio State University.

-----------------. Jewish Philanthropy and Communal Democracy: In Pursuit of a Phantom. Response, 11, No. 2, Fa. pp 55-82.

ROTH, S. The Jewish Idea of a Community. New York, Yeshiva U.P., 164p.

SILVERMAN, Ira. How Much Democracy - and for Whom? The "Ins" and the "Outs". Present Tense, 4, No. 2, W. pp 59-63.

"The American Jewish community is kept under tight, undemocratic control because of the mistaken belief that it will thus be more effectively responsive to Israel's needs."

WOMEN

AGASSI, J.B. The Unequal Occupational Distribution of Women in Israel. Signs, 2, No. 4, pp 888-94.

Based on the 1972 Census.

BLUMENTHAL, Aaron H. The Status of Women in Jewish Law. Conservative Judaism, 31, No. 1, Sp. pp 24-40.

"Jewish men must realize the fact that the Halakhah often has been unfair, ungracious and discriminatory towards women. We cannot undo the past but we can measure up to the needs of the present by granting full equality to Jewish women under Halakhah."

FINKEL, Esther and LENCHNER, Edna. Conjoint Family treatment as an Adjunct to Group Treatment of Young Jewish Women. Journal of Jewish Communal Service, 53, No. 4, Ma. pp 289-93.

GORDIS, Robert. Women's Rights in Jewish Life and Law. United Synagogue Review, 33, No. 3, Ap. pp 4-5;29-31.

GREENBERG, Blu. Jewish Women: Coming of Age. Tradition, 16, No. 4, Su. pp 79-94.
Calls for the adaptation of Halakhah to the needs of women today.

HAZLETON, Lesley. Israeli Women: The Reality Behing the Myths. New York, Simon and Schuster, 235p.

ICHILOU, O. and RUBINECK, B. The Relationship Between Girls' Attitudes Concerning the Family and Their Perception of the Pattern Existing in the Family of Origin. Journal of Marriage and Family, 39, No. 2, pp 417-23.
Survey of 53 young Israeli women aged 16-18 of the underprivileged class.

JOHNSON, George E. The Lifestyle of Low Fertility: The Changing Needs of Jewish Women. Conservative Judaism, 31, no. 1, Sp. pp 15-23.
The changing role of women in Jewish society over the last three generations. Raises the issue of Jewish infertility within the context of Jewish history and experience in order to counteract Jewish zero population growth.

JOMIER, J. Le Coran et la guerre du 6 Octobre 1973 (10 Ramadan 1393) Bulletin d'Etudes Orientales, 29, pp 261-68.

KATZ, Barbara J. Liberated Kibbutz Women Return to Old Female Roles. Jewish Digest, 22, No. 8, Ap. pp 47-51. Condensed from The National Observer.
Explains that this is not a retrograde step.

LEHMANN, Linette. Femmes juives ... déplacées ou mal placées. Les Nouveaux Cahiers, 12, No. 47, W. pp 3-4.
The place of women in Jewish life.

LERNER, Anne Lapidus. "Who Hast Not Made Me a Man" The Movement for Equal Rights for Women in American Jewry. New York, American Jewish Committee, Institute of Human Relations, 38p.
Discusses the aims and objectives of the movement.

MONSON, Rela Geffen. Bringing Women In: A Survey of the evolving role of women in Jewish organizational life in Philadelphia, New York, The American Jewish Committee, 10p.

NEU, Irene D. Jewish Businesswoman in America. Jewish Digest, 22, No. 4, D. pp 39-48. Condensed from American Jewish Historical Quarterly, 46, No. 1.

ROSEN, Gladys. The Impact of the Women's Movement on the Jewish Family. New York, American Jewish Committee, 8p.

ROSEN, Ruth. (Historical Editor) and DAVIDSON, Sue. (Textual Editor). The Maimie Papers. Old Westbury, New York, The Feminist Press in cooperation with the Schlessinger Library of Radcliffe College, 439p.
Jewish prostitution in America.

ROSENBERG, Bernard. Women's Place in Israel. Dissent, 24, No. 4, Fa. pp 408-17.
Women's rights in Israel.

RUBIN, Barbara. On Women and War: An Interview with Marcia Freedman. Response, 7, No. 1, W. pp 41-47.
A leading Israeli feminist and Indendent Socialist Knesset memeber discusses the nature of the women's liberation movement.

SIEGEL, Rachel. The Jew as a Woman. Jewish Spectator, 42, W. pp 40-45.

STENDEL, Ori. The Status of the Arab Women in Israel. Middle East Review, 9, No. 2, W. pp 55-57.

TIGER, Lionel and SHEPHER, Joseph. Women in the Kibbutz. London, Penguin (Peregrine) x, 334p, Ind, Bibl.

Women in the Kibbutz are far from being downtrodden or mindless; they respond to a deeply rooted behavioural pattern.

ZUCKOFF, Aviva Cantor. Is Feminism Good for the Jews? Jewish Digest 23, No. 2, O. pp 60-62.

MARRIAGE/DIVORCE

HAUT, Irwin H. A Problem in Jewish Divorce Law: An Analysis and Some Suggestions. Tradition, 16, No. 3, Sp. pp 29-49.

Deals with the frequent problem in Jewish family law of the inability of an observant Jewish woman to obtain a get (religious divorce) following a civil divorce.

SABBATH, Jacques. La Famille juive. L'Arche, 20, Nos. 246-47. S-O. pp 51-93.

SCHLESINGER, Benjamin. Reflections on Family Breakdown among Jewish Families. Journal of Psychology and Judaism, 1, No.1, pp 45-54.

YOUTH

BLAU, Zena Smith, The Jewish Prince: Some Continuities in Traditional and Contemporary Jewish Life. Contemporary Judaism,

Provides evidence to "support the contention that it is Jewish boys, not girls, who enjoy singular advantages in socialization, relative to peers, from other religious backgrounds. To confer the title 'prince' upon them, therefore, would be consonant with empirical findings than is the fictional stereotype of the Jewish-American princess."

BRENNER, Marie. From Berkeley to Jerusalem: Last Stop on the 60s Express. The New York Times Magazine, 3 Ap. pp 71-73; 78.

Describes the Diaspora Yeshiva in Jerusalem, a very non-traditional setting for mostly young American Jews.

ICHILOV, Orit. Youth Movements in Israel as Agents for Transition to Adulthood. The Jewish Journal of Sociology, 19, No. 1, Ju. pp 21-32.

LEVINE, Herbert and Ellen Frankel. Havura in the Ivory Tower: A Letter from Princeton. The National Jewish Monthly, 91, No. 6, Ju. pp 24-27.

Two formerly non-observant graduate students at Princeton write of their new commitment to Jewish study and practice.

LEVINE, Norman and BROOKS, William C. The Effect of Outreach on Participation by Teens. New York, Florence G. Heller - JWB Research Center in Cooperation with Jewish Community Center of San Diego, v. 76p.

Study of special programmes for teenagers organised in American Jewish community centres, and their effect.

MAYER, Egon. Gaps Between Generations of Orthodox Jews in Boro Park, Brooklyn, N.Y. Jewish Social Studies, 39, No. 1, W/Sp. pp 93-104.

PORTNOY, Fern C. A Community Approach to Teen Service. New York, Florence G. Heller - JWB Research Center, Research Digest, A Research Project in Cooperation with the Jewish Community Center of Denver, 23p.

REISMAN, Bernard. The Chavurah: A contemporary Jewish experience. New York, Union of American Hebrew Congregations, xi, 234p.

The aims of this books are a) to explain this new phenomenon in American Jewry, b) to analyse the kind of people who join chavurot, their reasons for doing so, the pattern of organisation and c) provide practical informaion for forming chavurot and mapping out their programme.

----------------. Professional Leadership for the Chavurah. CCAR Journal, 25, No. 1, W. pp 51-63.

SKIDDELL, Elliot L. Pre-teen Attitudes Toward Prayer and Judaism. Reconstructionist, 43, No. 5, Ju. pp 21-27.

SOCIO/MEDICAL PROBLEMS

BAR-ZEV, Asher. Aberrant Behaviour in Jewish Tradition. Journal of Psychology and Judaism, 1, no. 1, Sp. pp 67ff.

--------------. Homosexuality and the Jewish Tradition, Jewish Affairs, 32, No. 9, S. pp 67-72.

BERGER, D. The Survivor Syndrome: A Problem of Nosology and Treatment. American Journal of Psychotherapy, 31, No. 2, pp 238-51

Berger discusses the post-trauma syndrome of concentration camp inmates noting that the persistent guilt - which has nothing to do with having identified with the aggressor - and the self-loathing seen in numerous patients is what has merited the distinction between "survivor syndrome" and regular traumatic neurosis. He feels that these two symptoms are not directly related to the holocaust trauma per se.

The Bio-Medical Revolution: Applying Jewish Values to Public Policy-Making. Analysis, Ap. pp 1-6.

"While Jewish authorities often avoided confrontation with accepted medical practices, today, the assertion of Jewish legal and ethical ideas is no less needed than when rabbinic decisions were accepted as binding by the entire community."

BLECH, Benjamin. Judaism and gerontology. Tradition, 16, No. 4, Su. pp 62-78.

The treatment of the aged in Judaism.

Calling Dr. Stress. Psychology Today, S. pp 93-94;96+

Journalist J. Robert Moslin talks with the chief national psychiatrist of Israel, Dr. Louis Miller, who discusses how tensions affect a people's character.

CASPER, Bernard. Tay-Sachs and Screening. Jewish Affairs, 32, No. 9, S. pp 61-66.

On the disease endemnic among Jews only.

GOODNICK, B. Mental Health from the Jewish standpoint. Journal of Religion and Health, 16, No. 2, pp 110-15.

The author sees Chapter 4 of Pirke Avoth as a pattern for everyday living and moral instruction.

LADER, Malcolm. Psychiatry on Trial. Harmondsworth, Pelican, Penguin Books, 202p, Bibl.

The author examines the problem of the abuse of psychiatry in the USSR in its historical-political context.

LAMM, Norman. Judaism and the Modern Attitude to Homosexuality. L'Eylah, 1, No. 3, Sp. pp 18-28.

LANDMAN, Leo. (Ed.) Judaism and Drugs. New York, Commission on Synagogue Relations of the Federation of Jewish Philanthropies, 2.e 269p, Ill.

LEIMAN, Sid. Z. Subsidized Abortion: Response to a Call. Sh'ma, 7, No. 9, D. pp 197-205.

Challenges the position expressed in "A Call to Concern" (Christianity and Crisis, 3 O.) in which some 200 ethicists and theologians issued a statement on the abortion issue. Identifying its target as those who maintain "that it is always wrong to terminate a pregnancy at any time after the moment of conception", the "Call to Concern" urges an alternative position. Followed by further discussion in "A Call for the Poor to Act on Conscience." by Eugene R. Borowitz. "Abortion: Moral Issues Beyond Legal Ones." by Seymour Siegel.

MACKTA, Jayne. Tay Sachs Risk: A Progress Report. Moment, 3, No. 2, D. pp 19-20; 51.

The editor of Breakthrough, periodical of the National Tay-Sachs and Allied Diseases Association, discusses the latest work being done in the screening and prevention of Tay-Sachs disease. This disorder is discussed further in: "One Family's Story" by Doris Goldberg. "Abortion Controversy" by the Editors in the same issue.

MARCUS, Jacob R. "Social Medicine" in the Ghetto. Jewish Spectator, 42, No. 3, Fa. pp 23-29.

Religion and Psychiatry. Federation of Jewish Philanthropies of New York. Task Force on Mental Health and Judaism. Jewish ethnopsychiatry; a manual of inservice and house staff education. New York, 80p.

SCHECHTER, Nathan. Pain and the Jewish Patient. Journal of Psychiatry and Judaism, 1, NO. 1, pp 35-54.

SCHWARTZ, Barry Dov. Homosexuality: A Jewish Perspective. United Synagogue Review, 34, Su. pp 4-5; 23ff.

In accepting homosexuals we need not sacrifice our traditional standards and the Jewish ideal of heterosexuality.

SMOLAR, Leivy. The Right to Die, the Bio-Ethical Frontier: Creating an Agenda. Journal of Jewish Communal Service, 53, No. 4, Su. pp 320-29.

SPERO, Moshe. On the Relationship Between Psychotherapy and Judaism. Journal of Psychology and Judaism. 1, No. 2, pp 15-34.

------------. Implications of Counter-Transference for the Religious Therapist and Client. Journal of Psychotherapy and Judaism, 1, No. 2, pp 39-52.

SPIEGEL, Marcia. Is Alcoholism the New Jewish Disease? Sh'ma, 8, 25 N. pp 189-91.

UNKOVICH, Charles M., ADLER, Rudolf J. and vILLER, Susan E. The Contemporary State of Jewish Alcoholism, Contemporary Judaism,

WIKLER, Marvin. The Torah View of Mental Illness: Sin or Sickness? The Journal of Jewish Communal Service, 53, No. 4, Su. pp 339-44.

DISCRIMINATION/
PREJUDICE

Bakke vs. The University of California: Special Section, Change,

Partial contents: The Case for Preference by Lee Daniels and Francesca E. Farmer. The Case Against Preference by Malcolm J. Sherman. In Search of a Just Outcome by Alfred B. Fitt.

BARSKY, Percy. How "Numerous Clausus" was ended in the Manitoba Medical School. Jewish Historical Society of Canada, 1, No. 2, pp 75-81.

BIRMINGHAM, Stephen. The Clubs Griffin Bell Had to Quit. The New York Times Magazine, 6 F. pp 20-21; 68-71.

A look at the private clubs that at least two of President Carter's Cabinet members belong to, the Capital City and the Piedmont Driving Club, which have no Black and few, if any, Jewish members.

GROSS, Barry R. (Ed.) Reverse Discrimination. Buffalo, New York, Prometheus Books, 401p.

HAAG, Ernest van der. Reverse Discrimination: A Brief Against It. National Review, 29, 29 Ap. pp 492-95.

"It would be too sweeping to say that categorical discrimination in hiring and college admissions is never justified; but before it can be justly imposed, we must consult both institutional purposes and historical circumstances more carefully than partisans of racial and sexual privilege seem to do.

HAGAN, John. Finding "Discrimination": A Question of Meaning. Ethnicity, 4, No. 2, Ju. pp 167-76.

Concludes that "the social attribution of discrimination deserves study. Such research, when combined with analysis of the antecedents and consequences of differential treatment, could ultimately produce the type of information that a social scientific approach to the study of discrimination can best provide.

JOHNSON, Doyle P. Religious Commitment, Social Distance and Authoritarianism. Review of Religious Research, 19, W. pp 99-113.

Investigates the relationship between religious commitment and social distance toward Latin Americans, Negroes and Jews and racial tolerance in a rural and small-town area undergoing the initial stages of industrial development.

LAVINSKY, Larry M. The Bakke Case. The Dilemma of Benign Racism. The National Jewish Monthly, 92, No. 4, D. pp 9-13.

"The Bakke case seeks to eliminate abuses in affirmative action programs that threaten to perpetuate the racism of the past, changing only the race of the victim."

LEVINE, Naomi. Bakke and Justice. Congress Monthly, 44, No. 7, O. pp 3ff.

Meritocracy and Its Discontents. The New Republic, 176, 15 O. Special Issue. pp 5-9; 12-26.

Issues raised by the Bakke case are discussed in: An Emerging National Consensus by Seymour Lipset and William Schneider. The War Inside the Jews by Leonard Fein. Race Certification by Eliot Marshall. The Conspiracy of Merit by Michael Kinsley.

National Invitational Conference on Adolescent Prejudice (15-16 Ja); Summary of the proceedings and recommendations. Sponsored by the U. of California., Berkeley and the Anti-Defamation League of B'nai B'rith. New York, ADL, 48p.

RASPBERRY, William. Race and Recompense. Skeptic, O. pp 42;58-60.
"The principle of affirmative action comes out of the realization that racial discrimination has become so institutionalized that merely to stop discriminating is, in effect, to continue discrimination."

SYRKIN, Marie. Falling Scores - Rising Quotas. Midstream, 23, No. 11, N. pp 58-61.

THOR, Mary Ten. (Ed.) The Bakke Symposium. Sacramento, Ca. Uncommon Lawyers Workshop, 283p.

RACE, RACIALISM, PREJUDICE

BANTON, Michael. The Idea of Race. London, Tavistock, 190p. Ind., Bibl.
Exploration of the first serious race theories and new approaches to the study of both racial and ethnic minorities. Refers to the Jews.

BROWN, S. White and Jewish. Jewish Affairs, 37, No. 1, pp 10-12.
Attitudes of South African Jews to Apartheid.

CHASE, Allan. The Legacy of Malthus: The Social Costs of the New Scientific Racism. New York, Knopf, xxvii, 686p., Ind., Bibl.
Examines the evolution of scientific racism from Thomas Malthus to the present.

GOLDSBY, Richard A. Race and Races. 2.e. New York, London, Collier Macmillan, x, 158p. Ind., Bibl.
Discusses race as a biological phenomenon. Deals i.e. with Jews.

MUHLEN, Patrick von zur. Rassen-ideologien. Geschichte und Hintergründe. Bonn, HHW, Dietz, 276p.
Discusses all manner of racialist ideologies, including Nazism.

Race and Integration. Society, 7, No. 3, Special Section, pp 32-48.
Includes: Population Stability and Equal Rights by James S. Coleman. Integrating Residential Neighbourhoods by Reynolds Farley. The Dangers of Forced Integration by David J. Armor. Stopping White Flight by Joan R. Harris.

RICHARDSON, Neville. The World Council of Churches and Race Relations: 1960 to 1969. Frankfurt/M., Bern, Lang, 78p. (Studies in the Intercultural History of Christianity, 9)
Analysis of documents and events.

SCHOEN, Douglas E. Enoch Powell and the Powellites. London, Macmillan, xviii, 317p.
Racial discrimination in England.

TINKER, Hugh. Race, Conflict and the International Order: From Empire to United Nations. London, Macmillan, 160p, Ind., Bibl. M. (The Making of the 20th Century)
Examines the race factor in international relations. Deals also with the Jews.

WHITE, J. and FRIDERES, J.S. Race Prejudice and Racism: a distinction. Canadian Review of Sociology and Anthropology, 14, No. 1, F. pp 81-90.

EDUCATION

Colloquium Papers on Jewish Education and Jewish Identity. New York, American Jewish Committee, 6 issues.

BLASI, Joseph R. The Kibbutz: Integrated Learning Environment and Informal Educational Experience. The Journal of Educational Thought, 12, No. 3, pp 231-42.

BRESLAUER, Daniel S. Abraham Joshua Heschel and Religious Education. Religious Education, 72, S-O., pp 484-90.

Education not merely for Jews but for all who take religious living seriously can be conceived as the process whereby a subject matter becomes the means through which primal issues of human existence are explored.

COHEN, Samuel I. Adult Jewish Education. 1976. Religious Education 72, No. 2, Ma-Ap. pp 143-55.

"In 1976 one rarely, if ever, comes across articles, studies, speeches, reports or predictions about the vanishing American Jew. The emergence of a wide-spread network of adult Jewish education programs in virtually every Jewish community in the United States may well be an important factor in this phenomenon."

DAVIS, Moshe. Expanding Horizons. L'Eylah, 1, No. 4, Aut. pp 33-35.

Jewish studies at various universities.

DONN, Hayim Halevy. To raise a Jewish Child: A Guide for Parents. New York, Basic Books, 250p.

DUCKAT, Walter. Which careers for Jews? American Zionist, 68, No. 1 O. pp 19-23.

Suggests a number of vocations, where the job outlook is considered to be favourable and opportunities for qualified persons are good.

FINKELSTEIN, Louis. The Ideals of the Founders. Judaism, 26, No. 3, Su. pp 265-67.

The beginnings of the Jewish Theological Seminary of America.

FUCHS-KREIMER, Nancy. Religious Education in Public Schools. What it means to the Jewish parents and child. Religious Education in Public Schools, 91,No. 5, Ja. pp 18-25.

GANNES, Abraham. Restructure Jewish Education? Congress Monthly, 44, No. 5, Ju. pp 15-17.

GORDON, H. Martin Buber's Impact on Religious Education: Reflections on the centennial of his birth. Religious Education, 72, No. 6, pp 580-97.

---------. Religious Education as Expressed in the Hasidic Stories of Martin Buber. Religious Education, 72, No. 6, pp 61-73.

HEIMREICH, William B. Wake Up, Wake Up, To the Work of the Creator. New York, Harper & Row, 210p.

An Account of Helmreich's year in a yeshiva, explaining orthodox Judaism and the all-enveloping ritual that permeates yeshiva life.

HENKOFF, Ronald. Do Oil and Education Mix? The Middle East Connection. Change, 9, No. 6, Ju. pp 25-29.

"The issues at stake here- political repression, discrimination, student selection, curriculum control - are too serious to be met by silence, either by students or faculty."

HIMMELFARB, Harold S. The Non-Linear Impact of Schooling: Comparing Different Types and Amounts of Jewish Education. Sociology of Education, 50, No. 2, Ap. pp 114-32.

Assesses the impact of different types and amounts of Jewish schooling in producing adult religiosity, using a sample from the Chicago area.

JANSSEN, H.G.A. De Israelitische Armenscholen in Gelderland (1836-1869) Studia Rosenthaliana, 11, No. 2, Jy. pp 157-97.

Jewish schools for the poor in 19th century Holland.

--------------. Staatsrechtelijke en culturele aspecten van het Israelisch onderwijs in Nederland tot 1869. (Juridicaland cultural characteristics of Jewish tuition in the Netherlands until 1869) Studia Rosenthaliana, 11, No. 1, Ja. pp 39-80.

Jewish Education: Jubilee Issue. Jewish Education, 47, No. 1, Sp. pp 1-48.

Includes: Jewish Education in America: Achievement and Challenge by Alvin I. Schiff. Jewish Pluralism and Jewish Education by Simon Greenberg. The Jewish Educator and Jewish Education - Four Myths by Norman Lamm. Facing the Future of Jewish Education by Eugene B. Borowitz.

Jewish Education Guide, New York, Hadassah, 27p.

KAMINETSKY, Edward Eliezer. Studies in Torah and Judaism. Sins of Omission: The Neglected Children. New York, Yeshiva U.P., 134p, Bibl.

The tasks of Jewish education.

LAWSON, E. Reward and Punishment: Patterns in Arab and Jewish Schoolchildren. International Journal of Intercultural Relations, No. 1, pp 105-7.

LIEGLE, Ludwig. Familie und Kollektiv im Kibbutz. Eine Studie Über die Funktionen der Familie in einem kollektiven Erziehungssystem. 4.e. Weinheim, Beltz, 248p.

MALKA, Salomon and ALLOUCHE, Jean-Luc. Les Maitres a Penser. L'Arche, 20, No. 239, F. pp 35-38.

MARCUS, Audrey Friedman. The Jewish Family as aodel for Christian Education. Living Light. 14, No. 2, Su. pp 208-18.

MASSARIK, Fred. Trends in the U.S. Jewish Education: National Population Study Findings. American Jewish Yearbook, 77, pp 240-50.

Facts and figures; forecasts a decline due to less Jewish children being born and mixed marriage.

Roundup of New programs in Jewish Education. The Pedagogic Reporter, 28, No. 1, Special Issue, W. pp 1-40.

Includes: Family, Parent and Adult Education - Jewish Civics and Community Involvement. Jewish Values. Teaching Bible. Teaching Hebrew. Teaching Israel.

ROSENZWEIG, Linda. Toward Universal Justice: Some Implications of Lawrence Kohlberg's Research for Jewish Education. Religious Education, 72, No. 6, N-D. pp 606-15.

"An educational approach designed to foster in young people a natural process of developing an increasingly more mature and adequate conception of principles of universal justice accords with the highest aims and teachings of Judaism."

ROSS, Saul. Jewish Ethics, Self Psychology and Sports. Journal of Psychology and Judaism, 2, No. 1, Fa. pp 13-30.

SARON, Gus. Jewish Education in Early Johannesburg. Jewish Affairs, 32, No. 9, S. pp 97-106.

----------, South Africa. American Jewish Yearbook, 77,pp 503-14.

SCHAFLER, Samuel. The Demographic Crisis and Jewish Education. Jewish Education, 47, No. 1, W. pp 13-15.

Decline in Jewish school enrolment is higher than the demographic decline.

SCHWARTZ, Lita S. and ISSER, Natalie. Attitudes Towards the Jewish Minority in Public Education. Jewish Education, 47, Su/Fa. pp 33-39.

"In the past mid-1970s there is some effort to integrate textbooks in both content and illustration, but there is frequently a 'forced' air about the effort that reduces its effectiveness."

SHEPHERD, Naomi. Going to School in Jerusalem. Present Tense, 4, No. 2, pp 8-11.

SHMUELI, Eliezer. Problems in educating Oriental Jewish Children in Israel. Integrated Education, 15, No. 3, My-Ju. pp 3-5.

Do we have the right to perpetuate a minority culture by subjugating the culture of the nation's majority?

SLESINGER, Zalman. Toward a Community Perspective of Jewish Education. Jewish Frontier, 44, No. 1, Ja. pp 23-26.

TAGLIACOZZO, A. L'education collective au Kibboutz. Connaissance d' Israel, 1, No. 1, Ja-Ju. pp 159-63.

TALMAGE, Frank (Ed.) Study Guide for "Sifron la-Student". U. of Toronto P., 2.r.e., 196p.

TELLER, Gerald A. A New Model for Jewish Education. Religious Education, 72, No. 3, My-Ju. pp 293-305.

The Winning of the Jewish Home: A New Frontier in Jewish Education. Special Issue. The Pedagogic Reporter, 28, Sp. pp 1-49.

Includes: Family Education: A New Frontier? by Isaac Toubin. Jewish Family Education by Bernard Reisman. Programs in Jewish Family Life Education by Murray Rockwitz. Annotated Biblio--graphy on the Jewish Family and Jewish Family Programming by Sunny Romer Oblath and Steven Huberman.

WITHNOW, Robert. Is There an Academic Melting Pot? Sociology of Education, 70, No. 1, Ja. pp 7-15.

The data analysed indicates that the under-representation of Catholics and the over-representation of Jews are likely to become less pronounced in the future.

STUDENTS

BLASS, Jerome H. ROle Preferences Among Jewish Seminarians. Sociological Analysis, 38, No. 1, Sp. pp 59-64.

Significant differences were found among the groups in the degree of preference for three of the eight rabbinical roles. There was also little agreement among the groups in their order of preference for, or interest in, the various ministerial activities associated with the rabbinate.

CAPLOVITZ, David. (et al) The Religious Drop-Outs: Apostasy Among College Graduates,Beverley Hills, Sage, 199p.

COWAN, Paul. World of our Children. The New York Times Magazine, 3 Ap. pp 64-70.
The author tells of his experience with several families on Manhattan's Upper West Side in starting a Hebrew School for their children, and of their reaction to its success.

GLANZ, David. An Interpretation of the Jewish Counter-Culture. Jewish Social Studies, 39, No. 1, W/Sp., pp 117-28.
"The Jewish counterculture may be seen as a 'third-generation return' which grows out of a particular set of historical circumstances and is essentially a search for Jewish identity."

LAVENDER, Abraham D. Studies of Jewish College Students: A Review and a Replication. Jewish Social Studies, 39, Nos. 1-2, W/Sp. pp 37-52.
Results of the author's 1971 study compared with Irving Greenberg's in 1949, using in both cases, the Jewish freshman student body of the University of Maryland.

-------------------. Jewish College Women: Future Leaders of the Jewish Community? The Journal of Ethnic Studies, 5, Su. pp 81-90.
"The American Jewish community deprives itself of many much needed talents to the extent that it does not encourage participation in its leadership positions of all individuals regardless of sex." Based on a 1971 study of 488 Jewish undergraduate students at the University of Maryland.

LAWRENCE, Charles III. The Bakke Case: Are Radical Quotas Defensible? Saturday Review, 15 O. pp 11-16.
"Will the Court be influenced by public cries of 'reverse discrimination' ignoring the fact that the vestiges of slavery cannot be eliminated unless descendants of salves are protected from institutionalized forms of racism."

MASON, Ruth (Et al) Guide to Jewish Student Groups. New York, North American Jewish Students' Network, 199p.

RAFAEL, E. Ben. L'étudiant israélien. Connaissance d'Israel, 1, No. 1, Ja.-Ju. pp 143-58.
Sociological study.

REINHARZ, Hehuda. The Origin and Development of the Bund Jüdischer Corporationen. The Wiener Library Bulletin, 30, Nos. 43-44, pp 2-6
Jewish student organisation in Germany, founded in 1910.

SACHS, Tony. The Jewish Student. Jewish Affairs, 32, No. 3, Ma. pp 45-47.

STEINBERG, Stephen. The Academic Melting Pot. Catholics and Jews in American Higher Education. N.e. New Brunswick, N.J. Transaction Books, xx, 183p, Ind, Bibl.
The purpose of the study was to assess the validity of the concept of "Jewish intellectualism" and the related concept of Catholic anti-intellectualism.

WALLACH, Charles. The Jewish Student in Britain. Jewish Affairs, 32, No. 12, D. pp 41-42.

WAXMAN, Chaim I. and HELMREICH,William B. Religious and Communal Elements of Ethnicity: American Jewish College Students and Israel, Ethnicity, 4, No. 2, Ju. pp 122-32.
"Whilst almost all expressed a positive identification with Israel, most had given no consideration to living there and,for the majority, their self-identities as Americans outweigh their Jewish identities."

WECHSLER, Harold S. The Qualified Student. A History of Selective College Admission in America. New York, John Wiley, xvii, 341p, Ind., Bibl.

Deals also with the admission of Jewish students to Colleges and Universities in the U.S.A.

JEWS AND SCIENCE

HALMOS, Pal: A Neumann-legenda. Termeszet Vilage, No. 1, pp 14-17.

On the inventor of computer science, John von Neumann, who because of his Jewish origin had to emigrate to the United States.

HOLLINGER, David A. Morris R. Cohen and the Scientific Ideal. Cambridge, Mass; London, MIT P., 262p.

REUBEN, Bryan G. Science and Religion Since David Hume. European Judaism, 11, No. 2, Su. pp 24-34.

LITERATURE

DYCK, Joachim. Athen und Jerusalem. Die Tradition der argumentativen Verknüpfung von Bibel und Poesie im 17. und 18. Jahrhundert. Munich, C.H. Beck, 203p, Ind.

Holds that European literature up to 1750 was historically determined by the relation of the judeo-Christian tradition to the antique world.

PHEIFFER, R. The Jew in Afrikaans Literature. Patterns of Prejudice 11, No. 1, Ja.-F., pp 23-27.

Antisemitism in Afrikaans literature.

JEWISH LITERATURE

ALTER, Robert. Defenses of the Imagination. Jewish Writers and the Modern Historical Crisis. Philadelphia, Jewish Publication Society of America, xv, 262p.

Essays on the contemporary Jewish writers in Israel, Europe and America whose work reflects the historical crisis in which they lived.

BANKS, Lynn Reid. Self-flagellation in Anglo-Jewish writing. Jewish Affairs, 32, NO. 6, Ju. pp 6-9; Congress Monthly, 44, No. 7, O. pp 15-16.

CASSUTO, Umberto. Storia della letteratura ebraica postbiblica. Rome, Carucci, xvi, 216p.

Geschichte der jüdischen Literatur. München, C.H. Beck, 257p.

HALPERIN, Irving. After the Schlemiel-American Jewish Literature Today. Jewish Affairs, 37, No. 1, Ja. pp 31-34.

KAHN, Lothar. German-Jewish Literature: An Overview. Judaism, 26, No. 4, Fa. pp 443-54.

KOLLIN, Ferenc. A Prager Könyvkiadó Törtenete. Budapest, Akad, Kiado, 170p. (Irodalom törteneti közlemenyeh 92)

The firm of Eugene Prager first published Hungarian exile literature in Czechoslovakia and later in England where it pioneered Jewish paperbacks.

LOCKER, Richard. The Literary View: Jewish American Fiction. The New York Times Book Review, 10 Ju. pp 3; 36-37.

MADISON, Charles A. Jewish publishing in America: The Impact of Jewish writing on American Culture. New York, Sanhedrin P., Hebrew Publ. Co., 294p.

SLOMOVITZ, Philip. Centennial of George Eliot's Daniel Deronda. The American Zionist, 67, No. 8, Ju. pp 28-30.

STEMBERGER, Günter. Geschichte der jüdischen Literatur: Eine Einführung. München, C.H. Beck, 257p, Ind.

Short introduction to Jewish literature from the Bible to the 20th century.

JEWISH WRITERS

ALEXANDER, Edward. Abba Kovner: Poet of Holocaust and Rebirth. Midstream, 23, No. 8, O. pp 50-59.

BAINES, Jennifer. Mandelstam. The Later Poetry. London, Cambridge U.P., xv, 253p, Ind, Bibl.

BERTHA, Bulcon. Interju Kardos G. Györggyel. Jelenkor, Ap. pp 311-20.

Kardos is a Jewish writer who returned to Hungary from Israel after World War II and whose books, many of Jewish themes, are best-sellers.

CARMILLY-WEINBERGER, Moshe. Censorship and Freedom of Expression in Jewish History. New York, Sepher-Hermon P., with Yeshiva U.P., 295p, Ind.

Censorship was never institutionalised in diaspora Jewish history, yet a form of inner censorship did exist, in the last 2000 years some 300 books were banned by Rabbinical authorities.

CHAMETZSKY, Jules. From the Ghetto. The Fiction of Abraham Cahan. Amherst Mass., U. of Massachusetts P., xiv, 160p, Ind, Bibl.

Cahan was founder and senior editor of the Jewish Daily Forward an essayist of considerable merit, author of The Rise of David Levinsky, and many other novels and short stories. He was a literary pioneer proving the duality of the American-Jewish immigrant experience.

CISMARU, Alfred. Ionesco as apologist of Jewish Causes. Jewish Affairs, 37, No. 1, Ja. pp 27-30.

CUKIERMAN, Walenty. Isaak Babel's Jewish Heroes and their Yiddish Background. Yiddish, 2, No. 4, Su. pp 15-22.

EPSTEIN, Joseph. Saul Bellow: AMerica's Major Novelist. Dialogue, 10, No. 3, pp 47-60.

FAIRLEY, Barker. Heinrich Heine: An Interpretation. N.e. Westport, Conn., Greenwood P., 176p.

FAIRLIE, Henry. Epistle of a Gentile to Saul Bellow. The New Republic, 5 F. pp 18-23.

Open letter discussing the author's thoughts on Israel provoked by reading Bellow's To Jerusalem and Back.

FINESTEIN, Israel. Israel Zangwill in His Day. Jewish Quarterly, 25, No. 1, Sp. pp 4-7.

GOSS, Isaac. Thus Spake Heinrich Heine. Jewish Affairs, 32, No. 11, N. pp 28-30.

GOTTGETREU, Erich. Heine and the Doctor of Kabbalah. Jewish Affairs, 32, No. 11, N. pp 31-33.

HERSCH, Marc. La condition juive d'oppression de Kafka revélée a travers ses écritures. Das Neue Israel,30, No. 3, S. pp 153-56.
Kafka's judaism as it appears in his writings.
HINDUS, Milton. (Ed.) The Worlds of Maurice Samuel. Selected Writings. Foreword by Cynthia Ozick. Philadelphia, Jewish Publication Society of America. xxxii, 445p.
Collection of essays by Maurice Samuel chosen from his over 20 books with an introduction by the editor.
HOLMQVIST, Bengt. (Ed.) Das Buch der Nelly Sachs. Frankfurt/M., Suhrkamp, 460p.
Collection of essays on the Nobel Laureate Jewish poetess.
JANS, Rolf-Peter and LAERMANN, Klaus. Arthur Schnitzler: Zur Diagnose des Wiener Bürgertums in Fin de siecle. Stuttgart, J.B. Metzler, xvii, 202p.
The authors present as a natural product of fin de siecle Viennese bourgeois society.
KAFKA, Franz. I am a Memory Come Alive. Autobiographical Writings. Ed. Nahum N. Glatzer, New York, Schocken; London, Wildwood House, 264p.
------------. Letters to Friends, Family and Editors. Tr. by Richard and Clara Winston, New York, Schocken, 640p.
KIENZLE, Siegfried. Ödön von Horvath. Berlin, Colloquium, 96p.
Monograph.
LYONS, Bonnie. Henry Roth: The Man and his Work. Cooper Square Publishers,
A critical analysis of Henry Roth's seven short stories and his novel'Call It Sleep'.
LYONS, John. Chomsky, 2.r.e. London, Harvester P., 192p.
MACCOBY, Hyam. Koestler's Racism. Midstream, 23, No. 3, Ma. pp 31-40.
Analytical critique of The Thirteenth Tribe.
MARKISH, Simon. La Litterature russo-juive et Isaak Babel. Cahiers du Monde Russe et Sovietique, 18, Nos. 1-2, pp 73-92.
MENASCE, Esther. Isaac Rosenberg, Poeta del Novecento Inglese, Verona, Libreria Internazionale, 213p.
Monograph.
MODIANO, Patrick. Emmanuel Berg interrogatoire. Paris, Gallimard, 198p.
NAULT, Marianne. Saul Bellow. His Works and His Critics. An Annotated International Bibliography. New York, Garland, 191p.
POLITZER, Heinz. Franz Kafka, der Künstler. Frankfurt/M., Suhrkamp, 536p.
REIF, Stefan C. Genizah Fragments at Cambridge. L'Eylah, 1, No. 4, Aut. pp 26-28.
Dr. Reif is the Director of the Genizah project at Cambridge, England.
ROTH, Henry. On Being Blocked and Other Literary Matters. Commentary 63, Au. pp 27-38.
Interview with John S. Freedman.
ROTH, Philip. Reading Myself and Others. New York, Bantam, 270p.
------------, and SINGER, Isaac Bashevis. On Bruno Schulz, New York Times Book Review, 13 F.
SLONIM, Marc. Soviet Russian Literature. Writers and Problems. 2.e. 1917-77. Oxford U.P., 446p.

TICKTIN, Harold. Koestler and the Jews. Congress Monthly, 41, No. 1, Ja. pp 14-17.
WACHTEL, Nili. A Portrait of Isaac Bashevis Singer: Freedom Through Slavery. Midstream, 28, No. 5, My. pp 75-80.
WADEPUHL, Walter. Heinrich Heine. Sein Leben, seine Werke, München, Wilhelm Heyne, xiii, 475p, Ind, Bibl, Ill. (Heyne Biographies 38)
Monograph.
WALDINGER, Albert. Abraham Cahan and Palestine. Jewish Social Studies, 29, Nos. 1-2, W/Sp. pp 75-92.
WEINZIERL, Ulrich. Er war Zeuge. Alfred Polgar. Ein Leben zwischen Publizistik und Literatur. Wien, Löcker & Wogenstein, 214p.
ZAFRANI, Haim. Poesie juive en Occident Musulman. Paris, Guenthner, x, 472p.

YIDDISH

FORMAN, Betty Yetta. From the American Shadchan to Annie Hall: The Life and Legacy of Yiddish Film in America. The National Jewish Monthly, 91, No. 11, N. pp 4-13.
HERTZBERG, Rabbi Arthur. Yiddish, the Language of our Soul. Yiddish, 2, No. 4, Su. pp 1-3; Congress Monthly, 44, No. 7, O. pp 4-5.
LIPSKY, Louis. Tales of the Yiddish Rialto: Reminiscences of Playwrights and Players in New York's Jewish Theatre. Westport, Conn., Greenwood P., N.e. 234p.
LUZATTO, Guido L. Il Teatro Yiddish di Varsavia nella sua Autenticita e nella sua Potenza. La Rassegna Mensile di Israel, 43, Nos. 1-2, Ja-F. pp 50-53.
The Yiddish State Theatre in Warsaw.
SANDROW, Nahma. Vagabond Stars. A World History of Yiddish Theatre. New York, Harper & Row, xii, 435p, Ind, Ill, Bibl. M.
Beginning with biblical dramas and Purim plays of 17th century. Special chapters on A. Goldfaden, J. Gordin and the Soviet Yiddish State Theatre.
SHATSKY, Natan. Yiddishe stenografie. (Jewish Shorthand) Sovietish Heimland, 17, No. 3, Ma. pp 164-73.
WEINREICH, Uriel. Modern English-Yiddish, Yiddish-English Dictionary, New York, Schocken, 789,16p.

YIDDISH LANGUAGE

ALLERHAND, Jacob. Yiddisch - Metamorphose einer Sprache. Studia Judaica Austriaca 4, Studien zur Literatur der juden in Osteuropa, pp 7-81.
Yiddish - metamorphosis of a language.

YIDDISH LITERATURE

BAUMGARTEN, Murray. Language, Luftmenschen, Catastrophe: themes of Sholem Aleichem. Yiddish, 2, No. 4, Su. pp 28-54.

BRAGINSKY, Yosef. Dos ort, vos die hebreishe literatur farnemt in der velt-literatur. Gedanken fun an orientalist). (The Place of Hebrew Literature in world literatur - thoughts of an Orientalist. Sovietish Heimland, 17, No. 7, Jy. pp 146-47.

Review article of V.1. Library of World Literature, containing ancient literature, and including excerpts from the Book of Ruth Isaiah and Jonah.

GITENSTEIN, R. Barbara. Fools and Sages: Humor in Isaac Bashevis Singer's The Fools of Chelm and their History. Yiddish, 2, No. 4, Su. pp 23-27.

GURALNIK, Aron. Di kunst, vos kukt arain in der tsukunft. (Art that looks to the future) Sovietish Heimland, 17, No. 11, N. pp 168-72.

Soviet Jewish literature after 60 years of the revolution.

HOWE, Irving,GREENBERG, Eliezer. (Eds.) Ashes out of Hope. Yiddish Stories. New York, London, Schocken, 340p.

Kurtser bibliografishe iberzicht fun di verk fun M. Grubian. (Short bibliography of the works of M. Grubian) Sovietish Heimland, 17, No. 8, Au. pp 172-75.

LEVENBERG, Shneier. The "Grandfather" of Jewish Literature. Jewish Frontier, 44, No. 7, Au-S. pp 20-21.

LYUBOMIRSKI, Yeshaie. Di yiddishe sovietishe dramaturgie in kamf kegn fashizm. (Soviet Jewish drama in the fight against fascism) Sovietish Heimland, 17, No. 11, N. pp 181-85.

MILLER, David Neal. Sholem Aleichem in English: The Most Accessible Translations. Yiddish, 2, No. 4, Su. pp 61-70.

PALMIERI, Franco. La letteratura della terza Diaspora - La Cultura ebraica della Yiddish all'Ameridish. Ravenna, Longo,

PRIZEL, Zoya. The Narrator in Sholem Aleichem's The Enchanted Tailor Yiddish, 2, No. 4, Su. pp 55-60.

RASKIN, Aron. Einike problemen fun der literaturantwiklung fun yisroel. (Some problems of the development of literature in Israel) Sovietish Heimland, 17, No. 1, Ja. pp 146-53.

Analysis of material published in the Hebrew journal Moznaim

A naie zamlung fun Peretzes verk ois russish (A new collection of Peretz's work in Russian) Sovietish Heimland, 17, No. 8, Aut. pp 141-44.

Review article.

REMENIK, Hersh. Der historisher goirl fun Mendele Moicher Sforim. (Mendele's historic fate) Sovietish Heimland, 17, No. 1, Ja. pp 136-45.

Di oktyober-revolutsie un di yiddishe literatur. (The October revolution and Yiddish literature) Sovietish Heimland, 17, No. 11, N. pp 173-80.

The six decades since the October Revolution enabled the multi-national literatures of the Soviet Union to make lasting contributions to the spiritual life of mankind.

STILLMAN, Gerald. A Defense of Nineteenth-Century Yiddish Literature. Yiddish, 2, No. 4, Su. pp 4-14.

----------------. Mendele Mocher Seforim, Our Zayde. Jewish Currents 31, No. 10, N. pp 5-9.

Z. Vendroff - tsu zain 100-ten geburtstog; Yoisef Opatoshu - tsum 90-ten geburtstog. Sovietish Heimland, 17, No. 1, Ja. pp 126-35.

On the centenary of Vendroff and the 90th birthday of Opatoshu.

VERGELIS, Aron. Di oktober revolutsie un die literatu (The October Revolution and literature) Sovietish Heimland, 17, No. 6, Ju. pp 138-42.

WEINER, Leo. The History of Yiddish Literature in the Nineteenth Century. New York, Sepher Hermon.

HEBREW

HEUMAN, Fred. S. The Uses of Hebraisms in Recent Bible Translations. New York, Philosophical Library, 154p, Ind, Bibl.

Shows the influences of Hebrew idioms on the English language.

SILVER, Ditsa. Di antimilchome-teme in der hainttsaitiger ivrit literatur. (Anti-war themes in contemporary Hebrew literature) Sovietish Heimland, 17, NO. 5, My. pp 156-64.

SIVAN, Gabriel. The Hebrew Element in Everyday English. Johannesburg, South African Zionist Federation. Information and Education Department, 16p.

SIVAN, Reuven and LEVENSTON, Edward A. The New Bantam-Megiddo Hebrew and English Dictionary. New York, London, Schocken,

HEBREW LITERATURE

ANDERSON, Elliott. (Ed.) Contemporary Israeli Literature. An Anthology. Philadelphia, Jewish Publication Society of America, 342p, Ill.

Anthology of Israeli poetry and prose in English translation.

BARZILAY, I. The Arab in Modern Hebrew Literature: image and problem Hebrew Studies, 18, pp 23-48.

BOCCATO, Carla. L'amor Possente, Favola Pastorale di Benedetto Luzzatto Hebreo Ventia Composta Durante la Peste del 1630. La Raseegna Mensile di Israel, 43, Nos. 1-2, Ja-F., pp 36-47.

A Hebrew pastoral poem written during the epidemic of 1630.

FRIEDLANDER, Yehuda. Uri Zvi Greenberg at 80. Jewish Quarterly, 25, No. 1, Sp. pp 8-11.

FRIEDLER, Egon. Aharon Megged on Hebrew Literature and Israeli Society. Israel Horizons, 25, No. 10, Fa/W., pp 20-22.

GILBOA, Yehoshua A. Tsvi Preygerzon - A Hebrew Writer in the USSR. Soviet Jewish Affairs, 7, No. 2, pp 62-68.

KABAKOFF, Jacob. The Arab Image in Hebrew fiction between World War I and World War II. Hebrew Studies, 18, pp 49-59.

SADAN, Dov. La littérature hebreique moderne. Connaissance d'Israel 1, No. 1, Ja-Ju. pp 33-46.

VARON, Miriam Laserson. Nathan Alterman - Poet and Playwright. Midstream, 23, No. 2, F..pp 53-57.

JUDEO-ARABIC, LADINO

BENAZERAF, Raphael. Recueil de refranes. (Proverbs) Judeo-Espagnols du Maroc. Réunis, traduits et commentés. Illustration by José Abad et Isaac Knato. Paris, Imprimerie Continentale, 150p, Ill.

BENOLIEL, José. Dialecto Judeo-Hispano-Marroquino Hakitia, Madrid, Copisteria Varona.

A Moroccan Judeo-Espagnol dialect.

MERZAGORA, Giovanna Massariello. Guido-italiano. Pisa, Pacini, 92p. (consiglio Nazionale delle Ricerche, Centro di studio per la dialettolgoia italiana No. 5)
The Italo-Jewish dialect, a variant of Ladino.

YARSHATER, E. The Hybrid Language of the Jewish Communities of Persia. Journal of the American Oriental Society, 97, No. 1, pp 1-7.

JEWS AND GENTILES

BENAMOZEGH, Elia. Morale ebraica a morale cristiana. Tr. Elio Piattelli, Assisi, Roma, Carrucci, 230p. (Collana di cultura ebraica 6)
Comparison between Judaism and Christianity.

BLUMENKRANZ, Bernhard. Juifs et Chrétiens: Patristique et Moyen Ages, London, Variorum Reprints, 368p.
Studies in Jewish-Christian relations in the works of the Church Fathers and medieval christian writings.

Christian Mission and Jewish Witness. Face to Face, 2, No. 1, Fa/W. pp 1-31.
Opinions by Catholics, Protestants and Jews on the new-old issue of the Christian mission to the Jews and its present-day relation to interreligious relations.

COSGRAVE, Patrick. Message d'un gentil aux Israéliens. France-Israel Information, 35, Ju. pp 12-13.
Pro-Israel.

DIPPER, Karl. Gerechtigkeit für Israel. Gottes Volk braucht sein Land. Wuppertal, Brockhaus, 271p.
Christian affirmation of the right of Jews to Jerusalem and Israel.

GOUTHRO, Arthur F. Opening address to the Conference on Jewish-Christian-Muslim Dialogue. Journal of Ecumenical Studies, 14, No. 3, Su. pp 405-6.

Juifs et Chretiens. Une brochure d'Information. Bruxelles, contacts interconfessionnels,
Jews and Christians - an information pamphlet.

KATZ, Jacob and HERSHKO, Moshe. Israel und die Völker. Tr. by H. Maor. Dusseldorf, Zentralrat der Juden in Deutschland. N.e. 312p.
German translation of "Israel ve-ha'amim", a survey of Jewish-Gentile relations throughout the ages.

LEWIS, Justin and KARBAL, Albert. On Sensitizing Youth to Moral Imperatives: The Holocaust as Case History. Religious Education, 72, No. 6, N-D., pp 657-63.
"Since the countries in which the Holocaust took place are all Christian, not only must a study of the destruction include a focus on the moral collapse of Western Civilisation, but also on the particular theological problems of Christianity vis-a-vis the Jews." Included a selected bibliography of material for teaching the Holocaust.

MARMUR, Dow. The Influence of Judaism on Christianity. The Liberal Catholic, 46, No. 1, Ma. pp 15-18; No. 2, Ju. pp 10-13.
Neither Jesus nor the Bible can be divorced from Judaism and the Gospels must be understood in terms of Jewish tradition, from which they originated.

MOORE, Donald J. Hope in Jerusalem. America, 134, 15 O., pp 236-39.
Report on a month-long seminar that brought Jews, Muslims and Christians together at the Hope Center for Phace and Interfaith Understanding in Ein Kerem, a suburb of Jerusalem.

OSMAN, Fathi, SHACHTER, Zalman M., SLOYAN, Gerard S. and LANE, Dermont A. Jesus in Jewish-Christian-Muslim Dialogue. Journal of Ecumencial Studies, 14, No. 3, Su. pp 448-54.

PARKES, James. Israel et le Monde Crétien. France-Israel Information, No. 35, Ju. pp 13.

PILON, Johan. Nes Amim: una aldea cristiana en Israel. El Olivo, No. 1, Ma. pp 36-44.
A Christian settlement in Israel.

REMAUD, Michel. Reflexions sur la permanence d'Israel. Nouvelle Revue Theologique, 99, No. 4, Jy-Au. pp 507-17.
The Church must face the permanence of the Jewish nation. Theologies which present Judaism as a decaying tradition, or in a negative fashion as a faith whose truth is made explicit in Christianity, neglect the origins of Judaism in the Covenant.

STAHL, Jerzy and KAREL, Piotr. Instytucje Religijne w Izraelu (Religious Institutions in Israel) Swieta Izraelskie i Zydowskie (Israelite and Jewish Holidays) Jednota, 21, No. 7, pp 11-19; No. 8, 20-28.

SWETNAM, James. Self-Discoveries in the Middle East. Several demonstrations of the lesson that biblical archaeology helps Christians learn about more than a dry and dusty past. America, 136, No. 13, 2 Ap. pp 292-95.

WEISS-ROSMARIN, Trude. (Ed.) Jewish Expressions on Jesus. An Anthology. New York, Ktav, xix, 421p.
Selection of writings by Jewish scholars on the Jewishness of Jesus and his crucifixion.

WERBLOWSKY, R.J. Zwi. Interfaith in Jerusalem. Face to Face, Vol. 11 W/Sp. pp 6-7.

YARON, Zvi. An Orthodox Jewish Israeli Views Interfaith. Face to Face, 11, W/Sp. pp 15-17.

DIALOGUE - GENERALLY

ANGELL, Charles. Difficult Days Ahead for Jewish-Christian Relations. Worldview, 20, No. 12, D. pp 29-32.
Charles will be leveled by Jews at the American churches when it becomes apparent that our views and theirs do not converge on the Middle East.

ANSARI, Zafar Ishaq. Some Reflections on Islamic Bases for Dialogue with Jews and Christians. Journal of Ecumenical Studies, 14, No. 3, Su. pp 433-47.

CRONER, Helga. Stepping Stones to Further Jewish-Christian Relations. An unabridged collection of Christian documents. Foreward by Edward A. Synan. New York, London, Stimulus Books, 157p. (Studies in Judaism and Christianity)

DENAUX, A. La pensée juive actuelle sur Jesus de Nazareth (In Dutch) Collationes, 39, No. 2, pp 287-313.
Historigraphical study of the problem exposing points of agreement and disagreement.

DITMANSON, Harold H. Judaism and Christianity: A Theology of Co-existence. Dialog, 16, No. 1, W. pp 17-24.
Despite recent improvement in Jewish-Christian relations, much remains to be done. To move beyond mere toleration, Christians must clarify their theological premises used in evaluating Judaism and must recognize its abiding autonomy.
DUBOIS, Marcel-Jacques. New Jewish-Christian understanding in Israel Face-to-Face, 11, W/Sp., pp 10-12.
FISHER, Eugene. Faith Without Prejudice. New York, Paulist Press, 179p.
On improving Christian-Jewish relations.
GASCOIGNE, Bamber. The Christians. London, Jonathan Cape; New York, Morrow; German ed. Wolfgang Krüger; Dutch ed. Elsevier; Norwegian ed. Grndahl; Finnish ed. Weilin Göös.
Discusses i.a. Christian attitudes to the Jews through the ages.
GIBEL, Inge Lederer. To a certain young Christian Radical. Worldview, 20, No. 6, Ju. pp 9-11.
Appeal for the same understanding for Israel as for Arabs.
HABERMAN, Joshua D. Universalism and Particularism in Inter-religious Dialogue. CCAR Journal, 125, Su. pp 59-74.
Turn of the dialogue to the 'positive' elements in inter-religious relations, namely a reexamination of cardinal doctrines in Judaism and Christianity.
HANN, Robert R. The Undivided Way: The Early Jewish Christians as a Model for Ecumenical Encounter? Journal of Ecumenical Studies, 14, No. 2, Sp. pp 233-48.
HELLWIG, Monika Konrad. Bases and Boondaries for Interfaith Dialogue: A Christian View. Journal of Ecumenical Studies, 14, No. 3, Su. pp 419-32.
HUCHET-BISHOP, Claire. Jules Isaac. Christian Attitudes on Jews and Judaism, No. 50, o. pp 7-10; 13. Condensed in Encounter Today, 12, No. 3, Su. pp 100-6.
Extract from a lecture delivered by the President of the Amitie Judeo-Chretienne de France at the summer coltoquium held by the International Council of Christians and Jews at Southampton University in July 1977 on the centenary of the birth of Jules Isaac, the French Jewish writer and historian, whose "Jesus and Israel" demonstrates that some of the Christian teaching has been responsible for creating a tradition of contempt toward Jews and Judaism.
IGLEHEART, Glenn. Why Bother with Christian-Jewish Relations? ADL Bulletin, Ap. pp 7-8.
"There are three reasons: Because of the scriptures, because of the times and because of God." By the director of the Southern Baptist Department of Interfaith Witness in Atlanta, Georgia.
Jewish-Christian-Muslim Dialogue. Journal of Ecumenical Studies, 14, No. 2, Su. pp 401-500.
Papers delivered at a May conference at the Graymoor Ecumenical Institute, Garrison, N.Y.
Judentum und Christentum. Paderborn Akademische Bonifatius Einigung. Lebendiges Zeugnis, Nos. 1-2, F.
LAFONTAINE, Charles V. To Trialogue and Back. Journal of Ecumenical Studies, 14, No. 3, Su. pp 401-4.
On Jewish-Christian-Muslim dialogue.

LAPIDE, Pinchas. Auferstehung. Ein jüdisches Glaubenserlebnis. München,, Kösel, Stuttgart, Calwer, 92p.
Explains the resurrection of Jesus to Jews.
LASKER, Daniel J. Jewish Philosophical Polemics Against Christianity in the Middle Ages. New York, Ktav, Anti-Defamation League of B'nai B'rith,xi, 286p, Ind, Bibl.
Study based on medieval Hebrew, Latin, and Arabic writings, many in manuscript.
McGARRY, Michael B. Christology after Auschwitz. New York, Ramsey; Toronto, Paulist P., 119p, Bibl.
The Catholic stand on the question of Judaism after World War II including the official statements.
MBITI, J. and ODUYOYE, M. African Christians and the Jewish Religion. Christian Attitudes to Jews and Judaism, No. 56, F. pp 1-5.
National Conference of Christians and Jews. Desegregation without Turmoil: the role of the multiracial community coalition in preparing for smooth transition; an experience guide based on a national conference co-sponsored by the Community Relations Service, U.S. Dept. of Justice and National Center for Quality Integrated Education, New York, Ap. 45p.
NEWBEGIN, L. The Basis, Purpose and Manner of Inter-faith Dialogue. Scottish Journal of Theology, 30, No. 3, pp 253-70. In German: in Theologie der Gegenwart, 20, No. 3, pp 159-66.
PAPENGUS, S.C. An Exploration of the Concept of 'Fidelity' (Faithfulne-s) in Interreligious Dialogue. Journal of Ecumenical Studies, 14, No. 1, W. pp 97-101.
PIERRARD, Pierre. Le centenaire de Jules Isaac. Rencontre, 11, No. 52, pp 201-5.
Isaac's centenary - a colleague recalling his fight for vindication of Jews in Christian theology, culminating in his encounter with John XXIII in 1960.
Is the Political Jesus Dead? Encounter, 47, No. 4, Ap. pp 83-92.
The Political Jesus, Thesis or Truth? by Samuel Sandmel. The Historical Jesus is 'Dead' by Trude Weiss-Rosmarin. Jesus or Christ by Joel Carmichael. The Jewish Jesus and Politics by Rosemary Radford Ruether, and a Reply by Hyam Maccoby.
ROTTENBERG, Isaac. Should There Be a Christian Witness to the Jews? The Christian Century, 94, 13 Ap. pp 352-56.
Considers an honest encounter between the church and the Jewish people as a priority concern.
SAND, A. Jesus im Urteil jüdischer Autoren der Gegenwart (1930-76) Catholica, 31, No. 1, pp 29-38.
Introduction and analytical bibliography to: Jesus in the Eyes of Jewish Authors 1930-76.
SANDMEL, Samuel. A Jewish Undertaking of the New Testament. Augmented Ed. London, SPCK, xxxiv, 366p, Ind, Bibl.
Applies scholarly criticism to the writings and historical background of the New Testament.
SCHACHTER, Zalman M. Bases and Boundaries of Jewish, Christian and Muslim Dialogue. Journal of Ecumenical Studies, 14, No. 3, Su. pp 407-18.
SCHONEVELD, J. Coos. Jews and Christians in Israel. Face-to-Face, 11, W/Sp. pp 13-14.

SCHONFIELD, Hugh Joseph. Passover Plot. N.e. London, Futura, 288p.
The trial of Jesus.
SCHULWEIS, Harold. Cairo trialogue: Christian, Moslem, Jew. Sh'ma, 7, 14 O. pp 161-66.
Implications of a 10-day visit in Egypt of a Moslem Imam, Presbyterian minister and a rabbi, during which time meetings were held with a number of key Egyptian religious and political figures.
SERRANO, Vincente. Conferencia de "The International Council of Christians and Jews" (ICCJ) El Olivo, No. 1, Ma. pp 68-74.
-----------------. El dialogo judeo-cristiano en Espana. Datos para una historia. El Olivo, No. 1, Ma. pp 9-18.
SHERMAN, Franklin. Report from Jerusalem. Dialog, 16, No. 1, W. pp 12-16.
A 14-week seminar of "Current Issues in the Jewish-Christian Dialogue" in the spring of 1976 at the Ecumenical Institute for Advanced Theological Studies in Jerusalem.
TALMON, Shemaryahu. Interfaith Dialogue in Israel. Face to Face, 11 W/Sp. pp 3-5.

JEWS AND CATHOLICS

Dialogue entre juifs et catholiques: données élémentaires. Les Nouveaux Cahiers, 12, No. 49, Su. pp 2-24.
Proceedings of a Jewish-Catholic dialogue.
Documentation: El Concilio Vaticano II sobre las relaciones con el judaismo. El Olivo, No. 1, Ma. pp 45-67.
EHRLICH, E.L. Gegen die Judenbekehrung. Judaica, 33, No. 2, pp 54-58.
Response to Professor Tommeso Federici's study presented at a Venice encounter between Jews and Catholics. Far from wishing to convert Jews, Christians should convert to the Jewish concept of "Sanctification of the Name."
FEDERICI, Tommaso. Mission und Zeugenschaft der Kirche. Freiburger Rundbrief, 29, No. 109-12, 12 D. pp 3-13.
German translation of a study outline presented in Venice in 1977 at the sixth meeting of the Catholic Jewish Contact Committee. Federici, presents a new proposal forreligious relations with Judaism. A review of current Catholic renewal in the wake of Vatican II leads to a clear vision of the particulars of the mission and witness mandates in the Old and New Testaments. For Catholic relations with Jews this means rejecting outright the mentality of proselytism and adopting the policy of dialogue. With commentary by Rabbi Klenicki of the A.D.L. in New York.
FERNÁNDEZ, Luis Suárez. Crónica de un seminario hispano-israel. El Olivo, No. 1, Ma. pp 75-78.
A Spanish (Catholic)-Jewish encounter.
FLEISCHNER, Eva. (Ed.) Auschwitz: Beginning of a New Era? Reflections on the Holocaust. New York, Ktav, The Cathedral Church of St. John the Divine, Anti-Defamation League of B'nai B'rith, xix 468p. Papers given at the International Symposium on the Holocaust held at the Cathedral of St. John the Divine, New York, 3-6 Ju.1974

The subjects discussed were: Theological Reflections on the Holocaust; The History of Christian Theology and the Demonization of the Jews; Christian Mission in Crisis; Judaism and Christian Education; Theological Reflections on the State of Israel in the Light of the Yom Kippur War; Radical Theology; The New Left and Israel; The New Romanticism and Biblical Faith; Auschwitz and the Pathology of Jew-Hatred; Blacks and Jews; Affinity and Confrontation on Common Theological Themes; Art and Culture after the Holocaust.

FLORIT, José Ribera. El mesianismo en la vision judía y cristiana. El Olivo, No. 3-4, Jy-D. pp 45-60.
Christian and Jewish concepts of messianism.

GARBER, George. Israel and the Catholic Church. The Impact of the establishment of the State of Israel on the attitude of the Catholic Church towards Israel during the years 1948-1975, as reflected in American Catholic periodicals. Ann Arbor, Mich., U. Microfilms, 203p.
Ph.D. thesis. New York University. Based on American Catholic Press.

GARZON, Baruj. Las relaciones Judeo-Christianas, Punto de vista de un judio. El Olivo, No. 1, Ma. pp 6-8.
The Chief Rabbi of Spain expresses his views on Jewish-Christian relations.

GRAYZEL, Solomon. The Church and the Jews in the 18th Century. New York, Sepher Hermon.

Le judaïsme. Documentation Catholique, 74, No. 1719, pp 421-26.
Official communique of meeting of the International Liason Committee between the Catholic Church and Judaism. Venice, 28-30 March.

KÜNG, Hans and LAPIDE, Pinchas. Is Jesus a Bond or Barrier? A Jewish-Christian Dialogue. Journal of Ecumenical Studies, 14, No. 3, Su. pp 466-83. As a Pamphlet: London, Collins, 44p.

SHEERIN, John B. Catholic-Jewish Relations. New Catholic World, Ju-Au. pp 173-8.
A Catholic view of the Christian-Jewish dialogue.

VALLINA, F. Javier Fernandez and PAYTANIM, Piyyut Y. Documentacion: Orientaciones del Episcopado frances sobre la actitud de los christianos con respecto al Judaismo. El Olivo, No. 3-4, Ju.-D. pp 83-94.

WILLEBRANDS, Cardenal Jan. Documentacion, Orientaciones y Sugerencias para la Aplicacion de la Declaracion Conciliar 'Nostra Aetate' El Olivo, No. 2, Ap.-Ju. pp 53-60.
Guidelines for the application of the Vatican Declaration on the Jews.

JEWS AND PROTESTANTS

HUDSON, Darril. The World Council of Churches in International Affairs. Leighton Buzzard, The Faith P., for the Royal Institute of International Affairs, 336p, Ind, Bibl.
The WCC takes an increasing interest in international affairs, not least in the Middle East.

MAURER, Marvin. Quakers in Politics: Israel, P.L.O. and Social Revolution. Midstream, 23, No. 9, N. pp 36-44.

Explains the Quaker's position in the light of their beliefs.

RAUSCH, David. American Evangelicals and the Jews. Midstream, 23, No. 2, F. pp 38-41.

Jewish heritage and history are seen as being extremely important to the Christian faith. After centuries of Christian 'gentilizing" of the Jewish people, it is refreshing that fundamentalist evangelicals have fought adamently against the idea that all Jews must be converted to Christianity and totally gentilized before the arrival of the Messiah.

-------------. "Evangelical Zionism": The Vicious Debate Among Evangelicals. Jewish Frontier, 44, No. 5, My. pp 28-30.

There is a gulf between the theology and philosophy of Fundamentalist-Evangelicals and Liberal-Evangelicals. The latter will never support Zionism or the right of the State of Israel to exist the way Fundamentalist-Evangelicals do.

-------------. Modern Eschatological Literature and the Jews. Jewish Frontier, 44, No. 2, F. pp 18-20.

Millions of American Protestant Fundamentalists hold an eschatological position (i.e. beliefs about the end of the world) that is favourable to the Jewish people.

-------------. True Friends: Evangelicals United for Zion. The American Zionist, 68, No. 2, N. pp 20-22.

Analyses the Fundamentalist-Evangelical proclamation of support for Israel, presented to Ambassador Dinitz at a meeting of Jewish and Evangelical leaders on 28th October 1976 in Washington, D.C.

RICE, Dan. Reinhold Niebuhr and Judaism. Journal of the American Academy of Religion, 45, No. 1, Ma. pp 101-46.

Among Niebuhr's many and varied contributions to the vital concerns of his era none surpassed in personal investment or impact those which grew out of his profound relationship with the Jewish people.

SUCHER, C. Lutners Stelling zu den Juden. Eine Interpretation aus germanistischer Sicht. viii, 316p. (Bibliotheca Human, et Reform, 23)

ORTHODOX

VAPORIS, Nomikos Michael and TANENBAUM, Marc H. Colloquium on Greek Orthodox-Jewish Relations, New York, 1872. Selected Papers and commentaries from proceedings 25-26 Ja. 1972. Brookline, Mass., Holy Cross Orthodox P., for the Holy Cross Greek Orthodox School of Theology, Hellenic College, 156p.

ISLAM

BEIT-HALLAHMY, Benjamin. In Search of the "Arab Character". Jewish Quarterly, 24, No. 3, Aut. pp 15-17.

"As traditional society breaks down, the fabric of Arab culture will become dramatically different. If there is such a thing as an Arab character, it will change with history and will reflect the new realities of new ways of life. Basing any theory or practice on the notion of an immutable 'national character' at such time will be not only futile, but also short-sighted and risky."

CRONE, Patricia and COOK, Michael. Hagarism. The Making of the Islamic World. Cambridge, Cambridge U.P., x, 268p, Ind, Bibl.

Origins and theory of Islam partly based on non-Muslim sources which point to a close link between the early form of Islam and Jewish messianism.

MERINO, Luis Diez. Judaismo e Islamismo: Perspectivas actuales de investigación. El Olivo, No. 1, Ma. pp 79-83.

The prospects of a Jewish-Muslim dialogue.

MUHAMMAD, Askia. Civil War in Islamic America: Behind the Washington Siege. The Nation, 216, 11 Ju., pp 721-4.

A former editor of Muhammed Speaks writes of the days preceding the Hanafi siege in Washington and also an introduction to the spread of Islam among the black citizens of the U.S.A.

QUADAFI, Muammar A. The Green Book. Parts 1 and 2. London, Martin Brian and O'Keefe. 96, 30p.

Arabic-English edition of Col. Quadafi's basic ideology.

RODINSON, Maxime. Islam and Capitalism. Tr. from French by B. Pearce. N.e. Harmondsworth, Penguin, xviii, 328p, Ind.

Social and economic development of the countries of Islam and the role of the Muslim religion in equating its precepts with the practices of modern capitalism.

WEISBORD, Robert. Islam, Black Nationalism and the Jews. Congress Monthly, 44, No. 5, Ju. pp 13-15.

YEHOSHUA, Yaakov. The Problems of an Islam-Jewish Dialogue in Israel Face to Face, 11, W/Sp. pp 18-19.

SECTS

HOPKINS, Joseph. The Children of God: Disciples of Deception. Christianity Today, 21, 18 F., pp 18-23.

Interview with two former members of the controversial sect about the group and its founder "Moses" Berg.

LYLES, Jean Caffey. Letting Go: Everybody Has the Right to be Wrong. Christian Century, 94, 11 My. pp 451-53.

Questions whether'Moonies' are entitled to the same religious liberties as mainstream churchgoers and concludes that "if young adults are to be assured of their civil liberties, they must be given one other freedom: the right to make the wrong choice."

ROBBINS, Thomas. "Deprogramming" the "Brainwashed": Evan a Moonie Has Civil Rights. The Nation, 216, 26 F.

"If persecution of deviant religions on obscurantist grounds of 'mind control' is institutionalized, its application to political dissidents may be inevitable. The Left has a stake in the liberties of Moonies and Krishnas."

RUDIN, A. James and Marcia. Onward (Hebrew) Christian Soldiers. Present Tense, 4, No. 4, Su. pp 17-26.

The "Hebrew Christians" a sect attracting young Jews in America.

--------------------------. Pied Pipers and Would-Be Messiahs. Keeping Posted, 22, F. pp 20-23.

Examines the various religious sects in America today and their influence on young Jews.

SPERO, Moshe.Halevi. Cults: Some Theoretical and Practical Perspectives. Journal of Jewish Communal Service, 53, No. 4, Su. pp 330-38.

STONER, C. and PARKE, J.A. All God's Children: The Cult Experience. Salvation or Slavery? Pittsburgh, Chilton, 324p.
Since 1965, over 1,300 new cults have emerged in the U.S.A.

HARAMGAAL, Ya'aqov. Deprogramming: A Critical View. The American Zionist, 67, eo. 7, My-Ju. pp 16-19.
The threat of cults to Jewish youth.

Unification Church. Dept. of Public Affairs. Response to A. James Rudin's report "Jews and Judaism in Reverend Moon's Divine Principle." New York, 13p.

WALLS, Dwayne. The Jesus Mania: Bigotry in the Name of the Lord. Saturday Review, 17 S. pp 13-18.
"Of concern to Jews is a nationwide 'buy Christian' campaign reminiscent of those they have been subjected to throughout their history, notably in Nazi Germany."

WALL, James M. Israel and the Evangelicals. The Christian Century, 94, 23 N. pp 1083-84.
"American Jews are going to argue their case in every possible forum of decision-making. But we would caution them to remember the important distinction between the strong empathy Christians feel with Isreel and the realistic awareness that political decision-making must be shaped by political and not religious guidelines."

WALSH, Richard. 'Moonies - Religious Converts or Psychic Victims? America, 134, 14 My. pp 438-40.
"The answer to that question, as well as its implications, are larger than any single sect and have to do with the quality of religious freedom for us all."

FISHMAN, Samuel Z. Comment on the Campus: The Moonies and the Response of the Jewish Community. Washington, B'nai B'rith Hillel Foundation, 5p.

NEGROES AND JEWS

DINER, Hasia R. In the Almost Promises Land: American Jews and Blacks, 1915-35. N.e. Westport, Conn., Greenwood P.; London, Westport P., xvii, 271p.
The period when Jews, led by Stephen S. Wise were in the fore-front of the fight for civil rights for blacks.

WILLIAMS, John A. The Boys from Syracuse. Blacks and Jews in the Old Neighbourhood. Present Tense, 4, No. 3, Sp. pp 34-38.

WILLIAMS, O. R. Jr. Historical Impressions of Black-Jewish Relations Prior to World War II. Negro History Bulletin, 40, No. 2, pp 728-31.

ZIONISM

ABRAMSKY, Chimen. Weizmann: A New Type of leadership in the Zionist Movement. Reprinted from Transactions Sessions 1973-75, 24 and Miscellanies Part 10. London, Jewish Historical Society of England, pp 137-49.

Lecture delivered to the Society on 9th April 1975.

ALCOTT, Amos. (Ed.) The American Republic and Ancient Israel. New York, Arno P., 250p.

ALEXANDER, Morris. Israel and me. A Behind-the-Scenes Look by a Longtime U.S. Zionist Leader and Returned Israeli Immigrant. New York, Schenkman, ix, 280p, Ill.

ALLOUCHE, Jean-Luc. Israel: Retour au judaisme. L'Arche, 20, No. 248, pp 23-27.

ALPERIN, Aaron. Historia del Primer Congreso Sionista. Tr. Isadora Niborski. Buenos Aires, Congreso Judio Mundial. Congreso Judio Latinoamericano, 40p, Ill. (Heohos de la Historia Judio, 91)

The first Zionist Congress.

ARKIN, Marcus. The Zionist Idea: A History of Evaluation. Johannesburg, South African Zionist Federation, Information Department, 42p.

ARNONI, S.M. Sionismen som Nasjonal Frigoringsbevegelse. Oslo, Norge-Israel Forening, 19p. (The Fundamentals of Zionism)

AVISHAI, Bernard. To Praise Zionism, and to bury it. Moment, 2, No. 10, O. pp 15-20.

Calls for a re-formulation of Zionist ideology.

BECK, Yoram and ZOHAR, David. (Ed.) A Zionist Anthology. New Brunswick, N.J. Transaction Books, 250p.

Essays on Zionism.

BOYER, A. Le sionisme de Hess en face des grands courants du judaisme du milieu du XIX siecle. Etude d'une lettre de Hess au rabbin Abraham Geiger, pamphlet contre la Reforme publiee en 1863. Yod, 2, No. 2, pp 7-32.

Hess's appeal to orthodox Jewry for a political Zionist engagement and for the preservation of Jewish religion for political ends.

BRESLAUER, Daniel S. Modernization and Zionism in America. Conservative Judaism, 31, No. 1, pp 70-78.'

"A new form of political religion can be devised which would take account of modernization in general and more specifically of the universalism associated with it. As in the case of Zionism such a political religion can overcome the danger of parochialism by providing a specific, cultural identity which includes within it a sense of universal concern and commonality with all human beings."

BUHEIRY, Marwan. Herzl and the Armenians. Journal of Palestine Studies, 7, No. 1, Aut. pp 75-97.

CATARIVAS, David. Why Israel? New York, EPM (Two Continents) 96p.

Argues the Zionist case.

The Contemporary Meaning of Zionism: New Definitions and New Directions. The 12th American-Israel Dialogue. Congress Monthly, 44, No. 3, Ma-Ap. 38p.

Contributors: Yehoshua Arieli; Arnold J. Band; Phil. Baum; Martin S. Bugun; Yossi Dan; Aryeh Dvoretsky; Abba Eban; Lova Eliav; Saul Farber; Nahum Goldmann; Murray A. Gordon; Arthur Hertzberg; Jacob Katz; Stephen Lerner; Naomi Levine; Janet O' Dea; Amnon Rafael; Michael Roeenak; Henry Rosovsky; Benjamin Schwartz; David Sidorsky; Ezra Spicehandler; Howard M. Squadron; Ephraim Urbach; David Vital; Walter Wurzberger; Zvi Yaron.

CROWN, Alan D. The Initiatives and Influences in the development of Australian Zionism, 1850-1948. Jewish Social Studies, 39, No. 4, Fa. pp 299-322.

Traces the motives, causes and influences which shaped the Zionist movement in Australia.

DAVIS, Moshe. (Ed.) With Eyes Toward Zion. Scholars Colloquium on America-Holy Land Studies, New York, Arno P., 252p, Ill.

Expanded papers delivered at the Colloquium organised by the American Jewish Historical Society and the Institute of Contemporary Jewry, Hebrew University, where significant relations between America and the Holy Land were discussed from many aspects.

FRIEDMAN, Isaiah. Germany, Turkey and Zionism, 1897-1918. New York, Oxford U.P., 488p, Ind, Bibl.

GOLDMANN, Nahum. Israel muss umdenken? Berlin, Rowohlt, 121p. German ed. of "Ou va Israel?"

GORNI, Yosef. The Jewishness and Zionism of Harold Laski. Midstream, 23, No. 9, N. pp 72-78.

------------. Zionism Socialism and the Arab Question. 1918-1930. Middle Eastern Studies, 13, No. 1, Ja. pp 50-70.

HALKIN, Hillel. Letters to an American Jewish Friend: Zionist's Polemic. Philadelphia, Jewish Publication Society of America, 246p.

HERMAN, Simon N. Zionisme en Pro-Israelisme. Amsterdam, Den Haag, Nederlandse Zionistenbond, Centrum voor Informatie en Documentatie Israel. 25p. (In Dutch)

Explains the difference between Zionism and just 'supporting' Israel.

HERTZBERG, Arthur. Some Reflections on Zionism Today. The 12th American-Israel Dialogue. Opening Session. Congress Monthly, 44, No. 3, Ma-Ap. pp 3-6.

The changing face of Zionism and the need for a re-assessment.

HOFFMAN, Gerard H. Reflections on Churchill. Jewish Affairs, 32, No. 4, Ap. pp 13-20.

Churchill's relations to Zionism and the Jewish problem.

KALMANN, Dov. Zionisme: van droom tot taat. Amsterdam, N.Z.B. Tarboetressort, 49p.

KAPLAN, Mendel. A New Zionism. Jewish Affairs, 32, No. 5, My. pp 16-19.

KATZ, Jacob. The Core of Zionism. The 12th American-Israel Dialogue. Fifth Session, Congress Monthly, 44, No. 3, Ma-Ap. pp 48-52.

-----------. Zionism and Jewish Identity. Commentary, 63, No. 5, My. pp 48-52.

KIERNAN, J. Poor and Puritan: An Attempt to View Zionism as a Collective Response to Urban Poverty. African Studies, 36, No. 1, pp 31-42.

KNEE, Stuart E. Jewish Non-Zionism in America and Palestine Commitment 1917-1941. Jewish Social Studies, 39, No. 3, Su. pp 209-26.

KODAMA, N. Herzl and the Zionist Movement. (In Japanese) Chuto sogo kenkyu, 6, No. 9, S. pp 79-89.

LADEMACHER, Horst. Moses Hess in seiner Zeit. Bonn, Ludwig Röhrscheid. 194p. (Veröffentlichungen des Stadtarchivs Bonn, 17)

LAMOUREUX, Charlotte, LEBOUTET, Laurent and GORIN, Michel. Le temps de vérité. Trois soinistes non-juifs parlent. Marseille, Librarie Pardesse, 24p.

M. Leboutet, one of the "Righteous Gentiles" his wife and a friend are non-Jewish Zionists who speak for Israel.

LANGER, Michael. Zionism and Reform Judaism. Responses to Modernity. Midstream, 23, No. 4, Ap. pp 28-55.

LAQUEUR, Walter. A History of Zionism. N.e. London, Weidenfeld and Nicolson, 656p, Ill, Ind, Bibl. M.

LATTES, Dante. Il Sionismo, Rome, Beniamino Carucci, 180p.

LEVENBERG, Shneier. Ahad Ha'am, the Father of Spiritual Zionism. Jewish Frontier, 44, No. 1, Ja. pp 8-9.

LEVIGNE, Catherine. Le Quai et les debuts du sionisme. Les Nouveaux Cahiers, 12, No. 50, Aut. pp 50-55.

The French Foreign Office's attitude to early Zionism.

LEWITTES, Mendell. The Religious Foundation of the Jewish State. New York, Ktav, 271p.

LITTMAN-OREBI, G. Le sionisme dans les pays islamiques: le cas de l'Egypte. Yod, 2, No. 2, pp 81-97.

Zionism among oriental Jews differed from European Zionism. The case of Egypt is a good illustration.

LUCAS, Noah. Is Zionism Dead? Interchange, 2, No. 5, Ja. pp 1;7-8.

"Israel in a state of permanent war is the definition of the political problem for which a new Zionism in the West must help to find the solution."

-----------. Zionism, Socialism and the Third World Movement. Olam. Jewish Themes and World Issues, No. 3, W/Sp. pp 17-21.

MANDEL, Neville J. Arabs and Zionism before World War I. Los Angeles U. of California P., 264p, Ill, M.

MARCUS, Michael. Bernard Lazare - An Anarchist's Zionism. Midstream 23, No. 6, Ju-Jy. pp 35-42.

MARMUR, Dov and POLISH, David. Toward a Zionist Ideology for Progressive Judaism. Ammi, Special Post-Conference Issue. No. 5, W. pp 1-5.

MARRUS, Michael R. The Idea of a Jewish State, 1896-1942. The Wiener Library Bulletin, 30, Nos. 43-44, pp 7-15.

METZER, J. The Concept of National Capital in Zionist Thought. 1918-1921. Asian and African Studies, 11, No. 3, W. pp 305-36.

MINTZ, Alan. The People's Choice? A Demurral on breira. Response, 10, No. 4, W.4p.

MONTEIL, Andre M. Notre amour d'Israël a des causes diverses mais egalement fortes. Perspectives France-Israel, 16, No. 73, N-D. pp 11-13.

Un neó-sionisme? *Les Nouveaux Cahiers*, 13, No. 50, Aut. Special *Issue.*

A symposium on Zionism in the contemporary world.

PERLMUTTER, Amos. Berl Katznelson and the Theory and Practice of Revolutionary Constructivism. *Middle Eastern Studies*, 13, No. 1, Ja. pp 71-89.

PILCH, Judah. Ahad Ha'am: His Ideology and His Legacy. *Jewish Frontier*, 44, No. 5,My. pp 15-20.

POLISH, David. Towards a Progressive Theology of Zionism. *Judaism*, 26, No. 4, Fa. pp 489-98.

-------------. Zionism is more than Pro-Israel Partisanship. *Jewish Frontier*, 44, 2F. pp 7-14.

POPPEL, Stephen M. Zionism in Germany 1897-1933: The Shaping of a Jewish Identity. Philadelphia, Jewish Publication Society of America, xviii, 234p, Ill, Ind, Bibl.

Zionist Ideology shaped Jewish identity in Germany, where the Zionism movement was originally only a philanthropic enterprise.

REITER, Alexandre. Le sionisme. Paris, Association France-Israël 20p. (Les Dossiers de France-Israël Information 2)

ROSENTHAL, David. The Proposal for a Jewish State Forty Years ago. *Jewish Frontier*, 44, No. 9, pp 8-10.

RUBENSTEIN, Amnon. To be a Free People. New York, London, Schocken,

SCHAUMANN, David. (Ed.) Pensieri e insegnamenti. Roma, Federazione Sionistica Italiana, 186p.

SCHOEPS, Julius H. Zur Geschichte des Zionismus. *Neue Politische Literatur*, 22, pp 62-70.

SELAVAN, I.C. A Pre-Herzlian Jewish State: Ralph B. Raphael's She' elat ha-Yehudim (The Jewish Question) *American Jewish Historical Quarterly*, 66, No. 3, pp 432-35.

Biography of Raphael, a Lithuanian Jew who came to the U.S.A. in 1871 and explanation of his ideas of a Jewish State.

SEMI, Emanuela Trevisan. La verità da'Eres Yisrael di 'Ahad Ha'am'. *Annali Dell'Instituto Orientale di Napoli*, 37, No. 1, Supplement No. 10, 83p.

SHAFIR, Shlomo. Taylor and McDonald: Two Diverging Views on Zionism and the Emerging Jewish State. *Jewish Social Studies*, 39, 39, No. 4, Fa. pp 323-46.

Essay on Myron C. Taylor and James G. McDonald, two American diplomats deeply involved in the problem of rescuing Jews from Nazi-occupied Europe.

SHATTAN, Joseph. Menahem Begin and the Demands of Honor. *American Zionist*, 68, No. 1, O.pp 15-18.

---------------. Why Breira? *Commentary*, 63, No. 4, Ap. pp 60-66.

SHIMONI, Gideon. Jan Christiann Smuts and Zionism. *Jewish Social Studies*, 39, No. 4, Fa. pp 269-98.

STANLEY, Maron. Reconstruction of Judaism. *Reconstructionist*, 42, No. 10, Ja. pp 12-16.

STEINHART, Milton J. Theodor Herzl the man; The Search for Identity and Zionism. Detroit, 4 parts, Reprinted from: *Bulletin, a Publication of the Sinai Hospital of Detroit*.

TSUR, Jacob. Prima Missione Par il Sionismo. *La Rassegna Mensile di Israel*, 43, Nos. 11-12, N-D., pp 638-59.

His first Zionist mission.

-----------. Zionism. The Saga of a National Liberation Movement. New Brunswick, N.J. Transaction Books, 112p. In French: Paris, Plon.

UROFSKY, Melvin I. Is Zionism Dead? Present Tense, 5, No. 1, Aut. pp 72ff.

VOGT, Ernst. Zionismus und Sozialismus - Zur Rolle der jüdischen Arbeiterbewegung bis zur Gründung des Staates Israel. Bonn., Schriften der Bundeszentrale für politische Bildung. 31p.

Study of the role of the workers' movements in the building of the Jewish State.

WILSON, N. Bernard Lazare et la sionisme de Theodore Herzl. Yod, 2, No. 2, pp 67-79.

Lazare's Zionism was more complex than a reaction to anti-semitism.

WIRNIK, Rachmiel. (Ed.) Zionism and Racism. New York, Zionist Information Service. 80p.

WISTRICH, Robert. Zionism - revolt against historic destiny. The Jewish Quarterly, 25, No. 2, Su. pp 6-12.

YE'OR, Bat. Zionism in Islamic Lands: The Case of Egypt. The Wiener Library Bulletin, 30, Nos.43-44, pp 16-29.

Zionisme, politiek en religieus zionisme, Zion: een belofte of een droom? Zionisme en de protestantse Kerken. Redactie: M. Kopuit, Nijkerk, G.F. Callenbach.

Zionism, politics and religious Zionism.

Zionismus: Befreiungsbewegung des jüdischen Volkes. Berlin, Kirche und Judentum, Kirchlichen Hochschulein, Berlin-Zehlendorf, 80p.

ANTI-ZIONISM

AGSTERIBBE, A.J. Antisemitisme, antisionisme, het huidige anti-seionisme in Nederland. Den Haag, Centrum vor Informatie en Documentatie Israel, 31p. (Publicatie 11)

Argues that anti-Zionism, at least in Holland, equals antisemitism.

AGURSKY, Mikhail. Arab Communists - Anti-Israel Extremists. Midstream, 28, No. 5, My. pp 14-18.

ALLOUCHE, Jean-Luc. Grande Bretagne: Montee de l'antisionisme dans les Universités. L'Arche, 20, No. 243, Ju. pp 29-31.

BERGER, Elmer. Genealogy of an American Tragedy. Reports, Nos. 30-31, New York, American Jewish Alternatives to Zionism. 85,99p.

Anti-Zionist essays.

BULAWKO, Henry. Du nouveau dans le debat entre la gauche et le sionisme. Regards, 12, No. 111, Ma. pp 11-14.

New facets of the debate between the Left and Zionism.

COHEN,M. Le quotidien Liberation et la guerre israëlo-arabe de 1973. Yod, 2, No. 2, pp 109-24.

The extreme left-wing paper launched into an anti-imperialistic, anti-Zionist campaign at the time of the Yom Kippur war and was accused of anti-semitism.

DARRAJ, F. Albert Memmi: Historical Objectivity and the Zionist Illusion. Shu'un Filastiniya, No. 65, pp 72-88. (In Arabic)

DAVIS, Uri. Israel: Utopia Incorporated. A Study of Class State and Corporate Kin Control. London, Zed, 182p, Ind. Bibl.

The author attacks Zionist ideology and the State of Israel.

DINER, Dani. Marché mondial, sionisme et violence: Thèses sur l' intégration capitaliste du Mashrek et ses conséquences politiques. Khamsin, No. 4, pp 66-87.
Contends that Zionism and capitalist influence in the Mashrek has engendered violence.
GARAUDY, Roger. Religious and historical pretexts of Zionism. Journal of Palestine Studies, 4, No. 2, W. pp 41-52.
GLUBB, F. Jewish Opponents of Zionism. Palestine, 3, No. 1, Ja. pp 68-73.
--------. Zionism and the Oriental Jews. Palestine, 3, No. 1, Ja. pp 74-77.
--------. The Zionist Race Concept. Palestine, 3, No. 15, Jy. pp 21-25.
The Holocaust Victims Accuse. Brooklyn, New York, Naturei Karta of U.S.A.
Anti-Zionist pamphlet.
KAYYALI, Abdul-Wahab. Zionism and Imperialism: The Historical Origins. Journal of Palestine Studies, 6, No. 3, Sp. pp 98-112.
KNEE, Stuart E. The King-Crane Commission of 1919: The Articulation of Political Anti-Zionism. American-Jewish Archives, 29, No. 1,
KRIEGEL, Annie. La Solitude de Kippour. L'Arche, 12, Nos. 246-47. S-O., pp 20-23.
UNESCO's anti-Israel policy.
LAMM, Bob. The Left Question and the Jews. Jewish Currents, 31, No. 1, Ja. pp 4-7.
Examines how far the anti-Zionism of the Left is antisemitism.
LOPEZ, G. Mexico and Zionism and Imperialism. Majallat Markaz al-Dirasat al-Filastiniya, No. 25, N-D., pp 22-43. (In Arabic)
MAKAI, György. Fajelmelet - fajuldozes. Budapest, Kozmosz Könyvek, 340p, Ill. (Racialism - racial discrimination)
In discussing racialism and racial persecution, the author also discusses Zionism which he equates with racism.
MEGGED, Aharon. A Word to the New Left - A Citizen's Diary. Midstream, 23, No. 4, Ap. pp 71-73.
Response to the anti-Zionism of the New Left.
NEUBERGER, B. Debatten om Israel. København, SDI, 40p. (In Danish)
Response to anti-Israel attitudes.
ORBACH, William. To Keep the Peace: The United Nations Condemnatory Resolution. Lexington, U.P. of Kentucky, 155p, Ind.
Discusses the effectiveness of UN resolutions and contends that UN standards are a mixture of the political situation and the moral standards operative in the international arena. Among the cases quoted are several resolutions condemning Israel.
PITTMAN, J. and KARKABI, Z. The True Face of Zionism. World Marxist Review, 20, No. 3, Ma. pp 119-29; Jewish Affairs, 7, No. 5, S-O., pp 9-12 and No. 6, N-D. pp 9-12.
Anti-Zionist view.
SCHNALL, David J. Native Anti-Zionism: Ideologies of Radical Dissent in Israel. Middle East Journal, 31, No. 2, Sp. pp 157-74.
SCHONFELD, Moshe. The Holocaust. The Victims Accuse. New York, Bnei Yeshivos, 128p.
Anti-Zionist trace accusing Zionists of collaboration with the Nazis.

SERFATY, Abraham. Lutte antisioniste et révolution Arabe. Préface Hani el-Hassan, Guervill, F. Della Suda, Quatre Vents, 84p.
Left-wing Moroccan, on the Arab anti-Zionist movement.
SHEHAB, Mounfid, YASSIN, El Sayed and RISK, Younan. Zionism and Racism: (Zionism as a form of Racial Discrimination) Cairo, the League of Arab States, Arab Educational, Cultural and Scientific Organisation, Institute of Arab Research and Studies, 111p.
SPATZ, Erwin. Romain Rolland contre la declaration Balfour. Yod, 2, No. 2, pp 103-7.
VARON, Benno Weiser. Nightmare in Black and White. Midstream, 23, No. 7, Au-S. pp 50-56.
The equation of Zionism with Apartheid at the UN.

ISRAEL

ALLON, Yigal. Israël: la lutte pour l'espoir. Paris, Stock, 299p.
Israel 1977-5737: Berichtsband über die Arbeits - und Studienfahrt der evangelischen Jugend Duisberg-Süd nach Israel (und in einige besetzte Gebeite Jordaniens und Syriens) vom 7, Juli bis 30 Juli (Jugendreferat des Kirchenkreises Duisburg-Süd, 55p, M.
A group of Protestant youth from Germany report on their visit to Israel.
Israël - Ombres et Lumières. Collection dirigée par Joseph Kessel. Paris, YCPA, Ed. Ramsey. 3 vols. 1108p, Ill.
Israkit. Israel Fact Sheets. London, Britain, Israel Public Affairs Committee (BIPAC) jointly with the Zionist Federation and the Board of Deputies, Unnumbered loose-leaf pages.
The subjects dealt with are:1 History of Zionism and Israel, Contemporary Israel, Arab Boycott of Israel, Arab Terrorism, Britain and the Middle East, the USSR and the Middle East, the Oil Weapon, the Arab World.
KAMEN, Charles S. Affirmation or Enjoyment? The Comemmoration of Independence in Israel. Jewish Journal of Sociology, 19, No. 1,Ju. pp 5-20.
NEUSNER, Jacob. Who is Israel? National Review, 29, 24 Ju. pp 714-16.
The State of Israel offers some challenges to American notions of the proper relation between politics and religion. That is because Americans tend to assume that all religions must be domesticated, denominational variants of a single model. But it is a model that Judaism doesn't fit.
The New Face of Israel. The New York Times Magazine, 17 Ju. pp 9-11; 49ff; 12-13; 33ff.
Two articles: Hawk on a Mission of Peace by William E. Farrell. A Journey Through a Land of Doubts by Marvin Kalb. A discussion of Menahem Begin, the new Prime Minister of Israel and how he and the Israeli people will react to the pressures coming from Washington regarding a Middle East Settlement.
RIQUET, Michel. L'existence d'Israël. Connaissance D'Israel. 1, No. 1, Ja-Ju. pp 5-22.
SALZ, Robert. The Evolution of the Partition Principle - Can It Work in 1977? Jewish Frontier, 44, No. 9, N. pp 11-15.
SAMUELSON, Arthur. Israel after Sadat: The End of the Beginning. Christianity and Crisis, 37, 26 D. pp 308-10.

SMITH, Terence. Reflections on a Troubled People - Israel Journal: 1972-76. Saturday Review, 5F, pp 8-20.

By the former New York Times Jerusalem correspondent.

Sovereignty, Ownership and 'Presence' in the Jewish-Arab Territorial Conflict: The Case of Bir'im and Ikrit. Comparative Political Studies, 10, No. 2, Jy. pp 155-76.

A Survey of Israeli Settlements. MERIP Reports, No. 60, S. pp 13-20.

TEEFFELEN, Toine van. Anthropologists on Israel: A case study in the sociology of knowledge. Amsterdam: U. of Amsterdam, Anthropologisch-Sociologisch Centrum, 79p. (Papers on European and Mediterranean Societies, 9)

ZOGBY, James. (Ed.) Perspectives on Palestinian Arabs and Israeli Jews. Wilmette, Ill., Medina P., 92p.

GENERAL DESCRIPTION

BREYDENBACH, Bernhard, von. Die Reise ins heilige Land. Ein Reisebericht aus dem Jahre 1483. Wiesbaden, Guido Pressler, 56p. Ill. M.

A journey to the Holy Land in the late 15th century.

COQUET, Evelyne. Wir ritten nach Jerusalem. Bergisch Gladbach, Lübbe, 350p, M. Ill.

ELLUL, J. Impressions d'Israël. Foi et Vie,76, No. 4, pp 1-72.

Accuses the Western press of ignorance of the Israeli reality. Holds that anti-Zionism is just a cover for antisemitism.

FODOR, Eugene. Israel. London, Hodder, 375p, Ill., Ind.

Guidebook.

GOLD, Herbert. Les Sables du désert. L'Arche, 20, No. 242, My. pp 51-59.

Travels in the Negev and Sinai.

LOUVISH, Misha. Israel. American Jewish Yearbook, 77, pp 481-502.

Diplomacy, politics, economics, demography, personalities.

MALKA, Victor. En Israël. Paris, Hachette, 166p, Ill, M.

MIKES, George. Grüsse aus Jerusalem. München, Drömer, Knaur, 192p.

German ed. of author's humorous travel book: 'Milk and Honey.

OWEN, Frederick. The Holy Land. New York, Baker, 327p.

RABINOWITZ, Louis I. Torah and Flora. New York, Hebrew Publ. Co. 208p.

Biblical flora in Israel.

SHINAR, Mordejái. Acco. Antiquísima Fortaleza Marítima de Israel. Condensed by Isidoro Niborski. Buenos Aires, Congreso Judío Latinoamericano, 40p, Ill. (Hechos de la Historia Judiá, 94)

HISTORY

ANGST, Doris. Nichtzionisten in Palestina: Die Rolle der Jewish Colonization Association, 1900-1924. Zurich, Universitat Zurich, Philosophische Fakultät 1., 156p, M.

BOWYER BELL, J. Terror Out of Zion. Irgun Zvai Leumi. LEHI and the Palestine Underground, 1929-1949. New York, St. Martin's P., 374p, Ill.

CAMERON, James. The Making of Israel. New York, Taplinger, 107p, Ill. M.

American edition of book published in England, 1976.

CLIFFORD, Clark. Reoognizing Israel: The 1948 Story. American Heritage, 28, No. 3, Ap. pp 4-11.

---------------. When Truman fought the State Department. Jewish Digest, 22, No. 8, Ap. pp 29-32.
From speech to meeting of American Jewish Historical Society and American Historical Association, Dec., 1976.

COHEN, Michael J. American Influence on British Policy in the Middle East during World War II: First Attempts at Coordinating Allied Policy on Palestine. American Jewish Historical Quarterly, 67, No. 1, S. pp 50-70.

----------------. Secret diplomacy and rebellion in Palestine, 1936-1939. International Journal of Middle East Studies, 8, No. 3, Jy. pp 379-404.

DONOVAN, Robert J. Conflict and Crisis. The Presidency of Harry Truman. 1945-1948. New York, W.W. Norton, xvii, 473p, Ind, Ill.
Includes Truman's role in the establishment of the State of Israel.

EBAN, Abba. Mein Land. Das Moderne Israel. München, Drömer Knaur, 446p, Ill.

----------. Present at the birth. Moment, 13, No. 1, N. pp 25-40.
On the circumstances of the establishment of the State of Israel.

GANIN, Zvi. The Limits of American Jewish Political Power: America's retreat from partition, November 1947-March 1949. Jewish Social Studies, 39, Nos. 1-2, W-Sp. pp 1-36.

GILBERT, Martin. Britain, Palestine and the Jews: Evolution of the 1939 White Paper. 1891-1939. Oxford, Oxford Centre for Post-graduate Hebrew Studies, 20p. (The Third Sacks Lecture)

---------------. The Jewish National Home: Whose Home? An historical enquiry. AJA Review, 19, No. 2, Aut. pp 8-10.

HATTIS, Susan Lee. Jabotinsky's Parity Plan for Palestine. Middle Eastern Studies, 13, No. 1, Ja. pp 90-96.

HAUGAN, Arne. Israels vej mod ar 2000. Israels historie og de aktuelle problemer i Mellemøsten. Haugan, som er norsk general-major, skriver et udførligt afsnit om de fire israelsk-arabiske krige. Copenhagen, Samleren, 160p. (In Danish)
Israel's history and present-day problems.

ILAN, Amitzur. Messianism and Diplomacy 1945-1948. The struggle for a Jewish State. The Wiener Library Bulletin, 30, Nos. 41-42. pp 36-46.
Partly based on material in the Central Zionist Archives.

Irgun Zvai Leumi: the story of a terrorist movement. Palestine, 3, No. 9, 30 Ju. pp 19-24.

JIRYIS, S. From the Balfour Declaration to the Partition of Palestine to Sadat's Visit. Shu'un Filastiniya, No. 73 D. pp 11-21. (In Arabic)

KARDOS, G. György. A Történet vége. (The End of the Story) Budapest, Magveto, 387p.
Third and final volume of the author's trilogy on Palestine, the first two treated the last months of the Mandate, this work is an autobiographical description of the period a year after the War of Independence.

LITVINOFF, Barnett. The Balfour Declaration: an accident of history. Jewish Quarterly, 25, No. 3, Aut. pp 12-14; 52.

MOSKOVITS, Shlomo. The United States recognition of Israel in the Context of the Cold War, 1945-1948. Ann Arbor, Mich., U. Microfilms, 294p. Bibl.
Ph.D. Dissertation, Kent State University.

NASHIF, Taysir. The Bases of Arab and Jewish Leadership During the Mandate Period. Journal of Palestine Studies, 6, No. 4, Su. pp 113-21.

NEUBERT, Friedrich Paul Harald. Die deutsche Politik im Palestina-Konflikt 1937-38. Bonn, 25p.
Ph.D. Dissertation, Rheinische Friedrich-Wilhelm University.

PODET, Alan H. The Unwilling Midwife - Ernest Bevin and the Birth of Israel. European Judaism, 11, No. 2, Su. pp 35-42.

POSTAL, Bernard. The Shaping of the UN Partition Plan. Congress Monthly, 44, No. 8, N. pp 9-12.

---------------. The Story of the Balfour Declaration. Congress Monthly, 44, No. 7, O. pp 12-14.

TIBAWI, Abdul Latif. Anglo-Arab Relations and the Question of Palestine 1914-1921. London, Luzac, xxvii, 523p, Ind,Bibl.

VARON, Benno Weiser. The History of One Yes. Midstream, 23, No. 9, N. pp 62-69.
The vote of Ecuador in the UN on 29th November 1947.

WASSERSTEIN, Bernard. 'Clipping the Claws of the Colonisers': Arab Officials in the Government of Palestine, 1917-48. Middle Eastern Studies, 13, No. 2, My. pp 171-94.

CULTURE/RELIGION

Interfaith in Israel: Special Issue. Face to Face, 2, W-Sp., pp 1-24.
Includes: Interfaith Dialogue in Israel by Shemaryahu Talmon. An Arab Christian Speaks Out by Elias Chacour. Jews and Christians in Israel by J. Coos Schoneveld. An Orthodox Jewish Israeli Views Interfaith by Zvi Yaron. The Problems of an Islam-Jewish Dialogue in Israel by Yaakov Yehoshua.

JAKOBOVITS, Immanuel. The National Idea - Differing Religious Attitudes. L'Eylah, 1, No. 3, Sp. pp 5-11.
A lecture by the Chief Rabbi to the Institute of Jewish Affairs, London.

LIEBMAN, Charles. The Rise of Militancy Among Religious Zionists. Hadassah Magazine, 59, No. 1, Ja. pp 14-15.
A major source of strength for Gush Emunim has been the fact that the Government has been so weak and divided that it has been unable to adopt any concerted policy with respect to them.

NOZICK, Robert. Orthodox Coercion in Israel. Moment, 2, No. 10, O. pp 60-64.

POLL, S. La religion en Israël. Connaissance d'Israel, 1, No. 1, Ja-Ju. pp 23-32.

RABINOWICZ, Harry. Hasidism and the State of Israel. London, Routledge & Kegal Paul, 250p. Ill. (Littman Library of Jewish Civilization)

RABINOVITCH, Nahum. The Religious Significance of Israel. L'Eylah, 1 No. 4, Aut. pp 14-17.

SCHIFF, Gary S. Tradition and Politics. The Religious Parties in Israel. Detroit, Mich., Wayne State U.P., 267p, Ind, Bibl.

SCHWARZFUCHS, Simon. Les heures supplémentaires. L'Arche, 20, No. 245, Au. pp 21-23.
Problems of religion in Israel.

TAL, Uriel. Signification de la Torah aujourd'hui: la Terre et l' Etat d'Israël dans la vie religieuse israelienne. Sidic, 10, No. 3, pp 4-16.
In the wake of the Yom Kippur War many young Israelis turned to religion as their Zionist expression.

YA'ARI, Meir. We Will Not Accept a Clerical Israel. Israel Horizons, 25, No. 8, pp 9-11.

INTERNAL POLITICS

ARONOFF, Myron J. Power and Ritual in the Israel Labour Party. Assen, Amsterdam, Van Gorcum, xiv, 184p, Bibl.
Analyses the history, inner structure and influence of the Israeli Labour Party.

AVISHAI, Bernard. The New Israel. The New York Review of Books, 23 Ju. pp 16-22.
A report from Israel in the light of Likud's victory in the election.

BEN, Philippe. L'opinion américaine face au 'Watergate' israélien. L'Arche, No. 242, My. pp 23-25.

BENAZON, Michael. Second Thoughts: Israel in 1977. The Canadian Forum, 62, No. 671, My. pp 9-15.

BENJAMIN, Gerald. Israel: too much democracy. Midstream, 28, No. 5, My. pp 3-13.

BRECHER, Michael and RAZ, M. Images and behaviour: Israel's Yom Kippur crisis 1973. International Journal, 32, No. 3, pp 429-51; 475-500.

BREWSTER, Charles E. Israel and its 'Bloc of Faithful' The Christian Century, 94, 23 F. pp 174-76.
A report on the rightist, religious-nationalist movement (Gush Emunim) which believes that Israel should keep all of the Arab land it occupied after the Six-Day War.

BRINKER, Menahem. A battle of interpretation: The last campaign in the Israeli elections. Dissent, 24, No. 4, Fa. pp 356-58.
"Elections in a representative democracy, in which each party has more than one position on a crucial issue, always leave room for varied interpretations. The struggle between these diverse positions and interpretations is very often the last battle in an election campaign." Followed by a supplementary report, "Israel: A Visitor's Notes", by Irving Howe.

CHANDLER, Harriette L. The Israeli Election and the Begin Victory. The Christian Century, 94, 20-27 Jy. pp 650-54.
"Israelis seem agreed that it is the duty of whoever leads their government to give away as little territory as possible for as much peace as possible."

COUBARD, J. Israël, L'échec d'une politique. Cahiers du Communisme, No. 9, pp 102-12.
Comments on the outcome of the Israeli election of May 1977.

DROR, Yehezkel. Are the Israel Labor Party and the Alignment Still Viable? Middle East Review, 10, No. 1, Fa. pp 49-53.
Answers in the affirmative, despite their election failure.

EBAN, Abba. Moment Interview: Moment, 3, No. 2, D. pp 15-18.
On the political situation in Israel.

EL-ASMAR, F. and KATZ, N. Israeli Elections. MERIP Reports, No. 58 Ju. pp 8-13.

ELMALEH, Elie. "Le second Israël": la victoire des paradoxes. Les Nouveaux Cahiers, 12, No. 50, Aut. pp 38-42.
Internal politics.

ETZIONI-HALEVY, Eva and LIVNE, Moshe. The response of the Israeli Establishment to the Yom Kippur War Protest. Middle East Journal, 31, No. 3, Su. pp 281-98.

EYAL, Eli. The Democratic Movement for Change: Origins and Perspectives. Middle East Review, 10, No. 1, Fa. pp 54-59.

FRIEDMAN, Theodore. Letter from Jerusalem: Israel's National Elections. Conservative Judaism, 31, No. 2, W. pp 75-79.

GAVRON, Daniel. Israel's mavericks. The Labor-Zionist who fell from grace. The National Jewish Monthly, 91, No. 11, Jy-Au. pp 13-20.

--------------. Israel's mavericks. Rabbi on the barricades. The National Jewish Monthly, 91, No. 11, Jy-Au. pp 12;21-26.

GILLON, Dan. Perilous Triumph for Begin. Middle East International, No. 75, S. pp 6-7.

GINZBURG, Eli. Israel: A look ahead to the 1980's. New York, Author,16p.

GORDON, Murray. Israel's government crisis. Midstream, 23, No. 3, Ma. pp 51-55.

HAREVEN, Shulamit. Opportunities for the Left. Israel Horizons, 25, No. 6, Ju. pp 14-17.
On the Israeli elections.

HARKAVI, Bernard. The Tasks Ahead for Americans. Israel Horizons, 25, No. 6. Ju. pp 7-8.
On the Israeli elections.

HOLLEY, C. Israel after Agranat. Journal of the Middle East, No.35, S. pp 25-33.
The after-effects of the Yom Kippur War in the light of the Agranat Commission report.

HOWE, Irving. Israel: A Visitor's Notebook. Dissent, 24, No. 4, pp 359-63.

HURWITZ, Ya'acov. Social Democracy Fails to Halt the Zionist Counter-Revolution. Israel Horizons, 25, No. 9, S. pp 7-11.
On the consequences of the Israeli elections.

ISAAC, Erich and Rael Jean. The "Earthquake" Israeli Elections, 1977. Midstream, 23, No. 7, Au-S. pp 3-10.

-------------------------. The Impact of Jabotinsky on Likud's policies. Middle East Review, 10, No. 1, Fa. pp 31-48.

Israel's Knesset. Koebenhavn, Sider,

Izrael Kommunista Pártjanak XVIII, Kongresszusa. (Részletek a központi bizottság beszámolojából) Az arab országok kommunista és munkaspartjainak közleménye. Nemzetkozi Zzemle, 21. No. 3, pp 13-20; 37-42.
The 28th Congress of the Israeli Communist Party. Extracts from the Central Committee's report.

JIRYIS, Sabri. The Israeli Elections; Dilemma and Challenge. Shu'un Filastiniya, No. 67, pp 7-19. (In Arabic)

KLUG, Tony. Israel - "end of an era" The Jewish Quarterly, 25, No. 2, Su. pp 13ff.
LEVINE, D. Les dernières élections israeliénnes. L'Afrique et L'Asie Modernes, No. 114, pp 42-52.
LOUVISH, Misha. The Consequences of Begin (Letter from Israel) Jewish Frontier, 44, No. 5, Ju-Jy. pp 3-5.
--------------. Last Lap in the Israeli Elections - and after (Letter from Israel) Jewish Frontier, 44, No. 5, My. pp 5-6.
MARSDEN, Eric. If Not Rabin, Who? Middle East International, No. 67 F. pp 6-7.
NACHMIAS, D. A Temporal Sequence of Adolescent Political Participation: Some Israeli Data. British Journal of Political Science. 7, No. 1, Ja. pp 71-83.
OZ, Amos. What Shall We Be? The Kibbutz Movement in Opposition. Jewish Frontier, 44, No. 10, D. pp 13-16.
PERETZ, Don. The Earthquake - Israel's Ninth Knesset Elections. The Middle East Journal, 31, No. 3, Su. pp 251-66.
PERLMUTTER, Amos. Cleavage in Israel. Foreign Policy, 27, Su. pp 136-57.

"Although the process of demobilization, the decline of central authority and the institutional decay of blocs, parties and groups have not left a political vacuum, uncertainty marks Israeli politics."

ROSENTHAL, David. The Historical Record of the Winners and the Losers: On the Results of the Recent Knesset Elections. Jewish Frontier, 44, No. 5, Ju-Jy. pp 6-8.
ROSSINI, F. and ROSENBLOOM, D. Antecedents of Public Bureaucracy: The Case of Israel. Administration and Society, 9, No. 1, My. pp 45-80.
SAMUELSON, Maurice. Likud Victory Clears the Air. Middle East International, No. 73, Jy. pp 12-14.
SCEMAMA, Andre. Israël: le "seisme" electoral. L'Arche, 20, No. 243, Ju. pp 17-19.
SHEPHERD, Naomi. Yadin's DMC - A New Force. Israeli Politics May Never Be the Same Again. Present Tense, 5, No. 1, Aut. pp 31-37.
SHLAIM, Avi. The Lavon Affair. Middle East International, No. 76, O. pp 12-14.
-----------. How Different is Begin? Middle East International, No. 75, S. pp 15-17.
-----------. Israel under Rabin: Three Lost Years. Middle East International, No. 73, Ju. pp 14-16.
SHOOR, Nahum. The Lessons and Challenges of the Elections in Israel. Israel Horizons, 25, No. 6, Ju. pp 4-6.
SIMON, Rita and WEST, J. Public Support for civil liberties in Israel. Social Science Quarterly, 58, No. 2, S. pp 283-92.
SMITH, Hanoch. Israel's Knesset elections: an analysis of the upset. New York, American Jewish Committee, 10p.
-------------. Israel's Knesset elections: popular attitudes and prognosis. New York, American Jewish Committee, 13p.
SOBOL, Yehoshua. To Break the Unholy Consensus on Borders. Elections in Israel. Israel Horizons, 25, No. 6, Ju. pp 11-13.
SZULC, Tad. How Carter Fouled the Israeli Elections. New York, 8 Ju pp 36-39.

VARON, Benno Weiser. As Begin Begins. American Zionist, 67, No. 8, Jy. pp 15-17.

VIORST, Milton. The Israelis Watch Begin: The Nation, 216, 24 D. pp 686-90.

"Israeli doves are gradually gaining the upper hand in Israel, though one does not know how much influence they can have within the framework of the Begin leadership."

WEISS-ROSMARIN, Trude. Ten Years After the Six-Day War. Jewish Spectator, 42, No. 2, Su. pp 3-10.

YAFFE, Richard. A Rallying Point Against Likud. Elections in Israel Israel Horizons, 25, No. 6, Ju. pp 9-11.

LEGAL SYSTEM

Judios y no judios ante la ley Israeli. Beunos Aires, Plus Ultra, 80p

Jews and non-Jews in Israeli law.

KLEIN, Claude. Le caractère juif de l'état d'Israël. Etude d'Israël Paris, Cujas, 183p, Bibl.

Juridical study on Israeli legislation designed to preserve the Jewish character of the State.

The Law of Return - Undermining Jewish Unity. Reconstructionist, 43, No. 6, S. pp 4-6.

On the question of "who is a Jew?"

LORCH, Natanael. and SAGER, S. Israel Parliament. - The Knesset. Parliamentarian, 58, No. 3, Jy. pp 172-76.

RICHTER-FRIED, Susanna. Das Notariat in Israel: Abriss seiner geschichtlichen Entwicklung bis zum Notargesetz von 1976. Zürich, Juris Druck. xiii, 145p, Bibl.

Ph.D. Dissertation, Zürich University.

RUBENSTEIN, A. Observations sur le droit israelien. Connaissance d'Israël, No. 1. Ja-Ju. pp 77-88.

SCHROETER, Leonard. Israel and Torture. Moment, 3, No. 1, N. pp 61-2

Answers some accusations.

MINORITIES

HALPERN, Ben. The Arabs of Israel: A Test of Jewishness. Judaism, 26, No. 4, Fa. pp 413-17.

KAHANE, Meir. The Arab Problem in Israel: Emigration is the Only Solution. Judaism, 26, No. 4, Fa. pp 393-404.

LENSKI, Robert G. An Israeli Dilemma. Mankind Quarterly, 17, No. 4, O-D. pp 97-118.

Expresses the racialist view that because of rising non-Jewish elements of the population, it will become a necessary innovation for Israeli governmental legislation to adopt birth control policies aimed at preserving the demographic power base.

MAYER, Egon. The Druze of Bet Ja'an. Modernization and the Activation of Minorities in Israel. Middle East Review, 9, No. 2, W. pp 16-29.

NAKLEH, Khalil. Anthropological and Sociological Studies of the Arabs in Israel: A Critique. Journal of Palestine Studies, 6, No. 4, Su. pp 41-70.

PRITTIE, Terence. Israel's Arab Minority. 1-2, Britain and Israel, No. 70, Jy. pp 1-4, No. 71, Jy. pp 1-4,

RYAN, Joseph. The Other Israelis. Commonweal,101, 7 Ja. pp 13-15.
"Arabs in Israel are becoming more numerous and more Palestinian."

SAMUELSON, Arthur H. There is Another Way - The Arab Problem in Israel. Judaism, 26, No. 4, Fa. pp 405-12.

SHAMEKH, A. Bedouin Settlements. Ekistics, 43, No. 258, My. pp 249-59.

SHMUELI, Avshalom. The Process of Nomadic Sedentarization in the Desert Frontier of the Jerusalem Vicinity. Plural Societies, 8, Nos. 3-4, Aut/W. pp 43-52.

SMOOHA, Sammy and HOFMAN, John E. Some Problems of Arab-Jewish Coexistence in Israel. Middle East Review, 9, No. 2, W. pp 5-16.

VARON, Benno Weiser. Israel's Reluctant Compatriots. American Zionist, 68, No. 2, N. pp 17-19.
The Jew knows that the Arab is his reluctant compatriot.

ZENNER, Walter and KASDAN, Leonard. The Israeli Druzes. Midstream, 28, No. 5, My. pp 34-47.

JERUSALEM/ HOLY PLACES

BAUMGARTEN, Sheila. 'Progress' threatens Jerusalem. Jewish Currents 22, No. 10, Ju. pp 61-64. Condensed from The Jewish Student Press Service.

BENVENISTI, Meron. Jerusalem: The Torn City. Minneapolis, U.of Minnesota P., 407p.

COHEN, Saul B. Jerusalem. Bridging the Four Walls. A Geopolitical Perspective. New York, Herzl P., 218p. Ind, Ill. Bibl.
Professor Cohen contends that, because of its unique geopolitical situation, Jerusalem can be a bridge between Jews and Arabs

-------------. Geopolitical bases for the integration of Jerusalem. Orbis, 20, No. 2, Su. pp 287-313.

COMAY, Joan. Jerusalem. Paris, Ed. Arthaud. 158p, Ill.

CRAMER, Francis. Lasst Friede sein! Zürich, Orell Füssli, xx, 144p. Ill.
A Swiss photographer's work on Jerusalem showing the harmony in which Jews, Moslems and Christians live together.

GILBERT, Martin. Jerusalem. Illustrated History Atlas. London, Martin Gilbert and the Board of Deputies of British Jews; New York, Macmillan, 128p, Ill, M.

Jerusalem, und seine grosse Zeit. Würzburg, Georg Popp, 288p, Ill.

KESSEL, Yoram. Past Glories Come to Life. Report on the Jerusalem Excavations. Jewish Chronicle Colour Magazine, S. pp 34-40.

KLIJN, A.F.J. Een Joodse Klacht over de Verwoesting van Jerusalem in het Jaar 70. Kampen, J. H. Kok, 31p.
Discusses the traditional literature bewaiting the destruction of Jerusalem in 70 C.E.

MOSKIN, Robert J. Report from Jerusalem. City at the Crossroads. New York, Institute of Human Relations P., A.J.C., 64p.

NANTET, Jacques. Mille et une Jerusalem. Essai, Paris, J.E. Lattes. 196p.
Objective essays on Jerusalem, holy city of three faiths, capital of a permanently endangered State.

RICHMOND, Diana and John. Jerusalem: Open City? Middle East International, No. 72, Ju. pp 21-23.
Maintains that Jerusalem is Arab.

SCEMAMA, André. Jerusalem devant l'Offensive de Paix Arabe. L'Arche, 20, No. 238, Ja. pp 23-25.

FOREIGN AFFAIRS

BROWNSTEIN, Lewis. Decision Making In Israeli Foreign Policy: An Unplanned Process. Political Science Quarterly, 92, No. 2, pp 259-79.
Contends that "foreign policy decision making in Israel has been characterized by a lack of planning and systematic process, that it has been dominated by a small elite, that its foreign policy institutions lack the capacity to implement a more systematic approach and that the government tends to resist input from those, particularly in academic institutions, who might be able to provide a somewhat different perspective on foreign policy issues."

DECTER, Moshe. The Arms Traffic with South Africa. Midstream, 23, No. 2, F. pp 14-25.

-------------. "To Serve, To Teach, to Leave." The Story of Israel's Development Assistance Program in Black Africa. New York, American Jewish Congress, 126p, M.
History and extent of Israel's assistance programme to Africa since its inception in 1957.

HERZOG, Chaim. Israel and South Africa: The UN's Hypocritical Report. Congress Monthly, 44, No. 9, D. pp 5-9.

HICKS, B. South Africa and Israel: An Historical and Continuing Alliance. Part 2, Middle East Perspective, 10, No.3, Ju-Jy. pp 5-6; 8.

Israel and the Third World: The Role of Oil and Mideast Politics. Analysis, Ja-F. pp 1-8.
The radical reversal of Israel-Third World relations and policies that might help restore a more balanced approach on the part of these nations to the Arab-Israeli conflict.

Israelske Studenerorganisationer i U.S.A. and Canada. Aspekter af Israels undenrigspolitik. København, SDI, orientering, 44p.
Aspects of Israeli foreign policy.

KATZ, Shmuel. The Basis of Israeli Policy. Appme Bulletin, 11, No. 4, Su. pp 2-4.

LUZZATTO, Guido L. Israele e il Mondo verso l'ultimo Quarto del Secolo. La Rassegna Mensile di Israel, 43, Nos. 1-2, Ma-Ap. pp 111-20.

SIMON, Merrill. Israel and Western Europe - a New Era, New Expectations. Jewish Frontier, 44, No. 3, Ma. pp 9-12.

NEUBERGER, Benjamin. Aspekter af Israels undenrigspolitik. København SDI, 12p (In Danish)
Israel's foreign policy.

RANZ, Sheldon. Skeleton in the Closet. Israel and South Africa. Jewish Currents, 31, No. 1, Ja. pp 8-10.

SLONIM, Shlomo. Israel and the New Scramble for Africa. Midstream, 23, No. 9, N. pp 30-35.
The bizarre great-power configuration has implications for America's global stance, and for its relations with the

principals in the Arab-Israeli dispute, in particular.

STEVENS, Richard P. Israel and South Africa. Middle East International, No. 69, Ma. pp 16-18.

-----------------. and ELMESSIRI, Abdelwahab M. (Eds.) Israel and South Africa: The Progression of a relationship. New York, New World P. 36p.

VARADI, M. Israele: bene o gravame per il mondo occidentale? Rivista di Studi Politici Internazionale. 44, No. 2, Ap-Jy. pp 263-72.

Israel and the Western World.

VERSCHOOR, J. Israel en de staten in Zwart Afrika: de ontwikkeling van een verhouding van circa 1960 tot 1976. Den Haag, Centrum voor Informatie en Documentatie Israel, 51p.

Israel and the Black African States 1960-76.

VOGEL, Rolf. 25 Jahre deutsch-israelischer Beziehungen. Bonn, Deutschland Berichte. 64p.

ZVINOVEMBER, Harvey. Israel and the Third World. Jewish Spectator, 42, No. 2, Su. pp 16-18.

ISRAEL-DIASPORA RELATIONS

ALTER, Robert. New York and/or Jerusalem. Commentary, 64, No. 2, Au pp 50-56.

Discussion of book by Hillel Halkin, Letters to an American Jewish Friend: A Zionist's Polemic. in which he makes his case for Zionism in six long letters to a hypothetical friend in New York, a younger contemporary who is an untypical American Jew in having a knowledge of Hebrew, a familiarity with Jewish culture and a strong commitment to Jewish life but who is typical in having chosen to relate to Israel personally as a tourist and nothing more.

BREIRA. Proceedings of Breira's First Annual Membership Conference. 20-22 F. 1977. New York, 27p.

A new group of committed Jews who maintain the right of diaspora Jewry to criticize Israeli policies.

COHEN, Jack J. The two-way stream: Israel and Diaspora. Reconstructionist, 43, No. 1, F. pp 17-21.

COOPER, Elias. The Jews and the Land of Israel. American Zionist, 68, No. 2, N. pp 8-16.

DAVIS, Moshe. (Ed.) World Jewry and the State of Israel. with foreword by Professor Ephraim Katzir. New York, Arno P., xix,372p. (Publications of a Continuing Seminar on World Jewry, vol. 2)

Scholars discuss Israel-Diaspora relations.

Dissent and the State of Israel: Special Section. Conservative Judaism. 31, No. 2, W. pp 15-44.

American Jewry and Israel: The Limits of Dissent by Mordecai Waxman. American Jewry and Israel: The need for Dissent by Arnold Jacob Wolf. Discussion on Dissent by Rabbi Judah Nadich and others.

EBAN, Abba. The Changing Moods of Zionism. The 12th American-Israeli Dialogue. Opening Session. Congress Monthly, 44, No. 3, Ma.-Ap. pp 7-9.

GILLON, Dan. Growing Concern Among American Jews. Middle East International, No. 67, Ja. pp 6-8.

Detects a sense of frustration, leading to dissent with Israeli policies.

-----------. U.S. Jews split on Begin. Middle East International, No. 73, Jy. pp 4-6.

GILLON, Philip. The image of the Jew in films. AMMI, No. 6, Ju. pp 5-7.

GLAZER, Nathan. American Jews and Israel: The Last Support. Jewish Digest, 22, No. 5, Ja. pp 68-73. Condensed from Interchange, 2, No. 3.

HOROWITZ, Irving Louis. Israeli-Diaspora Relations as a Problem in Center-Periphery Linkages. Contemporary Jewry, No. 1, Sp/Su. pp 28-38.

The arguments which have raged concerning divided loyalties of American Jews is largely chimerical if not entirely fictitious.

ISAAC, Rael Jean. Brêira: Counsel for Judaism. New York, Americans for a Safe Israel. 30p.

Explains the position of Breira, the organisation created in the aftermath of the Yom Kippur war, which seeks a peaceful solution to the Arab-Israel conflict.

----------------. and Erich. The Rabbis of Breira. Midstream, 23, No. 4, Ap. pp 3-17.

LIEBMAN, Charles S. Pressure without sanctions. The Influence of World Jewry on Israeli Policy. Rutherford, New Jersey. Farleigh Dickinson U.P., 304p, Ind, Bibl.

Deals with the policital aspects of Israel-Diaspora relations. with particular reference to American Jewry.

Le livre de la fidelite, 1977. Paris, Association France-Israel. 279p, Ill. France-Israël Information, Numero Special, Supplement au. No. 34, de Mai 1977.

Special issue of the journal dedicated to French support for Israel.

RABINOWITZ, Malka. Dropouts: Israel Versus Diaspora. News, Views, Reviews, 91, No. 5, Ja. pp 26-30.

SACHER, Howard. The Diaspora and Israel: A New Dimension of Support. Jewish Education, 47, No. 1, W. pp 32-38.

Calls for American Jewish restraint in criticism of the Israeli government and "restraint and discrimination in the techniques by which we express our support for Israel."

SAFRAI, Shmuel. The Diaspora and Israel. Jewish Spectator, 42, No. 1, Sp. pp 28-34.

SHAPIRO, Edward S. American Jewry and the State of Israel. Journal of Ecumenical Studies, 14, No 1, W. pp 1-16.

Contemporary pro-Israel sentiment is in marked contrast to the minority position which Zionism held in American Jewry as recently as a decade ago.

SIMON, Rita and KRAKOWER, James. Important and Desirable Characteristics and Qualities of a Jewish State as Viewed by Israelis and American Jews. Ethnicity, 4. No. 5, pp 189-200.

Israel-Diaspora relations.

VITAL, David. Israel en het wereld Jodendum. Amsterdam Nederlandse Zionistenbond. Centrum voor Informatie en Documentatie Israel. Den Haag, pp 26-43.

W.S. Israel and the Diaspora. Jewish Currents, 31, No. 5, My. pp5-9.

WAXMAN, Mordecai. American Jewry and Israel: The Limits of Dissent. Conservative Judaism, 31, No. 2, W. pp 15-28.

WEIDENFELD, George. The Seven Deadly Cliches. Address to the Anglo-Israel Assocaition A.G.M. on Tuesday 14th December 1976. London, Anglo-Israel Association, 14p.

On Israel-Diaspora relations.

WOLF, Arnold Jacob. American Jewry and Israel: The Need for Dissent. Conservative Judaism, 30, No. 2, W. pp 29-34.

ZUCKOFF, Murray. Israel-Diaspora Relations. A Diaspora View of the Israeli Press. Interchange, 2, No. 6, F. pp 2ff.

ISRAEL DEFENCE FORCES

AZMI, M. The Israeli Navy Before and After the 1973 War. Shu'un Filistiniya, No. 65, Ap. pp 103-16 (in Arabic.)

CREVELD, Martin van. Israel and nuclear weapons. The Wiener Library Bulletin, 30, Nos. 41-42. pp 57-61.

On Israel's nuclear capability.

DEACON, Richard. The Israeli Secret Service. London, Hamish Hamilton, 318p, Ind, Ill, Bibl.

The author intends to show how centuries of persecution helped to equip the Jews with a talent for espionage and how this played a vital role in the events leading up to the creation of Israel.

EISENBERG, Dennis. LANDAU, Eli and PORTUGALI, Menachem. Operation Uranium Ship: A True Story. New York, Athenium, 260p, Ill.

The disappearance of a ship carrying uranium and suspected of being hijacked by Israelis.

FABIAN, Larry L. and SCHIFF, Ze'ev. (Eds.) Israelis Speak (About Themselves and the Palestinians) Washington, D.C., Carnegie Endowment for International Peace, viii, 258p, M.

A group of 13 Israelis held a week's discussion on Israel and the Palestinian Arabs at the invitation of the Carnegie Endowment for International Peace. This is the transcript of the discussion.

GLAZER, Penina Migdal. and Myron. War Resisters in the Land of Battle. Dissent, 24, No. 3, Su. pp 289-96.

Conscientious objectors in Israel.

PIEKALKIEWICZ, Janusz. Israël a le bras long. Les services secrets d'Israel. Paris, Grancher, 290p.

TINNIN, David B. with Dag Christensen. The Hit Team. With Updated Final Chapter. New York, Little Brown; London, Weidenfeld & Nicolson, 256p. In German: Frankfurt/M., Goverts; In French, Paris, Laffont.

Israel's secret service operations against the Munich murderers.

ECONOMIC AND SOCIAL LIFE

ABU NIML, H. The Predicament of the Israeli Economy between Jewish and Arab Labor. Shu'un Filastiniya, Nos. 63-64, F-Ma. pp 57-84. (In Arabic)

ADLER, H. and KAHANA, R. Portrait social de la jeunesse israelienne. Connaissance d'Israel. 1, No. 1, Ja-Ju. pp 123-42.

ARIELI, Mordecai and KASHTI, Yitzhak. The Socially Disadvantaged Peer Group in the Israeli Residential Setting. The Jewish Journal of Sociology, 19, No.2, D. pp 145-56.
Compares Ashkenazim and Sephardim.

Bank Leumi at 75. Jewish Digest, 23, No. 2, D. pp 33-38.
Condensed from Jerusalem Post International Edition.

BEN DAVID, S., KLIGER, D., ESHEL, R., HEICHEL, H. and LEHMAN, D. The Adaptation of the older Prisoner in Israel. International Journal of Offender Therapy and Comparative Criminology. 21, No. 1, pp 57-65.
Based on interviews with 15 aged prisoners whose problems are the same as those of younger ones.

BEN PORATH, Y. and BRUNO, M. The Political Economy of a Tax Reform. Israel 1975. Journal of Public Economy, 7, No. 3, Ju. pp 285-307.

BENSIMON, Doris and ERRERA, Eglal. Israël et ses populations. Bruxelles, Ed. Complexe, (PUP) 419p. Ind, M. (Collection Pays et Populations)
Sociological study of Israeli society, including the non-Jewish population.

BERDICHEVSKY, N. The Persistence of the Yemini Quarter in an Israeli town. Ethnicity, 4, No. 3, pp 287-309.
In Rehovot.

BILLIS, D. Differential Administrative Capacity and Organizational development: A Kibbutz case study. Human Relations, 30, No. 2, pp 109-27.
Questions the administrative capacity of a classless society devoid of financial benefits for the individual.

BIASI, Joseph R. The Quality of Life in a Kibbutz Cooperative Community. Cambridge, Mass., Institute for Cooperative Community. 800p.

---------------. Is a common ideology critical to a Kibbutz. Ekistics, The Problems and Science of Human Settlements, 44, No.263, O. pp 231-35.

---------------. The Israeli Kibbutz as a Social Alternative. Cambridge, Mass., Institute for Cooperative Communities, 120p.

--------------- and MURRELL, Diana L. Adolescence and Community Structure: Research on the Kibbutz of Israel. Adolescence, 22, No. 46, Su.

CHEVALIER, Y. Les groupes ethniques en Israel. Connaissance d'Israel. 1, No. 1, Ja-Ju. pp 47-64.

DON, Y. Industrialization in advanced rural communities: The Israeli Kibbutz. Sociologia Ruralis, 17, Nos. 1-2, pp 59-74.

DUTTER, Lee E. Eastern and Western Jews: Ethnic Divisions in Israeli Society. The Middle East Journal, 31, No. 4, pp 451-68.
Ethnic divisions will persist into the future and they bode ill for the long-term stability of the Israeli political system and, derivatively, Israel's ability to deal effectively with her Arab neighbours, especially in adhering to the terms of a Middle East peace settlement.

EFRAT, Elisha. Développement urbain en Israël. Connaissance d'Israel 1, No. 1, Ja-Ju. pp 89-104.

ETZIONI-HALEVY, Eva and SHAPIRA, Rina. Political Culture in Israel: Cleavage and Integration Among Israeli Jews. Boulder, Praeger,xvi, 249p. (Praeger Special Studies in International Politics and Government)

GILBOA, Yehoshua A. Israel's Ethnic Gap. Jewish Spectator, 42, No. 2, Su. pp 19-25.

GLASS, Moshe M. Die Beeinflussung der israelischen Volkswirtschaft durch die Fiskalpolitik in den Jahren 1960-1974. Ver such einer strukturell-quantitativen Analyse. Zürich, Wirtschaftwissenschaftliches. Institut der Universität. 270p. (Reihe B/2)

Examines the fiscal policy of Israel 1960-1974 and its influence on the national economy.

GRADUS, Y. and KRAKOVER, S. The Effect of Government Policy on the Spatial Structure of Manufacturing in Israel. Journal of Developing Areas, 11, No. 3, Ap. pp 393-409.

GREENBERG, Harold I. and NADLER, Samuel. Poverty in Israel: Economic Realities and the Promise of Social Justice. New York, Praeger, 190p.

HANDELMAN, Don. Work and Play among the Aged: Interaction Replication and Emergence in a Jerusalem Setting. Assen/Amsterdam, Van Gorcum, xvi, 193p.

HASSIN, Y. Prisoners Furlough: A Reassessment. International Journal of Criminology and Penology. 4, No. 2, pp 171-78.

Negative results of an Israli experiment for the re-integration in society of prisoners and to reduce the adverse effects of prison life.

INBAR, Michael. Ethnic Integration in Israel. A Comparative Case Study of Moroccan Brothers who settled in France and in Israel. New Brunswick, N.J., Transaction Books, 144p, Bibl.

Results of an empirical study of 132 matched Moroccan Jewish Brothers, 66 each, who settled in France and in Israel to establish whether there was any discrimination against Moroccan Jews.

Industrial Democracy in International Perspective. Annals of the American Academy of Political and Social Science. No. 431, pp 1-140.

Collection of articles on industrialized countries (U.K., W. Germany, France, Holland, Scandinavia and U.S.A.) developing countries (India, Peru, Israel) and Socialist countries (U.S.S.R Yugoslavia and others.)

JAFFE, Eliezer D. Reorganisation of the Social Welfare Network in Israel; Proposed Conceptual Frameworks. Journal of Jewish Communal Service, 53, No. 4, Su. pp 362-45.

----------------. Manpower Supply and Admissions Policy in Israeli Social Work Education. Journal of Jewish Communal Service, 53, No. 4, Ma. pp 242-49.

KIRSCHENBAUM, A. and SHICOR, D. Immigrant Settlement and Delinquency in Israel. American Sociological Association, Annual Meeting, 6-9 S. Chicago, Papers on Migration and Ethnicity.

Analysis of the "Quality of Life" in Israeli new towns focuses on various socioeconomic indicators and the extent of juvenile delinquency. These towns were established for the purposes of population redistribution and absorption of immigrants. They have a lower educational background, larger families a lack of more sophisticated skills and lower income.

KLAFF, Vivian Z. The Impact of Ethnic Internal Migration Patterns on Population Distribution in Israel: Observed and Projected. *International Migration Review*, 11, No. 3, Fa. pp 300-25.

---------------. Residence and Integration in Israel: A Mosaic of Segregated Peoples. *Ethnicity*, 4, No. 2, Ju. pp 103-21.
Concludes that social integration in an ethnically heterogeneous society depends primarily on the institutional dispersion of ethnic groups on the socio-economic status dimension.

NACHMIAS, C. and SADAN, E. Individual Modernity. Schooling and Economic Performance of Family Farm Operators in Israel. *International Journal of Comparative Sociology*, 18, Nos. 3-4, pp 268-79.
Disparity between Oriental, European and Israeli-born farm workers.

Noget om Borneopdragelse i Kibbutz. København, DAKIV, 47p (in Danish)

POLITIS, Henele. Le Kibboutz dans la societe Israelienne. *Les Nouveaux Cahiers*, 13, No. 51, W. pp 34-36.

ROSENSTEIN, Eliezer. Worker Participation in Israel: Experience and Lessons. *Annals of the American Academy of Political and Social Science*. No. 431, My. pp 113-22.

SADAN, E. Developpement economique et composition ethnique des mochavim. *Connaissance d'Israël*. 1, No. 1, Ja-Ju. pp 65-76.

SALIM, M.A.R. Jewish Trade in Palestine Before the Establishment of the State of Israel. *Shu'un Filastiniya*, No. 72, N. pp 132-49. (In Arabic)

SHAPIRO, Anita. The Ideology and Practice of the Joint Jewish-Arab Labour Union in Palestine, 1920-39. *Journal of Contemporary History* 12, No. 4, O. pp 669-92.

SHUVAL, J.T. and ADLER, L. Processes of Continuity and Change During Socialization for Medicine in Israel. *Journal of Health and Social Behaviour*, 18, No. 2, pp 112-24.
Survey of medical students in two Israeli universities.

SILVER, Harold. Social Work in Kibbutzim. *Journal of Jewish Communal Service*, 53, No. 4, Ma. pp 235-37.

SIMON, Julian L., MYERSON, Charles and SPECHLER, Martin. Are Russian Olim Good for the Israeli Economy? *Jewish Frontier*, 44, No. 4, Ap. pp 23-32.

SITTON, Shlomo. Israel. An Economic Survey. New York, London, Praeger, 275p.

SOEN, Dan. Social Problems in the Metropolitan Area of Tel Aviv. An Analysis of Urban Problems against National Background. *Annales Internationales de Criminologie*, 15 (1976) No. 2, pp 195-213.

SZESKIN, A. La structure fonciere en Israel. *Connaissance d'Israël* 1, No. 1, Ja-Ju. pp 105-22.

WEBER, O. L'autosugestion au kibboutz. *Esprit*, 1, No. 3, pp 399-412.
Despite its egalitarianism, kibbutz society is bureaucratic and authoritarian.

WEINGROD, Alex and GUREVITCH, Michael. Who are the Israeli Elites? *Jewish Journal of Sociology*, 19, No. 1, Ju. pp 67-78.

YASSOUR, Avraham. Kibbutz Members analyze the Kibbutz. Cambridge, Mass., Institute for Cooperative Community, 400p.

MIDDLE EAST

The Arms Trade and the Middle East. Philadelphia. American Friends Service Committee, 34p.

Surveys arms supplies to the region, including Israel.

ASKARI, Hossein and CUMMINGS, John Thomas. Middle East Economies in the 1970's. A Comparative Approach. Boulder, Col., Praeger, 613p.

BULLOCK, John. Death of a Country. The Civil War in Lebanon. London, Weidenfeld & Nicolson, vi, 200p, Ind, Ill, M.

The war in Lebanon was not only a bitter civil conflict but also a struggle for the Arab leadership and a realignment of forces in preparation for a general Middle East settlement.

CHIBWE, E.C. Afro-Arab Relations in the New World Order. London, Julian Friedmann, x, 150p, Ind.

The former Director of the Bank of Zambia and Zambian Ambassador to West Germany, examines the consequences of the Afro-Arab Summit, political and economic co-operation between the Afro-Arab States, and their role with regard to the liberation of southern Africa and the resolution of the Middle East conflict.

EISENSTADT, S. Convergence and divergence of modern and analysing societies: indications from the analysis of the structuring of social hierarchies in Middle Eastern societies. International Journal of Middle East Studies, 8, No. 1, Ja. pp 1-28.

Includes Israel.

ERRARA-HOECHSTETTER, Irene. (Ed.) La course aux armaments au Proche-Orient. Paris, Documentation Francaise, 52p. Bibl. (Problemes Politiques et Sociaux 318)

Collection of articles and documentation on Middle East armaments.

ESCO Foundation for Palestine, Inc. Palestine, A Study of Jewish, Arab and British Policies. New Haven, London, Kraus Reprint, 2vols

First published in 1947 the book is considered as the definitive work on the political history of Palestine.

Ethnic and Religious Minorities in the Middle East: Special Issue - Part II. Middle East Review, 10, No. 1, W/Sp. pp 1-74.

Includes: Some Problems of Arab-Jewish coexistence in Israel by Sammy Smooha and John E. Hofman. The Druze of Bet Ja'an: Modernization and the Activation of Minorities in Israel by Egon Mayer. An Arab View of the Jews of Iraq by Eliahu Khazoum. The Status of Arab Women in Israel: "The Middle East Slave Trade." by Andrea Rosenberg.

EVRON, Yair. Role of Arms Control in the Middle East. London, International Institute for Strategic Studies, 43p. (Adelphi Papers 138)

The legal and strategic implications of arms control in the Middle East.

FREDERICK, Howard H. The Arms Trade and the Middle East: A Primer. Philadelphia, American Friends Service Committee, 34p.

GOMAA, A.M. The Foundation of the League of Arab States. London, Longman, 340p.

GONTHARDT, Walter. Arabiens Sprung in die Zukunft. Zürich, NZZ, 88p, Ill. Schriften zur Zeit. 37.

The Islamic revolution.

KEDOURIE, Elie. (Ed.) The Middle Eastern Economy. Studies in Economics and Economic History. London, Frank Cass, 185p.
Essays on current economic issues and the economic history of the Middle East by J. A. McCarthy, R.L. Tignor, M. Deeb, F. Newton, H. Askari and S. Majin, D.A. Roy and T. Ciller.

KOEHLER, W. Die Wiederöffnung des Suez-Kanals, Auswirkungen und Erwartungen unter politischen, wirtschaftlichen und strategischen Aspekten. München, Weltforum, 80p.
With the reopening of the Suez Canal a new era begins in the Middle East.

LEWIS, Bernard. Right and Left in Lebanon. The New Republic, 176, 10 S. pp 20-23.
"Religion explains more about the civil war than politics does."

--------------. The Arabs in History. London, Hutchinson, N.e. 200p Ind, Bibl., M. (Hutchinson U. Library)
Paperback edition of Professor Lewis's classical examination of the key issues of Arab development.

MANSFIELD, Peter. Arab Unity Still Out of Reach. Middle East International, No.78, D. pp 4-5.

Middle East Annual Review. London, Macmillan, 400p, Ind, Bibl.

The Military Blanace 1977-78. London, International Institute for Strategic Studies, 111p.
Annual survey witn a chapter on the Middle East and including comparisons of military strength of Middle Eastern countries.

Le monde arabo-islamique et l'Afrique. Numero special. Afrique Contemporaire, 16, No. 90, Ma-Ap. 63p.

Moutafakis, George. The Role of Minorities in the Modern Middle East Societies. Middle East Review, 9, No. 2, W. pp 63-72.

NAAMANI, Israel T. The Secret of Assad's Success. Jewish Frontier, 44, No. 5, Ju-Jy. pp 14-16.

OWEN, Roger. (Ed.) Essays on the Crisis in Lebanon. London, Ithaca P., 89p. M.

PALAZZOLI, Claude. Ly Syrie. le reve et la rupture. Paris, Le Sycomore, 293p. Ind.
Syria's role as the spearhead of aggression against Israel, mentor of the Palestinians, police force in Lebanon.

PATAI, Raphael. Society, culture and change in the Middle East. Philadelphia, U. of Pennsylvania P., 240p, Ind, Bibl.

PONOMARYOV, B. et al. (Eds.) History of Soviet Foreign Policy 1945-1970. Tr. D. Svirsky, London, Central Books, 554p.
Includes the Middle East.

PRANGER, Robert J. Nuclear War Comes to the Mideast. Worldview, 20, Nos. 7-8, Jy-Au. pp 41-44.
Followed by "Nuclear War in the Mideast - Part II: Ethical Questions to the Pranger Scenario" by Roger L. Shinn.

RABINOVICH, Itamar. From June to October. The Middle East Between 1967 and 1973. New Brunswick, New Jersey, Transaction Books, 550p, Ind, Bibl.

RADNAI, Zoltán. Milyen arab egység? Iarsadalmi Szemle, 32, No. 2, F. pp 81-88.
Hungarian view of Arab unity against the background of the Middle East conflict.

RICHMOND, John. Egypt in Modern Times. New York, London, Columbia U.p. 252p.

RIQUET, Michel. Une minorité chrétienne: Les Maronitès au Liban. Genève. C.I.D., 31p, Bibl.

The Maronite minority has suffered badly during the Lebanese civil war; Father Riquet explains their position and Fr. Michel Hayek, in an epiloque explains how their situation impinges on the Arab-Israeli conflict.

ROSENBERG, Adrea M. The Middle East Slave Trade. Middle East Review, 9, No. 2, W. pp 58-62.

Slavery still persists in Arab countries.

SCHIFF, Zeev. Setting a New Stage. Midstream, 23, No. 3, Ma. pp 14-19.

The implications of the Syrian invasion of Lebanon.

SCHOLCH, Alexander. Der Libanesische Bürgerkrieg. Aus Politik und ZeitGeschichte, B 14/77, 9 Ap. pp 3-21.

SINAI, Anne and POLLACK, Allen. (Eds.) The Hashemite Kingdom of Jordan and the West Bank. A Handbook. New York, American Academic Association for Peace in the Middle East. 371p, Ind., Bibl.

Collection of papers and documents on Jordan's past and present. Contributors include: B.C. Busch, E. O'Ballance, A. Melamid, E. Kanovsky, U. Dann, C. Bailey, T. Prittie, I. Gershuni, D. Dishon, R. W. Stookey, H. Chase, O.M. Smolansky, N. Olin, J.S. Migdal, M.S. Chertoff, S. Mishal, D. Tsimhoni, L. Bernstein A.L. Eliav, A. Rubenstein, A. Susser, T.A. Idinopulos, V.A. Bull and M. Benvenisti.

SOULIE, G.J.L. and CHAMPENOIS, L. La politique exterieure de l'Arabie Saoudite. Politique Etrangere. 42, No. 6, pp 601-22.

SPEARS, Sir Edward. Fulfilment of a Mission: Spears Mission to Syria and Lebanon. 1941-44. London, Leo Cooper, xi, 311p, Ind, Ill.

Contributes important background to the history of the Middle East; the author, head of the mission to the "Levant States" was involved in the reshaping of that area during World War II.

STILLMAN, Norman A. In his cousin's house: the Jew in the traditional Arab World. Middle East World, 9, No. 2, pp 37-40.

Strategic Survey 1976. London, Institute of Strategic Studies, 134p.

Includes the Middle East, with special chapters on Lebanon, Syria and PLO.

MIDDLE EAST
POLICY OF POWERS

AL-ASALI, B. French Political and Military Points of View on the Arab-Zionist Conflict. Al-Majalla al-Askariya, 29, No. 4, N. pp 3-15. (In Arabic)

ALLMAN, T.D. The Influence Game: Everybody Plays It in the Middle East, but Nobody Wins Except the Middlemen. The New Republic, 26 Ma. pp 25-27.

The real significance of the Hussein payoff, and Carter's ritual praise for him, is that the whole process of US-Arab relations has become corrupted by the ethic of the secret payment.

BALL, George W. How to Save Israel in Spite of Herself. Foreign Affairs, 55, No. 3, Ap. pp 453-571.

BARNEA, Nahum. Confessions of an Israeli Reporter: Dark Suspicions and Doomsday Prophecies. The National Jewish Monthly, 92, N. pp 14-16.

"The paradox is that as the flow of arms grows wider and deeper, Israel's confidence in the long-term American commitment to her survival diminishes. Israelis feel that if they were Americans they would be uneasy. So there are more arms and more suspicions, which in turn lead to demands for more arms."

Begin in the U.S.: Duplicity and confrontation. Events, No. 22, Jy. pp 13-14.

BEN, Philippe. USA: Surenchère à la modération. L'Arche, 20, No. 238, Ja. pp 25-27.

Americans call for moderation by Israel.

BENTOV, Mordechai. When Begin Calls on Carter, Bible in Hand. Israel Horizons, 25, No. 6, Ju. pp 19-21.

BRAUN, Ursula. Der europäisch-arabische Dialog - Entwicklung und Zwischenbilanz/The European-Arab Dialogue. A First Evaluation. Orient, 18, No. 1, Ma. pp 30-56.

The British Public and the Middle East: A New Opinion Poll. Middle East International, No. 75, S. pp 23-25.

BRUZONSKY, Mark. How to "Save Israel from Herself" Middle East International, No. 72, Ju. pp 8-10.

----------------. Middle East Policy: Carter's "year of decision". Dissent, 24, No. 1, W. pp 8-11.

"Numerous policy decisions regarding the Middle East will be required in the early months of the Carter administration, spanning issues of arms sales, foreign aid, and technology transfers. But all will be jeopardized without continuance of the American post-Yom Kippur War effort to bring about a deescalation of the Arab-Israeli conflict."

----------------. Peace in the Middle East: Mr. Carter grasps that nettle. The Nation. 23 Ap. pp 489-92.

"Months of political maneuvering lie ahead. A bruising confrontation between the United States and Israel is near unless one of the parties alters course. Yet real and lasting peace can be built only upon a solid and trusting American-Israel relationship."

----------------. Two Views of 'normalization'. Middle East International, No. 73, Jy. pp 10-11.

----------------. We Want the Israelis to Understand Us. Worldview, 20, Nos. 7-8, Ju-Au. pp 19-24.

Carter's Middle East peace plans.

----------------. and DINITZ, Simcha. Let Us talk face to face. Worldview, 20, Nos. 7-8, Jy-Au. pp 25-26.

----------------. and GHORBAL, Ashraf. We want the Israelis to Understand Us. Worldview, 20, Nos. 7-8, Jy-Au. pp 19-24.

BRYSON, Thomas A. American Diplomatic Relations with the Middle East. 1784-1975. Metuchen, New Jersey, Scarecrow; Folkestone, Bailey Bros. xiii, 431p, Ind, Bibl.

Written with the intention "to provide some understanding of the American problem" in the Middle East.

BÜTTNER, Friedemann. German perceptions of the Middle East conflict. Images and identifications during the 1967 War. Journal of Palestine Studies, 6, No. 22, F. pp 66-81, Bibl.

Analyses various public opinion surveys.

CAMPBELL, J. Soviet Policy in Africa and the Middle East. Current History, 73, No. 430, O. pp 100-4.

CEFKIN, J. Leo. United States Policy in the U.N. Context. Middle East Review, 11, No. 3, Sp. pp 60-67.

U.S. Policy as expressed in Middle East Debates and resolutions in the UN.

CHASE, Harold. United States - Middle East Policy: The Military implications. Middle East Review, 9, No. 4, Su. pp 43-49.

CHURBA, Joseph. The Politics of Defeat: America's Decline in the Middle East. Intro. by Admiral ElmoR. Zumwalt. New York, Cyrco; London, Eurospan, 224p, Ind, M.

Concludes that Israel "should not be viewed in the context of the problem of Palestine but rather in relation to the American strategic need for a strong asset in the region."

DISNEY, N. China and the Middle East. MERIP Reports, 7, No. 10, D. pp 3-18.

DOWTY, Alan. United States Foreign Policy and the current impasse: some observations. Middle East Review, 11, No. 3, Sp. pp 39-46.

DRINAN, Robert E. Honor the Promise: America's Commitment to Israel. Foreword by Elie Wiesel, New York, Doubleday, 250p.

EL-QAZZAZ. Marwan H. A Comparative analysis of the United States policy in the 1956 Suez war. Ann Arbor, Mich., U. Microfilms,284p.

Ph.D. Dissertation, Southern Illinois U.

FAYYAD, T. Issues of Difference between the US and Israel. Shu'un Filastiniya, No. 71, D. pp 213-19, (In Arabic)

Palestinian view of US-Israel realtions and US policies in the Middle East.

FEIN, Leonard. Carter, Israel and the Jews. Moment, 3, No. 2, D. pp 9-14.

"If the president and his advisors want us to believe in the decency of their intention and the wisdom of their behaviour, they must begin by understanding the depth of our fear."

Foreign Relations of the United States, Diplomatic Papers, Washington D.C., US Govt. Print. Off. 6, The Near East, South Asia and Africa, xi, 1852p.

FORRESTAL, F. The Sinai-American Connection. MERIP Reports, 7, No. 10, D. pp 19-22.

FRIEDRICH, Salomon M. Après une décennie d'amitié fervante dix dernieres annés d'épreuves. Perspectives France-Israël, 16, No.73, N-D. pp 8-10.

France-Israel relations.

GAZIT, Mordehai M. Malgre nos divergences comportons-nous en vieux amis. Perspectives France-Israël, 16, No. 73, N-D, pp 4-5.

The Israeli Ambassador to France on French-Israeli relations.

GOLAN, Galia. Soviet Policy in the Middle East: Growing Difficulties and Changing interest. The World Today, 33, No. 9, O. pp 335-42.

------------. Yom Kippur and After. the Soviet Union and the Middle East Crisis. London, Cambridge U.P.: Jerusalem, Hebrew U.P., x, 350p, Ind, Bibl.

GOTTHEIL, Fred. United States - Middle East Economic Relations. Middle East Review, 9, No. 4, Su. pp 50-62.

GRIFFITH, William E. Le Moyen-Orient. L'energie et les grandes puissances. Politique Etrangere. 42, No. 1, pp 5-20. Europa Archiv 32, No. 6, 25 Ma. pp 181-92.

Groupe Démocrate-Chrétien du Parlement Européen. Dialogue Nord-Sud et Dialogue Euro-Arabe. Chronologie et Documentation. Luxembourg, Centre Européen du Kirchberg. 264p.

Of special interest: Chronology and documentation of the Euro-Arab dialogue.

HASSNER, Pierre. Soviet Foreign Policy: Ideology and Realpolitik. Problems of Communism. 26, No. 5, S-O. pp 82-89.

Includes Soviet Middle East policies.

HATEM, N. Letter from Washington: The Soviet-American Joint Communique and the American-Israeli Working Paper. Shu'un Filastiniya, No. 73, D. pp 173-77. (In Arabic)

On the Sadat-Begin peace initiative.

HAUSER, Rita. Brookings Institution Report: Forecast of Carter's Mideast Policy. Hadassah Magazine, 59, No.1, Ja. pp 10-11.

President Carter can be the catalyst to facilitate the long-desired face-to-face negotiations between the parties.

HAYES, Stephen. Joint economic commissions as instruments of US foreign policy in the Middle East. Middle East Journal, 31, No. 1, pp 16-30.

HELLER, Joseph. Roosevelt, Stalin and the Palestine Problem at Yalta. The Weiner Library Bulletin, 30, Nos. 41-42, pp 25-35.

Their decisions did not entirely present the reality of the Middle East situation.

HOWE, Russell Warren and TROTT, Sarah Hays. The Power Peddlers: How Lobbyists Mold America's Foreign Policy. New York, Doubleday, vi, 569p, Ind, Bibl.

Discusses the various interest groups that "lobby" in America. In the chapters "The Mideast Conflict" and "East-West Trade" the "Jewish lobby" is treated in detail.

KAMPF, Herbert. The American Interest in Isreal's Security. Midstream,23, No. 6, Ju-Jy. pp 27-34.

KARAM, S. Permanent and Transitory Factors in the Principles of Soviet Policy. Shu'un Filastiniya, No. 72, N. pp 45-66. (In Arabic)

KAWAMOTO, K. Kissinger and Rogers: U.S. Middle Eastern Policy. 1969-73. Choto sogo kenkyo, 7, No. 3, pp 38-55.(In Japanese)

-----------. The Soviet Union and the October 1973 War. Chuto sogo kenkyo, 7, No. 9, pp 39-56. (In Japanese)

KEDOURIE, Elie. England and the Middle East: The Destruction of the Ottoman Empire, 1914-1921. Hassocks, Surrey, Harvester P., 236p.

Includes the creation of a Jewish national home in Palestine.

KHADER, B. and LUSIGNOLI, F. (Eds.) Riflessioni critiche sul dialogo euro-arabo. Un alternativa alla dipendenza. Politica Internazionale, No. 10, O. pp 25-33.

Objections to a Euro-Arab dialogue.

KHALAF, A.H. Britain's Colonial Designs in Palestine. Shu'un Filastiniya, No. 67, Ju. pp 82-89. (In Arabic)

Retrospective study.

KISSINGER, Henry A. America's continuing concerns in the Middle East. Department of State Bulletin, 76, No. 1962, 31 Ja. pp 90-91.

KONDRAKE, Morton. Begin, the Winner: Even if Sadat Gets the Prizes. The New Republic, 176, 24/31 D. pp 11-13.

"The Arabs wanted to use the United States to muscle Israel. The Carter Administration thought a 'crunch' would be necessary with Israel, in response, elected as prime minister its toughest most uncompromising hawk, and he seems on the verge of producing a peace that no dove could have."

LAQUEUR, Walter. Confronting the Problems. Commentary, 63, No. 3, Ma. pp 33-41.

Prospects of American Middle East Policy under Carter.

LIPSET, Seymour Martin. The Middle East: foreign policy and public opinion. Address at the 46th General Assembly, Dallas, 9-13 November 1977. New York, Council of Jewish Federations, 11p. (Assembly Papers)

----------------------. and SCHNEIDER, William. American opinion towards Israel and Jews. New York, American Professors for Peace in the Middle East. 57p.

--. Carter vs. Israel: What the Polls Reveal. Commentary, 64, No. 5, N. pp 21-29.

"Beyond whatever opinion the majority holds on specific issues like oil, Israel is fervently backed by a politically potent minority, including a very large number of non-Jews, who are prepared to punish at the ballot box those who seek to undermine the unique America-Israel relationship."

EL LOZI, Salim. Which is the real Carter? Events, No. 22, Jy. pp 10-12.

MAALOUF, Amin. Moyen-Orient: La Peur. Jeune Afrique, No. 862, Jy. pp 14-18.

African analysis of the conflict.

MACKINTOSH, Malcolm. Die sowjetische Aussenpolitik der siebziger Jahre. Europa Archiv, 32, No. 24, 25 D. pp 841-50.

Includes Soviet policy in the Middle East.

MCLAURIN, Ronald D. et al. Foreign Policy Making in the Middle East: Domestic Influences on Policy in Egypt, Iraq, Israel and Syria. Boulder, Col., Praeger, 325p.

MANSFIELD, Peter. Where do the Dutch Stand? Middle East International, No. 73, Jy. pp 23-24.

MATES, L. Critical Situation in the Middle East. Review of International Affairs, 28, No. 678, 5 Ap. pp 14-17.

The Middle East: Focal Point of Conflict, the Interests of the Powers, an Australian Perspective: Report from the Joint Committee on Foreign Affairs and Defence. Australia Parliament, Canberra, Australian Government Publ. Service, xxiii, 387p, Bibl.

Middle East Problems, Hearings, Subcommittee on Near Eastern and South Asian Affairs. Committee on Foreign Relations, U.S. Senate, 18-20 My. Washington, 79p.

Middle East Strategic Problems. Hearing before the Sub-committee on Near Eastern and South Asian Affairs of the US Senate Committee on Foreign Relations. 95th Cong. 1st Sess. on an evaluation of the main strategic problems of the Middle East. 3 O. Washington DC, USGPO, 128p.

MOSHER, Lawrence. Can the Lobby Stop Carter? Middle East International, No. 77, D. pp 4-5.

----------------. Carter: A waiting game? Middle East International No. 67, Ja. pp 4-5.

----------------. Carter's Patient Strategy. Middle East International, No. 75, S. pp 4-5.

----------------. Letter from Washington. Middle East International, No. 78, D. pp 12-13.

----------------. One in the Eye for Carter. Middle East International, No. 73, Jy. pp 6-7.

The Necessity for a Middle East pax Americana. Events, No. 15, 22 Ap. pp 12-13.

NIR, Y. US Involvement in the Middle East Conflict in Soviet Caricatures. Journalism Quarterly, 54, No. 4, W. pp 697-702;726.
Shows their antisemitic character.

OREN, Stephen. The Carter Administration and the Middle East. Middle East Review, 10, No. 1, Fa. pp 14-18.
To evolve a Middle East policy of its own the administration must take hard decisions.

The Prospects for Peace in the Middle East: a first-hand report. Report of a Factfinding mission to Israel. 30 Ju to 7 Jy. to the Committee on International Relations. House, 15 Au. Washington, 18p

QUANDT, William B. Decade of Decisions; American Policy toward the Arab-Israeli Conflict. 1967-1976. Berkeley, Ca.; London, U. of California P., viii, 313p, Ind., Bibl. M.

-----------------. Soviet Policy in the October Middle East War. International Affairs, 53, No. 3, Jy. and No. 4, O. pp 587-603.

REICH, Bernard. The Evolution of United States Policy in the Arab-Israeli Zone. Middle East Review, 11, No. 3, Sp. pp 9-18.

--------------. Quest for Peace. United States - Israel Relations and the Arab-Israeli Conflict. New Brunswick, New Jersey, Transaction Books, 495p, Ind, Bibl.
Analysis of US and Israeli policies since the June 1967 war by a Professor of Political Science at George Washington University

Reorganised Israel Lobby has lost none of its teeth. Events, No. 30,' N. pp 14-16.

ROSENFELD, Stephen S. The Pentagon Tilt. Present Tense, 4, No. 3, Sp. pp 18-20.
Pro-Arab attitudes in the American military administration.

ROSTOW, Eugene V. The American Stake in Israel. Commentary, 63, No. 4, Ap. pp 32-46.

----------------. (Ed.) Middle East: Critical Choice for the USA. Boulder, Col.; London, Westview P., 211p.

ROTHENBERG, Morris. The Role of the Soviet Union: The Impact of 1967. Middle East Review, 19, No. 4, Su. pp 37-42.

RUBENSTEIN, Alvin Z. Red Star on the Nile. The Soviet-Egyptian Influence Relationship Since the June War. Princeton, New Jersey; London, Princeton U.P., xxiv, 383p, Ind.
Study covering the period up to the October War and Sadat's immediate post-war shift towards Washington.

-------------------. Soviet-American Rivalry in the Middle East. Middle East Review, 11, No. 3, Sp. pp 33-38.

SHARIF, Regina S. Latin America and the Middle East Conflict. Journal of Palestine Studies, 7, No. 1, Aut. pp 98-122.

SHEEHAN, Edward F. The Arabs, Israelis and Kissinger: A Secret History of American Diplomacy in the Middle East. Commentary, 63, No. 1, Ja. pp 78-82.

SHLAIM, Avi, JONES, Peter and SAINSBURY, Keith. British Foreign Secretaries since 1945. Newton Abbot, Devon, David & Charles, 267p

Discusses British foreign policy from 1945 to 1974 with some emphasis on the various Foreign Secretaries' Middle East policy.

SIMON, Merrill. Israel and Western Europe - A New Era, New Expectations. Jewish Frontier, 44, No. 3, Ma. pp 9-12.

SLONIM, Shlomo. Sadat's American Strategy. Midstream, 23, No. 7, Au-S. pp 27-31.

SMART, Ian. Oil, the Super-Powers and the Middle East. International Affairs, 53, No. 1, Ja. pp 17-35.

SMOUTS, Marie Claude. French Foreign Policy: The Domestic Debate. International Affairs, 53, No. 1, Ja. pp 36-50.

Includes French policy in the Middle East.

SNIDER, Lewis W. Arabesque. Untangling the patterns of supply of conventional arms to Israel and the Arab states and the implications for United States policy on supply of "lethal" weapons to Egypt. Denver, Col., U. of Denver, Graduate School of International Studies, 151p. (Monograph Series in World Affairs, Vol. 15, Book 1)

Concludes i.a. that the U.S. is likely to have more political influence over Egypt and Israel if it becomes a major supplier of arms to both sides.

SPIEGEL, Steven L. Carter and Israel. Commentary, 64, No. 1, Jy. pp 35-40.

-----------------. The United States and the Middle East Crisis. Middle East Review, 11, No. 3, Sp. pp 25-32.

SUDFELD,Peter, TETLOCK, Philip E. and RAMIREZ, Carmenza. War, Peace and Integrative Complexity: UN Speeches on the Middle East Problem. Journal of Conflict Resolution, 21, No. 3, S. pp 427-40.

SZULC, Tad. Carter's Middle East Incompetence. New York, 26 D. pp 10-14.

TRICE, Robert H. Congress and the Arab-Israeli Conflict: Support for Israel in the US Senate, 1970-73. Political Science Quarterly, 92, No.3, Fa. pp 443-63.

Examines the voting behaviour of the U.S. Senate on issues directly related to the Arab-Israeli conflict.

The Truth About Russia's Middle East Motives and Manoeuvres. Events, No. 33, D. pp 34-37.

U.S.-Israel: How will Carter Deal with the Begin Problem. Events, No. 20, Jy. pp 8-11.

United States Policy Toward the Middle East: Middle East Review, 10, No. 1, Sp. pp 1-88.

Includes: The Evolution of United States Policy in the Arab-Israeli zone by Bernard Reich. A National Energy Policy - At Last? by S. Fred. Singer. Countering Terrorism: The United States and Israeli Approach by Charles Wise and Stephen Sloan. The Conditions of a General Settlement by Marver H. Bernstein. Statements on Middle East Policy by Jimmy Carter; Cyrus Vance; Zbigniew Brzezinski; James R. Schlesinger.

U.S., U.S.S.R. issue statement on the Middle East: joint U.S.-Soviet Statement. Department of State Bulletin, 77, No. 2002, 7 N. pp 639-40.
VANCE, Cyrus. Interviewed on "Meet the Press" Department of State Bulletin, 77, No. 2001, 31 O. pp 579-84.
Positions on U.S. Middle East Policy.
VERNANT, J. Politique et diplomatie: Moyen-Orient: le plan Carter. Revue de Défence Nationale, 33, My. pp 103-8.
WHETTEN, Lawrence L. Arab-Israeli Dispute: Great Power Behaviour. London, International Institute for Strategic Studies, 45p. (Adelphi Papers, 128)
Emphasises the role of the United States.
-------------------. (Ed.) The Political Implications of Soviet Military Power. London, Macdonald and Janes; New York,Russak & Co., ii, 183p, Ind.
William A. Griffith on "The Decline of Soviet Influence in the Middle East."
WILDAVSKY, Aaron. What's In It for Us? America's National Interest in Israel. Middle East Review, 10, No. 1, Fa. pp 5-13.
YANIV, Avner. Dutch Middle East Policy since 1973. The Wiener Library Bulletin, 30, Nos. 41-42, pp 47-56.

ARAB-ISRAELI CONFLICT

AL-ASIR, R. On the October War. Shu'un Filastiniya, No. 62, Ja. pp 98-115. (In Arabic)
AL-MAJDUB, M. The Feasibility of Expelling Israel from the UN. Fikr, Nos. 15-16, N-D. pp 53-62. (In Arabic)
APPME Study Mission visits the confrontation states. APPME Bulletin, 11, No. 4, Su. pp 5.
American Professors for Peace in the Middle East visited Jordan, Syria and Iraq.
The Arab World and Israel. World Affairs Report, 6, No. 4, Ja. pp 386-93; 7, No. 1, Ma. pp 49-54; 7, No. 4, D. pp 368-74.
ARONSON, Shlomo. Israeli Views of the Brookings Report. Middle East Review, 10, No. 1, Fa. pp 19-25.
"War in the Middle East, as the Brookings Group assumed in 1975, is not imminent (and could not be a reason for one-sided Israeli concessions in any event). The Arabs, rather, want the U.S. to press Israel on their behalf. Begin has decided not to be pressed, while using the positive Brooking demands from the Arabs to prove the fact of Arab intransigence to the American public."
BADRAN, Shaun. I Hold Nasser to blame for June war defeat. Events, No. 26, S. pp 11-14.
BADRI, Maj. Gen. Hassan el., MAGDOUB, Maj. Gen. Taha el., and DIN ZOHDY, Brig. Gen. M.D. El. The Ramadan War. 1973, Boulder., Col., Westview P., 250p. Ill.
BALLAS, Shimon. The Israeli image in Arab literature. The Jewish Quarterly, 25, No. 2, Su. pp 14-19.
The Israeli character has not yet found his place in contemporary Arab literature.
BEN-MEIR, A. Psychological Dimensions of the Arab-Israeli Conflict. Current History, 72, No. 423, Ja. pp 25-27.

BHUTZNI, Surendra. (i.e. Suendar Zahid.) The United Nations and the Arab-Israeli Conflict. Gurgaon, Academic P., x, 316p, Ind, Bibl.

BLUM, Yehuda Z. Grundzüge des arabisch Israelischen Konflikts. Aus Politik und Zeitgeschichte B17/77, 30 Ap.

Explains the roots of the Arab-Israeli conflict.

Can an Israeli State and a Palestinian State Co-exist? New York, American Friends Service committee, unnumbered papers, approx. 60, M.

Report of an AFSC symposium on 24 May 1977. The participants were Prof. Herbert C. Kelman (Harvard); James Jonah (UN Secretariat); Prof. Elias Tuma (Palestinian, U. of California, Davis); Edward sheehan (Harvard Research Fellow); Prof. Gidon Gottlib (U. of Chicago) and Samir Anabtawi (a Palestinian, Prof. at Vanderbilt U.) All the statements were heavily biased in favour of the Palestinians.

CAPLAN, Neil. Arab-Jewish Contacts in Palestine After the First World War. Journal of Contemporary History, 12, No. 4, O. pp 635-68.

CARMICHAEL, Joel. Arabs Today. New York, Anchor, Doubleday, xxiv, 218p, Ind, Bibl.

Among the questions discussed are: Arabs and Jews; Seeds of the present conflict; the response to Israel - and to oil.

CHURBA, Joseph. The War Option in the Middle East. Midstream, 23, No. 10, D. pp 3-5.

"Startling as it may appear to some, the war option still remains - but it is in Arab hands, not in Israel's hands, and would be exercised in accordance with the belief that the United States would once again impose limits on the Israeli riposte even as it dictates terms for a settlement in the Middle East."

Conflict in the Middle East. Social Praxis, 4, Nos. 3-4, pp 191-364.

Collection of articles: Zionism and the idea of a Jewish State 1896-1942; The State of Zionism; Religion and Nationalism in the Middle East; The Case of Lebanon; The Future of Nationalism; Canadian Middle East Policy after the October War 1967-1976; American and Soviet Conceptions of Middle East Peace 1967-1976; The Petrodollar Market.

CURTIS, Michael. Cause of the 1967 Arab-Israel War. Middle East Review, 9, No. 4, Su. pp 7-11.

---------------. The Use and Abuse of International Organisations. APPME Bulletin, Ja 1977, pp 1-12.

The double standard in international political organisations applied in regard to the Middle East conflict.

DARRAJ, F. Chomsky. War and Peace in the Middle East. Shu'un Filastiniya, No. 62, Ja. pp 116-32. (In Arabic)

DOWTY, Alan. Current Perceptions of the conflict: Cairo, Damascus, Amman. Middle East Review, 10, No. 1, Fa. pp 26-30.

The ultimate solution, in both moderate and non-moderate eyes, is the assimilation of Israel in the Middle East so that it ceases to be an alien element.

DÜRRENMATT, Friedrich. Sur Israël. Tr. Walter Weideli. Paris, Albin Michel. 192p.

French edition of work published in German. the Swiss writers thoughts of the Arab-Israeli conflict.

EBAN, Abba and AKZIN, Benjamin. To Israelske Synspunkter. Copenhagen, SDI, 9p. (In Danish)
Two views on the Middle East conflict.

EL-ASMAR, Fouzi. Israel Revisited 1976. Journal of Palestine Studies 6, No. 3, Sp. pp 47-65.

FINGER, Seymour Maxwell. the UN Security Council and the Arab-Israel conflict, 1967-1977. Middle East Review, 9, No. 4, Su. pp 18-24.

FRAENKEL, Jacob. What Are Israel's true boundaries? Midstream, 23, No. 3, Ma. pp 3-8.

FUCHS, Walter R. Die Araber und ihre Welt. Und Mohammed ist ihr Prophet. Munich, Knaur, 319p, Ill.
Study in Arab mentality and the historical background to the present Middle East conflict.

GOLDMANN, Peter. Historisk Kronologi. Copenhagen, SDI, 36p. (In Banish)
Handbook on the Arab-Israeli conflict.

Introduktion til konflikten i Mellemøsten. Copenhagen, SDI, 32p, M. (In Danish)
Survey of the causes of the Arab-Israeli conflict with a map by Martin Gilbert.

GORDON, Aharon David. On the Arab Question. Response, 11, No. 2, Fa. pp 39-54.
From the Socialist-Zionist's book "Nation to Nation"

HADDAD, W. Christian Arab attitudes toward the Arab-Israeli conflict. Muslim World, 67, No. 2, Ap. pp 127-45.

HALPERN, Manfred. The Morality and Politics of Intervention. New York, Council on Religion and International Affairs, 36p.
On the Middle East conflict.

HANDEL, M. The Yom Kippur War and the Inevitability of Surprise. International Studies Quarterly, 21, No. 3, S. pp 461-502.

HAREVEN, Alouph. theSix Day War in Retrospect: An Israeli View. Middle East Review, 9, No. 4, Su. pp 12-17.

HARKAVY, Robert E. Spectre of a Middle Eastern Holocaust: The Strategic and Diplomatic Implications of the Israeli Nuclear Weapons Program. Denver, Col., U. of Denver Graduate School of International Studies, 126p, (Monograph Series in World Affairs, 14, No. 4)
Concludes that Israel's nuclear capability enhances the probability of nuclear war in the Middle East.

HEYMONT, Irving. Bab el-Mandeb: A Potential New Factor in the Arab-Israel conflict. APPME Bulletin, 9, No. 3, Ma. pp 3-5.
The closure of the straits and its consequences.

HIRSCHMANN, Ira. Questions and Answers about Arabs and Jews. London, Bantam, xv, 125p, M.
A leading American authority on the Middle East gives a succinct explanation of the conflict and offers a solution.

HIRST, David. the Gun and the Olive Branch: the roots of violence in the Middle East. London, Faber; New York, Harcourt Brace, 367p, Ind.

HOLLEY, C. Can the Arabs go to War? Journal of the Middle East, No. 29, Ma. pp 23-25.

HOYT, Robert F. The Middle East: Unmuddying the Waters. Christianity and Crisis, 37, 21 Ma. pp 46-49.
Real clarity is not yet available in the Middle East.

HURNI, Ferdinand. Israel - von Arabern gesehen. Schweizer Monatshefte, 57, No. 8, N. pp 631-43.
The Arab view of Israel.

Den Arabisk-Israelske Konflikt. Israels Ambassade i København. 27p. (In Danish)

KARRUM, H. Treason and Coincidence in the Defeat of 1967. Dirasat' Arabiya, Nos. 10-11, Au-S. pp 100-103, (In Arabic)

KASTER, Heinrich L. Neues Spannungszentrum der Weltpolitik Die Sowjetpräsenz in Nahen Osten and Ostafrika. Politische Meinung, 22, pp 79-85.
Soviet presence in the Middle East and East Africa creates new tensions.

KATZ, Samuel. Inside Israel's Crisis. A Documentary History of the Arab-Zion Conflict. Spec. ed. Battleground. Fact and Fantasy in Palestine, London, Rex House, 24p.

KEDOURIE, Elie. The real T.E. Lawrence. Commentary, 64, No. 1, Jy. pp 49-56.
Lawrence's support for Arab nationalism and his inimical attitude to Jewish aspirations in Palestine.

KHOURI, Fred J. The Arab-Israeli Dilemma. 2 ed. Syracuse, New York, Syracuse U.P., xii, 466p, Ind, M.
The second edition has an additional chapter on the 1968-73 period, but omits the extensive bibliography of the first.

--------------. UN Peacekeeping in the Middle East. Journal of South Asian and Middle Eastern Studies, 1, No. 1, S. pp 97-117.

KIMMERLING, B. Sovereignty, ownership and "presence" in the Jewish-Arab territorial conflict: the case of Bir'im and Ikrit. Comparative Political Studies, 10, No. 2, Jy. pp 155-76.

This Land is my Land: The Israeli-Palestinian Conflict: Cover Story. Intellect, D. pp 198-200; 202-5.
Contents: The Palestinian Issue: Anatomy of a Slogan by Benjamin Akzin. Eluzive Boundaries of Peace in the Holy Land by Basheer K. Nigim.

LAVIV, Yigal. An Historical Parallel. Israel and Palestine. No. 63, O. pp 9-11.
Anti-Israeli - pro Arab view.

Lebanon: A high price for the Palestinian cause. Events, No. 15, 22 Ap. pp 22-25.

LEKACHMAN, Robert. The Middle East Conflict. Making Room for Reason. Interview with Wayne Cowan and Robert Hoyt. Christianity and Crisis, 37, No. 13, 15 Au. pp 180-89.
Lekachman is distinguished Professor of Economics at Lehman College, New York, and serves on the editorial boards of Dissent, The New Leader, Civil Liberties Review and others.

LEVY, Robert. Hostile "Friends". The American Zionist. 68, No. 2, N. pp 23-27.
The Report of the 1977 American Friends Service Committee National Conference on peace in the Middle East reveals that "A.F.S.C.'s doctrinal opposition to coercion as an instrument of national and international policy is suspended with regard to Israel."

LEWAN, Kenneth M. Der Nahostkonflikt. Kritisches zu Veröffentlichungen in dieser Zeitschrift. Aus Politik und Zeitgeschichte, B17/77 30 Ap.

Analyses and at times argues with articles on the Middle East conflict published in this supplementary periodical to the German government paper Das Parlament.

LEWIS, Bernard. Settling the Arab-Israeli Conflict. Commentary, 63, No. 6, Ju. pp 50-56.

Deals with the relations between the state of Israel and the Arab states, the relationship between the Israelis and the Palestinians, and the policies and actions of the greater powers.

LORCH, Natanel. One Long War. Arab versus Jew since 1920. New York, Herzl P., xvi, 254p, Ill, M.

Surveys the role of armed force, violence and war in thehistory of the Zionist enterprise in Palestine.

MARINSKY, Deborah. Background on Israel's Boundaries. Midstream, 23, No. 3, Ma. pp 9-13.

MEMMI, Albert. The Arab "Nation" and the Israeli "Thorn". The American Zionist, 67, No. 8, Jy. pp 10-14.

MILENKOVICH, M. Middle East: Sliding Towards a new war? Review of International Affairs, 28, Nos. 654-5, 5-20 Jy. pp 22-26.

MILLER, Arnold J. The Jewish Kingdom of the Arabs. Jewish Digest, 22, No. 4, D. pp 60-62. Condensed from Friday Forum, 26 Au. Supplement to The Philadelphia Jewish Exponent.

MORRIS, Ya'akov. Defensible boundaries of even greater importance. Kansas City, Kansas, American Educational League for a Secure Israel. 20p.

NIELSEN, Jorgen S. (Ed.) International Documents on Palestine 1974. Beirut, Institute for Palestine Studies, xi, 604p, Ind.

-----------------. International Documents on Palestine 1975. Beirut, Institute for Palestine Studies, xi, 561p, Ind.

1967-1977: A Ten Year Perspective of the Arab-Israel Conflict. (Special Issue) Middle East Review, 10, pp 3-73.'

The Six Day War in Retrospect: An Israeli View by Alouph Hareven. The Dilemma of the Occupied Territories by Steven J. Rosen. The Role of the Soviet Union: The Impact of 1967 by Morris Rothenberg. United States-Middle East Economic Relations by Fred Gottheil.

The Quiet War for Arab Land and Water Rights. Events, No. 33, D. pp 26-27.

Alleges that Israel deprives its Arab minority of water supply.

RAMIREZ, War, Peace and Integrative Complexity: UN Speeches on the Middle East problem 1947-1976. Journal of Conflict Resolution, 21, No. 3, S. pp 427-42.

RETI, Ervin. Véres évek, fekete hónápok (Bloody years, black months) Budapest, Zrinyi, 148p.

Background to the Middle East conflict - with pro-Arab bias.

ROSEN, Steven and INDYK, M. The Temptation to Preempt in a Fifth Arab-Israeli war. Orbis, 20, No. 2, Su. pp 265-85.

ROSENFELD, Alvin. The Plot to Destroy Israel. The Road to Armageddon. New York, Puttnams, 256p, Ind.

Expose of the Arab world's relentless drive to destroy the State of Israel.

ROSENFELD, Stephen S. From Washington: How the Arabs and Israel Make Their Case. Present Tense, 5, No. 1, Aut. pp 15-18.

SALIH, W. The theory of belligerency and its effects on Arab-Israeli relations. L'Egypte, 68, No. 369, Jy. pp 429-42.

Arab-Israeli Conflict. London, Holmes McDougall, 96p, Ill.
Syllabus for schools (ages 13-16)

SHARIF, Regina S. (Ed.) United Nations Resolutions on Palestine and the Arab-Israeli Conflict 1975. Beirut, Institute for Palestine Studies; Abu Dhabi, Center for Documentation and Studies, xv, 56p.

SHINN, Roger L. Nuclear War in the Mideast. Ethical Questions to the Pranger Scenario. Worldview, 20, Nos. 7-8, Jy-Au. pp 45-47.

SID-AHMED, M. Nach vier Kriegen im Nahen Osten. Thesen zu envier offensiven Friedenspolitik, Berlin, Rowohlt, 154p.
Considered as the most important Arab statement on the Middle East crisis in recent years. His chief argument is that the October 1973 war and detente have fundamentally changed the basis of the conflict.

United Nations Resolutions on Palestine and the Arab-Israeli Conflict 1976. Beirut, Institute for Palestine Studies, 54p.

VAN DAM, N. Israeli Sectarian Propaganda During the October 1973 War. Muslim World, 67, No. 4, pp 295-305.

Ww Want the Israelis to Understand Us: Interview. Worldview, 20, Jy-Au. pp 19-24.
Interview with Egypt's Ambassador to the U.S. Ashraf Ghorbal, by Mark Bruzonsky.

ZAREMBA, Alan Jay. An exploratory analysis of national perceptions of the Arab-Israeli conflict as represented through world newspapers: an international communication study. Ann Arbor, Mich. U. Microfilms, 294p, Bibl.
Ph.D. thesis, State U. of New York, Buffalo.

ARAB BOYCOTT

The Arab Boycott and Title VII. Harvard Civil Rights - Civil Liberties Law Review, W. pp 181-205.
"An illegal act does not become legal just because the stakes are very high, and if discriminatory employment practices are allowed by the courts to be imported into the United States in order to lower the risk of losing Arab business, the burden is upon Congress to amend Title VII (enacted as a general mandate to reduce employment discrimination in the United States, part of the 1964 Civil Rights Act)

Arab Boycott. Hearings, Subcommittee on International Finance, Committee on Banking, Housing and Urban Affairs, U.S. Senate on S.69 and S.92, 21 F.-15 Ma. Washington, D.C. 616p.

The Arab Boycott in Canada. Findings and Recommendations. Montreal, Report of the Commission on Economic Coercion and Discrimination. 11 Ja. 90p.

BARLAS, Stephen. Aiding and Abetting the Boycott. The Jewish Veteran, 81, No. 1, Ja-F. pp 6-10.
"If the hope of a true viddle East peace is indeed a diaphanous one, then the United States must approach its confrontation with the boycott in an affirmative fashion."

BRONFMAN, Edgar M. Anti-Boycott Legislation: How to Succeed in Business and Public Policy by Really Trying. The New Republic, 4 Ju. pp 17-19.

"From the community point of view the bill is not perfect but it is a good bill squarely putting the United States and its business community on record against boycott practices. From the standpoint of American business, the legislation may still cause some difficulties."

CLUTE, N. Van der. Legal Aspects of the Arab Boycott. New York, Practising Law Institute.

FEUSTEL, Sandy. America and the Arab Boycott. Middle East International, No. 74, Au. pp 8-9.

GUREN, George E. Breaking the logjam on the boycott. Up Ahead are new options. Present Tense, 4, No. 2, W. pp 44-51.

HOTALING, E. The Arab Blacklist Unveiled. Beverley Hills, Cal., Landa, 288p.

LEVINE, Naomi. Challenging Saudi Arabian Discrimination and American Involvement. Congress Monthly, 44, No. 1, Ja. pp 6-8.

The American Jewish Congress contends that the U.S. Saudi Arabian Technical Cooperation Agreement entered into by the U.S. in June 1974, involved the U.S. Government in constitutionally prohibited practices.

LOWENFELD, A.F. Sauce for the Gander: The Arab Boycott and United States Political Trade Controls. Texas International Law Journal, 12, No. 1, pp 25-39.

MASLOW, Will. The Struggle Against the Arab Boycott. A Case History. New York, American Jewish Congress, 30p. (Mimeo) Also: Midstream, 23, No. 7, Au-S. pp 11-26.

The role of Jewish organisations gaining enactment of effective legislation against the Arab boycott.

MOSES, Alfred H. Battling the Boycott: the achievement of Federal legislation. New York, American Jewish Committee, 15p.

NOONAN, John T.Jr. Bribes and the Boycott. The Responsibilities of American Lawyers. Reprinted from American Bar Association Journal, D. New York, AJC Institute of Human Relations, 4p.

PARRY, C. Defining Economic Coercion in International Law. Texas International Law Journal, 12, No. 1, pp 1-4.

RUZIE, David. The Frence Anti-Boycott Law. Patterns of Prejudice, 11, No. 4, Jy-Au. pp 4-6.

The French initiative will facilitate the task of the institutions of the Common Market to take a stand.

STANISLAWSKI, Howard. Canada and the Arab Boycott: Developments and Proposals. Montreal, Canada-Israel Committee, iii, 45p.

TURCK, Nancy. The Arab Boycott of Israel. Foreign Affairs, 55, No. 3, Ap. pp 472-93.

U.S. Congress. Senate. Committee on Banking, Housing and Urban Affairs. Arab boycott. Hearings before the Sub-Committee on International Finance ... on S.69 to amend and extend the Export Administration Act and S.92 to amend and extend the Export Administration Act of 1969 to improve the administration of export controls pursuant to such act, to strengthen the antiboycott provisions of such act, and for other purposes, 21-22 F. and 28 and 15 Ma. Washington, U.S. Govt. Print. Off. 616p.

OCCUPIED TERRITORIES

ADAMS, Michael. Israel's Treatment of the Arabs in the Occupied Territories. Journal of Palestine Studies, 6, No. 2, W. pp 19-40.

ARKADIE, Brian van. Benefits and Burdens: A Report on the West Bank and Gaza Strip Economies since 1967. Washington D.C., Carnegie Endowment foı International Peace. xi, 164p, M.

Compact history and interpretation of events in the West Bank and Gaza Strip since 1967.

------------------. The Impact of the Israeli Occupation on the Economies of the West Bank and Gaza. Journal of Palestine Studies, 6, No. 2, W. pp 103-29.

Maintains that Israeli occupation harmed the economy in these areas.

de BRISSAC, Marie-Pierre. Les Territoires de dieu. Paris, Fayard, 180p. (Une femme face aux passions israelo-palestiniennes)

The author was a member of the UNESCO team investigating discrimination in education in the Israeli occupied territories.

COLBI, Saul P. A Guide to the Christian Churches in the State of Israel and in the Administered Areas. Face to Face, 11, No. 1, W/Sp. pp 20ff.

DESTRO, Adriana. Villaggio palestinese. Mutamento sociale in territorio occupato da Israele. Milano, Angeli, 328p. (Collana di antropologia culturale e sociale, 2, 6).

Sociological study of a Palestinian village in the occupied territories, showing the beneficial changes.

EFRAT, Elisha. Changes in the Settlement Pattern of Judea and Samaria during Jordanian rule. Middle Eastern Studies, 13, No. 1, Ja. pp 97-111.

-------------. Settlement Pattern and Economic Changes of the Gaza Strip 1947-1977. Middle East Journal, 31, No. 3, Su. pp 349-58.

GERSON, A. War, conquered territory and military occupation in the contemporary international legal system. Harvard International Law Journal, 18, No. 3, pp 526-56.

Based on the author's forthcoming book: Israel, the West Bank and the Role of International Law.

GRUEN, George E. and BRANDRISS, Marc. Israeli Policy Toward the West Bank and Jewish Settlements. R.ed. New York, American Jewish Committee, 9p. (A background memorandum)

HAWARI, H. Remarks on the Uprising in the Occupied Territories. Shu'un Filastiniya, No. 67, Ju. pp 116-24. (In Arabic)

Israel and Torture: The "Sunday Times" report with replies and counter-replies. Journal of Palestine Studies, 6, No. 4, Su. pp 191-219.

Israel Restructures West Bank Economy. Interview with A. R. Husseini MERIP Reports, No. 60, S. pp 21-22.

Israeli Settlement Policy. MERIP Reports, No. 59, Au. pp 18-23.

Israeli Settlements in the Occupied Territories. Middle East International, No. 72, Ju. pp 17-20.

Israeli Settlements in Occupied Territories. International Commission of Jurists. D. pp 27-36.

"With the right to conquest the right to create settlements has disappeared, and what is left is the bare right to temporary military occupation where necessary in lawful self-defence.

This does not include a right to establish settlements of a civilian nature or settlements of a permanent character."

KAPELIOUK, Amnon. Who Owns the West Bank? Middle East International No. 78, D. pp 18-19.

LESCH, Ann. Israeli Settlements in the Occupied Territories, 1967-1977. Journal of Palestine Studies, 7, No. 1, Aut. pp 26-47.

MONROE, Elizabeth. 'Allon road' puts doubt on Carter's 'Homeland'. Events, No. 15, 22 Ap. pp 26ff.

Supports the Palestinians.

-----------------. The West Bank: Palestinian or Israeli? The Middle East Journal, 31, No. 4, Aut. pp 397-412.

Holds the view that it belongs to the Palestinians.

NIZAL, N.Y. Israeli Settlements on the West Bank. Shu'un Filastiniya, No. 67, Ju. pp 149-69 (In Arabic)

ROSEN, Steven J. The Dilemma of the Occupied Territories. Middle East Review, 9, No. 4, Su. pp 25-36.

U.S. Position on Israeli Settlements. Department of State Bulletin, 77, No. 2006, 5 D. pp 821-2.

PALESTINIANS

ABBOUSHI, W.F. The Road to Rebellion: Arab Palestine in the 1930s. Journal of Palestine Studies, 6, No. 3, Sp. pp 23-46.

ABDUL-LATEEF, S.M. The Palestine Question in the Literature of the Resistance. Al-Katib, No. 198, pp 151-53. (In Arabic.)

ABU-LUGHOD, I. PNC Maps out Palestinian Strategy. MERIP Reports, No. 57, My. pp 10-13.

-------------. Palestine Arabs in Israel. MERIP Reports, No. 58, Ju. pp 19-25.

-------------. The Palestinians Today. Palestine, No. 1, Ja. pp 85-89.

ADAMS, Michael. Peace and the Palestinians. Middle East International, No. 77, pp 28-31.

Argues that without the Palestinians no peace can be achieved.

AL-HOUT, Shafiq. Toward a Unitary Democratic State. Journal of Palestine Studies, 6, No. 2, W. pp 9-11.

Puts the Palestinian point of view.

Arabs Under Israeli Occupation, 1975. Beirut, Institute for Palestine Studies, 152p, (loose-leaf)

Folder of material.

BONDS, Joy, EMERMAN, Jimmy, JOHN, Linda, JOHNSON, Penny and RUPERT, Paul. Our Roots are Still Alive. The Story of the Palestinian People. San Francisco, Peoples Press, 192p.

Propaganda volume written for young people.

BRUZONSKY, Mark and KIPPER, Judith. Washington and the PLO. Middle East International, No. 67, F. pp 14-15.

CARRE, Oliver. Le Mouvement national palestinien, Paris, Gallimard-Julliard, 217p. (Collection Archives 68)

CHACOUR, Elias. An Arab Christian Speaks Out. Face to Face, 11, W/Sp. pp 8-9.

Anti-PLO.

CHAGNOLLAUD, Jean-Paul. Maghreb et Palestine. Paris, Sindbad, 268p.

PLO connections with Algeria, Morocco and Tunisia.

COHEN, Stephen P. and others. Evolving Intergroup Techniques for Conflict Resolution: An Israeli-Palestinian Pilot Workshop. Journal of Social Issues. 33, No. 1, W. pp 165-89.
"The workshop demonstrated that the Palestinians attached great significance to a statement of recognition, while the Israelis found it difficult to see that such a statement could be a matter of consequences ... The pilot workshop exceeded initial expectations that it would serve as an opportunity to evolve techniques; it also provided substantive clarification of some of the central dynamics of the conflict."

Le Conseil National Palestinien. Damascus: Office Arabe de presse et de documentation.

Detention of Palestinian Youths in East Jerusalem. Journal of Palestine Studies, 6, No. 2, W. pp 206-11.
Alleges torture.

DOWTY, Alan. The Phantom of a West Bank PLO State: Don't Bank on it. The New Republic, 20 and 27 Au. pp 15-18.
"The kind and degree of linkage between the two banks of the Jordan is something to be decided in due time, by the populations concerned. For this elemental right to be exercised the world at large must rid itself of the notion that a PLO State on the West Bank has anything to do with resolution of the Arab-Israel conflict or with the right of self-determination."

FARAH, Tawfic. Political Socialization of Palestinian Children in Kuwait. Journal of Palestine Studies, 6, No. 4, Su. pp 90-102.

GABBAY, R. Israel and the Palestinian Arabs. Australian Journal of Politics and History, 23, No. 1, Ap. pp 19-27.

GLUBB, F. The Israeli Black Panther Movement and the Palestinian People. Palestine Bulletin, 3, No. 16, N. pp 10-13.

GOLAN, Galia. Soviet Union and the Palestinian Liberation Organisation. London, International Institute for Strategic Studies 34p. (Adelphi Papers)
Based on a study prepared for a conference at Haifa University.

GOOD, Nancy. The PLO and the prospects for peace negotiations. APPME Bulletin, Ja. pp 4-6.

GREENFIELD, R. Note: The Abu Daoud Affair. Journal of International Law and Economics. 3, No. 3, pp 539-83.
Includes articles from the French law of 10 March 1927 on the extradition of aliens.

De grondslagen van de PLO, de tekst van het Handvest en van de tien ponten van 1974, vijftien punten 1977, overzicht van de samenstelling van de PLO, lijst van persoonlijkheden in de PLO. Den Haag, Centrum voor Informatie en Documentatie Israel. 30p.
Principles of the PLO, its structure and a list of PLO personalities.

GROSSMAN, Lawrence I. (Ed.) The Palestine Liberation Organization: A Documentary Handbook, Montreal, Canada-Israel Committee, 76p.

HAJJAJ, Aref. Der libanesische Bürgerkreig, seine palästinensischen und innerarabischen Faktoren sowie seine Auswirkungen auf den arabisch-israelischen Konflikt (The Lebanese Civil War, its Palestinian and Inner-Arabic Factors and its Effects on the Arab-Israel Conflict). Orient, 18, No. 1, Ma. pp 16-29.

HALPERIN, Emmanuel and CYGIELMAN, Victor. Israël face aux palestiniens. L'Arche, 20, No. 239, F. pp 16-20.

HARKABI, Yehoshafat. Arab Strategies and Israel's Response. New York, Free P.; London, Collier Macmillan, xiii, 198p.

The former chief of Israeli military intelligence identifies the main trends in Arab strategic thinking since the June 1967 war and offers suggestions for an Israeli initiative to secure peace.

-------------------. Israel ... and the Palestinians. How to end PLO Extremism. Interchange, 2, No. 6, F. pp 3-6.

-------------------. and LEWIS, D. Palaestinenserne og PLO. København 'Indsight', 24p. (In Danish)

The Palestinians and the PLO.

-------------------. Three Concepts of Arab Strategy. New York, Anti-Defamation League, 14p.

HARRIS, Lillian Craig. China's Relations with the PLO. Journal of Palestine Studies, 7, No. 1, Aut. pp 123-54.

HEFLEY, James and Marti. The liberated Palestinian. The Anis Shorrosh story. Foreword by Adrian Rogers. Wheaton, Ill, Victor Books, Scripture P., 172p, Ill, M.

Story of a Palestinian who, instead of becoming a member of a terrorist organisation, has become an international spokesman for the reconciliation between Jews and Arabs.

HERTZBERG, Arthur. Palestine: The Logic of Partition Today. Columbia Forum. pp 17-22.

Israels Ambassade. Den Palestinensiske Nationalpagt (1968) 10-Punkts Programmet (1974) Nationalradets 15 Resolutioner (1977) København, 30p. (In Danish)

The Palestine Covenant with commentary by Yehoshafat Harkabi.

JANSEN, G. The PLO after Cairo. Middle East International, No. 71, My. pp 8-11.

JIRYIS, S. The Palestine National Council: Towards an Independent Palestinian State. Shu'un Filastiniya, No. 66, My. pp 18-29. (In Arabic)

JUREIDINI, Paul A. and HAZEN, William E. The Palestinian Movement in Politics. Lexington, Mass., Lexington Books, vii, 139p, Ind, Bibl.

Explains the roots and raison d'etre of the Palestinian movement from its origins in the 1920s to the time preceding the Lebanon crisis in 1975.

KAHN, Arthur and MURRAY, Thomas F. The Palestinians. A Political Masquerade. London, Committee for a Safe Israel. 40p.

Exposes the PLO as dedicated to the destruction of Israel.

KILO, M. Palestine in Political Strategies. Shu'un Filastiniya, No. 71, O. pp 36-48. (In Arabic)

KIMCHE, Jon. The Saudi Connection. Midstream, 23, No. 8, pp 3-8.

KLUG, Tony. The Middle East Impasse: the only way out. London, Fabian Society, 38p, M. (Fabian Research Series 330)

Argues for the establishment of a Palestinian State centred on the West Bank, as the only solution to the conflict.

KYLE, Keith. The Palestinian Arab State: Collision Course or solution? The World Today, 33, No. 9, D. pp 343-52.

LANGER,Felicia. Tanuskodom. Budapest, Kossuth, 200p.
Hungarian translation of the author's account of her defence of accused Palestinian terrorists in Israel.
--------------. Ten Years of Palestinian Children's Resistance. Palestine, 3, No. 8, 1 Su. pp 25-28.
LOZI, Salim-el. Twists and turns on the PLO road to Geneva. Events, No. 26, S. pp 17ff.
LUSTICK, Ian. Israel and the Palestinians. The Jewish Spectator, 42, No. 3, Fa. pp 36-8.
The Malpractice of the National Lawyers' Guild. Moment, 2, No. 10, O. pp 9-14.
Comment on the Guild's biased report on the occupied territories
MANSFIELD, Peter. PLO: A Time for Decision. The Middle East International, No. 76, O. pp 4-5.
----------------. Will the PLO Miss the Tide. Middle East International, No. 77, D. pp 6-7.
MANSOUR, Sylvie. The Sense of Identity among Palestinian Youth: Male and Female Differentials. Journal of Palestine Studies, 6, No 4, Su. pp 71-89.
MAROUN, A. Liban - Palestine. De la libération nationale a l'aliénátion populaire. Esprit, 45, No. 2, pp 195-200.
MAZZAWI, Musa. Donpt We have Rights Too? Middle East International, No. 77, D. pp 14-16.
Speaks for the Palestinians.
MEGGED, Aharon. The Question of Territory: Coexisting with the PLO. Midstream, 23, No. 10, D. pp 44-46.
MIRHIJ. B. and AHMAD, T. Lebanon in the Palestinian Revolution. Shu'un Filastiniya, No. 62. Ja. pp 51-69. (In Arabic)
MOHSEN, A. Special Report: Palestinians agree on strategy but not on Tactics. Middle East, No. 31, My. pp 23-27.
MUHSIN, H. Critique of the DFLP political program. Shu'un Filastiniya, No. 65, pp 151-72 (In Arabic)
MURAD, A. Report on the International Debate on Peace and the Palestinians. Shu'un Filastiniya, No. 72, N. pp 57-66 (In Arabic)
MUSALLAM, M. The People's Republic of China and the Palestine Revolution: Twelve Years of Revolutionary Solidarity. Palestine, No. 3, No. 1, Ja. pp 42-49.
NISAN, Mordechai. Jordan is the Palestinian State. The American Zionist, 67, No. 6, F. pp 15-17.
No Meetings with the PLO. Statement by the Presidents' Conference. Congress Monthly, 41, No. 1, Ja. p 5.
Palestine and the Soviet Union. Palestine, 3, No. 1, Ja. pp 31-41.
The Palestinian National Council - Jumblatt's Session. Palestine, 3, No. 5, Ap. pp 4-11.
Palestinian Prisoners and Detainees in the Zionist Occupation Prisons Palestine, 3, No. 7, 15 My. pp 19-23.
Palestine: Acts du Colloque Palestine. Bruxelles, 13-15 My. Paris, Gembloux, 269p.
Palestine National Council 15 point program. MERIP Reports, No. 57, My. pp 12-13.
A Palestinian State on National Soil. (Interview with Farouq Qaddoumi) Review of International Affairs, 28, No. 645, 20 F, pp 5-6.

Peace and the Palestinians. Report on an international seminar. Middle East International, No. 77, D. pp 28-31.

PERERA, J. (Et al) PLO: One move forward but ... Middle East, No. 37, N. pp 28-41.

PERETZ, Don. Palestinian Social Stratification: The Political Implications. Journal of Palestine Studies, 7, No. 1, Aut. pp 48-74

The Palestinian Arab National Movement 1929-1939. Vol. 2, London, Cass, xii, 414p, Ind.

QUADDUMI, Farouq. The Chances of War are Greater than Peace. Shu'un Filastiniya, No. 67, Ju. pp 33-53. (In Arabic)

Interview.

RICHMOND, John. Palestine: A Crucial Decade. Middle East International, No. 77, D. pp 21-22.

RIEBENFELD, Paul S. The Palestinian Issue in the Middle East. London, Conservative Friends of Israel. 20p.

Statement, presented to the Special Sub-Committee on Investigations of the Committee on International Relations of the U.S. House of Representatives (94th Session)

RONDOT, Pierre. La 13e session du conseil national palestinien. Maghreb Machrek, No. 76, Ap-Ju. pp 19-22.

RUBIN, Trudy. Before Geneva: How the Arabs are Dealing with the PLO. Interchange, 3, My. pp 1;6-8.

The Palestinians are a problem for both Arabs and Israelis.

SAYIGH, Rosemary. The Palestinian Identity among Camp residents. Journal of Palestine Studies, 6, No. 3, Sp. pp 3-22.

----------------. Sources of Palestinian Nationalism: A Study of a Palestinian Camp in Lebanon. Journal of Palestine Studies, 6, No. 4, Su. pp 17-40.

SCHUEFTAN, Dan. Report on the Palestine National Council Meeting in Cairo. APPME Bulletin, 11, No. 4, Su. pp 8-9.

SHAATH, Nabil. The Democratic Solution to the Palestinian Issue. Journal of Palestine Studies, 6, No. 2, W. pp 12-18.

SHEEHAN, Edward F. R. A Proposal for a Palestinian State. The New York Times Magazine, 30 Ja. pp 8-11.

Argues that the time is ripe for a territorial bargain as the key to an Arab-Israeli settlement.

SHUFANI, E. Arabs of Galilee and the Palestinian Struggle. Shu'un Filastiniya, No. 65, Ap. pp 54-59. (In Arabic)

SMITH, Colin and ANDREWS, John. The Palestinians. London, Minority Rights Group, 23p, Ill, M.

STEPHEN, Robert. Palestine: The Roots of Violence. Middle East International, No. 77, D. pp 23-24.

SUWAYD, M. Galilee and South Lebanon: the Revolutionary Plan to Confront the Israeli-Isolationist Project. Shu'un Filastiniya, No. 65, Ap. pp 67-71.

SYRKIN, Marie. Sign Language from the PLO. Midstream, 23, No. 4, Ap. pp 53-56.

TESSLER, Mark A. Israel's Arabs and the Palestinian Problem. The Middle East Journal, 31, No. 3, Su. pp 313-30.

TOUMA, Emile. Palestinian Arabs and Israeli Jews. Journal of Palestine Studies, 6, No. 2, W. pp 3-8.

Views of the Palestinian problem by the editor of the Arab language Communist weekly Al-Hihad.

TURKI, Fawaz. The Future of a Past: Fragments from the Palestinian dream. Journal of Palestine Studies, 6, No. 3, Sp. pp 66-76.

The UN and Palestine - Major resolutions of the General Assembly and Security Council, 1947-1977. Middle East International, No. 77, D. pp 17-20.

U.S. Votes against UN Resolution on question of Palestine. Department of State Bulletin, 7, No. 1960, 17 Ja. pp 41.

Statement in UN General Assembly by US Representative William W. Scranton.

WAINES, David. A Sentence of Exile: The Palestine-Israel Conflict 1897-1977. Wilmette, Ill., Medina, 226p.

WARD, Richard J., PERETZ, Don., and WILSON, Evan M. The Palestine State, a rational approach. Port Washington, New York, Kennikat P. x, 206p, Ind.

The authors contend that a fair and rational approach to the establishment of a Palestine state contiguous with the West Bank of the Jordan and the Gaza Strip might provide a solution to the problem of a national home for the Palestinians.

WASKOW, Arthur I. The Need to Talk with the PLO: Don't Call it Treason. The Nation, 216, 12 F. pp 178-80.

"American Jewish leadership should be trying to encourage the doves in the PLO - who are struggling against their own hawks."

West Bank - Nucleus for a homeland? Events, No. 26, 23 S. pp 23-29.

YA'ARI, Arieh. A Third, Palestinian State will Not Be a Threat to Israel. Israel Horizons, 25, No. 1, Ja. pp 10-14.

ZUREIK, Elia. Towards a Sociology of the Palestinians. Journal of Palestine Studies, 6, No. 4, Sum pp 3-16.

ZYCHER, Augustine. Palestinian Arab Women and the Vote. Middle East Review, 9, No. 2, W. pp 52-54.

TERRORISM

ABU-NIDAL, N. Terrorism in Europe. Shu'un Filastiniya, No. 73, D. pp 156-66 (In Arabic)

ALEXANDER, Yonah. and FINGER, Seymour Maxwell. (Eds.) Terrorism: Interdisciplinary Perspectives. With a foreword by Hans J. Morgenthau. New York, The John Jay P.; London, McGraw-Hill. 377p.

Menahem Begin on extremism and terrorism. Congress Monthly, 44, No. 5, Ju. pp 5-7.

BLUMENWITZ, David. Die beiden Abu-Daud-Entscheidungen des Appellations-gerichtshofes, Paris, Grundrechte, 4, No. 6, Ma. pp 114-17.

Proceedings issued by Israel in the French court of appeal in January for the extradition of the terrorist Abu-Daud, which failed.

BOWDEN, Tom. The Breakdown of Public Security: The Case of Ireland 1916-1921 and Palestine 1936-1939. London, Sage, xiv, 342p, Ill., Bibl. (Sage Studies in Twentieth Century History)

CLUTTERBUCK, Richard L. Guerillas and Terrorists. London, Faber, 125p.

Includes the Arabs.

DEMARIS, Ovid. Brothers in Blodd. The International Terrorist Network. New York, Scribners, 448p, Ind, Bibl.

The international links between terrorist organisations.

DOBSON, Christopher and PAYNE, Ronald. The Carlos Complex. A Pattern of Violence. New York, Putnams; London, Hodder, 254p, Ind.

"Carlos" alias Ilich Ramirez Sanches stands at the centre of the terrorist activities that included the OPEC hijacking in 1975.

Eine neue Welle von Aktionen. Stern, No. 9, 17F, pp 152-56.

Dr. Georges Habash, leader of the PFLP explains why there will be more airplane hijackings and no peace in the Middle East.

FRIEDMAN, Benjamin. The war against terrorism. Arab Terrorism and Israel. Jewish Affairs, 32, No. 3, Ma. pp 59-63.

FUNKE, Manfred. (Ed.) Terrorismus. Untersuchungen zur Struktur und Strategie revolutionärer Gewaltpolitik. Kronberg, Athenaüm; Düsseldorf, Droste, 389p, Bibl.

Among the essays are: Interpretations of Terrorism: Facts, Fiction and Political Science by Walter Laqueur; The Palestinians and the net of International Terrorism by Rolf Tophoven; The United Nations and International Terrorism by Rainer Lagoni.

GINIEWSKI, Paul. Le lezioni dell'Affare Abu Daud. La Rassegna Mensile di Israel, 43, No. 718, Jy-Au. pp 392-98.

HOROWITZ, Irving Lewis. Can Democracy Cope with Terrorism? The Civil Liberties Review, No. 3, My-Ju. pp 29-37.

Programs to forestall terrorism should be examined closely to see what their costs are for individual privacy, group interest, political competition and social change.

International Terrorism. Hearing, Subcommittee on Foreign Assistance Committee on Foreign Relations, U.S. Senate, 14 S. Washington, 90p.

JOHNSON, Chalmers. Terror. Society, 15, No. 1, (Ill) N-D. pp 48-52.

KRUMM, Karl-Heinz. Probleme der Organisation und Koordination bei der Terroristen-Bakämpfund. Auspolitik und Zeitgeschichte, B41/77, 15 O. pp45-53.

Questions of how to fight terrorism on the local and international level.

LAGUNI, Rainer. Die Vereinten Nationen und der internationale Terrorismus. Europa Archiv, 32, No. 6, 25 M. pp 171-80.

LAQUEUR, Walter. Guerrilla. A Historical and Critical Study. London, Weidenfeld & Nicolson, x, 462p, Ind, Bibl.

The first three chapters are a historical survey of the development of guerrilla movements and the origins of the guerrilla doctrine. The latter part of the book deals with the twentieth century. In his introduction the author states that this is the first part of a wider study.

---------------. (Ed.) The Guerrilla Reader. A Historical Anthology. Philadelphia, Temple U.P., vii, 256p, Bibl.

Selections of writings by von Clausewitz, T.E. Lawrence, Mao-Tse-Tung, Che'Guevara and others.

---------------. Interpretations of Terrorism, Fact, Fiction and Political Science. Journal of Contemporary History, 12, No. 1, Ja. pp 1-42.

---------------. Terrorism. London, Weidenfeld & Nicolson; New York, Little Brown; Kronberg, Athenäum; Paris, PUF, 277p, Ind, Bibl.

Investigation into the roots of terrorism, its doctrine, the sociology of terrorist groups, its patterns, motives and effectiveness.

LISTON, Robert A. Terrorism: Nashville, Tenn., Nelson, 160p, Ind, Bibl.
Analysing the various types of terrorist organisations, the author offers means to combat such activities, drawing on the examples of the British in Northern Ireland and the Israelis at Entebbe.

RABINOWITZ, Dorothy. The Hostage Mentality. Commentary, 53, No. 6, Ju. pp 70-72.
Reaction to terrorist acts.

RAPOPORT, Sandra E. Abu Daoud and the Law. Commentary, 63, No. 3, Ma. pp 70-71.
The case of the Palestinian terrorist who organised the massacre of Jewish athletes at the Munich Olympics in 1972.

Reflections on Terror. Thoughts on being held hostage. The National Jewish Monthly, 91, No. 9, My. pp 16-23.
Eyewitness accounts of victims of the attack on B'nai B'rith headquarters in Washington, D.C.

SOBEL, Lester A. (Ed.) Palestinian Impasse: Arab Guerrillas and International Terror. New York, Facts on File, Oxford, Clio P., 282p, Ind.
Unbiased analysis of Arab terrorism and its effect on the Middle East conflict.

TOPHOVEN, Rolf. Der internationale Terrorismus - Herausforderung und Abwehr. Aus Politik und Zeitgeschichte, 6/77, 12 F. pp 28-38.
Challenge of international terrorists and the means to combat it.

U.S. Congress, Senate. Committee on the Judiciary. The Terrorist and his Victim. Hearing before the Subcommittee on Criminal Laws and Procedures. 21 Jy. Washington, US Govt. Print. Off, 33p.

WILKINSON, Paul. Terrorism and the Liberal State. London, Macmillan, xv, 257p, Ind.

WISE, Charles and SLOAN, Stephen. Countering Terrorism: The U.S. and Israeli Approach. Middle East Review, 11, No. 3, Sp. pp 55-59.

MIDDLE EAST OIL

BRUZONSKY, Mark A. (Ed.) Middle East: U.S. Policy, Israel, Oil and the Arabs. 3.e. Washington, D.C. International Association, 200p, Ind, Bibl.

CAMPBELL, John C. Oil power in the Middle East. Foreign Affairs, 56, No. 1, O. pp 89-110.

DESPRAIRIES, Pierre. Le Problème de l'energie trois ans après la crise petrolíere. Politique Etrangere. 42, No. 1, pp 21-34.
Maintains that the Yom Kippur war had only a small role in the Arab oil-blackmail.

DORAN, Charles F. Myth, Oil and Politics. Introduction to the Political Economy of Petroleum. New York, Free P.; London, Collier Macmillan, x, 226p, Ind.
Explodes the myths created as a result of the Arab oil embargo of 1973; unfair oil prices, association of Israel with oi, etc.

ENGLER, Robert. The Brotherhood of Oil. Energy Policy and the Public Interest. Chicago, London, U. of Chicago P., xi, 337p, Ind.
Uses the 1973-74 energy crisis as a case study and traces the efforts of OPEC members to integrate all available energy sources into their empire. Discusses the role of oil in the Middle East arms race.

EZRA, Sir Derek. Problems of Energy Policy. AJA Review, 19, No. 2, Aut. pp 3-7.
The Chairman of the National Coal Board against the Arab oil blackmail.
HAMILTON, Adrian D. OPEC Back in Step. Middle East International, No. 74, Au. pp 4-5.
HUREWITZ, J.C. (Ed.) Oil: The Arab-Israeli Dispute and the Industrial World. Boulder, Col., Westview P.; London, Benn, 244p.
ISSAWI, Charles and YEGANEH, Mohammed. Economics of Middle Eastern Oil. N.e. New York, Greenwood P.; London, Westport P., 320p.
KLINGHOFFER, Arthur Jay. The Soviet Union and International Oil Politics. London, Columbia U.P.,xi, 388p, Ind.
LOZI, Salim el. Geheimabkommen Zwischen Öl-lobby und Jerusalem? Jüdischer Presse Dienst. Nos. 5-6, S. pp 41-43.
MILLER, Aaron David. The Influence of Middle East Oil on American Foreign Policy: 1941;48. Middle East Review, 11, No. 3, Sp. pp 19-24.
National Jewish Community Relations Advisory Council. National energy policy: Recommended positions for the American Jewish Community, New York, 12p.
The Palestinian Mirage: Oil Conquers. The American Zionist, 67, No. 6, F. pp 5-8.
PAUST, Jordan J. and BLAUSTEIN, Albert P. (Eds.) The Arab Oil Weapon. Leiden, Sijthoff; Dobbs Ferry, New York, Oceans. 380p.
Experts discuss aspects of the Arab oil embargo of 1973. All the relevant documents are reprinted.
PRICE, David Lynn. Oil and Middle East Security. Los Angeles; London, Sage, 84p, M. (Washington Papers)
RUSTOW, Dankwart A. U.S.-Saudi Relations and the Oil Crisis of the 1980s. Foreign Affairs, 55, No. 3, Ap. pp 494-516.
SHWADRAN, Benjamin. Middle East Oil. Issues and Problems. Cambridge, Mass, Schenkman, 122p, Bibl. Ill.
TUCKER, Robert W. Oil and American Power - Three Years Later. Commentary, 63, No. 1, Ja. pp 29-36.
UDOVICH, A.L. Middle East Oil, Conflict and Hope. New York, Lexington Books, 586p, M. (Critical Choices for Americans, 10)
United States: Department of State Memorandum of law on Israel's right to develop new oil fields in Sinai and the Gulf of Suez. International Legal Materials, 16, No. 3, My. pp 733-53.
Why Oil Prices Go Up. 1. OPPENHEIM, V.H. The Past: We Pushed Them. 2. MORAN, Theodore H. The Future: OPEC wants them. Foreign Policy, 25, W. pp 24-77.

MIDDLE EAST
SETTLEMENT

AL-HUT, S. On the Present Session of the UN: War and Peace are Twins. Shu'un Filastiniya, No. 72, N. pp 6-13. (In Arabic)
On the Middle East Conflict.
AL-KHALILI, G. A Study of the Current Political Situation. Shu'un Filastiniya, No. 72, N. pp 29-44.(In Arabic)
Argues that there is no prospect of a settlement.
--------------. On the Horizon: Receding Peace. Approaching Revolution. Shu'un Filastiniya, No. 66, My. pp 30-40. (In Arabic)

Arafat to Rabin: Halt to fight in return for a Geneva seat. The PLO/ Israeli Dialogue. Events, No. 10, F. pp 7-11.

AVINERI, Shlomo. Israel's Dilemma. Commentary, 64, No. 6, D. pp 47-50.

"If the attempt to convene a Geneva conference now is not immediately successful, the alternative need not be a breakdown in the whole process of peacemaking in the Middle East, but a reversion to the much less ambitious but much more realistic attempt at a partial solution." Written before President Sadat's trip to Israel.

BEELEY, Sir Harold. The Case for 242. Middle East International, No. 78, D. pp 10-11.

Advocates the settlement of the Arab-Israeli conflict on the basis of UN Resolution 242.

BEGIN, Menahem. Peace and National Security. American Zionist, 68, No. 1, O. pp 12-14.

BEN, Phillippe. L'embarras americain. L'Arche, No. 249, D. pp 25-27

American's surprise at Sadat's Jerusalem visit.

BERGER, Marilyn. Golda Meir Speaks Her Mind. New York, 12 D. pp 10-12.

In an interview with Golda Meir, prospects for a Middle East peace settlement and the future of Jews both in Israel and abroad are discussed.

BERNSTEIN, Marver H. The Conditions of a general settlement. Middle East Review, 11, No. 3, Sp. pp 68-69.

BRUZONSKY, Mark. Let us talk face to face. Worldview, 20, Nos. 7-8, Ju-Au. pp 25-40.

On the resolution of the Middle East conflict.

DMITRIYEV, Y. Middle East: way to a peaceful settlement. International Affairs, No. 3, Ma. pp 47-52.

Soviet stand on the issue.

EAGLETON, Thomas F. 1977: Year of Opportunity in the Middle East? The Convening of a Peace Conference. Vital Speeches, 15 Ja. pp 201-4.

"A final solution to the problems of the Middle East is by no means assuredin 1977. But I remain somewhat optimistic."

FRADE, F. El sorprendente viaje de Sadat. Revista de Politica International, No. 154, N-D. pp 73-91.

The impact of Sadat's visit to Jerusalem.

FRIEDMAN, Richard. Geneva: Who will represent the Palestinians. Israel Horizons, 25, No. 8, N. pp 12-15; 26-29.

On the Geneva Conference for peace.

GILLON, Dan. A time for plain speaking. Middle East International,' No. 72, Ju. pp 6-7.

GORDON, Murray. The pitfalls of a Geneva Conference. Congress Monthly, 44, No. 7, O. pp 10 -11.

HERZOG, Haim. Peace in the Middle East: Who Speaks for the Arab States? Vital Speeches, 1 Ja. pp 170-73.

A call to resume negotiations by Israel's Ambassador to the UN, delivered before the General Assembly in December 1976.

HIRSCH, Zeev. Towards Peace in the Middle East. How Can Business Contribute? Tübingen, J.C.B. Mohr, 14p (Kieler Vorträge 83)

Israel Embassy, Washington. The importance of defensible borders. Washington, 29 Ma. Sp. (Policy background)

JABBER, Paul. Peace Proposals for the Arab-Israeli Conflict, 1967-76 - A Survey. Bulletin of Peace Proposals, 8, No. 2, pp 153-66.

JIRYIS, Sabri. Limited Demands, Future Probabilities. Shu'un Filastiniya, No. 65, Ap. pp 60-66. (In Arabic)

-------------. On Political Settlement in the Middle East: The Palestinian Dimension. Journal of Palestine Studies, 7, No. 1, Aut pp 3-25.

KNIGHT, Jonathan. American International Guarantees for the Straits: Prelude to the Truman Doctrine. Middle Eastern Studies, 13, No. 2 My. pp 241-50.

LIPSET, Seymour Martin. Toward Peace in the Middle East. APPME Bulletin, 11, No.4, Su. pp 1-2.

LOZI, Salim. Does Israel make compromises? Events, No. 28, O. pp 12-17.

-----------. Is an Imposed Peace the only answer to Arab-Israeli enmity? Events, No. 15, 22 Ap. pp 10-11.

McDERMOTT, Anthony. Sadat Running Out of Time. Middle East International, No. 75, S. pp 8-9.

Marking time in the peace moves. Events, No. 33, D. pp 23-24.
Arab view of the peace process.

MERGUI, Raphael. Egypte-Israël: ou vont-ils. Jeune Afrique, No.883, 9 D. pp 86-89.

---------------. Israël veut-il la paix? Un reportage en Israël. Jeune Afrique. No. 841, 18 F. pp 18-23.

Middle East Maneuvers. The New Leader, 50, 19 D. pp 4-11.
Contents: What Sadat's Initiatives Mean by Hans J. Morgenthau. A View from Israel by Moshe Navon. Normalising the Conflict by Eliahu Salpeter. The Saudi Connection by Jesse Zel Lurie.

MOHSEN, A. Ten Years after 1967 Six Day War: despite optimism Middle East peace prospects appear bleak. Middle East, No. 32, Ju. pp 50-53.

NE'EMAN, Yuval. The Limits of Compromise. London, Calmus, 11p.
Originally written in 1975 following the Interim Agreement with Egypt.

NES, David. No Common Ground. Middle East International, No. 78, D. pp 8-9.

ODEH, Adnan Abu. Bridging the Peace Gap in theMiddle East. Journal of Palestine Studies, 6, No. 2, W. pp 53-65.

PELED, Mattityahu. Israel ... and the Arabs. There is someone to talk to. Interchange, 2, No. 5, Ja. pp 3-4.

PERIC, M. A Step Towards Peace in the Middle East. Review of International Affairs, 28, No. 66, 20 O. pp 28-30.

PERRY, Glenn. Security Council Resolution 242: The Withdrawal Clause The Middle East Journal, 31, No. 4, Aut. pp 413-33.

The Question of Territory - Three Views: Alexandre REITER, A Mini-Palestine? PAULUS, Future and Purpose. Aharon MEGGED. Coexisting with the PLO. Midstream, 23, No. 10, D. pp 39-46.

ROSEN, Steven. Solutionist Delusions: Israel Knows Its Security Needs Better Than Its Saviors Know Them. The New Republic, 176, 26 N. pp 14-16.

-------------. A Stable system of mutual deterrence in the Arab-Israeli conflict. American Political Science Review, 71, No. 4, D. pp 1367-83.

-------------. and MOUSTAFINE, Mara. Does Washington Have the Means to Impose a Settlement on Israel? Commentary, 64, No. 4, O. pp 25-32.

There is a mood of profound impatience behind the proposals of George Ball and Edward R.F. Sheenhan for an immediate settlement of the Arab-Isareli conflict and their ideas for economic and military sanctions against Israel to achieve one.

ROTH, Sol. The Right to the Land. Tradition, 16, No. 5, Fa. pp 7-22

Sadat: hope and determination. Events, No. 33, D. pp 11-18.

SAMUELS, Gertrude. Revisiting Israel's 'Good Fence': An Experiment Branches Out. The New Leader, 50, 14 Ma. pp 10-12.

Israelis insist, peace in the Middle East will depend more on relations between people than on politicians.

SCEMAMA, Andre. Le Caire-Jerusalem: Km O. L'Arche, 20, No. 249, D. pp 20-23.

On the interim settlement.

SERFATY, Simon. The Kissinger Legacy: Old Obsessions and New Look. The World Today, 33, No. 3, Ma. pp 81-90.

SIMON, Merrill. Egypt-Bankrupt and Destitute. Can It Afford Peace? Jewish Frontier, 44, No. 4, Ap. pp 14-18.

SISCO, Joseph J. (Moderator) Prospects for Peace in the Middle East. A Round Table held on 26 September 1977 between George Ball, J. William Fulbright, Rita Hauser, Jacob Javits. Washington, American Enterprise Institute for Public Policy Research, 42p. (AEI Forum 11)

SUWAID, M. The (Middle East) Settlement Strategy. Shu'un Filastiniya, No 73, D. pp 29-45. (In Arabic)

USTYUGOV, A. The Road to Settlement in the Middle East. International Affairs, No. 6, pp 80-85. (Soviet View)

Secretary Vance reaffirms factors for Mideast Conference. Department of State Bulletin, 77, No. 2002, 7 N. pp 637-39.

WALLER, Harold M. A Look at the Brookings Report. APPME Bulletin, 11, No. 4, Su. pp 6-7.

WHITE, Ralph K. Misperception in the Arab-Israeli Conflict. Journal of Social Issues. 33, W. pp 190-221.

"Some consensus exists as to what a fair, peace-promoting settlement would be. Both sides reject it." Some nonrational reasons are considered.

WILNER, Meir. Peace in the Middle East: sheet anchor for Israel. World Marxist Review, 20, No. 4, Ap. pp 32-40.

YOUNIS, M. Israel's Position on Palestinian Representation at the Geneva Conference. Shu'un Filastiniya, No. 73, D. pp 219-24. (In Arabic)

JEWISH HISTORY

ARON, Robert, MALKA, Victor, NEHER, André. Le Judaisme: Hier-Demain Paris, Buchet-Chastel, 234p. (Collection: Deux Milliards de croyants 4)

Essays on the role of the Jewish faith in the history of mankind.

BARON, Salo W. and WISE, George S. (Eds.) Violence and Defence in the Jewish Experience. Philadelphia, Jewish Publications Society, xii, 362p, Ind.

Papers prepared for a seminar on violence and defence in Jewish history and contemporary life, Tel Aviv University, 18 August - 4 September 1974.

DÖBLIN, Alfred. Flucht und Sammlung des Judenvolks. Aufsätze und Erzählungen. N.e. Hildesheim, Gerstenberg, 232p, (Exilliteratur 1)
Reprint of essays on the Jewish question.

EBAN, Abba. Dies ist mein Volk. Die Geschichte der Juden. München Drömer Knaur, 480p, Ill.

FOHRER, Georg. Geschichte Israels. Von den Anfängen biz zur Gegenwart. Heidelberg, UTB Quelle & Mayer, 290p, Bibl. M.
History of the Jews and Israel from earliest time to the present

JOSEPH, Anthony. Anglo-Jewish Genealogy. AJA Review, 19, No. 2, Aut. pp 18-20.

KOESTLER, Arthur. The Thirteenth Tribe: Khazar Empire and its Heritage. London, Picador, 224p.
Paperback edition of work published in 1976.

MCCULLOGH, W. Stewart. History and Literature of the Palestinian Jews from Cyrus to Herod, 550 B.C. to 4 B.C. University of Toronto P., 262p.

NEUSNER, Jacob. The Judaic Factor in Western Culture. Theology Today, 34, No. 3, pp 277-84.
Contends that Jewish presence in Western Christian societies has contributed to tolerance of non-conformism.

NOTH, Martin. Storia d'Israele. Brescia, Paideia. 584p. (Biblioteca di cultura religiosa, 25)
Biblical history.

ROTTENBERG, Dan. Finding our Fathers. A Guidebook to Jewish Genealogy. New York, Random House, xiv, 401p.

SACHAR, Howard Morley. The Course of Modern Jewish History. New York, Dell, 669p, Ind, M.
An Updated expanded edition.

---------------------. A History of Israel. From the Rise of Zionism to our Time. Oxford, Blackwell and Mott; New York, Knopf. xviii, 883p, Ind, Bibl. M.
Traces the evolution of Jewish nationalism from its 19th century beginnings to the present political and social factors that influence Israeli policies.

SCHEIBER, Sandór. (Ed.) Magyar-Zsidó Oklevéltár. XVII. Kotel 1431-1770. (Monumenta Hungariae Judaica, Tomus, XVII 1431-1770) Budapest, Magyar Izraelitak Orszagos Kepviselete, 452p, Ind.
Contains documentary material from the Hungarian National Archives, the Archives of the County of Sopron and the collection of Vienna Hofkammer, selected and compiled by Jenö Hazi. The conscription of Jews in Tolna County is published by Mihaly Szilágyi. Other contributions include documents from the archives of the Chapter of Gyulafehervar (Alba Julia) and of the County of Szabolcs-Szatmár. Házi's essay and the documents published on "The Fate of the Jews of Buda in 1686" the liberation of the city from Turkish rule and the conscriptions are of particular interest.

SETON-WATSON, Hugh. Nations and States. An enquiry into the origins of nations and the politics of nationalism. London, Methuen, xv,563p, Ind, Bibl.

STERN, Malcolm H. Tracing your Jewish Roots. Cincinnati, American Jewish Archives, 15p.
Guide to genealogical studies.

ZABALA, A. Martin de. El puéblo judio, singular y universal. *El Olivo,* Nos. 3-4, Jy-D. pp 105-8.

HISTORIOGRAPHY

ABRAMSKY, Chimen. A National Jewish History. *The Jewish Quarterly,* 25, No. 1, Sp. pp 28-33.

BOKSER, Ben Zion. The interaction of history and theology. *Judaism* 26, No. 3, Su. pp 321-25.

KOCHAN, Lionel. The Jew and his History: the Model of the Exile. Basingstoke (Hants) Macmillan, 164p, Ind, Ill, Bibl.
Examines the reason for the scarcity of Jewish historians and the neglect by Jews of research of their own history of the last 2000 years.

LEVENBERG, Shneier. Karl Marx's Place in Jewish History 110 years since the publication of "Das Kapital". *Jewish Frontier,* 44, No. 4, Ap. pp 20-22.

LEVI, Moises Orfali. Los Albores de la Era Moderna en la Historia del Judaismo Europeo. *El Olivo,* No. 2, Ap-Ju. pp 43-52.
Jewish historians (Graetz, Dubnow, Jost and Baer)

MACCOBY, Hyam. Velikovsky and Jewish History. *Midstream,* 23, No. 9, N. pp 45-55.

RAPHAEL, Chaim. The Texture of Jewish History. *Commentary,* 63, No. 1, Ja. pp 64-68.

STERN-TAEUBLER, Selma. (Ed.) Aufsätze zur Problematik jüdischer Geschichtesschreibung 1908-1950. Tübingen, J.C.B. Mohr, xxiv, 63p. (Schriftenreihe Wissenschaftlicher Abhandlungen des Leo Baeck Instituts)
Essays on Jewish historiography by the co-founder and first director of the *Gesamtarchiv der deutschen Juden.*

ANCIENT HISTORY

AHARONI, Yohanan and AVI-YONAH, Michael. The Macmillan Bible Atlas. New York, Macmillan, 264p, M. Ind.

ALON, D. A Chalcolithic Temple at Gilath. *Biblical Archaelogy,* 40, No. 2, pp 63-70.
Excavations in the modern Negev.

AVIGAD, Nahman. Ancient Galilean Synagogues: Showplaces for Jewish Art. *Jewish Art,* 1, No. 1, Su. pp 33-37.

AVI-YONAH, Michael and BARAS, Zvi. (Eds.) World History of the Jewish People. V 8: Society and Religion in the Second Temple period. London, W.H. Allen, xxxiv, 414p, Bibl. Ind, Ill, M.
Contributors to this volume are in addition to Z. Baras, D. Flusser, H.D. Mantel, S. Safrai, J. Licht, J. Klausner, and M. Stern.

CLAMER, C. and USSISHKIN, D. A Canaanite Temple at Tell Lachish. *Biblical Archaelogy,* 40, No. 2, pp 71-76.
Excavations in the Lachish area revealed a Temple dating to the days of the Kingdom of Judea.

EISENBERG, E. The Temples at Tell Kittan. Biblical Archaelogy, 40, No. 2, pp 77-81.
Discovery of a middle bronze age temple in the Jordan valley, north of Beth Shean.

FLAVIUS, Josephe. La guerre des juifs. Tr. P. Savinel. Precede de, Du bon usage de la Trahison par P. Vidal-Naquet. Paris, PUF, 608p. Ind.

HAYES, John H. a-d MILLER, J. Maxwell. (Eds.) Israelite and Judean History. London, SCHP, 712p, (Old Testament Library)

Hérode à Jericho. Bible et Terre Sainte, No. 189, pp 2-21.
Survey of the principal monuments constructed by Herod in Palestine with an historical study of the ups and downs of his regime and his last days in the Jericho winter palace.

LEMAIRE, A. Inscriptions hébraïques. Les Ostraca. tome 1, Paris, Ed. du Cerf, 304p, Bibl, Ind. (Coll: Litteratures anciennes du Proche Orient, 9)
Describes the tablets found in Samaria, Lachish and elsewhere in Palestine, 1910-35.

MAGNUSSON, Magnus. The BBC Archaelogy of the Bible Lands. London, BBC, 272p, Ill.
Text and illustrations from a BBC TV Serial.

MAZAR, A. Additional Philistine Temples at Tell Quasile. Biblical Archaelogy, 40, No. 2, pp 82-87.

NEGEV, Avraham. Archaelogy in the Land of the Bible. New York, Schocken, 131p.

SEGAL, A. Das Herodium und Masada. Eine vergleichende Studie. Antike Welt, 8, No. 1, pp 21-28.
Architectural study of the Herodion and of Massada.

VERMES, Géza. Dead Sea Scrolls: Qumran in Perspective. London, Collins, 238p.

MEDIEVAL HISTORY

ASTRIAN, Jose Cabezudo. La expulsion de los judiós en Ejea de los Caballeros. Sefarad, 30, No. 2, pp 349-64.
the 15th century expulsion of Jews from a Spanish city.

BACHRACH, Bernard S. Early Medieval Jewish Policy in Western Europe. Minneapolis, U. of Minnesota P., x, 213p, Ind, Bibl.
Historical study of the status of Jews in medieval Western Europe.

BLUMENKRANZ, Bernhard. La synagogue de Rouen (env. 1100) Archives Juives, 13, No. 3, pp 37-44.
Excavated in the courtyard of the Palace of Justice in the medieval Jewish quarter. Hebrew inscription.

GOLB, N. The Forgotton Jewish history of medieval Rouen. Archaelogy, 30, No. 5, pp 314-25.

KOCH, Yolanda Moreno. La conquista de Granada y la expulsion de Sefarad, segun las cronicas hispanohebreas. El Olivo, Nos. 3-4, Jy-D. pp 71-82.
The expulsion from Spain in 1192 in the light of contemporary Hebrew documents.

MILANI, Celestina. Ininerarium Antonini Placentini - Un viaggio in Terra Santa del 560-570 d. C., Milano, Vita e Pensiero, 324p.
A 6th century voyage to the Holy Land.

OVRUT, Barnett D. Edward I and The Expulsion of the Jews. The Jewish Quarterly Review, 67, No. 4, Ap. pp 224-35.
PARRONDO, Carlos Carrete. Convivencia judeo-cristiana en Castilia antes de 1492. El Olivo, No. 2, Ap-Ju. pp 29-34.
Jewish-Christian coexistence in Castile before 1492.
STOCK, Mario. L'editto di Espulsione degli Ebrei dal Regno di Napoli (1510) a la loro Breve Riammissione nel Settecento. La Rassegna Mensile di Israel, 43, Nos. 1-2, Ja-F. pp 32-35.

1600-1914

ELIA, Paolo. I Fratelli Verri e L'editto di Pio VI. La Rassegna Mensile di Israel, 43, Nos. 1-2, Ma-Ap. pp 133-36.
The counts Pietro and Alessandro Verri criticised Pope Pius VI's edict against the Jews.
Judentum im Zeitalter der Aufklärung. Herausgegeben vom Vorstand der Lessing-Akademie. Bremen. Wolfenbüttel, Jacobi, 410p, Bibl. (Worlfenbütteler Studien zur Aufklärung 4)
Judaism in the enlightenment.
LEVI, Enzo. Lo "Jus Kazaga" in Piemonte. La Rassegna Mensile di Israel, 43, Nos. 1-2, Ma-Ap. pp 152-62.
Some interesting verdicts from the period 1796-1874 - the French occupation of Saxony.
LEVIN, Nora. While Messiah Tarried. Jewish Socialist Movements, 1871-1914. New York; London, Schocken, 554p, Ind, Bibl.
NOSEK, Bedrich, and SADEK, Vladimir. Sociali'nye protivorecija v evrejskich religiozhych obscestich religiozhych obscestrach v Moravii i ich ostrazenie v socinenijach Menachema Mendela Korchmala (okolo 1600-1661) Judaica B ohemiae, 13, No. 2, pp 59-73.
Social dissent in the Jewish religious communities of Moravia as reflected in the works of Menahem Mendl Krochmal.
OLSON, R.W. Jews, Janissaries, Esnaf and the Revolt of 1740 in Istanbul. Social unheaval and Political Realignment in the Ottoman Empire. Journal of the Economic and Social History of the Orient, 20, No. 2, pp 185-207.
Bezirgan Bashi, a powerful Jew, had an important role in the revolt.
RASKOWSKI, Yevgeni. Der sotsial-ekonomisher matsev fun di yidn in der russlandisher imperie noch der reforme fun 1861. (The social-economic situation of Jews in the Russian Empire after the1861 Reform). Sovietish Heimland, 17, No. 4, Ap. pp 150-54.
REUTLONGER, A.S. Reflections on the Anglo-American Jewish Experience: Immigrants, Workers and Entrepreneurs in New York and London, 1870-1914. American Jewish Historical Quarterly, 66, No. 4, Ju. pp 473-84.
Compares the evolution of the East European settlements in London and New York.
SALBSTEIN, Michael Charles Nathaniel. Emancipation of the Jews in Britain: An Essay on the Preconditions. Goring by Sea, W. Sussex, Author, 76p.
SAMUEL, Edwin R. David Gabay's 1660 letter from London. Transactions of the Jewish Historical Society of England, 25, pp 38-42.
A Portuguese Jew describes post-restoration life in London.

----------------. Was Moyse's Hall, Bury St. Edmunds, a Jew's House? Transactions of the Jewish Historical Society of England. 25, pp 43-47.

The building was not a synagogue but perhaps a Jewish dwelling.

SCHAPPES, Morris U. The Political Origins of the United Hebrew Trades, 1888. The Journal of Ethnic Studies, 5, Sp. pp 13-44.

An important factor in organizing Jewish workers into trade unions and bringing them into the American labor movement.

SCHULOF, Izsák. Budai krónika. Budapest, Europa, 103p, (Bibliothec Historica)

A 16th century chronicle of Turkish rule in Hungary, written by a Jew.

SCHULTZ, Hans Jürgen. (Ed.) Freiheit, Gleichheit, Brüderlichkeit. Die vergessene Parole. Stuttgart, DVA, 192p.

The contributions formed part of a broadcast series over Süddeutscher Rundfunk and include contributions by Heinrich Böll Friedrich Heer and Ernst Simon.

SCHWARZFUCHS, Simon. Les prisonniers de l'Ile d'Aix. L'Arche, 20, No. 238, Ja. pp 51-53.

Russian Jewish prisoners in France during the Crimean War.

SHAFTESLEY, John H. Jews in English Regular Freemasonry, 1717-1860. Transactions of the Jewish Historical Society of England, 25, pp 150-209.

STERN, Fritz. Gold and Iron: Bismarck, Bleichröder, and the Building of the German Empire. New York, Knopf; London, Allen and Unwin, xxiv, 620p, Ind.

Shows through the relationship between the Prussian Prince, the Iron Chancellor and theJewish Bankers, that the German empire was built on gold not only on blood and iron.

YOGEV, Gedalia. Diamond and Coral: Anglo-Dutch Jews and Eighteenth Century Trade. Leicester, Leicester U.P., 342p.

1914-1939

BRAHAM, Randolph L. The Jewish question in German-Hungarian relations during the Kallay era. Jewish Social Studies, 39, No. 3, Su. pp 183-208.

BROOK-SHEPHERD, Gordon. Anschluss: The Rape of Austria. N.e. Westport, Conn., Greenwood P.; London, Westport P., 222p.

FORNDRAN, Erhard and others. (Eds.) Innen-und Aussenpolitik unter Nationalsizialistischer Bedrohung. Determinanten internationaler Bezichungen in historischen Fallstudien. Opladen, Westdeutscher. 361p, Ind.

Foreign relations of the Third Reich including its opponents, allies, neutrals and the influence of foreign states on Nazi politicies. Separate articles deal with Austria and Czecho-slovakia.

GRELL, Heinz. (Ed.) Der Osterreich-Anschluss 1938, Zeitgeschichte im Bild. Leoni am Starnberger See, Druffel, 160p, Ill, M.

Right-wing publication recalling the Anschluss of Austria in 1938 through contemporary photographs and documents showing the "fulfillment of historical nostalgia in this reuniting of Germans on both sides of the border."

MICHAELIS, Meir. Il Conte Galeazzo Ciano di Cortellazzo qualle antesignano dell'asse roma-Berlino. Nuova Rivista Storica, 61, pp 116-49.
Ciano's pro-German line 1934-36, in the light of some unpublished documents.

MORELY, James William (Ed.) Deterrent Diplomacy. Japan, Germany and the USSR, 1935-1940. New York, London, Columbia U.P., ix, 376p. Ind, Bibl.

STADLER, Karl Rudolf, STEINER, Herbert, EXENBERGER, Herbert and MAIMANN, Helene. Österreicher im Elil 1934-1945. Linz, Kammer für Arbeiter und Angestellte für Oberösterreich, 40p, Ill.
Austrians who lived in exile from Nazism until 1945.

The Third Reich and Yugoslavia 1933-1945. Belgrade, Institute for Contemporary History. xv, 800p, Ind.
Reports presented at the Symposium on "The Third Reich and Yugoslavia 1933-1945" in Belgrade, October 1973. Many of the papers relate also to the Jews, especially "The Third Reich: Initiator, organizer and executant of anti-Jewish measures and Genocide in Yugoslavia" by Jasa Romano and Lavoslav Kadelburg.

1939-1945

ALMANSI, Dante. Attivita Svolta del Consiglio della Unione delle Communita Israelitiche Italiana dal 13 Novembre 1939 al 17 Novembre 1944. La Rassegna Mensile di Israel, 43, No. 10, O. pp 507-24.
The activities of the Council of the Union of Italian Jewish communities November 1939 to November 1944.

AMOUROUX, Henri. Quarante millions de petainistes (juin 1940-juin 1941) Paris, Laffont, 550p.
French collaboration with the Nazis.

BAUDOT, Marcel, BERNARD, Henri, BRUGMANS, Hendrick, FOOT, Michael R.D and JACOBSEN, Adolf. Encyclopedie de la guerre 1939-1945. Paris, Castermann, 440p, Ind, Ill, Bibl.
Concise encyclopaedia of World War II with a chapter on anti-semitism dealing also with the"final solution" and putting the number of Jewish victims between 4 million and 5,165,200.

BAUER, Riccardo. Peace, guerra e razzismo. La Rassegna Mensili di Israel, 43, Nos. 5-6, My-Ju. pp 179-90.

BUCK, Gerhard. (Ed.) Das Führerhauptquartier 1939-1945. Zeitgeschichte im Bild. N.e. Leoni am Starnberger See, Druffel, 160p, Ill.
The right-wing book on Hitler's General HQ.

ERICKSEN, Robert P. Theologian in the Third Reich: The Case of Gerhard Kittel. Journal of Contemporary History, 12, No. 3, Jy. pp 595-622.
The career of Gerhard Kittel, a German Protestant theologian whose anti-Semitic tendencies took shape only after the arrival of the Third Reich. Concludes with the contention that Kittel should not be condemned.

ESTI, Bela. (Ed.) Liberation of Hungary: Selected documents. Tr. K. Ravasz. London, Central, Books, xxx, 185p, Ill, M.
Includes the liberation of the Budapest ghetto.

GIBBONS, Robert. Allgemeine Richtlinien für die politische und wirtschaftliche Verwaltung der besetzten Ostbegiete. Vierteljahreshefte für Zeitgeschichte, 25, No. 2, pp 252-61.
Nazi measures for the political and economic administration of the occupied Eastern territories in World War II.

LIPMAN, Samuel. German Wartime Broadcasts. Commentary, 63, No. 3, Ma. pp 72-74.
Nazi antisemitic propaganda.

LUKACS, John. The Last European War, September 1939-December 1941. London, Routledge; Garden City, Doubleday, x, 562p, Ind, Ill.
The first phase of World War II, deals extensively with the Jews

NEUGEBAUER, Wolfgang. Politische Justiz in Österreich 1934-1945. Justiz und Zeitgeschichte, 1, pp 169-210.

PILZER, Jay Mervyn. The League of Nations and the Jewish Question. Ann Arbor, Mich., U. Microfilms, 252p, Bibl.
Ph.D. Dissertation, Duke University.

Polens Schuld am Zweiten Welkrieg. 1920-1939. Hamburg, Rudolf Trenkel, 96p, Ill.
Accuses Poland of being responsible for World War II.

POST-WAR
HISTORY

GOLDBERG, Harvey E. Rites and Riots: The Tripolitanian Pogrom of 1945. Plural Societies, 8, No. 1, Sp. pp 35-56.

JACOBMEYER, Wolfgang. Polnische Juden in der amerikanischen Besatzungszone Deutschlands 1946-47. Vierteljahrshefte für Zeitgeschichte. 25, No. 1, Ja. pp 120-36.
Survey of Polish Jews in the U.S. Zone of Germany 1946-47.

HOLOCAUST

ALPERT, Rebecca Trachtenberg. Survival Imperatives After the Holocaust. Reconstructionist, 43, No. 3, Ap. pp 7-10.

ARONSFLED, C.C. The Lies of Paul Rassinier. Jewish Affairs, 32, No. 12, D. pp 47-50.

--------------. The Path of Hate. Jewish Affairs, 32, No. 9, S. pp 73-78.

BARON, Lawrence. Surviving the Holocaust. Journal of Psychology and Judaism. 1, No. 1, Sp. pp 25-37.
"In contrast to Bruno Bettelheim's view on the concentration camp inmates 'identification with their oppressors, Terrence Des Pres' The Survivor focuses on the patterns of mutual aid and strategic compromise employed by prisoners in order to survive with a semblance of dignity in a dehumanizing environment Des Pres' analysis falters when he attributes survival behaviour to atavistic instinctual responses triggered by the constant danger of imminent death."

BETTELHEIM, Bruno. Le coeur conscient. Paris, Laffont, 384p, (Pluriel, Le Livre de Poche)
French edition of 'The Informed Heart' (1960) a psychological study of survival, based partly on the author's experience of concentration camps.

DACHSLAGER, Earl. The Holocaust as a "Subject". Sh'ma, 7, No. 11, N. pp 181-84.

The cheapest use of the Holocaust would be to have to defend its actual occurrence, yet, as we know, this is precisely something which we have had to do.

Dimensions of the Holocaust. Evanston, Ill., Northwestern U.P., 63p.

ECKHARDT, Alice and Roy. The theological and moral implications of the Holocaust. Christian Attitudes on Jews and Judaism, Nos. 52-53. pp 7-12.

Their view of what Christian attitudes should be to the Holocaust.

ECKSTEIN, Jerome. The Holocaust and Jewish Theology. Midstream, 23 No. 4, Ap. pp 36-45.

ELIAS, Joseph. Dealing with "Churban Europe". The Jewish Observer, 14, O. pp 10-18.

Reviews the ever-mounting popular and scholarly works on the Holocaust, highlighting the lessons to be learned and the pitfalls to be avoided.

EPSTEIN, Helen. Heirs of the Holocaust: The Lingering Legacy for Children of Survivors. The New York Times Magazine, 19 Ju. pp 12-15; 74-77.

The author, herself the daughter of survivors, reports on her discoveries of the impact of the Holocaust on the victims and their heirs.

FENELON, Fania. The Musicians of Auschwitz. London, Michael Joseph; New York, Athenaeum, ix, 262p.

The author, deported from France, was a member of the Birkenau orchestra set up by the Nazis who had to play while others were sent to the gas chambers.

FRIEDLANDER, Harry, HILBERG, Raul, WIESEL, Elie. The Holocaust: Three Views. ADL Bulletin, 33, No. 11, N. pp 1;4-6.

Excerpts of talks given at a three-day conference on teaching about genocide and the Nazi Holocaust.

GREENBERG, Irving. Holocaust: The Need to Remember. New York, Council of Jewish Federations and Welfare Funds, 26p. (Assembly Papers)

Address at the 46th General Assembly of the Council.

HILLEL, Marc. Les Archives de l'Espoir. Paris, Fayard, 257p.

Describes the work of the International Tracing Service in Arolsen, where on 42 million record cards, are kept records of deportees, either dead or still living.

HIRSCHFIELD, M. J. Care of the Aging Holocaust Survivor. American Journal of Nursing, Jy. pp 1187-89.

HUTNER, Yitzhok. Holocaust. The Jewish Observer, 24, No. 1, O. pp 4-9.

Examines the term and the tragic epoch it is meant to denote to Orthodox Jews.

The International Tracing Service. Concentration Camps Records of Service to Survivors. Geneva, International Committee of the Red Cross, 40p.

IRVING, David. Hitler's War. London, Hodder & Stoughton; New York, Viking P., xxxiii, 926p, Ind, M.

The author set out to show that Hitler was not as evil as previous historians claimed.

JACKEL, Eberhard. Hitler und der Mord an den europäischen Juden. Jüdischer Presse Dienst, Nos. 5-6, S. pp 13-14.
Hitler's personal responsibility for the murder of European Jews.

KANTER, Isaac. Social Psychiatry and the Holocaust. Journal of Psychology and Judaism, 1, No. 1, pp 55-56.

KATZ, Monique. The Central Tracing Agency of the ICRC. International Review of the Red Cross, 17, No. 199, O. pp 407-12.

KATZ, Robert. Halál a Katakombában (Death in Rome) Tr. D. Tandori. Budapest, Kossuth, 300p.
The shooting of Jews in the Ardaetine Caves.

KIMMEL, Eric A. Confronting the Ovens: The Holocaust and Juvenile Fiction. The Horn Book, 53, No. 1, pp 84-91.
The Holocaust must be made comprehensible lest it be forgotten and therefore repeated; yet writers of juvenile fiction also have responsibilities to avoid excessive violence and depression

KLARSFELD, Serge. (Ed.) Die Endlösung der Judenfrage in Frankreich. Deutsche Dokuments 1941-1944. Paris, Antler, 244p.
Maitre Klarsfeld edited this collection of documents on the Final Solution.

MELTZER, Milton. Never to Forget: The Jews of the Holocaust. New York, Dell, xvi, 217p, M.

MONTEFIORE, Alan. The Moral Philosopher's View on the Holocaust. European Judaism, 11, No, 2, Su. pp 13-23.

NICK, Ann L. Teachers' guide to the Holocaust. New York, ADL, 39p.

OSTERREICHER, John M. The Challenge of the Holocaust. America, 133, 11 Ju. pp 525-27.
A discussion of Auschwitz: Beginning of a New Era? a collection of papers given at the International Symposium on the Holocaust, held at the Cathedral of St. John The Divine, in New York City, 3-6 Ju. 1974

ORY, Pascal. Les Collaborateurs 1940-1945. Paris, Seuil, 316p.
Documentation of French collaboration with the Nazis.

PIERRARD, Pierre and KAPLAN, Jacob. Etre rabbin sous l'occupation. Rencontre, 11, No. 52, pp 181-95.
Chief Rabbi Kaplan under Nazi occupation, first in Vichy, then in Lyon.

RANZ, John. The Relevance of the Holocaust: Misconceptions and Truths. Israel Horizons, 25, No. 10, Fa/W. pp 23-25; Jewish Frontier, 44, No. 4, Ap. pp 11-14.
The roots of our misconceptions of the Holocaust, particularly among survivors, stems from their not having been politically informed or active before the War.

REICHEK, Mortan A. The Savage World of Marcel Ophuls: The Holocaust, Algeria, Vietnam. Present Tense, 4, Aut. pp 52-57.
Reviews his film The Memory of Justice acclaimed as a masterpiece. It has also been strongly attacked by Jewish critics, disturbed by the film's failure to focus on Jewish suffering under the Nazis, a tendency to suggest equivalence between the Holocaust and postwar atrocities like Vietnam.

ROSENSAFT, Menachem. The Holocaust: History as Aberration. Midstream 28, No. 5, My. pp 53-55.

SZAJKOWSKI, Zosa. An Illustrated Sourcebook on the Holocaust. New York, Ktav, 155p.

WYSCHOGROD, Michael. Auschwitz: Beginning of a New Era? Reflections on the Holocaust. Tradition, 16, No. 5, Fa. pp 63-78.
Critique of the views of Dr. Irving Greenberg on the role of the Holocaust in Jewish theology.

PERSECUTION

BILLIG, Joseph. La solution finale de la question Juive. Essai sur ses principes dans le IIIe Reich et en France sous l'occupation. Paris, Serge & Beate Klarsfeld, 207p, Bibl.

BRAHAM, Randolph L. The Hungarian Labor Service System 1939-1945. New York, London, Columbia U.P., x, 159p, Ind, Bibl. (East European Monographs 31)
Professor Braham made a special study of the forced labour system in which tens of thousands of Hungarian Jews perished, using documents and interviews with survivors.

DAVIDOWICZ, Lucy. The War Against Jews 1933-1945. Harmondsworth, Pelican, 552p.
Paperback edition of her major work.

DOBOSIEWICA, Stanislaw. Mauthausen Gusen - oboz zaglady. Warszawa: Ministerstwo Obrony narodowej. 452p.
Polish work on the death camps of Mauthausen/Gusen.

DURAND, Pierre. Les armes de l'espoir. Les Francais a Buchenwald et a Dora. Paris, Eds. Sociales, 318p.
French prisoners, including Jews, in the two camps.

KENEZ, Peter. White Pogroms in the Ukraine, 1919. The Wiener Library Bulletin, 30, Nos. 41-44, pp 2-7.

RICHMAN, Leon. Why? Extermination Camp Lwow. (Lemberg) 134 Janowska Street, Poland. New York, Sepher Hermon, 273p.

Sachsenhausen: Dokumente, Aussagen, Froschungsergebnisse und Erlebnisberichte über das ehemalige Konzentrationslager Sachsenhausen. VEB Deutscher V. der Wissenschaften Berlin, 155p, Ill, M.

SCHRAMM, Hanna. Menschen in Gurs. Erinnerungen an ein französisches Internierungslager (1940-1941) Mit einer Dokumentation zur französischen Emigrantenpolitik von Barbara Vormeier. Worms, Georg Heintz; 384p. (Deutsches Exil, 13) French ed: Paris, Maspero.
Memoirs of a French concentration camp with an essay on French policy on refugees from Nazi Germany after 1933.

SKOCHOVA, Jarmila. Büchlein über die kleine Festung Theresienstadt, Prague, Nase vojsko.
Little book on Theresienstadt.

SUZMAN, Arthur and DIAMOND, Denis. Six Million Did Die. The Truth Shall Prevail. Johannesburg, South African Jewish Board of Deputies, xiii, 119p, Ill.
Documents and material to refute the attempt to deny the Nazi guilt of exterminating the six million Jews.

TREGENZA, Michael. Belzec Death Camp. The Wiener Library Bulletin, 30, Nos. 41-42, pp 8-24.

TRUBAKOV, Zachar. Viazoi mir hobn zich geratevet funem Babi Yar. (How we escaped Babi Yar) Sovietish Heimland, 17, No. 6, Ju. pp 83-117.
Eyewitness account of the massacre at Babi Yar.

WOLOWSKI, Alexandre. La vie quotidienne a Varsovie - sous l'occupation Nazie. Paris, Hachette, 370p.

ZAOUI, Andre. A Rome en juin 1944. Les Nouveaux Cahiers, 13, No 49, p27

RESCUE

BAUER, Yehuda. "Onkel Saly" - die Verhandlungen des Saly Mayer zur Rettung der Juden 1944-1945. Vierteljahrshefte für Zeitgeschichte, 25, No. 2, pp 188-219.
Mayer was the "Joint" representative in Switzerland during the war and engaged in the rescue of Jews from occupied countries.

BELYAEV, Vladimir. Der Mirtopolit Andrei Sheptitsky un der Rov Dovid Kahane. (The Metropolitan Andrei Sheptitsky and Rabbi David Kahane) Sovietish Heimland, 17, No. 12, D. pp 3-13.
In his description of experiences on the liberation of Cracow, recounts that the Metropolitan saved a rabbi from the Nazis and that the Rabbi, a Zionist, emigrated to Israel and was, at the time of writing, Chief Rabbi of Buenos Aires. Both the Metropolitan and the Rabbi are accused of collaboration with the Nazis.

COHEN, Albert and ASSA, Anri. Saving the Jews in Bulgaria, 1941-44. Sofia, State Publishing House "Septemvir" Prepared jointly with the Central Board of the Public Cultural and Educational Organisation of Jews in Bulgaria. (Originally published in Bulgarian) Ill.
This album reproduces part of the materials of the permanent exhibition on the experiences of Bulgarian Jewry during World War II - the only Jewish population in occupied Europe which survived as a whole in their own country.

DIRKS, G.E. Canada's Refugee Policy, Indifference or Opportunism? Montreal, McGill-Queen's University P., 316p, Ind, Bibl.
Relates to Canadian attitudes to the plight of refugees from Nazi-occupied Europe.

DRUKS, Herbert. The Failure to Rescue. New York, Robert Speller & Sons, ix, 108p, Ind, Bibl.
Documentary sutdy of US and UK governmental policies resulting in the failure to rescue Jews from Nazi persecution, partly based on the Archives of the World Jewish Congress.

FOOT, M.R.D. Resistance: An Analysis of European Resistance to Nazism. N.e. 1940-1945. London, Paladin, xx, 346p, Ind, Bibl.
Comprehensive study of all forms of resistance to Hitler including the Jewish resistance inside and outside of Palestine.

VOGEL, Rolf. Ein Stempel hat gefehlt. München, Droemer Knaur, 367p, Ind.
Documented study on the rescue attempts to save German Jewry before the outbreak of World War II.

WAR CRIMES

ALLEN, Charles R. Jr. Obstacles to Nazi-Hunting: USA. Jewish Currents, 31, No. 4, Ap. pp 35-40.
On the Nazi criminals who escaped to the USA.

--------------------. Odyssey of a Nazi Collaborator. Jewish Currents, 31, No. 11, D. pp 4-18.
A Nazi who escaped to the U.S.A.

ARONSFELD, C.C. The Extermination of the Jews was no "War Crime" Jewish Frontier, 44, No, 7, Au-S. pp 18-19.

BOLLE, Pierre Henri. La Suisse et l'imprescriptibilite des crimes de guerre et des crimes contre l'humanite. Schweizeriche

Zeitschrift für Strafrecht - Revue Penale Suisse, No. 2, pp 224-40.
Switzerland and the statute of limitations on War crimes and crimes against humanity.

DAN, Uri. The Eichmann Syndrome. New York, Leisure Books, 251p.
The effect of the Eichmann trial on young Israelis.

DRUKS, Herbert. Belated Hunt for Nazi criminals in America. The American Zionist, 67, No. 6, F. pp 9-12.

DUMAS, Francois Ribadeau. Les Danmes de Nüremberg, ou les possedes du Nazisme. Paris, Pierre Belfond, 314p, Ill.
By analysing the testimonies of the twelve major war criminals tried at Nuremberg, the author tries to answer the question whether the diabolic origins of Nazism have really been revealed in Nuremberg.

GEROSA, Guido. Il caso Kappler. Dalle Ardeatine a Soltau. Milan, Sonzogno, 206p, Ill.
Herbert Kappler was convicted to life imprisonment for crimes committed by him in Italy and was smuggled out of prison hospital in August 1977.

GETLEIN, Frank. Return of the Native. Commonweal, 10, 16 S. pp 580-82.
The recent escape of Herbert Kappler and war criminals in general.

GILBERT, Gustave M. Nürnberger Tagebuch. Gespräche der Angeklagten mit dem Gerichtspychologen. Hamberg, Fischers, 456p, Ind,
Conversations with the accused at Nuremberg conducted by the psychologist appointed by the Court.

HAREL, Isser. Kuca u ulici Garibaldi (uzbudljiva prica bivseg sefa izraelske tajne sluzbe sigurnosti o havtanju Adolfa Eichmana) Zagred, Prosvjeta, 320p.
Serbo-croatian edition of the author's book on the capture of Adolf Eichmann.

HAUSNER, Gideon. Justice in Jerusalem. New York, Schocken, 560p,Ill
American edition of the Israeli prosecutor's book on the Eichmann trial.

KARSAI, Elek. Itél a nép. Budapest, Kossuth, 296p, Ill. (Népszerú Tórtenelem, 5)
In "Verdict of the People" Dr. Karsai documents the trials of the major Hungarian war criminals using also hitherto unpublished material. The book is part of a series designed for the younger generation who know little or nothing about the Nazi era.

KLAIDMAN, Stephen. The Nazi Hunters, Justice, Not Vengeance. Present Tense, 4, No. 2, W. pp 21-26.

MASER, Werner. Nürnberg, Tribunal der Sieger. Wien, Düsseldorf, Econ, 702p, Ind, Ill, Bibl.
Hitler's biographer has researched for 25 years to produce this critical study of the international Military Tribunal. He claims that the trial was conducted along the lines of Anglo-Saxon law unfamiliar to the accused and to the defending counsel

PODGORECZNY, Marian. Albert Forster - gauleiter i oskarzony. (Albert Forster - le gauleiter et l'assuse) Gdansk, Ed. Maritimes, 436p, Ill.
Life and activities of the Gestapo chief in Gdansk and Pomerania the trial before a Polish tribunal ending in a death sentence.

RUCKERL. Adalbert. Nationalsozialistische Vernichtungslager im Spiegel deutscher Strafprozesse. Belzec, Sobibor, Treblinka, Chelmno. With a foreword by Martin Broszat. Stuttgart, DTV, 359p, Ind, Bibl. M.

The extermination camps of Belsec, Sobibor, Treblinka and Chelmno in light of the German trials.

SAUER, Karl. Die Berbrechen der Waffen-SS. Eine Dokumentation. Frankfurt/M., Röderberg, 88p.

SCHWARTZ, Martin. The Search for Nazis in America. Jewish Digest, 22, No. 9, My. pp 3-6. Condensed from The Jewish World.

SEGRE, Augusto. L'inutile fuga di Kappler. La Rassegna Mensile di Israel, 43, Nos. 7-8, Jy-Au. pp 315-28.

On the escape of the war criminal Kappler.

SELZER, Michael. The Murderous Mind. The New York Times Magazine, 27 N. pp 35; 111-17.

"Adolf Eichmann's psychological test drawings show that beneath his 'banal'exterior showed violent aggression, extreme anxiety and sadomasochism."

SERENY, Gitta. Into That Darkness: From Mercy Killing to Mass Murder. London, Picador, 380p, (Pan Books)

The concentration camp at Treblinka.

SMITH, Bradley F. Reaching Judgment at Nuremberg. London, Andre Deutsch; New York, Basic Books, xviii, 349p, Ind, Ill, Bibl. German ed: Frankfurt/M, Fischer.

SYDNOR, Charles W. Jr. Soldiers of Destruction: The SS Death's Head Division, 1933-1945. Princeton, N.J. Princeton U.P., xvi, 371p, Ind, Ill, Bibl. M.

Including their treatment of Jews.

SZULZ, Tad. A Nazi Hunter Takes on the Russians. New York, 19 D. pp 44-45.

Interview in Vienna with Simon Wiesenthal.

Das Urteil von Nüremburg 1946. 3.e. With a foreword by Lothar Gruchman. Münich, DTV, 306p, Ind.

The Waffen-SS. A History in 1115 Pictures. Brighton, Munin, 598p.Ill

WIESENTHAL, Simon. Why the Search for Nazis Must Go On. Jewish Digest, 23, No. 1, S. pp 83-88. Condensed from Canadian Zionist, 46, no. 5.

RESISTANCE

BERNARD, Henri. L'autre Allemagne, la resistance allemande a Hitler 1933-1945. Bruxelles, La Renaissance due Livre, 300p, Ind, Ill.

The German and Austrian resistance to Hitler and their contact with the resistance in Belgium.

CHICCO, Francesco. La Resistenza in Italia e in Europa. Torino, Paravia, 64p.

DILIO, Mario. Puglia antifascista. Bari, Adda, 316p,

Resistance in Puglia, Italy.

ECKMAN, Lester and LAZAR, Chaim. The Jewish Resistance: The History of the Jewish Partisans in Lithuania and White Russia during the Nazi Occupation, 1940-1945. New York, Shengold, 282p.

HAESTRUP, Jorgen. Secret Alliance: A Study of the Danish Resistance Movement 1940-1945. Odense, Odense, U.P. 1976-1977, 3 vols.

Includes the rescue of Danish Jews.

LIPSCHER, I. Jewish Participation in the Slovak Resistance Movement. Soviet Jewish Affairs, 7, No. 2, pp 40-42.
Of 140,000 Jews in Slovakia only 5,000 survived Nazi persecution. In 32 out of 46 partisan units 1,566 Jews served.

LOKER, Z. Radicalism, Heroism and Martyrdom in the Balkans. Jewish Quarterly Review, 68, No. 2, O. pp 104-16.
Jewish resistance in Yugoslovakia.

MILLER, David M. The Holocaust and Jewish Resistance. Jewish Currents, 31, No. 4, Ap. pp 15-19.

MOSCATI, Gianfranco. The Jews in the Fight Against Neofascism. Napoli, Author, 230p. (Mimeo)
Collection of documents, letters and stamps of the Holocaust.

RUBINSONOS, M. A heldisher kemfer kegn fashizm un reaktsie. Tsum 70-tn geburtstog fun Itsik Vitenberg. (A heroic fighter against fascism and reaction) Sovietish Heimland, 17, No. 4, Ap. pp 73-75.
Tribute to a Jewish underground fighter who fell in the Vilna ghetto.

SCHUDDEKOPF, Otto-ERnst. Der deutsche Widerstand gegen den Nationalsozialismus. Seine Darstellung in Lehrplänen und Schulbüchern der Fächer Geschichte und Politik in der Bundesrepublik Deutschland. Im Auftrag der Forschungsgemeinschaft 20 Juli. Frankfurt/M., Diesterweg, xiv, 55p.
Handbook for the teaching of German resistance.

SYRKIN, Marie. Blessed is the Match. The Story of the Jewish Resistance. N.e. Philadelphia, Jewish Publication Society of America, xviii, 366p.
A paperback edition.

The Warsaw Ghetto Uprising. New York, Congress for Jewish Culture,47p

INDIVIDUAL JEWISH COMMUNITIES

AFRICA

GITELSON, Susan Aurelia. A Guide to Africa South of the Sahara. New York, American Jewish Congress, World Jewish Congress, 38p, M.
Includes Jewish populations where they still exist and each country's relations with Israel.

ARAB COUNTRIES

GOLDMAN, Peter. (Ed.) Jøder og andre minoriteter i de arabiske lande Copenhagen,SDI, (In Danish)
Jews and other minorities in Arab countries.

GOUTALIER, M. Musulmans et juifs au Maghreb. In: L'idee de race dans la pensee politique francaise contemporaine. Paris, RS, pp 238-41.

SZONYI, David. The 'Other' Middle East Refugees. Jewish Digest, 23, No. 2, O. pp 13-15. Condensed from Jewish Student Press Service Features.
Jews from Arab countries.

ARGENTINA

BENGIO, Josef. Juifs d'Argentine: À la recherce d'une identité. Les Nouveaux Cahiers, 13, No. 48, Sp. pp 38-52.
Argentinian Jews in search of an identity.

BONO, Agostino. The troubled Jews of Argentina. Worldview, 20, No. 11, N. pp 10-13.
"Many Jewish leaders agree privately that government officials oppose anti-semitism but say that it exists in sectors of the police and military at a time when the government cannot afford deep divisions because of its self-styled 'dirty war' against the guerrillas."

LIEBMAN, Seymour B. Argentine Jewry: Ethnicity and Problems. Contemporary Jewry. Fa/W. pp 5-12.
"Apathy, anti-Semitism, disinterest, and radicalism may bring about a decimation of Argentine Jewry comparable to the toll taken by the Holocaust."

St. JOHN, Robert. The Most Southerly Jewish Congregation on Earth. Jewish Digest, 23, No. 1, S. pp 36-38.

SOFER, Eugene F. Argentinian Jewry: What Do We Need To Know? Interchange, 3, S. pp 1, 12-15.

---------------. Terror in Argentina. Jews Face New Dangers. Present Tense, 5, No. 1, Aut. pp 19-25.

TREASTER, Joseph B. Argentina: A State of Fear. The Atlantic Monthly, 32, No. 11, N. pp 16ff.
Recent political developments in Argentina and the current anti-semitic campaign.

AUSTRALIA

BRASCH, R. Australian Jews of Today. Sydney, Cassel, xiv, 233p, Ill.

ISRAEL, Alec. Australian Jewry: Fighting Against the Stream. Ammi No. 6, Ju. pp 8-9.

PORUSH, Israel. The House of Israel - A History of the Great Synagogue. Melbourne, Hawthorn P., 347p, Ill.

AUSTRIA

WERNER, Alfred. Forty Years After The Anschluss. Jewish Frontier, 44, No. 10, D. pp 21-24.
Visit to Austria.

BRAZIL

FRIEDLER, Egon. The Jews of Brazil. Jewish Digest, 22, No. 8, Ap. pp 67-70. Condensed from Israel Horizons, 24, No. 9,

BULGARIA

Annual V. 10. Sofia, Social Cultural, Educational Organisation of the Jews in the People's Republic of Bulgaria, Central Board, Publ. 1977, 271p, Ill.
Essays on the history of Bulgarian Jews.

VIDAS, Samuil. From the history of the Jewish Choir of the Capital (Sofia) Bolgarskaya Musica, No. 5, My. 4p.

CANADA

CHIEL, Arthur A. Manitoba Jewish History - Early Times. Jewish Historical Society of Canada, 1, No. 2, O. pp 55-74.

HAYES, Saul. Are Jews of Quebec an Endangered Species? Jewish Historical Society of Canada, 1, No. 1, Ap. pp 24-34. Congress Monthly, 44, No. 5, Ju. pp 11-13.
Versions of a Research Report, published by the Institute of Jewish Affairs.

KAYFETZ, Ben G. A Look at Jewish Canadiana. Jewish Historical Society of Canada, 1, No. 1, Ap. pp 35-42.

KORENBLUM, Toba. Quebec Separatism: Good or Bad for the Jews? Jewish Digest, 22, No. 6, F. pp 8-11. Condensed from The Canadian Jewish News.

MALKA, Victor. La grande peur des juifs du Quebec. L'Arche, 20, No. 238, Ja. pp 19-22.

PEREL, Shlomo. Quebec's Nationalist Movement and the Future of Its Jews. Israel Horizons, 25, No. 4, Ap. pp 23-28.

WEINFELD, Morton. The Jewish Question in Quebec. Midstream, 23, No. 8, O. pp 20-31.
The future of Jews after the victory of the Parti Quebecois in the provincial elections of November 1976.

WISSE, Ruth R. and COTLER, Irwin. Quebec's Jews: Caught in the Middle. Commentary, 64, No. 3, S. pp 55-59.

CANARY ISLANDS

BEINART, Haim. The Jews in the Canary Islands: A Re-Evaluation. Transactions of the Jewish Historical Society of England, 25, pp 48-86.

CARIBBEAN

MOSKIN, J. Robert. Lost Colony of the Caribbean. Present Tense, 5, No. 1, Aut. pp 7-10.
History and eventual disappearance of the Jewish community of St. Eustatius, a small island in the Caribbean.

CHINA

GLASSGOLD, Cook. The Last of the Jews in China. Jewish Digest, 22, No. 5, Ja. pp 74-76. Condensed from China and U.S.

CURACAO

ZUCKER, Norman and Naomi. Survivors on a Desert Island. "In Curacao, God knows what's going on." Present Tense, 4, No. 4, Su. pp 32-38.

CZECHOSLOVAKIA

SADEK, Vladimir. The Progress of the Restoration Work at the Old Jewish Cemetery in Prague. Judaica Bohemiae, 13, No. 1, pp 3-6.

DOMINICAN REPUBLIC

HOCHHAUSER, Jack. The Forgotten Colony of Sosua. Dominican Republic. Jewish Digest, 22, No. 4, D. pp 52-54. Condensed from "Westchester-Rockland Newspapers Feature."
The colony was founded by German Jewish refugees stranded there.

EGYPT

MIZRAHI, Maurice. L'Egypte et ses juifs: le temps revolue (XIXe et XXe siecles) Lausanne, Author, 267p, Bibl.
Egyptian Jewry in the 19th and 20th Centuries.

ETHOPIA

SHERMAN, Arnold. Rahamim. A Falasha Odyssey. American Zionist, 68, No. 1, O. pp 24-26.

FRANCE

COHEN, D. Les cimetières juifs de Marseille. Marseille, No. 108, pp 78-86.
History of Jewish cemeteries from 1783.
--------. L'image du juif dans la société française en 1843 (d'après les rapports des préfets) Revue des Etudes juives, 136, Nos. 1-2, pp 163-69.
Jews in France in 1843 as presented to the Minister of Interior by prefects, showing the effects of emancipation.
DERCZANSKY, Alex. Le creuset francais. Les Nouveaux Cahiers, 13, No. 50, Aut. pp 11-13.
The Jewish vote in France.
DEUTSCH, Emeric. Qui sont les juifs de France. L'Arche, 12, No. 241 Ap. pp 33-36.
Demographic picture of French Jewry.
DOSSAT, Y. Les Juifs à Toulouse: un demi-siècle d'histoire communautaire. Cahiers de Fanjeaux, No. 12, pp 117-39.
History of the second largest Jewish community in the South of France.
French Jewry in the City. Encounter Today, 12, Nos. 1-2, W/Sp. pp 24-28.
HILDESHEIMER, F. Negociants - juifs à Marseille au XVIII siècle. Archives Juives, 13, No. 1, pp 11-18.
It appears that despite numerous documents, there were only few Jews in 18th century Marseilles.
ISRAEL, Gerard. Regards sur une histoire. Les Nouveaux Cahiers, 13, No. 50, Aut. pp 3-7.
French Jewish history.
KRIEGEL, Annie. Le project communautaire. Les Nouveaux Cahiers, 12, No. 50, Aut. pp 14-17.
French Jewish communal life.
LERCH, D. and RAPHAEL, Freddy. Le colportage juif en Alsace au XIX siecle. Revue des Sciences Sociales de la France de L'est. 7, Special Issue. pp 102-19.
Jewish peddlars in 19th century France.
POUGATCH, Isaac. Les Juifs de France. Paris, 128p, Bibl.

RANGER, Jean, et al. Les élections à Paris de 1965 á 1977. Structures urbaines et géographie électorale. Revue Francaise de Science Politique, 27, No. 6, S. pp 789-959.
Six articles on the influence of demographic distribution of ethnic groups on elections in France.

RAPHAEL, Freddy. Stéréotype du juif dans un village D'Alsace en 1976 Revue des Sciences Sociales de la France de l'Est. Special Issue, pp 142-53.

ROTHSCHILD, David de. French Jewry: Part of the Jewish People: Address at the 46th General Assembly, Dallas, 9-13 N. 1977. New york, Council of Jewish Federations, 4p (Assembly Papers)

TAPIA, Claude. Propositions méthodologiques pour l'etude des comportements religieux. Communautes et pratiques religieuses dans le judaïsme francais. Archives des Sciences Sociales des Religions 44, No. 1, pp 93-101.
Survey among North African Jews who settled in the Paris region.

-------------. and GDALIA, Janine. Politisation des juifs de France Les Nouveaux Cahiers, 12, No. 50, Aut. pp 18-26.

VICAIRE, Marie-Humbert and BLUMENKRANZ, Bernard. Juifs et Judaisme en Languedoc. XIIIe siècle-début XIVe siècle. Paris, Commission Francaise des Archives Juives, 422p, Ind, Ill. (Collection France-Judaica 6)
Illustrated, documented history of the Jews of Languedoc in the 13th and 14th centuries.

WEINBERG, David H. Community on Trial: Jews of Paris, in the 1930s. Chicago, London, U. of Chicago P., xvi, 239p, Ind, Bibl.
Examines the Jews in the second largest community between 1933 and 1939. Discusses i.a. the attitude of Parisian Jews to the World Jewish Congress.

WEYL, R. and RAPHAEL, F. Organisation civile et religieuse des Juifs en Alsace (1648-1793). Revue des Sciences Sociales de la France de l'Est. No. 6, pp 73-99.
The secular and religious organisation of Jews in Alsace 1648-1793)

GERMANY

BARLEV, Jehuda. Juden und jüdische Gemeinde in Güterslah 1671-1943. Gütersloh, Stadt Gütersloh Kulturamt, 105p, Ill.
History of the Jews in Gu"tersloh from the late seventeenth century to the destruction of the community.

GRAUPE, Heinz Mosche. Die Entstehung des modernen Judentums: Geistesgeschichte der deutschen Juden, 1650-1942. N.e. Hamburg, H. Buske, 380p.
Spiritual history of German Jewry 1650-1942.

GRUNWALD, Kurt. Three chapters of German-Jewish Banking History. pp 191-208. Offprint from Yearbook of the Leo Baeck Institute, 21.

LIEBESCHÜTZ, Hans and PAUCKER, Arnold. (Eds.) Das Judentum in der Deutschen Umwelt 1800-1850. Studien zur Frühgeschichte der Emanzipation. Tübingen, J.C.B. Mohr, xii, 448p. Ind, Bibl. (Schriftenreihe Wissenschaftlicher Abhandlungen des Leo Baeck Instututs 35)
Fourth volume of series of studies on German Jewry between Emancipation and Nazism. Studies in this volume are:

Jews and German Environment in the Age of Restoration by Hans Liebeschutz. German Jews and the Process of Secularization in Education by Julius Carlebach. Late Nationalism in German Political Thought of the 19th century by G. Schulz. The Entry of Jews into the Bourgeoisie by J. Toury. Ludwig Phillippson and the Allgemeine Zeitung des Judentums by J. Phillippson. Samson Raphael Hirsch His Thought and Influence by P.E. Rosenblüth. Encounter of Germans and Jews in the Era of Romanticism by H. G. Reissner. The 1848 Revolution as an Internal Jewish Turning Point by J. Toury.

MELICHAR, E. Zur Rechtsstellung des Wahlausschusses einer Israelitischen Kultusgemeinde. Österreichisches Archiv für Kirchenrecht. 28, Nos. 1-2, pp 99-101.

Explains the individual status of the Jewish community in the light of a constitutional court judgement of 29th January 1977.

SEIVERS, Leo. Juden in Deutschland. Die Geschichte einer 2000 Jährigen Tragödie. Hamburg, Stern, 282p, Ind. Bibl. Ill. (Ein Sterm Buch)

First published in the form of a series of articles published in Stern magazine.

VOGEL, Rolf. Ein Stück von uns 1813-1976. Deutsche Juden in deutschen Armeen. Mit einem Vorwort von Verteidigungsminister Georg Leber, Mains, Hase und Köhler, 2.e. 400p, Ind.

Documentary on the participation of Jews in the German Army.

ZIMMERMAN, Moshe. Zwischen deutschen Nationalismus und hamburgischem Patriotismus. Die Juden in Hamburg 1930-1965. Hamburg, Hans Christian. (Hamburger Beiträge zur Geschichte der deutschen Juden, 6) 266p.

GERMAN DEMOCRATIC REPUBLIC

KIRCHNER, Peter. The Jewish Community in the Capital of the GDR. European Judaism, 11, No. 1, W. pp 14-15.

GREECE

BARZILA, Esther. De Diable blue. Les Nouveaux Cahiers, No. 49, pp 61-73.

Memoirs of a Salonika Jewish woman on Jewish life in Greece in the 1930s.

HUNGARY

CHERNUSH, AKosh. Hungary's Jewish Renaissance. The National Jewish Monthly, 91, No. 6, F. pp 16-24.

Official slogans notwithstanding, Jewish identity and a re-examination of the Jewish past are popular literary themes.

INDIA

LORD, James Henry. Jews in India and the Far East. Westport, Conn., Greenwood P; London, Westport P., iii, 137p.

Facsimile of the 1907 edition.

ORIN, Yosefa Bat. Odyssey through Jewish India. Ammi, No. 6, Ju. pp 1-4.

WALLACH, Michael. Where Caste Once Ruled. On the ancient and exotic Jewish community of Cochin. Jewish Chronicle, Colour Magazine, S. pp 20-26.

ZIEGLER, M. Ancient Jewish Settlement in India. Jewish Frontier, 44, No. 5, Ju-Jy. pp 26-27.

IRAQ

KHAZOUM, Eliahu. An Arab View of the Jews of Iraq. Middle East Review, 9, No. 2, W. pp 31-36.

LUKS, Harold P. Iraqi Jews during World War II. The Wiener Library Bulletin, Nos. 43-44, pp 30-39.

ITALY

CANEPA, Andrew M. L'atteggiamento degli ebrei italiani davanti all loro seconda emancipazione: premesse e analisi. La Rassegna Mensile di Israel, 43, No. 9, S. pp 419-36.

The attitude of Italian Jews before their second emancipation - premises and analysis.

CHIUPPANI, Giovanni. Gli ebrei a Bassono. N.e. Bologna, A. Forni, 119p.

Reprint of a monograph of the Jews of Bassano, first published in 1906.

COLOMBO, Dino. Il Ghetto di Biella. La Rassegna Mensile di Israel. 43, Nos. 11-12, N.-D. pp 672-77.

LEDBEN, Michael. The Unknown Catacombs. Commentary, 64, No. 3, S. pp 64-66.

Newly discovered Jewish catacombs in Italy.

LUZZATTO, Aldo. L'Insediamento degli Ebrei in Peimonte Durante il Secolo XV. La Rassegna Mensile di Israel, 43, Nos. 5-6, My-Ju. pp 279-92.

The first Jewish settlements in 15th century Piedmont.

MICHAELIS, Meir. Riflessioni Sulla Recente Storia dell'Ebraismo Italiano. La Rassegna Mensile di Israel, 43, Nos. 5-6, My-Ju. pp 191-211.

MILANO, Attilio. Gli Ebrei in Italia nei Secoli XIe E XIIe. La Rassegna Mensile di Israel, 43, Nos. 11-12, N-D. pp 567-637.

PALMIERI-BILLIG, Lisa. Jews of Rome. Hadassah Magazine, 59, No. 10. O. pp 14-15, 35-38.

RAVENNA, Alfredo. Ricordi Pugliesi. La Rassegna Mensile di Israel, 43, Nos. 1-2, Ja.-F. pp 48-49.

STOCK, Mario. Il Posto della Risiera di Trieste nel Martirologio Ebraico. La Rassegna Mensile di Israel, 43, Nos. 7-8, Jy-Au. pp 376-78.

VITTA, Eduardo. L'apporto Culturale di Una Minoranza. La Rassegna Mensile di Israel, 43, Nos. 1-2, Ja-F. pp 3-11.

Instituto regionale Toscano di cultura ebraica - established in December 1976. Survey of Jewish culture in the region.

JAPAN

FREUND, Judith and William. A Minyan in Tokyo. Jewish Digest, 23, No. 1, S. pp 71-72. Condensed from The Light.

KENYA

ROSENBERG, Diana B. Nairobi Hebrew Congregation Archives. A descriptive list. Nairobi, 40p. (Mimeo)

LATIN AMERICA

ANCZELEWITS, Natalie. Vegn dem yiddishn yishuv in Latein-Amerike. (The Jews in Latin America). Sovietish Heimland, 17, No. 2, F. pp 162-68.

SCHERS, David and Hadassa. The Jewish Communities of Latin America: External and Internal Factors in their Development. Jewish Social Studies, 39, No. 3, pp 241-58.

"While trends of assimilation are strong and dominant, there are other factors, which may permit the majority of the Jewish population to preserve their Jewish identity despite widespread views to the contrary.

MEXICO

KOLACK, Shirley and Sol. The Ambiguous Status of Jews in Mexico. Conservative Judaism, 30, No. 4, Fa/W. pp 79-85.

The community's large investment in Jewish identity has not necessarily made committed Jews and the roots of Mexican citizenship are shallow. There is evidence that most young people are not strongly committed to or involved in Jewish communal affairs.

RUBENSTEIN, Robert E. Strangers Among Each Other: The Jews of Mexico City. The American Zionist, 67, No. 6, F. pp 18-20.

MOROCCO

MALKA, Victor. La politique juive du roi Hassan II. L'Arche, 20, No. 244, Jy. pp 28-29.

NETHERLANDS

FUKS, L. Oost-Joden in Nederland tussen beide wereldoorlogen. Studia Rosenthaliana, 11, No. 2, Jy. pp 198-215. (In Dutch)

There was a large influx of East European Jewish refugees in Holland, whose isolation resulted in a number of new organisations.

GANS, Mozes Heiman. Memorboek. History of Dutch Jewry from Renaissance to 1940. Baarn, Bosch and Keuning; London, George Prior, 850p, Ind, Ill, U.S. ed: New York, Abner Schram.

English edition of monumental historical work on Dutch Jewry, first published in Dutch in 1971.

KOEN, E.M. Notarial Records Relating to the Portuguese Jews in Amsterdam up to 1639. Studia Rosenthaliana, 11, No. 1, Ja. pp 81-96 and No. 2, Jy. pp 216-27.

LAANSMA, S. De Joodse gemeente te Zutphen. Zutphen, De Walburg P. 80p.
Monograph of a Dutch community.

TESTEMALLE, A. Mary. Amsterdam, la Jerusalen del Norte en tiempos de Baruj de Spinoza. El Olivo, No. 2, Ap. Ju. pp 35-42.

NORTH AFRICA

STILLMAN, Norman A. Recent North African Studies in Israel: A Review Article. International Journal of Middle East Studies, 8, No. 3, Jy. pp 405-7.

PANAMA

Kol Shearith Israel: a hundred years of Jewish life in Panama 1876-1976. Panama City, Centennial Book Committee, 487p. (English and Spanish)

PERU

ARONSFELD, C.C. In the Land of the Incas. Jewish Affairs, 32, No. 11 N. pp 38-41.
Jews in Peru.

POLAND

DOBROSZYCKI, Lucjan. A Photographic History of the Jews of Poland 1865-1939. New York, Schocken; YIVO Institute for Jewish Research, xviii, 269p, Ind, Ill, Bibl.

HELLER, Celia S. On the Edge of Destruction. Jews of Poland between the Two World Wars. New York, Columbia U.P., xi, 369p, Ind, Ill.

ROSENTHAL, David. Commemorating Warsaw Jewry. Jewish Frontier, 44, No. 4, Ap. pp 6-10.

Seyfer Laskarzew und Sobolew (The Book of Laskarzew and Sobolew) N.p. 714p.
A collection of articles and recollections of two 'shtetls' situated south of Warsaw on their history, everyday Jewish life and the Holocaust.

VINECOUR, Earl. Polish Jews: The Final Chapter. New York, McGraw Hill, 122p, Ill, Bibl.

PORTUGAL

STEINBERG, Harry. 59 Rua Alexandre Herculano. Present Tense, 4, No. 3, Sp. pp 9-12.
Jewish life in Lisbon (Portugal)

RHODESIA

GERBER, Israel J. The Jews of Rhodesia. Reconstructionist, 43, No. 2, Ma. pp 7-10.

ROMANIA

KIRSHBAUM, Mordecai. O, Rumania, Rumania. Jewish Veteran, 81, My-Ju pp 14-16.
Jewish life in Rumania during a visit on the High Holy Days.

KORN, Itzhak. With the Jews of Bucharest. Jewish Frontier, 44, No. 10, D. pp 24-26.
MALKA, Victor. Voyage En Roumanie. L'Arche, 20, No. 245, Au. pp 23.

SOUTH AFRICA

Agonizing Choice for South African Jews. Congress Monthly, 44, No. 9 D. pp 13-14.
ARKIN, Marcus. South Africa, its Jews and the Israel Connection. South Africa International, 8, No. 2, O. pp 83-90.
FELDBERG, Leon. (Ed.) South African Jewry 1976-77. A Survey of the Jewish Community: Its Contributions to South Africa; Directory of Communal Institutions and a Who's Who of Leading Personalities in Johannesburg. 560p, Ill.
MELAMET, Max. South Africa: Racial Problems and Jewish Reaction. Congress Monthly, 44, No. 2, F. pp 4-8.
MOSS, Rose. Return to South Africa. Some Care, Many Don't. Present Tense, 4, No. 2, W. pp 33-37.
Jewish attitude to apartheid.
What Future for South African Jews? Jewish Affairs, 32, No. 8, Au. pp 4-7.

SPAIN

DIEZ MERINO, L. El judaismo español en Al-Andalus a través del Primer Congreso de Historia de Andalucia (14-19 dic. 1976) Ciencia Tomista, 104, No. 2, pp 319-28.
Summarises the papers relating to Jews in Andalusia.
GORDON, Annabelle. Spain Today. Jewish Affairs, 32, No. 10, O. pp 29-31.
LACAVE, Jose Luis. Pleito judio por una herencia en aragones caracteres hebreos. Sefarad, 30, No. 2, pp 25-38.
Jews in Aragon.
LEWIS, Rose. Muslim Glamour and the Spanish Jews. Midstream, 23, No. 2, F. pp 26-37.
Jewish historians have too frequently bought into viewing Spanish Islamic tolerance toward the Jews. Some authors now see this as a ploy by Jewish scholars to have a stick with which to beat their Christian neighbours. There is a form of religious bigotry and anti-Semitism which is traditionally Arab: the envy and the violence,the assertive self-esteem, the deep need to dominate and to feel superior. This was present in Muslim Spain and continues to persist today in the Arab world.
MASJUAN, Carolina Nonell. Una antiqua sinagoga en Cifuentes. Wad-Al-Hayara, No. 4, pp 245-57.
An Ancient synagogue in Cifuentes.
ROMANO, David. Cementerios judios dé Lerida. Sefarad, 30, No. 2, pp 365-66.
Jewish cemeteries in Lerida (Spain)
SEPHIHA, Haim Vidal. Reviving Mediaeval Spanish Jewry. An Interview with ... Encounter Today, 12, No. 1-2, W/Sp. pp 16-19.
Spanish Jewry in 1977. Encounter Today, 12, Nos. 1-2, W/Sp. pp 29-31

SYRIA

MORTON, Michael. Syrian Jewry Today. Jewish Affairs, 32, No. 11, N. pp 17-19.

TUNISIA

LITTMAN, David. Quelques aspects de la condition de Dhimmi. Juifs d'Afrique du Nord avant la colonisation. (D'apres des documents de l'Alliance Israelite Universelle). Geneve, Centre de Documentation et d'information, 32p.

Nineteenth century Jews in the Maghreb.

UGANDA

ODED, Aryeh. 'Black Jews' of Uganda. Jewish Digest, 22, No. 9, My. pp 69-70. Condensed from Bi-Tfutzot Ha-Gola.

UNITED KINGDOM

The Second Conference on Jewish life in Modern Britain, London, 13th March, 1977. London, The Board of Deputies of British Jews. Institute of Jewish Affairs, 1 vol. (various pagings)

Discussion of various aspects of Anglo-Jewish society.

DAICHES, David. Glasgow. A vivid and illuminating portrait of a vigorous city. London, Andre Deutsch, xiv, 243p, Ind, Ill, M.

The book contains interesting information on Glasgow Jewry, past and present.

FISHER, Samuel. (Lord Fisher of Camden) British and American Jews: Comparisons. Congress Monthly, 41, No. 1, Ja. pp 9-11.

------------------------------------- Expectations. L'Eylah, 1, No. 4, Aut. pp 6-10.

On Anglo-Jewry.

GOLDWATER, Raymond. Anglo-Jewry in crisis. L'Eylah, 1, No. 3, Sp. pp 33-36.

GOULD, Julius. Jews in the British Establishment. Jewish Affairs, 32, No. 8, Au. pp 8-11; Jewish Digest, 22, No. 8, Au. pp 73-77.

GUTTENTAG, G.D. The Beginnings of the Newcastle Jewish Community. Transactions of the Jewish Historical Society of England, 25, pp 1-24.

Covers the period from the 17th century to 1880.

NEWMAN, Aubrey. Provincial Jewry in Victorian Britain: A Report. Transactions of the Jewish Historical Society of England, 25, pp 222-29.

Report of a Symposium.

SHAW, Paul. Gateshead: A Powerhouse of Judaism. A Unique Jewish Community and its Neighbour in Newcastle-upon-Tyne. Jewish Chronicle, Colour Magazine, S. pp 8-19.

U.S.A.

American Jewish Ephemera; a bicentennial exhibition from the Judaica collection of the Harvard College Library. Introductory lecture on impressions of Jewish daily life in the past one hundred years, by Oscar Handlin. Catalogue of the exhibition by Charles Berlin, Cambridge, Mass., Various Pagings.

APPELBAUM, Joy Zacharia. The history of the Jews of Teaneck. Teaneck, N.J. Author, 249p.

ARON, S. William. The Lower East Side is Dying. Jewish Digest, 22, No. 5, Ja. pp 77-80. Condensed from Jewish Student Press Service.

DANIELS, Doris Groshen. Colonial Jewry: Religion, Domestic and Social Relations. American Jewish Historical Quarterly, 66, No. 3, Ma. pp 375-400.

Presents a picture of the many faceted activities of New York Jewry in the Colonial period.

DUBROVSKY, Gertrude. Farmingdale: New Jersey: A Jewish Farming Community. American Jewish Historical Quarterly, 67, No. 2, Ju. pp 485-97.

EISENBERG, Azriel and GOODMAN, Hannah Grad. (Eds.) Eyewitness to American Jewish History: a history of American Jewry; Part Two The German Immigration 1800-1875. New York, Union of American Hebrew Congregations. 148p.

EVANS, Eli. Southern Jews and Baptists and Jimmy Carter. Jewish Digest, 22, No. 5, Ja. pp 58-61. Condensed from The New York Times.

FLUER, L. The Birth of the Jewish Lobby: A Renaissance. American Jewish Archives, 28, No. 2, N. pp 107-18.

The "Jewish Lobby" was created in the early '40s with the object of pressing the U.S. Government to rescue Jews from Nazi oppression.

GOLDSTEIN, Israel. The Role of American Rabbis in World Jewish Affairs. Zionism and the State of Israel. New York, Ktav, 116p.

Reprint from "The American Rabbi: A Tribute on the Occasion of the Bicentennial of the United States and the Ninety-Fifth Birthday of the New York Board of Rabbis." Edited by Gilbert S. Rosenthal.

GORDON, Suzanne. The Jews of San Francisco. Moment, 3, No. 5, pp 14-18;53-55.

GRINSTEIN, Hyman B. Rise of the Jewish Community of New York, 1654-1860. New York, Porcupine P.; London, Eurospan, xiii, 645p.

Facsimile of 1945 edition.

HANSEN, Niels. Der Einfluss ethnischer Minderheiten auf die Aussenpolitik der Vereinigten Staaten. Europa Archiv, 32, No. 17, S. pp 551-60.

Their quest for identification.

HERTZBERG, Arthur. The American Jewish Intelligentsia. Midstream, 23, No. 2, F. pp 45-46.

-----------------, and BAUM, Phil. The Credibility of the American Jewish Community. Congress Monthly, 44, No. 8, N. pp 4-5.

The refusal to face the real Jewish challenges.

HERTZBERG, S. Unsettled Jews:Geographic Mobility in a Nineteenth Century City. American Jewish Historical Quarterly, 62, No. 2, pp 125-39.

HOLLI, Melvin C. and JONES, Peter d'A. (Eds.) The Ethnic Frontier. Grand Rapide, Mich., Eardmans, 422p.

Writings about ethnic group survival and identity in Chicago and the Midwest includes an essay by Victor Greene on the role of the Jewish communal leaders, and one by Edward Mazur on the History of "Jewish Chicago" till 1940.

HORNUNG, Clarence P. The Way It Was: New York, 1850-1890. New York, Schocken,xi, 212p, Ill.
Includes the impact of the great wave of Jewish immigration.

Indiana Jewish Historical Society. 9th Publication. Fort Wayne,51p.
Contents: A Brief History of the Lafayette Orthodox Hebrew Free Loan Society by Chester E. Eisinger. Preface to the History of the Jewish People and a Sketch of the Jewish Congregation in the city of Muncie, Indiana by Alexander L. Schonfield. The American Heritage - Roots of Greatness by Joseph Levine.

LANDESMAN, Alter F. The History of New Lots, Brooklyn to 1887: Including the Villages of East New York, Cypress Hills and Brownsville. Port Washington, N.Y. Kennikat P., 258p.
A Jewish populated area.

LAVENDER, Abraham D. (Ed.) Coat of Many Colours: Jewish Subcommunities in the United States. Westport, Conn., Greenwood P.; London, Westport P., xii, 324p, Ind.
Essays on small Jewish community life in the USA.

-------------------. Shalom Y'all: Accent on Southern Jewry. Contemporary Jewry, 3, No. 1, Sp/Su. pp 37-53.
Describes some of the values basic to the Southern and Jewish subcultures.

LEVINSON, Robert E. Jews in the California Gold Rush. New York, Sepher Hermon.

LEWIS, Evelyn. The Jewish Vote: fact or fiction. Trends in Jewish voting behaviour. Ann Arbor, Mich. U. Microfilms, 172p.
Ph.D. Dissertation, Ball State University, Muncie, Indiana.

LIEBMAN, Charles S. American Jews: Still a Distinctive Group. Commentary, 64, No. 2, Au. pp 57-60.
"American Jews have not only transformed their environment in some instances, and resisted it in others, but have even remained utterly indifferent to it in areas that touch their deepest concerns and values as Jews. Therein, perhaps, lies some basis for a hope for distinctive Jewish survival."

MALLER, Allen S. Class Factors in the Jewish Vote. Jewish Social Studies, 39, No. 1, W/Sp. pp 159-62.
The May 1969 mayoral campaign in Los Angeles. The extent to which class factors may be operating to differentiate the standard Jewish voting pattern. Concludes that Jewish voting patterns remain unique but, Jews, too, react to issues in the context of their social structure.

MAYER, Egon and WAXMAN, Chaim I. Modern Jewish Orthodoxy in America. Toward the Year 2000. Tradition, 16, No. 3, Sp. pp 98-112.
Discusses a number of basic issues for the future of modern Orthodox Judaism in America.

MENENDEZ, Albert J. Religion at the Polls. Philadelphia. The Westminster P., 248p, Bibl.
Analyses the so-called religious vote, including the Jews in the USA and the specific issues that move members of religious groups to vote one way or another.

MILLER, Alan W. God of Daniel S.: In Search of the American Jew. New York, Dell, 245p.

MILLER, Randall M. and MARZIK, Thomas D. (Eds.) Immigrants and Religion in Urban America. Philadelphia, Temple U.P., xxii, 170p.
Includes: Western Impact on East European Jews: A Philadelphia

fragment by Maxwell Whiteman.
POLNER, Murray. Rabbi: The American Experience. New York. Holt, Rinehart and Winston, 244p.
RAVITCH, Diane. Brouhaha in Brooklyn: Is Anti-CIA Hysteria Turning into McCarthyism of the Left? The New Republic, 176, 12 Ma. pp 18-21.
The case of Michael Seltzer, assistant professor of political science at Brooklyn College, whose colleagues voted overwhelmingly in January to ask the college president to dismi-s him because of his involvement with the CIA.
RICHIN, Moses. The Promised City: New York's Jews. 1870-1914. N.e. Cambridge, Mass, Harvard U.P., xv, 342p, Ind, Ill. (Harvard Paperback)
Work first published in 1962, identifying the currents of humour and institutional vitality that converged on the Lower East Side of New York.
ROSENTHAL, Gilbert S. The American Rabbi. New York, Ktav, x, 200p.
A tribute on the occasion of the Bicentennial of the United States and the Ninety-fifth Birthday of the New York Board of Rabbis.
RUBIN, Ronald. Brooklyn's Hasidim: The Yiddish Connection. New York 28 Ma. pp 7-8.
RUZIN, Robert H. The Jewish Farmer and the Small-Town Jewish Community: Schoharie Country, New York. American Jewish Archives, 29, No. 1, Ap. pp 3-21.
Efforts of a group of American Jews living in a rural environment, without sacrificing their Jewish identity.
SCULT, Melvin. Mordecai M. Kaplan:Challenges and Conflicts in the Twenties. American Jewish Historical Quarterly, 66, No. 3, Ma. pp 401-6.
Studying the reactions to Kaplan's challenges reveals much about the tensions within the Jewish community at that time.
STEIN, Leon. (Ed.) Out of the Sweatshop. The Struggle for Industrial Democracy. New York, Quadrangle, 367p.
Essays on the struggle for improved conditions for immigrants, among them Jews.
SZONYI, David. American Jewish Community. What Happened When the PLO Came to Town. Interchange, 2, No. 5, Ja. pp 5-8.
Time of Renewal for U.S. Churches. U.S. News and World Report. Special Section, 11 Ap. pp 54-72.
Includes: Judaism: Ancient Faith Looks to a New Kind of Challenge.
WAGNER, Stanley M. (Ed.) Traditions of the American Jew. New York, Ktav ,161p.
WARSHAW, Mal. Tradition: Orthodox Jewish Life in America. New York, Schocken, 144p, Ill.
WEISS-ROSMARIN, Trude. The Cultural Tradition of the American Jew. Jewish Spectator, 42, No. 3, Fa. pp 3-10.
WIERNIK, Peter. History of the Jews in America. New York, Sepher Hermon. (Reprint)
WOLPIN, Nisson. Who's Saving American Jewry. The Jewish Observer, 13, D. pp 3-7.
"The Orthodox community can, to the best of its ability,

devote its resources to strengthening its own members while reaching out to others."

USSR

ALTSHULER, Mordecai. La culture juive en Géorgie. Istina, 22, Nos. 3-4, Jy-D. pp 411-31.
Describes the Jewish community in Georgia after the establishment of the Soviet regime in 1921: the schools, synagogues, the Jewish library in Tiflis, the committee of assistance to Georgian Jews, and the historical and ethnographical museum.

BARON, Salo. Jews under the Tsars and Soviets. 2.e. New York, London, Macmillan, xvii, 468p, Ind.
An updated edition of a classic work by one of the Jewish people's most prominent historians.

BLEICH, David J. Jews in Russia Today: Fact and Fiction. The Jewish Observer, 13, No. 3, D. pp 8-10.
Report on Russian Jews based on a 'three-week visit involving extensive and unsupervised contact with Jews of all walks of life."

FISHBANE, Michael. The Jews of Russia and Poland: Recollections of a Journey. Midstream, 23, No. 7, Au-S. pp 41-49.

GORSHMAN, Shira. A raize kein lite un kein veissrussland. (Travels in Lithuania and Belorussia). Sovietish Heimland, 17, No. 2, F. pp 3-42.

ILLES, Béla. Kárpáti rapszodia. (Carpathian Rhapsody) Mora, Diakkönyvtar. 572p.
Autobiographical novel by Illes who was born in Berehovo, Carpatho-Russania later Hungary, then Czechoslovakia and after World War II Soviet Union. The novel was written in Moscow 1937-39 when the author had been living there since his deportation from Czechoslovakia after the fall of the Proletarian Dictatorship.

PATTERSON, Jose. The Diary of a Long Weekend in Moscow. B'nai B'rith Journal, Sp. pp 4-5;12.

SOBOL, Richard. Faces of Soviet Jewry: A Photo-essay. The National Jewish Monthly, 92, No. 4, D. pp 4-7.

TSHERNOWITS, 1976. Sovietish Heimland, 17, No. 3, Ma. pp 3-12.
Report on the life of Jews in Tchernowicz.

YUGOSLAVIA

MELNICK, Norman. Dubrovnik. Present Tense, 4, No. 4, Su. pp 10-11.
Photos and article on the local synagogue and tiny community.

ROTBART, Vladislav. Novosadski Jevreji U Ratu I Revoluciji. Jevrejski Pregled, 28, Nos. 3-4, Ma-Ap. pp 15-17.
The Jews of Novi Sad in war and revolution.

MISCELLANEOUS

GRAND, Samuel and Tamar. Jews in Distant Lands. Ed. by Daniel Syme and designed by Martin Gordon and Ralph David. New York, Union of American Hebrew Congregations, 63p, Teachers' Guide.

JEWISH ORGANISATIONS

Proceedings of the American Jewish Committee. Seventieth Anniversary meeting. 13-16 May 1976. Washington, New York, 149p.

Dossiers du mois: Le Conseil Général du C.J.M.

- Une nouvelle prise de conscience, discours de Nahum Goldmann.
- Raduire la méfiance, discours du président Carter.
- Résolutions du Conseil Général.

Regards, 13, No. 116, D. pp 7-19.

Report of the World Jewish Congress, General Council, November 1977, Washington, DC.

COHEN, Stuart A. The Conquest of a Community? The Zionists and the Board of Deputies in 1917. Jewish Journal of Sociology, 19, No. 2, D. pp 157-184.

COLE, Diane. 39 Hours - The Siege Remembered. The National Jewish Monthly, 91, No. 9, My. pp 6-15.

The attack on B'nai B'rith headquarters in Washington, DC.

Conference of Presidents of Major American Jewish Organisations. Report for the Year ending March 31. New York, 32p, Ill.

La charte du C.R.I.F. Les Nouveaux Cahiers, 12, No. 50, Aut. pp 8-10.

Diamond Jubilee Canadian Hadassah - WIZO, 1917-1977. (Sixtieth Convention held in Jerusalem) 1977, Montreal, 59p, Ill.

DUNKER, Ulrich. Der Reichsbund jüdischer Frontsoldaten 1919-1938. Geschichte eines jüdischen Abwehrvereins. Düsseldorf, Droste, 354p Bibl.

The Federation of Jewish Veterans was one of the major Jewish organisations in Germany which, during the Hitler regime, fought against antisemitism.

GILDESGAME, Pierre. Maccabi Past and Present: A survey and summary for the information of leaders and members of the largest Jewish Youth Movement. London, 14p.

GOLDIN, Milton. Plaques and flattery will get you nowhere. Present Tense, 4, No. 3, Sp. pp 25-28.

On Jewish fundraising in America.

--------------. The UJA: Losing its appeal? Interchange, 2, No. 8, Ap. pp 1;6-8.

Fundraising erodes Jewish communal life.

KING. Sandra, KLEINROCK, Stella S., ROKAW, Irene, STECKEL, Julie and WASSERMAN, Harry. The Havurah Experience. Reconstructionist, 43, No. 4, My. pp 15-19.

MANOR, Y., SHEFFER, G. United Jewish Appeal. ou la metamorphose du don. Revue Francaise des Sociologie, 18, No. 1, pp 3-34.

Sociological study of the American United Jewish Appeal, originally a philanthropic institution which later enabled the donors to achieve pride, social status and personal satisfaction

Moment Interviews Alex Schindler. By the Presidents: He's a President. Moment, 2, No. 5, F-Ma. pp 14-17.

President of the Conference of Presidents of Major American Jewish Organisations.

NEWMAN, Aubrey. The United Synagogue 1870-1970. London, Henley, Boston, Routledge & Kegan Paul, xv, 240p, Ind, Ill, M.

History of one of Britain's most important Jewish institutions on the occasion of its centenary.

SHAROT, Stephen. Intrumental and Expressive Elites in a Religious Organization. The United Synagogue in London. Archives des Sciences Sociales des Religions,43, No. 1, pp 141-55.

SHERER, Moshe. What is Federation Doing with the Jewish Charity Dollar? The Jewish Observer, 13, F-Ma. pp 4-6.
Calls for a special commission of distinguished Jews, to throroughly publicaly air Federation policies and priorities.

Synagogue council of America. The American Jewish Experience: Excerpts from the celebration of the Bicentennial of the American Revolution and the Jubilee Anniversary of the Synagogue Council of America. New York, 40p.

TOBIAS, H.J. and WOODHOUSE, C.E. Political Reaction and Revolutionary Careers: The Jewish Bundists in Defeat 1907-10. Comparative Studies in Society and History, 19, No. 3, pp 467-96.
The reasons for the failure of the Bund after 1905.

WEISS-ROSMARIN, Trude. The National Foundation for Jewish Culture. Jewish Spectator, 42, No. 1, Sp. pp 5-9.

World Jewish Congress. Office of the Secretary General. Activities of the World Jewish Congress, February 1975 - October 1977. Report of the Secretary General to the General Council of the World Jewish Congress at its Meeting in Washington, 30 October - 3 November, Geneva, 55p.

SEPHARDI AND ORIENTAL JEWS

BARNETT, Richard D. Diplomatic Aspects of the Sephardic Influx from Portugal in the Early Eighteenth Century. Transactions of the Jewish Historical Society of England, 25, pp 210-21.
Immigration of "New Christians" before 1720.

FAUR, J. Sephardim in the Nineteenth Century: New directions and old values. Proceedings of the American Academy of Jewish Research 44, pp 53-80.
Jewish identity was very important in multi-national Yugoslavia.

HECHT, Abraham B. Is There a New Wind Blowing on the Sephardi Horizon? Jewish Frontier, 44, No, 5, Ju-Jy. pp 23-24.
The social and economic status of Sephardic Jews seems to improve.

MALINO, Frances. The Sephardic Jews of Bordeaux. U. of Alabama P., viii, 166p, (Judaic Studies 7)

MATHEWS, R. Israel's Oriental Jews: prejudices remain. Middle East, No. 32, Ju. pp 57-60.

MERON, Ya'akov. The Legitimate Rights of 'Arabian' Jews. Congress Monthly, 44, No. 8, N. pp 7-9.
Abolition of racial prejudices against the Jews from Arab countries is a prerequisite of any peace settlement in the Middle East.

MESNIL-AMAR, Jacqueline. Nous étions les juifs de l'oubli. Les Nouveaux Cahiers, 22, No. 50, Aut. pp 43-49.
Oriental Jews.

Oriental Jews: Waiting for a miracle. Flash of Damascus, No. 59, Ma-Ap. pp 26-29.

ORIN, Yosefa Bat. Closing the Social Gap: From Wadi to Haifa U. Hadassah Magazine, 59, No. 12, D. pp 12-13.

PELEG, Ilan and Sima. The Ethnic Factor in Politics: The Mobilization Model and the Case of Israel. Ethnicity, 4, No. 2, Ju. pp 177-87.
"Despite considerable governmental efforts, multi-dimensional discrepencies between European and Oriental Jews still exist."
SEPHIHA, Haim Vidal. L'Agonie des Judéo-espagnols. Paris, Ed. Entente, 131p, Bibl, M.
The decline of Sephardi and especially Judeo-Espagnol (Ladino) culture.
SOEN, Dan. Orientals, Westerners and Ethnic Stratification in Israel Mankind Quarterly, 17, No. 1, Ja-Ma. pp 182-200.
"On the basis of all the data analysed one may expect the tension along ethnic lines to continue growing in the near future."
WEIL, S. Verbal Interaction among the B'nai Israel. International Journal of the Sociology of Language, No. 13, pp 71-85.
Study of a group of Indian Jews in Lod, Israel.

LEADERSHIP

BELLIN, Lowell E. Jewish decision making. Jewish Digest, 22, No. 4, D. pp 55-59. Condensed from United Synagogue Review, 30, No. 1.
GLAZER, Nathan. American Jewish Leadership. Contemporary Jewry, 2, Sp/Su. pp 3-16.
Raises questions about ethnic leadership and considers how they have been resolved within the American Jewish community.
GOLD, Bertram H. Pressures Facing the American Jewish Community. Waltham, Mass., Philip W. Lown Graduate Center in Contemporary Jewish Studies, Brandeis U., 15p. (The Milender Seminar in Jewish Communal Leadership Address)

LEGAL PROBLEMS

BRÜCKNER, Jens A. Das Handbuch der Berufverbote. Rechtsfibel zur berufsverbotspraxis. Berlin, Nicholaischer V. 288p.
Handbook to the Federal German Law governing the employment of right and left radicals in the Civil Service.
FORSYTHE, David P. Humanitarian politics. The International Committee of the Red Cross, Baltimore, Johns Hopkins P., 298p.
Analysis of the International Red Cross Conference in humanitarian law.
de GEOUFFRE de la PRADELLE, Paul. Les perspectives d'avenir du droit humanitaire. Berlin, Duncker and Humblot. In: Um Recht und Freiheit. Fesctschrift für Friedrich August Freiherr von der Heydte, pp 461-70.
Discusses the International Red Cross Conference on Humanitarian Law.
Origin and Development of International Humanitarian Law. 2.e. Geneva, International Committee of the Red Cross, 18p.
PICTET, J.S. Fresh Aspects of International Humanitarian Law. International Review of the Red Cross, 17, No. 199, O. pp 399-401.

JEWISH LAW

KLINGENBERG, Eberhard. Das israelitische Zinsverbot in Torah. Misnah und Malmud. Wiesbaden, Franz Steiner, 102p. (Akademie der Wissenschaften und der Literatur Mainz. Abhandlungen der geistes - und sozialwissenschaftlichen Klasse, 7)
The prohibition of charging interest in Jewish law.

SIEGEL, Seymour and GERTEL, Elliot. (Eds.) Conservative Judaism and Jewish Law. New York, Rabbinical Assembly, 364p. (Studies in Conservative Jewish Thought 1)

WEXLER, Stanley B. Should Orthodox Jews Fight for Legislating Morals: A Rabbi Says No. Jewish Life, 32, Su. pp 21-24.
Believes that "it is unwise for Jewish groups to advocate actively for state endorsement and codification of Jewish moral values in the body of contemporary law." Followed by an opposing point of view by Reuben E. Gross.

INTERNATIONAL LAW

MUTHARIKA, A. Peter. The Regulation of Statelessness under International and National Law. Text and Documents. Dobbs Ferry, New York, Oceans. 1 loose-leaf volume, Bibl.

HUMAN RIGHTS

BERGER, Peter L. Are human rights universal? Commentary, 64, No. 3, S. pp 60-63.

DERSHOWITZ, Alan. The Carter human rights initiative. Moment, 2, No. 5, F-Ma. pp 68-70.

Document: Déclaration sur les droits de l'homme des juifs en Union sovietique et en Syrie. Regards, 12, No. 112, Ap-My. pp 16-19.

Documents: La défence des Droits del'homme en Pologne. Istina, 22, Nos. 3-4, Jy-D. pp 289-329.

HENEGHAN, Thomas E. Human rights protests in Eastern Europe. The World Today, 33, No. 3, Ma. pp 90-100.
Includes Jewish activists.

HUBNER, Peter. Analyse neuer sowjetischer Aussenungen sur Menschenrechtsproblematik. Köln, Bundesinstitut fur ostwissenschaftliche und internationale Studien, 62p. Berichte des b-ndesinstituts fur ostwissenschaftliche und internationale Studien, 59)
A study of Soviet attitudes to Human Rights' problems.

KOREY, William. UN Human Rights: Illusion and Reality. Freedom at Issue, No. 2, S-O. pp 27-34.
An examination of the promise and performance of the world organisation.

LAPENNA, Ivo. Human Rights: Soviet Theory and Practice. Helsinki and International Law. London, Institute for the Study of Conflict, 16p.

LAQUEUR, Walter. The Issue of Human Rights. Commentary, 63, No. 5, My. pp 29-35.

MOWER, A Glenn. Implementing United Nations Covenants. Society, 15, No. 1, N-D. pp 76-80.

MOYNIHAN, Daniel P. The Politics of Human Rights. Commentary, 64, No. 2, Au. pp 19-26.
Against double standards of the UN and governments on this issue.

PELIKAN, Jiri and WILKE, Manfred. Menschenrechte. Ein Jahrbuch zu Osteuropa. Berlin, Rowohlt, 478p.

Review of human rights in Eastern Europe.

PERETZ, Don. The Middle East: Unabated Unrest. Freedom at Issue. No. 1, Ja-F. pp 24-26.

Survey of basic rights, including freedom of press, political organization, assembly and individual expression of dissent.

REISMAN, Michael. The Pragmatism of Human Rights: Diplomacy of the Possible. The Nation, 216, 7 My. pp 554-58.

Report of the League Conference on Implementing a Human Rights Commitment in United States Foreign Policy. 40 recommendations to President Carter. New York. International League for Human Rights.

RÉVÉSZ, László. Menschenrechte in der UdSSR. Bern, SDI, 320p (Tatsachen und Meinungen, 38)

Violations of human rights in the USSR.

RIESMAN, David. Prospects for Human Rights. Society, 15, No. 1, N-D pp 28-33.

The Status of human rights in selected countries and the U.S. Response. Prepared for Subcommittee on International Organisations Committee on International Relations, House, by the Foreign Affairs and National Defense Division. Washington, DC, Library of Congress, 79p.

VASEK, Karel and LISKOFSKY, Sidney. (Eds.) The Right to Leave and to Return. Papers and Recommendations of the International Colloquium held in Uppsala, Sweden, 19-20 June 1972. New York, The American Jewish Committee, The Jacob Blaustein Institute for the Advancement of Human Rights, the International Institute of Human Rights, Uppsala University, Faculty of Law, xi, 570p.

WEINGARTNER, Erich and Marilyn. Human Rights is more than Human Rights. A Primer for Churches on Security and Cooperation in Europe. Rome, IDOC, Europe Dossier Five, 290p, Bibl.

What is the Council of Europe doing to protect human rights? Strasbourg, Council of Europe, 75p, Ill.

GENOCIDE

U.S. Congress. Senate. Committee on Foreign Relations, Genocide Convention. Hearings before the ... On Ex. O, 81st Cong., 1st Sess; International Convention on the prevention and punishment of the crime of genocide, 24 and 26 May, Washington, U.S. Govt. Print. Off., 154p.

CIVIL RIGHTS

COMMISSION ON LAW, SOCIAL ACTION AND URBAN AFFAIRS, AMERICAN JEWISH CONGRESS. Discrimination, Segregation and Affirmative Action. 20 recent Civil Rights Decisions Affecting the Jewish Community. New York, AJC, 109p, (Mimeo)

Includes the Bakke case.

DERSHOWITZ, Alan M. Brief amici curiae: Regents of the University of California. v Bakke, U.S. Supreme Court, Oct. 1977 term, no 76-811, for American Jewish Committee, American Jewish Congress, et al. New York, 70p.

Discusses the test-case for reverse discrimination.

DWORKIN, Ronald. Why Bakke Has No Case. The New York Review of Books, 24, No. 48, 10, pp 11-15.

"It is hardly Bakke's fault that racial justice is now a special need - but he has no right to prevent the most effective measures of securing that justice from being used."

KONVITZ, Milton R. Civil Rights in Immigration. N.e. London, Greenwood P., 216p.

U.S. Commission on Civil Rights. Statement on affirmative action. Washington DC, 12p, (Clearinghouse, 54)

RELIGIOUS RIGHTS

BALL, William B. Religious Liberty in Education. Journal of Ecumenical Studies, 4, No, 4, Fa. pp 94-108.

GORDIS, Robert. Judaism and religious liberty. Journal of Ecumenical Studies, 4, No. 4, Fa. pp 25-34.

HELBLING, Hanno. (Ed.) Religionsfreiheit im 20 Jahrhundert. Zürich, Interfnom, 89p. (Text und Thesen 94)

Essays on freedom of religion in the 20th century.

HENNESEY, James. An American Roman Catholic Tradition of Religious Liberty. Journal of Ecumencial Studies, 4, No. 4, Fa. pp 35-39.

HESBURGH, Theodore M. The American Responsibility for Fostering Religious Liberty Internationally. Journal of Ecumenical Studies, 4, No. 4, Fa. pp 135-45.

KELLY, Dean M. Deprogramming and Religious Liberty. Civil Liberties Review, Jy-Au. pp 23-33.

"Deprogramming is a bsic and fundamental violation of the constitutional guarantees to freedom of speech and association. It is the encroachment upon the individual's religious freedom, the very right to think and to believe, that is most repugnant in the Jesus movement."

LITTELL, Franklin H. Foundations and Traditions of Religious Liberty: Keynote Address. Journal of Ecumenical Studies, 4, No. 4, Fa. pp 4-19.

METZ, R. Eglises et Etat en France. Situation juridique actuelle. Paris, Le Cerf, 146p, Bibl.

Treatment of religious organisations under French law.

PFEFFER, Leo. Church-State Relations Today. Congress Monthly, 44 No. 2, F. pp 8-10.

------------. Fair Employment for Sabbath Observers. Congress Monthly, 44, No. 4, My. pp 8-10.

------------. The Supreme Court and Religion. Congress Monthly, 44, No. 6, S. pp 9-12.

RAINES, John C. Religious Liberty and Social Inequality. Journal of Ecumenical Studies, 4, No. 4, Fa. pp 109-12.

Review of Pre-Slaughter Stunning in the EEC. Brussels, Luxembourg, Commission of the European Communities, Information on Agriculture No. 30, Ma., 90p.

Relates also to ritual slaughter (Shechitah)

SACERDOTI, Giorgio. Ebraismo e Costituzione: Prospettive di Intesa tra Comunita Israelitiche e State. La Rassegna Mensile di Israel, 43, Nos. 7-8, Jy-Au. pp 329-55.

SMYLIE, Robert F. The U.S. and the USSR: Religious Liberty as a Human Right. Worldview, 20, No. 9, S. pp 33-35.

TANENBAUM, Marc H. Contemporary Issues of Church/State Relations. Journal of Ecumenical Studies, 14, 4, Fa. pp 82-93.

Although committed to the principle of separation of church and state, is not happy with that stance which is an inadequate response to the human issues that are raised by aid-to-parochial school issues.

WEDEL, Cynthia C. The Prospects for Religious Liberty. Journal of Ecumenical Studies, 4, No. 4, Fa. pp 158-61.

RACIAL DISCRIMINATION

Affirmative Action in Higher Education: Special Issue. The Urban League Review, Su. pp 4-64.

Includes: The Status of Affirmative Action by Betty Adams. Affirmative Action Reconsidered by Thomas Sowell. The Case for Affirmative Action in Higher Education by Marcus Alexis. The Bakke Case: Worrisome Wrinkle or Wholesale Retreat by Fran Farmer.

MACDONALD, Ian A. Race Relations and the New Law. London, Butterworth, xvii, 246p, Ind.

Commentary to the 1976 Race Relations Act (UK) the third such Act which completely replaces the Acts of 1968 and 1965. The author shows the changes since 1968.

Report of the UN Preparatory Sub-Committee of the Council for the World Conference to Combat Racism and Racial Discrimination. Ap. 19p. 3 annexes.

MINORITY RIGHTS

ALLWORTH, Edward. (Ed.) Nationality Group Survival in Multi-Ethnic States. Shifting Support Patterns in the Soviet Baltic Region. New York, London, Praeger, xiv, 299p, Bibl.

The Jewish interest is dealt with substantially in the chapter entitled Resources of Ethnically Disenfranchised by Eli M. Lederhandler as well as in the clearly-arranged tables and the Appendix.

CHYET, Stanley F. The document that guaranteed political equality to Jews. Jewish Digest, 22, No. 8, Ap. pp 52-54.

HALLIDAY, Fred. Britain's Arab Communities. Middle East International, No. 67, Ja. pp 28-29.

LITTMAN, David G. and MEMMI, Albert et al. Jøder og Andre Minoriteter I Arabiske Lande. SDI Orientering arabiske lande før og efter oprettelsen af Israel. Copenhagen, SDI, 32p. (In Danish)

Jewish and other minorities in Arab countries.

----------------. and YE'OR, Bat. Peuples Proteges en Terre d'Islam Geneve, Centre d'Information et de Documentation sur le Moyen-Orient, 13p.

Jews now living in some Muslim countries of North Africa are still protected by Islamic law.

VEITER, Theodor. Nationalitätenkonflikt und Volksgruppenrecht im 20 Jahrundert. München, Internationales Institut für Nationalitätenrecht und Regionalismus, 236p, Ind.

The position of ethnic minorities in international law.

POLITICAL PROBLEMS

SEGRE, Dan V. Jewish Political Thought and Contemporary Politics. Shefa Quarterly, 1, No. 2, Au. pp 76-92.

PERLMUTTER, Amos. The Military and Politics in Modern Times. London, Yale, U.P., xix, 335p, Ind.

Includes a chapter on Israel.

NAZISM

ACH, Manfred. and PETROP, Clemens. Hitlers "Religion". Pseudoreligiöse Elemente im nationalsozialistischenSprachgebrauch. St. Augustin, Asgard Verl. 116p. (Asgard Edition 3)

Analyses the pseudo-religious elements in Nazi speech.

ADAM, Uwe Dietrich. Hochschule und Nationalsozialismus. Die Universität im Dritten Reich. Tübingen, J.C.B. Mohr. x, 240p. Ind. Bibl. (Contubernium. Beiträge zur Geschichte der Eberhard-Karl-Universität Tübingen 23)

The author took the University of Tübingen as an outstanding example of Nazi policy in higher institutes of learning.

AUERBACH, Hellmuth. Hitlers politische Lehrjahre und die Münchener Gesellschaft 1919-1923. Vierteljahrshefte fur Zeitgeschichte, 25, No. 1, Ja. pp 1-45.

Hitler's early years in Munich.

BAHR, Rudolf. Grundlagen für Karl Kraus' Kritik an der Sprache im nationalsozialistischen Deutschland. Köln, Bohlau, vi, 156p. Bibl. (Böhlau Forum Litterarum 8)

Systematic analysis of Kraus' critique of national socialist jargon.

BARKAI, Avraham. Das Wirtschaftssystem im Nationalsozialismus. Köln, V. für Wissenschaft und Politik, 290p. Bibl.

The national-socialist economic order.

BAUMGARTNER, Raimund. Weltanschauungskampf im Dritten Reich. Die Auseinandersetzung der Kirchen mit Alfred Rosenberg. Mainz, Matthias-Grünewald, xxiii, 275p.

The ideological struggle between the churches and Nazis, notably Alfred Rosenberg.

BEYERCHEN, Alan D. Scientists under Hitler. Politics and the Physics Community in the Third Reich. New Haven, London, Yale U.P. xii, 287p, Ind, Bibl.

Based on interviews with German physicists who suffered under the Nazis and went into exile because their main concern was the protection of their autonomy against political encroachment.

BLUM, Howard. Wanted: The Search for Nazis in America. Greenwich, Conn., Fawcett Books, 285p.

Traces the fate of ex-Nazis who were allowed to immigrate into the U.S.A.

BOSSMAN, Dieter. (Ed.) "Was ich über Adolf Hitler gehört habe." Folgen eines Tabus: Auszüge aus Schüler-Aufsätzen von heute. Frankfurt/M. Fischer Taschenbuch, 360p.

Excerpts from over 3000 essays of students in all kinds of schools in 121 German cities in answer to the question "What I have heard about Adolf Hitler" - showing abysmal ignorance of Nazism.

BROSZAT, Martin. Politische Denunziationen in der NS-Zeit. Aus Forschungserfahrungen im Staatsarchiv München. Archivalische Zeitschrift, 75, pp 221-38.

Political denounciation under the Nazis. Based on documents in the Munich (Bavarian) state archives.

---------------., FRÖHLICH, Elke and WIESEMANN, Falk. (Eds.) Bayern in der NS-Zeit. Soziale Lage und politisches Verhalten der Benölkerung im Spiegel vertraulicher Berichte. München, Wien, R. Oldenbourg, 712p, Ind, Bibl. M.

Documented history and analysis of the political behaviour of the population of Bavaria during the Nazi era. Part V deals with the persecution of the Jews.

BULLOCK, Alan. Hitler. Eine Studie über Tyrannei. Tr. by Wilhelm and Modeste Pferdekamp. Nachdruck der Vollständig überarbeiteten Neuausgabe 1971. Mit einem Vorwort des Verfassers 1977. Kronberg, Athenäum; Düsseldorf, Droste, 886p, Ind, Bibl.

German editions of Hitler, A Study in Tyranny.

COWAN, Wayne H. Nazis in America? Process, Due and Overdue. Christianity and Crisis, 37, 7 Ma. pp 34-36.

"There can be no doubt about the difficulty of conducting these investigations almost 30 years after the fact. Nevertheless, they must be pursued with diligence and care. Overdue process can mean only one thing for everyone involved: Justice delayed is justice denied."

COWLING, Maurice. The Impact of Hitler. British Politics and British Policy. 1933-1940. Chicago, London, U. of Chicago P., N.e. 445p, Ind.

Originally published in 1975. The paperback edition does not contain the footnotes referred to in the text.

DAMMEYER, Manfred. Nationalsozialistische Filme im historisch-politischen Unterricht. Aus Politik und Zeitgeschichte, No. 16, 23 Ap. pp 3-24.

DAVUDSIBM Eugene. The Making of Adolf Hitler. New York, Macmillan, 408p.

Psycho-historical study.

DESCHNER, Günther. Reinhard Heydrich. Statthalter der totalen Macht. Biographie. Esslingen, Bechtle, 368p.

Biography of the SS-leader, Nazi Governor of Bohemia and Moravia, murdered by the Czech resistance.

DOMARUS, Max: Mussolini und Hitler. Zwei Wege, gleiches Ende. Wurzburg, Author, 512p.

Compares the Duce with the Fuhrer.

EARLEY, George and Roberta. Bavarian prelude. 1923: A Model for Nazism. The Wiener Library Bulletin, 30, Nos. 43-44, pp 53-59.

Hitler's first breakthrough.

ELLERIN, Milton. American Nazis - Myth or Menace? New York, Trends Analyses Division, American Jewish Committee, 12p.

FEST, Joachim C. Das Geschichte des Dritten Reiches. N.e. Munich, Piper, 516p. Ind. Ill, Bibl.

New edition of book first published in 1963 to accompany the author's film "Hitler - eine Karriere."

---------------. Hitler. Tr. R. and C. Winston. N.e. Harmondsworth, Penguin, 1248p.

---------------. and HERRENDÖRFER, Christian. Hitler - eine Karriere. Berlin, Wien, Ullstein, 190p, (Ullstein Buch 3412)

Text and photography from the controversial film "Hitler - a Career", made in Germany in 1977.

FLEMING, Gerald. Germany 1933-1945: A Teaching System in Pictures, Texts and Documents. European Judaism, 11, No. 1, W. pp 9-12.

Report on an experimental project in the University of Sussex.

FLESSAU, Kurt-Ingo. Schule der Diktatur. Lehrpläne und Schulbücher des Nationalsozialismus. With a foreword by H.J. Gamm. München, Ehrenwirth, 228p, Bibl.

Detailed critical analysis of school textbooks used in the Third Reich.

FRANZ WILLING, Georg. Entstehungs - und Frühgeschichte der Hitlerbewegung 1. Ursprung der Hitlerbewegung, 1919-1922, 2. Krisenjahr der Hitlerbewegung, 1923, 3. Putsch und Verbotszeit der Hitlerbewegung November 1923 - Februar 1925. Pr. Oldendorf, Schük, Ind, Bibl.

Basic work on the origins of the Nazi movement up to 1925.

GROSSER, Alfred. Wie war es möglich. Die Wirklichkeit des Nationalsozialismus. Zehn Studien. Tr. Anneliese Botond, München, Hanser, 184p.

Tries to answer the question, how it was possible that the Nazis were able to take over Germany and perpetuate their crimes. Rita Thalmann's study "Das Protokoll der Wannseekonferenz: von Antisemitismus. Zur Endlösung der Judenfrage" is of special interest.

HAAS, Karl, HAHN, Manfred, SPANN, Gustav and AICHINGER, Wilfried. Osterreichische Schulbuchwirklickeit. Die Republik, 13, No. 3, Jy-S. pp 16-50.

Examines how the Nazi era is taught in Austria.

HANISCH, Ernst. Zur Frühgeschichte desNationalsozialismus in Salzburg 1913-1925. Offprint from: Mitteilungen der Gesellschaft für Salzburger Landeskunde, V.117. pp 371-410.

Beginnings of the Nazi party in Salzburg, Austria.

HANISCH, Ernst. Verbände, Opposition, Emigration der deutschen Katholiken in der Zeit des Nationalsozialismus. Zeitgeschichte, 4, No.8, My. pp 297-304.

HEARTFIELD, John. Photomontages of the Nazi Period. London, Gordon Fraser with Universe Books. 143p. Ill.

Heartfield was an important anti-Fascist artist.

HENNIG, Eike. Bürgerliche Geselleschaft und Faschismus in Deutschland. Ein Forschungsbericht. Frankfurt, Suhrkamp, 430p.

Attempts to show the relationship between bourgeois society and Nazism in Germany, which has still not been completely understood.

Adolf Hitler. Hamburg, Jahr, 130p, Ill. (Das III Reich Sonderdokumentation 1)

Articles by Werner Maser, Walter Görlitz, Hans Kehrl, Joachim Fest, etc.

JETZINGER, Franz. Hitler's Youth. Tr. L. Wilson. N.e. Westport, Conn., Greenwood; London, Westport P., 200p. Ill.

KÜHNL, Reinhard and HARDACH, G. (Eds.) Die Zerstörung der Weimarer Republik. Köln, Pahl-Rugenstein, 292p, (Kleine

Bibliothek, 88)
History of the collapse of the Weimar Republic, the rise of the NSDAP and increasing antisemitism in Germany 1917-1933.

LANG, Jochen van. Der Sekretär. Martin Bormann: der Mann, der Hitler beherrschte, Stuttgart, DVA, 512p, Ill, Bibl.
Documented biography of Martin Bormann: Hitler's secretary and later named as his successor.

LEVIN, Nora. The Humanizing of Hitler. Reconstructionist, 43, No. 5 Ju. pp 28-31.
On the attempts to whitewash the Nazis.

LOSEMANN, Volker. Nationalsozialismus und Antike. Studien zur Entwicklung des Faches Geschichte 1933-1945. Hamburg, Hoffman und Campe. 280p, Ind, Bibl. (Historische Perspektiven, 7)
Analyses the National-Socialist attitude to the teaching of the ancient history which mirrored also the attitude of the bourgeoisie brought up in the humanist tradition.

LUZA, Radomír V. Nazi Control of the Austrian Catholic Church. 1939-1941. Catholic Historical Review, 63, No. 4, O. pp 537-72.

---------------. Österreich und die grossdeutsche Idee in der NS-Zeit. Tr. Doris Haubner. Wien, Köln, Böhlau, 396p, Ind, Bibl. (Forschungen zur Geschichte des Donauraumes, 2)
Austria and the idea of a greater Germany in the Nazi era.

McKALE, Donald M. The Swastika Outside Germany. Kent, Ohio, Kent State U.P., xvi, 288p, Ind, Bibl.
The German-American Bund, directed by the NSDAP Auslands-Organisation, was the main propaganda vehicle of the Nazis in the USA. Based on official documents.

---------------. The Nazi Party in the Far East, 1931-1945. Journal of Contemporary History, 12, No. 2, Ap. pp 291-311.
The Nazi Party in the Orient was of highly racial orientation, it relied on propaganda and subversion, made efforts to mobilise the German communities for Nazi aims. But the Party had a far more negative than positive impact on Germany's efforts in the Far East and on her relations with Japan.

MANVELL, Roger. S.S. and Gestapo: Rule by Terror. Ballentine Books, Future, 160p, Ill.
Shortened version of the author's study of the Nazi system.

MARTINI, A. Un guidizio sconosciuto di Pio XII sul nazismo. La Civilta Cattolica, 128, No. 2, My. pp 324-38.
An unknown statement of Pius XII against Nazism.

MAZZERELLA, Mario Dominic. The British Catholic Press and the Rise of Nazi Germany. 1933-1940. Ann Arbor, Mich., U. Microfilms, 329p, Bibl.
Ph.D. Dissertation, American University.

MOSSE, George L. Intervista sul nazismo. A cura di Michael A. Ledeen. Rome, Laterza, vii, 160p, Ind, (Saggi Tascabili Laterza 35)
Questions put by Ledeen to Professor Mosse on Nazism during a long interview. In shorter form: Society, 7, My-Ju. pp 69-73.

NEUMANN, Franz. Behemoth - Struktur und Praxis des Nationalsocialismus 1933 bis 1944. Ed. with an afterword "Franz Neumanns Behemoth und die Heutige Faschismusdiskussion" by Gert Schäfer. N.e. Köln, Europäischer V. 784p.
A new edition of a classic work on Nazism.

PACHTER, Henry. Heidegger and Hitler. Boston University Journal,25.

PILET, Jacques. Le Crime Nazi de Payerne. Paris, Favre, 192p, Bibl.
Describes the murder by Swiss Nazis of a Jew called Bloch in the Canton of Vaud and analyses local antisemitism then and now.

POMMERIN, Reiner. Das Dritte Reich und Latein Amerika. Die Deutsche Politik gegenüber Süd - und Mittelamerika 1939-42. Düsseldorf, Droste, 390p.
The extent of Nazi influence in Latin and Central America during the first three years of World War II.

PORTER, Jack Nusan. A Nazi Runs for Mayor. Dangerous Brownshirts or Media Freaks? Present Tense, 4, No, 4, Su. pp 27-31.
U.S. Nazis.

RAPPAPORT, Ernest A. Notes on Blindness and Omniscience: From Oedipus to Hitler. Psychoanalytic Review, 63, W. pp 281-90.

REIMANN, Viktor. The Man Who Created Hitler - Joseph Goebbels. Tr. Stephen Wendt. London, William Kimber, 352p.

ROBINSON, Hans. Justiz als politische Verfolgung. Die Rechtsprechung in 'Rassenschandefällen' beim Landgericht Hamburg 1936-43. Stuttgart, 168p, Bibl. (Schriftenreihe der Vierteljahreshefte, 35)
Study of the cases of 'Rassenschande' adjudicated before the Hamburg Court.

ROGOWSKI, R. The Gauleiter and the Social Origins of Fascism. Comparative Studies in Society and History, 19, No. 4, pp 399-430.

ROZNYÓI, Agnes. A Szálasi-puccs. 2.r.e. Budapest, Kossath, 107p. Ill, Bibl. (Nepszerü Törtenelem S.)
Popular work on the Arrow-Cross take over of power in Hungary in October 1944. The first edition was published in 1962.

RUBIN, Arnold P. The Evil That Men Do. The Story of the Nazis. New York, Mesorev, 223p.

Schüler über den Hitler-Film. Judischer Presse Dienst, No. 5-6, S. pp 18-21.
A survey of schoolchildren in Germany, who watched a film about Hitler, and revealed their ignorance of the Nazi era.

SCHWARZWÄLLER, Wulf. Rudolf Hess. Der Letzte von Spandau. Eine Biographie. Wien, Molden, 304p, Ind.
Biography of Hitler's Deputy, the last of the major war criminals in Spandau prison.

SINGER, David G. The Prelude to Nazism: The German-American Press and the Jews 1919-1933. American Jewish Historical Quarterly, 66, No. 3, Ma. pp 417-31.

SKLAR, Dusty. Gods and Beasts: The Nazis and the Occult. New York, Crowell.

SMELSER, Ronald M. Nazis Without Hitler: The NSDAP and the First Czechoslovak republic. East Central Europe, 4, No. 1, pp 1-19.

STACHURA, Peter. (Ed.) Adolf Hitler and Nazi Germany. London, Croom Helm, 240p.

STEINBERG, Michael Stephen. Sabres and Brown Shirts. The German Students' Path to National Socialism, 1918-1935. Chicago, London, U. of Chicago P., vii, 237p, Ind.
Includes the attitude to Jews.

SUDHOLT, Gert. (Ed.) Adolf Hitler's drei Testamente - Für den Fall meines Todes verfüge ich. Leoni, Druffel, 108p.
Edited version of Hitler's three wills, published in the wave of nostalgia for the Third Reich.

SUTTON, Antony. Wall Street and the Rise of Hitler. Seal Beach, Calif. P., 210p, Ind, Bibl.
An influential sector of American business was not only aware of the nature of Nazism but, for its own purposes, aided it wherever possible.
TOLAND, John. Adolf Hitler. Tr. Uwe Bahnsen, 1200p. Ill, M.
WAAENER, Hans. (Ed.) Gegenwarts-literatur und Drittes Reich. Deutsche Autoren in der Auseinandersetzung mit der Vergangenheit. Stuttgart, Reclam, 342p, Ind.
A number of German scholars discuss how contemporary literature deals with the Nazi past.
WAITE, Robert G.L. The Psychopathic God, Adolf Hitler. New York, Basic Books, xx, 482p, Ind, Ill.
Psychological study.
WISHNER, Maynard. American Nazis and the First Amendment. Jewish Affairs, 32, No. 12, D. pp 43-46. Sh'ma, 7, No. 2, S. pp 134-36.

NEO-NAZISM

American Nazis: Are They More Than Just A Curiosity? U.S. News and World Report, 7 N. pp 57-58.
"With militaristic zeal and a 'whites only' policy, U.S. brown shirts are seeking political power - and also stirring widespread opposition."
ARONSFELD, C.C. The National Front - Britain's Neo-Nazi Force. Congress Monthly, 44, No. 9, D. pp 9-10.
"The 12 year old National Front draws its inspiration from Germany but its practice is all homemade. It is avowedly racist, its virulant 'anti-Zionist' more and more drops the pretense of differing from anti-Semitism and it leads the international campaign to whitewash Hitler."
BINGHAM, Richard, FRENDREIS, John P. and RHODES, James M. The Nominating Process in Non-partisan Elections and Right-wing Candidates: Nazi support in Milwaukee. Prepared for delivery at the 1977 annual meeting of the Southwestern Political Science Association, Statler Hilton Hotel, Dallas, Texas, 30 Ma - 2 Ap. 1977. Milwaukee, Urban Research Center, University of Wisconsin, 30p.
CHAIROFF, Patrice. Dossier Néo-Nazi. L'Arche, 20, No. 249, D. pp 54-63.
Extracts from the book.
-----------------. Dossier Néo-nazisme. Paris, J.P. Ramsey, 468p.
History of the development of the Neo-Nazi movements since the end of World War II, a country by country description of activities and their international connections.
DESSARRE, Eve. Les Nostalgiques du Reich millenaire. L'Arche, 12, No. 242, My. pp 41-43.
On the revival of Nazism.
DEUTSCH, Zvi. Milwaukee Jews counter Nazi Threat. Jewish Currents,' 31, No. 8, S. pp 5-7.
EDGAR, David. Racism, Fascism and the Politics of the N.F. London, Institute of Race Relations, 30p. (Race and Class Pamphlet 4). Reprinted from Race and Class 19, No. 2.

EYRES, Stephen. The National Front is a Socialist Front. London, Aims for Freedom and Enterprise. 18p. (Studies of the Left 1)

HARROP, Martin and ZIMMERMAN, Gary. The Anatomy of the National Front. Colchester, Essex U. Dept. of Govt. 5p.

HERETH, Michael. Der Fall Rudel oder Die Hoffähigkeit der Nazi-Diktatur. Protokoll einer Bundestagsdebatte. Hamburg, Rowolt,107p

Edited minutes of the debate in the Bundesstag on 16.3.1977 when the German Parliament debated the cases of the dismissed General Krupinski and Franke and their contacts with the Right-wing Col. Rudel.

HUSBANDS, Christopher T. The National Front Becalmed? The Wiener Library Bulletin, 30, Nos. 43-44, pp 74-78.

JÄCKEL, Eberhard. Literaturbericht. Rückblick auf die sogenannte Hitler-Welle. Geschichte und Wissenschaft im Unterricht, 28, pp 695-710.

Surveys the literature of the Hitler-nostalgia of the early 70s.

KADAN, Albert. Neofaschismus - ein aktuelles Problem in Osterreich? Die Republik, 13, No. 3, Jy-S. pp 4-15.

Balanced view of neo-fascism in Austria.

KOSCHNICK, Wolfgang J. Return of "The German Menace." Worldview, 20, Nos. 1-2, Ja-F. pp 19-22.

The Hitler nostalgia.

LAZZARO, Claudio. El resurgimiento nazi en Europa. Informativo, 13, No. 94, N-D. p p 18-21.

LESHNIK, Lawrence S. West Germany's Neo-Nazis. ADL Bulletin, 34, No 5, My. pp 7-8.

Nayer oisbruch fun neonatsizm un antisemitizm in mizrach eirope un amerike. (Outbreak of neo-Nazism and antisemitism in Western Europe and America) Sovietish Heimland, 17, No. 12, D. pp 14-24.

Mentions i.a. publication of 'The Hoax of the Twentieth Century' by A. Butz.

Neofaschismus - ein aktuelles Thema der Zeitgeschiche Osterreichische Schulbuchswirklichkeit. Graz, Styria.

Neofascism, though a topical subject of contemporary history is not touched upon in Austrian schoolbooks.

NEUBEBAUER, Wolfgang. Aktuelle faschistiche Strömungen in Osterreich. Zeitgeschichte, 4, No. 8, My. pp 280-91.

On the subject of neo-Nazism in Austria.

PEROTTI, Berto. La notte dei cristalli, Milano, Mu-sia, 200p.

On the Nazi atrocities of 10 November 1938.

POLKE, Bernd. Täglicher Faschismus in der BRD. Nachrichten aus einer belagerten Gesellschaft. Tübingen, Initiative, 244p.

Neo-nazism in the Federal German Republic.

SKIDELSKY, Robert. The Return of Mosley: A Reply. The Wiener Library Bulletin, 30, Nos. 43-44, pp 79-80.

South Africa's Jews Combat Neo-Nazi Propaganda. Congress Monthly, 44 No. 9, D. pp 11-13.

WALKER, Martin. The National Front. London, Fontana, 224p.

FASCISM

ARONSFELD, C.C. The Day the Nazis Banned B'nai B'rith. B'nai B'rith Journal, 1, Su. pp 8-10.

BADER, William C. The return of Mosley. The Wiener Library Bulletin, 30, Nos. 41-42, pp 62-67.

CARSTEN, Francis L. Faschismus in Österreich. Von Schönerer zu Hitler. München, Wilhelm Fink Verlag, 373p, Ind, Bibl. In English: Beverley Hills, Ca. Sage, 360p.

DOS SANTOS, T. Socialismo y fascismo en America Latina hoy. Revista Mexicano de Sociologie, 39, No. 1, pp 173-90.

FELICE, Renzo de. Der Faschismus. Ein Interview. Tr. Jens Petersen Stuttgart, Klett Cotta, 166p, Ind.

Mussolini's biographer and Italy's greatest expert on Fascism answers questions on Fascism.

----------------. Interpretations of Fascism. Tr. Brenda Huff Everett. Intro. by Charles F. Delzell. London, Harvard U.P., xvi, 248p, Ind, Bibl.

First English edition of work published in 1969. Differentiating between the fascist "regime" and the "movement" the author holds that fascism was born "on the left" and stands in the political and cultural tradition of the Enlightenment and the French Revolution.

LAQUEUR, Walter. (Ed.) Fascism. A Reader's Guide. Analyses. Interpretations. London, Wildwood House; Los Angeles, U. of California P., 541p, Bibl.

NOLTE, Ernst. Marxismus, Faschismus, Kalter Krieg, Vorträge und Aufsätze 1964-1976. Stuttgart, Deutsche Verlags-Anstalt, 399p, Ind.

PERFETTI, Francesco. Il nationalismo italiano delle origini alla fusione col fascismo. Bologna, Cappelli, 292p, (Storia dei partiti politici, 8)

PURCELL, Hugh. Fascism, London, Hamish Hamilton, 95p. Ind, Ill, Bibl. (People and Politics)

Book for Youth, on Fascism. Including the Nazi persecution of Jews.

RABINBACH, Anson G. Marxistische Faschismustheorien. Ein Uberblick. Asthetik u. Kommunikation, 8, No. 27, pp 89-103.

RABINOVICH, Abraham. Jerusalem: 1967-1977. Congress Monthly, 44, No. 5, Ju. pp 7-11.

SAAGE, Richard. Faschismustheorien. München, C.H. Beck, 2.e. 184p. Bibl.

Analyses the current discussion on Fascism.

SALVATORELLI, Luigi. Nazionalfascismo. Pref. Giorgio Amendola. Torino, Einaudi, xxv, 124p, Ind. (Piccola Biblioteca Einaudi 320)

Essay on the origins and development of Fascism.

SALVEMINI, Gaetano. Italian Fascist Activities in the United States. Ed. with intro. by Philip V. Cannistraro. New York, Center for Migration Studies, iii, 267p, Ind.

Study of the major organisations, methods and personalities in the Italian Fascist movement in the USA from 1922-1936.

SZÉKELY, Gábor: Kommunista vezetök elemzései a fasizmusról a huszas evek elejen. A Politikai Föiskila Közleményei, No. 4, pp 219-34.

Analysis of fascism by Communist leaders in the early 1920s.

THAMER, Hans Ulrich. Ansichten des Faschismus. Der italienische Faschismus in der politischen und wissenschaftlichen Diskussion. Neue Politische Literatur, 22, No, 1, pp 19-35.

-------------------. and WIPPERMAN, Wolfgang. Faschistische und neofaschistische Bewegungen. Darmstadt, Wissenschaftliche Buchgesellschaft, xiii, 268p, Ind. (Berträge der Forschung, 72)

Analysis of all forms of fascism and neo-fascism in Spain, Argentina, South-East Europe, France and Italy with a concluding essay in establishing a typology of Fascism.

VREE, Dale. A Fascism in our future? Worldview, 20, No. 11, No. pp 14-23.

WEISS, John. Fascism in Czechoslovakia 1919-1939. East Central Europe, 4, No. 1, pp 35-43.

WISTRICH, Robert S. Fascist Movements in Austria. The Wiener Library Bulletin, 30, Nos. 43-44, pp 60-64.

ANTI-FASCISM

AMENDOLA, Giorgio. Der Antifaschismus in Italien. Ein Interview von Piero Melograni. With an afterword by Jens Petersen. Tr. from Italian by Traute Rafalski. Stuttgart, Klett Cotta, 256p, Ind.

The author, a veteran antifascist, member of the Central Committee of the Italian Communist party was the organiser of the partisans action in the liberation of Rome and Milan.

ANDREOLI, Annamaria. (Ed.) Memorie dell'antifascismo in Emilia-Romagna. Fra cultura e ideologia. Firenze, La Nuova Italia, 222p.

FERRAROTTO, Marinella. L'Accademia d'Italia. Intellettuali spotere durante il fascismo. Napoli, Liguori, 163p, Ill. (Le Istituzioni culturali, 1)

The relation of Italian intellectuals to the Fascist regime.

HAUG, W.F. Der hilflose Antifaschismus. Zur Kritik der Vorlesungsreihen über Wissenschaft und NS an deutschen Universitäten. 4.e. Köln, Pahl Rugenstein, 168p, Bibl. (Kleine Bibliothek, S 79)

The role of the universities in Nazi Germany and their attitude to Nazism after the fall of the Third Reich.

KOEHLER, Manfred, SALLFELD, Wolfgang and SCHILLER, Klaus. (Eds.) Antifaschistische Literatur 1933-1945. Frankfurt/M. Diesterweg, iv, 136p, (Texte und Materialien zum Literaturunterricht)

Anthology of German exile literature, includes many Jewish authors with explanations, as a teaching aid.

RADICAL RIGHT

Anti-Defamation League of B'nai B'rith. The Extreme Right in West Germany. New York, 9p. (Fact Finding Report)

BORNE, Dominique. Petits Bourgeois en Révolte? Le Mouvement Poujade, Paris, Falmmarion, 249=.

The Right-wing Poujade Movement had antisemitic elements.

BRIGOULEIX, Bernard. L'Extrème Droite en France. Les "Fachos". Paris, Fayolle, 235p.

Survey of the newly rising extreme right neo-fascist antisemitic movements in France.

GERMANI, Gino. Authoritarianism, National Populism and Fascism. New Brunswick, N.J. Transaction Books, 350p.

JELINEK, Yeshayahu. The The Slovak Right: Conservative or Radical? A Reappraisal. East Central Europe. 4, No. 1, pp 20-34.
With many references to antisemitism.

MAIER, Gerhart. Extremisten im öffentlichen Dienst? Bonn: Bundeszentrale F. Polit. Bildung, 90p.
Official publication on extreme Right and Left oriented members of the civil service in W. Germany.

POLLACK, Martin. Die Neue Rechte. Stossrichtung Schulen. Wiener Tagebuch, 7, Nos. 7-8, Jy-Au. pp 7-9.
The "New Right" infiltrates schools in Austria.

"Rechts-Staat" - links der Elbe. Geneva, Marva, 205p.
The Right-Radical contributors to this volume of essays are right-wingers and attack the Federal German Republic i.a. for restitution payments, censorship and defence.

TIXIER VIGNANCOUR. Le contre-mal Francais. Paris, Albin Michel, 288p, Ill.
A French extreme rightist's view of his society.

VERFASSUNGSSCHUTZ 1976. Bonn, Der Bundesminister des Innern, 178p. Ill. (27)
Right and Left Radical movements and publications in the Federal German Republic.

Verfassungsschutzbericht Bayern 1976. München, Bayerisches Staatsministerium des Innern, 72p.
Bavarian Minister of the Interior's Report on extreme Right and Left-wing activities in Bavaria in 1976.

Who's Left, What's Right? Symposium. Encounter, 48, No. 3, Ma. pp 18-32.

COMMUNISM

BAGRAMOV, E. Di internatsionale farbridertkait fun di boier funem komunism. (The International brotherhood of the builders of Communist) Sovietish Heimland, 17, No. 11, N. pp 186-90.
Discusses i.a. the'historical experience of the CPSU's struggle with Zionism and fascism'.

BEINEN, J. The Palestine Communist Party 1919-1948. MERIP Reports, No. 44, Ma. pp 13-15.

DAWISHA, A. Communist Parties Remain Peripheral Forces in Middle East Politics. Middle East, No. 33, Jy. pp 30-32.

----------. Soviet Union in the Middle East. Setback or Comeback? Middle East, No. 33, Jy. pp 25-39.

Konstitutsie (grund-gesets) funem farband sovietishe sotsialistishe republikn. (Constitution of the USSR) Sovietish Heimland, 17, No. 11, N. pp 5-32.
Full text in Yiddish.

Di "Morgen Freiheit" af fremde vegn fun antisovietizm un protsionism. (The Morgen Freiheit on the road to antisovietism and pro-Zionism) Sovietish Heimland, 17, No. 5, My. pp 140-47. No. 6, pp 157-66.
Two comments castigating the split in the Israeli communist party.

RAKOWSKA-HARMSTONE, Teresa. Ethnicity in the Soviet Union. Annals of the American Academy of Political and Social Science, No. 433, S. pp 73-87.

RASKOVSKI, Yevgeni. Fun der geschichte vegn dem onteil. fun di yidn in der revolutsioner-folkistisher bavegung. (The History of Jewish participation in the revolutionary-popular movement). Sovietish Heimland, No. 6, Ju. pp 130-37.

SCHNEIDER, Eberhard. Politische Aspekte des neuen sowjetischen Verfassungentwurfs. Köln, Bundesinstitut für ostwissenschaftliche und internationale Studien. 47p. Berichte des Bundesinstituts, 42)

Political aspects of the new Soviet Constitution; some affect Jews.

SHRAIBER, Y. Di kommunistn fun yisroel in kamf far sholem, demokratie, far die recht fun di arbetendike. (Israel's communists in the struggle for peace, democracy, for the rights of the workers.) Sovietish Heimland, 17, No. 7, pp 109-14.

SZAJKOWSKI, Zosa. Kolchak, Jews and the American Intervention in Northern Russia and Siberia. 1918-20. New York, S. Frydman, 218p. Ind, Ill. (Jews, Wars and Communism, 3)

----------------. The Mirage of American Jewish Relief in Soviet Russia, 1917-39. New York, S. Frydman, 259p, Ill, Ind, (Jews, Wars and Communism, 4)

TCHERNIS, Yoshe. Soldatn funem leninishn batalion. (Soldiers of the Leninist Battalion). Sovietish Heimland, 17, No. 8, Au. pp 4-15.

Data on Jewish participation in the October Revolution.

COMMUNIST POLICY ON JEWS

COHEN, Steven M. and GOLDMAN, Marshall. The Kremlin and the Jews. The Shcharansky Affair - the case for moderation. Moment, 2, No. 10, O. pp 48-51.

Documents touchant la situation culturelle et religieuse en Union Soviétique:
XV. Appel à la conscience chrétienne contre la discrimination dont les Juifs sont victimes en URSS.
XVI. Appel de F. Dektor en vue d'obtenir l'existence d'une revue juive en langue russe.
XVIII. Le Symposium sur la culture juive en Union Soviétique.
Istina, 22, No. 1, Ja-Ju. pp 88-108.

FELDBRUGGE, F.J.M. The Legal Position of Jews in the Soviet Union. Lecture delivered at the International Association of Jewish Jurists in Holland, The Hague, 12 June, 13p.

FLEISHMA, Lazar, RONEN, Omry and SEGAL, Dmitri. (Eds.) Slavica Hierosolymitana, V. 1. München, Wilhelm Fink, 335p.

With articles by scholars from Israel, the Soviet Union, the United States and Great Britain.

GITELMAN, Zvi. Characteristics of Soviet Jews. Jewish Spectator, 42, No. 4, W. pp 35-39.

-------------. Jews in the USSR: Prospects and Policies. New York, National Jewish Conference Center. 16p.

-------------. The Struggle for Soviet Jewry. New York, Council of Jewish Federations, 25p. (Assembly Papers)

Address at the 46th General Assembly of the Council.

GREENBERG, Blu. Encounters in Russia. Moment, 2, No. 5, F-Ma. pp 26-36.

HAZARD, John N, BUTLER, William E, MAGGS, Peter B. The Soviet Legal System, Fundamental Principles and Historical Commentary, Dobbs Ferry, N.Y., Oceana, xvii, 621p.

Important from the point of view of the position of Jews in USSR.

HIRSZOWICZ, Lukasz. Jewish Cultural Life in the USSR - A Survey. Soviet Jewish Affairs, 7, No. 2, pp 3-21.

"Direct and indirect evidence provided by official Soviet sources indicate the existence of a public interest in Jewish culture in the USSR. Given reasonable conditions it can be concluded that a substantial Jewish cultural activity could emerge in that country."

------------------. and SZAFAR, Tadeusz. The Jewish Scapegoat in Eastern Europe. Patterns of Prejudice, 11, No. 5, S-O. pp 7-11.

ISRAEL, Gerard. Juifs d'URSS· Un problème désormais universel. Les Nouveaux Cahiers, 13, No. 48, Sp. pp 1-5.

Sees the Soviet Jewish problem as a universal one.

KOREY, William. From Moscow: The "Socialism of Fools". The American Zionist, 67, No. 7, My-Ju. pp 8-11.

Soviet antisemitism.

--------------. The Silent Screams of Babi Yar. Hadassah Magazine, 59, No. 1, Ja. pp 12-13; 36-39.

"The Kremlin has chosen to plunge the Jewish torment at Babi Yar down history's 'memory hole'."

--------------. Soviet Anti-Semitism Since the Six-Day War. Insight, Soviet Jews, 3, No. 11, N. pp 1-8.

--------------. Soviet Jewry: Plight and Prospect. Midstream, 23, No. 4, Ap. pp 18-27.

--------------. The Soviet Protocols of Zion. Hadassah Magazine, 59, No. 12, D. pp 10-11.

Report on the recently published book entitled International Zionism, issued by Soviet Academy of Sciences, a blatent example of officially sponsored anti-Semitism.

LAWRENCE, John. Soviet Jews. Religion in Communist Lands, Su. pp 76-80.

What the practice of the Jewish religion means to Soviet Jews.

LEVENBERG, S. Karl Marx's view on the 'Jewish Question'. The Jewish Quarterly, 25, No. 1, Sp. pp 37-40; Jewish Affairs, 32, No. 10. O. pp 24-28.

LEVIN, Nora. The Murder of Jewish Culture in the USSR. Jewish Frontier, 44, No. 8, O. pp 30-32.

The period from 1948 to the year of Stalin's death, in 1953.

-----------. Soviet Jewry: Problems and Policies. Congress Monthly, 44, No. 2, F. pp 11-12.

LIPSON, Leon and CHALIDZE, Valery. (Eds.) Papers on Soviet Law. No. 1, New York, Institute on Socialist Law. 200p.

Collection of articles, including the Human Rights Covenants of the United Nations and the Constitutional Law of the USSR by Henn-Juri Uibopuu. Some Remarks on Jews and other Prisoners of Conscience in teh USSR by Leon Lipson. Documents are appended, i.a. on the internal passport system and 'anti-parasite' measures.

MAIDAN, Michael. Marx on the Jewish Question. Olam, Jewish Themes and World Issues, No. 3, W-Sp. pp 11-16.

MAYER, Daniel. La Situation des Juifs en URSS: Defense et Esperance. L'Arche, No. 241, Ap. pp 13-24.

MEISSNER, Boris. Die politischen Aspekte der neuen Bundesverfassung der Sowjet-Union. Europa Archiv, 32, No. 22, 25 N. pp 800-810.
    Deals i.a. with the rights of minorities in the Soviet Union in the new Constitution.

PERAKH, Mark. Solzhenitsyn and the Jews. Midstream, 23, No. 6, Ju-Jy. pp 3-17.

PONTILLON, Robert. Les Juifs d'URSS, L'Arche, 20, Nos. 246-47. S-O. pp 12-13.

SCHENKER, Jonathan. In Commemmoration: 12 August 1952. Congress Monthly, 44, No. 6, S. pp 13-15.
    In memory of the martyred Soviet Jewish writers.

------------------. The Shcharansky Commission, Congress Monthly, 44 No. 8, N. pp 12-14.
    Anatoli Shcharansky is a refusenik who has been jailed.

Soviet Jewry and the Implementation of the Helsinki Final Act. Report. Prepared on behalf of the ongoing Presidium and Steering Committee of the World Conference on Soviet Jewry in co-operation with the Jewish communities concerned, eondon, 64p.

TAS, Luciano. 1948/1952: la distruzione della cultura ebraica nell' URSS. Rome, della Voce, 23p. (I quaderni de la Voce Repubblicana 2)

VERGELIS, Aron. Azoi lebn mir, un undzer lebn in opgeshpiglt in undzer verk. (This is how we live and our life is mirrored in our work). Sovietish Heimland, 17, No. 10. O. pp 179-87.
    To mark the 60th anniversary of the Revolution the issue brings 26 articles depicting life in the USSR. Vergelis analyses these and concludes that Soviet Jews 'consider themselves a vital part of the Soviet people'.

ZALOMAN, Moshe. La véridique histoire de Moshé ouvrier juif et communiste au temps de Staline. Tr. Halina Edelstein. Fontenay-sous-bois. Ed. Recherches, 288p.
    The author, of Polish origin, was arrested in Kiev in 1937 and spent ten years in the Gulag.

A zsidó kultúra a Szovjetunióban: tények és koholmányok. Szputnyik, No. 6, Ju. pp 70-74.
    Jewish culture in the Soviet Union: facts and trumped up charges.

COMMUNIST POLICY ON ZIONISM AND ISRAEL

AGURSKY, Mikhail. L'Union Soviétique et Israël. France-Israel Information, No. 35, ju. pp 10ff.

ASTAKHOV, S. Alliance Between Tel Aviv and Pretoria. International Affairs, No. 8, Au. pp 62-66.
    Accuses both of racialism.

BONDAREVKS, Grigori. Der emes vegn di batsiungen tsvishn di tsionistn un natsismi. (The truth about the connections between Zionists and Nazis.) Sovietish Heimland, 17, No. 9, S. pp 149-58.
    Reprints a document allegedly in 'secret archives' in London, dated 1941 being 'proposals by the Irgun Zvei Leumi on the

settlement of the Jewish question in Europe and the active participation of Irgun in the war on the German side. This document was allegedly handed to a Nazi intelligence officer in Istanbul.

-------------------. In a nets fun vidershpruchn tsvishn di imperialistishe meluches. (In a net of contradictions between the imperialistic powers) Sovietish Heimland, 17, No. 2, F. pp 154-6)
Accusations against the Zionist movement for its handling of the European situation in the late 20s and 30s and for 'collaborating' with theNazis.

-------------------. Der tsionism un der kamf far Palestine. (Zionism and the struggle for Palestine). Sovietish Heimland, 17, No. 3, Ma. pp 141-48.
Includes accusations of Zionist-Nazi collaboration during the war.

-------------------. Triumf fun koruptsie. (The triumph of Corruption). Sovietish Heimland, 17, No. 8, Au. pp 113-20.
Analyses the result of the Israeli elections and ascribes Begin's victory to corruption in every aspect of Israeli public life.

DEUTSCHER, Isaac. Die ungelöste Judenfrage. Zur Dialektik von Antisemitismus und Zionismus. Vorwort und Ubersetzung by Eike Geisel and Mario Offenberg. Berlin, Rotbuch, 144p. (Rotbuch 159)
Deutscher's eight essays on the Jewish question and on Israel which appeared in English under the title The non-Jewish Jews and Other Essays. Part of the book is taken by a postscript by two new-leftists who try to show the relevance of Deutscher's ideas for the shaping of the attitudes of the West German New Leftists, to Antisemitism, Zionism and the Middle East conflict.

PORATH, Yehoshua. The Palestine Communist Party 1929-1939. Olam, Jewish Themes and World Issues, No. 3, W-Sp. pp 22-27.

Remarks of CPSU on Palestine. MERIP Reports, No. 55, Ma. pp 21-33.

RICHMOND, Diana. Soviet Jews and Israel. Middle East International, No. 78, D. pp25-26.
Anti-Zionist view.

SHARIF, Walid. Soviet Marxism and Zionism. Journal of Palestine Studies, 6, No. 3, Sp. pp 77-97.

COMMUNIST TRIALS AND PURGES

LOEBL, Eugen. My Mind on Trial. New York, Harcourt Brace, Jovanovich, xiii, 235p.
Leobl was accused in the Slansky Trial in Prague.

STERN, August. The Soviet Union v. Dr. Mikhail Stern. New York, Urizen; London, Pluto, 330p. German ed: Berlin, Ullstein.
Dr. Stern, falsely accused was tried and convicted for malpractice.

Treatment of Anatoly Shcharansky and Yuri Orlov. Report. Committee on Foreign Relations, Senate, to accompnay Senate Res. 198, 30 Ju. Washington, 2p. (Senate Report 90-318)

COMMUNIST POLICY ON RELIGION

BORDEAUX, Michael, MATCHETT, Kathleen and GERSTENMAIER, Cornelia. Religious Minorities in the Soviet Union. London, Minority Rights Group, 1977, 3.r.e. 28p, Bibl. (MRG Report 1)

MARICHAL, R. Un appel au EEC a propos de la nouvelle legislation religieuse en URSS. Istina, 22, No. 1, pp 26-31.
Includes the Jews.

OSIZMADIA, Andor. Kétoldalú szerződesek. Az állam és az egyházak kapcsolatának jogi rendezése. (Bilateral agreements, Juridicial relations in Hungary) _Világosság_, 18, No. 3, Ma. pp 129-33.
Includes the Jews.

PASZTOI, Margit. Egyházi müemlékek védelme Magyarország gon. (Protection of Clerical Monuments in Hungary) _Vilagossag_, 18, No.7 Jy. pp 427-34.
Deals with Jewish monuments, only one per cent of the total.

A Propaganda World Conference of Churchmen in Moscow. _East-West Digest_, 13, No. 14, Jy. pp 552-54.

RAPACKI, Zbigniew. Un autre mesure du temps. _Istina_, 22, Nos.3-4, Jy-D. pp 280-83.
The Vatican's policy on religious liberty in Eastern Europe.

TOMKA, Miklós. A felekezeti arányok és a szekularizáció Magyarországon. (Religious distribution and secularization in Hungary) Világossag, 18, No. 4, Ap. pp 235-38.
Includes the Jews.

VAMOS, Imre. Az egyházak es az enyhülés. (The Churches and Detente) _Vilagóssag_, 18, No. 10, O. pp 651-55.
Hungarian view.

Views of a Communist Patriarch. _Insight_, 3, No. 8, Au. pp 3-7.

DISSENT - USSR and EASTERN EUROPE

BARGHOORN, Frederick C. Detente and the Democratic Movement in the USSR. London, Collier Macmillan, 192p.

BLOCH, Sidney and REDDAWAY, Peter. Russia's Political Hospitals. The Abuse of Psychiatry in the Soviet Union. London, Victor Gollancz; New York, Basic books, 510p, Ind, Ill.
Fully-documented volume on an increasingly controversial aspect of Soviet society.

GELB, Barbara. Ten Days That Shook Me In Russia. _The New York Times Magazine_, 18 S. pp 21;48-54;58-63.
"Though the plight of Soviet dissidents seems familiar, it is a moving experience to enter their tormented world ... This time the Jews are vocal; this time they will not permit themselves to be marched quietly into oblivion."

GENDIN, Lev. Revenge. A Record of an encounter with Soviet Repression. Tr. Si Frumkin with ed. assistance by Louis Rosenblum. Cleveland, Ohio, Union of Councils for Soviet Jews. Action-Central for Soviet Jews, 32p, Ill.
Gendin, a Jewish activist, describes his clashes with the Soviet authorities at the turn of 1974-75.

GERSTENMAIER, Cornelia. Die Bürgerrechtsbewegung in der Sowjetunion. Studiengesellschaft für Information und Fortbildung, 111p.

GREENBERG, Blu. The Children of the Jews of Silence Launch a New Jewish Cultural Resistance. Hadassah Magazine, 59, No. 6, Ju-Jy. pp 10-12;32.

Discusses Tarbut, a new Jewish cultural movement developing in the USSR.

HOTZ, R. I dissidenti dell'Est europeo. La Civiltà Cattolica, 128, No. 2, My. pp 339-50.

HÜBNER, Peter: Sowjetische Dissidenten 1975-1977. 1. Ziele und Aktivitäten. 2. Reaktionen der Behorden. Osteuropa, 27, Nos. 1 and 2, pp 743-52; 860-78.

Includes the Jewish activists among the dissidents.

MEERSON, AKSENOV, Michael and SHRAGIN, Boris. (Eds.) The Political Social and Religious Thought of Russian 'Samizdat' - An Anthology. Tr. Nikolas Lupinin. Belmont, Mass., Nordland, 624p, Ind, Bibl.

PLIOUCHTCH, Léonide. Dans le Carnival de l'Histoire. Paris, Le Seuil, 442p.

Memoirs of a Soviet dissident.

RIESE, Hans-Peter. (Ed.) Bürgerinitiative für die Menschenrechte. Die tschechoslowakische Opposition zwischen dem "Prager Frühling" und der "Charta 77". Foreword by Heinrich Böll. Conclusion by Arthur Miller. Köln, Frankfurt/M. Europäischer V. 320p. (Demokratischer Sozialismus in Theorie und Praxis)

The dissident movement in Czechoslovakia.

TALMON, Jacob L. Andrei Sakharov's Ordeal. Midstream, 23, No. 2, F. pp 3-13.

White Paper on Czechoslovakia. Paris, International Committee for the Support of Charter 77 in Czechoslovakia, 269p.

Extensive documentation of the struggle for human rights in Czechoslovakia.

WIESEL, Elie. Freedom of Conscience - A Jewish Commentary. Journal of Ecumenical Studies, 14, No. 4, Fa. pp 70-81.

EMIGRATION - USSR

A brif tsum generalsekretar fun der organizatsie fun die varainikte natsies h'Kurt Waldheim. (A letter to the Secretary-General of the United Nations Organisation, Mr. Kurt Waldheim) Sovietish Heimland 17, No. 5,My. pp 3-6.

Letter signed by 300 Soviet Jews in Vienna asking for help in their repatriation to the USSR.

BROWNFIELD, Allan C. Where is home for Soviet Jews? Middle East International No. 69, Ma. pp 19-20.

Against the immigration of Russian Jews to Israel.

CHALIDZE, Valery. How Important is Soviet Dissent? Commentary, 63, No. 6, Ju. pp 57-62.

"Apart from theissue of the extent of dissent, the Soviet dissident movement - and I specifically include the human-rights movement - has contributed over the past decade to transforming the Soviet Union into a somewhat more open society"

Crossroads to Freedom. Marking Time in Rome. Soviet Jews, 3, No. 3, Ma. pp 1-8.

Report on the position Soviet Jewish emigrants are in whilst waiting for overseas visas in Rome.

DINNERSTEIN, Leonard and JAHER, Frederic Cople (Eds.) Uncertain Americans. New York, Oxford U.P. x, 325p.
Contains essays by Dinnerstein on East European Jewish migration
DUBLIN, Richard A. Some observations on resettling Soviet Jews. Journal of Jewish Cŏmmunal Service, 53, No. 4, Ma. pp 278-81.
The fact that Soviet Jews are immigrants and not refugees makes a profound difference in their level of experience. They are not basically struggling for survival but people hoping for a better future.
ELBAUM, M., NAGIEL, I. and GRIGORIEFF, V. Le grand detour. Regards 12, No. 114, Au-S. pp 6-21.
Russian Jewish emigrants talk to Leopold Unger.
FEIN, Leonard. Let my people go. Moment, 2, No. 4, Ja. pp 7-12.
For Jewish emigration from Soviet Russia.
FELDMAN, William. Social Absorption of Soviet Immigrants. Integration or Isolation. Journal of Jewish Communal Service, 53, No. 3, Fa. pp 62-68.
The Jewish Family Service Association of Cleveland, Ohio surveyed its caseload of Soviet immigrants who were sponsored by the Cleveland Jewish community from 1972 through 1976.
FISHER, Max. What to Do About Soviet-Jewish Dropouts. Israel Horizons, 25, No. 1, Ja. pp 6-8.
GIDWITZ, Betsy. But Still Unsettling. Moment, 3, No. 1, N. pp 15-18.
On Russian immigrants to the U.S.A.
GILISON, Jerome M. (Ed.) The Soviet Jewish Emigre. Proceedings of a National Conference held at the Baltimore Hebrew College in December 1976. Baltimore, Ma.Baltimore Hebrew College, Center for the Study of Soviet Jewish Emigration and Resettlement, 167p, Bibl.
GITELMAN, Zvi. Soviet Jewish Emigrants: Why are they Choosing America? Soviet Jewish Affairs, 7, No, 1, pp 31-46.
-------------. Soviet Political Culture: Insights from Jewish emigres. Soviet Studies, 29, No. 4, O. pp 543-64.
GREENBERG, Irving. Crossroads at Vienna: Olim and Noshrim. Response 10, No. 4, W. pp 11-24.
"Upgrading the inner quality and dynamism of Israeli society and of American Jewish community is the key to attracting and holding the commitment not only of Soviet Jews but of native Israeli and American Jews."
HARRIS, David A. Entering a New Culture. A Handbook for Soviet Migrants to the United States of America. Vstuplenie v noviyu zhizn. Kratky ocherk o SShA v pomosch emigrantam iz Sovetskogo Soyuza. Tr. Marina Rappoport, 3.r.e. New York, HIAS, 148p.
Bilingual booklet with basic information on the US.
HAWKS, Irene K. The New Immigrant: A Study of theVocational Adjustment of Soviet Jews. Journal of Jewish Communal Service, 54, No. 2, D. pp 161-65.
Examines the resettlement of the Soviet Jew in New York City.
Hostages: the Plight of Veteran Refuseniks. Insight, 3, No. 12,D. pp 1-7.
JACOBS, Paul. Let My People Go - But Where? The Dilemma of Soviet Jews. Present Tense, 4, No. 2, W. pp 15-20.
JELEN, Christian and UNGER, Leopold. Le Grand Retour. Preface by Golda Meir. Paris, Albin Michel, 348p, Bibl..

KAMENETSKY, Thor. (Ed.) Nationalism and Human Rights: Processes of Modernisation in th USSR. New York Libraries Unlimited; London, Eurospan, 246p.

A collection of studies aiming at the presentation of dissent in the multi-national Soviet State, Soviet nationality policies in their theoretical and practical aspects are discussed. The development of the dissident movement in analysed.

LEVENFELD, Barry. Recent Soviet Immigration to the United States. Contemporary Jewry, 2, No. 1, Sp/Su. pp 17-27.

The issues examined: "1. The reasons and reactions to the sharp increase in Soviet immigration to the United States and 2. the degree of these immigrants' success in adjusting to life in America." Based on the results of a questionaire administered to 97 Soviet immigrants in Boston and Chicago.

NOVAK, William. American Roulette - The Ups and Downs of Russian Immigrants. Moment, 3, No. 1, N. pp 9-18; 51-56.

Conversations with Soviet Jews in Boston reveal that their adjustment has been relatively easy.

RAYMIST, Malka. Russian Peasants who are Jews. Jewish Digest, 23, No. 2, O. pp 65-67. Condensed from World Zionist Organisation Feature.

SEVALA, Efraim. Au revoir. Israël. Juifs Russes et Israël. Paris, Autier, vii, 245p.

STIEF, William. The Refuseniks of Kiev. Saturday Review, 17 S. pp 21-26.

The plight of Ukrainian Jews, to whom the Soviet authorities have refused visas for several years.

TAFT, Ethel. The Absorption of Soviet Jewish Immigrants. Their Impact on Jewish Communal Institutions. Journal of Jewish Communal Service, 54, No. 2, D. pp 166-71.

WEISS-ROSMARIN, Trude. Neshirah. Jewish Spectator, 42, No.1, Sp. pp 3-5.

Soviet Jewish emigrants fail to go to Israel.

Welcome to New York, NYANA orientation manual. New York, Association for New Americans, New York, 37p.

In English and Russian.

EAST-WEST RELATIONS

Basket III: implementation of the Helsinki Accords, Hearings, Commission on Security and Cooperation in Europe. Congress, Washington, 1. Human rights. 23-24 F. 1977; Human contacts, family reunification and binational marriages. 15-17 Ma. 1977. 233p. 2. Religious liberty and minority rights in the Soviet Union, 27-28 Ap. 1977; Helsinki compliance in Eastern Europe, 9 My. 1977. 439p. 3. Information flow, and cultural and educational exchanges, 19-25 My, 1977. 193p. 4. Soviet Helsinki watch. reports on repression, 3 Ju. 1977; US policy and the Belgrade Conference, 6 Ju. 1977,104p.

BUERGENTHAL, J. (Ed.) Human Rights, International Law and the Helsinki Accord. New York, Universe Books, Montdair Allanheld, Osmun & Co.

Discusses the issues of Basket Three of the Helsinki Final Act.

Commission on Security and Cooperation in Europe. Report to the Congress of the United States on implementation of the Final Act of the Conference on Security and Cooperation in Europe: findings and recommendations two years after Helsinki. Washington, Au. 254p.

DUPUY, B. La "troisieme corbeille" d'Helsinki. *Istina*, 22, Nos. 3-4, Jy-D. pp 276-79.
Discusses the Third Basket of the Helsinki Final Act.

East-West Institute. Implementation Conference on Security and Cooperation in Europe - CSCE II. The Hague, East-West Institute, 102p.

Entre Helsinki et Belgrade. *Istina*, 22, No. 1, pp 3-6.
Editorial on the Belgrade Review Conference.

Final Act of the Diplomatic Conference on the Reaffirmation and Development of International Humanitarian Law Applicable in Armed Conflicts ... Geneva, 20 F-10 Ju. London, HMSO, 109p. (Cmnd 6927)
This Red Cross Conference was an example of politization of International organisations.

FINOCCHIARO, Gianni. La Conferenza per la sicurezza europea. Il dibattito internationale fino al 1972. 2.r.e. Prefazione di Roberto Ducci. Padova, Cedam, 195p. (Publicazioni della Societa italiana per l'organizzazione internazionale)
On the debate leading to the Conference on Security and Cooperation in Europe.

Helsinki: Human Rights - Policy of Detente. The Realisation of the Final Act of Helsinki in the countries of the East bloc. München, Hanns-Seidel-Stiftung; Luzern, Europäische Konferenz für Menschenrechte und Selbstbestimmung, St. Gallen, Communio Nova Bohemica, 2 vols.

From Helsinki to Belgrade: Issues and Perspectives. Report of the fourth Williamsburg Conference. Washington, D.C., Center for Strategic and International Studies, 46p, Ill.

Implementation of the Final Act of the Conference on Security and Cooperation in Europe: debate on the general policy of the Council of Europe (27,28 and 29 Ap) Strasbourg, Council of Europe, Parliamentary Assembly, 195p.

Implementation of the Final Act of the Conférence on Security and Cooperation in Europe: findings and recommendations two years after Helsinki. Report transmitted to the Committee on International Relations, House, by the Commission on Security and Cooperation in Europe, 23 Washington, 194p.

Report to the Congress of the United States on implementation of the Final Act of the Conference on Security and Cooperation in Europe: findings and recommendations two years after Helsinki. Washington, Commission on Security and Cooperation in Europe, 230p.

JACOBSEN, Hans Adolf, MALLMAN, Wolfgang, MEIER, Christian. (Eds.) Sicherheit und Z-sammenarbeit in Europa. KSZE 1973-75. Köln, Wissenschaft und Politik. 700p.
Surveys the aims and prospects of the Conference on European Security and Cooperation.

KOREY, William. Final Acts and Final Solutions. *Society*, 15, No. 1, N-D. pp 81-86.
"While the Helsinki Declaration requires the recognition of religions and specifically allows for 'contacts and meetings' to 'exchange information' Soviet authorities have done nothing since 1 August 1975 to provide the essentials for freely observing the Judaic faith."

--------------. Soviet Jewry's Desperate Cry: Honor the Helsinki Pact's Guarantee of Human Rights. Hadassah Magazine, 59, No. 5, My pp 14-15; 33-36.

Extensive documentation of non-compliance by the Communist countries is currently being accumulated by Congressman Dante Fascell's Commission on Security and Cooperation.

Die KSZE und die Menschenrechte. Politische und rechtliche uberlegungen zur zweiten Etappe. Mit Beiträgen von Dieter Blumenwitz, George Brunner, Rupert Dimecke, Wilhelm Greve, Jens Hacker, Boris Meissner, Hans-Peter Schwarz, Berlin, Duncker and Humbolt, 143p. (Studien zur Deutschlandfrage, Band 2)

The second phase of the Conference on Security and Cooperation in Europe - the Human Rights Issue.

NEAGU, Romulus. European Security: A Romanian Point of View. Bucharest, Meridiane, 151p.

NORTON, A. Detente: the implications of October 1973. Military Review, 57, No. 9, S. pp 21-27.

Note of the month. Procedural wrangles in Belgrade. The World Today 33, No. 9, D. pp 321-25.

Soviet procrastinations at the Conference on Security and Cooperation in Europe.

NOWAK, Jerzy. Miedzynarodowe kontakty osobowe po KBWE (Die internationalen privaten kontakte nach der KSZE) Sprawy Miedzynarodowe, 30, No. 4, Ap. pp 7-24.

Private international contacts after the Conference on Security and Cooperation in Europe.

OSADCZUK-KORAB, B.A. Osteuropa unterwegs nach Belgrad. Folgen der KSZE Konferenz in Helsinki. Osteuropa, 27, No. 5, My. pp 371-77.

East European countries between Helsinki and Belgrade.

ROTH, Stephen J. Facing the Belgrade Meeting: Helsinki - Two Years After. Soviet Jewish Affairs, 7, No. 1, pp 1-16.

SCHEINERT, D. Le doigt sur la detente. Regards, 12, No. 111, Ma. pp 15-18.

SCHULZ, Eberhard. Konsolidierung der Entspannung nach Helsinki. Osterreichische Zeitschrift für Aussenpolitik, 17, No. 2, pp 77-84.

----------------. Unorthodoxe Gedanken zwischen Helsinki und Belgrad Versuch einer Bilanz über ein Kapital Entspannungspolitik. Osteuropa, 27, No. 5, My. pp 378-88.

SCHWAB, George and MORGENTHAU, Hans J. Detente in Historical Perspective. 2.r.e. New York, Cyro P., 175p.

SCHWARZ, Hans-Peter. Azischenbilanz der KSZE, Stuttgart, Seewald, 136p.

-------------------. Zwischen Helsinki und Belgrad. Chancen und Gefahren für Gesamteuropa. Die Politische Meinung, 22, No. 172, My-Ju. pp 5-22.

SCHWEIGLER, Gebhard. Die amerikanische Entspannungspolitik: Wandel oder Kontinuitä? Europa Archiv, 32, No. 22, 25 N. pp 791-99.

SEDIVY, Jaroslav. Grundfragen des Friedens und der Sicherheit in den internationalen Beziehungen. Europa Archiv, 32, No. 24, 25 D. pp 851-58.

Selected Documents Relating to Problems of Security and Cooperation in Europe. 1954-77. Miscellaneous No. 17. London, HMSO, S. x, 362p, (Cmnd 6932)

FUR Sicherheit und Zusammenarbeit in Europa. Die DDR und die Schlu-sakte von Helsinki.Berlin, Staatsverl. der DDR, Hrsg. Institut für Internationale Beziehungen an der Akademie für Staats - und Rechtswissenschaft der DDR, 79p.

VYSOCKY, Martin. Ceskoslovaksko a Konferncia a bespecnost ... v Europe (Czechoslovakia and CSCE) Bratislava, Obzor, 108p.

WAJSMAN, Patrick. L'Illusion de la detente. Presses universitaires de France, 285p.

MIGRATION AND REFUGEES

BERKMAN, Ted. J.F.K., Fanny Holtzman and the refugees. Jewish Digest, 22, No. 8, Ap. pp 22-25.
    Excerpted from the book The Lady and the Law, Boston, Mass. Little & Brown, 1976.

I Campi di Concentramento Italiani per Ebrei Profughi. Milano, Israele Kalk, 500p, Ill.
    Italian concentration camps for Jewish refugees.

FRAGOMEN, Austin T. 1976 Amendments to the Immigration and Nationality Act. International Migration Review, 11, No. 1, Sp. pp 95-100.

GENIZI, Haim. James G. McDonald: High Commissioner for Refugees. 1933-35. The Wiener Library Bulletin, 30, Nos. 43-44, pp 40-52.
    McDonald resigned his post seeing the futility of trying to save Jews from Nazi persecution.

GOLDNER, Franz. Die österreichische Emigration 1938 bis 1945. Wien, München, Herold, 364p.
    Includes the Jewish migrants from Austria.

HANISCH, Werner and VOGL, Dieter. Helsinki - Ergebnisse und Perspektiven. Berlin, Staatsverl. der DDR 126p. (Blickpunkt Weltpolitik)
    East German view of the CSCE.

HAWKINS, Freda. Canadian Immigration: A New Law and a New Approach to Management. International Migration Review, 11, No. 1, Sp. pp 77-94.

IRIS, Mark. Immigration without Integration. New Brunswick, N.J. Transaction Books, 221p.
    Immigrant communities which maintain their ethnicity.

JACOBSON, Gaynor I. The International Migration Factor: Causes and Consequences. Journal of Jewish Communal Service, 53, No. 4, Su. pp 371-78.

KAYSER, Bernard. European Migrations: The New Pattern. International Migration Review, 11, No. 2, Su. pp 232-40.

KESSNER, Thomas. The Golden Door. Italian and Jewish Immigrant Mobility in New York City 1880-1915. New York, Oxford U.P., xxvi, 224p, Ind.
    Sociological study of two major groups of immigrants during the period of the mass immigration to the U.S.A.

SALT, John and CLOUT, Hugh. (Eds.) Migration in Post-War Europe. (New Geographical Essays) London, Oxford U.P., 238p.
    Includes Jews.

SUTHERLAND, D.E. On the Migration of Sociological Structures 1933-41 A Forgotten Episode in the History of American Sociology and a Case Study in the Sociology of Migration. Sociologie Contemporaine, 22,

Nos. 1-3, (1977) pp 87-121.
WAKIN, Edward. The Immigrant Experience. Faith, Hope and the Golden Door. New York, Our Sunday Visitor.
Focuses on Roman Catholics, with an additional chapter on Jews.

ALIYAH/YERIDAH

ADLER, Seymour. Maslow's Need Hierarchy and the Adjustment of Immigrants. International Migration Review, 11, No. 4, W. pp 444-51.
Uses the need hierarchy theory of Abraham Maslow (1970) to describe the stages in the adjustment process of new immigrants. This notion is then developed and applied to interpreting some longitudinal data on the changing needs of immigrants to Israel during the first two years after their arrival.
FERON, James. The Israelis of New York. New York Times Magazine, 16 Ja. pp 14-15;17.
"Back home, they are considered deserters. But, they reply, don't Jews have a right to emigrate from their homeland?"
HANDELMAN, Ira and KUSHNAN, Moshe J. The New Immigrants: Israelis and the Los Angeles Jewish Community. Davka, No. 19, pp 9-11.
Investigates the ambivalent relationship between Israelis who have resettled in Los Angeles and LA's American Jews.
JONES, Kenneth. Thoughts on the Reverse Exodus. Davka, No. 19, pp 12-23.
Speculates on the reasons Israelis leave Israel and what might induce them to remain.
LUFT, Gerda. Heimkehr ins Unbekannte. Eine Darstellung der Einwanderung von Juden aus Deutschland nach Palastina vom Aufstieg Hitlers zur Macht bis zum Ausburch des Zweiten Weltkrieges. 1933-1939. Wuppertal, Peter Hammer, 141p.
Immigration of German Jews to Palestine 1933-1939.
SABBATELLO, Franco E. L'immigrazione dall'italia in Israele (1969-1974): Caratteristiche ed Integrazione. La Rassegna Mensile di Israel, 43, No. 5-6, My-Ju. pp 215-42.
SELIGMAN, Ruth. An Untapped Source of Aliyah from America. The American Zionist, 67, No. 8, Jy. pp 18-20.
Retired American Jews settle in Israel.
SHAMA, Avraham and MARK, Iris. Immigration without Integration: Third World Jews in Israel. Cambridge, Mass., Schenkman, xii, 225p, Ind, Bibl.
TABORY, E. and LAZERWITZ, B. Motivation for Migration: A Comparative Study of American and Soviet Academic Immigrants to Israel. Ethnicity, 4, No. 2, Ju. pp 91-102.
This study suggests that both Soviet Jews and some American Jews are "pushed' to leave because of a feeling of uneasiness based upon their relations with the larger society.
TAMARIN, Georges R. Israeli Migratory Processes Today: Does Israel Really Want all its Immigrants? Plural Societies, 8, Nos. 3-4, Aut/W. pp 3-32.
UROFSKY, Melvin I. American Aliyah: A Dialogue Between the Deaf? Midstream, 23, No. 4, Ap. pp 57-63.

VIEST, Agnes. Identität und Integration dargestellt am Beispiel mitteleuropäischer Einwanderer in Israel. Frankfurt/M. Peter Lang, 158p, Bibl. (Europäische Hochschulschriften)
Integration of Central European immigrants to Israel.
ZUCKERMAN-BARELI, Chaya. Aspirations for Out-migration in an Israeli Development Town. Plural Societies, 8, Nos. 3-4, Aut/W. pp 33-42.

ARAB REFUGEES

CHOUCRI, Nazli. The New Migration in the Middle East: A Problem for whom? Cambridge, Migration and Development Study Group, 30p.
Recent tenjencies in Middle East migration and its implications for Egypt and the other Arab states.
PRITTIE, Terence and DINEEN, Bernard. Det dobbelte flygtningeproblem København, SDI, 48p. (In Danish)
the dual refugee problem - Arab refugees and Jewish refugees from Arab countries.

NATIONALISM

SZULC, Tad. Nationalism is Rampant Again. Notes on a European Journey. Present Tense, 4, No. 2, W. pp 38-43.

ANTISEMITISM

L'Affaire Dreyfus. Annales Economics, Societes, Civilisations, 32, No. 2, pp 240-91.
Two articles on the problems raised by the Dreyfus affair (with English summary)
AGES, Arnold. Anti-Semitism versus Anti-Zionism. Conservative Judaism, 31, No. 3, Su. pp 7-12.
Discusses the ambiguities surrounding the question from a Communist viewpoint, the Arab propaganda field and Christian prejudice.
AGURSKY, Mikhail. Dmitrievsky and the Origins of National Bolshevism Soviet Jewish Affairs, 7, No. 2, D. pp 53-61.
Serge Dmitrievsky's antisemitism.
Antisemitismus noch immer ein Tabu. Zeitgeschichte, Part 8,
Discusses the way the question of antisemitism is swept under the carpet in Austria and Germany.
ARKIN, Marcus. The Dreyfus Affair in Historical Perspective. Jewish Affairs, 32, No. 3, Ma. pp 51-58.
AUGUET, Roland. Le Juif errant. Paris, Payot, 194p.
Traces the history of the 'wandering Jew' as an antisemitic prototype.
AVINERI, Shlomo. Neuvas Formas de Antisemitismo. Information, 12, No. 90, D-Ja. 1977. pp 6-8.
Anti-Zionism as a form of antisemitism.
BAYME, Steven Gilbert. Jewish leadership and antisemitism in Britain 1898-1918. Ann Arbor, Mich., U. Microfilms, 365p.
Ph.D. Dissertation, Columbia University.
BERK, S.M. The Russian revolutionary movement and the pogroms of 1881-1882. Soviet Jewish Affairs, 7, No. 2, pp 22-39.
The pogroms were, in some measure, supported by the movement.

CARDOZA, Elena P. de Argentina: Where Jewish Hopes Have Turned To Ashes. Hadassah Magazine, 59, No. 12, D. pp 18-19;26-28.

"Since the contemporary virulence of anti-Semitism in Argentina is a corollary to degredation of human rights for many Argentine citizens as well, anti-semitism will not abate until human rights are more sensitively regarded."

CHARLE, Christophe. Champ littéraire et champ du pouvoir: les écrivains et l'AffaireDreyfus. Annales, Economies, Sociétes, Civilisations, 32, No. 2, Ma-Ap.

COHEN, Naomi W. Pioneers of American Jewish Defense. American Jewish Archives, 29, No. 2, N. pp 116-50.

In pre-war America, Jews did not enjoy the services of an organised institutional response to anti-Jewish outrages at home and abroad. Protests against anti-Semitism and other anti-Jewish activities were delivered by three American Jewish periodicals of the time - The Occident, The Asmonean and The Israelite. Professor Cohen analyses the methods employed by them.

COHN, Robert. Anti-Semitism and the Jesus People. Reconstructionist 43, No. 1, F. pp 11-16.

COLOMBO, Anne. Esiste antisemitismo nella letterature Italiana? La Rassegna Mensile de Israel, 43, Nos. 7-8, Jy-Au. pp 387-91.

Antisemitism is not one of the main features of Italian literature.

EHRHARDT, A. A Travers l'affaire Dreyfus: Henry et Valcarlos. Paris, Klinchsieck, 214p.

FREI, Bruno. The Jewish Question: Before and after the Holocaust. Jewish Currents, 31, No. 2, F. pp 12-17; No. 3, pp 4-9.

GELTMAN, Max. On Socialist anti-Semitism. Midstream, 23, No. 3, Ma. pp 20-30.

GORMAN, Robert M. Racial antisemitism in England: the legacy of Arnold Leese. The Wiener Library Bulletin, 30, Nos. 43-44, pp 65-73.

GREENBURG, Sam. Through the years with Shakespear's Merchant. Reconstructionist, 43, No. 7, O. pp 19-26.

"In a truly civilised world, we might hope that an enlightened audience could savor Shakespeare's play while rejecting the bigotry with which he spiced his work for the taste of his contemporaries."

Ambassador Herzog says United Nations is World Center for Anti-Semitism. ADL Bulletin, 34, No. 10, O. pp 4-5;8.

In an interview, Israel's representative to the United Nations discusses present and reviews past General Assembly sessions.

HOLZER, Jerzy. The Political Right in Poland 1918-39. Journal of Contemporary History, 12, No. 3, Jy. pp 395-412.

Discusses official antisemitism of the period.

JAENEN, Cornelius J. Thoughts on French and Catholic Anti-Semitism. Jewish Historical Society of Canada, 1, No. 1, Ap. pp 16-23.

Relates to the French-Canadian scene.

Jüdisches Museum in Eisenstadt. (Ed.) Der gelbe Stern in Österreich. Katalog und Einführung zu einer Dokumentation. Eisenstadt, Rötzer, 134p, Ill. (Studia Judaica Austraica 5)

Antisemitism in Austria. Includes also articles: Der Weg zur

Katastrophe by Kurt Schubert. Die Katastrophe der Juden in Österreich 1938-1945 - ihre Voraussetzungen und ihre Überwindung. by Johnny Moser.

KNAPP, Betty L. Céline et ses obsessions. Les Nouveaux Cahiers, 12, No. 47, W. pp 18-28.
C.F. Céline's antisemitism.

KOLODNY, Ralph L. Father Coughlin and the Jews: A Reminiscence for Younger. Colleagues. Journal of Jewish Communal Service, 53, No. 4, Su. pp 309-19. Congress Monthly, 44, No. 8, N. pp 14-17.
Discusses the popular radio priest who was the most vicious antisemitic spokesman in America.

KÖLLUNG, Friedrich. Bei uns wie überall? Antisemitismus in der Schweiz 1866-1900. Zurich, SIG, 412p, Ill, Bibl, M.
Fundamental study of antisemitism in Switzerland 1866-1900.

LANDAU, Lazare. L'Europe malade de l'antisémitisme. Les Nouveaux Cahiers, 12, No. 47, W. pp 7-17.

LILL, R. Gli inizi dell'antisemitismo nella Germania bismarcklana. Storia Contemporanea, 8, No. 3, pp 415-39.
Antisemitism in the second half of the 19th century in Germany.

LOWRY, Richard. The Rejected-Suitor Syndrome: Human Sources of New Testament "Antisemitism" Journal of Ecumenical Studies, 14, No. 2, Sp. pp 219-32.

MARKISH, Simon. Jewish Images in Solzhenitsyn. Soviet Jewish Affairs, 7, No. 1, pp 69-81.
Solzhenitsyn is no antisemite, he just considers Jews as strangers in Russia. His views should be considered in the light of Jabotinski's ideas.

MAULKO, G. Les étrangers en France et le problème du racisme. Preface de P. Serre, Paris, La Pensée Universelle, 256p, Ill.
History of immigration to France since World War I. Second half discusses anti-Arab and anti-Jewish trends and counter-reaction to these.

MAURER, Harry. Anti-Semitism in Argentina: 'Jews and Leftists Tremble'. The Nation, 216, F. pp170-73.
Recent anti-semitic eruptions, Arab involvement, government toleration and the position of the Argentine Jewish 'establishment'.

MOGGE, Birgitta. Rhetorik des Hasses. Eugen Dühring und die Genese seines antisemitischen Wortschatzes. Neuss, Gesellschaft für Buchdruckerei. 243p. (Aus Zeit und Geschichte)

NEWMAN, J. A Noteworthy Misconception of Jews and Jewish Philosophy. Dialogue, 16, No. 3, pp 397-410.
Gibson's antisemitism in chapter III of The Philosopher and Theology.

NGUYEN, M. Note sur les problèmes de l'antisémitisme maurraissien. In: L'idée de race dans la pensée politique francaise contemporaine Paris, CNRS, 281p.
Discusses the ambiguities in the antisemitism of Charles Maurras.

NOLA, Alfonso. Ancora Antisemitismo. La Rassegna Mensile di Israel, 43, No. 5-6, My-Ju. pp 212-214.

-------------. Mircea Eliade e l'antisemitismo. La Rassegna Mensile di Israel, 43, Nos. 1-2, Ja-F. pp 12-15.

POLIAKOV, Leon. Der arische Mythos. München, Europa, Tr. Margaret Venjakob, 440p.
--------------. Geschichte des Antisemitismus. Tr. Rudolf Pfisterer Worms, Heintz. 1. Von der Antike bis zu den Kreuzzügen, xi, 95p.
--------------. Histoire de l'antisemitisme. L'Europe Suicidaire, 1870-1933. Paris, Calmann-Levy, 364p. (Liberte de l'esprit S)
From the revolutionary period to the rise of Ponty.
PONTY, J. Le Petit Journal et l'Affaire Dreyfus (1897-1899) analyse de contenu. Revue d'Histoire Moderne et Contemporaine, 24, No. 6, O-D. pp 641-56.
This newspaper was published in one million copies, and became one of the most vociferous antisemitic organs of the period.
PRITTIE, Terence. Antisemitism in Imperial Germany. AJA Review, 19, No. 2, Aut. pp 13-14.
RAPOPORT, Roger. The Marine Corps Builds Klansmen. New Times, 27 My. pp 21-32.
Recent Ku Klux Klan activities at Marine base Camp Pendleton, California.
RIOUX, Jean-Pierre. Nationalisme et conservatisme: la ligue de la patrie francaise, 1899-1904. Paris, Beauchesne, 118p.
Antisemitism in France, coinciding with the Dreyfus Affair.
ROGALLA VON BIEBERSTEIN, J. The Story of the Jewish Masonic Conspiracy. 1776-1945. Patterns of Prejudice, 11, No. 6, N-D. pp 1-8; 21.
Fully treated in the author's Die These von der Versenwörung 1776-1945, Berne, 1976.
ROME, David. Clouds in the Thirties. On Antisemitism in Canada. 1929-1939. A Chapter on Canadian Jewish History. Montreal, Canadian Jewish Congress, 3 sections.
A documented study of Canadian antisemitism in the pre-World War II period, with analysis of the major cases in which it manifested itself.
-----------. The Political Consequences of the Jewish School Question, Montreal 1925-1933. Jewish Historical Society of Canada, 1, No. 1, Ap. pp 3-15.
ROSENMAN, Stanley. Psychoanalytic Reflections on Antisemitism. Journal of Psychology and Judaism, 1, No. 3, pp 3-23.
SARACINI, Eugenio. Breve storia degli ebrei e dell'antisemitismo. Intro. by Umberto Terracini, Milan, Mondadori, 153p.
SHANKMAN, Arnold. Ronald Linden Loses a Job - Academic Anti-Semitism 1977. Jewish Currents, 31, No. 7, Jy-Au. pp 5-8.
SZÁRAZ, György. Egy Előítélet Nyomában. In the Footsteps of a Prejudice. Budapest, Magvető, 287p
Szaraz seeks to expiate the burden of collective crime perpetrated on Hungarian Jews by Hungarians.
VOIGT, Judith. Arabisk Antisemitisme. Genoptrykt fra 'Israel' København, 12p. (In Danish)
Arab antisemitism.
WEINZIERL, Erika. Antisemitismus. Journal Für Angewandte Sozial Forschung, 17, No. 3, pp 13-26; No. 4, pp 12-21.
WEISS, Hildegard. Antisemitismus. noch immer ein Tabu? Zeit-Geschichte, 4, No. 8, My. pp 292-96.
The Austrian scene.

WILSON, Stephen. Le Monument Henry: la structure de l'antisémitisme en France 1898-1899. Annales, Economies, Sociétes, Civilisations, 32, No. 2, Ma-Ap.

ZUIDEMA, Willem. How Prejudice is Passed On. Christian Attitudes on Jews and Judaism, No. 80, O. pp 11-13.

"It is not enough to expose the roots of antisemitism nor to describe them in terms of theology or history. We have to see how they function in a non-religious context. We have to analyse the mechanisms of prejudice in the first things our children learn about Bible and religion."

ANTISEMITIC PUBLICATIONS

APP, Austin J. Power and Propaganda in American Politics and Foreign Affairs. Speech delivered to the Members of the Washington Chapter of the Military Order of the World Wars who met at the Army and Navy Club in Washington, D.C. 10 Feb. 1977. Takoma Park, Boniface P., pp 11-16. (Reprinted from The Liberty Bell.)

Antisemitic.

BUCK, Pitman, Jr. American Freedom and Zionist Power. Seabrook, Texas, Author, 39p.

Antisemitic tract.

FREEDMAN, Ben, EPSTEIN, Max and KELSO, James Leon. Sionismen det Dolda Förtrycket. Sedan du studarat detkommer du aldrig att se pa världshistorien pa samma sätt igen! (Zionism the Hidden Tyranny: Presbyterian Clergymen of Note and Prominence challenge Jew-Control Report on the Middle East. Sweden, Bible Researcher, 30p.

Antisemitic tract.

HARWOOD, Richard. Dog Werkligne sex Mijoner? Sanningen Till Sist. (Did Six Million Really Die? The Truth at Last) Sweden, Bible Researcher, 46p, Ill, M.

Swedish edition of Did Six Million Really Die?

KAUFMANN, Theodore N. Deutschland muss ausgelöscht werden! Germany Must Perish. Witten, Witten, 96p.

Nationalist pamphlet, first published in the USA in 1941. Antisemitic.

The Six Million Reconsidered. Is the 'Nazi Holocaust' Story a Zionist Propaganda Ploy? Volume One: In an Examination of the Jewish Genocide Claim Versus the Disaster of the Twentieth Century by the Committee for Truth in History. Chapel Ascote, Historical Review P., Media Research Associates, 170p.

Sequel to the antisemitic tract Did Six Million Really Die?

SYKES, Christopher. The Protocols of the Elders of Zion. History Today, 26, No. 2, F. Condensed in Jewish Affairs, 31, No. 4, Ap. pp 43-45.

TOLLET, D. La littérature antisémite polonaise de 1588 à 1668. Auteurs et editions. Revue Francaise d'Histoire du livre. 46, No. 14, pp 73-105.

ANTISEMITIC
LEGISLATION

HACKER, Ivan. Judengesetze im Burgenland von Stephen dem Heiligen bix Maris Theresia (1001-1780). Offprint from Studia Judaica Austriaca III, pp 7-15.
Anti-Jewish legislation in Burgenland (Eastern Austria) from the time of St. Stephen to Maria Theresa. This part of Austria, before 1919, belonged to Hungary.

CHRISTIAN
ANTISEMITISM

Evangelican Survey Findings. New York, Anti-Defamation League of B'nai B'rith. 13p.
Surveys traces of antisemitism in Evangelical doctrine.

BEDARIDA, Renée. Témoignage Chrétien. 1941-44. Paris, Ed. Ouvrières 378p.
History and analysis of a French right-wing Catholic journal.

BLUMENKRANZ, Bernhard. Ecriture et image dans la polémique antijuive de Maître Emerngaud. Offprint from: Juifs et judaisme de Languedoc, Toulouse, pp 295-318.
The anti-Jewish polemics of Maître Emerngaud.

BOROWITZ, Eugene B. Antisemitism and the Christologies of Barth. Berkouwer, and Pannenberg. Dialog, 16, No. 1, W. pp 38-41.
Rosemary Ruether called antisemitism "the left hand of Christology" but did not apply this insight to modern theologies. Here are three test cases, Karl Barth has a negative theological evaluation of Jews, although fortunately (and consistently) he defends them against any social-political degradation that might result. Wolfhart Pannenberg"s book on Christology claims Jesus' resurrection in principle brought about the collapse of Judaism, and although he later apologized (1972) his forthcoming re-issue of the book has no modification whatsoever on this point. Ironically, the biblicism of G.C. Berkouwer is the most devoid of both theological and social prejudice against the Jews, which suggests that Ruether's thesis need not apply in every case.

BOXE, Piet Van and McGRATH, Margaret. Anti-Jewish Elements in Liturgy: A Challenge to Christians. SIDIC, 10, No. 2, pp 25-27.
The need for a revision of liturgical texts and customs has been recognized for some time in the Roman Catholic Church.

BUNTE, Wolfgang. Peter Rosegger und das Judentum. Altes und Neues Testament. Antisemitismus, Judentum und Zionismus. Hildesheim: G. Olms, 453p. (Judaistische Texte und Studien 6)

FRIEDLANDER, Albert H. Christliche Theologie und antijudaism: Die Kategoire "Alt-Neu" in der hebräischen Bibel und Tradition. Evangelische Theologie, 37, no. 6, N-D. pp 502-8.

IDINOPULOS, T.A. and WARD, R.B. Is Christology Inherently Anti-Semitic? A Critical Review of Rosemary Ruether's Faith and Fratricide. Journal of the American Academy for Religion, 45, No. 2. pp 193-214.
In her book, Ruether analyses the theological roots of antisemitism which is criticized.

IGLESIAS, Luis Garcia. Los canones del Concilio de Elbira y los judios. El Olivo, No. 3-4, JY-D. pp 61-70.

The Council of Elvira (Spain) in the 4th century regulated the relationship between Jews and Christians.

LANGMUIR, G.I. L'absence d'accusation de meurtre rituel à l'ouest du Rhône. Cahiers Fanjeaux, No. 12, pp 235-49.

Ecclesiastic authorities neglected the lay people's attempts to import blood-libel stories from the North.

LOTZ, Roy. Another Look at the Orthodoxy Anti-Semitism Nexus. Review of Religious Research, 19, W. pp 126-33.

Examines the most salient criticisms of the 1966 study Christian Beliefs and Anti-Semitism by Charles Glock and Rodney Stark and reanalyses the Bay Area data on which it rests.

Oberammergau passion play. Passio nova. Bitteres Leiden, obsiegende Tod und glorreiche Auferstehung des eingefleischten Sohn Gottes. Einer christlichen Versammlung vorgestellt durch P. Ferdinand Posner OSB Ettal 1750. Für Obberammergau bearbeitet von Alois Fink. Oberammergau, 199p, Eng. Tr. by George Saloman, New York, A.J. Committee, 104p.

Official text.

RUETHER, Rosemary. Brudermord und Nächstenliebe. Die Theologischen Wurzeln des Antisemitismus. München, Chr. Kaiser. 270p. (Abhandlungen zur christlichjüdischen Dialog, 6)

"Fratricide and Neighbourly Love" the theological roots of antisemitism.

RUPP, G. Martin Luther and the Jews. Nederlands Theologisch Tijdschrift. 31, No. 2, pp 121-35.

Lecture at Leiden, first given as a Robert Wayley Cohen Memorial Lecture in London, and published by the Council of Christians and Jews in 1962.

THE ARTS

JEWISH ART

CASSUTO, David. The Scuola Grande Tedesca in the Venice Ghetto. Journal of Jewish Art, 3-4, pp 40-57.

DOLEZELOVA, Jana. The State Jewish Museum Collection of Wedding Dishes and Plates. Judaica Bohemiae, 13, No. 1, pp 29-43.

EIS, Ruth. Hannukah Lamps of the Judah L. Magnes Museum, Berkeley, 137p. Ill.

EMMANUEL, Vera. The Visual Dimension - Aspects of Jewish Art. Jewish Quarterly, 25, Nos. 3-4, pp 5-8.

Fabric of Jewish Life. Textiles from the New York Jewish Museum Collection, N. 1977 - Ma. 1978. A Wealth of Material for all occasions and from many countries held at the Jewish Museum. Catalogue by Barbara Kirshenblatt-Gimblett and Cissy Grossman, 144p Ill.

FERBER, Stanley. Micrography: A Jewish Art Form. Journal of Jewish Art, 3-4, pp 12-24.

FOERSTER, Gideon. The synagogues at Massada and Herodion. Journal of Jewish Art, 3-4, pp 6-11.

FRIEDLER, Egon. Habima: A theatre that reflects its land and people. Israel Horizons, 25, No. 7, S. pp 12-14.

FUKS, Marian. Z Diariusza Muzycznego. Sylwetki eseje szkice. Warszawa, Zydowski Instytut Historyczny w Polsce. 398p, Ill.

Jewish musicians and their patrons during the Nazi occupation.

GARTENBERG, Egon. Mahler: The Man and His Music. New York, Schirmer Books (Macmillan); London, Cassel, 448p, Ind.

HORVATH, Bela. Czigány Dezsö Ady-képei. Budapest, Magveto", 88p. Ill. (Gyorsulo Idö)

Czigany, a noted Jewish painter of this century made many portraits of the poet Ady.

JOSEPHS, Z. Jewish Glass Makers. Transactions of the Jewish Historical Society of England, 25, pp 107-19. Ill.

KANIEL, Michael. Trees of Light: The Menorah and the Hannukah Lamp. Jewish Art, 1, No. 1, pp 14-27.

KLAGSBALD, Victor. From the Collector's Cabinet - Clay Lamps with Biblical Scenes. Journal of Jewish Art, 3-4, pp 122-31.

KRESH, Paul. From "Eli-Eli" to Bob Dylan. The Great Jewish Record Hunt. Present Tense, 5, No. 1, Aut. pp 40-48.

LAZAR, Hava. JOnah, the Tower and the Lions: An Eighteenth Century Italian Silver Book Binding. Journal of Jewish Art, 3-4, pp 58-73.

LEVIN, Michael. The Transformation of the Villa Savoye into the Jewish National Library: le Corbusier's Influence on Two Generations of Israeli Architects. Journal of Jewish Art, 3-4, pp 103-21.

PINSHAW, Israel. Synagogue Ark in Outshoorn Museum. Jewish Affairs, 32, No. 8, Au. pp 15-18.

South Africa.

PRIEBATSCH, Suzanne. Narkiss on Jewish Art. Jewish Affairs, 32, No. 9, S. pp 91-96.

On Bezalu Narkiss, Professor of Art History, The Hebrew University.

ROSENBERG, Louise. Bookplates of Jewish Interest. Australian Jewish Historical Society, 8, No. 3, pp 126-33.

SCHÜLER, Irmgard. Jewish Gold Glasses. Journal of Jewish Art, 1, No. 1, pp 28-32.

SCHWARTZ, Ora. Jewish Weaving in Kurdistan. Journal of Jewish Art, 3-4, pp 74-89.

Vilner yiddisher teater - 20 yor. (The Vilna Yiddish Theatre- 20 years) Sovietish Heimland, 17, No. 2, F. pp 174-76.

WALLACH, Charles. Art in Judaism. Jewish Affairs, 32, No. 9, S. pp 21-24.

WERNER, Alfred. Art in Suburbia. Jewish Quarterly, 25, No. 1, Sp. pp 21-24.

--------------. Through the Golden Door. American Jewish Archives, 29, No. 2, N. pp 95-106.

Between 1905 and 1945 a "Jewish School" of artists and sculptors maintained a discernible presence in the world of American art and especially in New York City.

JEWISH ARTISTS

AMISHAI-MAISELS, Zvi. Steinhardt's Call for Peace. Journal of . Jewish Art, 3-4, pp 90-102.'

BEIT-ARIE, Malachie. Joel Ben Simeon's Manuscripts: A Codicologer's View. Journal of Jewish Art, 3-4, pp 25-39.

COLE, Diane. The illusory images of Yaacov Agam. His works link abstract art to Kabbala. The National Jewish Monthly, 91, No. 8, Ap. pp 2-7.

Five American Sculptors: Calder, Flannagan, Lachaise, Lipschitz, Nadelman. N.e. New York, Arno P.; London, Art Book, 330p, Ill. (Museum of Modern Art S.)
HEIDER, Gertrud. Anatoli L. Kaplan - Keramik. Photos. by Klaus G. Geyer. Berlin, Union, 148p, Ill.
The ceramics of the Russian Jewish artist.
KAHANE, Zalmen. Moise Apelbaum. - der Yiddisher Chaliapin. (Moshe Apelbaum - The Jewish Chaliapin) Sovietish Heimland, 17, No. 8, Au. pp 102-4.
LIEBERMAN, William S. Max Ernst. New York, Arno P.; London, Art Book, 166p, Ill.(Museum of Modern Art S.)
MENUHIN, Yehudi. (Ed.) My Favourite Music Stories. Guildford, London Lutt P., 160p, Ill.
Collection of stories about music, including Chassidic.
PETÉNYI, Katalin. Amos Imre apokalipszis-sorozata. Ars Hungarica, No. 2, pp 267-77.
The apocalypse drawings of Imre Amos, Jewish graphic artist of the Holocaust.
POPPER, Frank. Agam. New York, Abrams, 354p, 488 Ill.
Monograph of the Israeli artist, Yaakov Agam.
RICHARDSON, Joanna. Sarah Bernhardt and her World. London, Weidenfeld & Nicolson; New York, Putnam, 232p. Ill.
SHNEIDERMAN, S.L. Chaggal-Torn? Midstream, 23, No. 6, Ju-Jy. pp 49-62.
On Chagall for his 90th birthday - his works for churches.
Binyomin Shwartser - 85 yor. Sovietish Heimland, 17, No. 5, My pp 86-91.
Tribute to the Yiddish actor.
SKOTNES, Cecil. The renowned South African artist, opened a retrospective exhibition of the works of the late Matthew Whippman in the Pretoria Art Museum. Jewish Affairs, 32, No. 6, Ju. pp 11-14.
STEIN, Leonard. Schoenberg's "Biblical Way". Jewish Quarterly, 25, No. 2, Su. pp 33-34.
SWEENEY, James Johnson. Marc Chagall. N.e. New York, Arno P., 102p, Ill. (Museum of Modern Art S.)
TELEPY, Katalin. Iványi Grünwald Béla.Budapest, Corvina, 90p, Ill. (Művészet Kiskönyvtara)
Monograph of the noted Jewish painter, founder of the Nagybánya School.
WALDMANN, M. Le peintre Z. Schreter. Paris, Piranhas, Ed.
WERNER, Alfred. Chagall and Israel. American Zionist, 67, No. 7, My-Ju. pp 12-15.
--------------. Chagall at Ninety. Journal of Jewish Art, 1, No, 1 pp 4-13.
--------------. The Glory of Chagall. Jewish Digest, 23, No. 1, S. - pp 13ff.
--------------. Abraham Rattner: Color Magician. Reconstructionist 43, No. 4, My. pp 20-25.
--------------. Soutine. 1893-1943. New York, Abrams, 160p, Ill.
--------------. Hermann Struck: Still Unforgotten, Jewish Frontier, 44, No. 5, My. pp 21-24.
WEYL, Martin. Jacques Lipschitz. Jewish Affairs, 32, No. 11, N. pp 24-27.

FOLKLORE

BEIT-HALLAHMI,Benjamin. Sacrifice, fire and the victory of the sun: A Search for the origins of Hanukkah. Psychoanalytic Review, 63, No. 1, W. pp 497-510.

BLUE, Lionel and ROSE, June. A Taste of Heaven. Adventures in Food and Faith. London, Darton, Longman and Todd, 138p. Ind, Ill.

The authors discuss the food of Christians, Jews, Muslims, Hindus, Sikhs and other faiths.

KATZ, P. and F.E. Symbols as Charters in Culture Change: The Jewish Case. Anthropes, 72, Nos. 3-4, pp 486-96.

Comparison of traditions of circumcision, Passover and the Synagogue in North America, Eastern Europe and Israeli kibbutzim

LANDMANN, Salcia. Jüdische Witze. Nachlese 1960-1976. München, DTV, 259p.

The author's second collection of Jewish anecdotes with an introductory essay on Jewish humour.

LINZER, Norman. (Ed.) Understanding Bereavement and Grief: Proceedings of Two Interdisciplinary Educational Conferences in 1974 and 1975, co-sponsored by the Jewish Funeral Directors of America, Yeshiva University and allied professions. Co-edited by Harriet Feiner and Adelaide Jablonsky, New York,KTAV Publishing House, Yeshiva U.P. and Jewish Funeral Directors of America, xvi, 253p.

SPALDING, Henry D. A Treasure-Trove of American Jewish Humor. New York, Jonathan David, 446p.

ABBREVIATIONS

Ap.	April
App.	Appendix
Au.	August
Aut.	Autumn
Bd.	Band
Bibl.	Bibliography
Col.(s)	Column(s)
Comp.(s)	Compiler(s)
D.	December
Ed.(s)	Editor(s) Edition
F.	February
Fa.	Fall
f.	following page
ff.	following pages
Fr.	Front
Hrsg.	Herausgegeben
Ill.	Illustrated, Illustrations
Ind.	Index
Ja.	January
Ju.	June
Jy.	July
M(s)	Map(s)
Ma.	March
Mimeo.	Mimeographed
My.	May
N.	November
N.D.	No Date
n.e.	new edition
n.p.	no place of printing
N.S.	New Series
O.	October
P.	pages (books)
pp.	pages (articles)
r.e.	revised edition
S.	September
Sp.	Spring
Su.	Summer
s.	series
tr.	translated
U.	University
U.P.	University Press
V.	Volume
Verl.	Verlag
W.	Winter

PERIODICALS

Adam International Review (London)
ADL Bulletin (New York)
Administration (Dublin)
Administration and Society
Administration Science Quarterly (Ithaca)
Adolescence (New York)
Adult Education (New York)
Aesthetik und Kommunikation (Berlin)
African Report (Washington (DC)
African Studies (Johannesburg)
L'Afrique Contemporaine (Paris)
L'Afrique et L'Asie Modernes (Paris)
Air Force Magazine (Washington DC)
AJA Quarterly (London)
AJA Review (London)
Alföld (Hungary)
America (New York
American Academy of Jewish Research (New York)
American Bar Association Journal (Chicago)
American Heritage (New York)
American Jewish Archives (Cincinnati)
American Jewish Historical Quarterly (New York)
American Journal of International Law (Washington DC)
American Journal of Nursing (New York)
American Journal of Sociology, The (Chicago)
American Political Science Review (Washington DC)
American Sociological Review (Washington DC)
American Zionist, The (New York)
Analysis (New York)
Angelicum (Rome)
Annales Economies, societes, civilisations (Paris)
Annales internationales de criminologie (Paris)
Annali dell'Instituto Orientale di Napoli (Naples)
Annals of the American Academy Political and Sociel Science, The (Philadelphia)
Annual of the Swedish Theological Institute (Leiden)
Anthropos (Freiburg)
Antike Welt (Zurich)
L'Arche (Paris)
Archivalische Zeitschrift (Köln)
Archives Juives (Paris
Archives des Sciences Sociales des Religions (Paris)
Armed Forces and Society (Chicago)
Army Quarterly and Defence Journal (Tavistock)
Ars Hungarica (Budapest)
Art Forum (New York)
Asian Affairs (London)
Asian and African Studies (Jerusalem)
Asian Profile (Hong Kong)
Asien, Afrika, Latinamerika (Berlin)
Atlantic Monthly, The (Boston)
Atlas World Press Review (New York)
Aus Politik und Zeitgeschichte (Das Parlament) (Bonn-Godesberg)
Aussenpolitik, Zeitschrift für Internationale Fragen (Freiburg)
Australian Journal of Politics and History (Sydney)

Bible et Terre Sainte (Paris)
Biblical Archaelogist, The (Chicago)
Bild der Wissenschaft (Stuttgart)
Blätter für Deutsche und Internationale Politik (Cologne)
B'nai B'rith Journal (London)
Bookseller, The (London)
Boston University Journal (Boston)
Britain and Israel (London)
British Journal of Political Science (Cambridge)

Bulletin de la Societe Francaise de Sociologie (Paris)
Bulletin D'Etudes Orientales (Damascus)
Bulletin des Leo Baeck Instituts (New York)
Bulletin of the American Schools of Oriental Research (Cambridge)
Bulletin of Peace Proposals (Oslo)

Cahiers du Monde Russe et Sovietique (Paris)
Canadian-American Slavic Studies (Pittsburg)
Cahiers de Fanjeaux (Toulouse)
Candian Review of Sociology and Anthropology, The (Toronto)
Catholica (Münster)
Catholic Historical Review (Washington DC)
Catholic Mind, The (New York)
Catholic World, The (New York)
CCAR Journal (New York)
Central European History (Atlanta)
Change (New Rochelle)
Christian Attitudes on Jews and Judaism (London)
Christian Century, The (Chicago)
Christianity and Crisis (New York)
Christian Scholar's Review (Wenham)
Christianity Today (Washington DC)
Chuto Sogo Kenkyu (Tokyo)
Chuto Tsuko (Tokyo)
Ciencia Tomista (Salamanca)
Civil Liberties Review, The (USA)
Civil Rights Digest (Washington DC)
La Civilta Cattolica (Rome)
Coexistence (Oxford)
Collationes (Ghent)
Commentary (New York)
Common Ground (London)
Commweal (New York)
Community Development Journal (London)
Comparative Political Studies (Beverley Hills)
Comparative Politics (Chicago)
Cooperative Studies in Society and History (London)
Community (Milano)
Congress Monthly (New York)
Connaissance d'Israël (Paris)
Conservative Judaism (New York)
Contemporary Jewry (Philadelphia)
Council Woman (USA)
Criterion (Chicago)
Culture et Development (Louvain)

Davka (Los Angeles)
Department of State Bulletin (Washington DC)
Deutsche Jugend (Munich)
Diakonia (Mainz)
Dialog (St. Paul)
Dialogue (Kingston)
Dissent (New York)
Documentation Catholique (Paris)
Documenti e Fatti (Rome)
Les Dossiers de L'Archeologie (Dijon)

East Central Europe (Tampa)
Ecrits de Paris (Paris)
Ecumencial Review, The (Geneva)
Ekistics (Greece)
Elet es Tudomany (Budapest)
Eletünk (Budapest)
Emuna/Israel Forum (Rottenberg)
Encounter (London)
Encounter Today (Issy-Les-Molyneux)
Engage/Social Action (Washington DC)
Esprit (Paris)
Esquire (New York)
Ethnicity (Chicago)
Etudes Theologiques et Religieux (Montpelier)
L'Egypte Contemporaine (Cairo)
Europa Archiv (Bonn)
European Judaism (London)
Evangelische Theologie (Munchen)

Face to Face (Washington DC)
Facts (Washington DC)
Fizikai Szemle (Budapest)
Flash of Damascus (Damascus)
Foi et Vie (Paris)
Foreign Affairs (New York)
Foreign Policy (New York)

Foundations (Rochester)
France-Israël Information (Paris)
France-Palestine (Paris)
France - Pays Arabes (Paris)
Freedom at Issue (New York)
Freiburger Rundbrief (Freiburg)

Geschichte in Wissenschaft und Unterricht (Stuttgart)
Grundrechte (Kehl)

Hadassah Magazine (New York)
Harper's Magazine (New York)
Hebrew Studies (Louisville)
Hegel Studien (Bonn)
Ter Herkenning (The Hague)
Hispanic Review (Philadelphia)
Historian, The (Allentown)
History of Education (New York)
History Today (London)
Horizons (Quebec)
Horn Book Magazine, The (Boston)
Humanitas (Broscia)
Human Relations (London)

Index of Censorship (London)
Indian Political Science Review (New Dehli)
India Quarterly (New Delhi)
Industrial Relations (Quebec)
Informations Bulletin (Prague)
Insight (London)
Integrated Education (Evanstown)
Intellect (New York)
Inter-American Economic Affairs (Washington DC)
Interchange (Toronto)
International Affairs (London)
International and Comparative Law Quarterly (London)
International Journal (Toronto)
International Journal of Comparative Sociology (Toronto)
International Journal of Criminology and Penology (New York/London)
International Journal of Intercultural Relations (Elmswood)
International Journal of Middle East Studies (London)
International Journal of Offender Therapy and Comparative Criminology (London)
International Journal of the Sociology of Language (The Hague)
International Migration Review (New York)
International Review of Modern Sociology (De Kalb)
International Review of the Red Cross (Geneva)
International Studies (Detroit)
Irodalmi Szemle (Budapest)
Irodalomtörtenet (Budapest)
Israel Horizons (New York)
Israelitisches Wochenblatt für die Schweiz (Zurich)
Istina (Paris)

Jednota (Yugoslavia)
Jeune Afrique (Tunis)
Jewish Affairs (Johannesburg)
Jewish Affairs (New York)
Jewish Art (New York)
Jewish Chronicle Colour Supplement (London)
Jewish Currents (New York)
Jewish Digest (Houghton)
Jewish Education (New York)
Jewish Frontier (New York)
Jewish Historical Society of Canada (Montreal)
Jewish Journal of Sociology (London)
Jewish Life (New York)
Jewish Observer (New York)
Jewish Quarterly, The (London)
Jewish Quarterly Review (Philadelphia)
Jewish Social Studies (New York)
Jewish Spectator (New York)
Jewish Veteran (Washington DC)
Jewish World, The (London)
Journal des Savants (Paris)
Journal for the Scientific Study of Religion (Notre Dame)
Journal for the Study of Judaism in the Persian, Hellenistic and Roman Period (Leiden)
Journal für Angewandte Sozialforschung (Vienna)

Journalism Quarterly (Iowa)
Journal of Conflict Resolution, The (Ann Arbor)
Journal of Contemporary History (London)
Journal of Developing Areas (Macomb)
Journal of the Economic and Social History of the Orient (Leiden)
Journal of Ecumenical Studies (Pittsburgh)
Journal of Educational Thought (Calgary)
Journal of Ethnic Studies (Bellingham)
Journal of Geological Education (Austin)
Journal of Health and Social Behaviour (Waltham)
Journal of the History of Ideas (Lancaster)
Journal of Intergroup Relations, The (Louisville)
Journal of International Law and Economics (Washington DC)
Journal of Jewish Communal Service (New York)
Journal of Jewish Studies (London)
Journal of Marriage and Family (USA)
Journal of Palestine Studies (Beirut)
Journal of Psychology and Judaism (Ottowa)
Journal of Public Economics (Amsterdam)
Journal of Religion and Health (New York)
Journal of Social Issues (Ann Arbor)
Journal of Social Psychology, The (Provincetown)
Journal of South Asian and Middle Eastern Studies (Villanova)
Judaica (Zurich)
Judaica Bohemiae (Prague)
Judaica Post (Detroit)
Judaism (New York)
Jüdischer Presse Dienst (Dusseldorf)
Justiz und Zeitgeschichte (Graz)

Kairos (Vienna)
Keeping Posted (New York)
Khamsin (London)
Kortars (Budapest)
Kosmos & Oekumene (Hertogenbosch)
Kritika (Budapest)

Latohatar (Budapest)
Law and Society Review (Minneapolis)
Learning With (Minneapolis)
Lebendiges Zeugnis (Paderborn)
Lettre (Paris)
Leviathan (Wiesbaden)
L'Eylah (London)
Liberal Catholic, The (London)
Link (New York)
Living Light, The (Huntingdon)
Lumen Vitae (Bruxelles)

Maandelijke Tijdschrift (Antwerp)
Maghreb-Machrek, Monde Arabe (Paris)
Magyar Könyvszemle (Budapest)
Mankind Quarterly (Edinburgh)
Medio Oriente Informa (Mexico C.)
Melanges de Science Religieuse (Lille)
Menorah (London)
MERIP Reports (Washington DC)
Merkur (Munich)
Middle East International (London)
Middle East Journal (Washington DC)
Middle East Perspective (New York)
Middle East Review (New York)
Middle East Studies (New York)
Military Review (Fort Leavenworth)
Mirovaia Ekonomika I Mezhdunarodnye Otnosheniia (Moscow)
Mitteilungen der Geographischen Gesellschaft in München (Munich)
Moment (New York)
Monde Juif, Le (Paris)
Monthly Review, (New York)
Muslim World (Hartford)

Nachrichtenblatt (E. Berlin)
Nagyvilag (Budapest)
Narody Azii i Afriki (Moscow)
Nation, The (U.S.A)
National Jewish Monthly (Washington DC)
National Review (New York)
Naval War College Review (Newport)
Nederlands Theologisch Tijdschrift (Wageningen)
Negro History Bulletin (Washington DC)
Nemzetközi Szemle (Budapest)
Neue Israel, Das(Zurich)
Neue Politische Literatur (Villingen)
New Catholic World (New York)
New Community (London)
New Elul (London)
New Leader, The (New York)
New Left Review (London)
New Politics (New York)
New Republic (Washington DC)
New York (New York)
New York Review of Books, The (New York)
New York Times Magazine, The (New York)
Nietzsche Studien (Berlin)
Nouveaux Cahiers, Les (Paris)
Nouvelle Revue Theologique (Louvain)
Nuova Rivista Storica (Rome)

Olam (London)
Omega: The Journal of Death and Dying (Farmingdale)
Orbis (Philadelphia)
Orient (Hamburg)
Österreichische Zeitschrift für Aussenpolitik (Vienna)
Österreichisches Archiv für Kirchenrecht (Vienna)
Osteuropa (Stuttgart)

Pai News (London)
Pakistan Horizon (Karachi)
Palestine (New York)
Palestine Bulletin
Palestine Exploration Quarterly (London)
Parliamentarian (London)
Partisan Review (New Brunswick)
Patterns of Prejudice (London)
Pedagogic Reporter (New York)
Perspective (New York)
Phyton (Atlanta)
Pioneer Woman (New York)
Plural Societies (The Hague)
Pluriel-Debat (Paris)
Politica Internationale (Milan)
Political Science Quarterly, The (New York)
Political Studies (London)
Politico (Pavia)
Politique Etrangere (Paris)
Politische Meinung (Bonn)
Present Tense (New York)
Problems of Communism (Washington DC)
Proceedings of the American Academy of Jewish Research (New York)
Progressive, The (Madison)
Provence Historique (Aix-en-Provence)
Przeglad Historyczny (Warsaw)
Psychology Today (New York)
Publishers Weekly (New York)
Public Opinion Quarterly (Princeton)

Race and Class (London)
Readers Digest (London)
Recherches de Science Religieuse (Paris)
Reconstructionist, The (New York)
Regards (Brussels)
Religion in Communist Lands (Keston)
Religious Education (New Conn.)
Religious Studies (London)
Rencontre Sous le Signe de la Langue Francaise (Paris)
Republik, Die (Vienna)
Response (Waltham)
Review of International Affairs (Belgrade)
Review of Religious Research (New York)
Review of Socialist Law (Leiden)
Revista Mexicana de Sociologia (Mexico)

Revista Politica International (Madrid)
Revue de Defence Nationale (Paris)
Revue de Droit Penal Militaire et de Droit de la Guerre (Bruxelles)
Rebue des Etudes Juives (Paris)
Revue des Etudes Cooperatives (Paris)
Revue des Sciences Religieuses (Strasbourg)
Revue des Sciences Sociales de la France de L'Est (Strasbourg)
Revue d'Histoire de la Medicine Hebrai"que (Paris)
Revue Egyptienne de Doirt International (Cairo)
Revue Francaise d'Histoire du Livre (Bordeaux)
Revue Francaise de Sociologie (Paris)
Revue Generale de Droite International Public (Paris)
Revue d'Histoire Moderne et Contemporaine (Paris)
Revue Internationale de Sciences Sociales (Paris)
Revue Militaire Suisse (Laussanne)
Revue Philosophique de la France et de L'etranger (Paris)
Revista di Archeologia Cristiana (Rome)
Rivista di Studi Politici Internationali (Firenze)
Romantisme (Paris)
Rassegna Mensile di Israel, La (Rome)

Saeculum (Munich)
Saturday Review (New York)
Schweizer Monatshefte (Zurich)
Schweizerische Zeitscheift für Soziologie (Geneva)
Schweizerische Zeitschrift für Strafrecht Revue Penale Suisse (Berne)
Science and Society (New York)
Scottish Journal of Theology (London)
Sefarad (Madrid)
Sens (Paris)
Shalom (Sao Paolo)
Sh'Ma (New York)
Sidic (Rome)
Signs (Chicago)
Situations Moyen Orient (Paris)
Social Casework (New York)
Social Compass (Louvain)
Social Forces (Chapel Hill)
Sociological Analysis (Sheffield)
Social Praxis (Ontario)
Social Science Quarterly (Baton Rouge)
Socialist Society (Bombay)
Society (New Brunswick)
Sociologica Ruralis (Assen)
Sociology of Education (Albany)
Sociology of Work and Occupations (London)
Soedinenye Shtaty Amerika: Ekonomika, Politika, Idiologia (Moscow)
South Africa International (Johannesburg)
South Atlantic Quarterly, The (Durham)
Soviet Jewish Affairs (London)
State Department Bulletin (Washington DC)
Storia Contemporanea (Bologna)
Studia Patavina, Rivista di Scienze Religiose (Padova)
Studia Rosenthaliana (Amsterdam)
Studies in Bibliography and Booklore (Cincinnati)
Studies in Literary Imagination (Atlanta)
Studium Legionense (Leon)
Survey (London)
Survival (London)
Szazadok (Budapest)

Tarsadalmi Szemle (Budapest)
Termeszet Vilaga (Budapest)
Texas International Law Journal (Austin)
Texas Law Review (Austin)
Theologie der Gegenwart (Frankfurt)
Theology Today (Lancaster)
Third World Review (Cortland)
Törtenelmi Szemle (Budapest)
Tradition (New York)
Transactions of the Jewish Historical Society of England

(London)
Tsukunft, Di (New York)

Uj Forras (Budapest
Uj Iras (Budapest)
Un Sancta (Meitingen-Freising)
United Synagogue Review (New York)
Unzer Tsait (New York)
Urban Affairs Quarterly (Ann Arbor)
Urban League Review (New Brunswick)

Victimology (Washington DC)
Viewpoints (Montreal)
Vigilia (Budapest)
Vilagossag (Budapest)
Voenno-Istoricheskii Zhurnal (Moscow)

Western States Jewish Historical Quarterly (Santa Monica)
Wiener Library Bulletin (London)
Wiener Tagebuch (Vienna)
World Affairs (Washington DC)
World Affairs Report (Washington DC)
World Marxist Review (London)
World Politics (Princeton)
World Today (London)
Worldview (New York)

Yiddish (Flushing)
Yiddishe Shprakh (New York)
Yod. Revue des Etudes Hebraiques et Juives Modernes et Contemporaines (Paris)
Youth and Society (Beverley Hills)

Zeitschrift für Deutsches Alterum und Deutsche Literatur (Wiesbaden)
Zeitschrift für Religions-und-Geistesgeschichte (Köln)
Zwingliana (Zürich)

NAME INDEX